Quick Reference Card

General Rules

Save your documents in the My Documents folder.

Create lots of folders for specific types of files or projects within the My Documents folder.

Use the SETUP or INSTALL program to add new software to your system. Do not drag icons to install software.

Install programs into the Program Files folder.

Do not save your documents or install programs in the Windows folder. Exceptions exist (wallpaper graphics and cursors, for example), as noted elsewhere in this book.

Never delete any file you did not personally create.

Never delete any program file; always use the Uninstall option in the Control Panel's Add/Remove Programs icon.

File-Naming Rules

A filename can contain letters, numbers, and spaces.

Yes, filenames can start with numbers.

A filename cannot contain any of these characters: " * / : ? \ ¦ < >

A filename can be from 1 to 255 characters long.

Short, descriptive names work best.

Windows treats uppercase and lowercase letters the same, although it displays them in both upper- and lowercase.

A period followed by as many as three characters at the end of a filename is the filename's extension. It tells Windows the file type. In the standard Windows setup, registered file extensions are not displayed.

Folders are named like files.

Windows Mouse Shortcuts

Copy	Ctrl+drag
Shortcut	Ctrl+Shift+drag
Move	Shift+drag
Display menu after drag	Right+drag

Internet Explorer

Drop a bookmark	Ctrl+D
Open a new window	Ctrl+N
Open a Web page	Ctrl+O
Beginning of document	Home
End of document	End
Refresh or reload	F5

Outlook Express

Forward a message	Ctrl+F
Go to Inbox	Ctrl+I
Send and receive mail	Ctrl+M
New message	Ctrl+N
Reply to a message you're reading	Ctrl+R
Next unread message	Ctrl+U
Spell-check your message	F7

Bizarre Shortcut Key Combinations

Close a window	Alt+F4
Display a shortcut menu	Alt+F10
Display the system menu	Alt+Spacebar
Move up one folder	Backspace

Important Phone Numbers

Your computer dealer: ______________________________

Your computer guru: ______________________________

Your Internet service provider's support line: ______________________________

Your computer manufacturer's support line: ______________________________

Your computer's serial number may be required; write it here: ______________________________

____

Microsoft support line: ______________________________

The number you dial to connect to the Internet: ______________________________

Alternative Internet number: ______________________________

Other support lines: ______________________________

Your Internet Account Information

You might want to keep your password information on a separate piece of paper in a safe place.

Internet account logon name: ______________________________

Internet account password: ______________________________

Email logon name: ______________________________

Email password: ______________________________

Email address: ______________________________

Your ISP's domain name: ______________________________

Searching for Something on the Web

Your first choice: `http://www.yahoo.com`

A good second choice: `http://www.excite.com`

A gaggle of search engines is listed in the Yahoo! catalog: `Computers & Internet:Internet:World Wide Web:Searching the Web:Search Engines`

To find links for sounds on the Web, look in the Yahoo! catalog: `Computers & Internet:Internet:World Wide Web:Searching the Web:Search Engines`

Search newsgroups at `http://www.dejanews.com`.

To locate shareware software, visit `http://www.shareware.com`.

Get the WinZIP unzipping program at `http://www.winzip.com`.

Common Shortcut Key Combinations

Windows/My Computer/Windows Explorer

Select All	Ctrl+A
Copy	Ctrl+C
New	Ctrl+N
Open	Ctrl+O
Print	Ctrl+P
Save	Ctrl+S
Cut	Ctrl+X
Paste	Ctrl+V
Undo	Ctrl+Z
Delete	Delete
Really delete	Shift+Del
Start Thing	Ctrl+Esc
Switch tasks	Alt+Tab
Choose menu item	Alt+[underlined letter]
Properties	Alt+Enter
Help	F1
Rename	F2
Find	F3
Look in/Address	F4
Refresh a window	F5
Switch to the left or right panel in Windows Explorer	F6
Activate menu	F10
Cancel	Esc
OK	Enter
Next field	Tab

DAN GOOKIN

TEACHES

WINDOWS 98

201 West 103rd Street,
Indianapolis, Indiana 46290

Dan Gookin Teaches Windows 98

International Standard Book Number: 0-7897-1688-7

Library of Congress Catalog Card Number: 98-84861

Printed in the United States of America

First Printing: October, 1998

00 99 98 4 3 2 1

Trademarks

All terms mentioned in this book that are known to be trademarks or service marks have been appropriately capitalized. Que cannot attest to the accuracy of this information. Use of a term in this book should not be regarded as affecting the validity of any trademark or service mark.

Warning and Disclaimer

Every effort has been made to make this book as complete and as accurate as possible, but no warranty or fitness is implied. The information provided is on an "as is" basis. The authors and the publisher shall have neither liability nor responsibility to any person or entity with respect to any loss or damages arising from the information contained in this book.

Executive Editor
Grace Buechlein

Acquisitions Editor
Angela Wethington

Development Editor
Rebecca Whitney

Project Editor
Katie Purdum

Copy Editor
Rebecca Whitney

Indexer
Rebecca Hornyak

Proofreaders
Benjamin Berg

Technical Editor
Craig Arnush

Interior Design
Ruth Lewis
Louisa Klucznik

Cover Design
Mike Freeland

Layout Technicians
Michael Dietsch
Ayanna Lacey
Heather Hiatt Miller

Contents at a Glance

Table of Contents

III Printing and Faxing

IV Disks, Folders, and Files

VII Problem Solving

Acknowledgments

This book would not have been what it is without the caring assistance of my beloved, Sandy. She was my tester. I would write a chapter and pass it off to her for review and evaluation. If she "got it," I figured that I was on the right track, and then the chapter was edited and sent to the publisher for butchery. If Sandy didn't get it, I wasn't doing my job and went back to rewrite stuff. Because of her input, I rewrote this book's first chapter (from scratch) three times. Thanks, wife-unit!

To the gang at Macmillan, thanks go to Grace, Becky, Katie, Craig, and the rest of the crew for making things so very fun. Thanks especially to the suits upstairs, who realize and admit to the value of the author's contribution. Thank you for letting me participate in the *Teaches* author-driven project.

Oh, and thanks to Angie, even though she's in another department.

Thanks to my agent, Matt Wagner, for whatever it is he does, without which I would be utterly lost. I suppose.

Thanks to *Hamlet*. And thanks to Michael Fietsam, for bailing me out of set-building duties.

Tell Us What You Think!

As the reader of this book, *you* are our most important critic and commentator. We value your opinion and want to know what we're doing right, what we could do better, what areas you'd like to see us publish in, and any other words of wisdom you're willing to pass our way.

As the Executive Editor for the Operating Systems team at Macmillan Computer Publishing, I welcome your comments. You can fax, email, or write me directly to let me know what you did or didn't like about this book—as well as what we can do to make our books stronger.

Please note that I cannot help you with technical problems related to the topic of this book, and that due to the high volume of mail I receive, I might not be able to reply to every message.

When you write, please be sure to include this book's title and author as well as your name and phone or fax number. I will carefully review your comments and share them with the author and editors who worked on the book.

Fax: 317-581-4663

E-mail: `opsys@mcp.com`

Mail: Executive Editor
Operating Systems
Macmillan Computer Publishing
201 West 103rd Street
Indianapolis, IN 46290 USA

Introduction

Good morning, student!

Welcome to *Dan Gookin Teaches Windows 98*, a book designed to infuse you with knowledge about your computer and its operating system, Windows 98.

Through a very sneaky and entertaining process, this book teaches you how to become a clever and insightful computer user. After you discover how Windows works, you'll quickly find yourself boldly doing amazing things with your PC—all on your own. It's painless, and it's fun.

Are you ready for the next step?

About This Book

This book shows you how to use your own brain to make sense of Windows 98. If you've been using other books, references, and the online Help system to struggle through Windows, this book's lessons and real-life examples will be a welcome and beneficial relief. It's a tutorial. It's a training guide. It's entertaining and educational.

In the chapters and lessons in this book, you learn about Windows not from vague, out-of-context references, but rather from useful, real-life examples. Each chapter contains several tutorials that show you how Windows works. Eventually you'll be able to anticipate what Windows does and place yourself firmly in the driver's seat.

If you've been stuck in computer kindergarten, welcome to the next level! I believe that you'll find this text an enjoyable relief.

Organization

This book has seven major parts:

Part I: Windows Orientation and Review

Part II: Working in Windows

Part III: Printing and Faxing

Part IV: Disks, Folders, and Files

Part V: Somewhere, Out There

Part VI: The Tweak Master

Part VII: Problem Solving

Part I offers a gentle introduction to Windows—a brush-up and quick review. It's designed for folks new to Windows 98 who might need some extra help.

Parts II through VII speed up the pace a bit. It's not rocket science; it's just that I figure that you appreciate it when an author understands when you "get it." The chapters in this book don't tell you how to click a mouse over and over again, and they assume that you, as a smart person, eventually understand how Windows works. (If you're new to this idea, I believe that you'll enjoy my approach.)

Each part of this book has chapters about a specific subject related to the title of that part of the book. For example, printing is covered in Part III, and the Internet is covered in Part V.

Where to Start

You can start reading any chapter in any part at any time and in any order. The book is cross-referenced so that you can read related information in any order you like. Most folks will probably read the book from front to back. No problem there.

It's important that, after you start a chapter, you work it all the way through. Many of the lessons in each chapter build on each other. Also, some of the files created in Part I are used throughout the rest of the book.

Conventions

When you're asked to do something in a tutorial, it appears in an action-step that looks like this:

▶ **Close the My Documents window.**

This line is a directive for you to do something. In this example, you're told to close a window onscreen. Notice that you're told to do something but are not told how to do it. Part I tells you how; the other parts of this book merely tell you what to do without the boring details (although occasionally I give you details, primarily to show you alternative ways to do things).

The following action-step tells you to choose the Save As command from the File menu:

▶ **Choose File ➡Save As.**

The ➡ symbol indicates a menu item, command, or submenu.

When you see a directive with underlined letters, as shown here, you can press the Alt key with that underlined letter as a shortcut: Alt+F in *F*ile, for example.

If you're required to type something, it looks like this:

▶ **Type** My Computer **in the Address box.**

The plain text *My Computer* is what you type. Or it might look like this:

▶ **In the Filename box, type** My Icon File**.**

This directive tells you two things: You can press Alt+N to activate the Filename box, and you have to type the text *My Icon File* in that box.

If the typing command is explained in the main text, the stuff you type is shown in boldface type, as in "Type **My Icon File,** and press the Enter key."

You're always told when to press the Enter key.

Be sure to read everything. In fact, it's a good idea to preview all the steps so that you know where the tutorial is headed.

Gotta Have Icons

This book uses the following icons to flag various important points:

The fabulous Tip icon details a shortcut or handy tidbit of information worthy of note. Unlike some other authors, I do not overuse this icon. When you see the Tip icon, you can be assured that the text mentioned in that box is truly a handy tip.

The Watch Out icon indicates something you should stand up and pay attention to. It's a warning—an alert to be on your toes.

The Important Point icon flags something to remember or a note of interest that affects more than what you would think. For example, an Important Point icon in Chapter 31 flags text that tells you what the Search button in Internet Explorer *really* does.

I can't help it. Once in awhile I lapse into nerdspeak or have to give some speech about the historical significance of, for example, a red hard drive light versus a green hard drive light. I thought that I would be nice and flag those items with a Yawn icon.

This is shouting text!

Sometimes I have to blurt something right out. To make that point, I show you my comments as the preceding "shouting text."

Assumptions, Silly and Sensible

It's hard to write a computer book, let alone *teach* something, without making a few assumptions. Up front, I assume that you're using a computer running Windows 98. You might have purchased a new PC with Windows 98 already installed, or you might have upgraded from an earlier version of Windows. Whatever. Windows 98 is on your computer now.

This book does not cover installing Windows 98.

This book does not cover the Windows 98 Plus! package, although I might mention it from time to time.

I do not assume that you have any specific software packages, such as Microsoft Office. However, this book does use Internet Explorer exclusively. I don't cover other Internet programs (Netscape and Eudora, for example) in this book.

In Part V, I assume that you have a modem installed on your computer. Chapters in Part VI assume that your PC has a sound card. If your PC is missing a modem or sound card, just skip the affected chapters.

This book assumes that you've graduated from computer kindergarten. Even if you're a new computer user, you most likely understand some basic Windows concepts. This book respects you for that. You know how to use your software. You know how a window works. You know what a mouse is, and you know how to use it to point-and-click and drag-and-choose menu items.

Finally, this book assumes that you're willing to *learn*. Windows is not that hard to use. You just have to be taught how to think like Windows. This book does a good job of that, transforming even the meekest computer user into someone who can truly get the most from his or her computer and its operating system.

About Me, the Gentle Author

Hello! I'm Dan, and I'll be your author this evening. Would anyone like to start with a cocktail?

Wait—it's a flashback! Okay. I'm over it. Come to think of it, I was never a waiter. I cooked in a restaurant for six years but left when I started writing magazine articles and eventually books about computers. Even so, I still cook up a mean steak. (And I know exactly what medium rare means.)

I began writing computer books in the mid-1980s. Although most of my titles were about computer programming and other advanced topics, I'm perhaps best known for a book that took me only three little weeks to write: *DOS For Dummies* (published by IDG Books, Worldwide, Inc.). That book woke a sleeping giant and introduced computers to millions of ignored readers.

When I found out that Macmillan is publishing an author-driven computer book series, I went nuts. Most computer book series are "created" by the publisher, and content is dictated to the author. The *Teaches* series is the opposite of that concept. It's a nutty idea: The author creates the content, and the publisher heeds the author's wisdom. (You would think it would be that way all the time, but no.) I was dying to try this, and I feel very fortunate that Macmillan chose me to go berserk with its *Teaches Windows 98* title.

My idea was simple: There are lots of users who are beyond the beginner level—the same people who needed a book like *DOS For Dummies* but who now want something more. I assume you're one of these readers, that you want to *learn* and grow. No book now on the market helps you do that. Rather than have you buy something less, I wrote this book to help lift you to the next level. Not only that: I got a chance to run amok again (just like in the old days!) because this series is author-driven. I'm quite sure that I drove many an editor insane during this project.

On a personal note, I own no stock, nor do I have any personal interest, in any of the products mentioned or recommended in this book. I name the products I know about, and I recommend stuff I use and trust. Notice that this book has no companion CD for me to shill and no ad-choked Web page you must visit. I'm not under pressure to steer you one way or the other. Also, I've paid for all shareware programs mentioned in this book. If you use shareware products, you should pay for them.

Finally, I'm open to answering any questions you might have about Windows or this book (see my email address after this paragraph). I personally answer every email question I get, although I admit that I'm not a genius and cannot help everyone. If you feel like writing just to say "Hi!" I answer those letters too.

Have fun!

Dan Gookin, 1998

`dgookin@wambooli.com`

Part I

Windows Orientation and Review

Chapters in This Part

Part I

Visual Topic Reference A.

1. Desktop.
2. My Computer; access to your disk drives and files (Chapter 6).
3. My Documents, where your creations are stored (Chapter 6).
4. Start Thing, used to start programs and other things (Chapter 2).
5. Taskbar, for switching programs.
6. Get on the Internet (Chapter 7).
7. Quick Launch bar.
8. System tray; miscellaneous stuff.

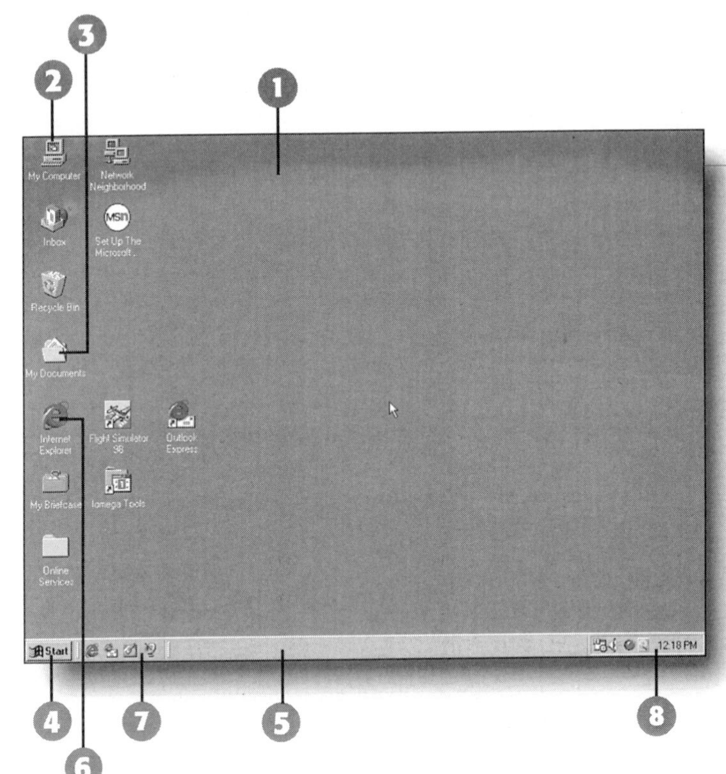

Part I

Visual Topic Reference B.

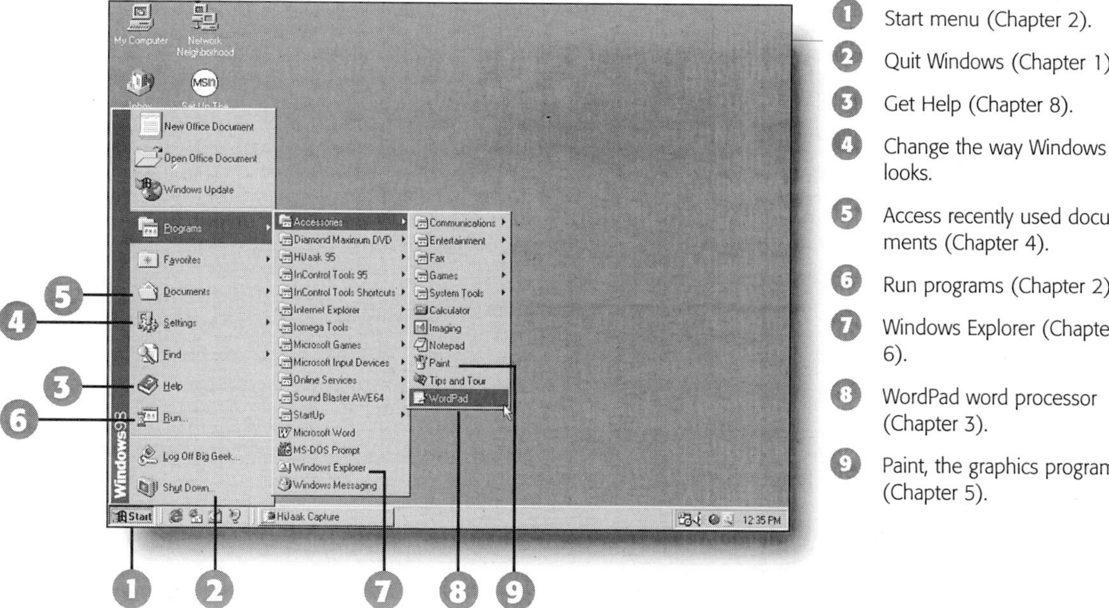

1. Start menu (Chapter 2).
2. Quit Windows (Chapter 1).
3. Get Help (Chapter 8).
4. Change the way Windows looks.
5. Access recently used documents (Chapter 4).
6. Run programs (Chapter 2).
7. Windows Explorer (Chapter 6).
8. WordPad word processor (Chapter 3).
9. Paint, the graphics program (Chapter 5).

Chapter 1

Windows On and Off

Questions Answered and Thoughts Inspired

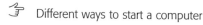

 Different ways to start a computer

 Important parts of the desktop

 How and when to turn a computer off

With all the buttons you could imagine on a computer, only one turns the thing on and off. Oh, if only it were that simple. The truth is that turning a computer on and knowing when and how to turn it off is a big deal. That's what is covered here, in the first chapter of this book.

Ladies and Gentlemen, Start Your Computers

Although your computer is friendly, don't try to swoon it with love poems or flowers. To truly turn the thing on, you have to supply it with electricity.

You can turn on a computer and all its peripherals in three ways. Choosing the way you turn it all on depends on whether you have a power strip, an Uninterruptible Power Supply (UPS), or neither.

"I Don't Have Any Power Strips or Nuthin'—All My Stuff Plugs Right In to the Wall"

To turn on your computer when everything just plugs in to the wall, heed these steps:

▶ **Turn on everything except the main computer box.**

▶ **Turn on the main computer box.**

Always turn on the computer box (the *console*) last. That way, it recognizes all the goodies plugged in to it.

- Most computer devices have a push button On-Off switch. It's labeled with the line-and-circle hieroglyph shown in the margin.
- The On-Off switch on some computers is labeled with a crescent moon.

"I'm Smart, and I Bought a Power Strip"

I guarantee that your computer room probably lacks the number of wall sockets you need in order to plug in every part of your computer system. To make things easier, buy a power strip.

▶ **Plug everything in to a power strip.**

The power strip has several sockets in which you plug the various parts of your computer system. Plug the power strip in to the wall socket, and you're set.

▶ **Turn on your computer by turning on the power strip.**

I know that I said (in the preceding section) to turn on the computer box last; turning everything on at one time, however, works just as well.

- Try to get a power strip that has line filtering or noise suppression. If the power strip offers spike or surge protection, that's even better. This feature ensures that the electricity flowing into your computer is clean and prevents the electricity from harming any of the computer's electronic components.

I recommend the Kensington SmartSockets power strips. The sockets are arranged in such a way that the bulky transformers (on the ends of most computer plugs) don't get in the way of each other. Also, the sockets are color coded and come with corresponding color stickers so that you can easily identify what plugs in to what.

"I Spent the Big Bucks, and I Have a UPS"

The acronym UPS in this book stands for Uninterruptible Power Supply, not the initials of the shipping company. A *UPS* is a special type of power strip, one that continues to give your computer juice even when the power is out. If you have a UPS (and I recommend that you do), do the following:

- **Plug the monitor and computer in to the UPS.**
- **Plug everything else in to a power strip.**

You don't have to plug everything in to the UPS. You want primarily to keep the monitor and console (the computer box) alive during a power outage. Everything else—especially printing—can wait until the power comes back on.

To turn your computer on with a UPS, do the following:

- **Turn on the power strip.**
- **Turn on the UPS.**

Again, you want to turn the computer on last so that it "sees" everything connected to it.

If you have a UPS and the power goes out, save your work immediately! Then shut down Windows as described at the end of this chapter. Do not try to continue working, because the UPS battery eventually drains—and it usually drains much faster than its manufacturer claims.

- Most computer and office supply stores sell UPSs.
- A typical UPS has two sockets: one for your monitor and the other for the computer box.

If your UPS has extra sockets, you can also plug in your modem, which prevents it from being disconnected if a power outage strikes while you're online.

Do not plug in a laser printer to a UPS. Laser printers draw down too much power to justify that action. Besides, you can always print when the power comes back on.

The Startup Sequence, or "Messages From Beyond"

As your computer starts up, you're assaulted with a series of messages onscreen. First, you see some text messages, and then a beep, and then Windows itself flashing its graphical glory.

▶ **Sit back and watch.**

When Windows is done loading, you either see the desktop or are asked to log on.

- If you see a message about a "non-system disk" or some such nonsense, it means that you've left a floppy disk in your PC's drive A. Remove the disk, press the Enter key, and continue staring at your PC.
- Other messages might appear during the startup process. If they concern you, see Chapter 10 for information about startup troubleshooting procedures.

Log In, Mystery Guest

Sometimes, when Windows starts up, it needs to know who you are. You need a name and a password, which were probably set up when you first used Windows.

You log in (or log on—I don't know the difference) in the logon dialog box, as shown in Figure 1.1.

▶ **If you see the logon dialog box, type your password.**

▶ **Click OK to start using Windows.**

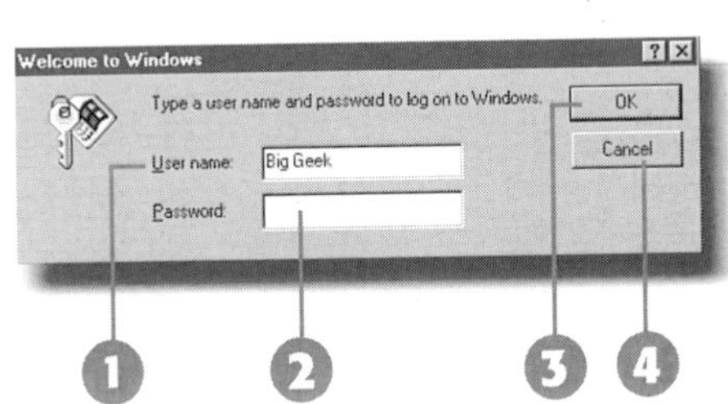

Figure 1.1
The logon dialog box.

1. Who you are.
2. Type your password here.
3. Start using Windows.
4. Start using Windows.

- If you don't see the logon box, you don't need to log on!
- If you type an incorrect password, Windows doesn't let you in! You can click Cancel, of course, and Windows lets you in. So much for security. (If you're into security, Microsoft wants you to use Windows NT.)

- If you're on a network and you click Cancel rather than log in, Windows doesn't let you make any new network connections.
- Chapter 8 has detailed information about logging on.

The Desktop

Figure 1.2 shows the main Windows screen, the *desktop*. Several important goodies are flagged for your viewing pleasure.

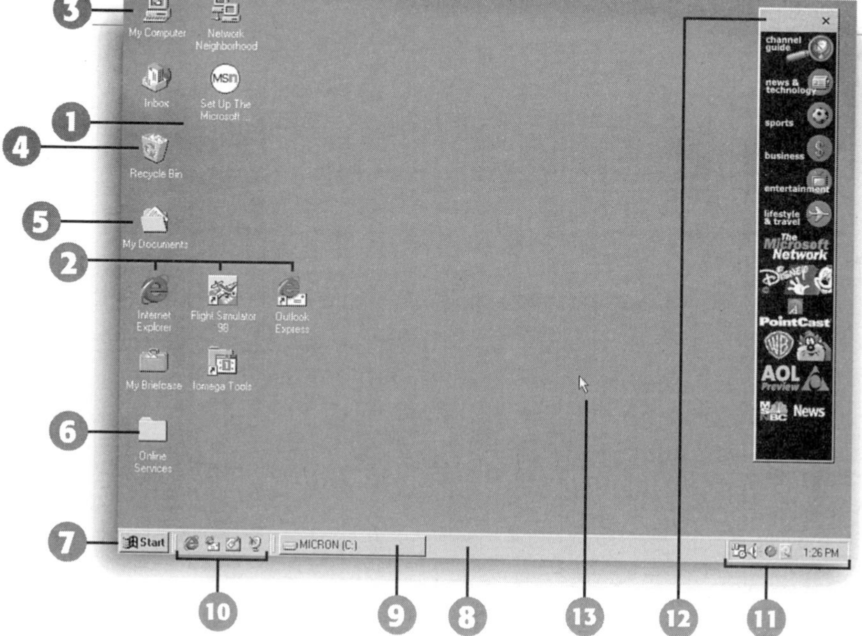

Figure 1.2
The desktop.

1. Wallpaper.
2. Icons.
3. My Computer.
4. Recycle Bin.
5. My Documents folder.
6. A folder.
7. Start Thing.
8. Taskbar.
9. Button on the taskbar.
10. Quick launch bar.
11. System tray.
12. Active Desktop Channel bar.
13. Mouse pointer.

The *desktop* is considered the main level at which you use Windows. Just about everything you can see or do on your computer can be visited from the desktop.

Other items on the desktop are discussed in various spots throughout this book. Use the index or table of contents to find something you're curious about.

You have much to be curious about in Windows.

Be sure that you find the Start button, which I call the *Start Thing*. It's the key to doing just about everything in Windows.

The Start Thing lives on the *taskbar*, which is another important doohickey.

Escaping from Windows

You have no real way to just quit Windows. Because Windows is your computer's operating system, quitting Windows is the same thing as turning off your computer. You can do it in one of several ways, depending mostly on what you plan to do after you're done with your computer.

Never just turn off your PC!

You can shut down Windows in several ways, and you can find all the methods in one place—the Shut Down Windows dialog box, as shown in Figure 1.3.

The following sections tell you more about the options in the Shut Down Windows dialog box, such as how and when to use them.

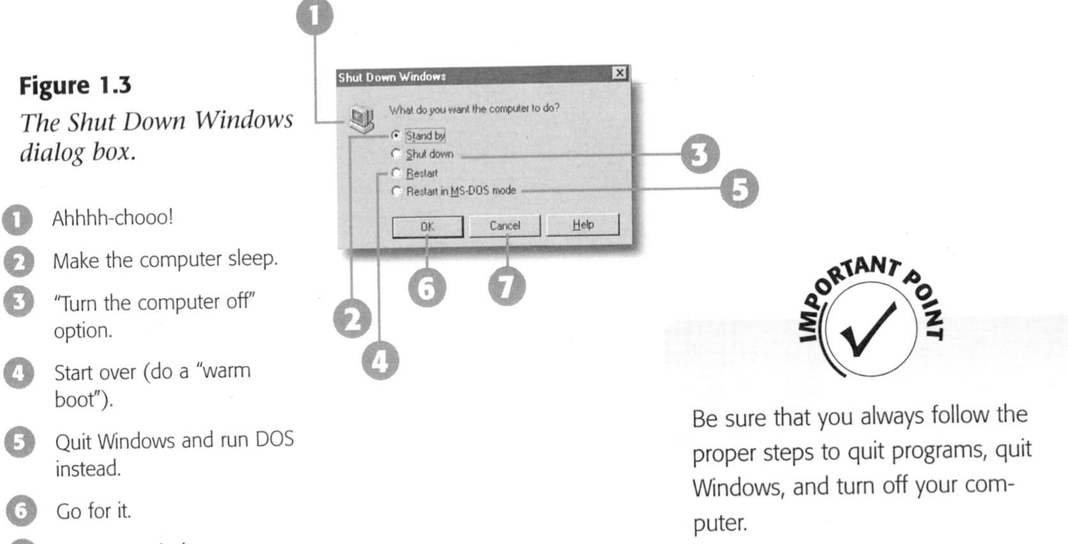

Figure 1.3
The Shut Down Windows dialog box.

1. Ahhhh-chooo!
2. Make the computer sleep.
3. "Turn the computer off" option.
4. Start over (do a "warm boot").
5. Quit Windows and run DOS instead.
6. Go for it.
7. Return to Windows.

Be sure that you always follow the proper steps to quit programs, quit Windows, and turn off your computer.

Putting Your PC to Sleep

Newer PCs come with the capability to "sleep." That is, they can go into a special low-power mode in which, technically, they're still on, although all the computer's electronics are, well, sleeping. Sleeping is not the same as turning the computer off because, although it looks off, it's still very much on.

I never turn off a computer unless I know that I will be out of town for more than a weekend. When I do get up and leave for a while, I put my PC to sleep.

▶ **Pop up the Start Thing menu.**

Click the Start button with your mouse, or press Ctrl+Esc.

▶ **Choose the Shut Down command.**

▶ **Click the Stand By item.**

This action fills the circle (the *radio button*) next to that option, which tells Windows that that's the way you want to shut down your computer.

▶ **Click OK.**

Zzzzz....

The screen goes blank. Your hard drives might warble to a smooth stop. Although you can't see it happening, the microprocessor has gone into low-power mode. Electricity still flows through the computer, which helps it, when you wake the thing up, remember what you were doing. Speaking of which:

▶ **To wake your PC up again, press the Ctrl key or wiggle the mouse.**

When the computer is awake again, everything looks just the way you left it.

If you see the screen saver, press the Ctrl key or wiggle the mouse again to get back into Windows.

Only a few of the newer PCs have the capability to sleep. If you don't see the Stand By option in the Shut Down Windows dialog box, your PC probably can't sleep. (It has insomnia!)

- A killer giveaway that your PC can sleep is the "moon" button on the computer box. Pressing that key also puts the computer to sleep—and wakes the system up after it has been asleep.
- You can "sleep your PC" by pressing the moon button on the computer box without having to use Windows Shut Down command.
- I like having my computer sleep because it gives me instant access to it. It takes too long to shut down and then turn on a computer.
- Another advantage of your computer's sleeping: You don't have to quit programs. You should save your work before you leave for the day, of course, but you don't have to quit anything.

Starting Over (Resetting, or the "Warm Boot")

Windows has to be restarted more often than you think. You have to restart it after adding programs or new software to help Windows work with your hardware or when your computer starts acting screwy and (honestly) you have no other way to get it to pay attention.

To restart or reset your computer, follow these steps:

▶ **Pop up the Start Thing menu.**

▶ **Choose the Shut Down command.**

The Shut Down Windows dialog box appears (refer to Figure 1.3).

▶ **Choose the Restart item.**

▶ **Click OK.**

Windows shuts down, closing open programs and windows.

If you have any unsaved documents open, Windows asks you to save them.

If you have any DOS programs or games running, Windows stops and asks you to close them properly. Then you have to repeat the preceding steps all over again.

After shutting everything down, Windows starts your computer up again, just as though you have turned it on for the first time.

- Resetting is often necessary when you install new hardware or software. The computer tells you to reset or does it on its own.
- Resetting is also known as a *warm boot*.
- Turning the computer off, waiting, and then turning it on again is called a *cold boot*. To fix some problems, you might have to do that rather than reset.

TIP

Resetting can sometimes fix strange bugs. For example, if you lose the mouse pointer or the desktop starts acting weird, resetting can fix it.

Never reset your computer by pressing the Reset button on the computer box. Always try the Shut Down Windows command first. Only if you cannot move the mouse and your situation seems hopeless should you resort to punching the computer's Reset button. Otherwise, you might lose information or damage important files.

Shutting Down

To turn off your computer, follow these steps:

- **Bring up the Start Thing menu.**
- **Choose the Shut Down command.**
- **Choose the Shut Down item in the Shut Down Windows dialog box.**
- **Click OK.**

As with resetting, Windows asks you to save any unsaved documents; if you have DOS programs open, the shutdown operation stops and you're asked to quit your DOS programs.

Eventually you see the screen that says "It's now safe to turn off this computer."

- **Turn off your computer.**

Switch off the power. Turn off all your computer goodies.

If you have a power strip, turn it off to turn everything off at one time.

If you have a UPS, you can just turn off the monitor and the computer box. It's a good idea to keep the UPS turned on so that its battery doesn't discharge.

Be patient. Sometimes it takes awhile for Windows to shut down, say two or three minutes.

- **You're done.**

Now walk away. Do something physical. Enjoy the nice weather. Breathe fresh air. Look up and see the pretty sky.

- Only when you see the message "It's now safe to turn off your computer" should you turn off your PC.
- Some computers might turn themselves off automatically. With these computers, you never see the "It's now safe to turn off your computer" message because the computer is already turned off. That's okay.

Chapter 2

Running Your Programs

Questions Answered and Thoughts Inspired

- Starting programs painlessly
- Toying with a window
- Quitting your programs
- Using a handy way to get at recently saved stuff

Windows is not the reason you use your computer. Really, who wants Windows? No, you bought your computer to do certain tasks, for which you also bought programs. It's those programs you want to use when your computer is on. This chapter shows you how that can happen.

Starting Any Old Program

Most programs you run are on the Programs menu, off the main Start Thing menu. Fishing a program from that menu is how you start using just about any program you run in Windows.

▶ **Bring up the Start Thing menu.**

Click the Start button to pop up the menu. Figure 2.1 shows you what's important and what's not.

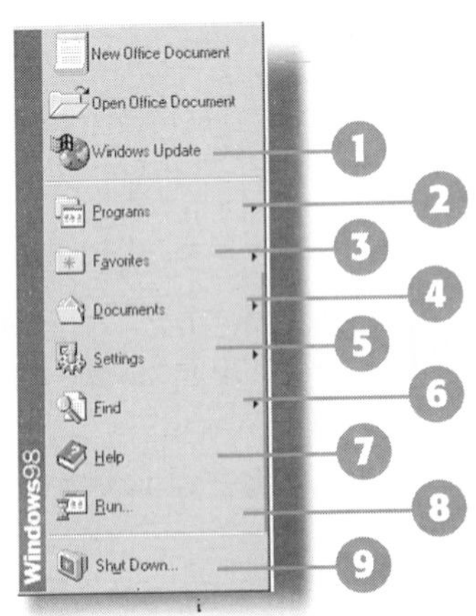

Figure 2.1
The Start Thing menu.

1. Programs sometimes appear here.
2. See the submenu for programs.
3. Favorite Web pages.
4. Recently opened documents.
5. Change settings and stuff.
6. Find files or programs or lost keys.
7. Get help, sometimes.
8. A boring way to run programs.
9. Options for leaving.

▶ **Choose Programs.**

Point the mouse at Programs, near the top of the menu. You don't have to click the mouse—just point. A submenu appears! Figure 2.2 shows what's up with the submenu.

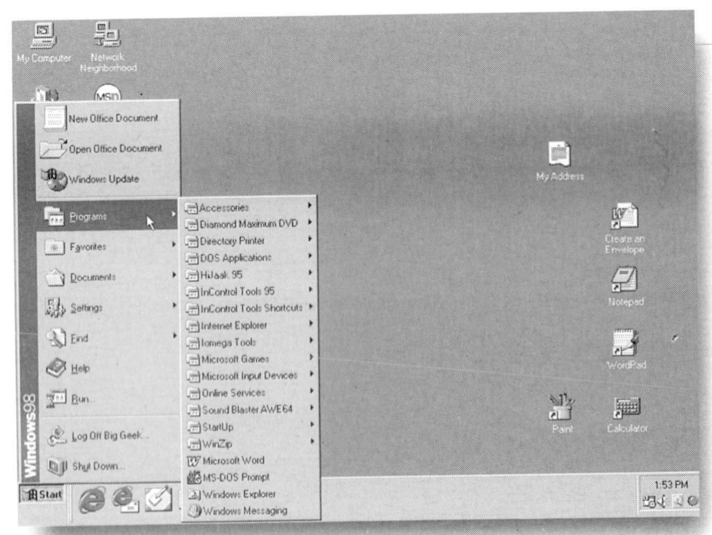

Figure 2.2
A submenu.

▶ **Look for your program.**

Now you look for your program. The submenu has two parts: The top shows additional submenus, and the bottom lists programs. If the program you want to run is right there at the bottom of the Programs submenu, click the program's name to start it.

If you don't see your program right away, you have to fish through the submenus. Fortunately, most of the submenus are named descriptively.

After you choose a program to run, the Start Thing menu and its submenus vanish, like the waiter in a restaurant after you order. Eventually your program appears on the desktop in its own window.

- Most of your favorite programs should be on the main Programs menu. If not, you can move them there by editing the Start Thing menu. Chapter 10 tells you how.
- If you don't see your program right away, look for it on one of the submenus.
- Press the Esc key to back up to the preceding submenu.

Be careful with the mouse! Those submenus are slippery; any subtle mouse movement causes them to flit in and out.

"I'll have the Number Four with chow mein."

Browsing the Submenus for the Calculator Program

Suppose that you want to start the Calculator program. The jet you're flying in is 150 miles from Denver, and the pilot says that you're landing in 20 minutes. About how fast are you going? Impress your seatmates with the answer to that trivia before the flight attendant beckons you to turn off your laptop!

▶ **Pop up the Start Thing menu.**

▶ **Choose Programs.**

▶ **Choose Accessories.**

The Accessories submenu appears, showing even more submenus and programs.

▶ **Choose Calculator.**

Click Calculator with your mouse. The Calculator program starts and displays itself onscreen, as shown in Figure 2.3.

Figure 2.3.
The Calculator.

1. Control menu.
2. Title bar.
3. Minimize button.
4. Maximize button.
5. Close button.
6. Menu bar.
7. Calculator window.

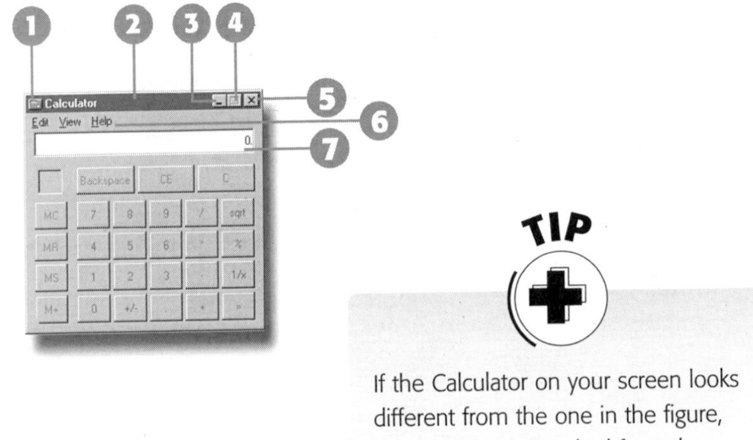

TIP

If the Calculator on your screen looks different from the one in the figure, choose View ➡Standard from the menu.

▶ **Enter** 150.

Use the mouse to click the 1, 5, and 0 buttons.

▶ **Click** /.

The / is the division symbol (the ÷ thing doesn't appear on your keyboard).

▶ **Enter** 20.

▶ **Click** *.

The * is the multiplication symbol. On a computer keyboard, X represents the letter *X*, not the multiplication symbol.

▶ **Enter** 60.

▶ **Click** =.

You have your total. The plane is traveling approximately 450 miles per hour. Better not stick your head out the window.

Keep the Calculator onscreen for the rest of this chapter.

- You can also enter numbers into the Calculator by typing them from your keyboard.

YAWN

Speed is measured in miles per hour. Dividing 150 miles by 20 minutes gives you a speed of 7.5 miles per minute. That value is then multiplied by 60 to get 450 miles per hour.

What Is and Is Not Important in a Program's Window

Figure 2.3 described the basic parts of any Windows program. All programs appear in a similar window, which means that after you figure out how one window works, you can work them all.

- *Title bar*—Use the title bar to drag the window to a new position on the desktop.
- *Close button*—Click this button to close the window.
- *Menu bar*—The program's commands are listed here. Click on a menu title to display the commands.
- *Window contents*—The bulk of the program. In a word processor, that's where you type. In a graphics program, it's where you draw.

▶ **Move the Calculator window around.**

Point the mouse at the Calculator window's title bar, and then drag the window to another spot onscreen. The window follows the mouse around like a homesick puppy. Release the mouse to keep the window in its new position.

In Windows, you can have lots of windows open at a time. Often you move a window to see what's beneath it.

The Toying-with-a-Window Tutorial

You can't do much with the Calculator program; its window is of a fixed size, and its contents are just buttons. A more typical program is Notepad, the wee li'l text editor in Windows.

Start Notepad by obeying these steps:

▶ **Pop up the Start Thing menu.**

▶ **Choose Programs ➡Accessories ➡Notepad.**

The Notepad window appears onscreen, as shown in Figure 2.4.

Any text you type appears where the insertion pointer is blinking.

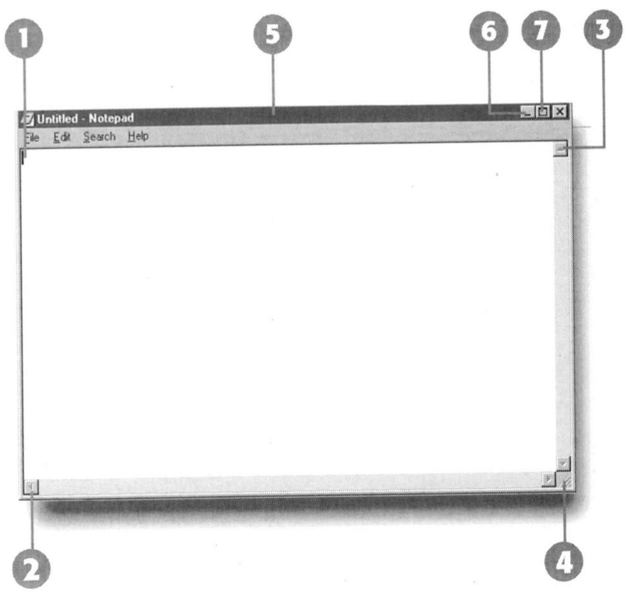

Figure 2.4
The Notepad window.

1. Insertion pointer.
2. Horizontal scrollbar.
3. Vertical scrollbar.
4. Drag here to resize the window.
5. Drag here to move the window.
6. Minimize button.
7. Maximize (and restore) button.

▶ **Type** Here I am in a jet plane whizzing along at **(with a space at the end).**

Use your keyboard to type the text *Here I am in a jet plane whizzing along at*

Make sure that you type a space after the word *at*. Use your keyboard's spacebar.

▶ **Resize the Notepad window to a tiny box.**

Point the mouse at the lower-right corner of the window, and drag up and to the left until the window is about the same size as shown in Figure 2.5.

Had there been more text, the scrollbars would be available to let you scroll up or down or left or right to see more text.

▶ **Click the Maximize button.**

This step makes the window fill the screen.

You should run most applications maximized because that method gives you more room to see what you're doing.

Notepad doesn't really need to be maximized, so just follow the next step.

The Restore button is available only when a window is maximized.

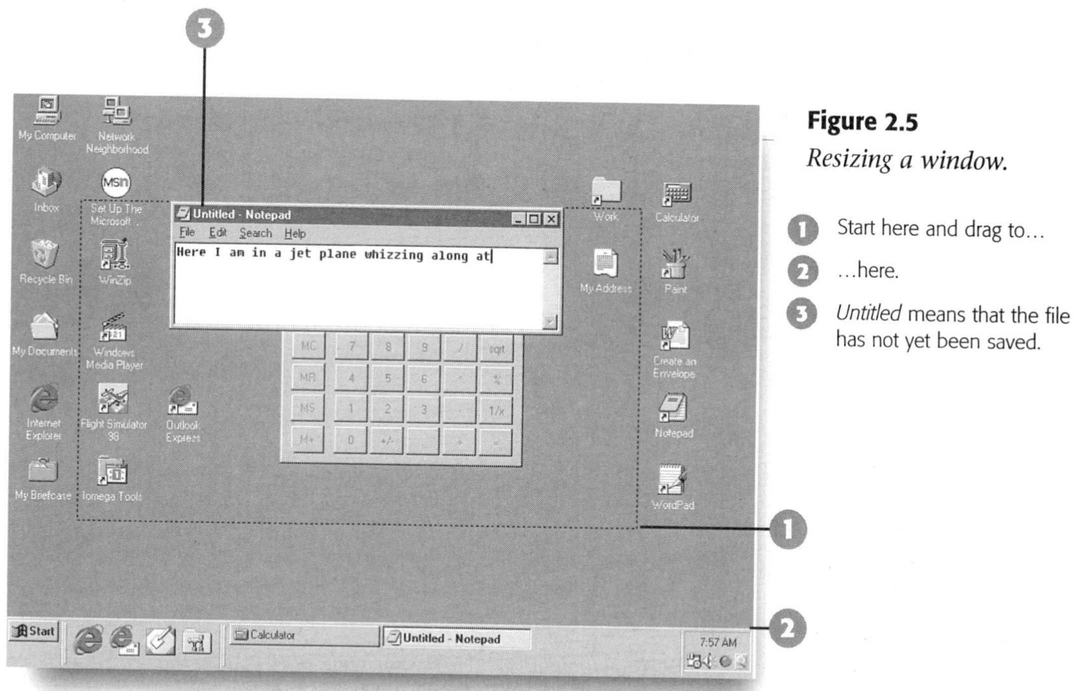

Figure 2.5
Resizing a window.

1. Start here and drag to...
2. ...here.
3. *Untitled* means that the file has not yet been saved.

▶ **Click the Restore button.**

The window resumes its previous size and location.

▶ **Minimize the window.**

Click the Minimize button to shrink the window to a button on the taskbar. Notepad is now tucked away, out of view. You didn't quit it. The program is still "running," and your text is still intact. You will visit the program again in just a few steps.

You don't really have to quit a program until you're done with it.

With the Notepad out of the way, you should now see the Calculator.

▶ **Choose Edit from the menu.**

Click the Edit option on the Calculator's menu bar, and the Edit menu drops down into view.

▶ **Choose Copy.**

Click the mouse on the word *Copy*. The value stored in the Calculator (450) is copied to the Windows Clipboard. You can now paste that value into Notepad.

▶ **Restore Notepad.**

Locate the Notepad button on the taskbar, at the bottom of the screen. Click it with the mouse. The Notepad window resumes its size and position onscreen.

▶ **Choose Edit ➡Paste from the menu.**

This step pastes in the value 450, which you just copied from the Calculator.

▶ **Type** miles per hour **(with a space at the beginning).**

Type the text *miles per hour*. You have to start that phrase with a space so that 450 doesn't butt up against the word *miles*.

▶ **Press the Enter key.**

Although you can't see all that you've typed, you can use the bottom (horizontal) scrollbar to view all the text. Better still, do this:

▶ **Choose Edit ➡Word Wrap.**

Now everything's tidy. It's time to save your work so that you have a copy of it to admire later.

▶ **Choose File ➡Save As.**

The Save As dialog box appears. The text in the File Name input box is highlighted. It says *Untitled*, so you need to name your document something else.

▶ **Type** Jet Trip.

Type the words *Jet Trip* in the File Name box.

▶ **Press Enter.**

This step saves your text to disk and ends the tutorial.

- After the file has been saved, you see its name, Jet Trip, appear on the window's title bar.

Use the Minimize button when you want a program out of the way but you don't want to quit. You can use the taskbar to switch between any number of programs you're using at one time. (See Part V of this book for more information about switching programs and cut-and-paste.)

- More information about the Save As dialog box is in Chapter 3.
- Files saved to disk can be opened later for editing, printing, or whatever.

Quitting a Program

You can quit any Windows program in several ways. The best way is to click the Close button, the little X, in the upper-right corner of just about every window. That thing works every time.

Close the Calculator window now with these steps:

▶ **Switch to the Calculator window.**

If you can see the window on the desktop, click the mouse on the window. That brings the window up front and ready for action, if it's not already.

If you cannot see the Calculator window, click the Calculator button on the taskbar.

▶ **Click the Close button.**

Click the mouse on the Calculator window's Close button. *Floop!* The window goes away.

Now close Notepad with these steps:

▶ **Switch to the Notepad window.**

▶ **Choose File ➡Exit.**

The File ➡Exit command closes most major applications. (It doesn't close everything, however; the Calculator program doesn't have a File menu.)

Had you not saved your work in the preceding section, a warning dialog box would appear, prompting you to save. Otherwise, the Notepad window vanishes from the screen. You're done.

Using the Documents Menu

Suppose that after finishing this chapter's tutorial, you realize that you want to add another line to the Jet Trip file. Like all files you've recently created or modified, that file appears on the Documents menu. Here's how to get back at it really quickly:

▶ **From the Start Thing, choose Documents ➡Jet Trip.**

The Notepad program starts again, this time with the Jet Trip file loaded and ready for editing.

▶ **Work on your document.**

Or, if you don't have anything to add, follow the next step.

▶ **Close Notepad.**

Now you're really done.

- The Documents menu holds the last 15 files you've opened.
- Some older DOS and Windows programs do not put their files on the Documents menu. When that happens or whenever you can't find a document on the menu, you have to start the program and open the document the old-fashioned way.
- Chapter 4 contains information about using the Open dialog box for opening files.

You can use the Documents menu to instantly access any file you've been working on recently. This technique is a great way to start your Windows day if you're immersed in some huge project.

Chapter 3

Saving Your Stuff

Questions Answered and Thoughts Inspired

- Basic file saving
- Using the Save As dialog box
- Saving with a different name
- Saving files as a different type
- Making a new folder for your stuff

Some dialog boxes you see all the time when you're using Windows. No, I'm not talking about the error messages. These main dialog boxes are associated with the main things you do in any program. Chief among them is the Save As dialog box, which you should be using all the time to save your stuff. This chapter covers that basic operation.

Hello, Save Dialog Box

Always save your stuff. Well, except for silly stuff, which you don't have to save. Considering that less and less time is available to create silly stuff, however, you probably create useful documents and such with your computer. And you want to keep them. To do that, you need to save.

- With a computer, saving is a central part of the creative process.
- You save documents as files on disk. That way, you can access the document later for reviewing, editing, or whatever.
- You save stuff with the File ➡Save command.
- The Ctrl+S key combination usually also saves stuff.
- Many programs sport a Save button, which you can click to save your stuff.

Save

The Save Tutorial

Writing is the main thing most people do with a computer. In Windows, you probably use a full-horsepower word processor, something like Microsoft Word or WordPerfect. Windows comes with a low-horsepower word processor called WordPad.

IMPORTANT POINT

Always save your stuff. Most people save only when they think that something is worth saving. Wrong! Save every few minutes or so; you never know when a computer will spaz out or cousin Jimmy will trip over the power strip.

▶ **Open WordPad.**

From the Start Thing menu, choose Programs ➡Accessories ➡WordPad. The WordPad window appears onscreen, as shown in Figure 3.1.

▶ **Type some prose.**

There's no point in trying the Save command unless you have something worthy of saving. If you're dry, type this text:

> **I have to reluctantly say that our mission has not been a success. Two miles from camp, Bradley stepped on a bee and went into anaphylactic shock. Dr. Jockson ran up to help, but he tripped and fell. The spoon in his iced tea gouged his eye, although he did not lose the eye. We tried to make camp, but Purvis parked the supply wagon too close to the fire and it burned, consuming all our food. We attempted to rescue the food, but by then the ammunition boxes caught fire, and everyone was ducking for cover. Then it began to rain. A vote was taken the following morning, ending our mission. We would have been back yesterday if it weren't for the stampede.**

You don't have to type all that—you can type something you made up yourself. Just make sure that you type something in the document window.

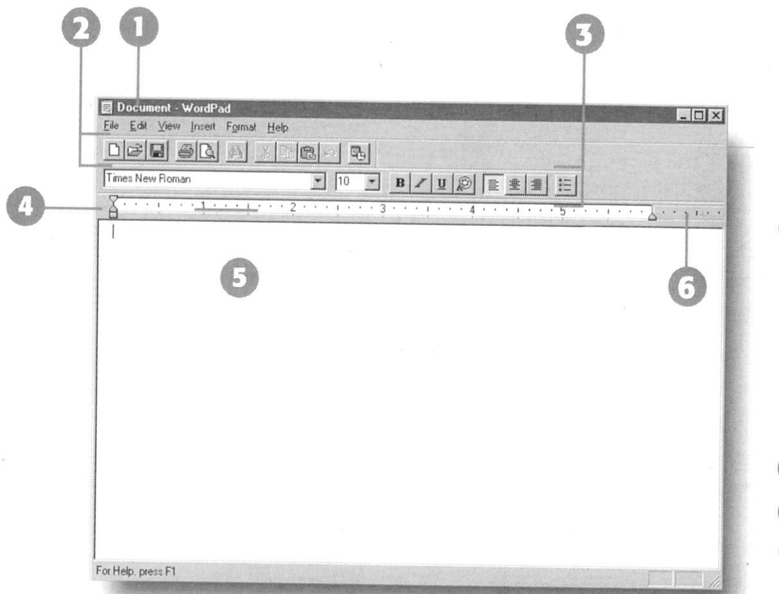

Figure 3.1
WordPad.

1. *Document* means that nothing has been saved.
2. Toolbar, with buttons for New, Open, Save, Print, and other commands.
3. Format bar (formatting commands).
4. Ruler.
5. Document window.
6. Resize the window so that you see the right margin on the ruler.

▶ **Choose File ➡Save As.**

The Save As dialog box appears, as shown in Figure 3.2. Your duty there is to assign your document a name.

▶ **Find a folder for your document.**

The Save As dialog box is showing you the My Documents folder, which is where WordPad likes to save its documents unless told otherwise. That's fine for this tutorial. For other projects, you doubtless want to save your stuff elsewhere, in a specific folder.

Folders help you stay organized.

▶ **Find *Document* in the File Name input box.**

In the File Name input box, you type your file's name. Right now it says *Document*. That's the name WordPad gives all its unsaved documents. (Notepad and Paint use *Untitled* instead.)

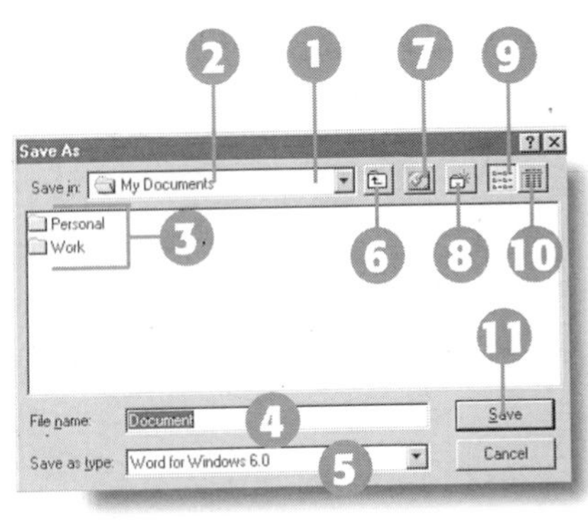

Figure 3.2
The Save As dialog box.

1. Choose another folder or disk drive from here.
2. The folder in which you're saving this document.
3. Contents of the current folder.
4. Your file's name.
5. The type of file you're saving.
6. Go "up" one directory.
7. Go to the desktop.
8. Create a new folder.
9. Icon view.
10. Detailed file list view.
11. Click to save.

You need to give your document its own name—hopefully, something more clever and descriptive than *Document*.

▶ **Type** Our Journey **in the File Name box.**

Type *Our Journey* in the File Name box. *Document* is highlighted, so your text replaces it.

If *Document* is not highlighted, press Alt+N. That keystroke focuses the attention of Windows on the File Name input box.

If you make a typing mistake, press the Backspace key to back up and erase.

▶ **Click the Save button with the mouse.**

Or you can just press the Enter key. This step saves the document to disk.

▶ **Notice the file's name on the title bar.**

That's your clue that the file has been saved.

Keep WordPad and this document open for the remaining tutorials in this chapter.

- After you save your document, you can continue working and saving, print, open or create another document, or quit the program.
- Continue to save your document as you work on it. The next section tells you how.

Save It Again, Sam

Get used to saving a document over and over. I save about every ten minutes or so. That way, if anything bad happens, I have a recent copy of my work saved to disk. Saving again is easy; Windows gives you several options for saving your stuff as you go:

▶ **Choose File ➡Save to save your document again.**

Or

▶ **Press the Ctrl+S key combination.**

Or

▶ **Click the Save button on the toolbar.**

Save all the time! Save! Save! Save!

▶ **Return to your WordPad document.**

As you continue the tutorial from the preceding section, you see that the Our Journey document needs a new paragraph. You have nothing to write this time; you just split the existing paragraph in two.

▶ **Position the insertion pointer at the end of the fourth sentence.**

Filenames Good, Bad, and Ugly

Windows allows you to name your files just about anything. You can use numbers, letters, spaces, and a smattering of symbols to creatively endow your document (or graphics image or whatever) with a proper name. Even so, the best filenames are short and descriptive.

Here are some good filenames:

Report 5/99

Cancellation notice

Umberto's restaurant review (yuck)

More useless charts for the meeting

Personal

Filenames can be in upper- or lowercase, they can start with a number or letter, and can be as long as 255 characters (although shorter is better).

You can use just about any symbol on the keyboard for a filename, although you cannot use the following characters:

" > * ? / : \ ¦ <

If you try to use one of these characters, Windows does not let you save the file; either you see an error message telling you what's wrong or Windows just becomes stubborn and doesn't save the file without telling you what you've done wrong.

Click the mouse after the word *eye* and the period. The cursor should be blinking at the beginning of the space between the fourth and fifth sentences.

▶ **Press the Delete key.**

This action deletes the space between the two sentences.

▶ **Press the Enter key.**

This action creates a new paragraph, starting with "We tried to make..."

▶ **Press Ctrl+S to save.**

The changes in your document are saved to disk.

- You don't have to rename the document when you save again; Windows saves your changes to the document already on disk.
- Had you not already saved the document, the Save As dialog box would appear. Because you've already given the document a name, however, the Save As command is not necessary.

Saving the Same File with a New Name

Some people save a document by using the same name over and over. Others feel compelled to save a document in drafts. For example, they might save a first go-through as First Draft or DOC01, the second draft, as Second Draft or DOC02, and so on. This method is easy.

▶ **Choose File ➡Save As.**

The Save As dialog box appears, which allows you to resave any document to disk with a new name. Figure 3.3 shows what the Save As dialog box should look like.

If you're following the WordPad tutorial, you see the file's current name, Our Journey, in the Save As dialog box.

▶ **Type a new filename.**

Rename the file **Failed Journey**.

▶ **Click Save.**

Rather than type over the original name, edit the text in the File Name text box: Press the Home key and type **Failed**. Then press the Delete key to remove the word *Our*, and you're left with *Failed Journey*.

The document is saved to disk under a new name.

Now two documents are on disk: The first is the original draft, Our Journey, and the second is a copy or second draft, Failed Journey.

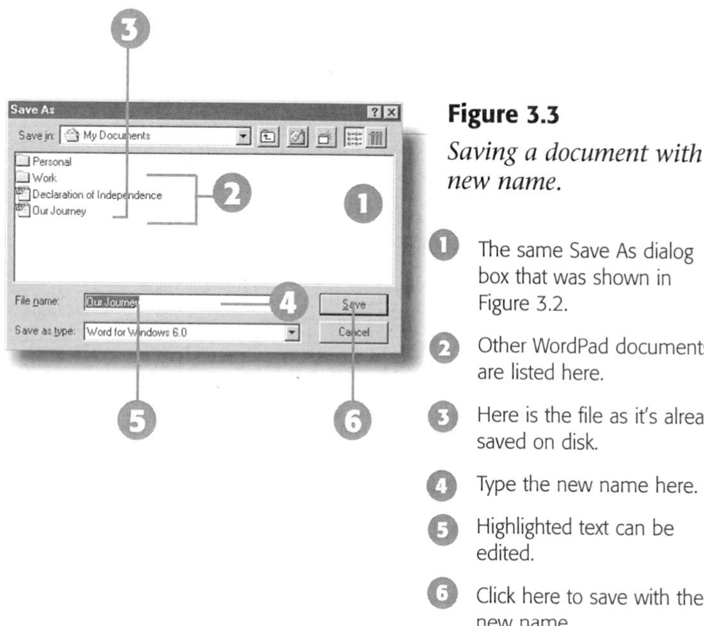

Figure 3.3

Saving a document with a new name.

1. The same Save As dialog box that was shown in Figure 3.2.
2. Other WordPad documents are listed here.
3. Here is the file as it's already saved on disk.
4. Type the new name here.
5. Highlighted text can be edited.
6. Click here to save with the new name.

Saving a File As Another Type

Different programs create different types of files. WordPad saves files, unless you tell it otherwise, in the Microsoft Word 6.0 file format. However, suppose that you're exchanging files with someone using MacWrite on a Macintosh. You have to save your document in a common file format, something both WordPad and the other guy's program can digest.

Most Windows applications enable you to save a document as another file type. You use the Save As dialog box to change the format to something else.

Continue this chapter's WordPad tutorial:

- **Summon the Save As dialog box again.**

Choose File ➡Save As from the menu.

- **Drop down the Save As Type list.**

Click the down arrow by the Save As Type drop-down box (where it says "Word for Windows 6.0"). You see the smattering of file formats WordPad allows you to use for saving documents, as shown in Figure 3.4.

Figure 3.4
File types for WordPad.

1. Select the format for saving the file.
2. Standard format for all WordPad documents.
3. A text format with formatting information included.
4. Plain text.
5. Plain text (again).
6. A format no one uses.
7. This window shows only those files matching the file type listed.

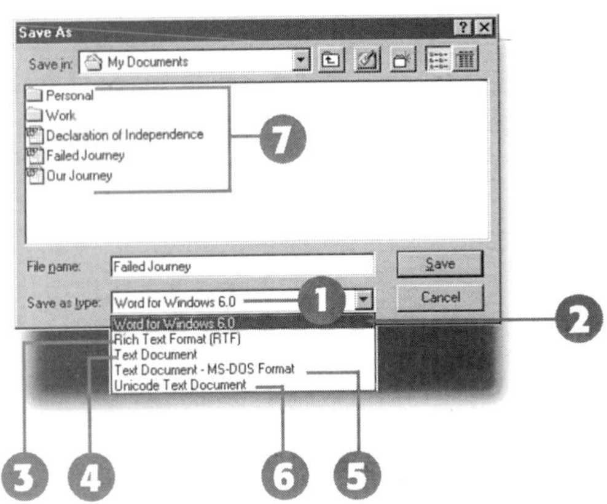

Suppose that someone on the Internet wants you to send him a copy of your file, but as a text message:

▶ **Choose Text Document.**

WordPad prepares to save only your document's text; no formatting information (bold, italics, justification, colored text) is saved.

Also, notice that the file list in the Save As window changes to show only those files that match the type you've selected (text files, in this case).

▶ **Click Save.**

A warning dialog box appears, explaining that the document will overwrite the one you already have on disk. Whoops! Better change the name.

▶ **Click No.**

It's always a good idea to enter a new filename when you change the file type.

▶ **Type** badtrip **as the filename.**

▶ **Click Save.**

More warnings! This time you're told that saving a text file removes all formatting. That's what you want.

▶ **Click Yes.**

The file is saved to disk as text only, which just about any computer anywhere in the world can digest.

Notice that the text appears in the WordPad window as one or two long lines. That's okay; text files are unformatted, which means that they lack right margins.

▶ **Close WordPad.**

Choose File ➡Exit from the menu.

- The only time you need to save a file in a specific format is when you're directed to do so, either by a manual, unconscious compulsion or under other circumstances, such as when you share a file with another human. This situation happens most often with graphics programs. For example, my painting software saves files in the RIFF file format, yet I must save my images in the GIF file format if I want to put them on a Web page.
- The file *format*, or type, normally used by a program is referred to as the native, or *default*, format. For WordPad, it's the Microsoft Word for Windows 6.0 file format.
- The Microsoft Word format is also known as the "doc" file format.
- The *RTF* file format is very common. It's a plain-text format, which means that any computer can read those files, and the RTF document retains formatting information. If you want to exchange files with someone who uses another type of word processor, RTF format is the best one to choose.
- Text formats save files as text only; letters, numbers, and other characters are saved, but no formatting information is saved.
- Honestly, I can't tell any difference between Text Format and MS-DOS Format. I just choose Text Format.
- *Unicode* format is used in some countries that have specialized alphabets, such as the Kanji alphabet in Japan. Normally, you never save anything in this format.

Saving a File in a New Place

A typical PC has tens of thousands of files stored on it. Some of those files are yours. Although finding them can be a challenge, Windows sets itself up with folders in which you can, fortunately, save the things dear to you. (All this stuff is covered in Part III of this book.)

Normally, Windows stores your documents, without specifying otherwise, in a folder called My Documents. Makes sense.

After working awhile, you might notice that the My Documents folder becomes a busy place. To cut down on the clutter, you should start saving your documents elsewhere, in new folders for specific projects, for example. All that can be done in any Save As dialog box.

On your way home from tap dance lessons, an idea hits you for the Great American Novel. You rush home and create your masterpiece:

▶ **Fire up WordPad.**

Choose Programs ➡Accessories ➡WordPad from the Start Thing menu.

▶ **Write your novel.**

Or just type a few random sentences because this section is a tutorial and there's no sense in wasting time being creative here.

▶ **Choose File ➡Save As.**

The Save As dialog box appears, allowing you to save your stuff. Because this project is a big one, you want to save your work in a *new* folder. No point in cluttering the My Documents folder with something *really* good.

▶ **Click the Create New Folder button.**

A new folder appears in the Save As dialog box's window (see Figure 3.5). The new folder is named New Folder. Although that's like naming your dog Dog, I don't dwell on that.

Notice that the New Folder name is highlighted, which is your clue that it can be edited. In fact, anything you type now becomes the name of the new folder. That's always a good idea because New Folder isn't very descriptive (aside from the obvious).

▶ **Give the folder a new name, such as** Great American Novel.

If you make a mistake, press the Backspace key to back up and erase. Then press the Enter key.

The folder now has the name Great American Novel.

▶ **Open the folder.**

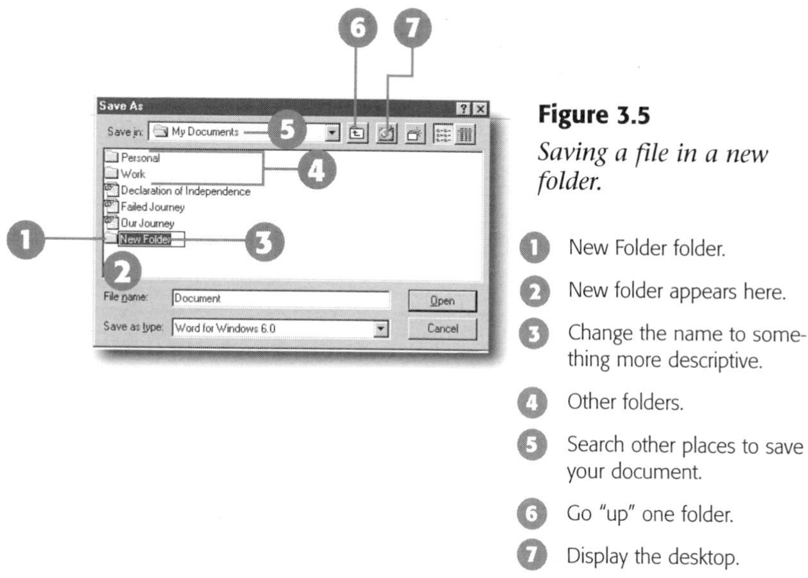

Figure 3.5

Saving a file in a new folder.

1. New Folder folder.
2. New folder appears here.
3. Change the name to something more descriptive.
4. Other folders.
5. Search other places to save your document.
6. Go "up" one folder.
7. Display the desktop.

Double-click on the folder in the Save As dialog box window. This step opens the folder, displaying its contents. Now you're ready to save your file in the new spot.

▶ **Type** Chapter 1 **for the filename.**

Type it in the File Name text box as the name for your document, the first chapter in the next *New York Times* best-selling page-turner.

▶ **Click Save.**

The file is saved in a new folder on disk.

- It's a wonderful idea to put related files in the same folder.
- Part III of this book discusses folders and file organization in great depth.
- The rules for naming folders are the same as for naming files. See the sidebar "Filenames Good, Bad, and Ugly," earlier in this chapter.
- You can use other buttons and controls in the Save As dialog box to save your document anywhere on your computer, on any hard drive, on a network computer, or on the desktop.

Chapter 4

Opening Documents

Questions Answered and Thoughts Inspired

- Working the Open dialog box tutorial
- Opening a file of another type
- Using the Open dialog box to browse
- Using the Document menu
- Opening icons
- Cheating with the recent file list

When you save a document or file to disk, Windows carefully lays it out, giving the file a name and a pretty icon for you to remember it by. When you want to use the file again—to review, edit, modify, print, or whatever—you open it. This action loads the file from disk back into your program for reviewing, editing, modifying, printing, or whatevering.

Another term for opening a document on disk is *loading*. Although no Load command exists, you might see the word used in computer manuals and nerdy books.

- *Open* is the opposite of *save*. *Close* is the opposite of *open*, and *squander* is the opposite of *save*, but try to avoid falling into the illogical maze of computer semantics.
- Really geeky trivia: The original Microsoft Word program (for DOS) used the

command Transfer File Load to open a document on disk. Microsoft has come a long way.

Opening a File You Once Knew

As long as you're careful to save your stuff to disk, you can get at it again.

(The files mentioned in this chapter were created in the tutorials from Chapter 3.)

▶ **Fire up WordPad.**

▶ **Choose File ➡Open.**

The Open dialog box appears, as shown in Figure 4.1.

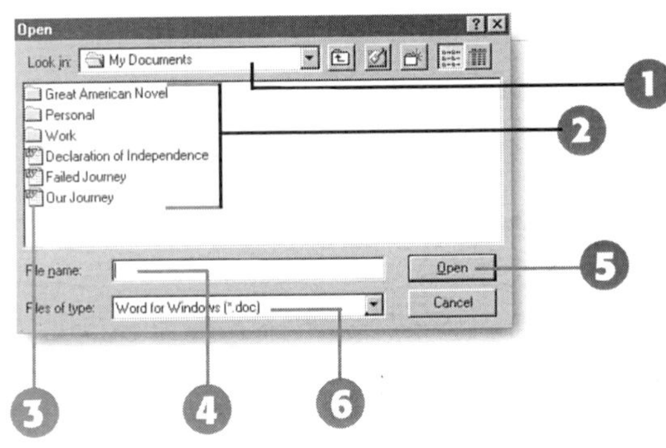

Figure 4.1
The Open dialog box.

1. Files and folders stored in the My Documents folder.
2. WordPad documents displayed.
3. Double-click any file to quickly open it.
4. You would be crazy to type a filename here.
5. Opens any selected file.
6. Files of this type are displayed.

WordPad automatically chooses the My Documents folder, displaying in the Open dialog box any WordPad files that might exist in that folder.

▶ **Select the file you want to open.**

For example, click the Failed Journey document. Click that document's name once with the mouse. It becomes highlighted, ready for action.

Use the vertical scrollbar to see more documents if they don't all fit in the Open dialog box's window.

▶ **Click Open.**

The document appears in WordPad, ready for reviewing, editing, printing or whatevering.

You can quit WordPad, if you want.

- Notice that opening a document requires less thinking than saving one.
- The common keyboard shortcut for opening files is Ctrl+O. This keystroke works in most Windows applications—but not all of them.

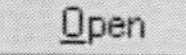

- A better shortcut is to click the Open button on the toolbar, if one is available.

Opening a File of a Strange and Alien Type

Suppose that you have this text file you just *need* to open in WordPad. (Work with me here.) Although WordPad can easily open a text file, you have to use the Open dialog box to find a file of that type. Here's how you do that:

- ▶ **Summon the Open dialog box in WordPad.**
- ▶ **Choose Text Documents (*.txt) from the Files of Type drop-down list.**

The Open dialog box displays only text files, as shown in Figure 4.2.

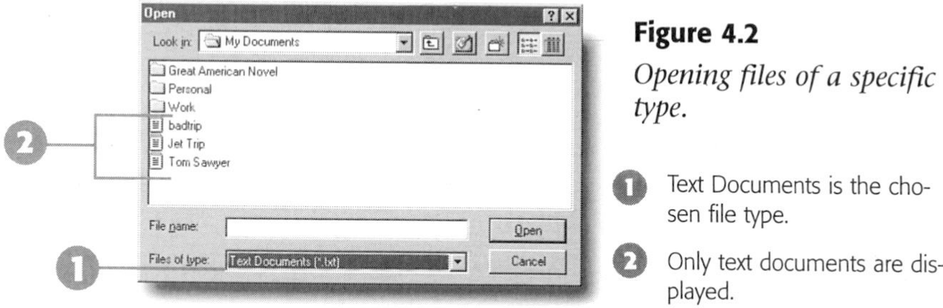

Figure 4.2

Opening files of a specific type.

1. Text Documents is the chosen file type.
2. Only text documents are displayed.

- ▶ **Find the file you want to open.**

Suppose that you find the file named Tom Sawyer that was shown in Figure 4.2. (On your computer you might or might not see text files. Work with me here.)

- ▶ **Double-click the document to open it.**

Double-clicking the filename is quicker than clicking the file once to select it and then clicking the Open button.

You can close WordPad if you want, even though I didn't say that this was a tutorial.

- Some text files are in the C:\Windows folder, although nothing as interesting as the Tom Sawyer file.
- On the Internet, visit `http://www.literature.org/` for interesting text files, now out of copyright, from famous authors.

- Not every program can read every file format. If the format you want isn't listed in the Files of Type drop-down list, you either are out of luck or must use some other application to read the file.
- The WordPad format bar and ruler don't appear when you edit or create plain-text documents. You can, however, see those items if you choose them from the View menu.

Most Windows programs remember which file type has been opened and automatically saves the file again as that type. If you want to save the file as another type (for example, to save a text document as a WordPad document), choose that type from the Save As dialog box.

Browsing for a File

You can use the Open dialog box to visit various disk drives or folders anywhere on your computer—or even on network computers. This process is known as *browsing*. The Browse dialog box is, in fact, essentially the same as the Open dialog box, except that the Browse dialog box is used to find program files.

The Search for Tips

Microsoft includes a file named TIPS with every version of Windows 98 it sells. The file is in the Windows folder on your computer's drive C. Here's how you can read that file by using WordPad:

▶ **Start WordPad.**

▶ **Choose File ➡Open.**

The Open dialog box appears.

▶ **Choose Text Documents (*.txt) from the Files of Type list.**

▶ **Click the desktop button.**

The contents of the desktop are displayed.

▶ **Open My Computer.**

Double-click the My Computer item to open it and display its contents.

▶ **Open drive C.**

No matter what its name, drive C has `(C:)` after it. On most PCs, it's the second item in the list (see Figure 4.3).

Open drive C by double-clicking its icon.

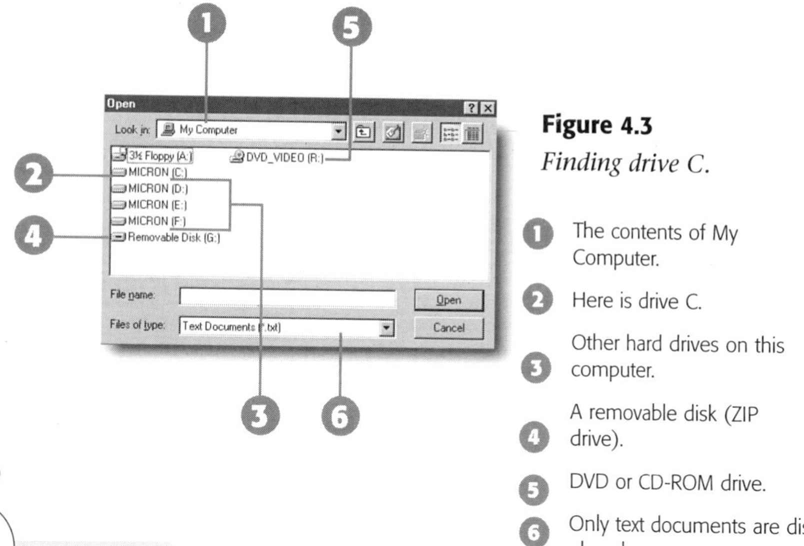

Figure 4.3
Finding drive C.

1. The contents of My Computer.
2. Here is drive C.
3. Other hard drives on this computer.
4. A removable disk (ZIP drive).
5. DVD or CD-ROM drive.
6. Only text documents are displayed.

TIP

A faster way to find the file is just to type **TIPS** in the File Name text box. That method is fast because you know the name of the file and it's easy to type. Most of the time, finding the file in the Open dialog box's window is simpler.

▶ **Open the Windows folder.**

Lots of files are in the Windows folder. Use the horizontal scrollbar to view the files lurking off to the right.

▶ **Open the TIPS document.**

Eventually, you should find the TIPS document. Double-click to open it.

▶ **Read the tips.**

Some are useful, some are strange, some might raise your eyebrows.

Not all the tips are for everyone. Some are for advanced Windows users or people with specific hardware. *Everything* listed in there, in fact, should be in a manual—if Microsoft ever decides to print one again.

▶ **Close WordPad when you're done.**

- Opening any folder in the Open dialog box displays the contents of that folder.
- To see the contents of the preceding ("parent") folder, click the Up One Level button.

A Faster Way (The Look In List)

Using the Open dialog box to find a document is called browsing. Browsing is okay for finding something when you don't know where it is. If you do know where a file is, you're better off using the Look In list.

As an example, Windows stores a bunch of graphics files in its own Windows folder. Here's how you can peruse them:

▶ **Open Paint.**

You can find the Windows painting program off the Start Thing menu, by choosing Programs ➡Accessories ➡Paint.

▶ **Maximize Paint.**

Click the Maximize button in the window's upper-right corner. It's easier to see the images when Paint bursts out to full-screen size.

▶ **Choose File ➡Open.**

The Open dialog box appears.

▶ **Choose drive C from the Look In list.**

Click the down arrow on the Look In drop-down list to display its contents (see Figure 4.4). Choose drive C: from that list.

▶ **Open the Windows folder.**

Double-click the Windows folder icon in the Open dialog box. Lo, the Open dialog box displays a whole lista graphics files.

You have to use the horizontal scrollbar to see the files; lots of subfolders are in the Windows folder.

▶ **Open the Clouds file.**

Find Clouds in the list, and double-click its icon to open the file. You see one of the Windows desktop wallpaper images, the one with white clouds against a blue sky—which is normal if you live on Planet Earth.

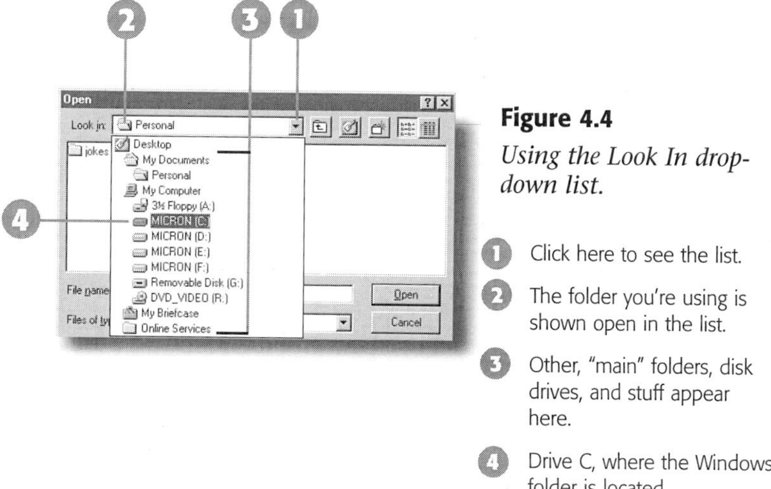

Figure 4.4

Using the Look In drop-down list.

1. Click here to see the list.
2. The folder you're using is shown open in the list.
3. Other, "main" folders, disk drives, and stuff appear here.
4. Drive C, where the Windows folder is located.

▶ **Quit Paint.**

Close the Paint program's window or choose File ➡Exit from the menu.

- Using the Look In drop-down list is faster when you know exactly where a file is located.
- Only major items appear in the Look In drop-down list: disk drives, the desktop, the My Documents folder, Network Neighborhood, and any folders on the desktop.
- One of the best times to use the Look In drop-down list is when you're in some folder deep, deep, deep down in your hard drive somewhere. It saves having to click the Up button a zillion times.

Don't mess with anything in the Windows folder. It's okay to open the graphics files there for a look-see, but don't modify the graphics files until after you've read through some of this book.

Opening Files Without the Open Dialog Box

The Open dialog box isn't the only way to open a file or document in Windows. In fact, if you haven't yet started your program, a faster way to get at your work is to open a document icon instead. This method works because Windows remembers which icons belong to which programs. Opening the icon is the same as starting the program and opening that file for editing.

Now, opening a document icon isn't always the fastest or most convenient way to get at your documents. It can be, though. The following sections detail these shortcuts that few people bother to remember.

(These examples assume that you've been working through the tutorials in this and the preceding chapters.)

Using the Documents Menu

If you're like me, you can't finish your work in one sitting. I'm too much of a fidgeter to get stuff done that quickly. Fortunately, Windows keeps track of the last several documents you've been messing with. Getting back to them is a snap, thanks to the Documents menu.

For example, to reopen the Clouds file mentioned earlier in this chapter, follow these steps:

▶ **Choose the Documents menu from the Start Thing.**

▶ **Choose Clouds from the Documents menu.**

The Paint program starts and automatically loads the document. At this point, you could busy yourself with work, if you were doing something other than working this tutorial.

▶ **Quit Paint.**

The tutorial is over.

- The Documents menu remembers only the last 15 documents you've opened.
- Some older Windows and DOS programs do not put the files you open on the Documents menu.
- Some files might be associated with programs other than those you used to open the files. For example, if you have Microsoft Word, it opens any WordPad documents you create. The reason is that Word takes ownership of the WordPad document file type (Word for Windows 6.0).

Finding a Document to Open

Opening documents in Windows is the same as starting a program and then opening that document in the program. This method is a time-saver:

My Documents Open the My Documents folder on the desktop.

▶ **Find the Failed Journey icon.**

You created this file in Chapter 3 by using WordPad.

▶ **Open the Failed Journey icon.**

Double-click the icon to open it. WordPad (or Microsoft Word) should start up, automatically opening the file and displaying it for review or editing.

▶ **Close WordPad (or Word).**

Lesson's over, point's made.

Using the Recent File List

Most programs (the better ones, at least) keep track of the last several documents you've worked on. Reopening a file is as easy as choosing it from a list.

▶ **Open WordPad.**

▶ **Drop down the File menu.**

Click on the File menu to display its contents. You see a list of commands, and near the bottom of the list you see items 1 through 4—the files you've most recently opened or saved (see Figure 4.5).

▶ **Choose Our Journey from the list.**

The Our Journey file is opened for editing. No Open dialog box needed, no browsing or hunting for a file.

▶ **Close WordPad.**

Thus endeth the tutorial.

TIP

Whenever I work on a project, I create a new folder and then paste on the desktop a shortcut to that folder. (Part III of this book explains how it's done.) Opening that folder displays a window full of the files I'm working on. Starting anything that way is a cinch; I just double-click whatever icon to open the file and get myself busy.

- A program's recent file list remembers the last four things you opened in that program, unlike the Start Thing's Documents menu, which remembers whatever you opened in *any* program.

Figure 4.5
The recent file list.

1. File menu.
2. The last four files opened or saved in WordPad.

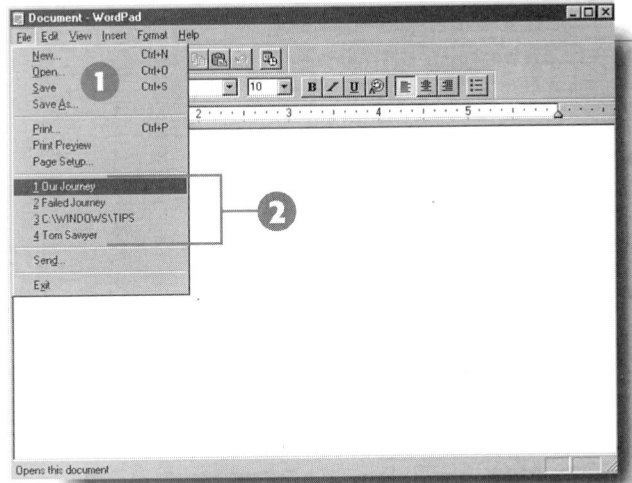

Some programs, such as Microsoft Word, allow you to set the number of items you want on the recent file list. In Word, choose Tools ➡Options, click the General tab, and use the Recently Used File List entries box.

Chapter 5

The Printing Chapter

Questions Answered and Thoughts Inspired

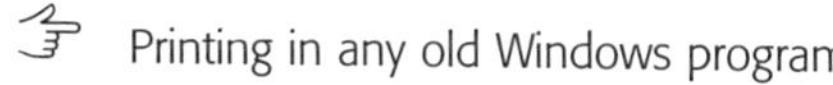

- Printing in any old Windows program
- Making more than one copy
- Doing an envelope in Windows

The computer supposedly ushered in the era of the paperless office. With everything on the screen, no one would really have a reason to print anything. Of course, this prediction was wildly wrong. (I still keep a notepad, card file, and calculator by my PC, proving at least to myself that the era of the traditional office isn't quite over.)

Everyone needs to print, and every application—even those that do 3D animations—has the capability to print. In Windows, all this printing is easy because the basic Print dialog box doesn't change from program to program. This chapter shows you the basics of the Print dialog box, plus a few other printing tricks. It's everything you need for the paperless office of the future.

Printing a Something-or-Other

Printing is almost as important as saving. Well, not really. Saving should be done all the time. Printing should be done only when you have something worthy to print. This philosophy is new for most people. (I have an old computer buddy who still prints rough drafts of his papers.)

The following tutorial drags you through the basic printing process using the Paint program that comes with Windows.

▶ **Start Paint.**

From the Start Thing menu, choose Programs ➡Accessories ➡Paint. The Paint program's window appears, as shown in Figure 5.1.

Figure 5.1
The Paint program.

1. Selection tools.
2. Eraser and Fill tools.
3. Color grabber and Magnifier tools.
4. Other drawing tools.
5. Color palette.
6. Left-click to pick foreground color.
7. Right-click to pick background color.
8. Draw the image here.

▶ **Create a silly picture.**

Figure 5.1 shows what I've drawn. Use the pencil or paintbrush tool to create something crude or interesting in Paint.

Color images print on a noncolor printer but not, of course, in color.

▶ **Save the silly picture.**

Give it the name **Silly Picture** in the Save As dialog box.

TIP

If you have a color printer, use some colors in your drawing. Choose colors from the color palette at the bottom of the Paint program's window.

Now you're ready to print.

▶ **Make sure that your printer is turned on and ready to print.**

Turn on your printer if it's not on already. Ensure that it has an adequate stock of paper and that it has enough printing ink or toner. (The printer warns you if it's low.)

▶ **Choose File ➡Print.**

The standard Print dialog box appears, as shown in Figure 5.2. Although some programs might use a subtly different Print dialog box, the general theme is the same.

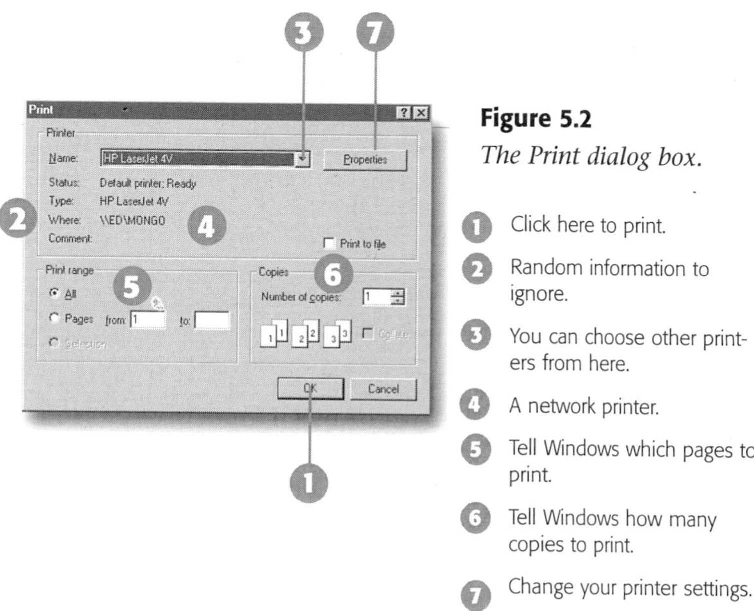

Figure 5.2
The Print dialog box.

The Print dialog box has way too much information in it. The settings there are handy when you need them, but now you don't.

▶ **Click OK.**

A "now printing" dialog box appears, although it might vanish too quickly for you to read it.

The printer whirs to life, sucks up a sheet of paper, and prints your masterpiece.

You're done, but keep the Silly Picture document and Paint available for the next section's tutorial.

- The Print dialog box keyboard shortcut is Ctrl+P.
- If your application has a Print button on the toolbar, you can click it to instantly print your document; the Print dialog box is not displayed.
- No, the Paint program does not have a Print button on its toolbar.
- I leave my printers on all the time. The newer printers have special power-saving modes that allow you to leave them turned on without wasting a bunch of electricity.

Printing Several Copies

Your masterpiece is just too brilliant not to share. Now that you have your own copy, why not make two more to send to your mom and best friend?

Continue from the preceding section's tutorial:

▶ **Choose File ➡Print.**

The Print dialog box appears.

▶ **Set the number of copies to 2.**

Find the Copies area in the lower-right corner of the dialog box. Type **2** in the Number of Copies box. You want to print two copies.

▶ **Click OK.**

Two more copies of the silly picture emerge from the printer, suitable for framing.

▶ **Quit Paint.**

Now that you have your wonderful artwork ready for distribution, you need to print an envelope in which to send it. The next section tells you the magic secret.

- You don't have to use the Print dialog box to print multiple copies. Heck, most of the time I forget about that option! Instead, just choose the Print command again to print a second copy. No biggie.
- Oh, by the way: The subject of stopping a printer run amok is covered in Chapter 6, "Digging Through Your Computer."

Generally speaking, print one copy first just to confirm that everything looks right. When you're satisfied, print your multiples as described in this section. That way, you won't freak when you notice the printer spewing out 120 Christmas letters with your spouse's name misspelled.

Printing an Envelope

Back in the early 1980s, when computer printers were coming into their prime, the following was a common statement: "Now the only thing you need a typewriter for is addressing envelopes." Things have, fortunately, changed.

Lots of envelope-printing programs are available, as well as envelope-printing features in most major word processors. Also, most printers have an envelope slot or feeder. Together, these features make the process of printing envelopes a snap. The following tutorial is really about changing the paper size and orientation for a printer, although it does show you how to print a simple envelope by using WordPad.

▶ **Start WordPad.**

The WordPad window appears onscreen, blank and beckoning for something to be written.

▶ **Type an address.**

For example, use my publisher's address:

Macmillan Publishing USA
201 W. 103rd Street
Indianapolis, IN 46290-1097

Or you can type your own address or any other address.

Don't worry about formatting or type size; just enter three lines of text, as shown.

▶ **Choose File ➡Page Setup.**

The Page Setup dialog box appears (see Figure 5.3). Although this dialog box doesn't seem like a printer dialog box, it has a great deal to do with where and how text is printed on the page.

You have to configure WordPad to print the address on an envelope.

▶ **Choose Envelope #10 4 1/8 x 9 1/2 In from the Size drop-down list.**

The #10 envelope is the most common size used in the United States. The preview changes to look like an envelope, although it's pointing the wrong way.

▶ **Choose Landscape.**

Ahhh. Better. The address is still not in the right spot, though.

▶ **Enter** 3 **for the Left margin.**

▶ **Enter** 1.75 **for the Top margin.**

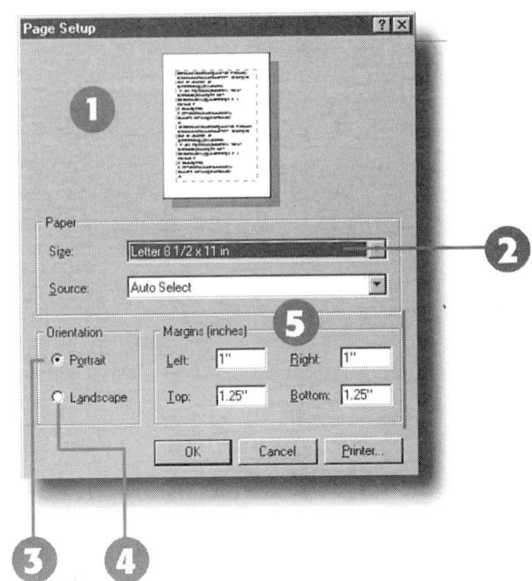

Figure 5.3
The Page Setup dialog box.

1. Preview of what the printed page will look like, kinda.
2. Choose paper size here.
3. Print tall (normal).
4. Print wide (sideways).
5. Set the margins from the edge of the paper.

The new margin values set the address more toward the spot where the people at the post office want to see it.

▶ **Click OK.**

Now WordPad knows that you're printing an envelope. The preview window in the Page Setup dialog box doesn't *really* show you what you're about to print, however. To see that, you have to use the Print Preview command.

▶ **Click the Print Preview button.**

Figure 5.4 shows what you might see. Although the envelope is close to being finished, the text needs formatting so that it looks a little less shabby.

▶ **Click Close.**

In WordPad again, adjust the size and style of your text.

▶ **Choose Edit ➡Select All.**

All the text in your document (well, the address) is selected.

▶ **Choose 14 from the Font Size drop-down list.**

▶ **Select the first line of text.**

▶ **Make it bold.**

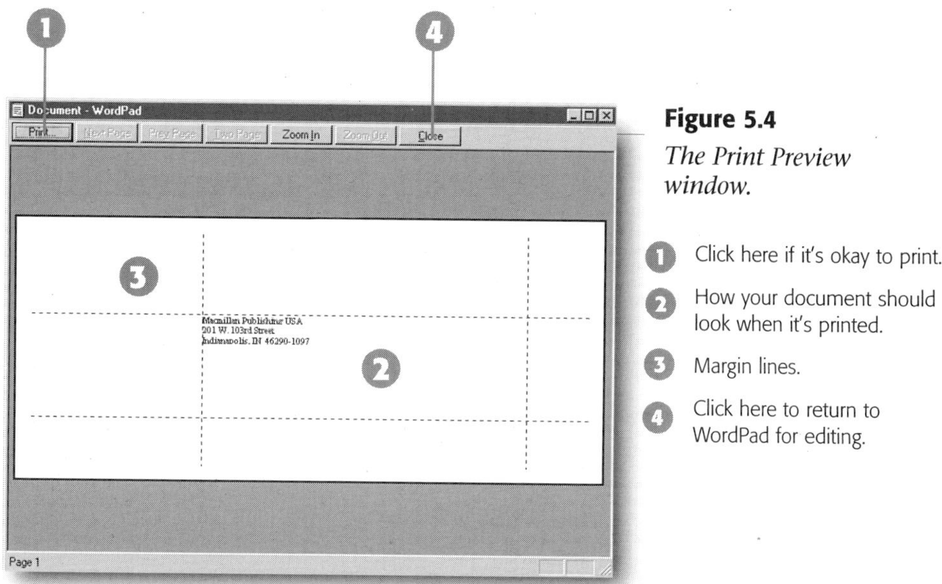

Figure 5.4
The Print Preview window.

1. Click here if it's okay to print.
2. How your document should look when it's printed.
3. Margin lines.
4. Click here to return to WordPad for editing.

Click the Bold button on the formatting toolbar or press Ctrl+B.

▶ **Click the Print Preview button.**

Now it should look much better—ready for printing.

▶ **Make sure that you have an envelope handy.**

Although this step seems rather obvious, if you don't have an envelope ready for printing, your printer might sit (and sit and sit), waiting for one to be inserted.

▶ **Locate the spot where the envelope feeds into your printer.**

The envelope should have a specific place to sit. You might have to open the front cover on some printers to find the envelope slot or feed tray.

▶ **Note how the envelope sits in the tray.**

You can stick an envelope into your printer in one of eight ways: four sides of the envelope times up and down.

▶ **Stick the envelope into the tray.**

▶ **Choose File ➡Print, and then click OK.**

Some printers might print your envelope right away, all neat and nice, as you expected.

Some printers might require you to press the On-line, Select, or Go button to print the envelope.

Some printers might not print the envelope correctly at all.

If the address prints fine but on the wrong side of the envelope or in the wrong orientation, try printing it again. This time, however, put the envelope into the printer in a different way: right side up or whichever orientation fixes the problem.

Most printers have a little picture on them that tells you how to stick the envelope into the slot or tray. The envelope's top flap goes in either up or down and left or right. If the envelope's flap is a dashed line, it means that it goes in face up; otherwise, you insert the envelope face down.

If the address is printed in the wrong spot on the envelope, adjust the margins from the Page Setup dialog box.

If the address is printed up-and-down on a left-and-right envelope (or vice versa), try sticking the envelope into the printer in the other direction.

Finally, if the envelope just doesn't print correctly, accept the fact that your printer can't print envelopes. (This statement is not a cop-out on my part: Some printers just can't print well on envelopes. You've done your best; your printer just isn't up to the task.)

▶ **Save your file.**

This step is optional, of course. You don't have to save the document; however, if you plan to print envelopes this way, this step can come in handy. Name the document **Envelopes.**

Whenever you want to print an envelope, open the Envelopes document, type the proper address, and print the envelope. You're set.

▶ **Close WordPad.**

- Most applications that have a Print command also have a Page Setup command. Sometimes Page Setup is available as a button in the Print dialog box.

After you get the envelope orientation down, tape the proper envelope-inserting instructions on your printer. For example, write "Envelopes go in face down, flap to the right." All my printers have instructions such as these.

- If the Page Setup command isn't available, you can select the paper size by clicking the Properties button in the Print dialog box.
- It helps to use the File ➡Print Preview command before you print your document to see how it will look—especially if you're messing with page sizes and margins.
- Another way to print envelopes is to print mailing labels first and then peel and stick the labels on the envelope. Most major word processors have the capability to print mailing labels. Or, if you want a specific mailing-label printing program (which is always better), I recommend Avery Label Pro.

Which printers do envelopes the best? I don't know. I can tell you, however, which printers are the *worst* for printing envelopes: the old dot-matrix printers. For printing envelopes, many dot-matrix models required a special (and expensive) envelope-feeding mechanism. Fortunately, those days are gone.

Chapter 6

Digging Through Your Computer

Questions Answered and Thoughts Inspired

- Browsing around with My Computer
- Reading your computer's disk storage statistics
- Visiting folders on the disk drives
- Using Windows Explorer
- Previewing the contents of a graphics file
- Opening a project window

The amount of information (files, programs, folders, documents, and all that) stored on your computer is massive. One of the main jobs of Windows is to ensure that all that information is easily available and stays organized. That role is handled by My Computer, which you can see on your desktop. This chapter tells you how the program works.

- *My Computer* is really Your Computer. It's represented on your desktop by an icon that shows you some basic goodies stored inside your computer.
- You use My Computer whenever you need to work with files or folders. It's an organizational tool.
- No, you don't have to organize your files and folders. Then again, you don't have to clean your house or take a bath, either.

- Gallant organizes his hard drive, and Goofus does not.
- My Computer has two modes of operation: *Window mode* and *Explorer mode*. Window mode is easier to use, although Explorer mode is faster when you know what you want. This chapter covers both methods.

Basic My Computer

My Computer lives as an icon on the desktop, right there with the Recycle Bin, My Documents, and other standard desktop icons.

▶ **Open My Computer.**

Double-click the My Computer icon to open it, displaying the hard drives your computer has and some special folders. Figure 6.1 shows the details.

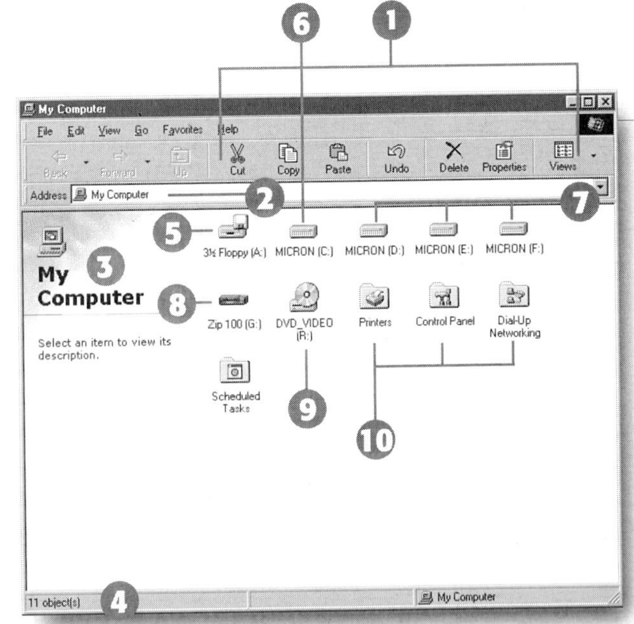

Figure 6.1
Stuff in My Computer.

1. Standard buttons.
2. Address bar.
3. My Computer contents window.
4. Status bar.
5. Floppy drive.
6. Main hard drive (C:).
7. Additional hard drives.
8. ZIP removable disk.
9. DVD or CD-ROM drive.
10. Special folders.

The contents of your My Computer window are probably different from what you see in Figure 6.1. For example, you might have only one or two hard drives, whereas four are listed in Figure 6.1. You might not have a ZIP drive, or you might have a second floppy drive. Every PC is different.

- The Printers and Control Panel folder you see in My Computer are the same ones you can get to from the Start Thing menu and its Settings submenu.

- You can also get to the Printers folder from inside the Control Panel folder. (Thank goodness it isn't anyone's family tree!)
- The Address bar is similar to the Look In drop-down list in the Open and Save As dialog boxes. In addition to using the Address bar to peek at a certain disk drive or network computer, however, you can also type a Web page address in it. (Read more about this subject in Chapter 7.)

Setting Things Up Just So

Rather than say, "This is the way I want you to do things," Windows gives you several mediocre options. Although that's okay, it can be confusing. For example, the My Computer window (the same one shown in Figure 6.1) can also look like Figure 6.2.

Microsoft just can't make up its mind when it comes to designing Windows.

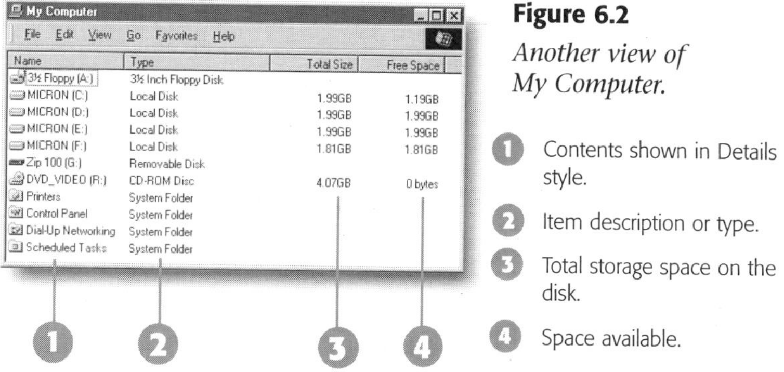

Figure 6.2

Another view of My Computer.

1. Contents shown in Details style.
2. Item description or type.
3. Total storage space on the disk.
4. Space available.

It's nice that Microsoft gives you those options. Still, I've found that some ways to view the contents of My Computer are better than others. To configure your system to match the way mine works, which is the way I figure works best and which is shown throughout this book, follow these steps:

▶ **In the My Computer windows, choose View ➡Large Icons from the menu.**

It helps, in addition to using large icons, to view the window contents as a Web page and to display the standard buttons, Address bar, text labels, and status bar. You choose each of these items from the View menu.

If an item is already selected, it has a check mark or black dot by it; selecting the item again removes it from the screen. Accordingly, do not select an item if a check mark is already there. If it has no check mark, however, choose the item.

- **Check to see whether As Web Page is chosen on the View menu.**
- **Check to see whether Standard Buttons is chosen on the View ➡Toolbars submenu.**
- **Check to see whether Address Bar is chosen on the View ➡Toolbars submenu.**
- **Check to see whether Text Labels is chosen on the View ➡Toolbars submenu.**
- **Check to see whether Status Bar is chosen on the View menu.**
- **Adjust the window's size so that the Views button is visible on the Standard Button bar.**

Drag the window's right edge to the right until you can see the Views button (refer to Figure 6.1).

If the Standard Button bar appears on the same line as the menu bar, drag the Standard Button bar down. Figure 6.3 shows you what to do.

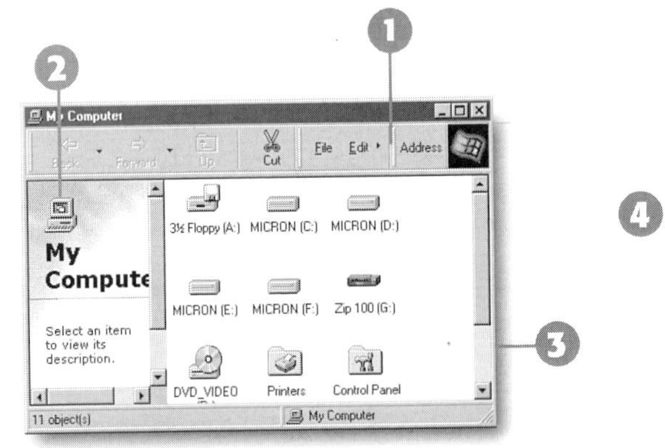

Figure 6.3
Adjusting the window.

1. Point the mouse here to drag a toolbar down.
2. Drag down to here.
3. Grab this edge to make the window wider.
4. Drag the window edge this way.

- **Choose View ➡Arrange Icons ➡By Drive Letter.**
- **Choose View ➡Folder Options.**

The Folder Options dialog box appears.

- **Choose Custom ➡Based on Settings You Choose.**
- **Click the Settings button.**

The Custom Settings dialog box appears.

- **Make sure that Open Each Folder in the Same Window is selected.**

If not, choose that item.

- **Make sure that For All Folders with Html Content is selected.**

If not, choose that item.

- **Make sure that Double-Click to Open an Item (Single-Click to Select) is selected.**

If not choose that item.

- **Click OK.**
- **Click Close to close the Folder Options dialog box.**

Selecting this command always rearranges the icons in the window to match whatever size you've resized the window. (It works with any window in My Computer.)

Now your system is set up in a way that I figure is ideal. You can always change these options later as you grow comfortable (or uncomfortable) with them. From now on, though, your My Computer window will behave the same way as described in this chapter and most of this book.

- The only option you might not want to select is Open Each Folder in the Same Window. Some people prefer to see a different window for each folder, although the screen gets cluttered after awhile.
- You might want to make more adjustments to the window's size, depending on how much real estate it occupies onscreen. The bigger the window, the more files and other information you can see at one time.

Getting Disk Information

An advantage of setting up My Computer as described in the preceding section is that you can get lots of information about an icon just by clicking it.

- **Click (once) on the C: drive icon.**

The icon has (C:) after its name, if it has a name. (Chapter 20 covers disk drives and their names.)

What you see looks sort of like Figure 6.4. Windows displays useful information about the disk drive.

- **Click (once) on the Printers folder.**

Windows displays on the left side of the window some information about the Printers folder.

Figure 6.4
Information about your drive C.

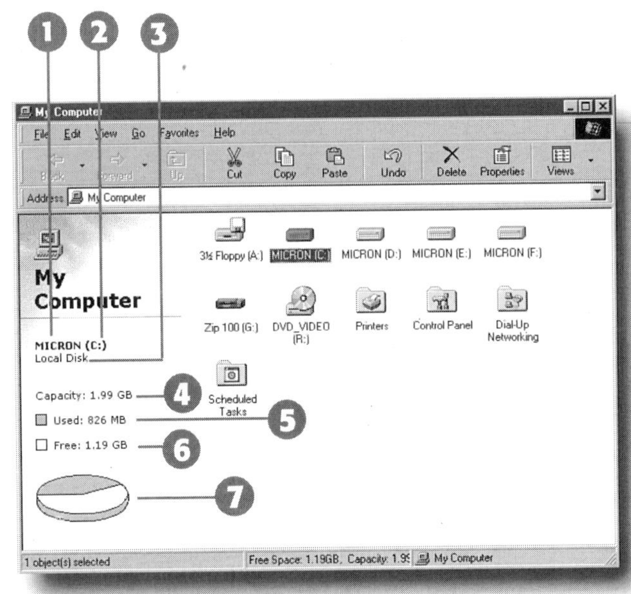

1. The disk's name.
2. Drive letter.
3. Type of disk (local, network, removable, or CD-ROM, for example).
4. Total disk capacity (2 gigabytes, for example).
5. Used disk space.
6. Available disk space.
7. Handy pie chart of disk use (not actual size).

You can click any item in the window, and Windows displays information about what it is or how it works. It might not all make sense to you, although it's certainly much more obvious than a silly little icon with a terse description.

Seeing What Lurks on a Disk Drive

To view the contents of a disk drive, you must open it.

▶ **Open drive C.**

Double-click the drive C icon to see which files and folders live there.

On drive C you find a score or so of files and folders, as shown in Figure 6.5. The files and folders you see aren't exactly the same, of course, as those shown in Figure 6.5.

▶ **Select the Command icon.**

Click the Command icon once to select it.

Information about the Command icon appears on the left side of the window. It's an MS-DOS application (a program), and you can see the date it was last modified and its size in kilobytes. It's interesting trivia but stuff that's not apparent or obvious from just looking at the icon.

The first folder on any hard drive—what you see when you open a disk drive in My Computer—is called the *root folder* or often the *root directory*.

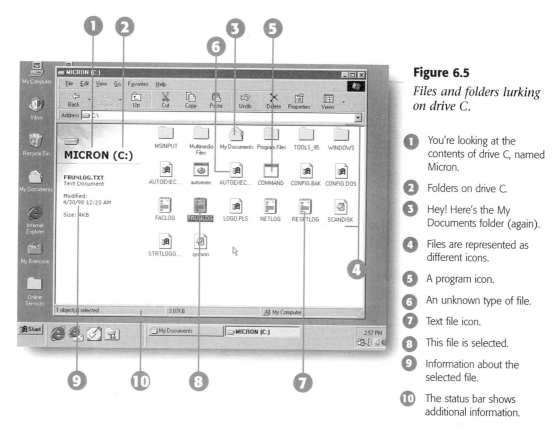

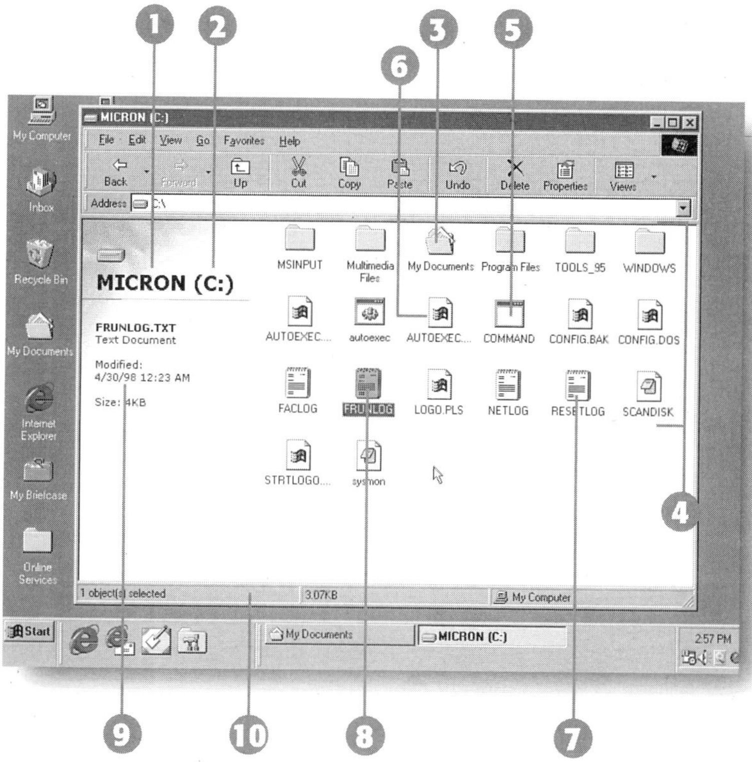

Figure 6.5
Files and folders lurking on drive C.

1. You're looking at the contents of drive C, named Micron.
2. Folders on drive C.
3. Hey! Here's the My Documents folder (again).
4. Files are represented as different icons.
5. A program icon.
6. An unknown type of file.
7. Text file icon.
8. This file is selected.
9. Information about the selected file.
10. The status bar shows additional information.

▶ **Unselect the command icon.**

Click in the My Computer window, but don't click an icon. Notice how the *status bar* (at the bottom of the window) displays information about the files and folders. The total number of *objects* (files and folders) is displayed. Because the "hidden" files are basically programs and other files you shouldn't mess with, they're not displayed in the window.

The size value shown on the status bar (in the center area) tells you the total size of all the files in the window. The value does not include the size of the files in any folders that are displayed.

▶ **Click the Up button.**

This step takes you "up" one level in My Computer, back to the main window.

Opening a Folder

Folders open just like disk drives do: To open a folder, you double-click it. The contents of that folder then appear in the My Computer window.

▶ **Open drive C.**

▶ **Open the My Documents folder.**

The contents of the My Documents folder are displayed in the window. Figure 6.6 shows the contents of My Documents on my PC.

Figure 6.6

The contents of the My Documents folder.

1. Contents of the My Documents folder.
2. More folders!
3. Files created or saved in the folder.
4. Paint document.
5. Text document.
6. WordPad or Microsoft Word document.

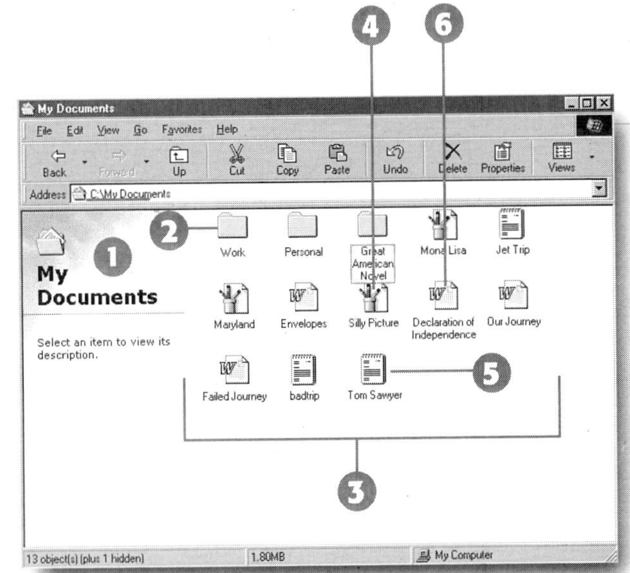

Suppose that you want to return to the My Computer window. Although you could click the Up button a few times, it's faster to use the Address drop-down list:

▶ **Choose My Computer from the Address drop-down list.**

The contents of My Computer are displayed again in the window.

To go back to the My Documents folder, you could open drive C and then the My Documents folder again—but you can use a faster way:

▶ **Click the Back button.**

The Back button returns you to the previously viewed folder, which is My Documents.

TIP

The easiest way to get to a main folder—a disk drive, My Computer, or even My Documents—is to choose that folder from the Address drop-down list.

If you click the down-pointing triangle to the right of the Back button, a list of recently visited folders appears. Choose any folder from that list to display its contents.

A list of recently visited folders also appears on the File menu.

- You can also start Windows Explorer by choosing Programs ➡Windows Explorer from the Start Thing menu.
- You can also start Windows Explorer by right-clicking the Start button and choosing Explorer from the pop-up menu. (This technique is the shortcut for editing items on the Start Thing menu, as described in Chapter 10.)
- In addition to the tree-structure thing, the Windows Explorer window has a Tools menu, which My Computer lacks.
- Unlike My Computer, Windows Explorer has only one window. Whereas you can configure My Computer to open a new window for every disk drive or folder you view, Explorer does not behave that way.

Locating a Specific File with Windows Explorer

An advantage of Windows Explorer over My Computer is that it lets you see how disk drives and folders are arranged in an overview style. That way, you can quickly dig deeply into folders on your hard drive, especially if you know right where they are.

▶ **Right-click My Computer.**

▶ **Choose Explore from the pop-up menu.**

An Explorer window appears.

▶ **Click the plus sign (+) by drive C.**

Clicking the plus sign opens drive C in the tree-structure thing and displays all folders available on that drive. Note that the contents of the right side of the window have not changed.

▶ **Click the + by the Program Files folder.**

This step opens the Program Files folder, displaying additional folders—lots of them.

The + by the Program Files folder changes into a – (minus), which means that the folder is open. Also, notice how the little folder icon next to Program Files is now open. Cute.

▶ **Click the Accessories folder.**

Selecting the folder displays its contents on the right side of the window, similar to what you see in Figure 6.8.

At any time, you can access files, open folders, or run programs from the right side of the Windows Explorer window. Remember that the Explorer works just like My Computer does and that anything you can do in one you can do in the other. The only difference—and the advantage—is that you see the tree-structure thing.

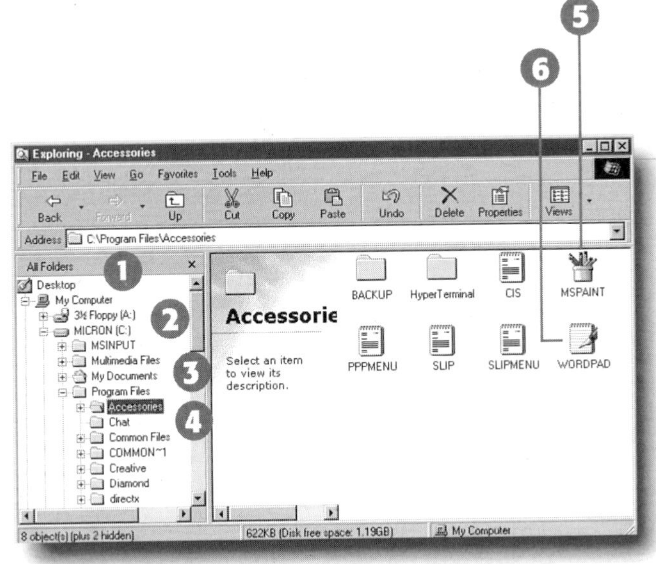

Figure 6.8
Contents of the Accessories folder.

1. You're looking in My Computer.
2. You're looking on drive C.
3. You're looking in the Program Files folder.
4. The folder you're looking at.
5. The Paint program; double-click to run.
6. WordPad; double-click to run.

▶ **Click the minus sign (–) by drive C.**

Clicking the minus sign by the drive C icon closes the tree-structure thing for that drive. The contents part of the window displays the root folder on drive C.

To get back to the Accessories folder, you could open the Program Files folder on the right side of the window. I believe, however, that you'll find the tree-structure thing handier to use:

▶ **Click the + by drive C.**

▶ **Click the + by the Program Files folder.**

▶ **Select the Accessories folder.**

Voilà! There you are again.

Now visit the My Documents folder:

▶ **Choose My Documents from the Address drop-down list.**

If the Address bar isn't visible in the window, choose the My Documents folder by scrolling all the way down the tree-structure thing.

▶ **Select the Silly Picture icon.**

Click the Silly Picture icon once to select it.

You should see a preview of that image below the My Documents title page, as shown in Figure 6.9. If a scrollbar appears, scroll down so that you can see the image preview.

(Alas, this trick doesn't work for plain text or WordPad documents.)

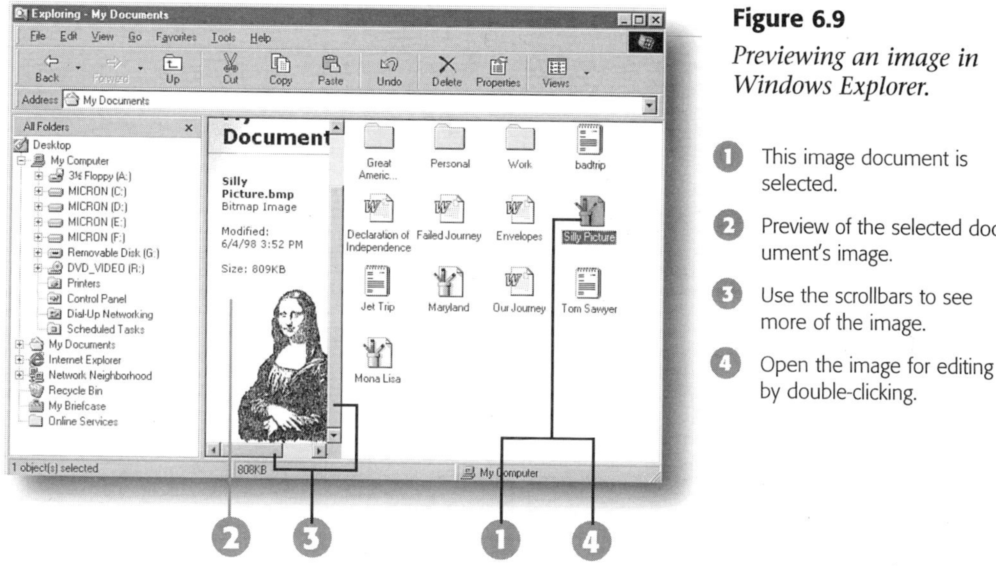

Figure 6.9
Previewing an image in Windows Explorer.

1. This image document is selected.
2. Preview of the selected document's image.
3. Use the scrollbars to see more of the image.
4. Open the image for editing by double-clicking.

- Clicking a plus sign opens a folder "branch" in the tree-structure thing.
- Clicking a minus sign closes a folder branch.
- Selecting a folder from the tree-structure thing displays the contents of that folder on the right side of the window.
- You can still open folders by double-clicking their icons on the right side of the window—although that's a great deal of clicking when you can just use the tree-structure thing instead.
- The image preview trick works in both My Computer and Windows Explorer windows. It works for the graphics files created by Paint and for JPEG and GIF format images (popular on the Internet).

Opening a Folder in Another Window

Whenever I'm working on a large project, I like to keep a window for the project's folder open and available. Browsing through My Computer as covered in this chapter just doesn't cut it. For browsing it's fine, although Windows has a better way to keep a window open if necessary.

Continue from the preceding tutorial (assuming that you're looking at the contents of the My Documents folder in Windows Explorer):

▶ **Right-click the Great American Novel folder.**

You created this folder in Chapter 3. Point the mouse at the folder and click the right mouse button—the button you normally don't press. A shortcut menu appears.

▶ **Choose Open.**

A new window appears. It's a My Computer window, and it displays the contents of the Great American Novel folder.

This method is how I typically work in Windows. If I were writing the Great American Novel, I would keep that folder available on the desktop so that I could access the files there. It's not a "you must do this" type of order. No, it's merely a suggestion for how to organize yourself while you work.

Because you're not working on the novel right now, put the Great American Novel window away by minimizing it.

▶ **Click the Great American Novel button on the taskbar.**

This step minimizes the window, keeping it out of the way for now.

▶ **Exit Windows Explorer.**

Close the window by clicking the X button in the upper-right corner.

- The window you open is another My Computer window, just like the one you opened by using the My Computer icon.
- You can run more than one instance of Windows Explorer at a time. Choosing Explore when you right-click on a folder, however, does not start another copy of Explorer; start Explorer as described earlier in this chapter, in the section "Starting Windows Explorer."

Chapter 7

Your Internet Orientation Chapter

Questions Answered and Thoughts Inspired

- Understanding basic Internet setup information
- Knowing what to look for in an Internet service provider (ISP)
- Using the Internet Connection Wizard
- Connecting to the Internet
- Disconnecting from the Internet

Oh, succumb to the hype. Join the Internet! It's the future. This is, after all, the communications age. (The information age ended with a hard drive crash in 1993.) This chapter is your Internet orientation. It covers background and setup and gives you a brief peek into the Internet to get you started.

What You Need to Get on the Internet

The Internet is not a computer, nor is it software. No, the Internet consists of thousands and thousands of computers all over the world. These computers send, receive, and store information. The draw of the Internet is all that information, which you can access instantly. To do that, you need five things:

- ✓ *A computer*—You should already have one.
- ✓ *A modem*—Your computer must scream across the phone lines at the Internet. Modems make that happen. The faster, the better.

✓ *Special Internet software*—You should already have this item; it's called Windows 98. No other software is needed. (If it is, you can use Windows' own software to grab even more software from the Internet. Neat-o.)

✓ *An Internet service provider (ISP)*—An ISP is a company that gives you access to the Internet. It supplies you with the phone number your computer calls to connect with the Internet.

✓ *Money*—Unless you have access through your business or school, you pay for using the Internet. The cost varies from a few dollars to several hundred a month, depending on which services you're getting. The average cost is less than $20 a month.

Of these five items, you probably need only two: the ISP and the money. Finding an ISP is easy. The money you have to find on your own.

- Setting up your computer to connect with the Internet isn't as tortuous as it was in the early days. Thanks to the Internet Connection Wizard, Windows makes it easy.
- Chances are that your PC is already configured to use the Internet; Windows asks you to set things up when it's first installed.
- You might already have Internet access through your company or university. If so, you don't have to worry about getting an ISP or the money (although, in a way, you're still paying for access—just not directly).
- *ISP* is one of many Internet acronyms. It stands for Internet service provider, the outfit your computer calls to connect you to the Internet.

TIP

I do not recommend connecting to the Internet through an online service such as AOL. Although AOL is popular, it's much better to have an ISP and access the Internet directly. (I don't even go into the subjects of busy signals and disconnects and junk email...)

Configuring Your PC for the Internet

You have a computer, and you have Windows 98. Now you have to confirm that your PC has a modem, and then you have to find an ISP and configure Windows to connect to that ISP.

If you are accessing the Internet from your office or school computer or you think that your PC is already configured for the Internet, please skip to the section "Confirming That Everything Is Okee-Doke," later in this chapter.

Checking to See Whether Your PC Has a Modem

A modem is not standard equipment on any computer, although most PCs are sold right from the computer box with modems already installed. If you're unsure, you can use one of two ways to check to see whether your PC has a modem installed.

- **Look 'round back, behind your PC.**
- **Locate the two phone jacks in the expansion slot area.**

If your computer has an internal modem installed, the computer has two phone jacks (plugs) on its backside. One of the plugs might even have a phone cord attached and plugged into the wall. If so, you're set.

The second way to tell (without looking behind your PC) is by using the Control Panel:

- **Open the Control Panel.**

From the Start Thing menu, choose Settings ➡Control Panel.

- **Open the Modems icon.**

The Modems Properties dialog box is displayed (see Figure 7.1). If you don't see any modems listed, your PC doesn't have a modem.

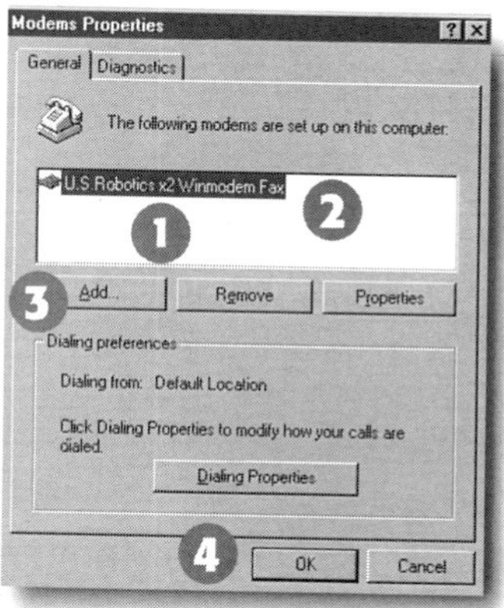

Figure 7.1
The Modems Properties dialog box.

1. Any modems you have are listed here.
2. My PC's U.S. Robotics modem is ready for action.
3. Click here if you add an external modem.
4. OK!

If you see a modem there, you're set. Make sure that a phone cable is attached to your PC and connected to the phone plug in the wall.

- **Close the Modems Properties dialog box.**
- **Close the Control Panel.**

If you don't have a modem, buy one!

Finding an ISP

Although the Windows Internet Connection Wizard can find an ISP for you, chances are that it doesn't list all that are available in your local area. For example, my hometown (population 30,000) has nine ISPs. (Nine!) None of them are listed when I use the Internet Connection Wizard to find an ISP.

My advice is to first search the yellow pages or ask at a local computer store or Radio Shack for a list of ISPs. Then shop for the best deal.

Find an ISP that offers the most service for the best price. The following items are a must:

- ✓ A personal email account
- ✓ Access to the Web (a PPP or SLIP dial-up account)
- ✓ Newsgroups
- ✓ Telephone support (so that you can get help)
- ✓ Lots of available phone lines (most ISPs have hundreds)
- ✓ A setup or "getting started" booklet

The following items are also good to have:

- ✓ Hard disk storage space
- ✓ Web space (for creating your own Web pages)
- ✓ Classes that teach you how to use the Internet
- ✓ Unlimited access

Unlike with your cable company, you have a choice when it comes to getting an ISP. Find a friendly one! Find the best price. Above all, find *people* you can deal with. If the folks who work there seem rushed or rude or self-absorbed, take your business elsewhere.

- ✓ I prefer an ISP that offers a "getting started" booklet.
- ✓ Free classes are a must.

TIP

My advice is to buy an external modem. (Although internal modems are cheaper, they're more difficult to install.) Buy the fastest modem you can afford; a model that runs at 56Kbps is just dandy. Also buy a serial cable to connect the modem to a serial port (COM1) on your PC. The modem should come with instructions on how to set everything up; Chapter 46 has additional information to help you.

- ✓ Unlimited access means that you can call at any time of the day and on any day of the week. It can also include unlimited connect time.
- ✓ Try to avoid ISPs that charge by the minute or hour or that limit your access to 20 minutes (or whatever) per month.
- ✓ If you cannot find an ISP in your area, check around where you live. For example, a nearby town or large city might have an ISP that offers access through numbers local to your area or even toll-free numbers.

TIP

Try to sign up for a flat monthly rate. That way, you can switch providers if the first one doesn't meet your needs. (The second provider I found offered me a great deal, and we negotiated a nice yearly contract.)

- ✓ If you can't find an ISP or detest paying long-distance charges, you need to use an online service, such as AOL. At least it gives you Internet access. (It also changes your configuration, as described in the following section. I do not cover that topic in this book.)

Running the Internet Connection Wizard

The Internet Connection Wizard configures Windows and your modem to talk with the Internet. To complete this task, you need some tidbits of information. Your ISP should provide you with this information:

- ✓ The phone number your computer needs to connect to the Internet
- ✓ Your Internet logon name
- ✓ Your Internet password
- ✓ Your email address (if it's different from your Internet logon name)
- ✓ Your email password (if it's different from your Internet password)
- ✓ The type of email server (POP3 or IMAP)
- ✓ The name of the incoming and outgoing (SMTP) email server (or servers)
- ✓ The name of the news (NNTP) server
- ✓ Your news server logon name and password (optional)
- ✓ The Internet Directory Service (LDAP) name, logon, and password (very optional)

You might need other information too, all of which you should keep in a handy place.

Don't try to understand any of this stuff! Lots of weird names, numbers, and acronyms are involved in setting up a connection to the Internet. You have to do this setup only once, so there's no point in stumbling over those things now. Just swallow, nod, and smile big as you work your way through this process. Type the names and numbers when the Internet Connection Wizard asks for them.

- **Choose Programs ➡Internet Explorer ➡Connection Wizard.**

The Wizard appears. Ho-hum.

I recommend getting a local ISP, which you should have already done.

- **Choose the option I Have an Existing Internet Account.**

It's the middle option.

- **Click Next.**

If you're using a local area network, you might see a dialog box warning you about your TCP/IP connection blah, blah, blah. Click OK if that happens. Your computer resets. Click OK again. Sorry for the inconvenience.

- **Choose Select This Option If You Are Accessing.**

It's the first one because you're using a modem to connect to the Internet (which I recommend).

- **Click Next.**
- **Choose Connect Using My Phone Line.**
- **Click Next.**

Ah, the infamous Phone Number phase, as described in Figure 7.2.

Enter the area code (if necessary) and phone number to connect to the Internet. Your ISP should have given you this information.

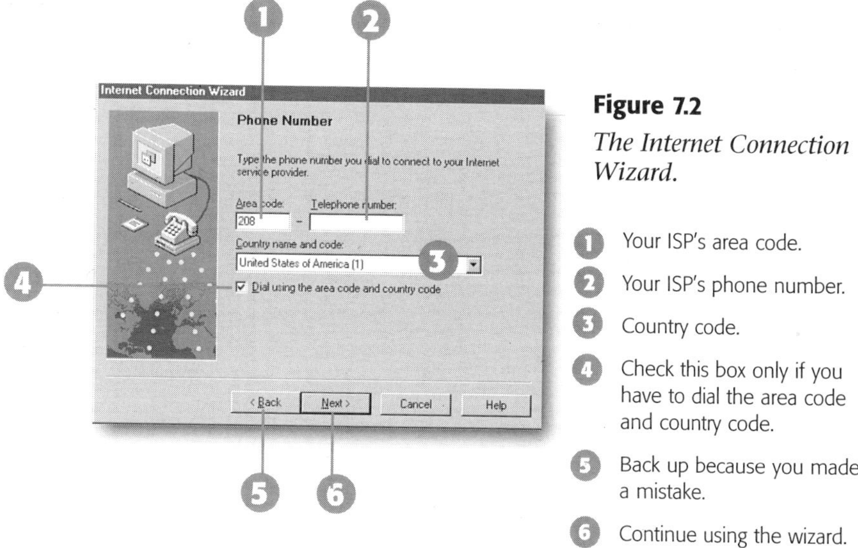

Figure 7.2

The Internet Connection Wizard.

1. Your ISP's area code.
2. Your ISP's phone number.
3. Country code.
4. Check this box only if you have to dial the area code and country code.
5. Back up because you made a mistake.
6. Continue using the wizard.

▶ **Uncheck the box next to Dial Using the Area Code and Country Code.**

Keep the box checked only if you have to dial the country *and* area code to connect. If you've followed my instructions, you should have a local ISP and not have to dial an area code.

▶ **Click Next.**

▶ **Enter your Internet username.**

▶ **Enter your Internet password.**

▶ **Click Next.**

In the Advanced Settings dialog box, make sure that No is selected. (Your ISP lets you know whether you have to mess with this area. Most likely, you do not.)

▶ **Click Next.**

▶ **Enter a connection name.**

For example, my ISP is named CompuTech, so that's what I type in the box. If your ISP is named CTS or something strange like that, type **CTS** (or **something strange like that**).

If you live in one of those places where you must dial an area code or you have to dial 1 when you phone someone across the street, you have to configure your modem's dialing properties. This subject is covered in Chapter 48, in the section "Long-Distance Dialing Hassles."

The name you type is used whenever you connect to the Internet. For example, Windows says, "Do you want to disconnect from CTS?" If you name your ISP connection Life Support, Windows says, "Do you want to disconnect from Life Support?"

Your Internet username and password might be different from your email username and password. Sometimes they're the same. Review the information your ISP gives you.

- **Click Next.**

The next series of steps lets you set up your Internet email account.

- **Click Yes to set up your email account and click Next.**
- **Choose Create a New Internet Mail Account and click Next.**

If you don't see this option, continue with the next step.

- **Enter your name in the Display Name box (if it's not there already) and click Next.**
- **Enter your email address in the Email Address box (if it's not there already) and click Next.**

Your ISP should have assigned you an email address.

- **Choose the mail server type.**

Your ISP should have given you this information.

- **Enter the incoming and outgoing email server names.**

Again, your ISP should have given you this information.

- **Click Next.**
- **Enter your email account name.**
- **Enter your email password.**
- **Click Next.**

You can enter an email account name in the Friendly Name phase of the Internet Connection Wizard, although I just leave whatever the computer has put there. Feel free, of course, to enter silly or misleading names if you want.

- **Click Next.**

The next few steps set up your Internet newsgroup (also called *Usenet*) accounts.

▶ **Choose Create a New Internet News Account and click Next.**

If you don't see this option, continue with the following step:

▶ **Enter your name in the Display Name box and click Next.**

This name appears whenever you post a news message on the Internet. It identifies you to others so that they can write back something like this: "Dan Gookin, you don't know squat about Warp Factor 2!"

▶ **Enter your email address in the Email Address box and click Next.**

▶ **Enter the news server name.**

Remember that this name and password might be different from your main Internet name and password. For example, you might be cute and log in to Windows as Lord Megabyte, although your ISP has given you the email account name WilburDoofus. Ensure that you use the correct name and password.

Your ISP supplies this NNTP name.

If your news server requires you to log in, click in the box next to the line My News Server Requires Me To Log On. After clicking the Next button, you're asked to enter the logon and password names for that account.

▶ **Click Next.**

Enter a friendly name if you want. I just leave this one as is.

▶ **Click Next.**

The next series of steps deals with an Internet Directory Service, which is an utterly new concept to me (and my ISP!), so I chose No.

▶ **Click Next.**

▶ **Click Finish.**

TIP

You can always come back later, rerun the wizard, and set up something like the Internet Directory Service.

- Believe it or not, you're done setting up your connection to the Internet on your computer.
- Your ISP might also supply you with a DNS name or server number. Windows no longer requires this thing, although other Internet software programs might need to know it. Better keep track of it, just in case.
- If you ever have to change any information, just run the Internet Connection Wizard again. For example, I recently added another news (NNTP) server by running the wizard again and skipping over the parts I didn't need to change.

You can access from several places in Windows the information you enter in the wizard: the Dial-Up Networking folder in My Computer, which contains connection information; the Internet icon in the Control Panel, which contains information about your Internet accounts and connection; and the Modems icon in the Control Panel, which contains general modem information. See the Index to find these items if you ever have to review your Internet settings.

Confirming That Everything Is Okee-Doke

Your computer gives you a good, telltale sign that the Internet Connection Wizard has done its job and you're ready to visit the world electronically:

- **Open My Computer.**
- **Open the Dial-Up Networking folder.**
- **Select your connection icon.**

Click the icon once to select it, as shown in Figure 7.3. Information about your Internet connection is shown on the left side of the window.

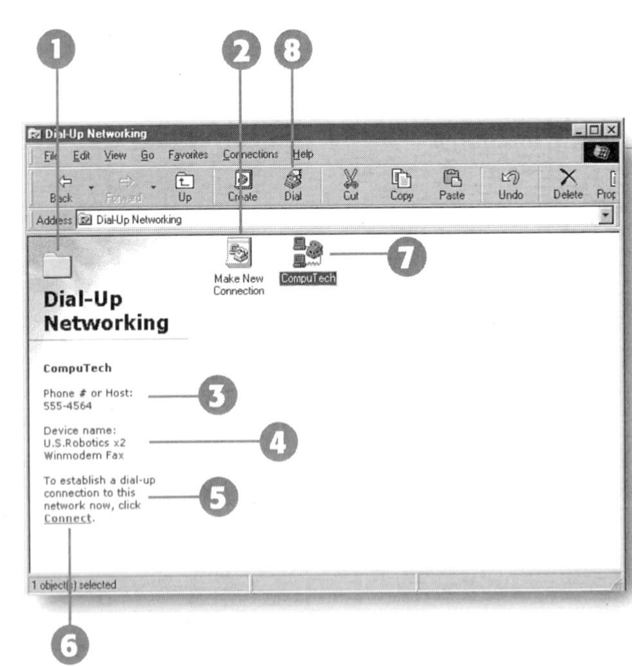

Figure 7.3
The connection icon is ready to dial up Mr. Internet.

1. Dial-Up Networking folder.
2. Connection icon.
3. Phone number.
4. Your modem.
5. Click here to connect.
6. Click here to connect.
7. Open this to connect.
8. You can click here to connect, too.

If you don't see a connection icon (refer to Figure 7.3), you either connect to the Internet in some other odd way or you have to run the Internet Connection Wizard to set things up. (I assume in this book that you connect to the Internet through a modem, which is done through the Dial-Up Networking folder.)

Connecting to the Internet

Connecting to the Internet is easy: Just run an Internet program or type an Internet address in an Address box. Cinchy.

▶ **Open the Internet Explorer icon on the desktop.**

The Dial-up Connection dialog box appears, as shown in Figure 7.4.

Type your logon ID and password, if necessary.

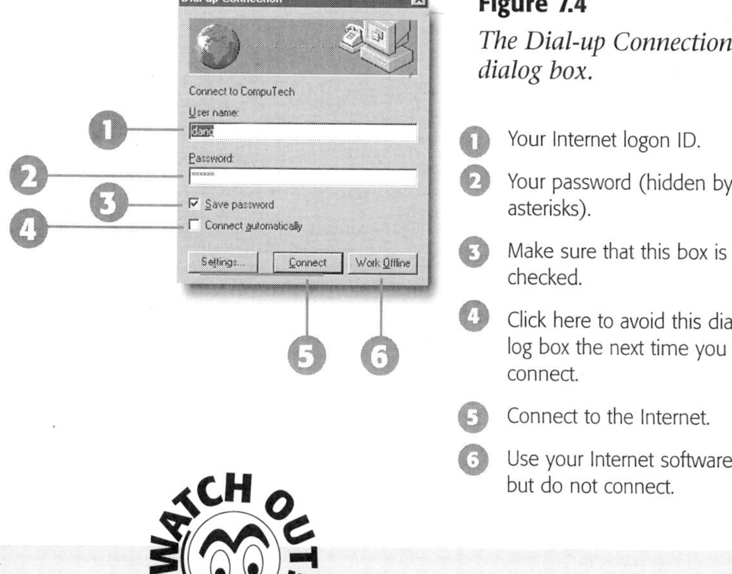

Figure 7.4

The Dial-up Connection dialog box.

1. Your Internet logon ID.
2. Your password (hidden by asterisks).
3. Make sure that this box is checked.
4. Click here to avoid this dialog box the next time you connect.
5. Connect to the Internet.
6. Use your Internet software, but do not connect.

WATCH OUT!

Putting a check mark by the Save Password option means that you don't have to type your password every time you connect to the Internet. It also means, unfortunately, that anyone who has access to your computer can log on to the Internet and pretend that he's you. Better be careful with this one.

Putting a check mark by the Connect Automatically option means that Windows connects to the Internet whenever you or some program requests online information. This option is a good one and not as devious as it sounds. Windows never dials up the Internet without your knowledge; a Connecting To dialog box always appears.

▶ **Click Connect.**

Windows attempts to connect to your ISP and the Internet. If Windows is successful, you see the online thing on the system tray on the taskbar (see Figure 7.5). If Windows cannot connect, it redials a few times before giving up. Just try again later.

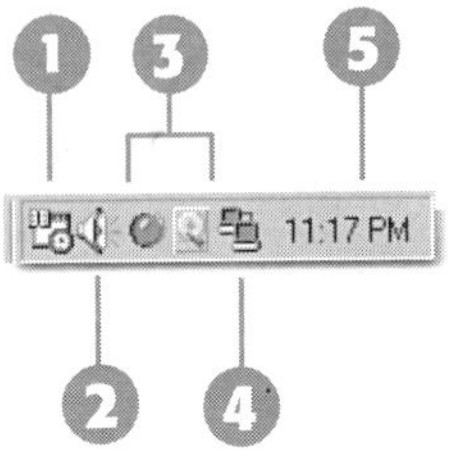

Figure 7.5
The online thing on the taskbar.

1. Task scheduler.
2. Volume control.
3. Other doohickeys.
4. Online thing (double-click to access).
5. Gads! It's late!

Now you're on the Internet, probably viewing the Microsoft home page on the World Wide Web. Whatever.

▶ **Close the Internet Explorer window.**

You might see a dialog box now, asking whether you want to disconnect or close your connection. Don't click Yes! In real life, you probably do, but this time click No. I want to show you how to use the online thing on the taskbar:

▶ **Double-click the online thing on the taskbar.**

The Connected to Your ISP dialog box appears, full of trivia.

▶ **Click Disconnect.**

You're offline, no longer connected to the Internet.

- Remember that your Internet logon ID and password might be different from other logon names and passwords you use in Windows and on the Net.
- The Save Password option in the Dial-up Connection dialog box might not be available if you're using a laptop PC or any computer used by more than one person.

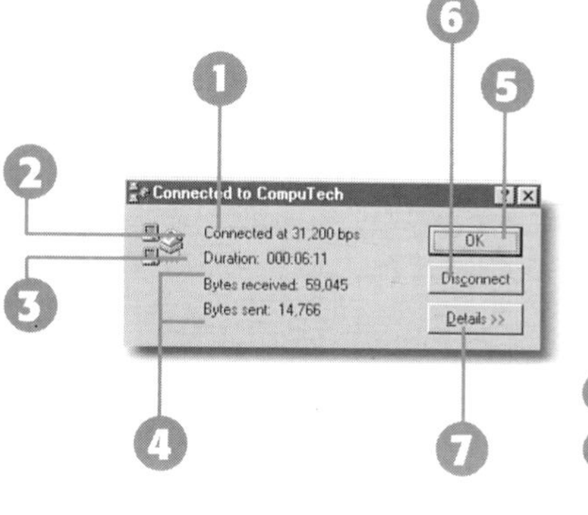

Figure 7.6
Disconnecting from the Internet.

1. Trivia!
2. The modem is talking at 31,200 bps (that's slow—must be the weather).
3. I've been online for 6 minutes.
4. Trivia!
5. Click to rid yourself of the dialog box and stay online.
6. Click to disconnect.
7. More trivia!

- You can also connect to the Internet by opening the ISP's icon in the Dial-up Networking folder in My Computer. The only advantage here is if you have several ISPs and want to connect to one in particular.

Keep an eye out for the online thing on the taskbar. If it's there, your computer is connected to the Internet. If that's not what you want, follow the preceding steps to disconnect.

Checking Out the Rest of the Internet

People primarily do two activities on the Internet: read email and browse Web pages. That's not the limit of what you can do, although it's what most people wander on the Net for.

Some people live only for email.

In Windows, you can read and compose email in the Microsoft Outlook Express program. You can browse the Web by using the Internet Explorer program, although you can also browse from any My Computer window or use the desktop as a Web browser. (Heck, if the mouse had a tiny video screen, Microsoft would let you browse with it too.)

More details about Outlook Express and Internet Explorer are provided in Part VII of this book, which goes into detail about the Internet and all the fun you can have there.

If you want to use Internet software but don't want to go online (to read old email, for example), choose the Work Offline command from the program's File menu. That action disconnects you without exiting the program.

- You can use programs other than Outlook Express and Internet Explorer to do your Internet duties. This book, however, covers only the programs that come with Windows.
- You can use Outlook Express to read newsgroups also.
- Windows comes with software you can use to create your own Web page on the Internet, which is covered in Part VII.
- The only software Windows does not come with is Internet chat software. Or does it? I'm not sure. Better check Part VII.

Yes, you can use Netscape to conquer the Internet. Windows is configured, however, to naturally use Internet Explorer rather than Netscape. Don't be surprised if Windows automatically starts Explorer whenever you want to visit the Internet, even if you've told Windows that Netscape is your preferred Web browser.

Chapter 8

Help Me!

Questions Answered and Thoughts Inspired

- Getting help for Windows
- Understanding the Help system
- Using the F1 key
- Finding help on the menu
- Using the ? button in a dialog box
- Learning the joys of point-and-shoot help

Believe it or not, Windows can be quite helpful. Computer programs are notoriously cryptic and confusing and don't offer help. You should appreciate any form of help, even if it's vague. And pointless. And written by a foreigner. Or a cyborg. Uh...

This chapter discusses the Windows Help system, which you can turn to in times of woe. The help that's offered isn't as good as the soothing voice of a friend or as appropriate as the wisdom of a computer guru, although it's better than nothing.

Windows Wants to Help You

Windows no longer comes with a manual. Instead, what's left of the manual is combined with the Windows Help system. After all, you need the manual to look up something you want help with, anyway.

For Windows itself, the Help system provides helpful information.

▶ **From the Start Thing menu, choose Help.**

Lo, the Help system window appears, as shown in Figure 8.1. This window is the same for all Windows programs, although the one you're looking at now is specific to Windows.

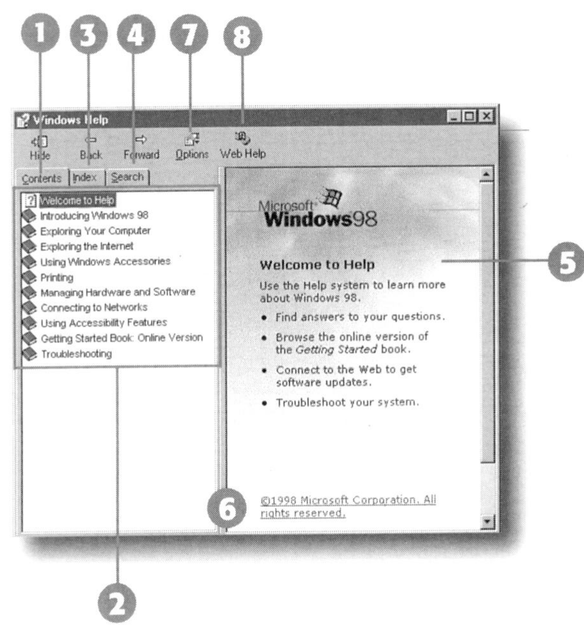

Figure 8.1
The Windows Help system.

1. Contents panel (similar to the manual).
2. Open these book icons and display more book icons, chapters, or text pages.
3. Index of all topics (use this option first).
4. Search for a word or topic in the Help system.
5. Help contents, which is where you see the Help information.
6. Click underlined links for more information.
7. Display a menu of additional options.
8. Venture out to the Web for even more help.

Suppose that you've grown annoyed with the sound the computer makes every time it starts:

▶ **Click the Index tab.**

If you haven't yet used the Windows Help system, you see the Preparing to Use Index for the First Time dialog box. A magic pencil writes secret messages in a book.

▶ **Type** sounds **in the text box.**

Type the word *sounds* in the text box below the Index tab. The list below the box highlights the word *sounds*, below which you see a half-dozen related topics.

▶ **Double-click the Assigning to Events topic.**

A Topics Found dialog box appears, which tells you that more than one topic is associated with that Help item.

▶ **Select the To Assign Sounds to Program Events option.**

▶ **Click Display.**

The right side of the window shows you the information you need to know.

If you click the underlined words *Click here*, the Sounds Properties dialog box appears, where you can change the sound.

▶ **In step 2 (on the right side of the screen), click the underlined word *event*.**

A pop-up window appears, explaining what the word *event* refers to. This feature is different from the *Click here* underlined text, which runs a program.

▶ **Click the mouse in the pop-up window to remove the window from the screen.**

How about some truly useful information:

▶ **Click the Search tab.**

▶ **Type** shortcut keys **in the text box.**

▶ **Click List Topics.**

Every instance of the phrase *shortcut keys* in the entire Windows Help system is displayed in a list. This information is handy.

Print all the shortcut key lists. The combinations are just too bizarre to memorize.

▶ **Select the topic Using Shortcut Keys for Windows Explorer.**

You have to scroll down the list to find this topic. When you do, click it once.

▶ **Click Display.**

The list of shortcut keys is displayed on the right side of the window.

▶ **Click the Options button on the menu bar.**

▶ **Choose Print.**

▶ **Click OK.**

The document is printed, giving you a handy list of shortcut keys.

▶ **Close the Help window.**

Getting Help Just About Anywhere

All Windows programs offer some type of help. Although the quality of help that's displayed varies, the methods for getting help are fairly consistent.

The Help Key on Your Keyboard

The best way to get help anywhere is to press the F1 key, which displays information about whatever you happen to be doing in Windows, as shown in the example in this section.

▶ **Start WordPad.**

Wait until the WordPad screen is staring you in the face.

▶ **Press the F1 key.**

The WordPad Help system is displayed. It works just like the Windows Help system, although the information is geared toward WordPad.

▶ **Close the Help window.**

Keep WordPad open for the next few sections in this chapter.

General Help from the Menu

Most Windows applications have a Help menu, the last menu on the right. (Sometimes the Help menu is off to the far right, away from the other items on the menu bar.)

▶ **Choose Help from the menu.**

The Help menu drops down, as shown in Figure 8.2.

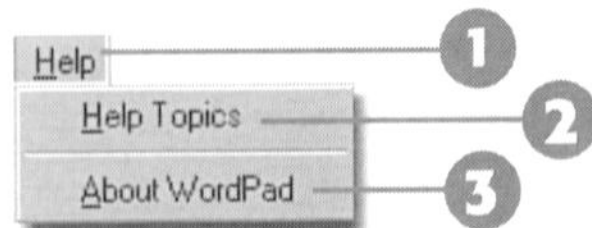

Figure 8.2
The Help menu in WordPad.

1. Help menu.
2. Same as pressing F1; displays the Help system.
3. Displays trivia about WordPad.

Some programs have an extensive array of items in the Help system. Figure 8.3 shows the Help menu for Microsoft Word.

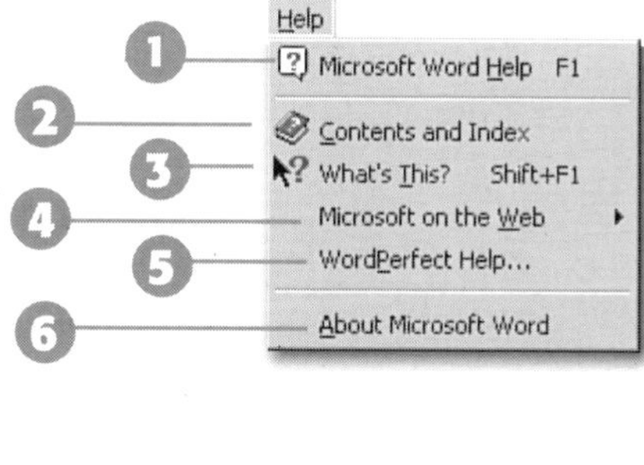

Figure 8.3
The Microsoft Word Help menu.

1. Displays Office Assistant help, where you can type a question.
2. Normal Help-system-style help.
3. Point-and-shoot help.
4. Help you can visit on the Internet.
5. Help for WordPerfect users who have just switched to Word.
6. Trivia.

Help is just a program like any other on your computer. You should remember to close its window when you're done reading the Help information.

- The Help system works the same way no matter which program you're using.
- Okay, some programs have a different type of Help system, maybe not as organized or thorough as the one Windows offers.
- If you haven't used the Help system, you might have to wait a few moments while Windows indexes the Help information.
- You can also get Windows help by pressing the F1 key whenever you see the desktop or when you're using My Computer or Windows Explorer.

The last item on the Help menu is usually About, which displays information about the program—although it's next to useless. In my opinion, the About dialog box should explain exactly what a program does. For example, the About dialog box for WordPad should say something along the lines of "This program is a little word processor no one ever uses."

▶ **Close the menu.**

Press the Esc key twice to close the WordPad Help menu. Keep WordPad open for the next section's tutorial.

The ? Button Help

In some dialog boxes, you can get help by clicking the ? button in the upper-right corner of the dialog box. WordPad has this type of feature.

▶ **Choose Format ➡Font.**

The Font dialog box appears.

▶ **Click the ? button.**

The cursor changes to a pointer/question mark. Now you can point at any item in the dialog box to get a description or helpful information.

▶ **Click in the Sample area.**

A pop-up window appears, giving you more information.

▶ **Click the mouse in the pop-up window to make the window go away.**

▶ **Click Cancel to close the Font dialog box.**

Keep WordPad open for the next, final installment in this tutorial.

Point-and-Shoot Help

The final type of help you encounter in Windows is what I call "point-and-shoot," although sometimes you don't have to shoot.

▶ **Point the mouse at the Save button on the WordPad toolbar.**

Just point the mouse—don't click. Eventually the word *Save* appears. That's what I call point-and-shoot help (official name: ToolTip). It's available for most toolbar buttons or just about any tiny icon. Even if it doesn't work, it's worth a try.

▶ **Point the mouse at the time on the taskbar.**

Just point the mouse, and eventually the full date and time are displayed. You have to hold the mouse still long enough for the date and time to pop up.

▶ **Quit WordPad.**

Another type of point-and-shoot help is available in some of the more sophisticated programs, such as Microsoft Word. You can press the Shift+F1 key combination to get the mouse pointer/question mark. Then you can click any item in the window to get help.

A similar point-and-shoot option on the Help menu exists: Named What's This in Word and Excel, it lets you click the mouse on any item in the window to display a pop-up description.

Not everything offers help, of course. If you click something and don't see a message or you see a "No help available" message, either it's not worth worrying about or it's something Windows is, frankly, clueless about.

Part II

Working in Windows

Chapters in This Part

Part II

Visual Topic Reference A.

1. Desktop.
2. Shortcut icons pasted on the desktop (Chapter 9).
3. Arrange icons on the desktop (Chapter 9).
4. Start Thing (Chapter 10).
5. Quick Launch bar (Chapter 11).
6. Click once on these program icons to start them up.
7. Scrap copied to desktop (Chapter 13).

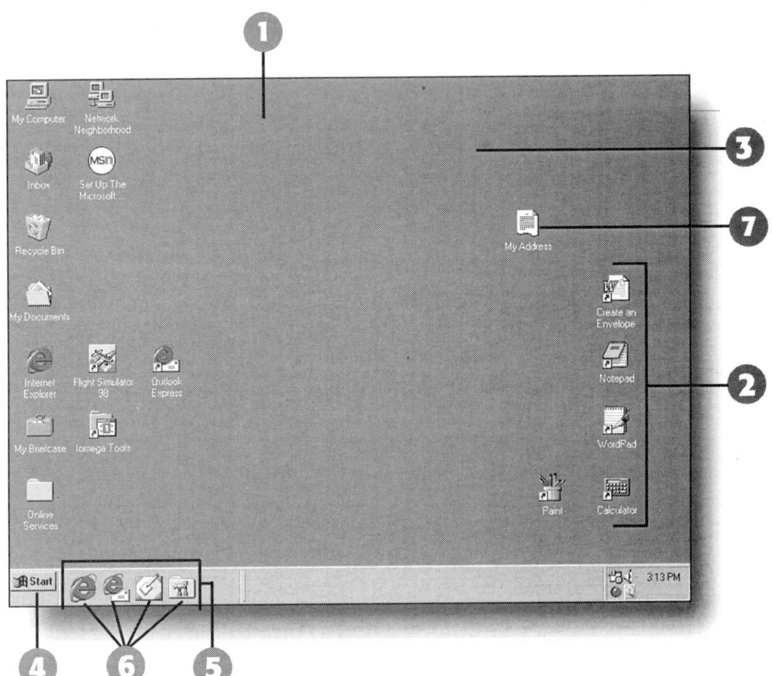

Part II

Visual Topic Reference B.

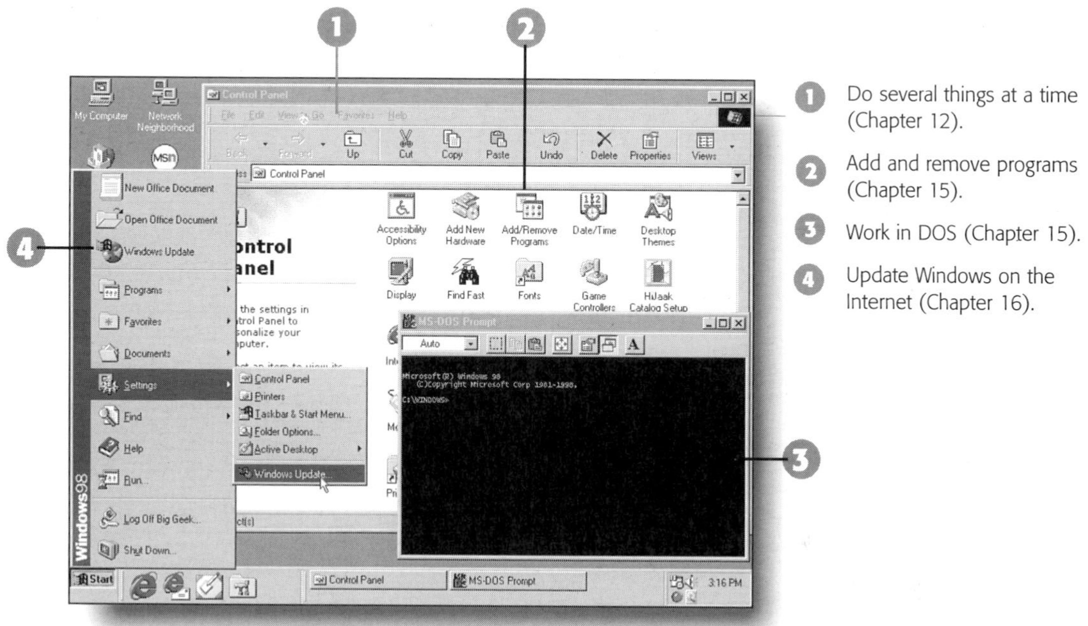

1 Do several things at a time (Chapter 12).
2 Add and remove programs (Chapter 15).
3 Work in DOS (Chapter 15).
4 Update Windows on the Internet (Chapter 16).

Chapter 9

Lurking and Working on the Desktop

Questions Answered and Thoughts Inspired

- Determining which icons should live on the desktop
- Putting a favorite program icon on the desktop
- Dragging and dropping on the desktop
- Putting a document shortcut on the desktop
- Adding folders to the desktop
- Arranging the desktop

If Windows had a face, it would be the desktop. And, boy, could that face use some makeup....

Almost everything you do in Windows starts at the *desktop*, which is the main level of storage on your PC. Windows has lots of things to put on the desktop, some of which can be handy as you wander through Windows. This chapter offers the lowdown on what's up with the desktop.

- Actually, you *can* apply makeup to the desktop. Chapter 37, "A New Face on the Interface," shows you how.
- Because the desktop is also a place to store stuff, it ties into the disk-file-folder scheme of things. Part IV of this book expands on all that.

What Belongs on the Desktop?

The desktop is the first thing you see when Windows is done starting itself and you're ready to work. The desktop is also your home base; after any Windows program quits, Windows closes the program's window and displays the desktop again.

The desktop is a starting place.

Obviously, the desktop makes an ideal place to put icons you commonly use. It's true that you can start every program you have from the Start Thing menu. By putting an icon on the desktop, however, you have a quick shortcut to just about any program you use.

Microsoft has already placed a few important icons on the desktop for you. Figure 9.1 shows a basic Windows setup you might find on a new computer or one with Windows 98 freshly installed. Table 9.1 tells you what these icons do.

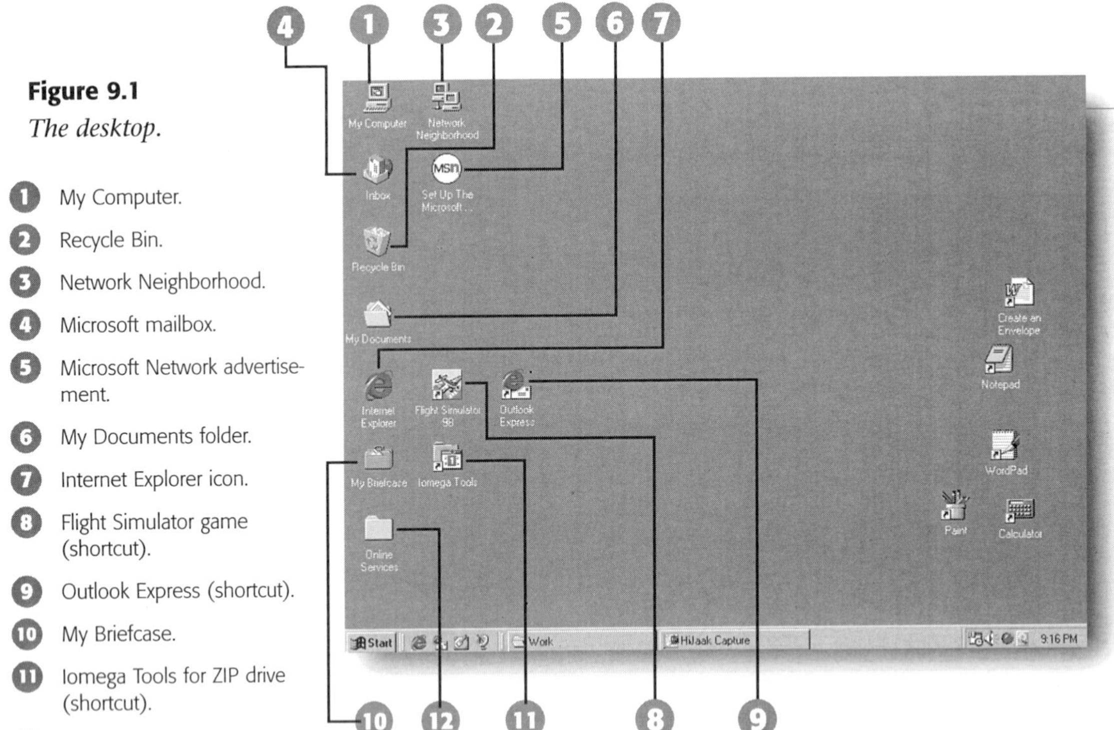

Figure 9.1
The desktop.

1. My Computer.
2. Recycle Bin.
3. Network Neighborhood.
4. Microsoft mailbox.
5. Microsoft Network advertisement.
6. My Documents folder.
7. Internet Explorer icon.
8. Flight Simulator game (shortcut).
9. Outlook Express (shortcut).
10. My Briefcase.
11. Iomega Tools for ZIP drive (shortcut).
12. Online Services folder.

Table 9.1 Items Microsoft Sticks on the Desktop for You

Icon	What It Does
My Computer	Provides access to your disk drives and files as well as other important aspects of your computer. You cannot delete this icon from the desktop.
Recycle Bin	The system trashcan, where files are deleted (thrown away). You cannot delete this icon from the desktop.
Network Neighborhood	Appears only on network computers to grant you access to other computers on the network. You cannot delete this icon from the desktop.
Inbox	The old Microsoft Exchange (or Messaging) program from Windows 95. This icon was probably retained when you upgraded to Windows 98. It's okay to delete this icon if you've never used the Inbox.
Set Up The Microsoft Network	A cheesy ad for the Microsoft online service. You don't suppose that it's there just because Microsoft also makes Windows, do you? Okay to delete.
My Documents	A shortcut icon (although it doesn't look that way) to your My Documents folder. A keeper.
Internet Explorer	Another shortcut icon; it starts Internet Explorer, which lets you browse the World Wide Web. Keep this one.
Outlook Express	Another shortcut, this one to Outlook Express, the email companion to Internet Explorer. Okay to keep.
My Briefcase	A program no one uses. Okay to delete.
Online Services Folder	Most likely was added by your computer dealer. It provides sign-up information for America Online (AOL), CompuServe, Prodigy, and others. Okay to delete.

Keep on the desktop the icons you use; delete icons you don't use. This topic is covered in the section, "Deleting an Icon from the Desktop," later in this chapter.

- Any icon you delete can easily be replaced later, if you want.
- You cannot delete My Computer or the Recycle Bin icons. They belong on the desktop.
- The Network Neighborhood icon might not appear on non-networked PCs. (It might appear on a non-networked PC as a fluke, in which case you just have to live with it.)
- A *shortcut* is a way to reference an icon, program, or folder elsewhere on your computer. This subject is covered in Chapter 24. For now, know that it's safe to remove a shortcut because doing so doesn't delete the main program; it deletes only the shortcut reference.

Some Handy Things to Have on the Desktop

As you would suspect, Windows doesn't automatically come with the handiest things you need placed on the desktop. Eventually you place your own favorite icons on the desktop for quick access. This section shows you the best way to put an icon on the desktop. I also give you suggestions about what to put there.

Placing a Program Icon on the Desktop

Any program you start at least once a month probably should have a place on the desktop. Why? Because it's just much handier to start up things from the desktop than from the Start Thing menu. Heck, I know people who have their desktops *filled* with icons. Maybe that's going overboard, but you get the idea.

One handy item to have on the desktop is WordPad, the li'l Windows word processor:

- ▶ **Open My Computer.**
- ▶ **Open drive C, then Program Files, Accessories folder.**

The Accessories folder is inside the Program Files folder on drive C. The WordPad program lives there. You should see in the window the icon labeled WORDPAD.

- ▶ **Drag the WordPad icon to the desktop.**

Figure 9.2 shows you the details. Releasing the mouse button creates a shortcut—a kind of tiny copy, or *alias*—to the real WordPad program.

Dragging any icon to the desktop creates a shortcut to the original icon. Dragging does not copy the entire program.

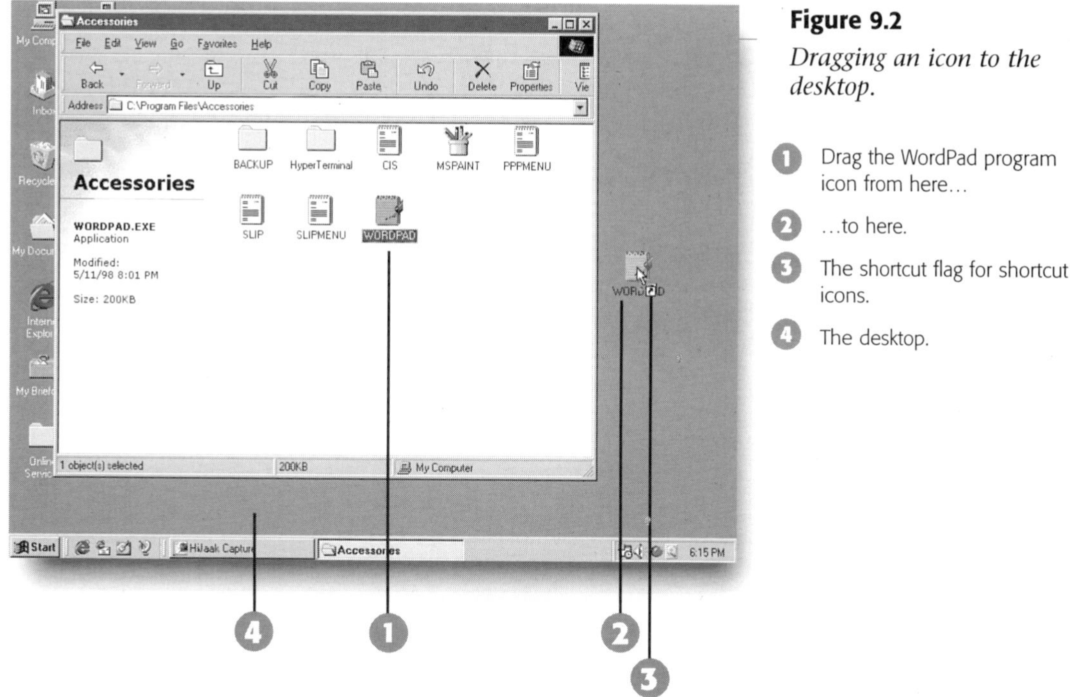

Figure 9.2

Dragging an icon to the desktop.

1. Drag the WordPad program icon from here…
2. …to here.
3. The shortcut flag for shortcut icons.
4. The desktop.

▶ **Press the F2 key.**

The F2 key is the Rename command for any highlighted icon. You, like me, probably hate the name Shortcut to WordPad. Changing it to just WordPad eliminates the redundancy. (The tiny arrow on the icon indicates that it's a shortcut already.)

▶ **Type** WordPad **and press Enter.**

Now you have on the desktop a shortcut to the WordPad program. Starting WordPad is a cinch:

▶ **Open WordPad.**

Double-click the WordPad icon on the desktop to start WordPad—no more Start Thing menu required.

Write something if you're inspired; otherwise:

▶ **Close WordPad.**

You might want to move the icon over to the right side of the desktop. That way, you can have a My Computer or Windows Explorer window open and still see your program icon on the desktop. You see in the next section how this technique can be handy.

Keep the My Computer window open for the next tutorial.

- For more information about shortcuts, see Chapter 24.
- Windows might not rename an icon on the desktop as Shortcut To. If so, you're lucky.
- See Chapter 24 for information about the F2 Rename command.

If Windows doesn't let you drag the icon around on the desktop, you might have the Auto Arrange option set: Right-click the desktop and choose Arrange Icons ➡Auto Arrange from the menu to remove the check mark and allow your icons to move freely about the desktop.

Copying a Program from the Start Thing Menu to the Desktop

Rather than swim through My Computer looking for program icons to paste on the desktop, you can just steal them from the Start Thing menu. Although this technique is sneaky, it works:

- ▶ **From the Start Thing menu, choose Programs ➡Accessories.**
- ▶ **Press and hold the Ctrl (Control) key.**
- ▶ **Drag the Calculator item from the submenu to the desktop.**
- ▶ **Release the Ctrl key.**

Holding down the Ctrl key while you drag forces Windows to copy the program's icon from the Start Thing menu to the desktop. If you don't press the Ctrl key, the icon is moved from the Start Thing menu to the desktop. Figure 9.3 describes this process.

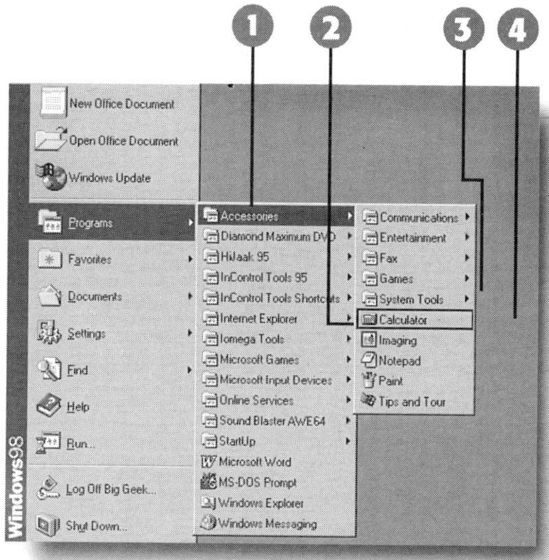

Figure 9.3
Stealing a program from the Start Thing menu.

1. Find a program on the Start Thing menu.
2. The Calculator is selected.
3. Dragging and dropping the Calculator icon on the desktop while pressing the Ctrl key.
4. The shortcut icon is placed wherever you let go of the mouse.

Use the preceding technique to place your favorite programs on the desktop. Here are some files you might find handy to keep there:

Notepad—Although WordPad is a good mini-word processor, sometimes you might just need a text editor. Better put Notepad on the desktop with WordPad.

Microsoft Imaging—Although I'm not sure whether this program comes with Windows or Microsoft Office, it's a great program for viewing and manipulating graphics images. You can find it, if you have it, on the Accessories submenu.

You don't need to rename the shortcut icon in this case; the icon carries the same name it had originally on the Start Thing menu. The only difference is that, rather than have to wade through various menus and submenus, you can now start the Calculator directly from the desktop.

WinZIP—You need this program, which you must purchase separately, if you plan to get files from the Internet. WinZIP has a nice drag-and-drop interface for unzipping program files. (See Chapter 33 for more information about WinZip.) After you get the program, place a copy of its icon on the desktop.

Paint—I must have several thousand dollars worth of graphics programs, although Paint is one icon that always finds its way to my desktop. It's just handy, especially for dragging and dropping various graphics files.

Backup program—Although I don't run my backup program all the time, having its icon on the desktop reminds me that I need to back up my hard drive. Soon.

Microsoft Word—Even though Microsoft gives you a trillion ways to start Word, I prefer to keep a Word icon on my desktop for quick access. Do the same for your word processor, even if it's not Word.

Microsoft Excel—The same information for Word applies to Excel or any other program you want easy access to.

Another quick way to start any program is to use the Quick Launch bar, which is covered in Chapter 11. Unlike the desktop, however, the Quick Launch bar has room for only so many icons. The desktop you can fill to your heart's content.

- Many icons on the desktop are capable of doing the drag-and-drop for loading documents. In many instances, that technique is kind of silly; dragging a WordPad document to the WordPad icon takes more time than just opening the document (which opens WordPad). Sometimes, however, you need to drag-and-drop something. For example, dragging a document to the WinZIP program begins the process of creating a new archive. Or, you might want to drag to the Microsoft Imaging program an image that would otherwise open in another program.

Putting a Document Shortcut on the Desktop

In addition to placing programs on the desktop, you might consider placing special data files there. For example, my Rolodex database file lives on my desktop, where I can always get at it in a hurry.

The following tutorial shows you how to place a document icon on the desktop, using the Envelopes document you created in Part I of this book:

▶ **Open the My Documents folder.**

An icon for My Documents should be on the desktop.

▶ **Drag the Envelopes document to the desktop.**

You created this document in Chapter 7.

When you drag the Envelopes document, you're *moving* it from the My Documents folder to the desktop. Notice how the icon lacks the little swooshy arrow in the lower-left corner?

Nothing is wrong with moving, or even creating, a file on the desktop. However, I prefer to have shortcuts rather than the original files on the desktop. (That's just me; you can do whatever you want. Remember that this is a tutorial.)

▶ **Press Ctrl+Z.**

The Ctrl+Z key combination is the Windows undo key. This example undoes the last file command you made, moving the Envelopes icon from My Documents to the desktop. If you look on the screen, you see Envelopes back in the My Documents folder.

▶ **Right-drag the Envelopes icon to the desktop.**

When you *right-drag*, you drag an icon by using the right mouse button rather than the left. When you release the mouse button, a pop-up menu appears, as shown in Figure 9.4.

Right-dragging always displays a pop-up menu, giving you a choice for copying a file.

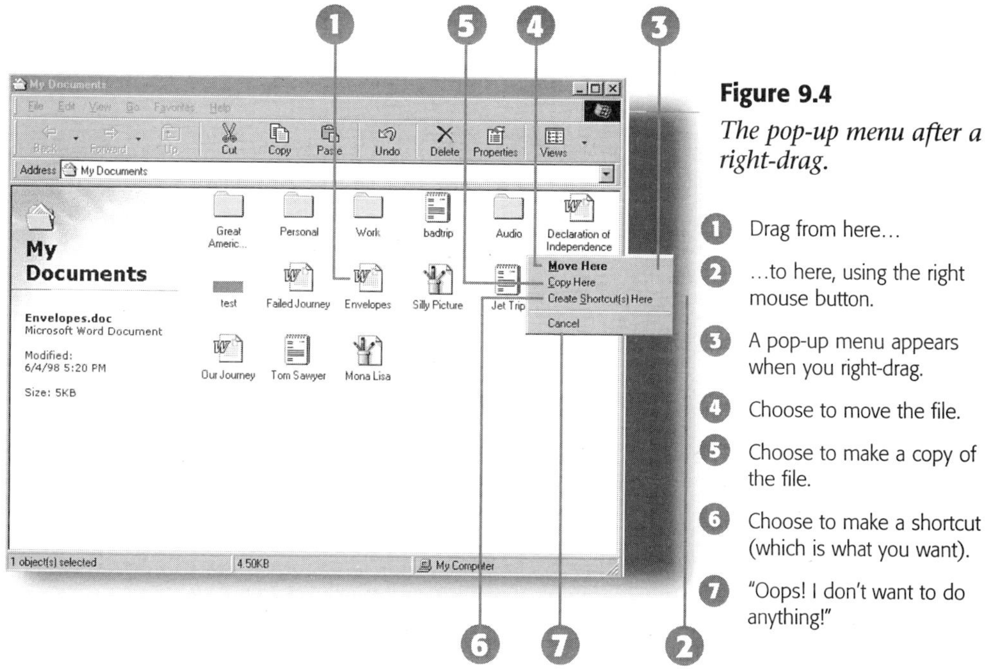

Figure 9.4
The pop-up menu after a right-drag.

1. Drag from here…
2. …to here, using the right mouse button.
3. A pop-up menu appears when you right-drag.
4. Choose to move the file.
5. Choose to make a copy of the file.
6. Choose to make a shortcut (which is what you want).
7. "Oops! I don't want to do anything!"

▶ **Choose Create Shortcut(s) Here.**

Plop! A shortcut copy of the Envelopes document is placed on the desktop. It's handy for whenever you need to print a quick envelope.

That filename stinks!

▶ **Press F2.**

▶ **Type** Create an Envelope **and press Enter.**

It's a more descriptive name than Shortcut to Envelopes, don't you think?

Keep the My Documents window open for the next tutorial.

- Placing a shortcut on the desktop keeps the original file wherever it was on your hard drive. For example, if the Envelopes document is saved in a folder full of related files—stuff you want to keep together—then creating a shortcut on the desktop makes more sense than moving the file away from its friends.
- Shortcuts don't take up the same amount of space as a copy of the original file. For example, the size of the Envelopes document is 5KB. (Click the Envelopes icon in the My Documents window, and read the size on the left side of the window.) The size of the shortcut copy, however, is only about 500 bytes—90 percent smaller. Shortcuts save disk space.

The right mouse button is the one you don't normally press. For all right-handed people, who normally click the mouse's left button, the right button ***is*** the right button. If you have your mouse configured for your left hand, however, a right-click involves the left button. Confused? Don't sweat it.

Putting a Project Folder Shortcut on the Desktop

I organize my personal projects by placing them in folders under the main My Documents folder. In fact, I often have folders within folders for various projects, depending on how organized I'm feeling at the moment. Having a shortcut to one of those folders on the desktop—especially one buried deep down—is entirely handy.

The following tutorial uses the Great American Novel folder you created in Chapter 3. (Make sure that you're looking at the My Documents folder, which is where you left off in the preceding section.)

▶ **Right-drag the Great American Novel folder to the desktop.**

A pop-up menu appears.

▶ **Choose Create Shortcut(s) Here.**

Ploop—there's your folder shortcut.

▶ **Close the My Documents window.**

To quickly get at the project, just open the shortcut icon on the desktop. That action displays the project window, easy as pie. (This technique is the way I start my own Windows day.) From there, you can open any document and get right to work.

Creating a Project Folder on the Desktop

Project folders are a great idea. If you want, you can create a project folder right on the desktop. This task involves no crime, no wasted space. It's just that the folder is right there on the desktop as opposed to being in My Documents or elsewhere on your hard drive.

▶ **Right-click the desktop.**

The desktop's shortcut menu appears, as shown in Figure 9.5.

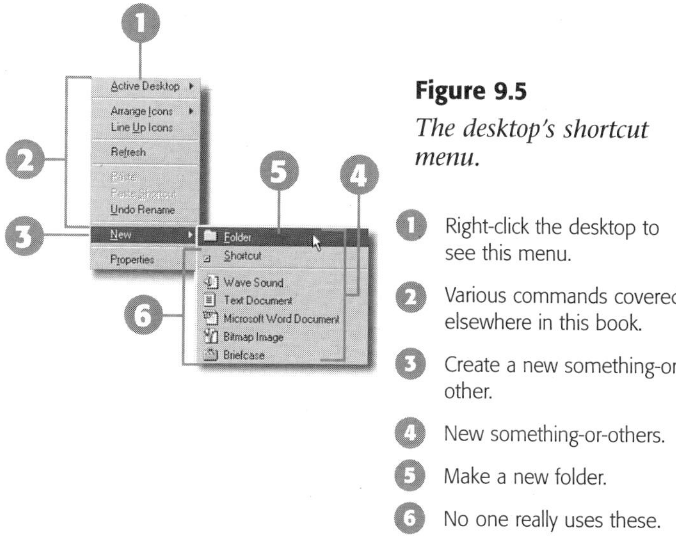

Figure 9.5
The desktop's shortcut menu.

1. Right-click the desktop to see this menu.
2. Various commands covered elsewhere in this book.
3. Create a new something-or-other.
4. New something-or-others.
5. Make a new folder.
6. No one really uses these.

▶ **Choose New ➡Folder.**

▶ **Type** Plans to Invade Fredonia **and press Enter.**

You have no need to press F2 to rename the folder. Windows most likely knows that New Folder is a stupid name, and you'll doubtless want to change it to something more descriptive of its contents.

Lining Up Icons on the Desktop

I keep my folders in the upper-right corner of the desktop, program icons in the lower-left corner, and what Windows originally put on the desktop over on the left.

Over time, you learn to like desktop icons in a certain place. Until then, you can move them around on the desktop however you want.

▶ **Drag your new icons to a proper place on the desktop.**

The positioning of icons is up to you. You can follow my example or create your own. Or you can change your mind later.

▶ **Right-click the desktop.**

▶ **Choose Line Up Icons.**

Windows arranges your icons, lining them up to a predefined grid. This process keeps things neat if you're a neatnik and hate to see one icon jostled out of line.

The pop-up menu has other commands you probably don't want to mess with. Anything on the Arrange Icons submenu lines up the desktop's icons in an orderly manner, from top to bottom and from left to right.

If you're having trouble moving the icons on the desktop, the Auto Arrange option has probably been set. Right-click the desktop and choose Arrange Icons ➡Auto Arrange to remove the check mark by that item.

Deleting an Icon from the Desktop

It's your computer. If you see on the desktop an icon you figure you'll never use, delete it. You can do it in one of two ways.

First, for most of the icons you create and for all shortcuts, drag the icon to the Recycle Bin:

▶ **Drag the Plans to Invade Fredonia folder to the Recycle Bin.**

You might see a dialog box asking you to confirm the deletion. If so, click Yes.

Second, you can press the Delete key.

▶ **Click the Notepad shortcut icon once to select it.**

▶ **Press the Delete key on your keyboard.**

You might be asked to confirm. If so, click Yes.

Deleting a shortcut does not delete the original file. In fact, you probably didn't really want to delete Notepad. So:

Press Ctrl+Z.

Notepad is back. Although it might not be in the same spot onscreen (look around for it), it's back.

Move the Notepad icon back to where you want it if Windows restored it to another location. Then choose Line Up Icons from the desktop's pop-up menu to straighten things out.

You can delete some of the Microsoft icons, although you see a *nasty* warning:

▶ **Drag the Set Up the Microsoft Network icon to the Recycle Bin.**

Perhaps *the* nastiest dialog box is displayed, as shown in Figure 9.6.

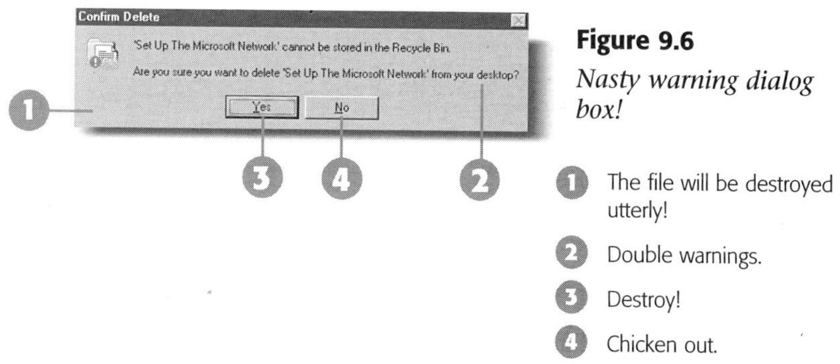

Figure 9.6
Nasty warning dialog box!

1. The file will be destroyed utterly!
2. Double warnings.
3. Destroy!
4. Chicken out.

The notion of this message is twofold: First, Microsoft wants you to feel a pang of guilt if you delete the icon, even though you'll probably never sign up for the service. Second, it's true: If you delete the icon, you cannot get it back.

Ponder for a moment.

▶ **Click Yes.**

Seriously, using the Internet with an ISP, as described in Chapter 7, beats the pants off using the Microsoft Network. Gadzooks!

You can also delete the My Briefcase folder because, honestly, no one uses it. If you need to coordinate files between a laptop and desktop PC, programs are out there, primarily Laplink and pcANYWHERE, that you can get at any software store.

Refer to Chapter 28 for more information about using the Recycle Bin.

You usually can easily restore later anything you delete to the Recycle Bin. Some icons, however, cannot be recovered. That's when Windows gives you the nasty warning that was shown in Figure 9.6.

Chapter 10

Ode to the Start Thing

Questions Answered and Thoughts Inspired

- Adding programs to the Start Thing menu
- Dragging and dropping on the Start Thing menu
- Editing the Start Thing menu
- Exploring the Start Thing menu
- Creating submenus

The Start Thing menu is where you should put all the programs you can run on your computer. *All of them*. That way, you can start *any* program you want to start by using the handy Start Thing menu. You don't have to find the program, fish through windows, or guess where it is. Every program on your PC should be on the Start Thing menu.

Another important point: The Start Thing is *yours*. You should customize it the way you want, by putting the programs you use right there, where they're handy. You can move stuff you never use to some other part of the menu, out of your way.

This chapter is all about the Start Thing, telling you how to put programs on its Programs submenu and how to organize everything.

- No program has to be in any certain place on the Start Thing's Programs submenu.
- Even if you're one of several people who use your computer, you can have your own custom Start Thing menu.

The Official Way to Add Something to the Start Thing Menu

Programs are added to the Start Thing menu as you install them. This process happens automatically: You install Microsoft Office, and it places a bunch of icons on the menu. You're done.

Unfortunately, not everything gets put on the Start Thing menu. Windows has, therefore, ways to add programs to the menu manually. The first way, the "official way," is demonstrated in this section. The unofficial, drag-and-drop method, is covered later in this chapter.

The following tutorial adds the Winver program to the Start Thing menu. Winver is a silly little program that displays the Windows version number. Everyone has it. (You delete it from the Start Thing menu later in this chapter.)

▶ **From the Start Thing menu, choose Settings ➡Taskbar & Start Menu.**

The Taskbar Properties dialog box appears.

▶ **Click the Start Menu Programs tab.**

▶ **Click the Add button.**

The Create Shortcut dialog box appears, as shown in Figure 10.1.

▶ **Click the Browse button.**

Use the Browse/Open dialog box to find your program on the disk. For this example, the Winver program is stored in the Windows folder on drive C, so you open drive C (if it isn't open already) and then the Windows folder in the Browse/Open dialog box.

▶ **Browse to drive C, Windows folder.**

▶ **Select the WINVER program and click Open.**

All the items on the Start Thing menu are shortcuts, or *aliases*, for the real programs that live elsewhere on the computer's disk drives. Deleting the shortcut on the menu does not delete the program. Likewise, moving the shortcut does not move the program.

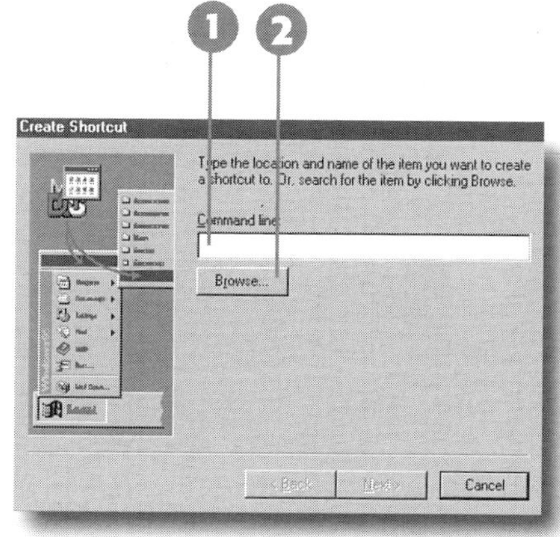

Figure 10.1
The Create Shortcut dialog box.

1. Type the command or pathname here (only for the nerdy folks).
2. Click here to use a Browse/Open dialog box to find your program.

You have to scroll the window to find the program; it's on the far right. (The programs are listed in alphabetical order.)

Clicking the Open button puts the text `C:\Windows\Winver.exe` in the Command Line box. You could have typed it yourself, had you known the exact filename and location. (Like anyone would...)

▶ **Click Next.**

Now you get to pick where on the menu the program lives. Figure 10.2 shows you how to work the dialog box.

▶ **Select the System Tools menu/folder.**

Locate the System Tools menu/folder on the list and click it once to select it.

▶ **Click Next.**

▶ **Type** Windows Version **in the box.**

This name is the one you want to appear on the menu. Without asking, Windows uses the program name, WINVER, which is dorky. Windows Version is much more descriptive.

▶ **Click Finish.**

▶ **Click OK to close the Taskbar Properties dialog box.**

You're done. To make sure that everything turned out okay, check the Start Thing menu.

TIP

You can name programs anything, although keeping the names short makes the menus easy to read. (You can even change a name later so that Microsoft Word becomes just Word.)

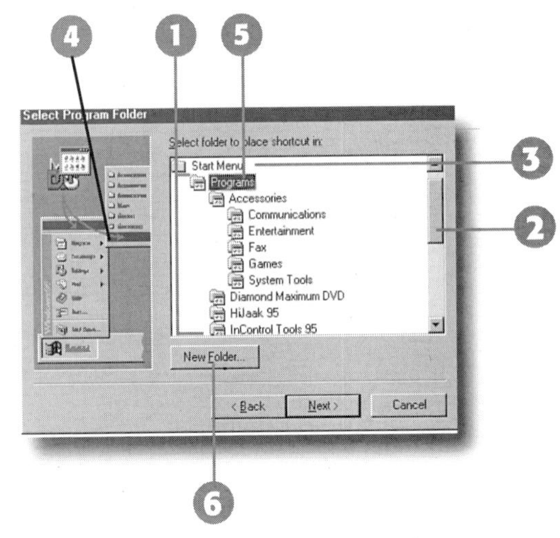

Figure 10.2
Choose a menu for your program.

1. Menus on the Start menu.
2. Scroll down to see more menus.
3. Click a menu name to select it.
4. Menus are essentially special folders.
5. Choose a menu from the list; the highlighted menu is where your program goes.
6. Click here to create a new submenu on the highlighted menu.

▶ **From the Start Thing menu, choose Programs ➡Accessories ➡System Tools.**

You see *Windows Version* down there at the bottom of the menu.

▶ **Choose Windows Version.**

Ah! The program runs. Impressive, no?

▶ **Click OK.**

You're using Windows 98. Although you should already know that, you can never be certain.

I call this method the "official" way because it's deliberate. It's also slow, however. The following section discusses the quicker way to mess with the Start Thing menu. It's sloppy, though, so the decision is yours.

Messing with the Start Thing

You can do much of your menu organization on the Start Thing with the mouse. You can drag menus and menu items around and place them in a new position or drag them off the menu completely.

Although this technique is cinchy and makes a great deal of sense, it can be sloppy. Be careful!

Adding a Program to the Start Thing

You can add any program to the Start Thing via a quick drag-and-drop of the mouse. It works like this:

1. **Find a program by using My Computer, the Explorer, or the Find command.**
2. **Drag the program's icon to the Start menu.**
3. **Drop the program's icon on the proper submenu.**

The following tutorial adds the old Windows File Manager to the Start Thing's Accessories menu. The first step is to find the old File Manager program, which is named Winfile. To find that file, you use the Windows Find command.

The Find command can locate any file on disk, as long as you know something about the file, such as its name.

▶ **From the Start Thing menu, choose Find ➡Files or Folders.**

The Find dialog box appears, as shown in Figure 10.3.

▶ **Type** WINFILE **in the Named box.**

The name of the program you want to find is Winfile. Not very romantic.

▶ **Choose drive C:\ from the Look In box (if it's not chosen already).**

Winfile is most likely on drive C. In fact, I'd guess that it's in the Windows folder, but then again, what do I know?

▶ **Put a check mark next to Include Subfolders (if one isn't there already).**

You want Windows to scan for the file on the *entire* hard drive. If you don't put a check mark by Include Subfolders, Windows looks only in the root folder of drive C.

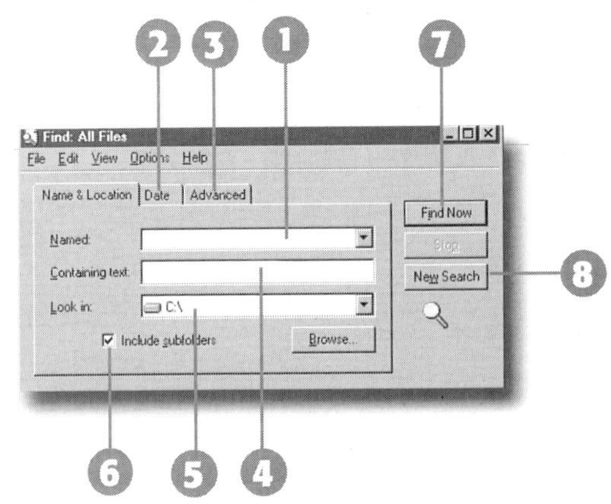

Figure 10.3

Finding a program for the Start Thing.

1. Type the program name here.
2. You can search by the file's date as well.
3. Or search by the file's type or size.
4. Files containing a certain bit of text.
5. Choose a disk drive or folder to look in.
6. Always click this box to look for files in subfolders (all over the hard drive).
7. Find that file!
8. Reset all the options for starting a new search.

▶ **Click Find Now.**

The results of the search are displayed in the bottom half of the window.

You might want to stretch the Find window to the right so that you can see all the columns.

You're looking for the Winfile icon that's an application or program. WINFILE is listed in the Type column, where the Find command displays its results. The file you want is probably the first one on the list.

Now that you've found the file, it's time to put it on the Start Thing menu.

It doesn't matter *where* on the Start Thing menu you put the icon. It's usually best to put the programs you use most often directly on the main Programs menu for easy access. Any other programs can go anywhere else you want. No rules apply here; the Start Thing is yours to mess with.

For this tutorial, you put the Winfile prog ram on the Programs ➡Accessories menu. (I have no special reason for choosing that menu; you can put it anywhere.)

▶ **Drag the Winfile icon to the Start Thing (do *not* release the mouse button yet!)**

The Start Thing pops up. (Although you might have to wait a few moments for it to pop up, it eventually does.)

▶ **Continue dragging to the Programs ➡Accessories menu.**

As you drag the icon through the menus, a horizontal insertion bar appears on the menus. It shows you where the icon will be added to the menu when you release the mouse button.

Keep the mouse button held down!

▶ **Continue dragging until the Winfile icon is near the bottom of the Accessories submenu.**

▶ **Release the mouse button to drop the icon on the menu.**

You see Shortcut to WINFILE on the menu.

▶ **Choose Shortcut to WINFILE.**

The old Windows File Manager starts. Ho-hum.

▶ **Close the File Manager window.**

▶ **Close the Find window.**

This tutorial is continued in the following section.

- You can add any program to the Start Thing menu by using this technique. You can drag the program's icon from the Find window or from any My Computer or Windows Explorer window.
- You can put a program *anywhere* on the Start Thing menu. Put programs you use most often on the main Programs menu.
- You can even create new submenus for your programs. A tutorial for that task appears later in this chapter.

TIP

In addition to placing programs on the Start Thing menu, you can place documents and even folders. Choosing a document runs the program which created that document (which can be handy). Choosing a folder opens that folder as a window.

- Dragging an item to the Start Thing menu always creates a shortcut. It does not move the entire program to the menu.
- More information about the Find command is in Chapter 27.
- See the section "Renaming a Menu Item," later in this chapter, for information about naming the Shortcut to WINFILE menu item something more descriptive.
- The shortcut to WINFILE (or whatever) might not appear when you drop the icon on the menu; it might just have the program name. If so, great.

Moving a Program Around on the Start Thing Menu

Just as you can drag a program to the Start Thing menu you can drag menu items from the menu to someplace else. Suppose that the Shortcut to WINFILE menu item (added in the preceding section) would work better for you if it were on the main Programs menu.

▶ **From the Start Thing menu, choose Programs ➡Accessories.**

This action displays the Accessories submenu.

▶ **Drag the Shortcut to WINFILE item from the Accessories submenu to the Programs menu.**

An insertion bar appears wherever you drag the menu item, as shown in Figure 10.4.

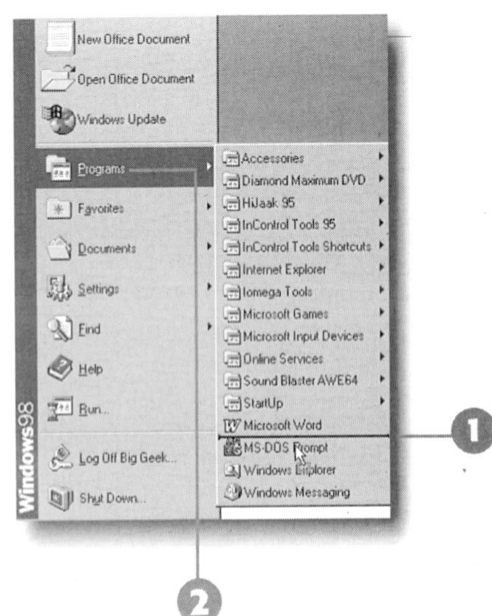

Figure 10.4
Dragging a menu item.

1. The insertion bar shows where the menu item will be dropped.
2. Point the mouse at a menu item to open that menu.

- **Drop the Shortcut to WINFILE item on the Programs menu, somewhere near the bottom.**

Release the mouse button to place the menu item.

Removing a Program from the Start Thing

It's *your* Start Thing menu. If you see on it an item you never use, delete it! This action doesn't delete the program, although it sure cleans up the Start Thing menu by paring it to be very efficient.

- **From the Start Thing menu, choose Programs ➡Accessories ➡System Tools.**

This action displays the System Tools submenu.

- **Right-click the Windows Version item.**

You added this item in a tutorial earlier in this chapter.

Right-clicking a menu item displays a pop-up menu.

- **Choose Delete.**

A warning dialog box might appear. Click Yes to trash the menu item.

It's gone!

You can also delete an item from the Start Thing menu by dragging it to the Recycle Bin. Unfortunately, because the Start Thing usually covers the Recycle Bin, you cannot see it to drag the icon.

- Deleting an item from the Start Thing menu deletes only the shortcut to that item; the program still exists on your hard drive and can always be added to the Start Thing again later.
- Many applications install "readme" files on the Start Thing menu. You definitely can remove these files after you've read them.

TIP

I also recommend removing any Uninstall commands from the Start Thing menu. For example, one slip of the mouse can run the Uninstall command, which means that you have to reinstall your program from scratch.

The Top of Start Thing

After you use Windows for a while, you see that quite a few programs like to stick icons at the top of the Start Thing menu. If you use those items, *great*! It's handy to have them there. If you don't use those items, they get in the way and can make the Start Thing taller than your screen. (Maybe.)

You place items on top of the Start Thing by dragging them there.

- **Open My Computer.**
- **Open drive C.**
- **Open the Windows folder.**

If you don't see any contents, click Show Files on the left side of the window.

- **Scroll down to find the WINVER icon.**
- **Drag the WINVER icon to the Start button.**

Drop the icon on the Start button; don't wait for the Start Thing to pop up.

It looks like nothing happened—yet.

- **Click the Start button.**

There, on top of the Start Thing menu, you see the WINVER command.

That's the cinchy way to put something at the top of the Start Thing menu. You can also drag any menu item to that position.

- **Close the My Computer window.**

Now comes cleanup time.

To remove any item from the top of the Start Thing menu, right-click that item and choose Delete from the pop-up menu. Or, if you want to keep the item elsewhere, just drag it to the Programs menu and then whatever other submenu you want to put the item on.

To delete the WINVER program right now, right-click it and choose Delete from the pop-up menu. Click Yes if you're asked whether you really want to delete the file. It's gone.

Why the Windows Folder Doesn't Display Its Files

The reason you have to click Show Files to see icons in the Windows folder is that Microsoft doesn't want you messing with those files. Quite a few people, especially novices, go "cleaning" though the Windows folder and unintentionally remove important files. This practice is a no-no.

Messing with the files in the Windows folder can botch things up. Windows puts a number of programs and folders there, however, that you do access occasionally. Running the programs isn't a problem. Deleting them is, though; hence the warning message.

Don't delete files in the Windows folder!

Viewing the Start Thing Menu with Windows Explorer

The drag-and-drop method of menu organization (demonstrated earlier in this chapter) can get out of hand. Especially if you're moving a menu item from one submenu to another, it's just too easy to slip up and get frustrated. For that reason, I recommend using the Windows Explorer for major Start Thing updates or overhauls.

Keep the Explorer window open for the next few sections in this chapter.

Using the Explorer to manipulate folders and icons is covered in detail in Part IV of this book.

Making a New Submenu

Because submenus are folders and vice versa, to make a new submenu on the Start Thing, you just create a new folder.

▶ **Open the Programs submenu/folder.**

Click the Programs icon on the left side of the Explorer window to display its contents on the right side of the window. You should see a bunch of submenus and folders listed and some program items and shortcuts.

▶ **Choose File ➡New ➡Folder.**

The New Folder icon appears on the right side of the window, ready for you to christen it with a decent name.

▶ **Type** DOS Applications **and press Enter.**

Press the Backspace key to back up if you make a typing mistake.

You might have to scroll the window down to see the entire icon.

Lo, you've created the DOS Applications submenu. Prove that it exists:

▶ **From the Start Thing menu, choose Programs ➡DOS Applications.**

Shhhh! The Start Thing is really a folder on your hard drive. The items are shortcut icons, and the submenus are folders inside folders. If you're handy with folders and icons, you might prefer the Windows Explorer method of working with the Start Thing:

▶ **Right-click the Start button.**

▶ **Choose Explore from the menu.**

A Windows Explorer window appears, with the Start Thing's folder and submenus splayed out for easy file editing, as shown in Figure 10.5.

Figure 10.5

Exploring the Start Thing.

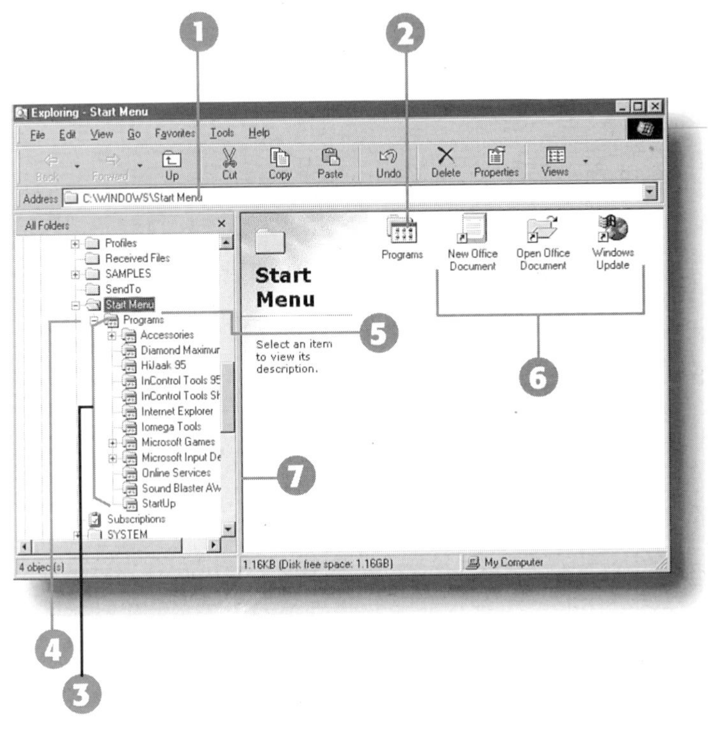

1. The Start Menu exists as the Start Menu folder inside the Windows folder on drive C.
2. Submenus, such as Programs, are all really folders.
3. Other folders and submenus.
4. The Programs submenu.
5. Choosing a folder displays its contents on the right side of the window.
6. Items on top of the Start Thing.
7. You can drag this divider left or right to see more of the tree-structure thing.

If the submenu doesn't appear, keep trying. Sometimes Windows is pokey and takes awhile to wake up.

The new menu is "empty" because no program items are there. But it lives!

Notice that the new submenu appears at the bottom of the list. This placement is tacky. However, you can drag the folder up to a more prominent place; use the dragging techniques demonstrated in the first half of this chapter if you want to move the folder.

▶ **Click in the Exploring-Programs window.**

This action makes the Start Thing menu go away if it's still open all over the desktop, and it returns the focus to the Explorer window for the next few steps.

▶ **Select the COMMAND folder in the WINDOWS folder.**

You might have to scroll up the left side of the window until you can see the COMMAND folder, just under the WINDOWS folder.

Selecting the folder (clicking it once) displays its contents on the right side of the window.

▶ **Select the EDIT program.**

Select the EDIT program shown in the margin, the one named EDIT.COM, which you can see displayed under the word *COMMAND* on the right side of the Explorer window.

The EDIT icon is the DOS text editor program, which you'll probably never use, but keep in mind that this is a tutorial.

▶ **Choose Edit ➡Copy.**

▶ **Scroll the left side of the window back down to the Start menu folder.**

The Programs submenu/folder should already be visible. If not, click the + (plus sign) by the Start menu folder to open it.

▶ **Click the + by the Programs folder to open it (if it's not open already).**

▶ **Click the DOS Applications folder.**

▶ **Choose Edit ➡Paste Shortcut.**

A Shortcut to MS-DOS Editor icon appears. Yeah!

Prove it worthy:

▶ **From the Start menu, choose Programs ➡DOS Applications ➡ Shortcut to MS-DOS Editor.**

The MS-DOS Editor appears in a window onscreen. (DOS programs run in their own text-based window.)

▶ **Press Alt+F and then X to quit the MS-DOS Editor.**

This step quits the Editor and closes the MS-DOS window. So much for that. You might use the Editor once or twice but—let's face it—it's primitive.

Keep the Explorer window open for the next section's tutorial.

Renaming a Menu Item

If you go and add programs to the Start Thing menu as demonstrated in this chapter, you notice that they have dorky names, such as Shortcut To Blah-Blah. Those names are blemishes on an otherwise tidy menu, the pockmarked sign that a rank amateur has added a menu item. Better make amends.

The only way to rename a menu item is to use Explorer and rename the shortcut icon associated with that menu item. (Explore the Start Thing as described in the preceding section if you don't already have that window open.)

- **Open the DOS Applications menu/folder (if it's not open already).**
- **Click the Shortcut to MS-DOS Editor item once to select it.**
- **Press the F2 key.**

Now you can type a new name or press the cursor keys on your keyboard to edit the name:

- **Edit the name to just** MS-DOS Editor.

Press the arrow keys to position the insertion pointer at the beginning of the filename. Then press the Delete key to delete *Shortcut to* from the name. Press Enter to rename the file.

Any menu item can be renamed, and using Explorer is the only way to do it.

Using the Startup Folder

You can add or remove submenus and folders at your whim; one folder in particular is important to Windows. The Startup folder contains programs that automatically start every time you start Windows. This folder might already have a few programs in it which start up every time you turn on your computer or reset Windows.

If you want to start a program automatically when Windows starts, put the program's icon in the Startup folder. For example, if you always start your Windows day by running Outlook Express to check your email, put a shortcut to that program in the StartUp folder. Likewise, if you *don't* want a program to start automatically, remove it from the StartUp folder.

Windows also lets you set *how* the program runs when it starts: minimized as a button on the toolbar, normally, or full-screen. To set this option, right-click the menu item and choose Properties. In the Shortcut panel, look for the Run drop-down list. Choose Minimized, Maximized, or Normal Window to run your program in that respective mode. Click OK.

Even submenus and folders can be renamed. Use the F2 key as just described.

- **Close the Explorer window.**

The rules for renaming a menu item or icon are the same as for renaming a file. Generally speaking, stick to numbers, letters, and spaces, and you'll be okay.

Moving or Rearranging Menus

The folders and menus on the Start Thing can be rearranged, just as folders can be moved or "pruned and grafted" on your hard drive. Because the two processes are identical, if you want to move a submenu on the Start Thing, refer to Chapter 23, which covers the topic of moving folders. The rules and methods are the same.

Chapter 11

Other Ways to Start Your Stuff

Questions Answered and Thoughts Inspired

- Using the Quick Launch bar
- Adding a program shortcut to the Quick Launch bar
- Editing the Quick Launch bar
- Using the Run command

The Start Thing should contain every program on your computer, placed right on the menu for easy access. Some programs you run more than others, though. Because Microsoft can't make up its mind about how to start programs in Windows, you can start up your stuff by using ways other than the Start Thing. Quick ways. Fast ways. Easy ways.

This chapter introduces you to the Quick Launch bar, which is most likely the main way you will start your top few programs. Also, I review in this chapter two quick ways to start programs: from the desktop and by opening a recent document.

The Quick Launch Bar

Windows 95 introduced the *taskbar*, a handy place that shows you a button for every program or window you have open. That feature just wasn't good enough, though!

With Windows 98, you now have *four* toolbars you can view along with the taskbar, not including toolbars you can create yourself. Of all that rabble, the one you probably want to use most often is the Quick Launch bar.

- **The four toolbars are Quick Launch bar, Address bar, Links bar, and Desktop bar.**
- **Chapter 38, "Toolbars from Beyond Infinity," covers all the toolbars in depth.**

Where Is the Quick Launch Bar?

Windows 98 automatically configures itself to show the Quick Launch bar along with the taskbar. Figure 11.1 helps you identify things.

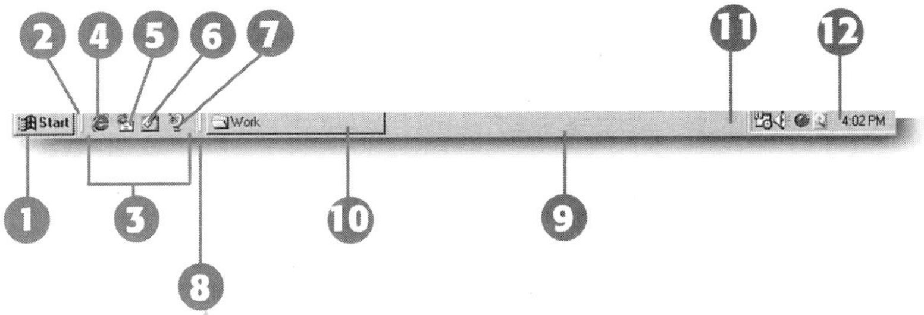

Figure 11.1
Important things around the taskbar.

1. Start Thing button.
2. Grab with the mouse to resize the toolbar (the "handle").
3. Quick Launch bar.
4. Internet Explorer.
5. Outlook Express.
6. View the desktop.
7. Channels.
8. Grab to resize or move the taskbar.
9. Taskbar.
10. Button on the taskbar.
11. Right-click to see the taskbar's pop-up menu.
12. System tray.

If you cannot see the Quick Launch bar, follow these steps:

▶ **Right-click the taskbar to display the taskbar pop-up menu.**

Right-click a blank part of the taskbar, not a button. If you can't manage that, right-click the time in the system tray. Although that action displays a different menu (with one extra option), it gets you to where you need to go.

Figure 11.2 shows the taskbar's pop-up menu.

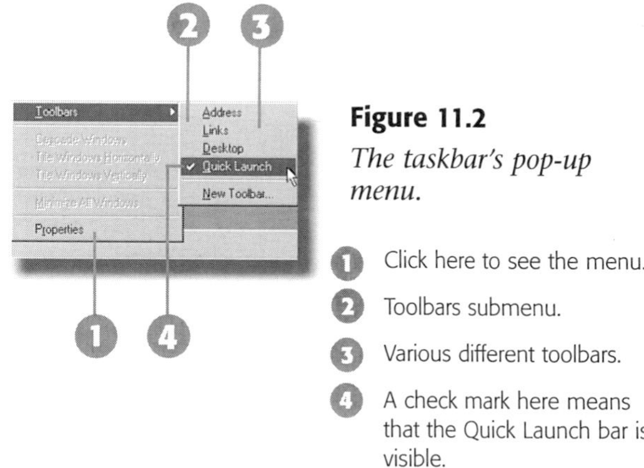

Figure 11.2
The taskbar's pop-up menu.

1. Click here to see the menu.
2. Toolbars submenu.
3. Various different toolbars.
4. A check mark here means that the Quick Launch bar is visible.

▶ **Choose Toolbars ➡Quick Launch if that item does not already have a check mark by it.**

The Quick Launch toolbar is visible.

To hide the Quick Launch toolbar, just repeat the preceding steps and *remove* the check mark. My advice, however, is to keep the guy visible because he is so very handy.

A Bigger Better Quick Launch Bar

Yes, the Quick Launch bar is probably too tiny on your screen. The following steps show you how to make it larger and how to reposition it for better access.

▶ **Right-click the Quick Launch bar's handle.**

The *handle* is that vertical "bump" on the left side of the toolbar (see Figure 11.3). Right-clicking the handle displays a pop-up menu, as shown in the figure.

▶ **Choose View ➡Large (if a check mark isn't next to Large already).**

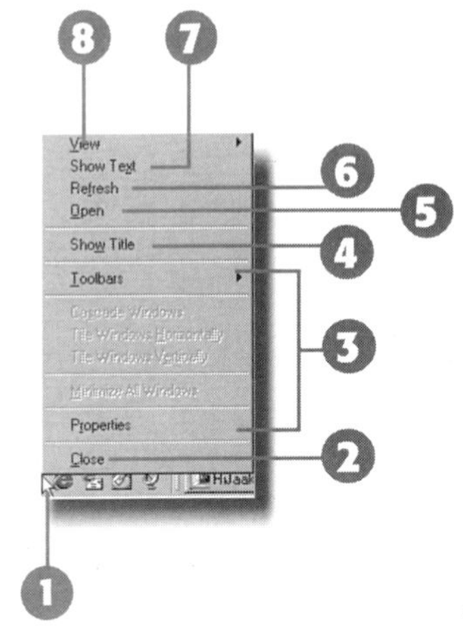

Figure 11.3
The Quick Launch bar's pop-up menu.

1. Right-click here.
2. Closes (removes) the Quick Launch bar.
3. Standard taskbar pop-up menu items.
4. Displays the text *Quick Launch* on the Quick Launch bar.
5. Opens folder containing the Quick Launch bar shortcut items.
6. Updates the Quick Launch bar after editing.
7. Displays text by each icon.
8. Sets icon size.

Hey boy! Nice, fat icons. They're the same size as other icons on the desktop, which means (depending on your screen setup) that you might not see any noticeable difference.

If you do see a difference, notice that the taskbar is now twice as high as before. (Changing the size of the icons on the Quick Launch bar does not change the size of buttons on the taskbar.)

If you start messing with the Quick Launch bar handle, however, you might end up with the taskbar and Quick Launch bar all discombobulated. Just use the grabber to carefully drag either the taskbar or the Quick Launch bar back to wherever you want it.

You can also use the handle on the left side of the Quick Launch bar to move the Quick Launch bar. You can drag the bar left or right, change its size, or even drag it up to the desktop, where it becomes a floating window.

Adding a New Program to the Quick Launch Bar

The Quick Launch toolbar, as it comes with Windows, has four buttons on it:

- Click this button if you want to start the Internet Explorer program.

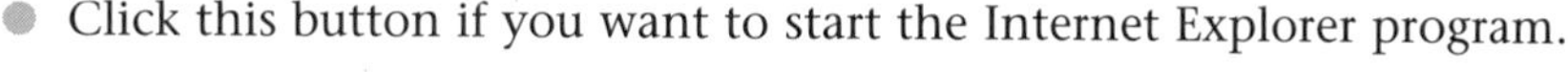

- Click this button if you want to start Outlook Express, the Internet email program.

- Click this button if you want to view the desktop and hide all open programs and windows.

- Click this button if you want to start the Internet Explorer program and visit the Channels Web page.

These four buttons are the ones Microsoft suggests for the toolbar. Of the four, you probably will use the two Internet icons. The Desktop icon is handy for hiding everything and getting a good look at the desktop. (The Channels icon I could do without.) In addition to those four, you want to put your own popular programs on the Quick Launch bar. Here's my advice:

Put your most commonly used programs on the Quick Launch bar.

Put on the bar only the programs you use every day—for example, Microsoft Word, Excel, a game, and whatever else you use *all the time*. Putting too many things there defeats the purpose and turns the Quick Launch bar into a copy of the desktop or Start Thing menu.

The following tutorial puts the FreeCell game on the Quick Launch bar (are you a FreeCell addict yet?):

▶ **From the Start Thing menu, choose Programs ➡Accessories ➡Games.**

This action displays the Games submenu, on which you find the shortcut to FreeCell.

▶ **Press and hold the Ctrl key.**

You're about do to a *Control+drag*, which means that you drag the mouse while holding down the control key (Ctrl) on the keyboard.

▶ **Drag the FreeCell menu item from the Start Thing menu to the Quick Launch bar.**

Notice the + (plus sign) attached to the mouse pointer as you drag the icon. It's your sign that the icon is being copied and not moved; a Ctrl+drag is a copy operation.

As you point the mouse at the Quick Launch bar, you see an insertion pointer, showing you exactly where the new icon will appear on the Quick Launch bar.

▶ **Release the mouse button.**

A copy of the FreeCell game is dropped on the Quick Launch bar.

- **Stop pressing the Ctrl key.**
- **Click the mouse on the desktop to hide the Start Thing menu.**

The Start Thing menu doesn't disappear after you drop the icon on the Quick Launch bar; clicking the mouse on the desktop makes the menu go away.

Look at the Quick Launch bar. Your icon lives there, easily and quickly accessible.

If more buttons are on the Quick Launch bar than can be displayed, a small triangle appears on the right side of the toolbar. Use the triangle to scroll left to see more buttons. Or you can rearrange the toolbar to a larger size, which is covered in Chapter 38, "Toolbars from Beyond Infinity."

- **Point the mouse at the FreeCell icon on the Quick Launch bar.**

The word *FreeCell* appears if you hold the mouse still. That's the icon's name, and you can change it:

- **Right-click the Quick Launch bar handle.**
- **Choose Open from the pop-up menu.**

A My Computer window is displayed, showing you the Quick Launch bar's contents as they're stored in a folder on disk. It's another way you can edit the Quick Launch bar; any shortcut icon pasted into this folder/window becomes a part of the Quick Launch bar.

- **Right-click the FreeCell shortcut icon.**
- **Choose Rename.**
- **Press the Home key and type** Maddening **and a space.**
- **Press the down-arrow key and type a space and then** game.
- **Press Enter.**

Don't bother junking up the Quick Launch bar. Windows 98 has other places (the desktop and the Start Thing menu, for example) to put programs you use occasionally.

Now the icon is named "Maddening FreeCell game."

- **Close the My Computer window.**
- **Point the mouse at the FreeCell icon on the Quick Launch bar.**

Cute. Accurate, but cute.

- Pressing the Ctrl (Control) key while dragging with the mouse copies an icon from one place to another. It's known as a *Ctrl+drag*.
- You can add any icon to the Quick Launch bar by dragging and dropping it.
- You can move any icon on the Quick Launch bar by dragging it right or left.
- Any shortcut icon pasted into the Quick Launch bar's window becomes part of the Quick Launch bar. (As with the Start Thing menu, paste only shortcuts to the bar.)

If you tweak Windows frequently, drag a Control Panel shortcut to the Quick Launch bar: Open My Computer on the desktop and drag the Control Panel's icon to the Quick Launch bar. Click Yes when you're asked whether you want to create a shortcut.

Running a Program from the Quick Launch Bar

Running a program from the Quick Launch bar is cinchy—one of the few times that happens in Windows. Click a program icon on the Quick Launch bar to run that program.

▶ **Click the FreeCell icon on the Quick Launch bar.**

Oops. Now you're *forced* to play a game of FreeCell. (Press the F2 key if you really want to.) Good luck!

The pathname for the Quick Launch bar's folder is

```
C:\Windows\Application
Data\Microsoft\Internet
Explorer\Quick Launch
```

Keep the FreeCell window open when you're done (or just keep it open if you're smart enough not to start playing).

▶ **Click the desktop button on the Quick Launch bar.**

The desktop button quickly displays the desktop for you, shrinking any open programs or windows to an icon on the taskbar. It's a handy way to redisplay the desktop if you need to access something there.

▶ **Click the FreeCell button on the taskbar.**

Oops! Now you have to play *another* game of FreeCell!

I'm sure that FreeCell somehow fits into Einstein's space, time, and black-hole theories.

▶ **Close the FreeCell window when you're done.**

If you ever get done!

Removing a Program

As usual, you can delete an icon from the Quick Launch bar in several ways. The most obvious is the drag-and-drop to the Recycle Bin:

▶ **Drag the FreeCell icon from the Quick Launch bar to the Recycle Bin on the desktop.**

If a warning dialog box appears, click Yes to trash the icon.

Remember that you're not deleting any program here; you're simply removing a shortcut icon.

The Desktop and Channels icons on the Quick Launch bar are special. Because they're not true shortcuts, deleting them is not a good idea. Instead, if you want to get rid of them, I recommend removing them from the Quick Launch bar and storing them somewhere handy:

Right-click the Quick Launch bar handle.

Choose Open.

The Quick Launch bar's window is displayed.

In this example, I'm having you remove the View Channels icon from the toolbar. Because it's a special icon, however, you're only *moving* it and not deleting it:

▶ **Right-click the View Channels icon.**

▶ **Choose Cut.**

The icon appears *dimmed*, which means that it has been cut but not yet pasted anywhere.

▶ **Click the Up button.**

This step takes you to the next-highest folder on your hard drive, which happens to be named Internet Explorer.

If you can't see the Up button in the My Computer window, press the Backspace key on your keyboard.

▶ **Click the Paste button.**

The View Channels icon is pasted into the window. If you were looking, you could see that at the same time it was removed from the Quick Launch bar.

The icon was deleted yet saved!

To put the icon back, simply repeat the preceding steps (without the cut-and-paste part) and then drag the icon in the Internet Explorer window back to the Quick Launch folder.

Repeat these special steps if you also plan to remove the Desktop icon from the Quick Launch bar. You can Ctrl+drag any other icon, including Internet Explorer or Outlook Express, from the Start Thing menu. The Desktop and Channels icons are special, however.

- You can also delete an icon by right-clicking it and choosing the Delete command from the menu.
- If you're using Netscape rather than Internet Explorer, you can delete the Internet Explorer icon on the Quick Launch bar and replace it with Netscape. The same goes for Outlook Express: Replace it with your preferred email program, if you have one.
- You can also delete an icon by opening the Quick Launch window and deleting the icon from there.

Other Ways to Start a Program

You should use the Start Thing menu for *every* program on your computer. The Quick Launch bar should be used for the things you use every day. What about other icons?

Use Shortcuts on the Desktop

If you don't feel like junking up the Quick Launch bar, consider making shortcut icons on the desktop instead. In fact, my personal desktop is littered with the icons of just about every major program I own. My desktop also contains shortcuts to project folders and even some shortcuts to documents I use frequently.

Refer to Chapter 9 for more information about putting shortcut icons on the desktop.

Use the Documents Menu

A second way to quickly start a program is to use the Documents menu on the Start Thing. The Documents menu contains the previous 15 documents you've opened. Choosing a document from this menu instantly loads the document into whichever program created it.

Use the Run Command

Also lurking on the Start Thing menu is the Run command. This command is not handy like the other ways of running programs. No, it's intended for typing a program name. Crude. Primitive. But effective.

▶ **From the Start Thing menu, choose Run.**

The Run dialog box appears, as shown in Figure 11.4, reminding many people of what the old days under DOS were like.

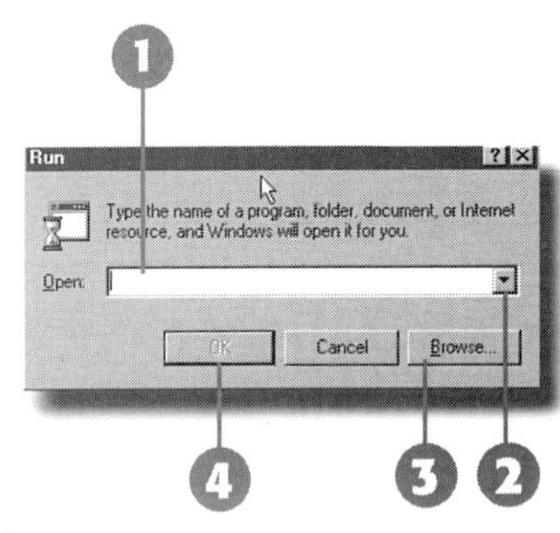

Figure 11.4
The Run dialog box.

1. Type the program name here.
2. Click to see previously typed program names (a whole list!)
3. Browse the hard drive for a program.
4. Run that program!

The idea is to type the name of the program you want to run—frequently an installation or setup program. Normally you're told *exactly* what to type in this dialog box. (There goes the mystery!)

Those are backslashes, not forward slashes.

Double-check to see that everything you've typed is kosher.

Click OK.

▶ **Type** c:\windows\media\bach's brandenburg concerto no. 3

Type the text exactly as shown here.

Ahh-ooo-gah! Oops. A warning dialog box points out that the program cannot be found.

I made that happen on purpose because I want to show you the nasty warning you see when you innocently forget to type something or make a common typo. That's why Windows was created: Typos and innocent mistakes drove DOS users mad.

▶ **Click OK to close the warning dialog box.**

Back in the Run dialog box, you have to edit the command so that Windows knows what to do with it.

▶ **Press the End key.**

The insertion pointer moves to the end of your command.

▶ **Type** .rmi

Type a period and then **rmi**.

▶ **Press Enter.**

If you see the warning dialog box again (this time not on purpose), you have to recheck your typing. Here's the full command you have to type:

c:\windows\media\bach's brandenburg concerto no. 3.rmi

If everything goes okay, you should be waking your neighbors with a rousing electronic version of J.S. Bach's Brandenburg Concerto no. 3.

It sings! I feel like da-a-a-ancing!

▶ **Close the Media Player window to stop the song.**

Or just let the song run out; the window closes automatically when the song is over. The music runs for a little longer than six minutes.

By the way, you can click the speaker icon in the system tray part of the taskbar to adjust your PC's volume level. Or refer to Chapter 41, "Sound Advice," which discusses volume in voluminous detail.

- You must type program names *exactly* when you use the Run dialog box.
- The Brandenburg Concerto in Windows 98 is not a program—it's a MIDI document. When you run it, Windows automatically loads the Media Player and plays the song for you.
- Your PC might have another MIDI program, in which case the Brandenburg Concerto is loaded into it for playback.
- Chapter 27, "Hunting Down Files," discusses how to use the Find command to locate MIDI music documents on your computer.

Chapter 12

Doing Several Things at a Time

Questions Answered and Thoughts Inspired

- How to use more than one program at a time
- How to switch programs with the taskbar
- How to switch programs with Alt+Tab
- How to arrange windows on the desktop

I watched an infomercial once where this guy actually made money while he slept. In fact, during the half-hour the infomercial ran, he made something like $12,000 in accrued interest. Amazing—not really the money part, but that the guy could do two things at one time.

Now you too can do two things at one time (three, if you take the guy's real estate advice). Windows blesses you with the ability to run several programs at the same time. It's called *multitasking*, and it really can save you time—if you know how it works, which is this chapter's topic.

- Don't close when you don't have to!
- Don't quit when you don't have to!
- Don't fall into the easy-money in real estate trap!

The Multitasking Demonstration

The idea behind multitasking isn't that you can use two or more programs at one time. You can't! Because you have only one head and one set of hands, you can work only one program at a time. The idea behind multitasking is that you don't have to quit one program to use another. You keep them all running and then switch between them.

▶ **From the Start Thing menu, choose Programs ➡ System Tools ➡ System Monitor.**

The System Monitor is a silly little program that shows how hard your computer is working (see Figure 12.1). It graphs various aspects of your computer—microprocessor usage and memory usage, for example—which is interesting to watch but trivial because it's nothing bad or worth remembering. The only reason I'm using it here is to show how your computer can do more than one thing at a time.

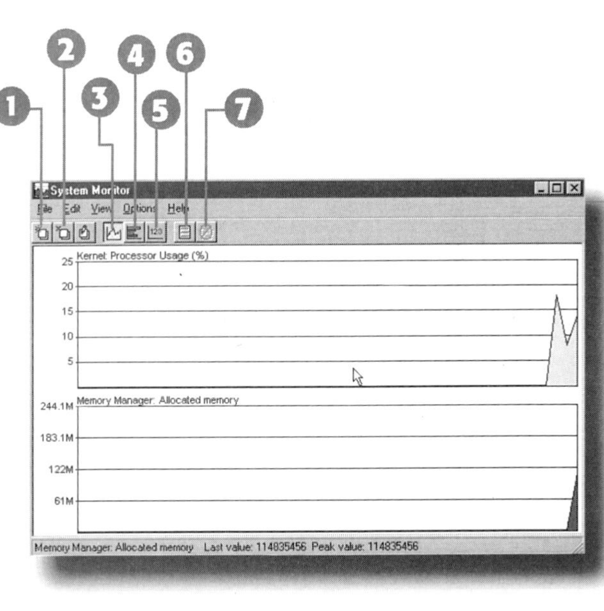

Figure 12.1

The System Monitor.

1. Use the Add button to add a new item to display.
2. The Remove button lets you remove an item from the display.
3. Line chart mode.
4. Bar chart mode.
5. Number chart mode.
6. Trivia.
7. More trivia.

▶ **Make sure that the Kernel Processor Usage and Memory Manager: Allocated Memory items are visible.**

If the items aren't visible (as shown in Figure 12.1), choose Edit ➡Add Item from the menu. In the Add Item dialog box, click Kernel, Processor Usage (%), and then OK. Then repeat these steps and, in the Add Item dialog box, click Memory Manager, Allocated Memory, and then OK.

Other items visible in the System Monitor are okay to add; I just want you to see something happening in the window during this demonstration.

▶ **Start WordPad.**

See? You have no reason to quit the other program; just start whatever you want to work on next.

> ***Don't quit a program until you're doggone done with it.***

▶ **Resize the WordPad window so that you can see the System Monitor window.**

Figure 12.2 shows what I'm getting at. You can position the WordPad window anywhere on the desktop; just make sure that you can still see the System Monitor in the background.

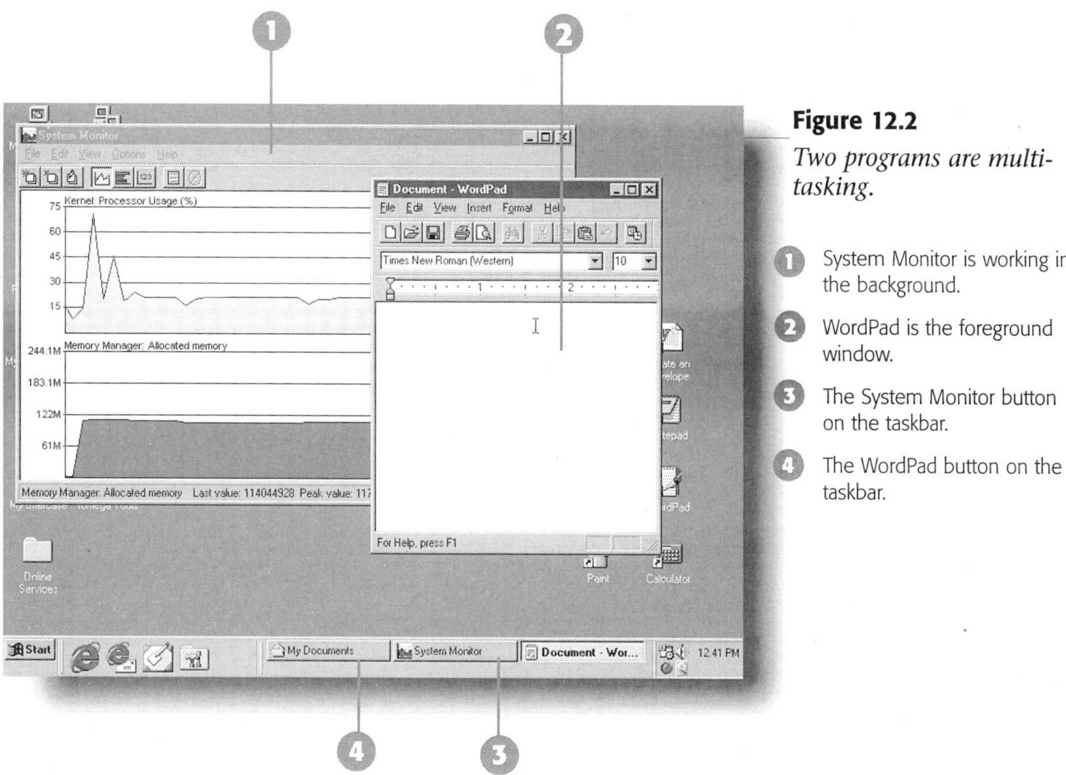

Figure 12.2
Two programs are multitasking.

1. System Monitor is working in the background.
2. WordPad is the foreground window.
3. The System Monitor button on the taskbar.
4. The WordPad button on the taskbar.

Keep both WordPad and System Monitor open for the following section.

- The program you're working on is in the *foreground.*
- Programs you have open are running in the *background.* It's a back-burner type of thing: Programs in the background continue to run just like a pot of soup on a stove's back burner continues to cook.
- Not every program runs in the background. Most programs require your input; when you switch that type of program to the background, it just sits and waits for you.

Switching Between Programs

Having two programs running is easy. Switching between them is easy too, after you learn the tricks:

- Bring any window to the foreground by clicking it.
- Click a window's taskbar button to bring the window to the foreground.
- Press the Alt+Tab key combination to switch windows.

To bring any window to the foreground, click it with the mouse.

▶ **Click on the System Monitor window.**

This step brings that window to the foreground. WordPad moves to the background.

▶ **Click on the WordPad window.**

Now you're back in WordPad.

▶ **Type some text in the WordPad window.**

Type this line:

```
System Monitor Report. At 12:40 PM, my System Monitor has shown the following:
```

▶ **Click the System Monitor button on the taskbar.**

▶ **Press Alt+Print Screen.**

Pressing the Alt+Print Screen key combination takes a snapshot of the foreground window. (You press Print Screen by itself to take a snapshot of the entire screen, as described in Chapter 17.)

▶ **Click the WordPad button on the taskbar.**

▶ **Press Ctrl+V.**

The graphics image is pasted into the WordPad window. (Ctrl+V is the shortcut for the Paste command.)

▶ **Maximize WordPad.**

Scroll up and down to see the entire image if you have to.

Most of the time you run your programs maximized, which is best. However, you cannot point-and-click at a window to bring it to the foreground. You have two options: Either use the taskbar or do this:

The Alt+Tab key combination switches you to the previously viewed window.

Press and hold the Alt key.

Tap the Tab key.

▶ **Press Alt+Tab.**

The System Monitor window is now up front.

You should see the Alt+Tab task window, as shown in Figure 12.3. Keep that Alt key held down!

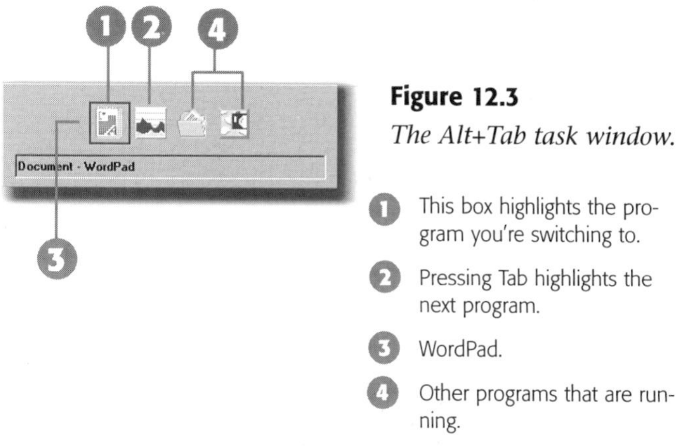

Figure 12.3
The Alt+Tab task window.

1. This box highlights the program you're switching to.
2. Pressing Tab highlights the next program.
3. WordPad.
4. Other programs that are running.

▶ **Tap the Tab key again.**

Keep that Alt key held down!

Notice that the highlight box moves to the next program in the list. Every time you press the Tab key, you select another program to run.

▶ **Press the Tab key until the WordPad icon is highlighted.**

▶ **Release the Alt key.**

You're back in WordPad.

Keep WordPad and the System Monitor open for the following section's tutorials.

- To switch to another program, simply click that program's window.
- To switch to another program, click that program's button on the taskbar.
- Pressing Alt+Tab returns you to the preceding window or program you were viewing.
- Pressing Alt+Tab and keeping the Alt key held down displays the task window, from which you can choose a program. Press Tab to choose an icon; release the Alt key to switch to that window.
- The Alt+Tab key combination works best when two or more programs or windows are open.
- Yes, Alt+Tab even switches to a program that has been minimized to a button on the taskbar.

Arranging Program Windows

Alt+Tab is officially known as the "cool switch."

I recommend that you run all your programs maximized. Unfortunately, you lose a little interactivity when you can see windows onscreen. Even with a small monitor, sometimes overlapping windows have advantages.

Arranging windows is a job given to the taskbar—specifically, the taskbar's shortcut menu.

▶ **Right-click a blank part of the taskbar.**

If you cannot find a blank part of the taskbar, right-click the current time in the system tray.

The taskbar's shortcut menu appears, as shown in Figure 12.4.

▶ **Choose Minimize All Windows.**

Floop! There's the desktop.

▶ **Open the My Documents window.**

You can find the My Documents icon on the desktop.

▶ **Restore the System Monitor window.**

Click the System Monitor button on the taskbar.

▶ **Right-click the taskbar and choose Tile Windows Horizontally.**

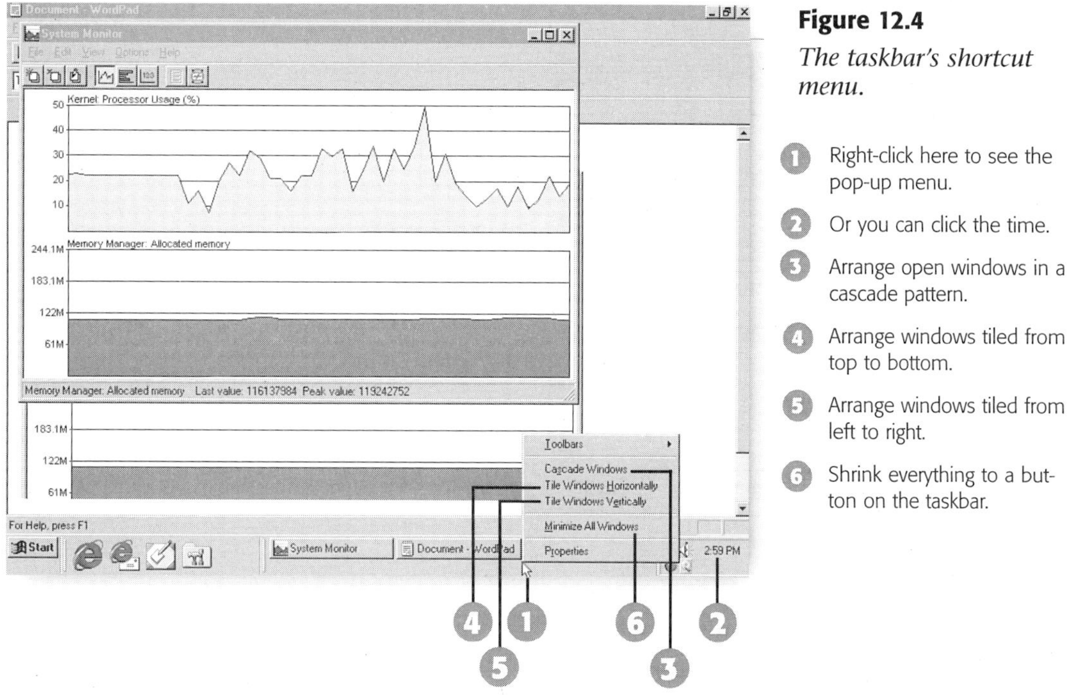

Figure 12.4
The taskbar's shortcut menu.

1. Right-click here to see the pop-up menu.
2. Or you can click the time.
3. Arrange open windows in a cascade pattern.
4. Arrange windows tiled from top to bottom.
5. Arrange windows tiled from left to right.
6. Shrink everything to a button on the taskbar.

Each window is displayed above the other. I find this arrangement highly useful for comparing two similar documents.

Notice that the WordPad window didn't get in the way. Only open windows are affected by the window-arranging commands.

- ▶ **Restore the WordPad window.**
- ▶ **Right-click the taskbar and choose Tile Windows Horizontally.**

That method doesn't really work, does it? Unless you have a large monitor with tiny windows, it's not useful.

- ▶ **Right-click the taskbar and choose Tile Windows Vertically.**

Better. Not many people use three windows at a time, however. Try this:

- ▶ **Right-click the taskbar and choose Cascade Windows.**

Each window is visible, if only by its title bar.

- ▶ **Minimize the System Monitor.**
- ▶ **Right-click the taskbar and choose Tile Windows Vertically.**

Now you can get a good view of two windows side by side; if you need the third window, click its button on the taskbar.

▶ **Close all windows.**

Because you have no need to save the file in WordPad, click No when you're asked. Close System Monitor—heck, close everything!

- Why mess with windows this way? Because you can run more than one program at a time.
- Only visible windows are affected by the commands on the taskbar's pop-up menu. Windows shrunk to buttons on the taskbar are not affected.

You don't really need to see all open windows at one time. When you're working between two programs, however, minimize all other windows and arrange the two windows by choosing Tile Windows Vertically from the taskbar's pop-up menu.

Chapter 13

Sharing with Cut and Paste

Questions Answered and Thoughts Inspired

- Understanding cut, copy, and paste
- Refusing to paste
- Viewing cut or copied stuff in the Clipboard
- Dragging to copy or cut
- Dragging to the desktop

Copying, cutting, and pasting should be old hat to you. You have, in addition to the kindergarten stuff, other ways to put information from one program into another program. This chapter covers all that.

A Basic Cut and Paste Review

Most *productivity* applications (programs that do stuff) enable you to cut and paste. Everything about cut and paste is kept on the basic Edit menu, as shown in Figure 13.1.

All these commands should be basic stuff for you, reviewed in Table 13.1. Oh—included with the Cut, Copy, and Paste commands are often Undo and Delete.

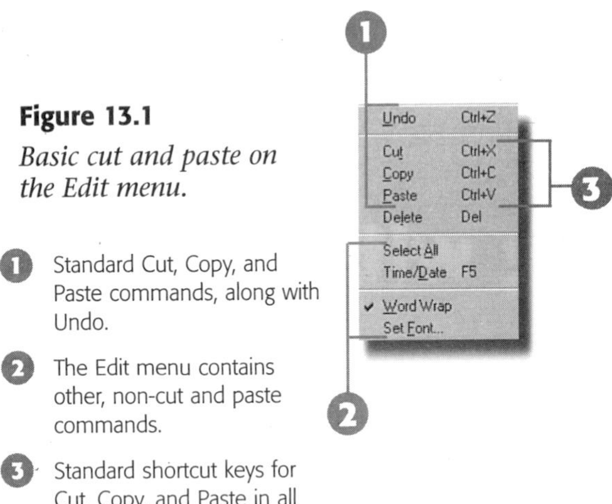

Figure 13.1
Basic cut and paste on the Edit menu.

1. Standard Cut, Copy, and Paste commands, along with Undo.
2. The Edit menu contains other, non-cut and paste commands.
3. Standard shortcut keys for Cut, Copy, and Paste in all Windows programs.

Table 13.1 Basic commands on the Edit menu.

Command	Shortcut Key	What It Does
Cut	Ctrl+X	Cuts the selected item, deleting it but also copying it to the Clipboard
Copy	Ctrl+C	Copies selected item to the Clipboard
Paste	Ctrl+V	Copies item from the Clipboard to your document
Undo	Ctrl+Z	Undoes your last edit or command
Delete	Del	Deletes selected item

- The selected item can be text or a graphics image.
- You can copy, cut, and paste within a document, across two documents, or between documents in separate programs.

"It Won't Paste!"

Cutting and copying are easy: You select the text or graphic you want to cut or copy and then cut it or copy it. You're done! Pasting can be a pain, though, primarily because many people forget this kindergarten admonition:

> You cannot paste text into programs that do not accept text, nor can you paste graphics into a text-only document. (This topic is discussed in the following section.)

- ▶ **Start Notepad.**
- ▶ **Type some text in Notepad.**

Type this line:

```
Here is what a red square looks like:
```

Press Enter two times to end the line.

Notice that you're typing *red square,* not *Red Square.* One is for Russians, and the other is a basic shape-and-color learning tool for 4-year-olds. Know the difference.

- ▶ **Start Paint.**
- ▶ **Draw a red square.**

Figure 13.2 shows you how.

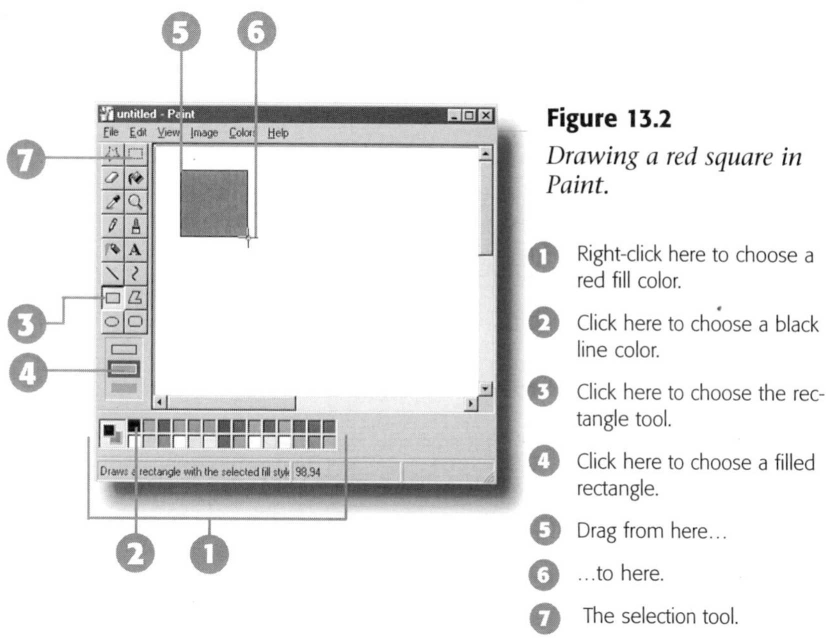

Figure 13.2

Drawing a red square in Paint.

1. Right-click here to choose a red fill color.
2. Click here to choose a black line color.
3. Click here to choose the rectangle tool.
4. Click here to choose a filled rectangle.
5. Drag from here…
6. …to here.
7. The selection tool.

- ▶ **Select the red square.**

Use the selection tool to drag a rectangle around the square.

- ▶ **Press Ctrl+C.**

The square is copied to the Clipboard.

▶ **Switch back to Notepad.**

You can press Atl+Tab or just click the Notepad button on the toolbar.

▶ **Press Ctrl+V to paste.**

Uh. Nothing happens, right?

If it won't paste, it won't paste. Don't keep pressing Ctrl+V and assume that the computer will change its mind.

Check the Edit menu:

▶ **Drop down the Edit menu.**

The Paste option is unavailable, right? The reason is that Notepad is a text-only application. It cannot accept graphics. You cannot paste the red square—a graphic—into a text-only application.

It doesn't work the other way, either:

▶ **Select the text in Notepad.**

Drag the mouse over the text *Here is what a red square looks like:* to select it.

▶ **Press Ctrl+C.**

The Copy command's shortcut key is Ctrl+C.

▶ **Switch back to Paint.**

▶ **Choose Edit ➡Paste.**

The Paste command is *dimmed*; it's unavailable. Why? Because Paint is a graphics program. You cannot paste text into it.

Keep both Paint and Notepad open for the next section's tutorial.

- Don't worry about knowing in advance which programs don't let you paste text or graphics. You know when you try to paste and nothing gets pasted.
- Quite a few advanced graphics programs don't let you paste graphics or text—unless the graphics or text were created in that program.
- The bottom line: If the Paste menu option is dimmed, you cannot paste, no matter how danged sure you are. That's just life in Windows.

Peeking at the Clipboard

Everything cut or copied in Windows is stored in the Clipboard. There it sits until something else is copied or cut.

If you do not want to add the Clipboard Viewer now, skip ahead to the following section.

▶ **From the Start Thing menu, choose Programs ➡Accessories ➡System Tools ➡Clipboard Viewer.**

The Clipboard Viewer appears. If you've been following along with this chapter's tutorial, the viewer should look somewhat like Figure 13.3.

You can view the contents of the Clipboard, but only if you install the Clipboard Viewer program. This program is normally not installed with Windows. Instead, you must add it yourself. To continue, see Chapter 15, "Adding More of Windows," to read how to add the Clipboard Viewer.

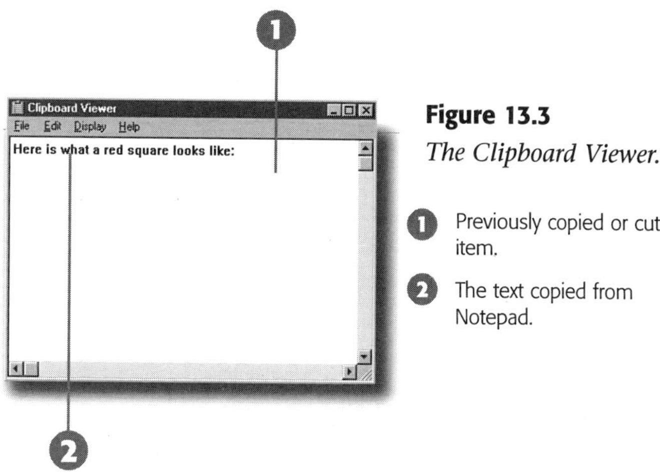

Figure 13.3
The Clipboard Viewer.

1. Previously copied or cut item.
2. The text copied from Notepad.

You can use the Display menu in the Clipboard Viewer to show how cut or copied items look to different programs. It might explain why something copied from one application might look different when it's pasted into another.

▶ **Switch back to the Paint program.**

It helps if you can position the Paint program's window so that you can still see the Clipboard Viewer.

▶ **Select the red square again (if you need to).**

▶ **Choose Edit ➡Copy.**

Lo, the red square appears in the Clipboard Viewer window.

The Clipboard Viewer proves that the Windows Clipboard is capable of holding only one item at a time. Many people forget this fact as they cut and paste.

Although you still can't paste the square into Notepad, the red square is available for pasting into any graphics-happy program.

Keep Notepad, Paint, and the Clipboard Viewer open for the following tutorial.

The Copy-Drag and the Cut-Drag

Copying and cutting are done much more easily by dragging with the mouse as opposed to using menu or keyboard commands. Here are a few general rules:

- Dragging a selected item is a cut-and-paste (move) operation.
- Dragging a selected item with the Ctrl key pressed is a copy-and-paste operation.

Not every program has drag-and-drop capabilities. Of all the freebies that come with Windows, WordPad is one of the few that enables you to copy-drag or cut-drag.

Dragging and Copying with WordPad

WordPad lets you copy and cut text within a document by using only your mouse and maybe the Ctrl key:

▶ **Start WordPad.**

▶ **Switch back to Notepad.**

Click the Notepad button on the taskbar.

▶ **Choose Edit ➡Select All.**

▶ **Choose Edit ➡Cut.**

All the text in the Notepad document has been selected and cut.

▶ **Close the Notepad window.**

If you're asked to save the document, choose No.

Better check to make sure that the text was properly cut and saved in the Clipboard:

▶ **Switch to the Clipboard Viewer.**

Yup. (Normally you would never need to do this step; Windows is very good about not losing anything that's copied. I'm just running a tutorial here.)

▶ **Switch to WordPad.**

▶ **Press Ctrl+V.**

Now the text is in WordPad.

▶ **Select the words *red square.***

Drag the mouse over the words *red square* to select them.

▶ **Drag the selected text down (but don't release the mouse button!).**

Point the mouse at the text, and then drag. Figure 13.4 details what you should see.

You have to be careful here; if you click too soon after selecting the text, you deselect the text and have to start over.

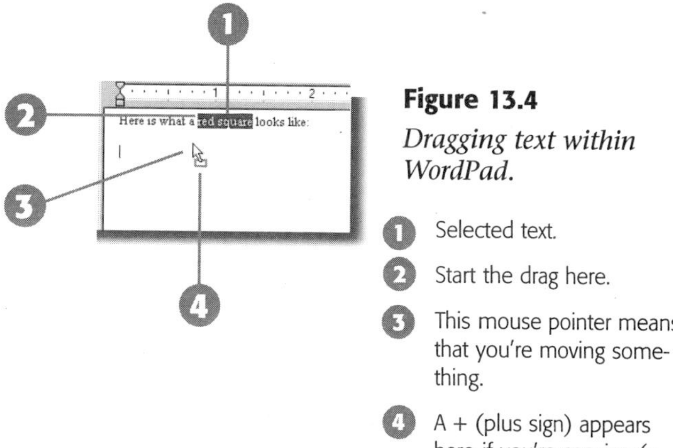

Figure 13.4
Dragging text within WordPad.

1. Selected text.
2. Start the drag here.
3. This mouse pointer means that you're moving something.
4. A + (plus sign) appears here if you're copying (a Ctrl+drag).

▶ **Press and release the Ctrl key (and keep the mouse button held down).**

A plus sign (+) appears along with the mouse pointer. When you press the Ctrl key, the drag operation becomes a *copy*, not a move.

The + by the mouse pointer means that you're copying (pressing the Ctrl key).

- **Keep the Ctrl key held down, and drag the text down two lines.**
- **Release the mouse button and then the Ctrl key.**

The text *red square* is copied on the third line in WordPad.

- **Switch to the Clipboard Viewer.**

The text does not appear because a copy-drag or move-drag operation within the same document doesn't involve the Clipboard. In fact, you should still see in the Clipboard the original text you copied from Notepad.

- **Close the Clipboard Viewer window.**

You're done with it for now.

- **From the taskbar's shortcut menu, choose Tile Windows Vertically.**

This command is covered in Chapter 12. Both WordPad and Paint should be positioned side by side on your screen.

- **Switch to Paint.**
- **Select the red square.**
- **Press Ctrl+C.**
- **Switch to WordPad.**
- **Press Ctrl+V.**

The red square appears in WordPad. Why? Because WordPad allows graphics to be pasted along with text.

The graphic appears with *handles* on it—eight total: one each on the corners and sides of the square. You can use the handles to resize the square, or you can drag the thing up or down in the document—just like you dragged text earlier.

If the text you copy-dragged *(red square)* was selected, the graphic you just pasted replaced the selected text.

- **Close Paint.**

You do not need to save the red square.

Dragging to the Desktop

WordPad is receptive to copying text and graphics in addition to dragging around text and graphics. In fact, you can drag items from the WordPad window and store them on the desktop.

▶ **Drag the red square to the desktop.**

Figure 13.5 shows how to drag an item of text or a graphics image from WordPad to the desktop.

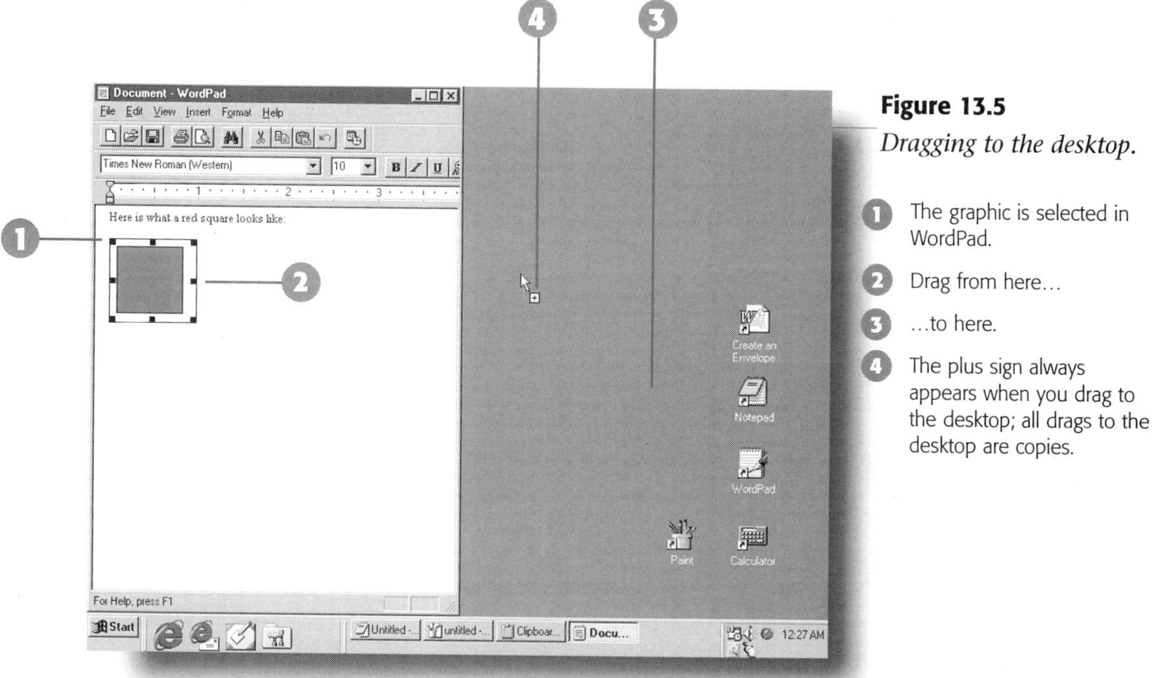

Figure 13.5
Dragging to the desktop.

1. The graphic is selected in WordPad.
2. Drag from here...
3. ...to here.
4. The plus sign always appears when you drag to the desktop; all drags to the desktop are copies.

The item copied to the desktop appears under the name Scrap. That name is dumb. It's like naming all your files File or something. If you want, press the F2 key to rename the Scrap icon to something more logical.

▶ **Press the F2 key and rename the Scrap icon** Red square graphic.

Type the new name, and press Enter to lock in the name change.

▶ **Click the WordPad window to reactivate it.**

▶ **Choose Edit ➡Select All.**

▶ **Press the Delete key.**

You now have a clean slate to work on.

▶ **Drag the red square graphic scrap back into WordPad.**

Lo, there's the graphic again. Notice that this technique was an automatic copy-drag; any scrap you drag in from the desktop is copied into the document.

Unfortunately, you probably have little need for a red square graphic (unless it's your company's not-very-creative logo). Something more interesting is your name and address, such as what you use at the end of a letter:

▶ **Press the Delete key to delete the red square graphic in WordPad.**

▶ **Type your name and address, as shown in this example:**

```
Julius Caesar
3570 Las Vegas Blvd. S.
Las Vegas, NV  89109
```

▶ **Select your name and address.**

Drag the mouse over the text to select it.

▶ **Drag it to the desktop.**

Aha! A different name. Text items from WordPad are given more detailed names than Scrap. The name is still confusing, though.

▶ **Press F2 and rename the Scrap icon** My Address.

Now you have a useful item on the desktop. Whenever you're writing a letter in WordPad (or Microsoft Word or WordPerfect), you can sign it off by dragging the My Address scrap into the document. No more typing!

▶ **Close WordPad.**

No need to save the document, so choose No if you're asked.

▶ **Delete the red square graphic icon if you want.**

Oh, you can keep the red square graphic scrap if it means something to you. No point in messing up the desktop with it, though. Keep the My Address icon; you'll probably use it quite a bit.

- Not every application enables you to drag to the desktop, nor can you drag stuff into all applications. WordPad is one of the few programs that comes with Windows that lets you do that (Notepad and Paint do not). All Microsoft Office programs and other major applications let you drag and drop to the desktop.
- If you drag the My Address icon into Notepad, it looks kind of disgusting. (What you're seeing is the Scrap file data format, which WordPad understands and Notepad does not.)

Here's a big clue about whether a program accepts drag-and-drop information from other programs: If the application has an Insert ➡Object command, you can drag and drop to it. (The Insert ➡Object command has to do with OLE, Object Linking and Embedding, which is an advanced form of cut and paste that few people use.)

- Dragging to and from the desktop works best if you do not maximize your program windows.
- You can copy a scrap item from the desktop by right-clicking the scrap icon and choosing Copy from the pop-up menu.

Chapter 14

Installing and Removing Software

Questions Answered and Thoughts Inspired

- Installing programs in Windows
- Using the Control Panel to install programs
- Installing programs the old-fashioned way
- Removing old cruddy programs
- Using third-party uninstall programs

Windows is only your PC's operating system; it's not the solution to all your computer problems. (Maybe it's the source, but I digress.) To get your work done, you use applications—real programs, not like WordPad or Paint. The process of copying those programs to your PC's hard drive is *installation*. This chapter covers software installation in addition to the process of removing software when you no longer need it.

Adding a New Program to Your PC

Software comes in boxes, shrink-wrapped all neat and tidy for you at the software store. Inside the box are a number of interesting and not-so-interesting items:

- ✓ The disk (or disks) containing the software
- ✓ The manual or a "getting started" guide

✓ A registration card

✓ Bonus stuff you can throw away

The most important item is the disk on which the software lives. Your installation task is to copy the files from that disk to your PC's hard drive. A special *Install* or *Setup* program does that for you, making sure that everything is done just so.

- The disk is most likely a CD-ROM, although some programs still come on floppy disks.
- Computer manuals are terrible, for the most part. They're also slim to non-existent in many packages. Don't fret: You can find most of the documentation in the Help system (refer to Chapter 8).
- You'll probably end up buying a book about the software to supplement any information that comes in the box.
- Sending in the registration card is optional. For some programs, you have to send it in to receive your "free" support. Most of the time, sending in the card just puts you on a junk-mail list.
- You can also register many applications over the Internet. Or you can have information printed on your printer, and then you can fax it if you want.
- Me? I never turn in registration cards. I get enough junk mail already. No matter how much a company promises, I've never received information about an update or next edition to any software package I've ever registered. (Microsoft doesn't like it when I write that, but it's true.)
- The "bonus stuff" you get often includes offers for add-on products, subscriptions to magazines, offers to join AOL, or some other way to waste your money. Sift through the offers lightly.

Installation Overview

I can't tell you exactly what happens during the installation process for every single program out there. The process generally goes like this:

1. **You stick the CD in your CD-ROM drive.**
2. **Windows recognizes the new software and asks whether you want to install it.**
3. **You run the installation program, which is usually a wizard that asks you a bunch of questions: You're asked how you want to install the program, choose options, and type your name, for example.**

4. **Files are copied to your hard drive.**
5. **Optionally, you might have to reset your PC.**
6. **You start using the program.**

The following section details the installation of a specific package. The following bullets highlight some exceptions to the preceding steps, plus some tips and pointers I've given people through the years:

- Before the installation, disable any antivirus programs you have. The antivirus programs might assume that the Install or Setup program is a virus and not a legitimate program. (See Chapter 46, "Tools to Help You," for more information about viruses.)
- If the Install or Setup program doesn't start automatically when you insert the CD or if you're installing from floppy disks, you have to use the Add/Remove Programs icon in the Control Panel. This subject is covered later in this chapter.

TIP

It's generally a good idea to quit all other programs before you start an installation. Doing so isn't a must—it's just that the installation program might restart your computer and, if you haven't saved a document in another window, slow things up.

- The Install or Setup program generally offers you choices, with one option suggested. Take the suggested option. Change something only if you really know what it's all about.
- Reset when the computer asks you to reset.
- After the installation, put the CD or other disks back in the box and store the box in a safe place. If you keep in a box all the goodies that come with the program, you can find them more easily later.
- If the program comes with a tutorial or workbook, do the exercises.

Using the Add/Remove Programs Icon in the Control Panel

You stuck the disk in the CD-ROM drive. Nothing. You stuck the floppy disk into drive A. Nothing. Yet you know that the program has to install somehow.

Time to try the Add/Remove Programs icon:

▶ **Make sure that your installation disk is in the floppy or CD-ROM drive.**

It would be nice if the computer could grow arms, open your software, insert the disk, and then install everything, but—alas—that won't happen.

▶ **Open the Control Panel.**

▶ **Open the Add/Remove Programs icon.**

The Add/Remove Programs Properties window is displayed, as shown in Figure 14.1.

▶ **Click the Install button.**

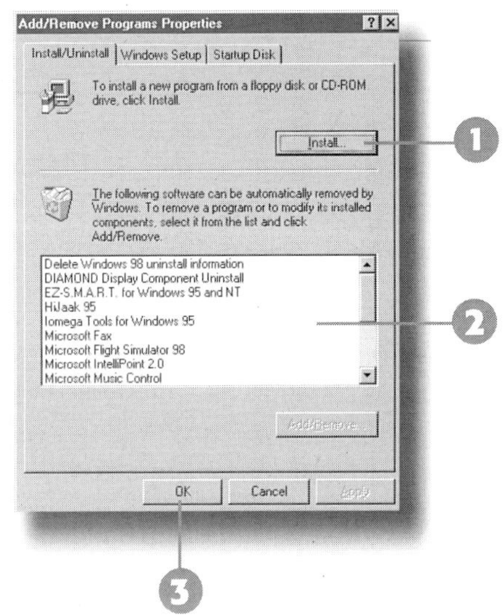

Figure 14.1
The Add/Remove Programs Properties window.

1. Click here to have Windows look for your Install or Setup program.
2. List of previously installed programs.
3. Click OK to start looking.

A wizard appears. Oh joy.

▶ **Click Next.**

Windows looks on drive A and then on your CD-ROM drive for a setup or installation program.

If Windows finds a program, you see its complex DOS pathname displayed in the Command Line for Installation Program input box. If that looks good, you're done—with this part, at least.

If no program is found, either nothing is available to install or Windows just failed again and is making you feel guilty. See the following section.

▶ **Click Finish to install the program (if any).**

Or click Cancel to rid yourself of the Add/Remove Programs Properties window.

At this point, your installation program takes over. Pay attention. Heed the advice I so lovingly gave you in the "Installation Overview" section, earlier in this chapter.

Doing It All Manually

Not every program installs automatically, and the Add/Remove Programs icon doesn't find every startup program. For example, older DOS programs or games might not follow the rules, and you have to set them up manually. Another exception: downloading software from the Internet.

The new rules for installing software: Hunt.

Open My Computer or use Windows Explorer, and locate the install file or the program you downloaded from the Internet. Find that icon and open it, and you're in business.

With some old, old DOS programs, you might have to do the installation yourself. In those cases, you have to copy all the files from the DOS floppy disk to a folder on your hard drive. Follow these steps:

TIP

What's the program's name? That's iffy. It could be Setup or Install. If the file was downloaded from the Internet, it could be *anything*. Pay attention! Read the instructions! Write down the installation filename!

- **Stick the DOS floppy disk in drive A.**

Likewise, stick the DOS program's CD-ROM into your CD-ROM drive.

- **Open My Computer.**

- **Open the drive A icon.**

This step works only if you have the disk in drive A; otherwise, you get an error.

Also, if you're installing from a CD-ROM drive, use its drive letter rather than drive A.

- **Select the file (or files) you want to copy.**

You might want to copy only one file, or you might need all of them. If a README or READ.ME file is available, open it in WordPad and read the instructions. It tells you which files to install or which program to run.

- **Choose Edit ➡Copy.**

- **Choose drive C from the Address drop-down list.**

The shortcut here is to press the F4 key and then the down-arrow key to select drive C. Press Enter.

- **Open the Program Files folder.**
- **Choose File ➡New ➡Folder.**

The new folder appears, named New Folder.

- **Type a name for the DOS game or program you're installing.**

To quickly select all files in the window, press Ctrl+A. That's the keyboard shortcut for the Edit ➡Select All command.

For example, if you're installing Commander Keen, type **Commander Keen** as the name.

Always give the folder a name befitting its contents.

- **Open the new folder.**
- **Choose Edit ➡Paste.**

The files are copied from drive A to the new folder on drive C.

When the files are done copying, the game is installed.

- **Close the Program Files window.**
- **Remove the disk from drive A.**

If it's a game or program you plan to use often, consider dragging it right now to the Start Thing menu or maybe even to the desktop or Quick Launch bar. Refer to Chapters 9, 10, and 11 for more information.

Place the disk in a safe spot so that you don't lose it.

- The subject of downloading software from the Internet is covered in Chapter 30, "Finding Stuff on the Web."
- Refer to the documentation that came with your program to discover its name. For example, you might have downloaded from the Web a file named NS32W405.EXE. If so, that's the file or icon you have to open to run the installation program.
- Also refer to Chapter 27, " Hunting Down Files," for information about finding specific files and icons on your hard drive.

Removing a Program

Who in his right mind would ever want to remove a program, especially considering how expensive software is? Even so, the desire to rid yourself of some old turkey comes around sooner or later. Most likely it's sooner if your computer dealer installed a bunch of junk on your hard drive.

It's a good idea to remove programs you don't use. Why? Because doing so cleans up your PC's disk space. Programs suck up disk storage. I had on my hard drive a 28MB monster of a program I used maybe once or twice and then never touched. Removing it gave me back that disk space.

Uninstalling a program isn't fatal. As long as you still have the original disks or CD-ROM, you can always reinstall the program later if you need it. If you don't use the program, however, there's no point in keeping it around.

The Absolutely 100% Wrong Way to Uninstall a Program

Never uninstall a program by removing its icon. You should never delete any icon or any file you personally did not create. Besides, long gone are the days when a computer program consisted of just one file. The typical program now consists of several dozen files located all over your hard drive.

I'm not telling you *never* to uninstall software. Obviously, if you don't use the software (like all that junk the dealer put on your hard drive), feel free to get rid of it. Make sure that you *uninstall* it, though; do not just delete the files, icons, and folders.

Another thing people goof up: Removing a program's menu item from the Start Thing does not remove the entire program from your hard drive. Likewise, removing a shortcut from the desktop or Quick Launch bar doesn't kill off the program. Use the Add/Remove Programs icon in the Control Panel, or run the proper Uninstall program.

Never delete program files. Always uninstall them.

- I wouldn't make such a big deal of this subject, but I get lots of letters from people who innocently try to delete a program by deleting icons on their hard drive. This no-no causes mountains of trouble and woe.

The Proper Way to Uninstall

Just about any program you've installed can also be removed by using the Control Panel's Add/Remove Programs icon. Although some exceptions exist, most of the main Windows applications you install can be plucked right out in nearly the same manner they were installed.

Never delete any file, icon, or folder you did not create. Just because you installed a program does not mean that you created it.

▶ **Open the Control Panel.**

▶ **Open the Add/Remove Programs icon.**

The Add/Remove Programs Properties window is displayed, which you've already seen in Figure 14.1. Figure 14.2, however, shows the bottom half of the box, which deals with removing programs.

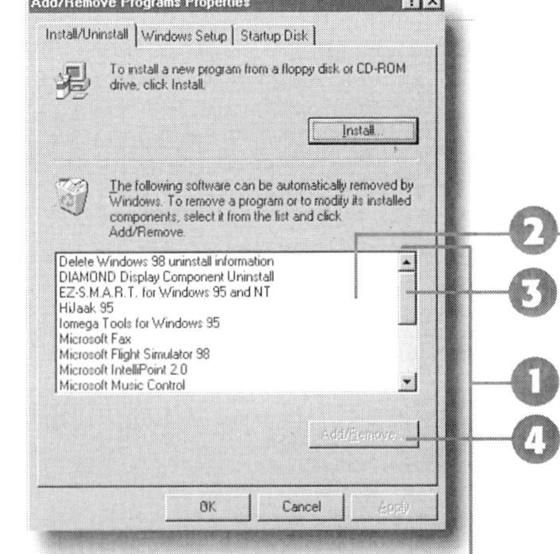

Figure 14.2

The Add/Remove Programs Properties window.

1. The bottom half of the window deals with removing programs.
2. A list of programs that are installed.
3. Use the scrollbar to see more programs.
4. Select a program, and then press this button to remove it.

If your program doesn't appear on the list, you have to use a third-party removal program. The one I recommend is covered in the following section.

Not every program you've installed appears on the list. In fact, the list might even include programs you've already removed.

▶ **Select the program you want to uninstall.**

Click that program's name on the list.

If you're working these steps as a tutorial, you have nothing to remove. (Please don't remove anything you're unfamiliar with just to try it out.)

If you want, you can remove any "uninstall Windows 98" type of programs. They appear if you've upgraded to Windows 98 from an earlier operating system. Although removing the "uninstall Windows 98" programs means that you cannot revert to your old operating system, it also frees up 80 or more megabytes of disk space.

▶ **Click Add/Remove.**

What happens next depends on which program you've chosen. What Windows does is run the program's Uninstall program or the Setup program with an Uninstall option. The next screen you see is probably your application's uninstall program, not Windows itself.

▶ **Continue working whatever steps are necessary to uninstall the program.**

Again, these steps vary, depending on the software.

If you're asked to restart your computer, do so.

- You can also use the Add/Remove button to add or remove individual components of a program. For example, you can add or remove programs from Microsoft Office by using the preceding steps. If you never use Excel, for example, you can remove it and leave the rest of Office intact.
- Why does the "uninstall Windows 98" program exist? For compatibility. Suppose that you have just upgraded and discover that your office's accounting program no longer works. Oops! Better uninstall Windows 98. Otherwise, if everything works (wait a few months to be sure), remove the "uninstall Windows 98" program to free up a few dozen acres of disk space.
- The list of programs in the Add/Remove Programs Properties window does eventually become inaccurate. Windows just can't keep track of all the programs you've installed or uninstalled. Don't let this inaccuracy bug you. If it does, do the following ***at your own peril***: Open the Registry Editor program (REGEDIT), and open the following key:

```
HKEY_LOCAL_MACHINE\SOFTWARE\Microsoft\Windows\CurrentVersion\Uninstall
```

TIP

You don't have to use the Add/Remove Programs icon in the Control Panel if you don't want to. Many applications install a Remove or Uninstall icon when they're first set up. You can open that icon and run the uninstall program manually if you want.

- You see a list of folders representing items displayed in the Add/Remove Programs Properties window. Select the folder for the program you no longer want to see, and press the Delete key to zap the program away. Close the Registry Editor when you're done.

The Best Way to Uninstall

When I uninstall programs, I do so with CleanSweep. It's not a part of Windows (so don't go looking for it). No, CleanSweep is a third-party utility from Quarterdeck. You have to buy it. Although you can get other uninstall utilities for Windows, all of which I'm sure work great, CleanSweep is the only one with which I'm familiar.

CleanSweep works best if you use the Install Monitor. If you don't, CleanSweep can guess about uninstalling programs, although it might not get all the program off your hard drive. For that reason, I recommend buying and installing CleanSweep before you install any other software on your PC.

CleanSweep has two parts: the Install Monitor and the CleanSweep program.

The Install Monitor tracks programs as they're installed. It checks every little jot and tittle the installation program makes or changes in your system, keeping track of everything. All that information is saved on your hard drive.

If you ever need to uninstall a program, you run the main CleanSweep utility. It finds all the pieces of any installed program (especially those the Install Monitor tracks) and then saves the program in a special backup file. That way, if something doesn't work right, you can un-uninstall the program to get your computer working properly. Otherwise, you just delete the backup file after awhile, and you're done.

- Yes, uninstalling programs is a big deal, and it should be done right. CleanSweep and other third-party utilities do a much better job of it than Windows.
- CleanSweep also comes with other disk space-saving utilities, which you can play with if you ever get the program.

Chapter 15

Adding More of Windows

Questions Answered and Thoughts Inspired

- Adding a new Windows component
- Removing a Windows component
- Updating Windows on the Internet

Windows is its own galaxy of programs. At the center is the operating system that controls your computer. Many other programs are in its immediate orbit—some of them useful, some interesting, some an utter waste of time.

Quite a few of those little programs are installed with Windows. Some of the programs are not. If you want to install the other programs, this chapter tells you how. If you want to remove some of the Windows galaxy of programs, this chapter tells you how to do that too.

Adding Something Windows Forgot

Windows 98 doesn't install all of itself on your computer. A few programs are always left on the CD. Most of the time, you don't need those programs. Occasionally, however, you might encounter a situation in which you need to add such-and-such a program from the CD. It's what I call "adding the rest of Windows."

For example, you might need the Clipboard Viewer program, which is covered in Chapter 13. The following tutorial details how to add that program, although you can follow along to add just about any component Windows forgot:

▶ **Insert your Windows 98 CD into your PC's CD-ROM drive.**

If you see (and hear!) the Windows 98 startup banner, just close that window.

▶ **Start the Control Panel.**

Add/Remove Programs

▶ **Open the Add/Remove Programs icon.**

▶ **Click the Windows Setup tab.**

You see a list of Windows components arranged by category, as shown in Figure 15.1.

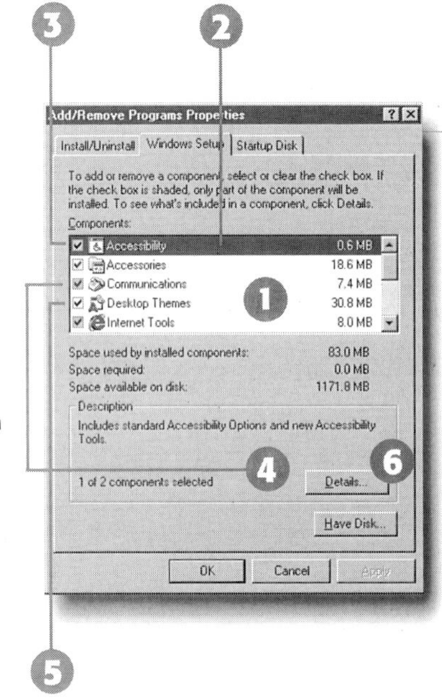

Figure 15.1
Adding Windows components.

1. List of component categories.
2. Choose a category from this list.
3. A check mark means that an item from that category has already been chosen.
4. A shaded check mark means that items from that category have not been chosen.
5. A check mark on a white background means that all items in that category have been chosen.
6. Click here to choose more items.

▶ **Scroll down and select the System Tools category.**

Or, if you were adding some other component, you would select its category.

▶ **Click Details.**

The System Tools dialog box appears.

▶ **Click in the box next to Clipboard Viewer.**

This step puts a check mark in the box.

It's entirely possible to browse the different categories, checking to see what you have (or have not) installed. Click the Details button, as described in the following step, to see which programs live in each category.

If a check mark is already in the box, you have nothing else to do; the Clipboard Viewer is already installed on your system.

▶ **Click OK to close the System Tools dialog box.**

▶ **Click OK to close the Add/Remove Programs dialog box.**

The program is then copied to your hard drive from the Windows CD.

You might sometimes add something heavy-duty that requires Windows to restart your PC. If so, restart it right away. If you don't, you might forget and your new program won't be installed properly until you do restart.

▶ **Close the Control Panel window.**

Now you can go nuts, if you want, and install every dang-doodle part of Windows on your PC.

- Installing *all*, or at least *more*, of Windows uses more disk space.
- Many of the programs that aren't installed are intended for special situations, such as using Windows in a bilingual setting or configuring your PC for easy access by disabled people. If you never use those programs, there's no sense in junking up your PC with them.
- Some programs aren't on the list. For example, I cannot manually install the DVD player, even though my PC has a DVD drive. Unfortunately, it's a DVD drive that Windows does not recognize, so I use another DVD player.

Removing a Piece of Windows

Removing a piece of Windows is cinchy: If you find yourself *not* using a part of Windows, you can easily remove that program from your PC's hard drive and save yourself oodles of space. Well, maybe not oodles.

To get an idea of how much space each part of Windows uses, look at the Add/Remove Programs dialog box:

- **Start the Control Panel.**
- **Open the Add/Remove Programs icon.**
- **Click the Windows Setup tab.**

On the right side of the scrolling window, you see a list of file sizes in megabytes (refer to Figure 15.1 too). For example, on my screen, the Desktop Themes item sucks down a whopping 30.8 megabytes of disk space. Jeez! My first PC's hard drive held only 20 megabytes.

Just as you can add a component, you can also remove a component. Why? Primarily to save disk space. If you're wishy-washy, there's no sense in removing anything.

Those Windows themes and sound schemes sure take up a bunch of disk space.

To remove a program component, click in its box to remove the check mark. Or you can select the component, click Details, and pluck out individual pieces.

- **Choose System Tools.**

Scroll down to find that item, and click it once to select.

- **Click Details.**

The top item in the list is Backup, the paradoxical Microsoft Backup program. The paradox: You can best use Backup in Windows if you have a tape drive, yet all tape drives sold for PCs come with their own, better-than-Microsoft's, backup program. Anyone is free to delete the Microsoft Backup program. In fact, I recommend it.

- **Click in the box by Backup to remove the check mark.**

See the new Space Freed Up item in the window? That item tells you how much disk space will be freed when you click OK.

- **Click OK.**

Nothing is deleted yet, so feel free to browse other components and delete things you might not need. If you don't know what you do not need, don't delete anything. My advice is to use Windows for a while and then review the component list again later. If you haven't used a program on the list, remove it. (If you make a mistake, you can always reinstall the program later, by following the instructions earlier in this chapter.)

Watch the Space Freed Up entry increase in size as you pluck out more unwanted stuff.

When you're finally ready to commit, click OK or Cancel to bail out. If you click Cancel, close the Add/Remove Programs dialog box and the Control Panel.

If you click OK, you'll probably be asked to restart your computer. Do so.

- I kind of lied. You can use the Windows Backup program to back up to a floppy disk or ZIP drive. Backing up to floppy disks, however, is truly insane. A typical 2GB hard drive, even if it's half full, requires almost 750 floppy disks for a full backup. How long are you planning on living?
- Besides, buying 750 floppy disks is much more expensive than buying a decent tape backup unit.
- ZIP drives come with their own backup software—another reason to rid yourself of the paradoxical Microsoft Backup program.
- Although you really shouldn't run out of disk storage space, if you do, removing some of the Windows programs can help. Another tip is to remove the "uninstall Windows 98" program, which is covered in Chapter 14. Also see Chapter 21 to read about several things you can do to free up disk space.

You can always reinstall later any of the Windows components you delete; a copy of every program is on the Windows CD-ROM.

Using the Online Windows Update

In addition to the copy of Windows that comes on the Windows CD-ROM, you can also update Windows through the Microsoft Windows Update Web site. You do it that way not so much to add new programs as to tune and tweak Windows 98 to perform better with your PC.

▶ **From the Start menu, choose Settings ➡Windows Update.**

You might also see a Windows Update icon at the top of the Start Thing menu or elsewhere.

If you cannot locate the icon on the Start Thing, run the program named WUPDMGR.EXE, located in the C:\Windows folder.

The Windows Update program connects you with the Internet. The Internet Explorer Web browser starts up, taking you to the update page out there in cyberspace.

The Windows Update Web page looks something like Figure 15.2.

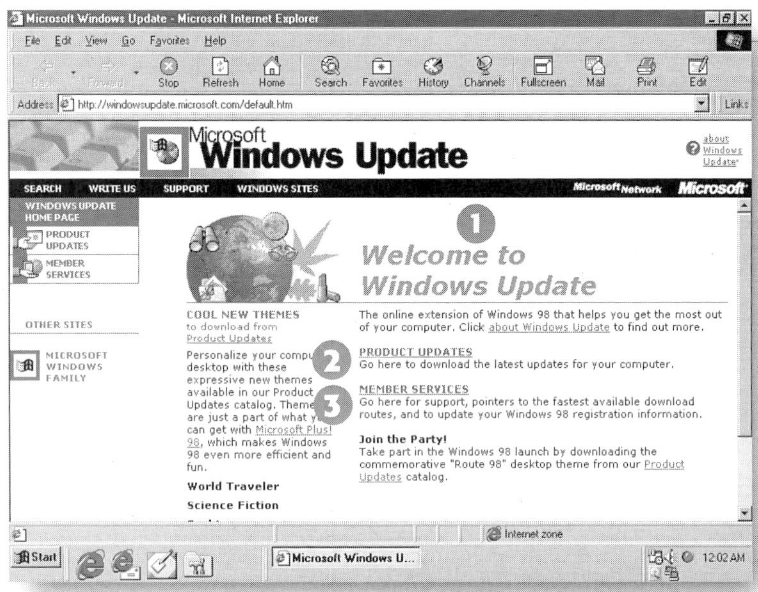

Figure 15.2

The Microsoft Windows Update Web page.

1. The content and layout of this Web page change over time.
2. Click here for a menu of product updates.
3. Click here to review your registration information.

▶ **Click the Product Updates item.**

The Product Updates item is a link on the Web page and is shown in Figure 15.2 as item B. (It might not be in the same location on your screen.)

Clicking Product Updates displays a menu of additional items for updating Windows. It also might prompt a program to be sent from the Microsoft computer on the Internet to your computer.

▶ **If you see the Security Warning dialog box, click Yes.**

Your computer needs a certain program in order to work with the Microsoft update program. Clicking Yes sends the program from Microsoft to you.

▶ **Click Yes in the Windows Update dialog box.**

Windows must scan your PC to see which files you need versus which you might already have. This process takes a few seconds.

Doh-dee-doh…

In a few moments, you see a list of items suggested for your computer. Figure 15.3 shows an example.

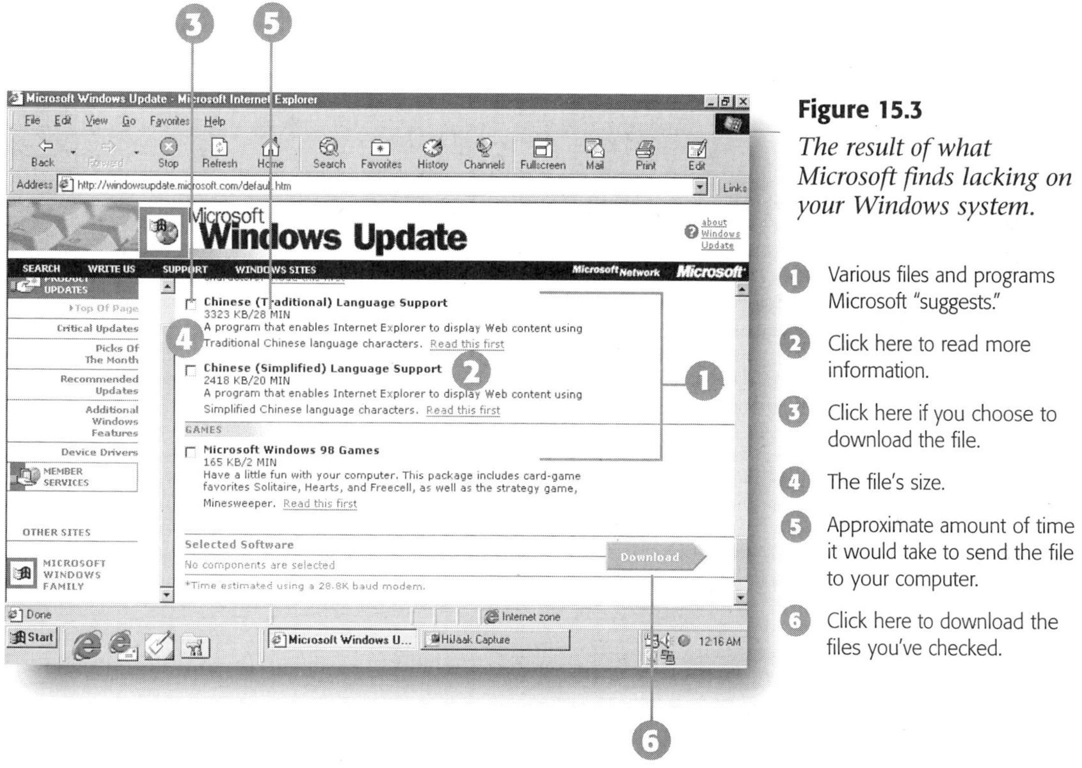

Figure 15.3
The result of what Microsoft finds lacking on your Windows system.

1. Various files and programs Microsoft "suggests."
2. Click here to read more information.
3. Click here if you choose to download the file.
4. The file's size.
5. Approximate amount of time it would take to send the file to your computer.
6. Click here to download the files you've checked.

Scroll through the suggestions. For each file, you see a brief description and an underlined Read This First link that displays more information.

Carefully pay attenion to the file size and download time.

For the tutorial, you can download the supplemental Web fonts, which are a collection of interesting fonts you can use on or off the Web.

▶ **Scroll down and find the Supplemental Web Fonts item.**

It's in the Additional Windows Features/Internet section.

▶ **Click the Read This First link for Supplemental Web Fonts.**

Definitely download the critical updates, if any. Choose from that category all the files that apply to your system.

A window describing additional information is displayed. (It includes uninstall information, in case you need it.)

For the fonts in this tutorial, no additional setup is involved.

▶ **Close the Microsoft Product Updates: Supplemental Web Fonts window.**

▶ **Click to put a check mark in the box by Supplemental Web Fonts.**

▶ **Scroll down to the bottom of the window.**

You see the large Download button looming on the right side of the window. To the left of the button, you see a summary of what you're downloading—how many bytes and how many hours (!) and minutes it should take to grab it all from the Internet.

If you want to print the information, click the Print button on the Internet Explorer toolbar or choose File ➡Print if you cannot see either the toolbar or the button. I recommend printing the information, especially if detailed instructions are involved with the program setup.

▶ **Click the large Download button.**

A multistep download checklist appears. Review the items on the list.

The Choose Download Site area lists several places around the universe where you can get the software. The site that's already chosen is probably best for you, so you really have nothing to do here.

▶ **Click the Start Download button.**

The Windows Update monitor window appears (see Figure 15.4).

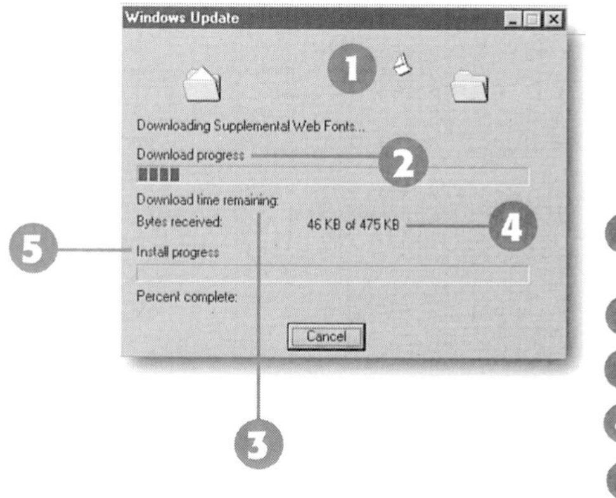

Figure 15.4

The Windows Update dialog box tracks your progress.

1. Files fling from the Internet to your PC.
2. Progress meter.
3. Time remaining.
4. Byte-by-byte blow-by-blow.
5. This meter monitors program installation.

Eventually it's done!

It doesn't take long to copy the supplemental Web font files from the Internet, and they take virtually no time to install:

▶ **Click OK in the Install Complete window.**

You can continue to browse the Windows Update Web site. Otherwise, you're done.

▶ **Close the Internet Explorer window.**

▶ **If you're asked to Disconnect, click Yes.**

Or you can click No to stay online and do, well, *whatever* on the Internet.

The Web fonts have been properly installed on your system. As the information online says, although you may or may not notice the fonts when you browse various Web pages, you can still use them in any Windows document that lets you change fonts.

- Refer to Chapter 7 and Part V of this book for more information about the Internet.
- Should you register Windows? Do you need to use the Upgrade service? No. As long as Windows works for you, you have no reason to bother with it. Especially if you fear that Microsoft might be snooping around in your

TIP

Check the Windows Update page at least once every few months to see whether any new files or updates are available for your PC and Windows.

computer (which it says it doesn't, but it doesn't stop newspaper articles from being written), don't bother with this service.

- More information about fonts in Windows is in Chapter 42, "More Fonts for You."
- You might be required to register your copy of Windows before you can use the Windows Update service. If so, you're prompted to register when you try to use the service.

Hey! Did you notice that opening the Windows Update icon always opens Internet Explorer? Talk about unfair competition. You cannot access the Windows Update page in any other way (especially from Netscape!) Sorry, but I didn't make up that rule.

Part III

Printing and Faxing

Chapters in This Part

Part III

Visual Topic Reference A.

1. The Print dialog box (Chapter 16).
2. Choose another printer (Chapter 16).
3. Print a range of pages (Chapter 16).
4. The Print Screen key takes a snapshot of the desktop (Chapter 17).
5. Alt+Print Screen takes a snapshot of a window (Chapter 17).
6. The Printers folder (Chapter 18).
7. Add a new printer (Chapter 18).
8. The default printer (Chapter 18).
9. Faxing (Chapter 19).

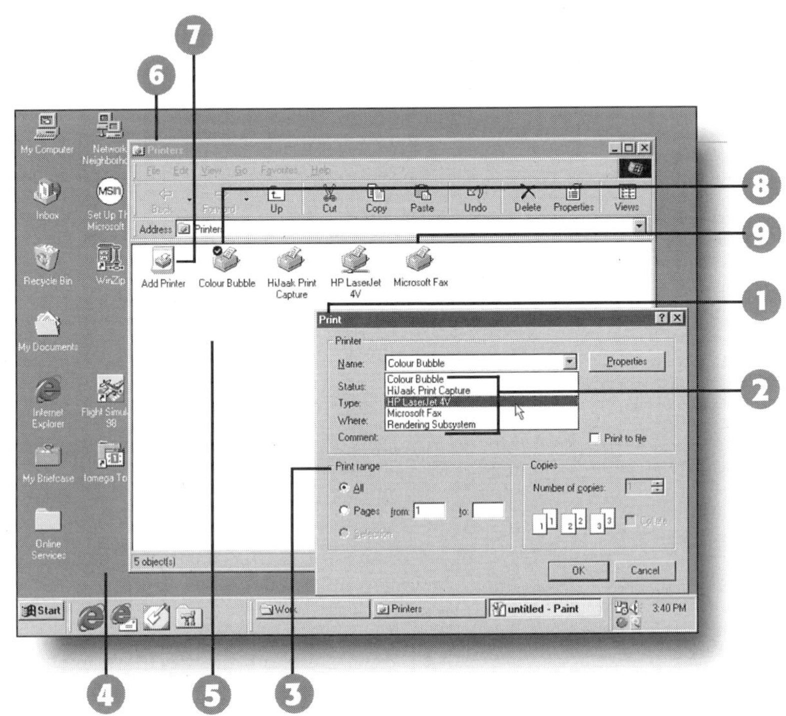

Chapter 16

Printing and Such

Questions Answered and Thoughts Inspired

- Using Page Preview
- Printing one page at a time
- Printing left and right rather than up and down
- Printing on different-size sheets of paper
- Using another printer (if you have one)

A computer without a printer is like a house without a front porch. My real estate guy said that a front porch on a house is like a smile. So, in a roundabout way, I suppose that a computer with a printer must be smiling.

Although I wouldn't normally write an entire chapter—let alone an entire *part* of a book—about printing, I get lots of email messages and questions about printing. Fortunately, in Windows, the printing process works in exactly the same way in every program. After you get the procedure down pat, printing should be a snap.

The Tao of Printing

I suppose that printing is a big deal because it involves two different pieces of hardware: a computer and a printer. It also involves paper. Normally, because you print on standard typing or photocopier paper, printing isn't a big deal. If you ever have to change anything, however—paper size, orientation, margins, whatever—printing becomes a pain. That's what this section tries to help you avoid.

To work the tutorials in this section, you have to create or open a document in WordPad:

▶ **Open WordPad.**

The document you create should be several pages long. Unless you have a head full of random thoughts you want to type right now, you're probably better off opening a document that's already on disk—something you can play with.

▶ **Choose File ➡Open if you would rather not type three pages of text now.**

The Open dialog box appears.

▶ **Use the Look In list to find drive C.**

▶ **Open the Windows folder.**

▶ **Choose Text Documents (*.txt) from the Files of Type drop-down list.**

Scroll to the left, and you should find a whole gaggle of text files stored in the Windows folder.

If you have the FAQ file, open it. It has lots of good information in it. Otherwise, choose the GENERAL file or any other file that's more than two or three pages long (about six screens full).

▶ **Choose your file from the list, and then click Open to open it.**

You now have something to print for the next several sections' tutorials.

▶ **Ensure that your printer is on and ready to print.**

You're ready to go.

- Using the FAQ file is a good idea for this tutorial. If you know of another large file you can open in WordPad, do so.
- Yes, it's a drag that WordPad gives you no page number clues. Microsoft Word didn't do that either, until about Version 3 or so.
- No, you have no other way in WordPad to get page number information than to use the Print Preview command (it's covered a few paragraphs from here).

Where Everything Lives

All Windows programs print from the File menu. It typically has three printing-related commands, as shown in Figure 16.1.

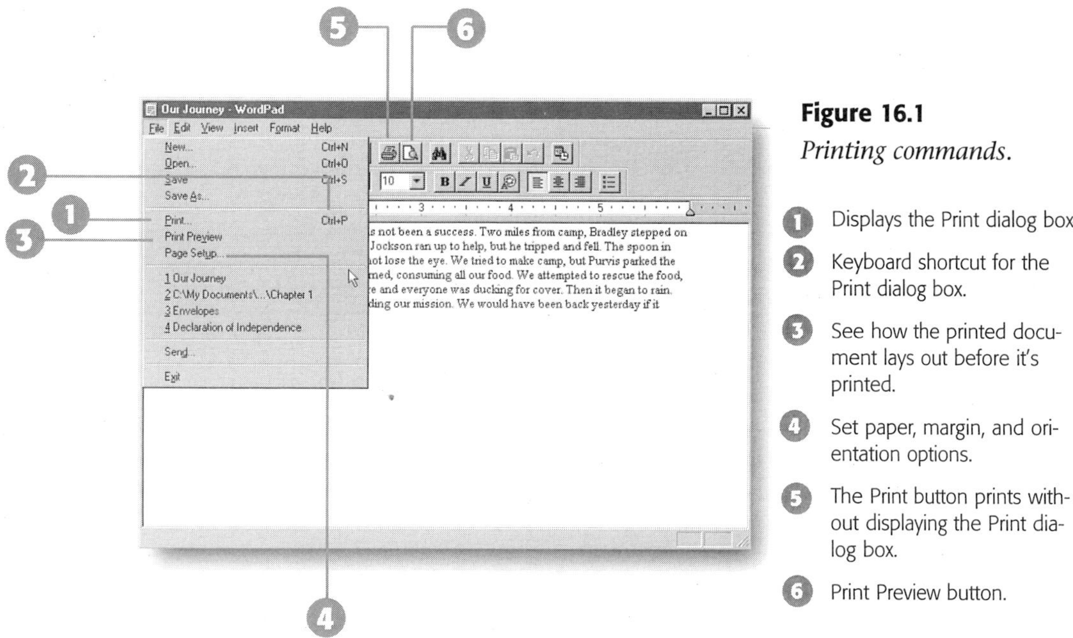

Figure 16.1
Printing commands.

1. Displays the Print dialog box.
2. Keyboard shortcut for the Print dialog box.
3. See how the printed document lays out before it's printed.
4. Set paper, margin, and orientation options.
5. The Print button prints without displaying the Print dialog box.
6. Print Preview button.

All the commands in Table 16.1 are on the File menu in most Windows programs (some programs might not have all of them).

Table 16.1

Commands on the File menu.

Command	*Shortcut*	*What It Does*
Print	Ctrl+P	Displays the Print dialog box
Print Preview	None	Shows the document layout as it will look when it's printed
Page Setup	None	Sets margins, paper size, and other printing options

Previews of Coming Printing Attractions

The Print Preview command is badly underused. Although the screen might show you fonts and layout and such, only the Print Preview command shows you what the whole page looks like. Using that command saves time over printing sample copies.

▶ **Choose File ➡Print Preview.**

The Print Preview window appears, as shown in Figure 16.2.

Figure 16.2
The Print Preview window.

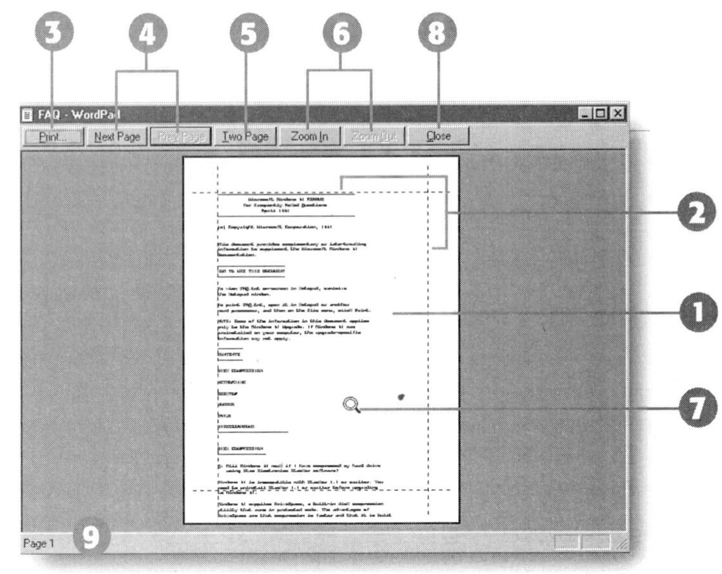

1. Your document as it will look when it's printed.
2. Margins.
3. Click to close this window and print.
4. Click to see the next or preceding page.
5. View two pages at a time.
6. Zoom in or out.
7. Click the mouse pointer to zoom in.
8. Return to your document.
9. Number of the page you're viewing.

Subtle differences exist in the way various programs display the Print Preview window. For the most part, the key elements shown in Figure 16.2 are always there.

▶ **Click the Close button.**

The Print Preview window is banished, and you return to WordPad.

- You can also click the Print Preview button on the toolbar to see a document preview.
- Only some applications let you edit text in the Print Preview window. In most applications, the Print Preview window is a look-only thing.

Printing Pages Individually or in Groups

The document you have loaded is probably several pages long. (The FAQ file is about eight pages long on my computer.) At times you probably don't need to print all the pages in a document. For example, if the printer chews up page 3, rather than reprint your whole document, just print page 3:

▶ **Choose File ➡Print.**

The Print dialog box appears, beautifully illustrated in Figure 16.3.

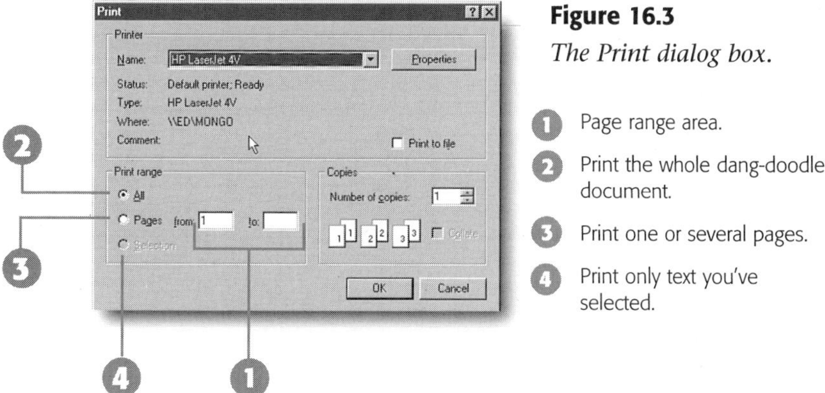

Figure 16.3
The Print dialog box.

1. Page range area.
2. Print the whole dang-doodle document.
3. Print one or several pages.
4. Print only text you've selected.

▶ **Click the Pages button.**

You want to tell Windows to print only page 3.

At first glance, the Pages button looks like it prints a range of pages, from 1 to whatever. You can use this item to print only one page, however.

▶ **Type** 3 **in the From box.**

▶ **Type** 3 **in the To box.**

Printing *from* page 3 *to* page 3 prints *only* page 3.

▶ **Click OK to print.**

Voom, voom, voom. Page 3 slides out of the printer.

Two things you probably didn't see: First, a dialog box said, "Now printing such-and-such a document on such-and-such a printer." Second, a little printer guy was (or maybe still is) in the system tray area of the taskbar. That guy appears only when you're printing, and he gives you access to the printer window. Unfortunately, he disappears after the document is printed (and sometimes before).

The printer window is discussed later in this chapter.

▶ **Inspect what you printed.**

Ensure that the proper page was printed, although you have no real way to tell in this tutorial because the pages aren't numbered. (That's why WordPad is free; when you paymoney for a word processor, you get automatic page numbering.)

▶ **Select the first seven lines of text in the document.**

Use the mouse to select the first seven lines of text. In the FAQ document, that includes all the information up through the copyright notice.

- **Press Ctrl+P to summon the Print dialog box.**
- **Click Selection.**
- **Click OK.**

Only the document's first seven lines—the selected text—are printed.

Keep WordPad open for the next section's tutorial.

- The Pages range can be any page number, from the first page to the last page number.
- No shortcuts or "wildcards" exist for the page numbers in the Pages range. For example, some programs might let you use the $ (dollar sign) as a symbol for the last page number, whatever it is. WordPad doesn't let you do that; you must know the exact page number.
- Yes, that's the only way to see page numbers in WordPad. Yes, it is rather lame.
- Printing selected text is one way to print part of a document that is either less than a page or some non-page-size amount, such as a page and a half.

TIP

You can use the Print Preview command to see how long your document is in WordPad. Just choose File ➡Print Preview and continue clicking the Next Page button until you get to the last page. The page number appears in the lower-left corner of the window.

Printing a Range of Pages in Microsoft Word

Microsoft Word (and possibly other programs) has a different method for printing a range of pages. Instead of the Pages item having a From and To box, it has just a text box. You type the range of pages you want by using a hyphen:

2-5 prints pages 2 through 5

9-10 prints pages 9 and 10

Print individual pages by specifying each one, separated by a comma:

3 prints page 3

3,5,7 prints pages 3, 5, and 7

Or you can combine the methods to print a document in all sorts of pieces:

1,5,9-12 to print pages 1 and 5 and pages 9 through 12.

Why this step is different, I'll never know. It's the only really weird exception (I haven't seen how WordPerfect does it in the current version). Excel and other Microsoft programs tend to stick with the standard Print dialog box, more or less. Whatever, just watch out for any oddities you might encounter.

Changing Orientation

Does *orientation* refer to how the paper is oriented (up and down versus left and right), or does it refer to how the words appear on the paper? Mankind might never know. Or you can at least take a guess after working this tutorial.

Continue to use WordPad from the preceding section as you print the first page of your document in landscape orientation.

Landscape orientation is "longways," or left to right. Portrait orientation is up and down, like you normally print.

- **Choose File ➡Print.**

Hey! There's no orientation option. Dang.

Well, there might be. It depends on the program. Some programs put the orientation item in the Print dialog box; most don't. WordPad doesn't. In fact, the page-orientation option shouldn't even be in the Print dialog box. Why? Because it's not a printing operation—it's a *formatting* operation.

- **Click Cancel to close the Print dialog box.**
- **Choose File ➡Page Setup.**

The Page Setup dialog box pops up, as shown in Figure 16.4.

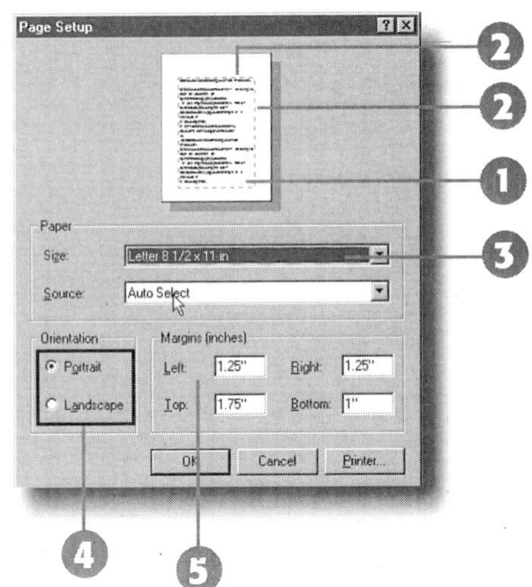

Figure 16.4
The Page Setup dialog box.

1. A preview of what the printed document layout will look like.
2. Margins.
3. Choose the paper size here.
4. Orientation is chosen here.
5. Set margins here.

▶ **Choose Landscape.**

Notice how the preview at the top of the dialog box changes? It reflects how a typical page in your document will be printed. Hey! In fact, those margins look dorky. Better change them all to one inch:

▶ **Enter** 1 **in the Left, Top, Right, and Bottom input boxes.**

A nifty shortcut for this step is to double-click in the Left input box first: Type **1** and press the Tab key, type **1** in the Right box and press the Tab key, type **1** in the Top box and press the Tab key, and then type **1** in the Bottom box.

Notice how your changes affect the preview.

▶ **Click OK.**

Back in WordPad it's hard to tell that landscape printing mode is active; the screen looks just about the same. However, because you adjusted your margins, you should notice that the ruler in WordPad is much longer now. That's always a good hint.

Don't worry about changing the paper in your printer! It's the *printer* that prints in landscape mode. You don't need to do a thing!

Now you're ready to print:

▶ **Choose File ➡Print.**

You want to print only one page, the first page.

▶ **Choose Pages.**

- **Type** 1 **in the From box.**
- **Type** 1 **in the To box.**
- **Click OK.**

The document should come out of the printer in landscape orientation.

The margins aren't affected if you're printing a text document, such as a FAQ; unlike a word processing document, the text document is "hard-formatted."

Keep WordPad open for the next section's tutorial.

- The changes you make in the Page Setup dialog box affect the *entire* document, not just one page.
- If I'm printing on three-hole punched paper (to put in a binder), I always set the left margin to 2 1/2 inches. That leaves enough room for the binding.

Your printer can print only so close to the edge of the paper. On most laser printers, it's a half-inch from the edge of the paper. Do not set your margins any wider than that, or else your text will not print.

- Some ink printers have a taller top margin than bottom.
- Landscape mode works best for things in a left to right display; for example, well—a landscape! On a computer, most often you print things such as spreadsheets and charts in landscape mode. In fact, I use the Print Preview command in Excel all the time to see whether I can save a page of paper by printing in landscape mode.

Changing Paper Size

Switching to a different-size sheet of paper isn't something you do often. In fact, it depends more on your printer than on anything the Print dialog box can do for you.

Most printers have the capability to accept any size sheet of paper *that fits*. For example, the printer tray on most laser printers can accommodate either American letter paper (8.5 by 11 inches) or European A4 paper (8.27 by 11.69 inches). For other sizes, however, you need another paper cartridge.

Ink and other types of printers might allow you to manually feed different-size sheets of paper. Still, they have limits, which depend mostly on the Print dialog box.

Writing a tutorial for this subject is rough because I have no idea what type of printer cartridge you have available. Still, I can show you where the decisions for paper size are made.

Assuming that you're still in WordPad:

- **Choose File ➡Print.**
- **Click the Properties button.**

The printer's properties dialog box appears, which is different for *every* printer on the market. The one you see in Figure 16.5 is for my Hewlett-Packard LaserJet 4V.

- **Click the Paper panel to bring it forward (if it isn't already).**

The Paper panel is where you choose various options for the paper in your printer.

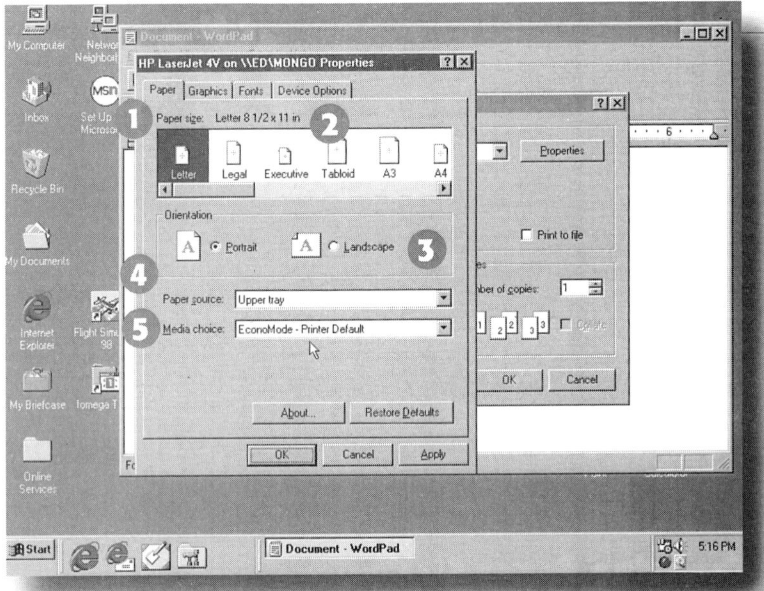

Figure 16.5

The Paper panel in the printer properties dialog box.

1. Paper panel.
2. Choose the paper size here (it might be a drop-down list in some dialog boxes).
3. Choose the orientation.
4. Other options (vary from printer to printer).
5. The paper source is important if you have other paper cartridges.

Note the paper-orientation area. It does the same job as the paper-orientation area in the Page Setup dialog box. Changes you make there are reflected here and vice versa.

The list of paper sizes you see is particular to your printer. For example, my printer comes with a cartridge for printing on tabloid-size paper (twice as wide as letter-size paper). You can see the Tabloid option in Figure 16.5.

Because the Tabloid size is a cartridge, I have to make sure that I choose the proper cartridge from the Paper Source list. In this case, it's the upper tray.

Many paper sizes obviously don't have their own cartridge. When you choose one, you have to select Manual Feed from the Paper Source list. Your printer then sits and waits for you to feed it the proper paper.

- **Click Cancel to close the printer properties dialog box.**
- **Click Cancel to close the Print dialog box.**
- **Quit WordPad.**

The tutorial ends!

- The paper options in the printer properties dialog box are duplicated in the Page Setup dialog box. A change made in either place is reflected in the other dialog box.
- Do not forget to change the paper source! If you're printing on a postcard, you probably want to use the manual feed.

If your printer has a separate cartridge for printing on legal paper, be sure, when you choose legal-size paper, to also choose the proper cartridge from the Paper Source list. Your printer then expects you to switch cartridges when you print, if the proper cartridge isn't already in place.

Choosing Some Other Printer

If your PC is blessed with more than one printer or you have access to printers on the network, Windows lets you make a snap decision about where to print your document.

Normally all the stuff you print goes to your PC's favorite printer (referred to by the ugly term *default printer*). That you should be familiar with. If you have another printer, however, you can print on it too.

The following tutorial assumes that you have more than one printer installed for your PC:

- **Open WordPad.**
- **Type** Hello alien printer!

Okay, it won't win a Hugo Award. If you feel more creative, however, or have something you *really* want to print, type it or open that document instead. I'm just running a tutorial here.

- **Choose File ➡Print.**

Some programs have advanced options for setting the paper size. For example, in the Microsoft Word Page Setup dialog box, you can specify an exact paper size. This process is ideal for printing invitations or other items of a weird size. As long as the paper fits in your printer's manual feeder, you can print. Trial and error is usually necessary, of course, to get everything looking right.

The Print dialog box appears. Notice the Name drop-down list. From that list you choose the other printer on which to print:

▶ **Drop down the Name list.**

Press Alt+N and then Alt+↓ (the down-arrow key) or click the down-arrow next to the list. You see all the printers available to your computer. Figure 16.6 shows what's available on my PC.

Figure 16.6

Choosing another printer.

1. Click here to see the list.
2. This computer's favorite printer is chosen automatically.
3. Other printers.
4. This printer is the only other one; the rest are special programs.

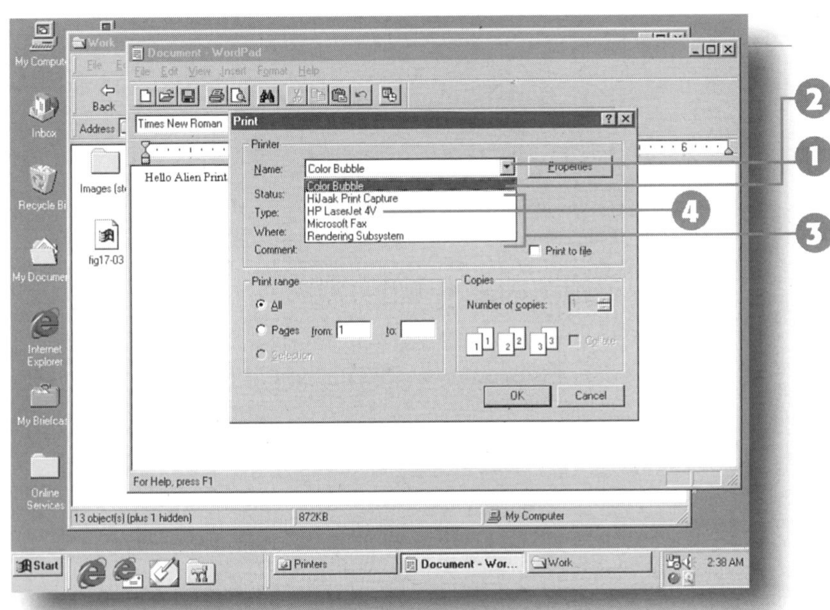

▶ **Choose another printer.**

Choose the printer by clicking its name on the list.

I can't tell you which printer to choose because I don't have your computer. Just choose any printer. In Figure 16.6, I chose the HP LaserJet 4V.

Make sure that what you choose is a printer and not some special printer-utility program. For example, in Figure 16.6, HiJaak Print Capture is a program designed to save a printed file as a graphics image. I have no idea what the Rendering Subsystem printer is, so I just don't choose it.

▶ **Click OK to print.**

The document is printed on the alien printer. If it's a network printer, you might have to lug your corpulent self over to the printer to retrieve your document.

Windows *remembers* which printer you chose. If you print in WordPad again, the document is printed on the last printer you've chosen. To prove this statement:

▶ **Choose File ➡Print.**

Lo, the alien printer is *still* selected. It stays selected until you do one of two things: Choose another printer *and print something* or quit that program.

It's always a good idea to check which printer you're using before you print.

After you quit a program in which you've changed printers, Windows forgets about the other printer and continues to use your favorite printer. Prove it:

▶ **Close the Print dialog box.**

Click Cancel to complete that step.

▶ **Close WordPad.**

You don't have to save the silly document if you don't want to.

▶ **Start WordPad.**

▶ **Choose File ➡Print.**

Ahhh. The universe is in balance. The favorite printer has been restored.

▶ **Click Cancel.**

▶ **Close WordPad.**

Ommmm...

The color printer in my office is "up for grabs" on the network. That way, if someone else (my wife or sometimes my son) wants to print a document in color, all she has to do is switch over to that color printer. Sharing a rare printer in that way gives everyone access to its fancy features. See Chapter 35 for more information about sharing printers on a network.

- Refer to Chapter 18, "Hello, Printers Folder!" for information about installing more printers.
- Setting one printer as your favorite is also covered in Chapter 18.
- The Hugo Award is the most prestigious honor in science fiction literature.
- Choosing a fax "printer" is how you send faxes in Windows. Windows 98 no longer supports its own fax printer, Microsoft Fax. You can still use it if you have it; otherwise, you'll probably use a third-party fax program.

Big tip: See how important your printer name is? Figure 16.6 shows some strange names. Giving your printer a good, descriptive name helps you choose it from a list of otherwise cryptic, hieroglyphic names. See the section "Changing a Printer's Name" in Chapter 18 if you've named your printer poorly.

Chapter 17

Printing Things on the Screen

Questions Answered and Thoughts Inspired

- Printing an image of the desktop
- Saving the desktop image
- Using Alt+Print Screen to print a window
- Printing a list of files

Ever go staring at your keyboard, mulling over the possibilities for some of the more bizarre names? SysRq? Scroll Lock? Break? (Why is it Break and not Brake?) Then there's the Print Screen key.

Fear not the Print Screen key! In Windows the Print Screen key has nothing to do with your printer. Well, not directly. This chapter shows you how to use the Print Screen key to take a snapshot of the desktop or a window. Also covered is the mysterious method for printing a list of files in a folder.

- Before Windows was DOS. In DOS the Print Screen key did send a copy of the text screen to the printer.
- The SysRq (System Request) key has no function in Windows. (SysRq shares a key cap with the Print Screen key.)

- The Scroll Lock key is used mainly in spreadsheets to switch between cursor and screen control, whatever that means.
- The Break key has no function in Windows, although in DOS, Ctrl+Break was used to halt a DOS program run amok.

Printing a Snapshot of the Desktop

The Print Screen button doesn't print the screen, although it does copy to the Clipboard the way the screen looks. From there you can paste whatever's onscreen into any program that accepts graphics—even save it to disk or print it to get a permanent copy of your desktop.

It doesn't matter what you have onscreen; whatever it is right now, Print Screen takes a picture of it.

▶ **Press the Print Screen key on your keyboard.**

Nothing happens! Actually, the Print Screen key has taken a snapshot of the desktop, saving it in the Windows Clipboard.

▶ **Start the Paint program.**

▶ **Maximize Paint.**

Click the Maximize button in the upper-right corner of the window.

▶ **Press Ctrl+V to paste the desktop image.**

If you see a warning dialog box explaining that the image in the Clipboard is larger than the bitmap, click Yes.

The desktop picture appears in the Paint program's document window. You can scroll down or left to see the full thing. It should all be there.

If you want to print, I recommend changing the image size; your desktop is probably twice as wide as your printer can print.

▶ **Choose Edit ➡Select All.**

This step selects the entire image for tweaking.

▶ **Choose Image ➡Stretch/Skew.**

The Stretch and Skew dialog box appears. Because you want to shrink your image by half, you change the horizontal and vertical size to 50 percent (the top boxes):

▶ **Type** 50 **in the Horizontal text box.**

▶ **Type** 50 **in the Vertical text box.**

Ensure that you've typed the values in the right boxes.

▶ **Click OK.**

Well...

Although the image is smaller, you lose a great deal of detail. Whatever.

If you're fussy, press Ctrl+Z to undo the resizing. Then go back to the Stretch and Skew dialog box and choose 75 rather than 50—and remember that your entire image still might not fit on a piece of paper.

▶ **Choose File ➡Print.**

Make sure that your printer is on and ready to print.

▶ **Click OK.**

You might not be pleased with the results. Keep in mind that Paint isn't the world's best graphics program. If you want a nice image of the desktop, get something with more oomph. I use the HiJaak 95 program (I'm sure that the Windows 98 version will be out by the time you read this book), which is great for manipulating and printing most types of graphics images.

You can also save the desktop image. You probably don't want to keep the small version, however:

▶ **Press Ctrl+Z.**

The Ctrl+Z key combination is the Windows undo key combination, which should undo the stretch and skew operation and restore your image to its real-life size.

▶ **Choose File ➡Save As.**

The Save As dialog box appears. It should be set to show the My Documents folder. If not, browse to that folder.

▶ **Type** Desktop Map **in the File Name box.**

▶ **Click Save.**

▶ **Quit Paint.**

TIP

I save an image of the desktop on all my Windows computers. (I usually minimize all the windows first, though.) The reason is that once upon a time Windows randomly reorganized my desktop for me. It hasn't happened in awhile, although if it does happen again or if one of the kids decides to rearrange my desktop, I have the Desktop Map file to help me arrange things to the way they were.

Printing a Window and Only the Window

The Print Screen key has two modes of operation. The first, in which you press Print Screen by itself, was demonstrated in the preceding section. That's full-screen mode. The second mode is top-window mode, which copies to the Clipboard the image of only the top window.

▶ **Double-click the time on the system tray.**

The system tray is on the taskbar and displays a hoard of tiny icons plus the current time. Double-clicking the time opens the Date/Time Properties dialog box, as shown in Figure 17.1.

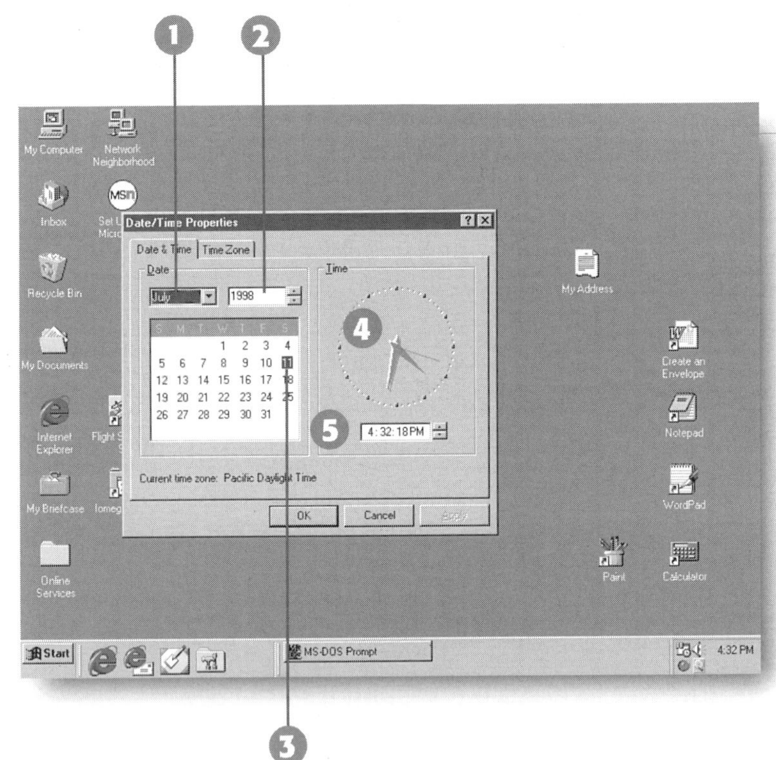

Figure 17.1
The Date/Time Properties dialog box.

1. Current month and change the current month.
2. Current year and change the current year.
3. Current calendar day and change the day.
4. Tick-tock time.
5. Change the time here.

Suppose that you work for a boss who *demands* to know what time you stop using your computer. Show him in style:

▶ **Press Alt+Print Screen.**

The Alt+Print Screen key combination captures only the topmost window onscreen, saving it as an image in the Clipboard.

- ▶ **Click Cancel to close the Date/Time Properties window.**

Now you get to write your memo to the bully boss:

- ▶ **Start WordPad.**
- ▶ **Maximize WordPad.**
- ▶ **Type** Here is when I quit work today:

Enter the text *Here is when I quit work today,* followed by a colon.

- ▶ **Press the Enter key twice.**
- ▶ **Press Ctrl+V to paste in the graphics image.**

You see an image of the Date/Time Properties dialog box pasted into the window. There! That'll show him!

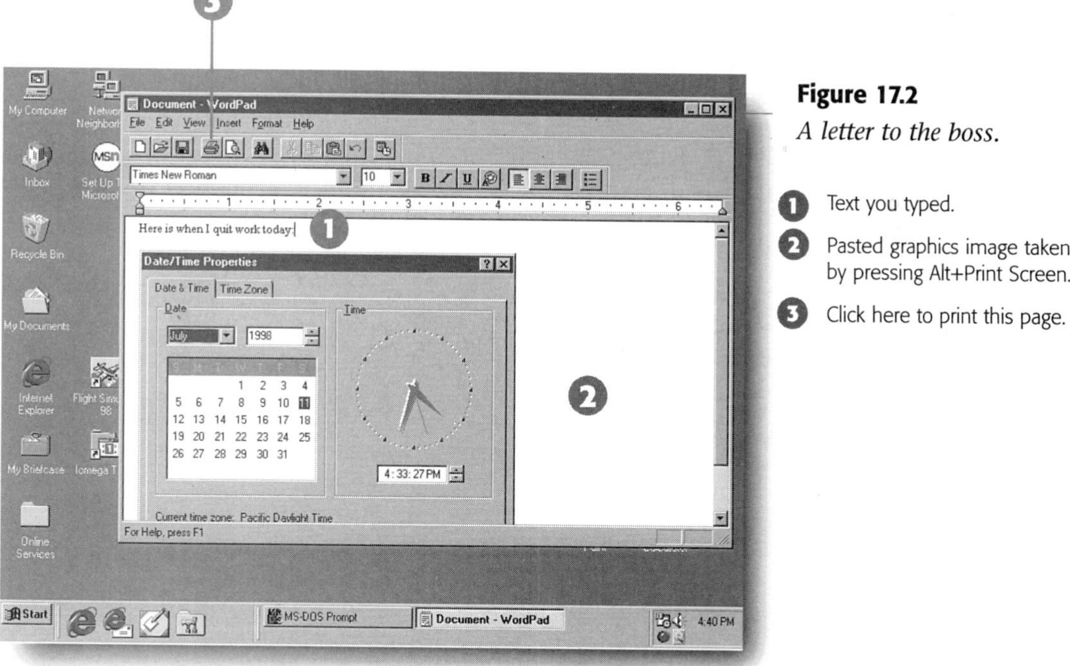

Figure 17.2
A letter to the boss.

1. Text you typed.
2. Pasted graphics image taken by pressing Alt+Print Screen.
3. Click here to print this page.

Figure 17.2 shows what I see on my screen.

▶ **Click the Print button on the toolbar.**

The image prints instantly; when you click the Print button on the toolbar, you don't see the Print dialog box.

If you don't see the toolbar, choose View ➡Toolbar from the WordPad menu.

▶ **Close WordPad.**

You can choose whether to save the file at this point. If it's meaningful to you, save it. (I didn't!)

I could have created every image in this book by using Alt+Print Screen. In fact, I've written books in which all the images were captured by a combination of Alt+Print Screen or just the Print Screen key alone. For this book, however, the publisher wanted all full-screen "screen shots," so I used only the Print Screen key (or the HiJaak 95 program, discussed earlier in this chapter).

Printing a List of Files in a Folder Can Be Done

Notice that pressing Alt+Print Screen captures only the visible part of a window. To prove it, try this test:

▶ **Open My Computer.**

▶ **Open drive C.**

▶ **Open the Windows folder.**

Click Show Files (on the left side of the window) if no files are displayed when you open the Windows folder.

The Windows folder contains a galaxy of files and folders, but does Alt+Print Screen show you the entire list?

▶ **Press Alt+Print Screen.**

The top window is captured, saved as an image in the Clipboard.

▶ **Start Paint.**

▶ **Press Ctrl+V to paste the image.**

If you're told that the image is larger than the bitmap (or something), click Yes.

Gander at the image. Use the scrollbars if you have to.

Notice that only the window was captured. Some 300 (or so) files are in the Windows folder. I'll tell you right now: You have no way in Windows to get a picture of *all* of them.

Sure, you can scroll the window down a chunk at a time and press Alt+Print Screen to paste into Paint and print. That kind of drudgery, however, is exactly what the computer is supposed to prevent.

Oy.

Windows has no solution to printing a list of files in a directory. You can cheat, however.

Prepare to cheat!

Whenever you want to print a list of files in a folder, you have to "cheat" and use DOS. The list of files might be necessary in order to compare files between two computers, print a summary of files required for a project, or do other types of record-keeping. (I suppose that it's not something you'll do all the time, which is probably why no File ➡Print command is available—although that's a lame reason.)

Rather than go to a DOS window to print the file list, you can use this shortcut:

▶ **Close Paint.**

You do not have to save the file; click No.

▶ **Use the Address bar to browse to the My Documents folder.**

A smattering of files, but not too many, should be in that folder. (If you see more than 50, browse on your own to another folder that has 50 or fewer files in it.)

To print the list of files, you have to use DOS—not the DOS prompt itself (although that method works), but rather an ingenious DOS command. See? Even though DOS is dead, it still does some things that beat the pants off Windows.

▶ **Choose File ➡New ➡Shortcut.**

The Create Shortcut dialog box appears.

▶ **In the Command line text box, type** command /c dir /o > prn.

You type this line:

```
command /c dir /o > prn
```

That's *command*, a space, slash *C*, a space, *dir*, a space, slash *O*, a space, a greater-than symbol, a space, and *prn*.

Those are all forward slashes; that character is on the ? key on your keyboard.

Make sure that the command looks *exactly* like it does in the preceding step. (That mandatory exactness is what frustrated so many people when they used DOS.)

- ▶ **Click Next.**
- ▶ **Type** Print a List of Files.

The name of the shortcut icon is Print a List of Files.

- ▶ **Click Finish.**

The icon appears in your My Documents window, as shown in Figure 17.3.

Figure 17.3

The new Print a List of Files icon.

1. Standard MS-DOS shortcut icon.
2. Other files in the My Documents folder.
3. It's always nighttime at `http://www.microsoft.com`

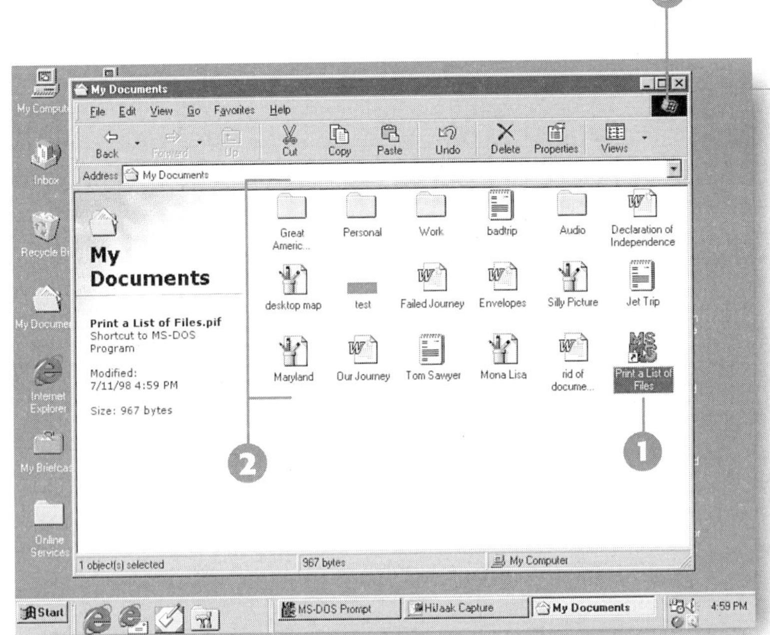

Don't try out the icon yet!

- ▶ **Right-click the Print a List of Files icon.**
- ▶ **Choose Properties from the pop-up menu.**

The Print a List of Files Properties dialog box appears.

- ▶ **Click the Program tab to bring that panel forward.**

You have to do a few things before you run the program, just to ensure that everything is working properly:

- **Erase any text in the Working text box.**

It probably says C:\Windows there now. Delete it! If you don't, the program prints only the files in the C:\Windows directory—not what you want.

A quick way to delete the text is to double-click in the text box and press the Delete key.

- **Put a check mark by Close on Exit (if one isn't there already).**

Them be all the modifications you need.

- **Click OK.**

The Print a List of Files Properties dialog box disappears.

You're ready to test the file. Make sure that your printer is online and ready to print.

- **Open the Print a List of Files icon.**

Blipvert! You might see a DOS window appear and then quickly disappear, or you might not.

The list of files prints on your printer.

- **Press your printer's Form Feed (FF) or Eject button.**

You might have to press the Online or Select button first and then press Form Feed to eject the page. On some printers you might have to press a Menu button and choose Eject or Form Feed from the menu. (See your printer's manual or refer to an office computer geek for help.)

If you have a laser printer, you don't see the list right away; laser printers do not print a page until you either fill up a page with text or press the Form Feed or Eject button.

Soon you have a crisp list of files in your eager hands. You might be baffled because the list looks something like this:

```
Volume in drive C is MICRON
Volume Serial Number is 2638-19F5
Directory of C:\My Documents

.              <DIR>          03-06-97  6:49p .
..             <DIR>          03-06-97  6:49p ..
LETTERS        <DIR>          03-27-97  2:33p Letters
WORK           <DIR>          03-20-97 11:35p Work
INTERNET       <DIR>          03-21-97  9:40a Internet
AUDIO          <DIR>          03-21-97 12:16p Audio
GRAPHICS       <DIR>          03-26-97  2:38p Graphics
PLAY           <DIR>          08-09-97 11:27p Play
SUREST~1 HTM         44,521  09-09-97  1:51p SureStore 6020 Error List.html
TEST1    VBS            110  02-08-98  4:38p TEST1.VBS
```

```
TEST     HTM           365  02-08-98  4:50p TEST.HTM
DUMBCRIM TXT         5,552  04-13-98  9:40p dumbcrim.txt
         4 file(s)          50,548 bytes
         8 dir(s)    1,392,508,928 bytes free
```

DOS displays the files, icons, and folders all in plain text. Everything is in a column:

- *First*—Describes the file's DOS name, which is cryptic
- *Second*—Displays the file's type as a three-letter extension
- *Third*—Displays <DIR> to flag directories or folders
- *Fourth*—Displays the file's size in bytes
- *Fifth*—Displays the file's date
- *Sixth*—Displays the file's time
- *Last*—Displays the file's long name—the name given to the icon or folder

Granted, this process is cryptic, although it's one of the few ways to see a list of all files in a folder. Compare them to what you see in the window.

▶ **Close the My Documents window.**

Or you can leave the window open, if you plan to tinker.

- To print a list of files for another folder, you have to copy the Print a List of Files shortcut to that folder.
- If the file list output is too long and cryptic for you, edit the DOS command. Right-click the Print a List of Files icon, choose Properties, and, on the Program panel, type the following line for the Cmd Line:

  ```
  command /c dir /o/b > prn
  ```

- The new command (which is only `DIR /O/B`) displays a list of only long filenames, which is often all you need.
- You can always use DOS to print a list of files in a folder. Of course, I don't elaborate on that subject here.
- The only Windows folder- and file-printing utility I can find is Directory Printer, by Glenn Alcott. You can download this $15 shareware program from his Web page:

  ```
  http://ourworld.compuserve.com/homepages/galcott
  ```

- Other folder- and file-printing utilities might exist. If so, I have yet to come across them.

What Does the DOS Command Mean?

Here's how the DOS command that's used to print a list of files works:

command /c—This part of the command runs the MS-DOS prompt program, although the /C option tells DOS to run only the following command and then quit.

dir /o—The DIR command displays a list of files, and the /O option sorts the files in alphabetical order.

>*prn*—This cryptogram sends the DOS command's output to the printer rather than to the screen. It does not spew the page from the printer when it's done, which is why you have to press the Form Feed button.

Chapter 18

Hello, Printers Folder!

Questions Answered and Thoughts Inspired

- Viewing the printers in your Printers folder
- Naming a printer
- Making a default printer
- Viewing and changing the printer queue
- Deleting a document in the queue
- Installing a printer
- Installing a network printer

You might think that the printer lives outside your computer, sitting by your desk. Physically that's true. To Windows, however, your printer lives in the Printers folder. It's one of those special folders that lives in Windows, showing you information about your printer and such. This chapter takes you on a cheap, one-day tour of the place where Windows thinks your printer lives.

Introducing Your Printers Folder

The Printers folder is one of the magic folders you can find all over Windows. The best way to get there is from the Start Thing:

- **From the Start Thing menu, choose Settings ➡Printers.**

Lo, the Printers folder appears, which looks something like Figure 18.1, except that it shows your computer's printers and not mine.

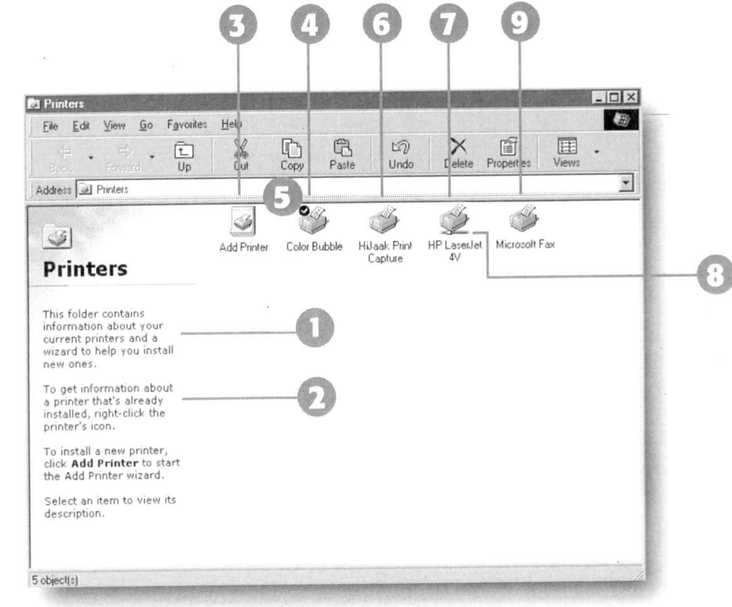

Figure 18.1

The Printers folder.

1. Hey! That's good information.
2. This isn't good information.
3. Run this thing when you add a new printer.
4. This computer's default printer, which is the one I use.
5. The wee li'l default check mark, telling me that this printer is my favorite.
6. A print-capture utility I don't use.
7. A printer on the network.
8. The network hose indicates a network printer.
9. The fax machine (see Chapter 19).

Keep the Printers folder open for the next few sections.

- Every printer attached to your computer, as well as printers you use on your network, appear in this window.
- Other icons appear in the window. If you have a fax modem, for example, you should see the Microsoft Fax printer and perhaps other fax printer icons.

- The window says to right-click a printer to get more information. Wrong! If you right-click the printer, you see a shortcut menu. If you choose the Properties command from the shortcut menu, however, you can see more information (don't expect *informative* information, though; it's more like raw data).
- You can also find the Printers folder in the Control Panel.
- A copy of the Printers folder lives in the main My Computer window.
- No matter how you get there, all Printers folders are the same.

Changing a Printer's Name

Naming a printer is important, but only if you have more than one printer or are sharing the printer on a network. After all, if you're the only one using your computer, you can name your printer Wandnolstalpian and no one would care.

If you have more than one printer or are sharing your printer on a network, you probably want something more descriptive than Wandnolstalpian. Maybe Color InkJet or Laser Printer with Business Letterhead would be better? Hmmm?

Changing a printer name in the Printers folder works the same way as renaming any icon in Windows:

▶ **Click the printer icon once to select it.**

If you have more than one printer showing, choose the *default* (favorite) printer. Look for the black circle with the check mark in it to find your favorite printer (refer to Figure 18.1).

▶ **Press the F2 key.**

F2 is the Rename command shortcut. I find it easier to use than the other ways of getting at the Rename command, primarily because your fingers are on the keyboard anyway in order to retype the new name.

▶ **Type** Honey Bun.

You can press the Backspace key to back up and erase or press the arrow keys to edit the text.

▶ **Press Enter to lock in the new name.**

There—you've renamed your printer as Honey Bun, which is utterly nondescriptive.

On your own, repeat the preceding steps and rename your printer to its original name—or something more descriptive, now that you have the chance.

- The other ways to rename a file after selecting it (other than pressing the F2 key) are to choose File ➡Rename from the menu or choose the Rename command from the icon's shortcut menu.
- A printer name is originally assigned when you install your printer. (Windows recommends using the printer's factory name. Gross.) Installing a printer is covered near the end of this chapter.

Picking Your Favorite Printer

Most PCs come with only one printer port. Even so, your PC is capable of handling as many as *three* honest-to-goodness printers (if you add two more printer ports). In addition to that, you can connect your computer to a network and use any printer that's "up for grabs" there. You always have a choice.

Rather than bombard you with printer choices every time you print, Windows lets you chose one printer as your favorite. That's the printer Windows always uses whenever you print something—unless you chose another printer temporarily.

I call it your "favorite printer," although Windows uses the ugly term "default printer." Yuck.

You can make any printer in the Printers folder the default. You might not have any printers or only one, but if you have more, it's a snap to make another printer the favorite, er, default.

Suppose that your PC is hooked up to a boring color printer and you have to use the faster laser printer for the next few months to print your novel:

▶ **Right-click the icon of the printer you want to make your favorite.**

For example, I could right-click the HP LaserJet 4V you saw back in Figure 18.1.

Right-clicking the printer icon displays a shortcut menu.

▶ **Choose Set as Default.**

The tiny check mark icon moves from your current favorite over to the new one (Figure 18.1 shows the check mark, which is next to the Color Bubble printer). Now Windows uses the new default printer as your favorite.

TIP

Remember that you can always switch printers on-the-fly in the Print dialog box. See the section "Choosing Some Other Printer," in Chapter 16.

- You can have three *physical* printers attached to your PC. That's a hardware limitation. Software-wise, Windows lets you connect to dozens of printers on a network. Also, the fax modem, which is kind of a printer, is listed on the list of printers, although it doesn't count as one of the three physical printers you can connect to a PC.
- Oh, and you can always switch back to another printer whenever you want.
- Some PCs come with two printer ports. Most of the newer models, however, come with one.
- To get the extra (or two extra) printer ports, you have to add an expansion card to your PC. Although they cost anywhere from $30 and more, they aren't too expensive. You would probably want a computer dealer or consultant to install the expansion card for you, to set everything up properly.
- You can choose a printer other than the default whenever you see a Print dialog box. See the section "Choosing Some Other Printer," in Chapter 16.

Checking the Print Queue

Let me put the print queue in perspective: About ten years ago, whenever you printed anything, your computer had to wait. Whether you were printing a single page or the equivalent of *War and Peace*, you could not use your computer until all the printing was done. Why? Because computers and printers back then were *slow*.

Welcome to today. Printers are fast. Not only that—Windows doesn't wait for the printer to finish printing before it lets you do something else. Before your document is printed, it sits in a sort of doctor's office and waits. That sort of doctor's office is called the *print queue*.

▶ **Open your default (favorite) printer.**

In the Printers folder, double-click your printer's icon to open it. A window is displayed, similar to the one shown in Figure 18.2.

If you have just printed something, you see that document listed in the printer's window. If you have just printed a bunch of documents, you see them all listed in the window as they wait to print. If your printer is shared on a network, you might even see documents from others waiting to print.

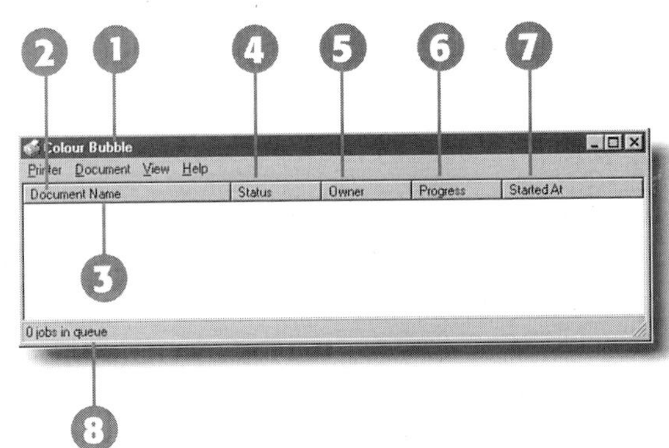

Figure 18.2

A printer's window, where the queue lives.

1. Printer's name.
2. Documents waiting to be printed are listed here, in the queue.
3. Document's name goes here.
4. Is it printing, waiting—what?
5. The computer that "owns" the document, or the user's name, might appear here.
6. The number of pages of the document that are already printed goes here.
7. The time the Print command was given for the document.
8. To see this information, make sure that a check mark is next to the View ➡Status Bar option on the menu.

TIP

Looking at the queue comes in handy sometimes. For example, you might print some huge document full of graphics and wonder why it's not printing yet. Fine: Check the printer's window, and look at the queue. The document might just be waiting. (Waiting for what, who knows?) At least the queue tells you that the Print command was successful.

As long as your document is in the queue, it will print. If a printer error occurs, Windows tells you so.

The following experiment may or may not work, depending on the speed of your printer:

▶ **Open Paint.**

▶ **Choose File ➡Open.**

▶ **Look in the C:\Windows folder.**

Choose drive C from the Look In list, and then open the Windows folder.

▶ **Open the Forest file.**

You might have to scroll right to find it. The Forest file is simply a graphics image of a bunch of pine leaves, or needles, as my wife calls them. I'm using a graphics image here because most printers take awhile to print them and you can see the image waiting in the queue.

▶ **Choose File ➡Print.**

▶ **Click OK.**

▶ **Switch back to your printer's window.**

Pressing the Alt+Tab key combination should accomplish this step right quick. What you should see is the file waiting to be printed, which looks something like Figure 18.3.

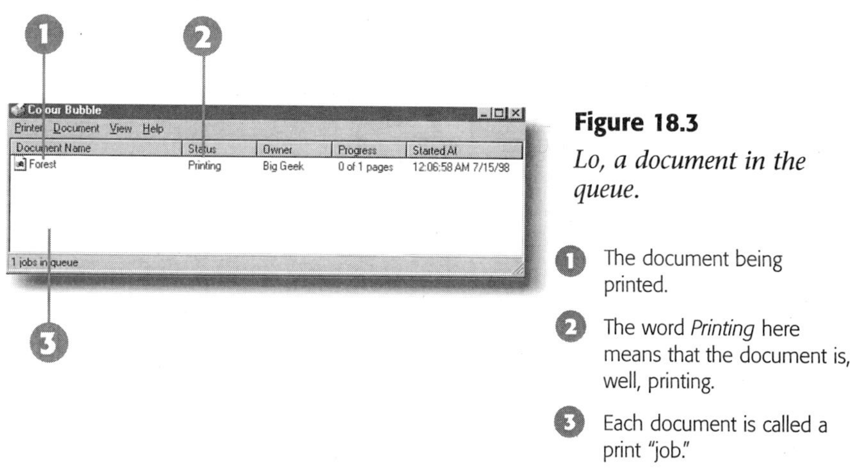

Figure 18.3

Lo, a document in the queue.

1. The document being printed.
2. The word *Printing* here means that the document is, well, printing.
3. Each document is called a print "job."

You might not catch your printer plugging away. In fact, some printers are too fast and you might never see *anything* in the queue. (My Color Bubble is pokey, so I see items in the queue even when I print text documents.)

▶ **Close Paint.**

Switch back to the Paint window by pressing Alt+Tab, and then close that window.

In addition to just looking at the queue, you can do other things to the documents waiting to be printed. You cancel a print job in the queue, which is covered in the next section. You can also move a print job, dragging it up in the list to print it ahead of other jobs. Again, this trick works only if you're printing a number of documents and can see them in the window.

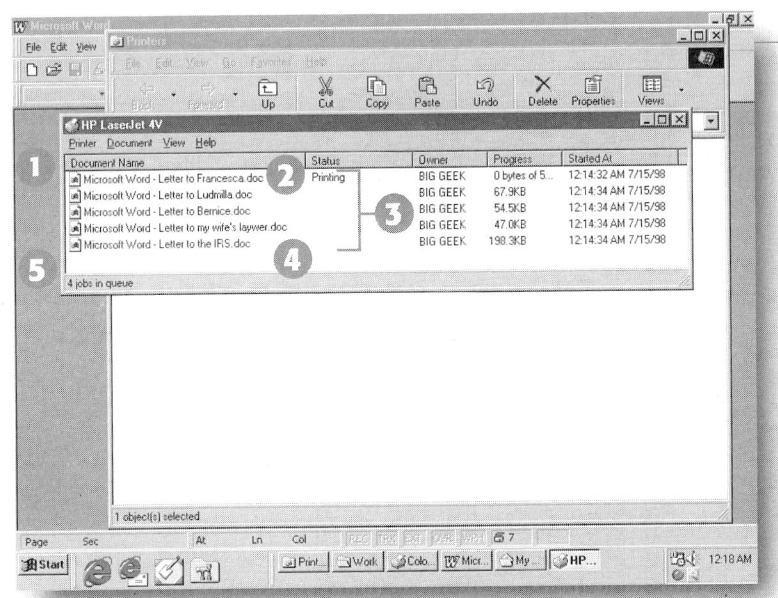

Figure 18.4

Moving a print job.

1. A ton of documents waiting to be printed (must be some sort of emergency).
2. Current document (the one that's printing).
3. Other documents are printed in this order.
4. Last document that will be printed.
5. Drag any of these files up or down the list to drop them in their new printing position.

Figure 18.4 shows a bunch of jobs sitting in the queue, waiting to print. If you want one of them to be printed before the others are printed, just drag it up in the list and drop it near the top. I've done it only a few times in my life—once as I was printing several long chapters with lots of graphics and I needed a short, little letter to be printed quickly.

▶ **Close your printer's window.**

▶ **Close the Printers window.**

No sense in wasting eyeball molecules staring at an empty queue.

- A *queue* (pronounced "Q") is a line. In England, they call a line a queue (which is actually more proper than *line*). Millions of Brits queue up to see *Star Wars*, for example.
- The name of the publisher of this book was adopted from the term *print queue,* although the extra ue was dropped to prevent Americans from calling the outfit "Q-E Publishing."
- Sometimes don't you just feel like going nuts and typing queueueueueueue?

Canceling a Print Job

Sometimes, if you're very quick, you can cancel what would seem to be "uncancelable." Although it seems as though choosing File ➡Print is a final act, it's not! You can stop a print job in several ways.

Suppose that because you think your computer is broken, you press Ctrl+P several dozen times. Then you look at the printer's window and see several dozen copies of the same document lined up in the queue. When that happens, follow these harried steps:

- **From the Start Thing, choose Settings ➡Printers.**
- **Right-click your default printer's icon.**

A shortcut menu appears. Hurry!

- **Choose Purge Print Documents.**

Bloop! They're gone. All documents are removed from the queue and disappear from the window.

Even though the documents are gone, don't be upset if your printer continues printing. Like a computer, a printer has memory. It might have stored the last few documents in memory and is printing them now.

- **Close the Printers window.**

Stopping your printer is another step; it's different for every printer.

With a dot-matrix or ink printer, just turn it off. You might have to manually remove or reset the paper feed before turning the printer on again.

With a laser printer, you may or may not be able to cancel. If your printer has a Reset button, that method works: Press the Online button to take the printer offline, and then press the Reset button. If that's not possible on your printer, you have to refer to its manual for detailed instructions about resetting the printer.

Installing a New Printer for Your Favorite PC

You can add a printer to your computer system in two ways, neither of which involves a shotgun or animal sacrifices: You can give your computer its own printer and connect it directly to the PC's rump. Or you can use a computer on the network, if you have a computer network.

The following two sections describe the details for both methods. Good luck!

Adding a Printer

Adding a printer to your computer is about 20 percent physical and 90 percent mental.

The physical part. This part might have already been done. If your printer is set up, plugged in, and ready to go, skip down a few paragraphs to read about the mental part.

▶ **Set the printer somewhere near your computer.**

A printer cable can be as long as 15 feet, although you want to keep the printer within arm's reach.

Unpack the printer or lure someone else into doing it for you. Remember that printers have lots of tape and plastic thingamabobs inside. An instruction sheet, often titled *Getting Started*, should tell you what to remove and where.

▶ **Plug the printer into the wall outlet.**

Make sure that the printer is turned off; if it pops on after you plug it in, it's no big deal. Just turn the printer off before you connect it to your computer.

▶ **Plug the printer cable into the printer and your computer.**

The printer cable has two distinctly different ends and can be plugged in at each end in only one way.

▶ **Stock the printer with paper.**

Buy the right kind of paper for your printer. Do not buy typing or bond paper.

For a laser printer, get photocopier paper. Buy it cheap, by the case. Thicker, better papers are available for more money.

For an ink or color printer, you have lots of paper choices, from standard photocopier paper to special papers that hold the ink better—even photographic-quality paper. As usual, you pay much more for the better stuff. (I just paid $15 for 10 sheets of photo-quality paper.)

Dot-matrix printers can use fanfold paper, which comes in various thicknesses. This type of printer is the only one that still prints multipart forms—in case that's what your business needs.

▶ **Turn the printer on.**

Ta-da!

The mental part. Concentrate on the printer. "You will work. You will work." Okay. Enough mental conditioning.

With the printer plugged in, turned on, and stocked with paper, you're ready to tell Windows and your entire computer about it. This process should be exciting, especially if it's a color printer and someone else paid for it.

▶ **Put your Windows CD-ROM into your PC's CD-ROM drive.**

Because Windows has to copy the printer's files from the CD-ROM to your PC's hard drive, you might as well have the disk ready to go.

▶ **From the Start Thing menu, choose Settings ➡Printers.**

The Printers dialog box is displayed.

▶ **Open the Add Printer icon.**

The Add Printer Wizard starts.

Unlike adding other hardware on your computer, adding a printer does not involve plug-and-play. In the future, Windows might be able to recognize and install a printer the second you plug it in. Today, you have to tell Windows all about your printer manually, er, mentally:

▶ **Click Next.**

Local printer and *network printer* are confusing terms. Obviously any printer in your office is local, and all printers can be used on a network.

▶ **Choose Local Printer.**

The printer you're adding is connected directly to your PC. I would have called it Open This Computer's Printer, but I'm too dumb to work for Microsoft.

▶ **Click Next.**

You might briefly see a window describing how Windows is building database driver whatever information. Okay. Fine. Wait it out.

Eventually the Add Printer Wizard displays a list of manufacturers and printers known to Windows, as shown in Figure 18.5.

▶ **Select your printer's manufacturer from the list on the left.**

For example, I'm using a Canon Bubble Jet printer, which is made by, surprisingly enough, Canon.

Clicking the manufacturer's name displays a list of printer makes and models on the list on the right.

▶ **Select your printer's make and model from the list on the right.**

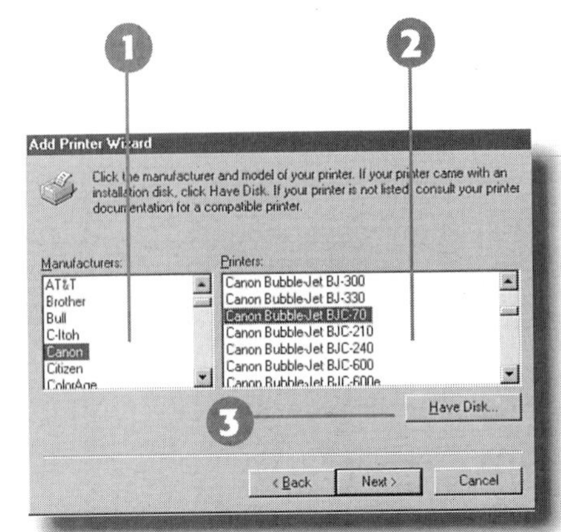

Figure 18.5
Choose a printer from this window.

1. Find your printer's manufacturer on this list.
2. Choose the printer model name and number from this list.
3. Click here if your printer doesn't appear or if it came with its own disk.

You should find this name and number on your printer somewhere. It's really obvious. For example, I have five printers in my office, and each one has its name and number on it, right up front:

- ✓ Canon Bubble Jet BJC-70
- ✓ Hewlett-Packard DeskJet 870Cse
- ✓ Hewlett-Packard LaserJet 4V
- ✓ Epson Stylus Color 600
- ✓ Hewlett-Packard LaserJet 4

TIP

If your printer name and number aren't listed, your printer probably came with one or more floppy disks. Put the first floppy disk in drive A, and click the Have Disk button. Click OK in the Install From Disk dialog box to continue.

Pay attention to the numbers and names. A definite difference exists, for example, between my LaserJet 4 and LaserJet 4V. Windows needs to know that difference.

▶ **Click Next.**

Windows needs to know how the printer is attached to your computer. It's probably guessing LPT1 onscreen, which is how 99 percent of printers are attached to PCs. Only if you *know* otherwise should you choose anything else.

▶ **Click Next.**

You can give your printer a new name or not, as shown in Figure 18.6. I always name my printers, so I typed *Color Bubble* in the box. It's more descriptive and fun than Canon Bubble Jet BJC-70 (which I got on sale, by the way).

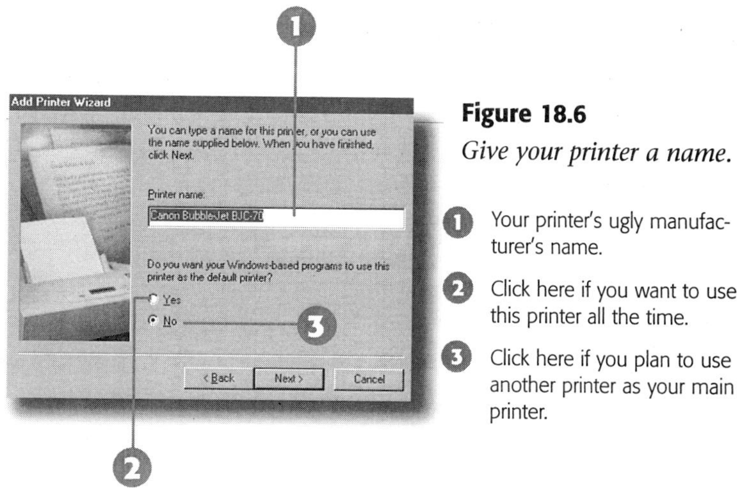

Figure 18.6
Give your printer a name.

1. Your printer's ugly manufacturer's name.
2. Click here if you want to use this printer all the time.
3. Click here if you plan to use another printer as your main printer.

▶ **Click Yes to make this printer your main printer (if Yes isn't chosen already).**

This step is an issue only if you have more than one printer connected to your PC. It's not a big issue because you can change favorite printers at any time, a subject that was covered earlier in this chapter, in the section "Picking Your Favorite Printer."

The name in the Printer Name text box is the name that appears in the Windows Printers folder as well as in all the Print dialog boxes in every program.

▶ **Click Next.**

Printing a test page is a good idea. It confirms that you've done everything correctly, and, well, it's fun.

▶ **Choose Yes (recommended).**

▶ **Click Finish.**

Files are copied from the Windows CD-ROM to your PC's hard drive.

The test page is printed, and a dialog box is displayed, asking you whether the page looks, well, okay.

▶ **Click Yes if the page looks, well, okay.**

If you click No, meaning that the page wasn't printed or looks bad, Windows runs the Printer Troubleshooter for you, which helps nail down exactly what went wrong.

Adding a Network Printer

With a network in your office, adding a printer involves no physical effort. Essentially you steal, uh, I mean *borrow* a printer that's already installed on another computer. No disks. No cables. Just a computer on the network is all you need.

▶ **From the Start Thing menu, choose Settings ➡Printers.**

The Printers dialog box is displayed.

▶ **Open the Add Printer icon.**

The Add Printer Wizard starts up. Yadda-yadda.

▶ **Click Next.**

▶ **Choose Network Printer.**

▶ **Click Next.**

Many printers have adjustments that can be made to improve the print quality or fine-tune other aspects of the printer. For example, the Canon Bubble Jet BJC-70 requires a color cartridge to be in place before it can print in color. Your color printer might be the same, so don't think that anything's wrong if it doesn't print in color.

In the next panel, you choose the computer whose printer you'll be using. Figure 18.7 explains.

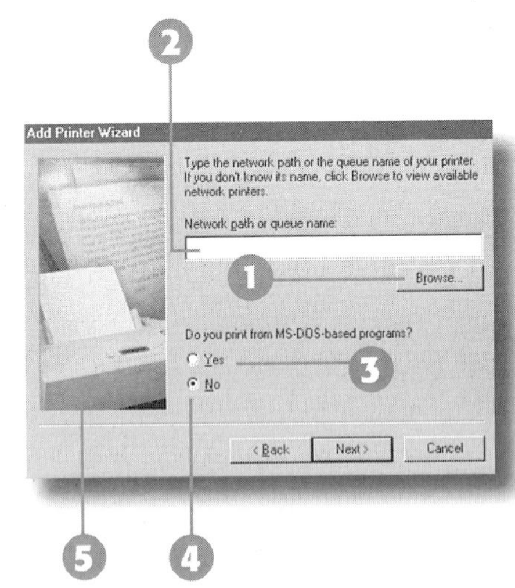

Figure 18.7

Locate the printer on the network.

1. Click here to find the printer on the network.
2. No one I know personally can remember the full pathname to a network printer.
3. Choose only if you use MS-DOS programs from which you'll be printing, such as the old WordPerfect or dBASE.
4. If you choose this option, you cannot print from any MS-DOS programs on the network printer.
5. Colorful graphic.

▶ **Click the Browse button.**

The Browse for Printer dialog box displays computers on your network that have printers up for grabs. Figure 18.8 explains things.

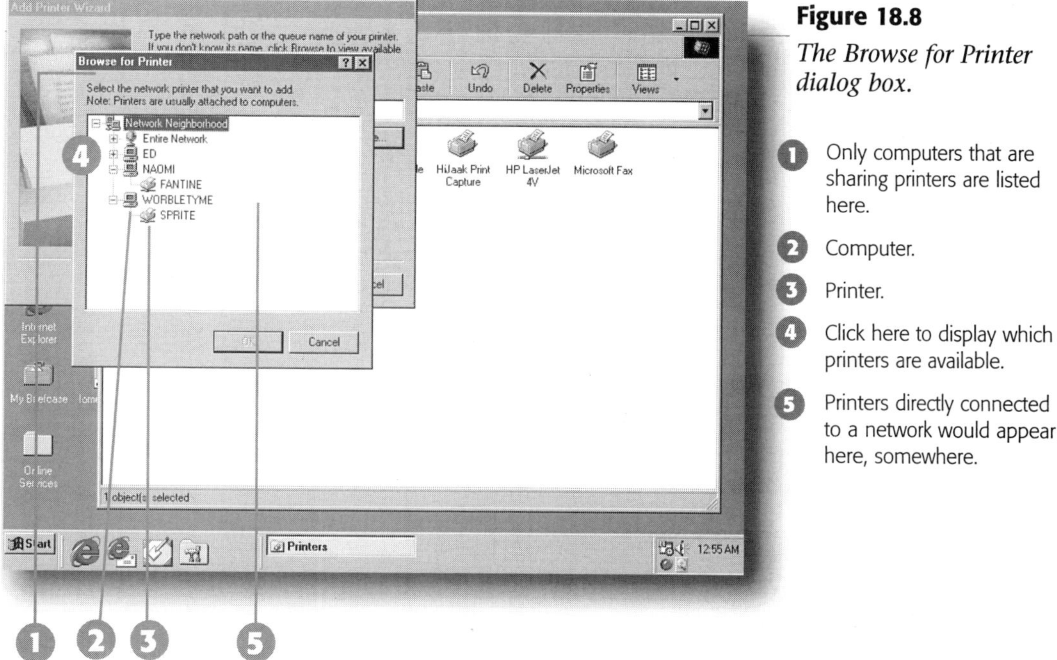

Figure 18.8
The Browse for Printer dialog box.

1. Only computers that are sharing printers are listed here.
2. Computer.
3. Printer.
4. Click here to display which printers are available.
5. Printers directly connected to a network would appear here, somewhere.

▶ **Select the printer you want to use.**

Open a computer in the list by clicking its plus sign. That step displays any network printers available for that computer.

Some printers are connected directly to the network, and they appear on the list right there with the computers.

Click the icon of the printer you want to use.

▶ **Click OK.**

You return to the Add Printer Wizard with your printer's complex and uninteresting pathname displayed in the Network Path *or* Queue Name text box.

▶ **Click Next.**

Give the printer a name, if you want. It's not necessary; the name that appears in the Printer Name text box is the one the sharing computer uses.

▶ **If this printer is your only one, choose Yes.**

At the bottom of the Add Printer Wizard dialog box, you're asked whether you want to use the network printer as your *default* printer (or the printer on which everything is printed unless you specify otherwise). If this printer is your only one, the answer is Yes.

An example of when you would choose No is if you add a specialty printer, one that's available only on your network (for example, a color printer or high-speed printer). In that instance, you might want to use another printer as the default instead.

▶ **Click Next.**

You want to print a test page, just to make sure that the network is operating properly, so choose Yes (Recommended).

▶ **Click Finish.**

Windows busily copies the necessary printer files from the network to your computer. Wocka-wocka-wocka...

If you see the Version Conflict dialog box, choose Yes to keep any current files on your computer; try not to overwrite files on your PC with older files elsewhere on the network.

Windows displays a dialog box asking you whether the test page was printed correctly.

▶ **Go grab the test page.**

If it looks okay, click Yes. You're in business.

If the document doesn't print or looks ugly (ugly as in "utterly wrong"), click No to run the Printer Troubleshooter.

- After adding the printer, the printer's icon appears in the Printer folder window.
- The default printer (the one your computer uses unless you say otherwise) has a check mark next to it. (That's a check mark, not the Nike swoosh thing.)
- Note that all network printers have plumbing; pipes below the printer indicate that it's on the network (either that, or it's a hydraulic printer).

Chapter 19

Sending a Fax (Which Is Like Printing)

Questions Answered and Thoughts Inspired

- Creating an OLE document to fax
- Faxing a document
- Using the Windows cover pages
- Configuring your PC to receive a fax
- Receiving and viewing a fax
- Sending yourself a fax (advice only)

Think about it: A fax machine is really a printer. It's not a printer connected to your PC, however. Instead, you must use the phone lines to call up the fax machine and then scream in the proper pitch to have the fax machine print. If you think of a fax machine in those terms, you can easily understand how to fax in Windows. This chapter gives you the details.

- This chapter covers the use of Microsoft Fax, which is really a Windows 95 program, although you might also have it with Windows 98. Other fax programs exist, and for the most part they work similarly to what's described here. Unfortunately, I don't have the space to cover every fax program.

- To send or receive a fax, your PC must have a fax modem installed. Almost all modems sold today have the capability to send and receive faxes. If your modem does not (if it's an older model or lacks fax modem smarts), you can't work the tutorials in this chapter.
- To confirm that you can send and receive faxes, look for the Microsoft Fax icon in the Printers folder. (From the Start Thing menu, choose Settings➡Printers.)

Having Your Computer Send a Fax

I use my computer to send faxes all the time. The computer is where I write the document I'm faxing, so sending the fax is as easy as printing.

Faxing works just like printing.

To fax a document, follow these steps:

1. **Compose the document you want to fax.**
2. **Choose File➡Print and select Microsoft Fax as your printer.**
3. **Enter information about who you want to send the fax to, choose a cover page, and perform other tasks.**
4. **Send the fax.**

The following tutorial works through the process of sending a fax; however, you can send a fax only if you have two things: a document to fax and the phone number of a machine to fax to.

- The following section helps you create a sample document for faxing.
- You have to locate the number of a fax machine on your own. You can use any fax machine: the one at the office, your club, your friend's house, wherever. You have to have a fax machine, however, to send the fax to.
- No, you cannot send the fax to yourself. I explain why at the end of this chapter.
- Even though being able to send faxes from your computer is nifty, a real fax machine might still come in handy. For example, a fax machine is good for sending things such as signed contracts, purchase orders, and other stuff you would have to retype or scan before faxing—which would be a hassle.

Creating a Document to Fax

The following tutorial creates a sample document to fax. It uses OLE (Object Linking and Embedding) to create a Paint graphics image inside a WordPad document. Freaky, huh?

- **Start WordPad.**
- **Type the following information (you can type this line):**

```
Here is exactly what I think of your proposal:
```

To make the word *exactly* appear in italics, highlight the word and then press Ctrl+I.

Press the Enter key twice at the end of the line to start a new paragraph (or two).

- **Choose Insert➡Object.**

The Insert Object dialog box appears, as shown in Figure 19.1. In this section you create a graphics image in the document. This method is the sneaky, non-cut and paste way to do it.

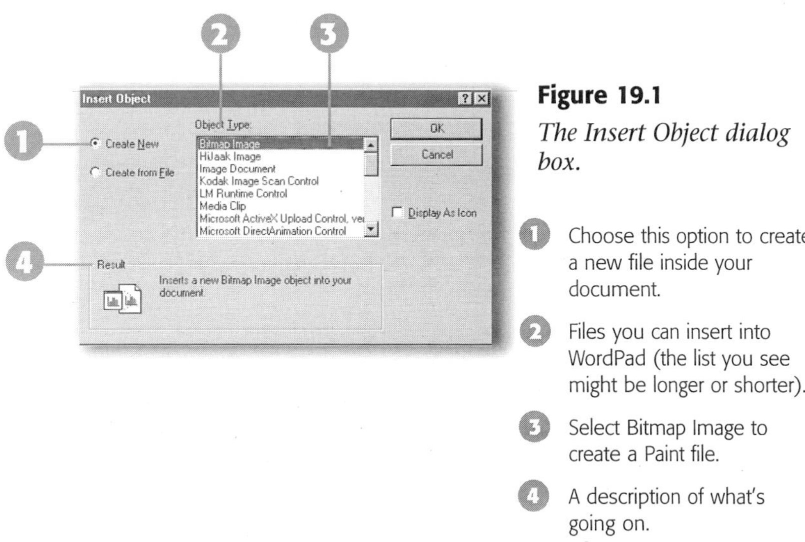

Figure 19.1
The Insert Object dialog box.

1. Choose this option to create a new file inside your document.
2. Files you can insert into WordPad (the list you see might be longer or shorter).
3. Select Bitmap Image to create a Paint file.
4. A description of what's going on.

- **Choose Create New (if it's not chosen already).**
- **Choose Bitmap Image from the Object Type list (if it's not chosen already).**
- **Click OK.**

Weird. The WordPad window changes. Even though you see *WordPad*, you're really in the Paint program creating an image. Figure 19.2 shows the possibilities.

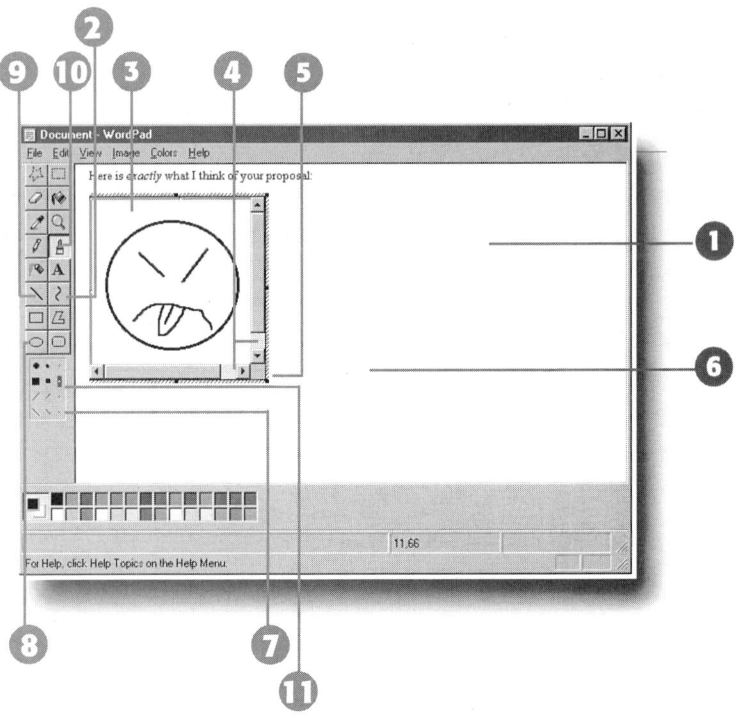

Figure 19.2

Creating a Paint image in WordPad.

1. The WordPad window.
2. Paint's palettes and tools.
3. Create the Paint image in here.
4. Use the scrollbars to see more of the image or…
5. …drag these handles to change the image size.
6. Click out here (in the WordPad window) to leave Paint.
7. Choose the line tool, and then select the line thickness from here.
8. Use the Ellipse tool to draw the head.
9. Use the Line tool to draw the eyes.
10. Use the Paintbrush tool to draw the mouth and tongue.
11. Choose the Paintbrush tool size from here.

▶ **Create an image.**

Use Figure 19.2 as your guide.

Your image doesn't have to look exactly like Mr. Yuck.

When you're done creating the image, you have to leave the Paint-inside-WordPad program.

▶ **Click the mouse outside the Paint image.**

The Paint image is inside the hashed box inside WordPad. Just click to the right of the box to return to WordPad.

The image appears in WordPad with the eight black handles around it, meaning that the image is selected. You can change the image's size by dragging a handle.

Because you should always save before you print, save the file in the My Documents folder as Nasty Fax:

▶ **Choose File➡Save.**

▶ **Change to the My Documents folder (if you're not there already).**

Choose My Documents from the Save In drop-down list.

▶ **In the File Name text box, type** Nasty Fax.

▶ **Click Save.**

Now you can send the fax, which works like printing.

Sending a Fax

If you have your document all created and ready to fax (and saved to disk), follow these steps to send the fax:

▶ **Choose File➡Print.**

The Print dialog box appears.

▶ **Choose Microsoft Fax from the Name drop-down list.**

If you don't see Microsoft Fax, you might be able to find another fax program listed, such as WinFax, which you can use to send faxes. If you're using another program, however, the following steps might not match the ones your fax program uses:

> **WATCH OUT!**
>
> You cannot fax by clicking the Print button on the toolbar. Only if you've chosen the fax as your default printer does that technique work. (See Chapter 18 for more information about the default printer.)

▶ **Click OK.**

Eventually you see the Compose New Fax Wizard, as shown in Figure 19.3.

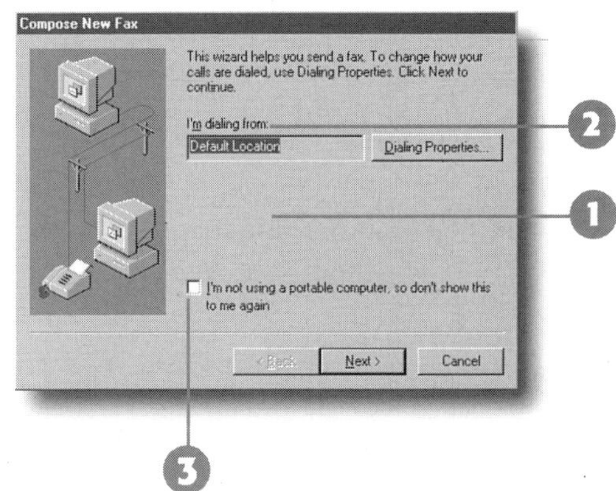

Figure 19.3
The New Fax Wizard starts up.

1. This screen is necessary only if you're using a laptop.
2. Enter your location here so that the modem knows how to dial the phone.
3. If you're using a desktop PC, click here and you'll never see this screen again.

▶ **Click Next.**

On the next screen, as shown in Figure 19.4, you enter the phone number of the fax machine to which you're faxing. The other information isn't required, although you can fill it in anyway, as shown in the figure.

▶ **Enter the person's name in the To box.**

This information is optional, although if you type a name, it appears on the cover page (if you elect to send one).

▶ **Choose a country, if necessary.**

This step is for dialing purposes. The fax needs to know which country code to dial.

▶ **Type the fax's phone number in the Fax # box.**

You can use your computer to send a fax anywhere that has fax machines. It makes no difference whether you're sending to a real fax machine or a computer with a fax modem; it's all the same to Windows.

You might also have to type a new area code; Windows uses your area code, as long as you set up your modem properly when Windows was first installed.

Be sure to put a check mark next to the Dial Area Code box if you have to dial your own area code to make a "local" call in your area.

If you want to send the fax to more than one person, click the Add to List button. The information you enter is put in the Recipient List area and the input boxes are emptied so that you can type information about another fax machine. That way, you can send the same fax to multiple people—such as when you send your resignation notice to the fax machine of every department in your company!

▶ **Click Next.**

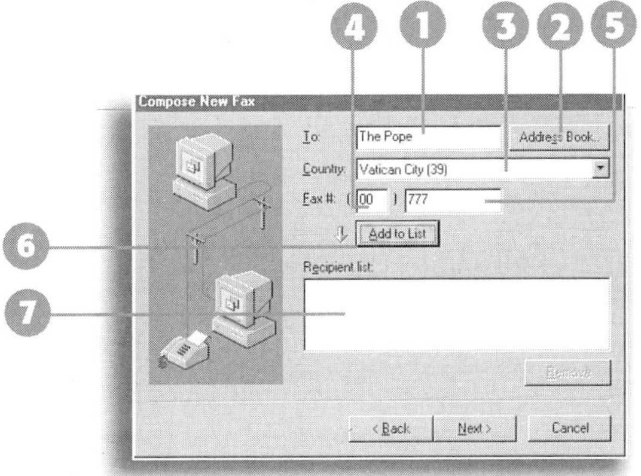

Figure 19.4

Enter information about the fax machine you're sending to.

1. Optionally enter the person's name here.
2. Don't bother with this button.
3. Choose a country here (other than the United States of America) if you're in the United States and sending something to another country.
4. Enter the area code here.
5. The fax phone number goes here.
6. Click to add the number to the fax list.
7. You can send the fax to multiple machines by entering new information after clicking the Add to List button.

You do not have to click the Add to List button if you're sending a fax to just one fax machine or recipient.

Now you get to select a cover page, if you want. Windows comes with several basic designs to choose from, all listed in the Fax Wizard, as shown in Figure 19.5.

The cover page is filled in based on the information you've already given the Fax Wizard plus information from the Address Book (if any). You enter additional cover page information in the following step:

▶ **Choose your cover page from the list.**

I typically use the Generic cover page whenever I send a fax, if I use a cover page at all.

▶ **Click Next.**

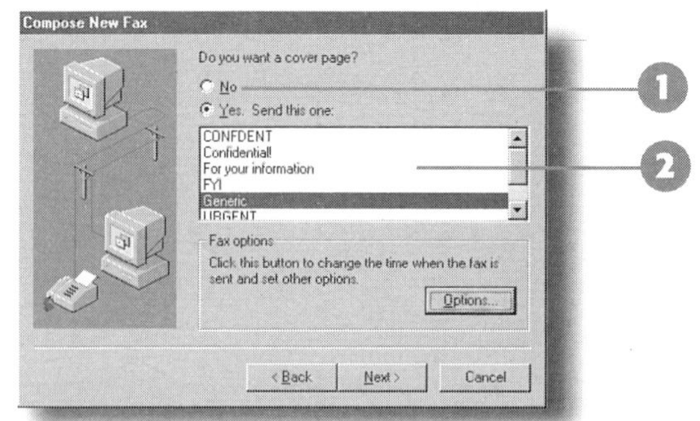

Figure 19.5

Choose a cover page—or not.

1. Click here not to send a cover page.
2. The list of available cover pages (although you can create your own).

The Wizard lets you type the fax's subject plus a brief note. This information appears on the cover page if you click the Start Note on Cover Page option. Otherwise, the note appears above the information you're faxing (on the first page).

▶ **Type a subject, such as Proposal Feedback.**

▶ **Type a note, if necessary.**

For this tutorial, a note isn't necessary. I believe that your message in WordPad (if you're following this chapter's tutorial) is sufficient.

▶ **Click Next.**

▶ **Click Finish.**

In a few moments, you should hear the fax modem dial up the other fax machine.

The other fax machine should answer. They sing for a while. Then your fax is sent. A Microsoft Fax Status dialog box appears while all this stuff is going on. You might also notice a little "fax guy" on the system tray.

The Microsoft Fax Status dialog box disappears when you're done sending the fax. Do not click the Hang Up button unless you hear a human answer the phone or some other circumstance that leads you to believe that you've dialed the wrong number.

Try to retrieve the fax, if possible. For example, if you're testing this process and are faxing to another fax machine in your office, get up and go take a look at it. Examine the cover page to see what you like. Experiment with other cover pages.

▶ **Close WordPad.**

The fax-sending tutorial is complete.

- See the following section for more information about cover pages.
- Don't bother with the Address Book button in the Fax Wizard. Sure, you can try using it, and I'm sure that someone else could write a whole book about it. The thing isn't intuitive, however, and is rather a pain to set up. No, I would just type the names and phone numbers manually if I were you. Saves time.

- The Start menu has an option called Compose New Fax (you choose Programs➡Accessories➡Fax➡Compose New Fax.) Don't bother with it. It runs the Fax Wizard as shown in this section but requires that you already have created the document to fax. Huh? That makes no sense to me. It's much better to use the Microsoft Fax in the Print dialog box because faxing resembles printing. Using the Compose New Fax command just doesn't make sense.

All About Cover Pages

Windows comes with about a half-dozen predesigned cover pages. You can use any of them when you send a fax, or you can create your own. It's all done with the Fax Cover Page Editor program.

▶ **From the Start Thing, choose Programs➡Accessories➡Fax➡Cover Page Editor.**

The Fax Cover Page Editor starts up, probably instilling a little wisdom in you with a tip of the day.

If you plan to create a cover page on your own, click the Next Tip button a few times to get some hints about things you can do.

Click OK to rid yourself of the Tips dialog box.

The Fax Cover Page Editor is really a Windows 95 program, although you might also have it in Windows 98.

▶ **Maximize the Cover Page Editor.**

Windows keeps its half dozen or so cover pages in the C:\Windows folder on your hard drive. You can use the Cover Page Editor to see what each one looks like, change them, or create your own.

▶ **Choose File➡Open.**

▶ **Browse to drive C.**

Choose your drive C from the Look In drop-down list.

▶ **Open the Windows folder.**

Slide the scrollbar to the right; you can see the list of cover pages to the right of all the folders shown in the Open dialog box.

▶ **Open the Generic cover page file.**

Double-click the word *Generic* to open that file.

The Generic Fax cover sheet appears in the Fax Cover Page Editor, as shown in Figure 19.6.

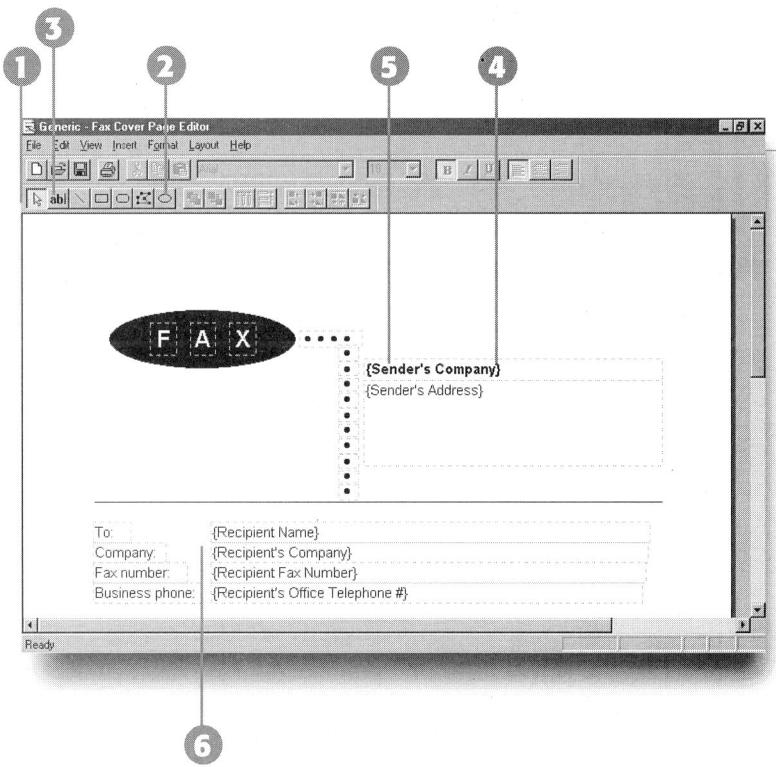

Figure 19.6

A generic cover page.

1. The toolbar shows elements you paste on the cover page.
2. This black oval was created by using the Ellipse tool. The color was selected by right-clicking the oval and choosing the Line, Fill and Color option.
3. The text tool creates text fields.
4. Use the Insert menu to put these braces (curly brackets) on the cover page.
5. Obtain this information from the Fax Wizard or Address Book.
6. The Fax Wizard fills in this information when you send the fax.

This program is *not* a word processor. It's more of a database that arranges information and graphics on a page.

The text in the curly brackets—such as {Recipient Name}—is replaced by information from the Fax Wizard when the cover page is printed. Those items (everything in curly brackets) are similar to fields in a database; the database is the information you enter in the Fax Wizard or that comes from the Address Book I told you not to use.

▶ **Choose File➡Print Preview.**

In the Print Preview window, you can get an idea of what the entire cover page looks like.

Notice the {Note} at the bottom of the page? That's replaced by whatever you type as a note in the Fax Wizard.

▶ **Close the Print Preview window.**

▶ **Click the Close button.**

You can open other cover page documents stored in the Windows folder and use the Print Preview command to see what they look like. Although each one has a different theme, they all display similar information.

If you want to create your own cover page, I recommend starting with one of the Windows examples: Use the mouse to drag the fields around, or use the tools on the toolbar to create your own graphics and text. Remember that you can copy and paste graphics from other programs on the cover page. (I don't have room in this chapter for a cover page tutorial.) Use the Save As command to save your cover page in the Windows folder under its own descriptive name. You see the cover page listed when you next use the Fax Wizard.

▶ **Close the Fax Cover Page Editor.**

Don't fret over the Cover Page Editor. If you have time, create your own cover page. Otherwise, be happy with what Windows provides. I use the Generic cover page for everything.

You can use the following bulleted items as tips if you decide to create your own cover page:

- Use the Insert menu to insert fields into your own cover page. The sidebar "About Them Thar Fields," later in this chapter, describes some of the more useful fields you can insert.
- Fields are inserted into a text box. Use the text tool to drag a rectangle that becomes the text box.
- You can also type text in a text box.
- The commands on the Insert menu insert not only the fields but also the corresponding prompt. For example, choosing Insert➡Recipient➡Name inserts two text boxes: To: and {Recipient Name}.
- You can resize the text boxes.
- You can delete the text boxes the Insert menu creates and leave just the fields.
- Click once on a text box to move or resize the text box, and click again to edit the text.
- Apply fonts by using the Format➡Font command or by using the Formatting toolbar. The font applies to all text in the box, so if you want to use another font, you have to create another text box.

- Use the Line, Rectangle, Rounded Rectangle, Polygon, and Ellipse tools to create graphics and other shapes on your cover page.
- Select a graphic by clicking it. You can then resize the graphic by dragging the eight tiny handles.
- You can "nudge" selected graphics by pressing the arrow keys on your keyboard.
- Right-click a selected graphic and choose Line, Fill and Color to change the graphic's appearance. (Color is kind of a misnomer; you have only shades of gray options because all fax machines print in black and white.)

Some items can appear in front of others, which might frustrate your editing. Use the Bring to Front and Send to Back buttons (to the right of the Ellipse button) on the toolbar to arrange graphics in front of or behind each other.

- If you have trouble lining things up, choose View➡Grid Lines. Various options on the Layout menu can also help you align two more selected objects.

About Them Thar Fields

A *field* is a placeholder for text to be filled in later. On the various cover pages are the fields enclosed in curly brackets. Of those listed, a handful are supplied by the Fax Wizard. When the cover page is created, the information from the Wizard is put on the cover page in place of the fields.

The pages have a number of fields, and much of that information comes from the Address Book. If you aren't using the Address Book, however, only a handful of the fields are filled in on the cover page:

{*Recipient Name*}—The To text box in the Fax Wizard (refer to Figure 19.4)

{*Fax number*}—The number entered in the Fax Wizard (refer to Figure 19.4)

{*Sender Name*}—Your computer's name, the name you use to log in to Windows

{*Sender Fax #*}—Your computer's modem number, which was entered when you installed the modem

{*Time Sent*}—The date and time the fax is sent, filled in by the computer

{*# of Pages*}—The total number of pages (including the cover page), which is filled in by Windows

{*Subject*}—The subject you enter in the Fax Wizard

{*Note*}—The note, if any, you entered in the Fax Wizard

Receiving a Fax

I do not use my computer to receive faxes. For that, I have a real fax machine. If you lack a real fax machine, however, or just want to use your computer to receive faxes, you can do it.

If you do use your PC to receive faxes, my best advice is to get it its own phone line. Sure, Radio Shack sells a gizmo that determines whether an incoming call is for you or a fax. A computer with its own phone line, however, can dial out to the Internet or send a fax whenever it wants, regardless of whether someone is on the phone.

The program used to receive faxes, Microsoft Exchange, is a Windows 95 program. You may or may not have this program in your copy of Windows 98.

Configuring Your Fax Modem to Answer Incoming Calls

To have your computer step up to the modem plate and wait for a fax pitch, you have to run the Microsoft Exchange program. It's a forerunner to the Outlook Express program that comes with Windows 98. (Exchange is a *beast* to set up, which is probably why it no longer ships with Windows 98.)

▶ **Open the Inbox icon on the desktop.**

The Inbox icon starts Microsoft Exchange. Or you might be able to find it on the Start Thing menu: Choose Programs➡Windows Messaging.

You have to configure your modem to answer incoming calls.

▶ **Choose Tools➡Microsoft Fax Tools➡Options.**

The Microsoft Fax Properties dialog box appears.

▶ **Click the Modem tab.**

This step brings the Modem panel forward, if it's not already.

▶ **Click the Properties button.**

The Fax Modem Properties dialog box is displayed, as shown in Figure 19.7.

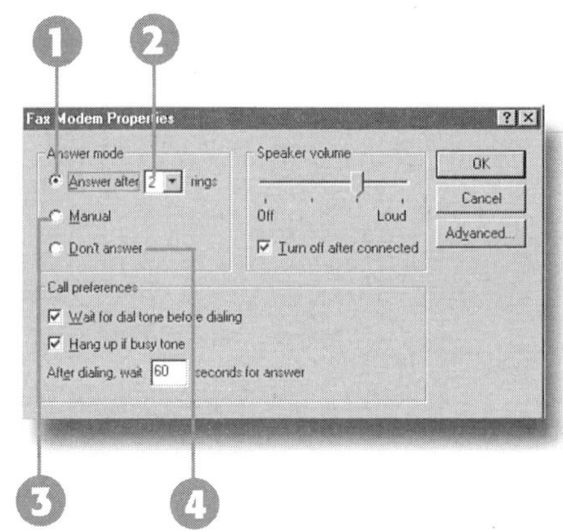

Figure 19.7

The Fax Modem Properties dialog box.

1. Check this option to have your computer automatically answer incoming phone calls.
2. Number of rings after which the computer answers.
3. Put a check here to answer manually.
4. Put a check by this item to prevent incoming faxes and allow the modem to be used for other purposes.

- **Choose Answer After.**
- **Set the number of rings to** 2.

You can set the number of rings to three or more by choosing another value.

- **Click OK to close the Fax Modem Properties dialog box.**
- **Click OK to close the Microsoft Fax Properties dialog box.**
- **Minimize the Inbox window.**

Now you sit and wait for a fax.

By the way, the fax modem answers the phone for you. However, that's just hardware. Windows provides the smarts (software) that reads the information from the modem and translates it into a fax you can see on your computer screen.

- **Double-click the wee li'l fax guy on the system tray.**

The Fax Status window appears, which tells you exactly what your fax modem is doing. (It's most likely idle, waiting for a fax right now).

If you've set your fax modem to the manual setting, you have to click the Answer Now button to receive a fax. Otherwise, you just wait. (Receiving a fax is covered in the next section.)

You should notice the wee li'l fax guy sitting on the system tray. It's your clue that Windows is sitting around and waiting for a fax.

▶ **Choose Options➡Display When Active.**

You want the Fax Status window to pop up when a fax comes in. Make sure that a check mark appears next to the Display When Active menu item.

▶ **Minimize the Fax Status window.**

You cannot quit the Microsoft Exchange program if you expect to use your PC as a fax machine. When you quit Microsoft Exchange, the Fax Modem is disabled and the wee li'l fax guy disappears from the system tray. Only while you're running Exchange can you receive a fax.

Receiving a Fax

The process of receiving a fax is obviously hard to do as a tutorial, so just follow along and pretend that your computer's modem line is ringing.

A-ha! A fax is coming in!

The Fax Status window appears right on top of whatever you're doing. It says *Answering Call*, and you hear the two faxes connect. Then it says *Connecting*.

As the fax starts coming in, the window looks like Figure 19.8.

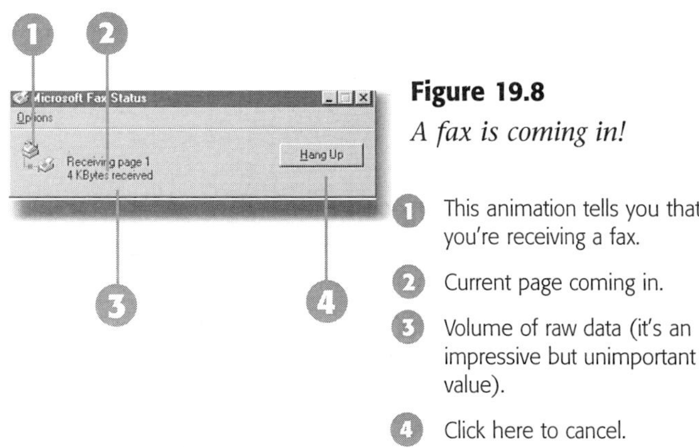

Figure 19.8
A fax is coming in!

1. This animation tells you that you're receiving a fax.
2. Current page coming in.
3. Volume of raw data (it's an impressive but unimportant value).
4. Click here to cancel.

Eventually the fax is received, and the Fax Status window goes away.

Your computer might play a tone or sound, indicating that a fax has been received.

On the system tray, you see a "new mail" notification; an envelope with a star on the corner indicates that you have a new piece of mail in the Microsoft Exchange Inbox. That's where you have to go to read the fax. (And it's the reason that you have to keep the Inbox open.)

▶ **Point the mouse at the li'l new-mail guy on the system tray.**

You see the text *You have new mail* appear.

▶ **Double-click the li'l new-mail guy.**

Your Inbox opens, and you can see the new mail item at the top of the list, as shown in Figure 19.9.

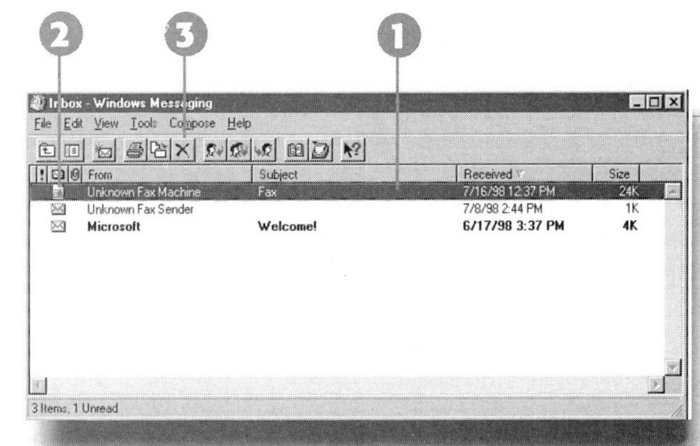

Figure 19.9
The fax sits in your inbox.

1. The most recent fax appears at the top of the list.
2. Double-click to open the fax.
3. Click here to delete the selected fax.

▶ **Double-click the new fax to view it.**

This step starts the Kodak Imaging program, which is used to view (and edit) complex graphics images. Figure 19.10 shows you some tricks.

Use the scrollbar to peruse your document.

If you want to print a copy, click the Print button on the toolbar.

You can use the File➡Save Copy As command to save the fax document to disk. Notice that the fax is saved as a *graphics* document; you cannot edit or copy the text. It's all an image.

▶ **Close the Imaging window when you're done viewing.**

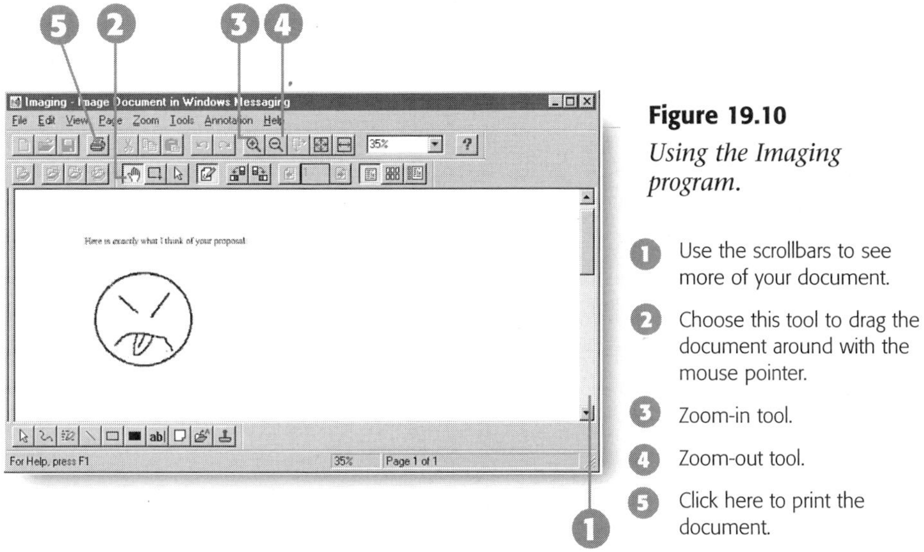

Figure 19.10
Using the Imaging program.

1. Use the scrollbars to see more of your document.
2. Choose this tool to drag the document around with the mouse pointer.
3. Zoom-in tool.
4. Zoom-out tool.
5. Click here to print the document.

The faxes stay in the Inbox until you delete them.

To delete the fax, click it once to select it, and then click the Delete button on the toolbar.

If you know that you're about to receive a fax, you can open the Inbox again and wait for the fax, closing it when you're done.

IMPORTANT POINT

Keep the Microsoft Exchange program open if you expect to receive more faxes. If not, you can close the Exchange window now.

Sending Yourself a Fax

No, you cannot send yourself a fax. Many people ask, and it's probably a legitimate question. Ask yourself this question: "Can I call myself on the phone?" Probably not.

To send a fax, you need both a sending and receiving machine on two different phone lines. If you have two computers or a computer and a fax machine and both are on different phone lines, you can send yourself a fax. Otherwise, you can't.

(For purposes of writing this chapter, I used my computer to call my office fax and then faxed from my office fax to my computer.)

It's possible to send a fax to someone and have her send it back to you. I don't know what that would prove, but it's possible.

Bottom line: You can't send yourself a fax.

Part IV

Disks, Folders, and Files

Chapters in This Part

Part IV

Visual Topic Reference A.

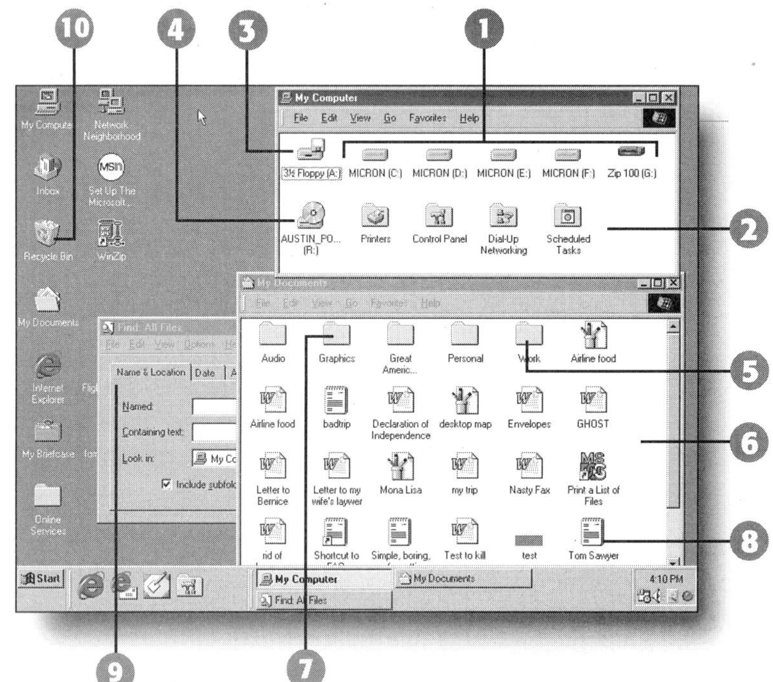

1. Work with these guys (Chapter 20).
2. Maintain your hard drives (Chapter 21).
3. Format a floppy disk (Chapter 22).
4. Use your CD-ROM drive (Chapter 22).
5. Make folders work for you (Chapter 23).
6. Manipulate files (Chapter 24).
7. Use the Send To command (Chapter 25).
8. Discover what this icon means (Chapter 26).
9. Find lost files (Chapter 27).
10. Empty the trash (Chapter 28).

Disk Drive 101

Questions Answered and Thoughts Inspired

- Understanding disk drives, letters, and names
- Recognizing disk icons
- Getting a different look at your disk drives
- Changing your disk's name

If a computer had only one type of long-term storage, no one would ever have to mess with disk drive names, letters, and types. Things just aren't that easy, though.

Your PC most likely has several types of long-term storage devices—called *disk drives*. You probably have a floppy drive, one or two hard drives, a CD-ROM or DVD drive, and maybe even a ZIP drive. Your computer needs to know the difference between these types of drives, and so do you. That's why this chapter is your basic disk drive orientation chapter, Disk Drive 101.

- *Long-term*, or permanent, storage is what your disk drives provide.
- *Short-term*, or temporary, storage is provided by your PC's memory, or RAM.
- You need both types of storage: short-term for creating or working on your stuff and long-term for saving your stuff for later.

Disk Drive Names and Letters

The disk drives inside your computer are named after famous letters of the alphabet, from A to Z. You can also give your drives their own names, called *volume labels*. The "volume" is the disk, and the "label" is its name. Even so, Windows and your software still refer to the drive by its letter, not by any volume label.

- A *volume label* is another name for a disk, a name you can give the disk and change at any time.
- Yeah, I hate the term volume label too, but I live with it.
- You cannot change the drive letter assigned to a disk. Well, you can't change it *much*. (More on that in Chapter 22.)

Drives A Through Z

Ever wonder why letters are assigned to disk drives? I don't. I'm just happy that they don't have strange names. With everything else in the computer biz named after a famous random number, be thankful that you have only letters of the alphabet to deal with when you're using disk drives. One letter per drive is enough for me, thanks.

▶ **Open the My Computer icon on the desktop.**

My Computer lists all the disk drives on your PC. Figure 20.1 shows my test computer's disk drives, which are similar to what you see but not exactly the same.

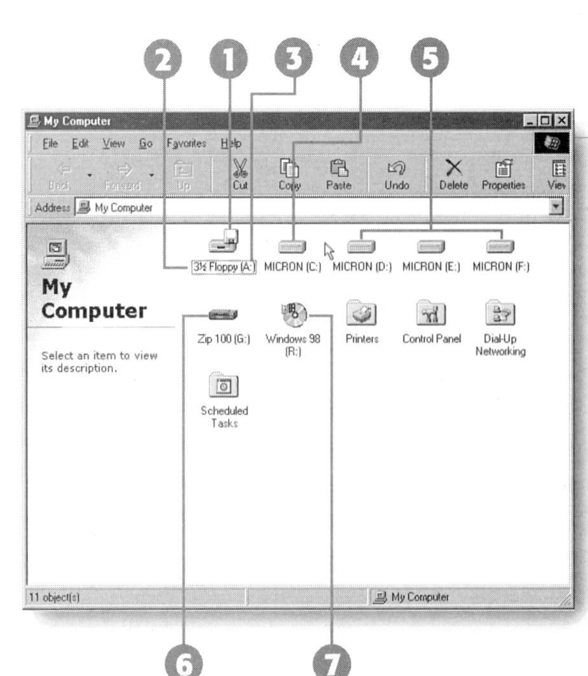

Figure 20.1
Disk drives on your computer.

1. Floppy drive A.
2. Disk's name.
3. Disk's drive letter, in parentheses.
4. Hard drive C, the first (main) hard drive.
5. Bonus hard drives D through F.
6. Removable ZIP drive.
7. CD-ROM drive.

Drive A. The first floppy drive on your PC is called *drive A*. For most PCs now sold, drive A is a 3 1/2-inch floppy drive capable of using 1.44MB floppy disks. (More on that in Chapter 22, "Removable Disks and Drives.")

Drive B. Where is drive B? Most PCs are sold without a drive B, although it would be a second floppy disk if you had one. Back in the old days (about 1982), having two floppy disks was the cat's pajamas. That was before hard drives were standard on a PC.

You cannot open drive A unless you have a floppy disk in the drive. Not only that, but the floppy disk must also be *formatted*. More on this subject in Chapter 22.

Drive C. The first hard drive on your PC is called *drive C*. This statement is true whether or not you have a drive B. Note in Figure 20.1 that the hard drive has a letter and a name. The name is optional, and you can change it, which I show you how to do in a few paragraphs.

Drives D and up. If you have any additional hard drives, they're given letters D and up. For example, my system has hard drives D through F. It's similar to having extra closet space: The more hard drives you have, the more room that's available for storing your stuff.

CD-ROM drive. Your PC most likely has a CD-ROM drive. That drive is typically given the next available drive letter after the last hard drive. On most systems, it's drive D, although it could also be drive E or even F, G, and up. In Figure 20.1, you can see that I've given my CD-ROM drive the letter *R*. Changing drive letters is explained in Chapter 22.

Removable drive. If you have any removable disk drives, they also appear in the My Computer window along with drive names and letters. You might find one, none, or several of the following:

> **ZIP drive.** The ZIP drive, as shown in Figure 20.1, is an option on many computers. It's basically a superduper floppy drive capable of storing 100 megabytes on a single disk.
>
> **JAZ drive.** The ZIP drive's big brother, the JAZ drive can store one or two gigabytes of information on a single disk. That's a great deal of storage space.
>
> **Magneto-optical (MO) drive.** This type of hybrid CD-ROM disk/floppy disk stores from 130 to more than 600 megabytes of information. It's used primarily by graphic-artist-types to hold their huge graphic-artist-type files.
>
> This type of removable drive (ZIP, JAZ, MO, or whatever else) is given a letter after your last hard drive or CD-ROM drive.

The sequence of disk drive letters after your last hard drive varies. The next letter could represent a ZIP drive or CD-ROM drive or whatever. The order depends on which drives Windows recognizes first when it starts up. You can assign specific letters to drives, which is shown in Chapter 22.

Network drive. Not shown in Figure 20.1 but visible on many systems is a network drive. This type of drive represents disk storage on other computers elsewhere on the network. You give them their drive letters when you set them up, which is covered in Chapter 35.

- You can add more hard drives to your PC, if you want. In fact, most PCs have room for a second hard drive. Adding one is a great way to get more storage space. (Have someone else install it, though.)
- Notice that the ZIP drive in Figure 20.1 has its own icon. Don't get jealous. That's just a feature of the ZIP software I'm using; your ZIP drive may or may not look the same.
- The icon shown for the CD-ROM drive also varies. If you have a special CD-ROM, it might show its own unique icon. Music CDs also show a unique icon.
- No special icon shows the difference between a DVD and CD-ROM drive—at least not right now.

Most newer computers have only one hard drive, C. Older computers with multiple hard drives (like mine) can be converted to a newer disk format that not only saves disk space but also eliminates many of the bonus disk drive letters. Chapter 21 tells you how.

Basic Disk Drive Icon Identification

Table 20.1 describes some of the icon types lurking in the main My Computer window, along with what they might represent.

Table 20.1 Icons in the My Computer Window

Icon	Represents
	A 3 1/2-inch floppy drive, either drive A or drive B.
	A 5 1/4-inch floppy drive, most likely drive B. Some computers keep this older drive format handy to remain compatible with older systems.

Icon	Represents
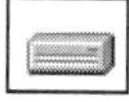	Your typical hard drive, drive C (and drives D, E, and up, depending on your PC).
	A CD-ROM or DVD drive (both use the same icon). The drive letter that's assigned depends on your PC. Some PCs might have more than one, in which case multiple icons appear in the My Computer window.
	Replaces the CD-ROM or DVD icon (see preceding entry) when you insert a musical CD in the drive. You can play the CD (see Chapter 22), thus turning your $1,000 computer into a $200 boom box.
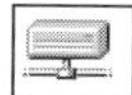	A hard drive (or even a CD-ROM drive) on the network. The drive letter is assigned when you *map* the network drive to your own computer. (See Chapter 35, which talks about mapping network drives.)
	Appears when the network is down or a network disk drive is unavailable.
	A weirdo icon for a *RAM drive*. That type of drive uses your computer's memory as a superfast disk drive. A RAM drive isn't necessary under Windows. In fact, the only time it's used is for the Windows emergency boot disk, which creates a RAM drive when your hard drive has gone south.

(I would include here the instructions for creating a RAM drive, but I don't recommend using one. If you really, *really* want to know how to create a RAM drive, email me at `dgookin@wambooli.com` with the subject line "RAM drive instructions," and I'll send you instructions.)

A Different View of Things

If you're puzzled by the contents of the My Computer window, you can change your view:

▶ **Adjust the My Computer window so that you can see the Views button.**

Drag the window's right side to the right until the Views button comes into view. (Choose View➡Toolbars➡Standard Buttons if you cannot see the buttons in the My Computer window.)

▶ **Click the down-pointing triangle by the Views button.**

A drop-down menu appears.

▶ **Choose Large Icons.**

What you see now is the way My Computer normally displays information. However, you have other ways to look at your disk drives:

▶ **Click the Views button.**

Click the button itself, not the down-pointing arrow.

Clicking the Views button changes the icon display in the window. Right now you're looking at Small Icons view. I suppose that if you have several hundred hard drives, this view would be a good way to see things.

▶ **Click the Views button again.**

I use List view primarily for wrangling files, which is covered in Chapter 24.

▶ **Click the Views button again.**

Aha! Details view looks like List view but adds a description after each disk drive (and after the folders). Figure 20.2 shows what you might see.

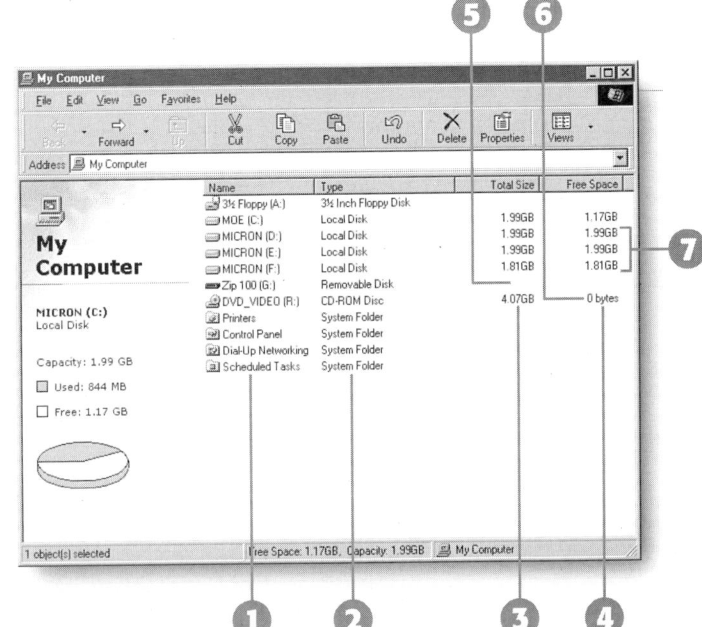

Figure 20.2

The Details view of your PC's hard drives.

1. Disk drives are listed here.
2. Type of disk drive.
3. Total storage space.
4. Amount of space available.
5. Because no disk is in the drive, a value is not displayed here.
6. A CD or DVD disk always has zero bytes available.
7. I haven't yet stored anything on these three disks.

▶ **Click the Views button once more.**

The window returns to the way it looked originally.

- Using the Views button is an excellent way to see which types of disks you have and how much storage is available.
- You can also directly select the view you like by choosing it from the Views button's drop-down menu.

Giving Your Disk a Name or Changing Its Old Name

All disks on your system have a drive letter. That's what's important. What's trivial is the disk's name, the volume label thing. You can add a name, change a name, or remove a name. It doesn't matter. The name appears in only a few places, and your software doesn't care whether you name a disk.

▶ **Open the My Computer icon on the desktop (if it's not open already).**

The main window shows all the disk drives on your computer. On my screen (shown in Figure 20.1), each of my hard disks is named Micron, probably because I bought the computer from Micron Electronics, although I remain suspicious.

▶ **Right-click drive C.**

A pop-up menu appears.

▶ **Choose Properties.**

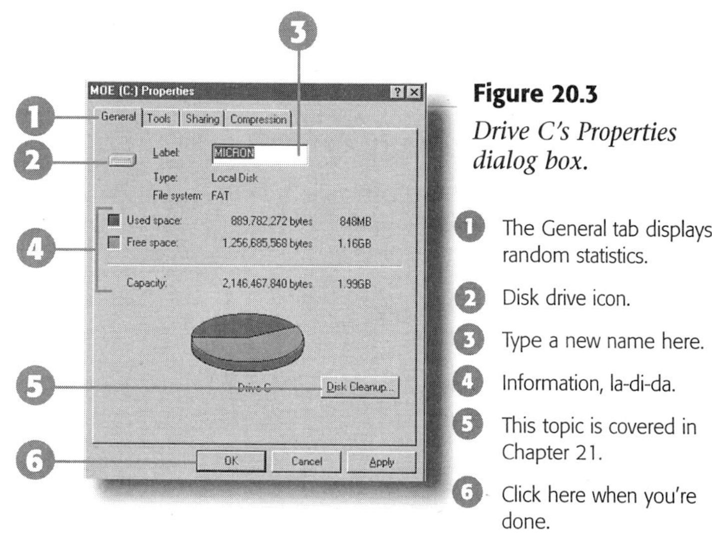

Figure 20.3
Drive C's Properties dialog box.

1. The General tab displays random statistics.
2. Disk drive icon.
3. Type a new name here.
4. Information, la-di-da.
5. This topic is covered in Chapter 21.
6. Click here when you're done.

The disk's Properties dialog box appears, as shown in Figure 20.3. Various tidbits of information are displayed, along with a text box showing the disk's name.

A-ha! It's a text box. You can change the name.

▶ **Type a new name in the Label box.**

Typing a new name erases the old name. Or you can just delete the old name, and the disk won't have a label. Or you can edit the existing name to something more personal (for example, Micron becomes Mike Ron).

You can type only as many as 11 characters, letters, numbers, and spaces. No, I didn't make up this rule. (It's an old DOS rule. Shows you how far we've come since 1981, huh?)

Press Backspace to back up and erase if you make a mistake.

▶ **Click OK to assign the new name.**

The new name appears whenever you reference the disk. However, the disk still retains its original drive letter.

▶ **Close the My Computer window.**

Thus endeth the tutorial.

- You cannot change the name of a CD-ROM or other write-protected disk.
- You must have a floppy disk in your floppy drive to assign it a name. Ditto for a ZIP drive; put the disk in the drive before you right-click its icon.
- If you remove the disk's label, only its drive letter appears (in parentheses) in the My Computer window.
- You can always go back and change the disk's label later. It's really no big deal.

Chapter 21

Caring for Your Hard Drive

Questions Answered and Thoughts Inspired

- Using Disk Cleanup to free up disk space
- Using the Defragmenter to tune up your disk
- Using ScanDisk to fix your hard drive
- Scheduling your disk maintenance chores
- Backing up (advice only)
- Explaining FAT32 (advice only)
- Compressing a hard drive (advice only)

Your hard drive should be very important to you—dear, in fact. All your data is stored there. All your programs. Your power supply can fry, the memory can pop and sizzle, the microprocessor can mess up math problems, and your monitor can melt, but your data survives on the hard drive. You should use every tool at your disposal to keep that data safe and happy. That's what this chapter tells you how to do.

- Personally, I find hard drives impressive: They spin at thousands of RPMs, hold billions of bytes of data, and can generally operate for five years or more without losing information. Wow.
- Lightning can strike your computer deaf, dumb, and blind, and as long as your data survives on the hard drive, you can get everything back.
- My first computer book (with my name on it) was about hard drives: *Hard Disk Management with MS-DOS and PC-DOS*, published in 1986.

Checking Your Hard Drive

Windows comes with an assortment of tools to help you manage your hard drive, to ensure that it's always in tip-top shape. Running these programs every so often is a regular part of using your computer, just like changing the oil is a regular part of using a car.

You do change your car's oil every so often, don't you?

Never mind. This section serves as an introduction to the various hard disk tools Windows provides. Later in this chapter, in the section "Scheduling Disk Maintenance for When You're Not There," you learn how you can automate these chores so that it's not so much of a pain in the butt to do them.

Cleaning That Hard Drive

Junky files accumulate on a hard drive like chocolate adheres to a 4-year-old's face. Even the most fastidious disk manager finds rogue files sucking up valuable disk space.

The last thing you need to do is wantonly delete files on your own to clean up disk space. Never do that, in fact. Delete only files you created yourself. Never delete program files (*uninstall* them instead). Other files? For them, you use the Disk Cleanup program:

- **Open the My Computer icon on the desktop.**
- **Right-click drive C.**
- **Choose Properties from the shortcut menu.**

In the drive C Properties window, you see various and sundry information about the hard drive. Blah, blah, blah. Figure 21.1 shows you the details because most of what happens in this dialog box is described in this chapter.

- **Click Disk Cleanup.**

Windows takes a few moments to examine your disk drives.

(Whistle aimlessly here.)

Finally, the Disk Cleanup for drive C dialog box appears, as shown in Figure 21.2.

To decide whether to delete a file, read its description.

- **Choose Temporary Files.**

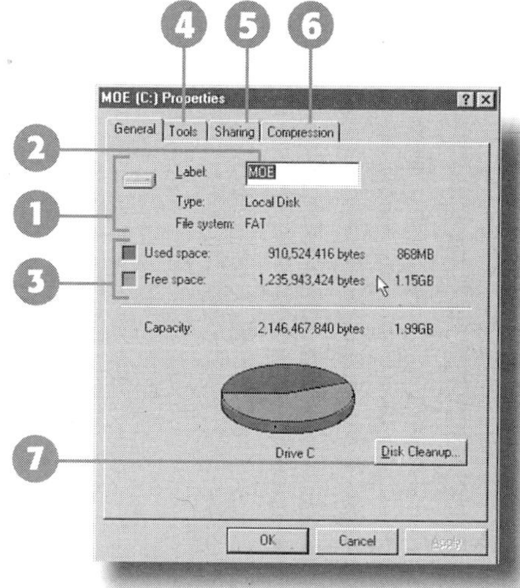

Figure 21.1
Drive C Properties dialog box.

1. Disk information.
2. Change the disk label here.
3. Drive usage stats.
4. Other disk tools: ScanDisk, Defrag, and Backup.
5. Networking information (see Part 5).
6. Disk compression—don't go here.
7. Disk cleanup happens here.

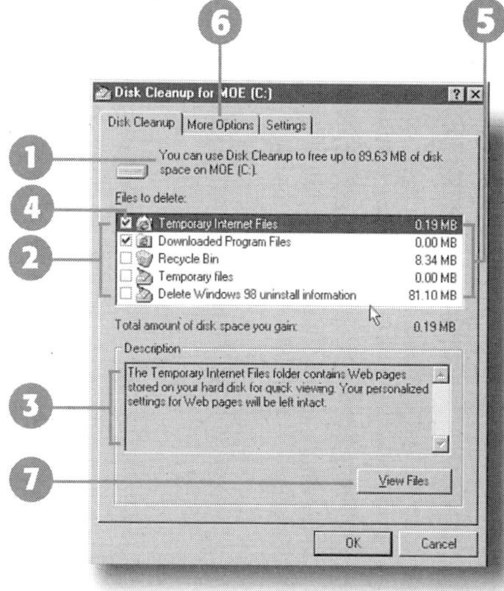

Figure 21.2
Disk Cleanup window.

1. Potential space you can clean up on this drive.
2. Select an item here, and...
3. ...see a description of it down here.
4. Put a check mark in this box to clean up the suggested item.
5. Amount of space each item uses.
6. Options for removing your software (refer to Chapter 14), parts of Windows (refer to Chapter 15), and converting your disk to FAT32.
7. Don't bother viewing the files; there's nothing you can do.

Just click that item; you don't have to put a check mark in the box just yet.

Read the description in the Description area. See? Temporary files are created in order to be destroyed. Why do they accumulate? Who knows?

▶ **Choose Temporary Internet Files.**

Read the description. Uh-huh.

▶ **Choose Downloaded Program Files.**

▶ **Click View Files.**

You see a list of program files Internet Explorer has grabbed from out yon. As long as all of them are flagged as Installed, you have nothing to worry about and can delete them. If one file is flagged otherwise, though, don't choose this option.

▶ **Close the Explorer Window.**

Notice that the Disk Cleanup program has already flagged Temporary Internet Files and Downloaded Program Files for removal. That's fine.

▶ **Choose other files to delete.**

My advice? Click *everything*. Put a check mark in *all* the little boxes:

✓ *Recycle Bin*—The Recycle Bin is emptied, removing any files there and preventing them from being undeleted. (See Chapter 28 for more information about the Recycle Bin.)

✓ *Temporary Files*—These can go, no problem.

✓ *Delete Windows 98 Uninstall Information*—If this item appears, you can remove it. However, if you've been using Windows 98 for less than two months, I'd keep this item around. (The information is necessary in case one of your applications is incompatible with Windows 98. Otherwise, you can delete the information.)

✓ *Other Types of Files*—Select the other types of files, and view the description or list of files. If in doubt, you don't have to remove them. Just keep in mind how much disk space they're using.

▶ **Click the box to put a check mark by the files you want to zap.**

▶ **Click OK.**

Windows warns you: "Are you sure you want to delete files?"

Of course you are! This process is disk cleanup! Those nasty files are sucking up precious bytes that your real programs and data crave!

▶ **Boldly click Yes.**

Disk Cleanup removes the files. You might see a tiny dialog box indicating Windows' progress. Then it disappears.

▶ **Click Cancel to close the Drive C Properties dialog box.**

If you want to clean up another hard drive, right-click the drive and choose Properties from its shortcut menu. Click the Disk Cleanup button, and you're on your way.

Keep the My Computer window open for the next section's tutorial.

- You should run the Disk Cleanup program at least once a month.
- Not every drive has stuff on it to clean.
- You can clean any hard drive or removable disk, such as a ZIP or JAZ drive, by using Disk Cleanup. You cannot clean CD-ROM drives; they're read-only. You cannot clean drives on other people's computers on the network.
- Don't bother with the View Files button in the Cleanup window. If you click that button, an Explorer window appears listing all the files scheduled for execution. Yet, even if you could tell what was in the files, you have no way to rescue one file from the lot, for example. All you can do is look. (Honestly, everything in the folder can go, and it saves you disk space.)
- Removing program files is covered in Chapter 14, "Installing and Removing Software."
- Removing tidbits of Windows is covered in Chapter 15, "Adding More of Windows." (Don't let the chapter title fool you.)
- You can also run the Disk Cleanup program from the Start Thing: Choose Programs➡Accessories➡System Tools➡Disk Cleanup. Select a disk to clean from the drop-down Drives list. Click OK.

Time for a Disk Tune-Up

The disk tune-up program is officially called Disk Defragmenter.

Yuck. What a horrid term. Although I prefer "tune-up," I have to use "defragmenter" because that's what Windows uses. I can live with that.

If you want a tired, old explanation of why defragmentation is necessary, read the sidebar, "A Tired, Old Explanation of Why Defragmentation Is Necessary," later in this chapter. Otherwise, just know that it's something you should do every so often that helps improve hard drive performance.

▶ **Open the My Computer icon on the desktop (if it's not open already).**

▶ **Right-click drive C.**

▶ **Choose Properties from the shortcut menu.**

▶ **Click the Tools tab to bring that panel forward.**

You see three tools listed, along with buttons to quickly access them:

✓ *Error-Checking Status*—Runs ScanDisk, the program that finds bad data and missing disk chunks. ScanDisk is covered later in this chapter.

✓ *Backup Status*—A tool no one uses, although it's kind of covered later in this chapter.

✓ *Defragmentation Status*—Aha! The option you want. It runs the Disk Defragmenter, which tunes up your disk's performance.

Notice how each item specifies the date that you last performed that disk maintenance job. Shame on you if any value is longer than a month. Double-dog shame if it says, "Windows was unable to determine when you last…" Egads!

Before you start: Note that this operation can take as long as one hour to complete, depending on how fragmented your hard drive is.

▶ **Click Defragment Now.**

Windows goes at it.

Although you can just sit there and watch, the Defragmenting Drive C dialog box is boring.

▶ **Click Show Details.**

What you see is a graphical "map" of files stored on your hard drive. Looks like a map of The City from Hell, right?

You see a row of squares turn green, flash, turn red, flash, and then reappear (see Figure 21.3). That's Windows moving files around, positioning them in a more logical and efficient manner on the disk.

Yes, you can do other things while the defragmenting operation is going on. Doing so, however, slows sown the defragmentation process. It's best just to sit and watch.

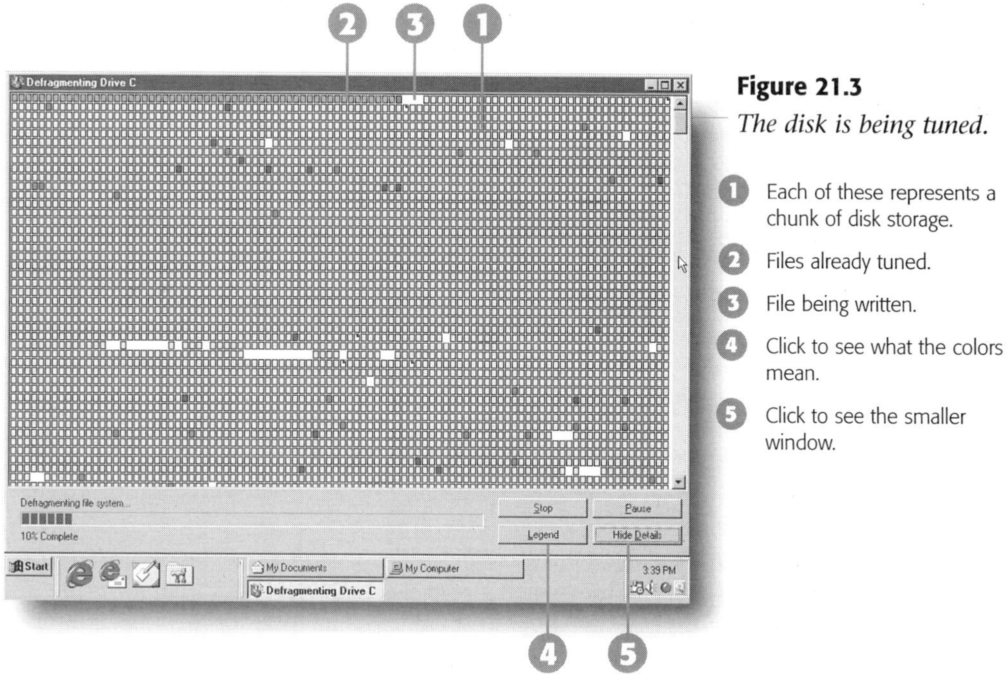

Figure 21.3
The disk is being tuned.

1. Each of these represents a chunk of disk storage.
2. Files already tuned.
3. File being written.
4. Click to see what the colors mean.
5. Click to see the smaller window.

▶ **Click Legend.**

A pop-up window appears telling you what each colored square represents. Read the legend. Then view the action onscreen to see how Windows is optimizing things.

▶ **Click Close when you're done looking at the Defrag Legend.**

Doh-de-doh. Wait. Wait. Wait.

Sometimes your drive defrags faster than at other times. It depends on how recently you've run the Defragmenter and how many new files you've added to your hard drive.

Eventually you see a dialog box telling you that you're done.

▶ **Click Yes to quit Disk Defragmenter.**

You're done.

Try not to use your computer while the Defragmentation program is running. If you do, it stops and takes even longer to complete. Just sit back and wait. Or go outside.

You can leave the Drive C Properties dialog box open for the next section's tutorial. Otherwise, click Cancel to close the Drive C Properties dialog box and close the My Computer window.

- To defragment any hard drive, right-click that drive, choose Properties from the shortcut menu, and continue as just described.
- You should run the Disk Defragmenter at least once a week or so.
- If no files need to be defragmented or you have a relatively new computer, you can still run Defragmenter. Although it doesn't take as long as it does on older, more fragmented hard drives, it still works.
- You can also run the Disk Tune-up program from the Start Thing: choose Programs➡Accessories➡System Tools➡Disk Defragmenter. Select from the drop-down list a disk to clean. Click OK.

A Tired, Old Explanation of Why Defragmentation Is Necessary

Suppose that you're going on a trip and you're packing your suitcase. You're almost done. The only thing left to pack is your son's teddy bear. But there just isn't room.

On one side of the suitcase is a tiny space, and you still have room in one of the outside pockets. To make the most of your suitcase space, you tear off the teddy bear's head. You put the body in the suitcase and the head in the outside pocket. What you've done is maximize the space by splitting Teddy in two.

On a computer you would say that Teddy was *fragmented*. That's what Windows does when it tries to make the most of your disk storage space. If a large file doesn't fit in one piece on the disk, Windows tears it up into tiny fragments and stores them where they fit.

You don't notice that your files have been fragmented. When you go to load or open a file, Windows reassembles it for you into one piece—just like you would sew Teddy back together for your son. However, keeping track of all the pieces—the fragments—leads to overhead.

When the files on a drive are more than 10 percent fragmented, you should run the Disk Defragmenter tool. That puts the files back together, which makes Windows access them more efficiently. In some cases, defragmenting a badly fragmented drive noticeably improves disk performance.

Fixing Your Hard Drive

In addition to other hard drive maladies is the category of file foul-ups. As long as you follow the advice in this book, you should never encounter any file weirdness. If you do, however, you have to fix those files, or at least have Windows discover what they are before they drive you nuts.

To fix files you run the ScanDisk program:

▶ **Open the My Computer icon on the desktop.**

(Do this step only if the My Computer window isn't already open.)

▶ **Right-click drive C.**

▶ **Choose Properties from the shortcut menu.**

This step displays the Drive C Properties dialog box if it isn't displayed already.

▶ **Click the Tools tab to ensure that that panel is brought forward.**

▶ **Click Check Now.**

ScanDisk fires itself up (see Figure 21.4).

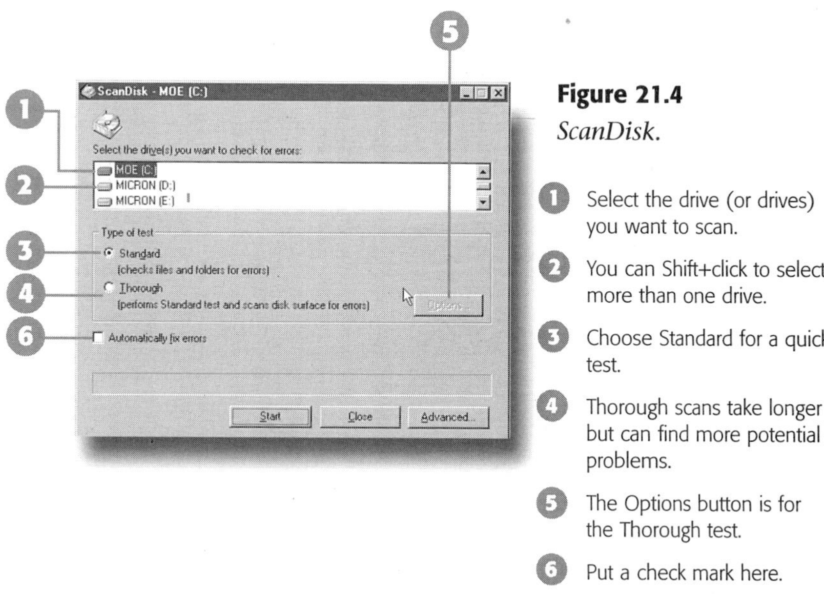

Figure 21.4
ScanDisk.

1. Select the drive (or drives) you want to scan.
2. You can Shift+click to select more than one drive.
3. Choose Standard for a quick test.
4. Thorough scans take longer but can find more potential problems.
5. The Options button is for the Thorough test.
6. Put a check mark here.

Drive C should already have been chosen from the list. If you want to scan other hard drives on your system, Shift+click them in the list. ScanDisk examines each drive you Shift+click.

▶ **Choose Standard if it's not chosen already.**

The Standard test does a quick check of your system. It's good enough for now.

The Thorough test checks every molecule of information on your hard drive, which takes awhile to run. You can rerun this tutorial after you're done and run the Thorough test.

▶ **Click to put a check mark by Automatically Fix Errors.**

You don't want to be bothered if an error is detected. After all, ScanDisk knows better how to handle it than you do.

To make sure that ScanDisk is set properly, especially if you're using it for the first time, see the nearby sidebar, "Setting 'Advanced' ScanDisk Options." If you've already done that, you have no reason to do it again here.

Setting "Advanced" ScanDisk Options

The Advanced button in ScanDisk doesn't contain complex or overwhelming options. Some choices there make ScanDisk easier to live with.

▶ **Click Advanced in ScanDisk to see the ScanDisk Advanced Options dialog box.**

The ScanDisk Advanced Options dialog box has five areas and lots of options to wade through. This sidebar has the options I feel are worth setting. If an item isn't listed, it doesn't matter either way.

▶ **Set Display Summary to Always.**

You want to confirm that ScanDisk did its job.

▶ **Set Lost File Fragments to Free.**

If you don't do it, your hard drive fills with files named FILE????.CHK, where the question marks are replaced by numbers. Those files are useless, and if you check the Free option, you never see them anyway.

▶ **Set Cross-Linked Files to Delete.**

A cross-linked file is hopelessly damaged and should be deleted. Not deleting it is frustrating. In fact, if this type of error happens frequently on your hard drive, get the Norton Utilities program, which fixes cross-linked files better than ScanDisk anyway.

All the other check mark items can be selected, except for Duplicate Name Check and Check Host Drive First. (If you're curious about an item, use the mouse to click the question mark in the upper-right corner of the dialog box, and then click one of those items for an explanation of what it does.)

The Duplicate Name Check item slows down ScanDisk (you see a warning if you choose it). It's not as crucial as other errors ScanDisk locates.

The Check Host Drive First item is necessary only if you're using disk compression, which I admonish you not to do in a few paragraphs.

▶ **Click OK to close the ScanDisk Advanced Options dialog box.**

ScanDisk remembers these settings so that you do not have to return to this dialog box and reset things again later.

▶ **Click <u>S</u>tart.**

ScanDisk checks your folders.

ScanDisk checks the File Allocation Tables (FATs).

It checks the folders again.

It checks files and folders.

If an error is found, it is repaired automatically. You've chosen all the proper options here and aren't bothered by ScanDisk as it busily fixes things.

Finally, a summary is displayed, as shown in Figure 21.5.

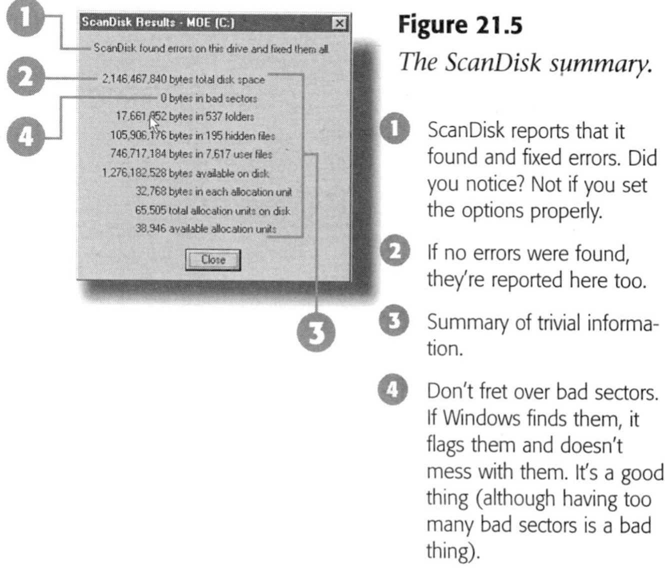

Figure 21.5
The ScanDisk summary.

1. ScanDisk reports that it found and fixed errors. Did you notice? Not if you set the options properly.
2. If no errors were found, they're reported here too.
3. Summary of trivial information.
4. Don't fret over bad sectors. If Windows finds them, it flags them and doesn't mess with them. It's a good thing (although having too many bad sectors is a bad thing).

▶ **Click Close to close the Results dialog box.**

You can scan more disks if you want (if you didn't select all the hard drives when you started). If not, you're done.

▶ **Click Close to close the ScanDisk window.**

▶ **Click Cancel to close the Drive C Properties dialog box.**

▶ **Close the My Computer window.**

Your disk is up to snuff.

- You should run ScanDisk at least once a week.

ScanDisk is an descendant of the old CHKDSK (Check-Disk) program in DOS. ScanDisk replaced CHKDSK in MS-DOS Version 6.0, and it has been a Windows program since Windows 95.

- ScanDisk is not magic. Some people used to run CHKDSK like they were incanting a spell. It doesn't work that way. If something is wrong, ScanDisk fixes it. If nothing is wrong, ScanDisk tells you so.
- ScanDisk produces a log file recording everything it did to your hard drive. The file, named SCANDISK.LOG, is kept in the root folder of drive C. If you open drive C in Windows Explorer, drag the SCANDISK.LOG file to the WordPad shortcut icon on your desktop for viewing. (See Chapter 9 for more information about having WordPad on the desktop.)
- ScanDisk can also be run from the Start Thing: Choose Programs➡Accessories➡System Tools➡ScanDisk. Select one or more drives to scan. Click Start.

The Thorough test ScanDisk does checks every cluster on your hard drive. Although this process takes time, it's a good test to perform every so often. Just start it when you know that you'll be away from your computer for a few minutes.

Scheduling Disk Maintenance for When You're Not There

The programs covered so far in this chapter—Clean Up, Defrag, and ScanDisk—aren't a major pain to run. Of course, you might forget to run them every so often. After all, you bought your computer to do work, not to be a hard disk maintenance operator. And, hey! Aren't computers supposed to make life easier?

Say hello to the Maintenance Wizard. This program automatically schedules routine disk operations. It's a time-saver.

▶ **From the Start Thing, choose Programs➡Accessories➡System Tools➡Maintenance Wizard.**

The Maintenance Wizard appears.

▶ **Choose Express.**

The Express option sets everything the way you need. (The Custom option doesn't do anything other than what is automatically chosen for you with the Express setting.)

▶ **Click Next.**

Choose a time that you want regular disk maintenance to occur.

You want to pick a time when you're not doing anything else. That's best.

The computer must be turned on for this program to work. If you're used to turning off your computer when you're done working (which I advise against in Chapter 1 anyway), these tasks never get done.

▶ **Choose Nights - Midnight to 3:00 AM.**

That should work for everyone, I hope. If not, pick something else.

▶ **Click Next.**

The final screen lists the tasks your computer will perform. Figure 21.6 explains what the little icons mean. You've already run all these programs if you've gone straight through this chapter's tutorials.

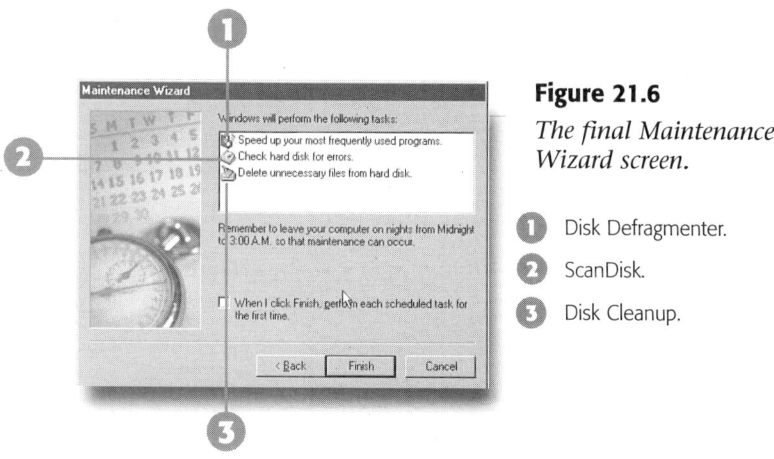

Figure 21.6
The final Maintenance Wizard screen.

1. Disk Defragmenter.
2. ScanDisk.
3. Disk Cleanup.

You do not need to put a check mark by When I Click Finish if you've already done the tutorials in this chapter.

▶ **Click Finish.**

The disk maintenance tasks are scheduled. You need not do a thing.

You might be prodded here to run the FAT32 converter. If you are, click No. The FAT32 converter is mentioned later in this chapter.

- Shhh! The Maintenance Wizard places certain disk tools into a program named Task Scheduler. That way, the tools run at specific times. You can examine or adjust in the Scheduled Tasks window what the Maintenance Wizard has done. Chapter 44, , "Scheduling Activities," has information about the Task Scheduler.
- The scheduled tasks take place even if your computer "goes to sleep" at night. If not, you can configure the tasks to wake the computer up; this subject is covered in Chapter 44.
- You can also use the Task Scheduler to adjust the time a task starts. For example, I'm usually up between midnight and 3:00 a.m, so I have my tasks start at 4:00 a.m. (Making this change is covered in Chapter 44.)
- You can confirm that the disk Maintenance Wizard has done its job. In a few days, open the Drive C Properties dialog box. Click the Tools tab to see that panel. Review the number of days that have passed since the drive was last checked for errors or defragmented. With the wizard doing its job, the number of days should always be small.

Some Backup Advice

I'm not gonna fool you: No one backs up their computer. We should, but we don't. Only in a business situation have I ever seen backups performed, and that's because of various threats and bonus checks.

I don't go into why people don't back up, and I don't bother telling you how important having a safety copy of your data is. Although you would agree with me, you still wouldn't back up your computer, so I don't waste time in this section carefully explaining how to do it.

I offer you, rather than the gory details, the following set of bullet points. The list has information you can use if you decide to back up, and it fulfills my contractual obligation to write about it:

- The best way to back up is to get a tape backup drive. The tape drive comes with its own backup software. Use that software rather than the Windows Backup program to back up your computer.
- The best type of tape backup to get is a DAT tape drive. Although it's very expensive, it's the best.
- Backing up your entire hard drive (all your hard drives) is a full backup.
- Do a full backup at least once a month. In a business situation, do a full backup once a week or every two weeks, depending on the value of your data.
- Backing up only those files that have been changed, added, or modified since the last backup is called an *incremental backup.*
- You should perform an incremental backup at least once a day if your data is valuable to you.

- Use at least three tapes to back up. Label them A, B, and C. Do a full backup to tape A. Put tape A in a fire safe or other place for safekeeping. Use the backup software to erase tape B. Perform incremental backups to tape B. Then do a full backup on tape B and store it away. Erase tape C and start the process over again. Rotate through each tape to ensure that you always have at least two full backups handy.
- If anything nasty happens to your data, you use the Backup program's Restore option to get the files from your backup tapes back to the hard drive.
- Failure to back up cost me three months' worth of work once. A hard drive crashed during a half-second power outage. My preceding backup (I'm glad I had one) was three months old. Although I restored from it, I've never been able to recover that three months' worth of missing data.
- Generally, only people who've lost an entire hard drive full of important files are those who religiously back up.

TIP

The best Backup programs have special Emergency Boot Disks that help you get your tape drive going and let you restore all your data.

Advice About Converting an Older Hard Drive to FAT32

Drop that image of Richard Simmons from your head. On your computer, FAT stands for *File Allocation Table*. It's a map on every hard drive that tells Windows where to find files. The FAT32 system is the latest version.

In a nutshell: Do you need to convert your old hard drive to the newer FAT32 system? No. (That's why this section is advice only.) I'm not opposed to converting hard drives; I just feel that you have better things to do with your PC.

First point: Chances are that you already have a FAT32 hard drive. If you've purchased your computer with Windows 98 already installed, your drives are probably converted already.

Second point: Converting a hard drive to FAT32 takes a long time. I recommend running the program at night or over the weekend if you ever decide to convert.

Third point: You risk screwing up and erasing your hard drive. The FAT32 Wizard even encourages you to back up before you start. That's just too scary for me.

Fourth point: It's just a hassle. I mean, why bother? Computers are supposed to make life easy, not interesting. Although Microsoft might push the FAT32 thing and it might be a boon to your hard drive, I'm not taking the risk.

You really have no need to mess with the FAT32 converter.

I'm not copping out here—I'm serious. Hey! Your computer works now, doesn't it? Why mess with things?

- The number one technical support issue with Windows 98 on the Internet during its first 90 days in release has been people who improperly convert their hard drives by using the Drive Converter (FAT32) program.

You don't have to convert your drives! Don't sweat this one.

- If you're curious, you run the converter from the Start Thing: choose Programs➡Accessories➡System Tools➡Drive Converter (FAT32).
- If you do not find the Drive Converter (FAT32) item on the menu, your drive has already been converted. Nothing to fear.
- I don't recommend compressing your hard drive, either. I rant about this subject next.

Advice About Compressing Your Hard Drive

An interesting fad hit computerdom in the early 1990s. At about that time, the size of programs ballooned, probably thanks to the dawn of the CD-ROM era. The typical hard drive was 40 to 90 megabytes big, and people left and right were running out of disk space.

Along came a company called Stac Electronics. It developed a program named Stacker that magically doubles your hard drive storage space—a process called *disk compression*. Although other programs did the same thing, Stacker got the fame and glory.

Stacker was the perfect solution back then: Big programs, small hard drives. It was a cheap solution. In my opinion, though, it was a solution whose time has passed.

Today, hard drives are huge: 2 gigabytes and more. Filling them up takes skill. You have to collect *huge* files and never delete anything for years before your 2 gigabytes are all used up. If you do use them up, installing a second hard drive is cinchy and cheap. Yet the legacy of Stacker hangs around.

Microsoft, not wanting to be left out of a good thing, developed DoubleSpace, a DOS disk expander that worked just like Stacker. DoubleSpace had problems and was replaced by DriveSpace, which is still available in Windows 98.

Do you need DriveSpace? No.

Compressing your hard drive with DriveSpace (or even Stacker) is now a bad idea. It's a software solution to a hardware problem. What you really need is a larger hard drive. It's cheap to add a second hard drive, and it doesn't give you the overhead or hassles of a disk compression program.

Please, please, don't bother compressing your hard drive! I get mail from people every few months or so who experience the nightmare of disk compression. Really, it was a great solution for 1992, but it's now a hazardous leftover.

- Compressing your disk adds overhead and slows down all disk operations. Although I realize that the literature might claim otherwise, it's physically impossible for disk compression not to slow down a hard drive.
- A compressed disk requires more maintenance from you. You have to deal with compressed drives, uncompressed drives, host drives, and all sorts of jargon. That's a pain in the butt.
- Even worse than compressing a drive is decompressing when you discover that you no longer like DoubleSpace. It's a major ordeal that no one has ever been happy to go through.
- No, I don't even recommend compressing removable drives, such as ZIP drives, to get more storage. Please, do not use DoubleSpace.

Chapter 22

Removable Disks and Drives

Questions Answered and Thoughts Inspired

- Using your floppy drive
- Formatting a floppy disk
- Inserting and removing CDs
- Auto-playing your CDs
- Playing a music CD
- Using a DVD drive

In addition to the hard disk, several other types of disks are used to store stuff on your computer: floppy disk, CD-ROM, DVD, ZIP, JAZ, MO—collect them all!

Seriously, each different disk has its own special purpose. This chapter clues you in to using each type of disk in the best manner possible.

- No, I'm not trying to be funny: JAZ and MO drives really do exist, in addition to WORM and CD-R drives.
- The disk is the device that goes into the drive: A floppy disk goes into a floppy drive; a CD goes into a CD-ROM drive; a DVD or CD can go into a DVD drive; and other types of disks go into their own drives.

- The hard disk is permanently fixed inside the hard drive; that disk cannot be removed. The terms *hard disk* and *hard drive* are interchangeable for most people.
- Only the most popular types of removable disks and drives are covered in this chapter.

The Original, Steadfast Floppy Drive

All PCs have at least one floppy drive. In the early days, that's how the IBM PC was sold. Me? I had a PC with *two* floppy drives. I was king of the block.

For the longest time, all computer software came on floppy disks. If you bought WordPerfect 4.1, you got a box with a real manual and four floppy disks. You could even run your entire computer—DOS and WordPerfect—from one floppy disk. Although it wasn't easy, it was possible.

Floppy disks are still used to install software, although most programs now come on CDs. You can use floppy disks to transport files between two computers—as long as the files aren't bigger than 1.4 megabytes. Although a floppy disk might seem unimportant, it really does have some handy uses. For most PCs, in fact, a floppy disk is the only way to get information from that PC to another computer.

- Floppy disks were also used for backing up hard drives, although they have pretty much been replaced by tapes for backups.
- The first IBM PC also had an option for a cassette tape to be used as file storage. I actually used one that way, back in 1984. I think I'm the only person who has.

Finding Your Floppy Drive

Your PC should have a slot right up front for the floppy disk. In Windows, the floppy drive is listed in My Computer with all your other disk drives.

▶ **Open the My Computer icon on the desktop.**

Your floppy drive appears on the list along with other drives in your system and the fancy folders, similar to what's shown in Figure 22.1 (it shows my computer, not yours).

▶ **Open your floppy drive A.**

Double-click the drive's icon to open it.

Ahh-oo-gah! The drive is not only not accessible but also not ready. Whoa.

Don't worry—it happens all the time. You can't use the drive unless it has a disk in it.

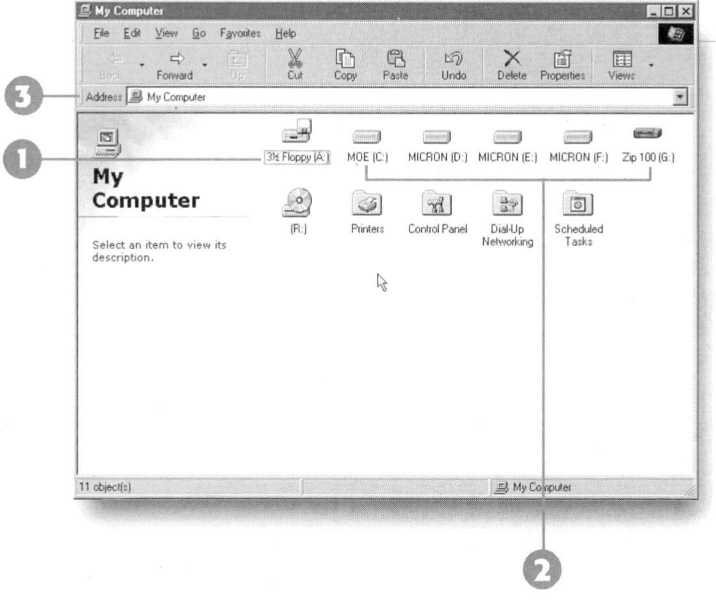

Figure 22.1
Drives in My Computer.

1. Floppy drive A.
2. Other disk drives in your system.
3. You can also choose drive A from the Address drop-down list.

- **Stick a floppy disk in drive A.**
- **Click Retry.**

Ahhh! Now it works. The computer reads the information from drive A, and soon the contents of that disk are displayed onscreen.

- **Close the My Computer window.**
- **Remove the disk from drive A.**

Most disk drives have a punch button you press to eject the disk. Unlike CD-ROMs and other drives, all floppy disks must be ejected manually.

You can access drive A only if you've put a disk in it.

- The disk in drive A must also be formatted before you can use it. Formatting is covered in the following section.

Formatting a Floppy Disk

All floppy disks must be formatted. Most of the time, you buy them that way, in the box. Some supercheap floppy disks are not preformatted, however, and you have to do it yourself. Formatting a floppy disk is a quick way to erase all the information on that disk.

▶ **Stick a floppy disk in drive A.**

Make sure that it's a new disk or else an old disk that doesn't contain any necessary data. (The process of formatting erases a disk's data.) Even if you have only preformatted disks, use one for this tutorial.

▶ **Open the My Computer icon on the desktop.**

▶ **Right-click drive A.**

A pop-up shortcut menu appears.

▶ **Choose Format.**

The Format dialog box appears, as shown in Figure 22.2. Generally, all the options you need are preselected for you.

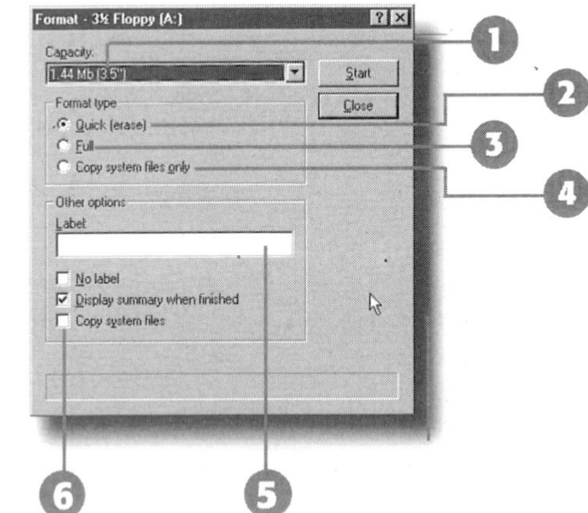

Figure 22.2
The Format dialog box.

1. The disk's size is shown here. Don't mess with it.
2. Reformat a disk.
3. Format a new disk.
4. Copy boot files to a formatted disk.
5. You can pretype a disk label here.
6. Create a boot disk.

▶ **Click Start.**

Windows formats the disk. It takes about a minute or so.

If any problems occur, Windows displays a dialog box telling you about the problem.

Notice that most disks are quick formatted. A quick format is quick because the disk is already formatted; Windows is basically just erasing the old disk's contents. A *full format*, on the other hand, takes longer because every part of the disk must be formatted.

If the disk cannot be quick formatted, you see a warning dialog box. Click OK and choose Full from the Format dialog box. Try again.

After a successful format, a summary screen is displayed, full of trivia. Whatever.

▶ **Click Close.**

The Format dialog box stays open onscreen, just in case you want to format another disk.

▶ **Remove the floppy disk from the drive.**

If you want to format another disk, stick it in drive A and click the Start button again. Otherwise, you're done.

If Windows cannot format the disk, a dialog box appears. Oh, well. Click OK and throw that disk away. I'm serious! It's trash. Try another disk.

▶ **Click Close to close the Format dialog box.**

▶ **Close the My Computer window.**

Yeah, it's not a happenin' time to format floppy disks.

The best advice I can give: Buy all your floppy disks preformatted in the box.

CD-ROM Drives

Once a multimedia gadget, the CD-ROM drive is now required equipment on all PCs. It stores megabytes of information and can be accessed just like a hard drive, and you can remove and insert new discs as you do with a floppy drive. Very handy.

You're probably quite adept at using your CD-ROM drive. Even so, I thought I'd toss in a few pointers in this section. Some stuff you might know; some might be new tricks to you:

- Almost all new software comes on a CD.
- You cannot write to a CD-ROM drive. The ROM part stands for **R**ead-**O**nly **M**emory, which cannot be changed.
- Some CD-ROM drives do have the capability to write CDs. These CD-R drives are more expensive than standard CD-ROMs. In fact, I know of no computer that comes with a CD-R drive; you generally have to buy it extra. CDs are written to in a special manner, not like hard drives or floppy disks.

CDs In and Out

Unlike the floppy drive, you can have Windows eject your CDs for you.

- **Open the My Computer icon on the desktop.**
- **Right-click your CD-ROM drive icon.**

Unlike with a floppy disk, it doesn't matter whether a CD is in the drive. Right-clicking the CD-ROM drive displays a pop-up shortcut menu.

- **Choose Eject.**

Your CD-ROM drive does one of two things, depending on the type of drive you have:

- ✓ If you have the sliding-tray type of drive, the tray slides out.
- ✓ If you have the caddy type of drive, the caddy holding the CD spits out the CD-ROM drive's mouth. (If no caddy is in the drive, nothing happens.)

Putting a CD back into the drive works differently, depending on which type of CD-ROM drive you have.

- ✓ *Tray CD-ROM drives*—Put the CD in the tray. Gently nudge the tray into the computer just a tiny bit. The mechanism should take over and slide the tray into the computer the rest of the way. You can also press a little button to insert the disc; it's the same button used to eject the disc (although it's hard to get to on some PCs when the tray is out).
- ✓ *Caddy CD-ROM drives*—Open the caddy's lid. (Pinch both sides of the caddy; it says *Open* on the clear lid.) Put the CD in the caddy so that you can see the CD's label through the clear side. Close the lid. Insert the caddy into the CD-ROM drive in the direction of the arrow.
- ✓ *Trayless CD-ROMs*—This type works like the single-play CD player in many cars. You just stick the disc into a slit in the computer. The CD-ROM drive "grabs" the disc and pulls it in the rest of the way. You use an Eject button to spew the disc back out.

- **Close the My Computer window.**

- You can also eject a CD by pushing the Eject button on the CD-ROM drive. This button is in a different spot on all CD-ROM drives.
- I prefer the sliding-tray type of CD-ROM drive. In fact, I thought that the caddy-type was obsolete, although they still make them.

After you insert the CD, Windows might "auto-play" it. If a window opens or a program starts, feel free to close it for now.

Caddy CD-ROMs are great when you have little kids. The caddy keeps chocolate, juice, and jelly off the CD when little hands go to insert a disk. For me, however, it just takes extra time to mess with the caddy.

Making Your CD Automatically Play Music or Software

Whenever you insert a CD, Windows automatically "plays" it. If it's a music CD, you should start hearing music. For data CDs, you might see a startup screen. This process is known as *auto-playing* a CD.

You can tell Windows whether you want it to auto-play your CDs. Why? Because it can be disruptive to change CDs and have Windows pop up some annoying startup banner.

You can disable auto-play as a permanent or one-time thing.

For a one-time thing, press the Shift key while you insert a CD-ROM. That prevents Windows from auto-playing the CD. Don't release the Shift key too quickly, or else the dern thing plays. Gads!

Pressing the Shift key while inserting a CD prevents auto-play.

To tell Windows to permanently disable auto-play for all CDs you insert (data, music, whatever), follow these steps:

- **Right-click the My Computer icon on the desktop.**
- **Choose Properties.**
- **Click the Device Manager tab.**

The Device Manager panel appears, as shown in Figure 22.3.

- **Open the CD-ROM type by clicking the + next to CDROM on the list.**
- **Click your CD-ROM drive to select it.**

Your CD-ROM appears in the tree-structure thing below the main CDROM title. Mine is a Hitachi GD-2000. Normally I wouldn't know that, but that's what it says onscreen (and in Figure 22.3).

Figure 22.3

The Device Manager panel in the System Properties dialog box.

1. Click here to open your CD-ROM type.
2. Click once to select your CD-ROM type.
3. Other hardware devices in your computer. It's best not to mess with them.
4. Click the Properties button here.

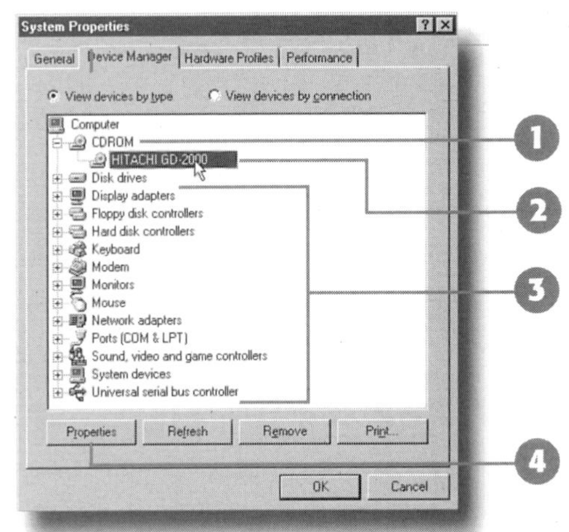

▶ **Click Properties.**

Your CD-ROM's Properties dialog box appears.

▶ **Click the Settings tab to bring that panel forward.**

The Settings panel shows its face, which you can also see in Figure 22.4.

Figure 22.4

The Settings panel for your CD-ROM.

1. Remove this check mark to disable auto-play.
2. Don't mess with anything else.
3. In this area you set the CD-ROM's drive letter, which is covered later in this chapter.

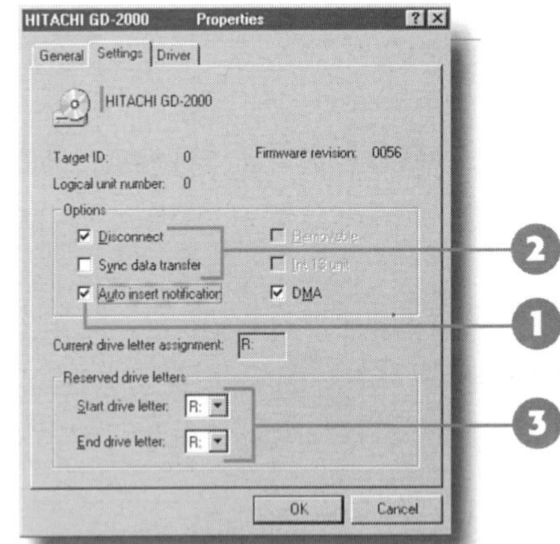

▶ **Remove the check mark by Auto Insert Notification.**

There. Now CDs no longer interrupt you while you're working. Or, if you'd rather that they did interrupt you (for example, because your kids rely on the auto-play feature to start up their Elmo game), leave this setting alone.

▶ **Click OK to close your CD-ROM's Properties dialog box.**

▶ **Click Close to close the System Properties dialog box.**

If you've made a change, Windows urges you to reset your computer. Click Yes to reset. When your system restarts, you should have a CD-ROM that no longer auto-plays. Insert a few CDs just to be sure.

- I don't know why they call it Auto Insert Notification rather than Auto-Play in the dialog box.
- Not every CD has auto-play capability. Music CDs do. A data CD has auto-play only if it has a file named AUTORUN.INF in its root folder.
- If you grow weary of not having CDs auto-play, repeat the steps in this section to put the check mark beside Auto Insert Notification again in the CD-ROM drive's Properties dialog box.

Lots of weird things are in the System Properties dialog box. Try not to mess with something you don't understand.

You can manually auto-run a data CD, even when you've turned off auto-run, by right-clicking the CD-ROM icon in the My Computer window and choosing the AutoPlay command. This command works whether or not you've turned off Auto Insert Notification.

Playing a Music CD on Your Computer

Playing a music CD is an easy task:

▶ **Put the music CD in your CD-ROM drive.**

Refer to the section "CDs In and Out," earlier in this chapter, for information about removing any CD already in the drive and inserting your CD-ROM.

If you have auto-play turned on (that is, if you didn't disable it in the preceding section), the CD just starts playing. Great!

If you don't have auto-play turned on, you have to start the CD-ROM player. From the Start menu, choose Programs➡Accessories➡Entertainment➡CD Player.

▶ **Maximize the CD Player window (if necessary).**

Click the CD Player button on the taskbar to maximize it, if necessary.

The CD Player window appears, looking like Figure 22.5.

You can use the buttons in the CD Player window to control how the CD plays, just as you use similar buttons on your boom box.

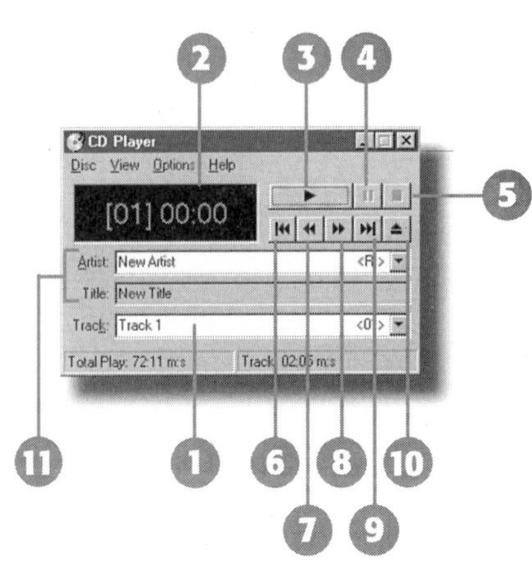

Figure 22.5
The CD Player.

1. Current track.
2. Timer.
3. Play button.
4. Pause button.
5. Stop button.
6. Previous track.
7. Rewind.
8. Fast forward.
9. Next track.
10. Eject disk.
11. Trivia.

The mess of drop-down lists at the bottom of the window is trivial. You can fill in the data, and Windows remembers it for each CD you use. I advise doing that only if you have a ton of time on your hands.

Listen for a while, if you like.

When you're done, the CD Player stops.

- **You can quit the CD Player by closing its window.**

If you want to listen to another CD, eject the current one and replace it with another.

If you want to listen to the current CD again, open the My Computer window, right-click your CD-ROM drive's icon, and choose Play from the menu.

- The CD Player program runs automatically, playing any music disk you insert—as long as you have Auto Insert Notification turned on.
- To have the CD play repeatedly, choose Options➡Continuous Play.
- To have the CD play tracks in a random order, choose Options➡Random Order.
- To adjust the CD's volume, you have to use the Volume Control window (see Chapter 41, "Sound Advice").

Changing Your CD-ROM Drive Letter

Windows assigns your CD-ROM drive letter based on how many hard drives are in your system and on how many other drives might "appear" before the computer sees the CD-ROM drive.

Normally the drive letter isn't a problem. If you ever plan to add more disk drives (of any type) to your PC, however, you should think about changing the CD-ROM drive letter now, before it becomes a hassle later.

Suppose that you add a removable disk (a ZIP disk, maybe) to your computer. You have hard drives C and D, and the CD-ROM is drive letter E. After you add the ZIP disk, however, it becomes drive E, and the CD-ROM is bumped down to drive F. None of your software can find the CD-ROM drive after that, and you have to reconfigure things. It's a pain.

That might never happen. Most people can merrily skip the tutorial in this section. It has happened to me enough, however, to urge me to tell you how to avoid the trouble.

Follow these steps only if you plan to add more disk drives to your computer later:

- **Right-click the My Computer icon on the desktop.**
- **Choose Properties.**
- **Click the Device Manager tab.**
- **Open the CD-ROM type by clicking CDROM on the list.**
- **Click your CD-ROM drive to select it.**
- **Click Properties.**
- **Click the Settings tab to bring that panel forward.**

The Settings panel appears, which should be familiar to you if you've worked the auto-play tutorial, earlier in this chapter (refer to Figure 22.4).

To set the CD-ROM to a specific letter, enter that same letter in both the Start Drive Letter and End Drive Letter boxes. I recommend using drive R.

- **Choose R from the Start Drive Letter box.**

This step should automatically choose *R* from the End Drive Letter box, although you might have to choose that drive letter manually.

You can choose another alphabet letter that comes before R if it isn't available.

- **Click OK to close the CD-ROM drive's Properties dialog box.**
- **Click OK to close the System Properties dialog box.**

Windows begs you to reset. Click Yes to do so.

When your computer starts up again, the CD-ROM is relettered to drive R (or whichever letter you chose). This relettering might cause some problems with programs expecting to find the CD-ROM drive at its old letter position. You should be able to work through those problems as you run each program.

You might have to reinstall some programs to make them recognize the new CD-ROM drive letter.

Some programs might merely ask you where the CD-ROM has gone. Specify the new letter, and everything should work.

DVD Drives

The successor to the CD-ROM drive is the DVD drive. Whereas a CD can store as much as 600 megabytes of information, DVDs can store more than 4 gigabytes of information. That's a bunch. It's enough, in fact, to store an entire 2-hour-movie on one side of the DVD disk.

- Although some newer PCs come with DVD drives, for now it's an item you must specifically request. Soon all PCs will have DVD drives.
- A DVD drive can read CDs just as well as a CD-ROM drive can. In fact, little visual difference exists physically between a CD-ROM drive and a DVD drive. The discs also look the same.
- DVD stands for Digital Versatile Disc for a computer, where the discs might contain movies or computer files. For the home, it's Digital Video Disc because it hooks up only to your TV set for playing movies. You can play both types of discs on your computer.
- DVD discs can contain data, music, or videos. Although I haven't seen any data or music DVDs yet, I have a few DVD videos. No porn.

Confirming That Your PC Has a DVD Drive

DVD drives look and work just like CD-ROMs. The only difference that applies to all makes and models is that it says *DVD* on the drive.

Some drives might say *DVD-ROM*.

Some drives might have a DVD light on the front, indicating that a DVD disk has been inserted.

Playing a Movie

Playing a movie on a DVD drive is the same as playing a music CD on a CD-ROM drive:

▶ **Put the DVD video in your DVD drive.**

The section "CDs In and Out," earlier in this chapter, describes how to do this step; it's the same for both DVDs and CDs.

Alas, Windows doesn't recognize my DVD, so the Windows DVD Player isn't displayed when I insert a video in my DVD drive. (Because Windows doesn't recognize my DVD player, I can't even install the program. Oh, well.)

As a new technology, DVD support in Windows is sparse.

Figure 22.6 shows my DVD drive's own player. My dealer installed this program, and it works okay. I have no idea how similar it looks to the Windows DVD Player, although the concepts are the same for both.

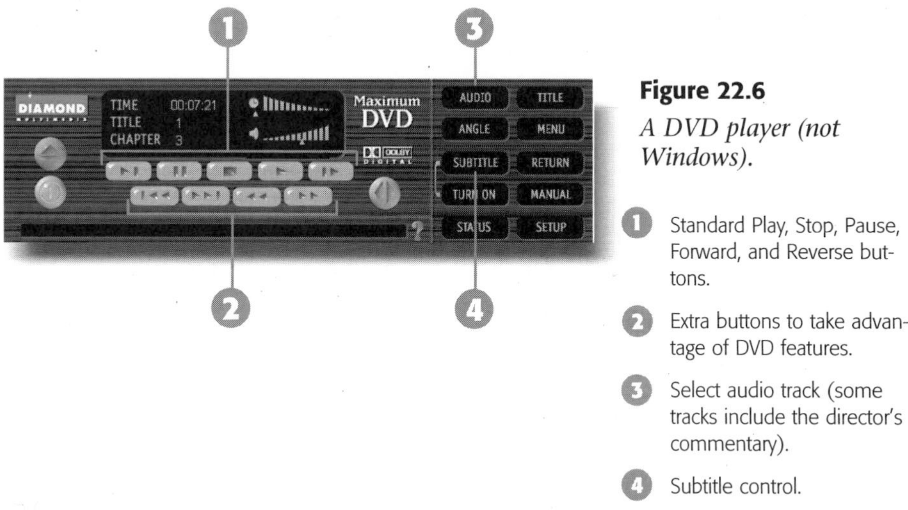

Figure 22.6

A DVD player (not Windows).

1. Standard Play, Stop, Pause, Forward, and Reverse buttons.
2. Extra buttons to take advantage of DVD features.
3. Select audio track (some tracks include the director's commentary).
4. Subtitle control.

Yes, playing the DVD is a great distraction. I mean, to see a movie on your computer screen—what could be more productive? (Don't get me started on Web TV.)

Shut down the DVD Player in about two hours, after you've watched the movie. Then get back to work.

Remove the DVD video from your DVD drive, and put it back in the box for safekeeping. (Or hide it from others in your office.)

- The newness of DVD players is what prevents Windows from supporting them in great numbers. CD-ROM drives had the same problems, back in the early 1990s.

- If you don't have auto-play turned on, you have to start the CD-ROM player. From the Start menu, choose Programs➡Accessories➡Entertainment➡DVD Player.
- Some DVD movies are on both sides of the disk. One side contains the TV-formatted version; the other side contains the wide-screen edition.
- At moments like this, you need the Windows Update program (refer to Chapter 15). Windows Update can locate new drivers, such as the one for my DVD drive (although it's not listed yet).

You cannot use the Print Screen key to capture an image from a DVD movie. It's not a bug—it's done on purpose to prevent movies from being copied illegally. See Chapter 17 for more information about using the Print Screen key.

ZIP Drives

Sure, other types of removable drives are available. Recently, however, I've noticed a trend among computer manufacturers: They seem to be installing a heck of a lot of ZIP drives on various PCs. Or should I say that a heck of a lot of PCs have ZIP drives? (I mean, having 200 ZIP drives in a single PC would be funny, but—oh, I'm rambling.)

ZIP drives are like beefy floppy drives. They swallow ZIP disks, which store as much as 100 megabytes in a hard plastic case about 4 inches square and a quarter-inch thick. Because these drives store a great deal of information (as much as 75 floppies' worth) and are removable, they're ideal for backing up data or sending files through the mail (as long as the other person has a ZIP drive) or moving files between two computers in two locations.

Odds are fairly good that your computer has a ZIP drive. And I should write about that, natch.

- **Open My Computer.**
- **Right-click your ZIP drive icon.**

You see a specialized pop-up menu relating to the ZIP drive, as shown in Figure 22.7.

The extra menu items come from Iomega, not from Microsoft. Your dealer installed them on your PC, and they're not part of Windows.

- **Choose Open.**

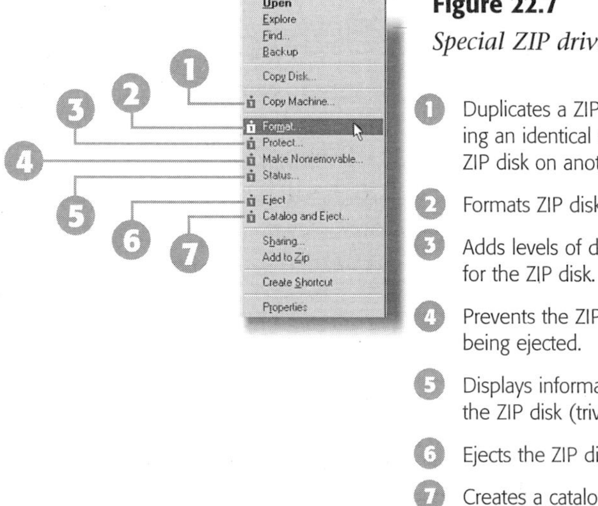

Figure 22.7
Special ZIP drive menu.

1. Duplicates a ZIP disk, creating an identical copy of one ZIP disk on another ZIP disk.
2. Formats ZIP disks.
3. Adds levels of data security for the ZIP disk.
4. Prevents the ZIP disk from being ejected.
5. Displays information about the ZIP disk (trivia!).
6. Ejects the ZIP disk.
7. Creates a catalog of files on the disk and then ejects the disk.

The ZIP disk's contents are displayed in a window. The disk works like any other hard disk, and it's removable, like a floppy disk.

Note that Windows uses the generic Removable Disk icon when it displays a ZIP disk's folder.

▶ **Close the ZIP disk's window.**

▶ **Close the My Computer window.**

I use my ZIP disk for backup files. I don't do full backups on them because that requires a large number of ZIP disks and the disks are more expensive than backup tapes. For backing up a day's work or important stuff I want to stick in the fire safe, however, they're ideal.

- ZIP drives have nothing to do with ZIP formatted files, which you'll probably download someday from the Internet. The two are entirely different things. For example, you *do not* have to put your ZIP files on a ZIP drive.
- Don't feel guilty about having a ZIP drive and not using it. Someday, when you have to take a huge graphics file to Kinkos for printing, you'll be thankful.
- ZIP disks are handy for moving large files between two PCs, both of which must sport a ZIP drive.
- On the downside, ZIP disks are expensive. Although they're cheaper than a box of 75 floppy disks (which store about the same amount of information), they're still pricey, about $13 apiece in bulk.

You can tweak ZIP disks similarly to CD-ROM drives: The sections earlier in this chapter about auto-play and changing the drive letter also apply to ZIP disks. For example, you could change your ZIP disk drive letter to Z. Follow the steps in the sections "Making Your CD Automatically Play Music or Software" and "Changing Your CD-ROM Drive Letter," earlier in this chapter; on the System Properties menu, however, open the Disk Drives item and choose IOMEGA ZIP 100 from the list.

- A ZIP drive is essentially a Bernoulli box, updated to fit in more compact and convenient cases. What's a Bernoulli box? It's an early type of removable hard drive that was like a large, bulky, and expensive ZIP drive. It works based on aerodynamic principles discovered by the eighteenth century Swiss mathematician Daniel Bernoulli. Now you know the $500 *Jeopardy* answer.

Chapter 23

Folders and Folders

Questions Answered and Thoughts Inspired

- Using the Windows Explorer
- Browsing to a specific folder
- Finding a folder with the Find command
- Working with pathnames
- Creating new folders and organizing them
- Renaming folders
- Moving folders
- Putting folder shortcuts on the desktop

Your disk drive is like the old Wild West. Beastly. Lawless. Desperadoes stealing cattle. Men drinking whiskey. Women- and childrenfolk afeared for their lives. Brazen hussies. Into this untamed land, you walk. You're the sheriff. It's up to you to clean up the place and get stuff organized.

Organizing folders is your job. It's up to you. Putting files into proper folders and keeping everything organized is the best way to run your computer. If you know how to work folder magic, your folders can keep you, your computer, and your files all neat and organized. This chapter gets you started on that road, with a few tips for swaggering and talking like John Wayne.

- Chapter 39, "A View to a Folder," contains additional folder information; specifically, about changing the way you view folders and their contents.
- You can work folders like files, in many respects. Chapter 24 covers basic file activities, each of which applies to folders too.
- John Wayne as John T. Chance in *Rio Bravo*: "'Sorry' don't get it done, dude."

Exploring Your Folders

If you're going to work with folders, you'll probably prefer the Windows Explorer way of displaying information over the My Computer type of windows. Windows Explorer displays files like a My Computer window and also shows you how folders are organized.

▶ **From the Start Thing, choose Programs ➡Windows Explorer.**

The Windows Explorer window appears, as shown in Figure 23.1. (To avoid serious typing injuries, I call it *Explorer* from now on; the other Explorer, Internet Explorer, I call *IE*, but not until Part V of this book.)

▶ **Resize the window so that the Views button on the toolbar is visible.**

Do this step so that the window looks like the one in Figure 23.1.

Notice in Figure 23.1 that I have Web Page view turned off. Although that mode is handy in some circumstances, it tends to get in the way when you're exploring folders or working with files.

▶ **Choose View ➡as Web Page to remove the check mark there (if necessary).**

Notice that Drive C is selected in the folder (left) half of the window. The contents of Drive C, the *root* folder, are displayed on the file (right) side of the window.

Folder side is the left side of the Explorer window, and file side is the right side.

Choosing a folder on the folder side displays that folder's files on the right side.

▶ **Choose the My Documents folder.**

Click the My Documents folder once on the left side of the window. Its contents appear on the right—including any folders inside the My Documents folder.

Keep the Explorer window open for the next tutorial.

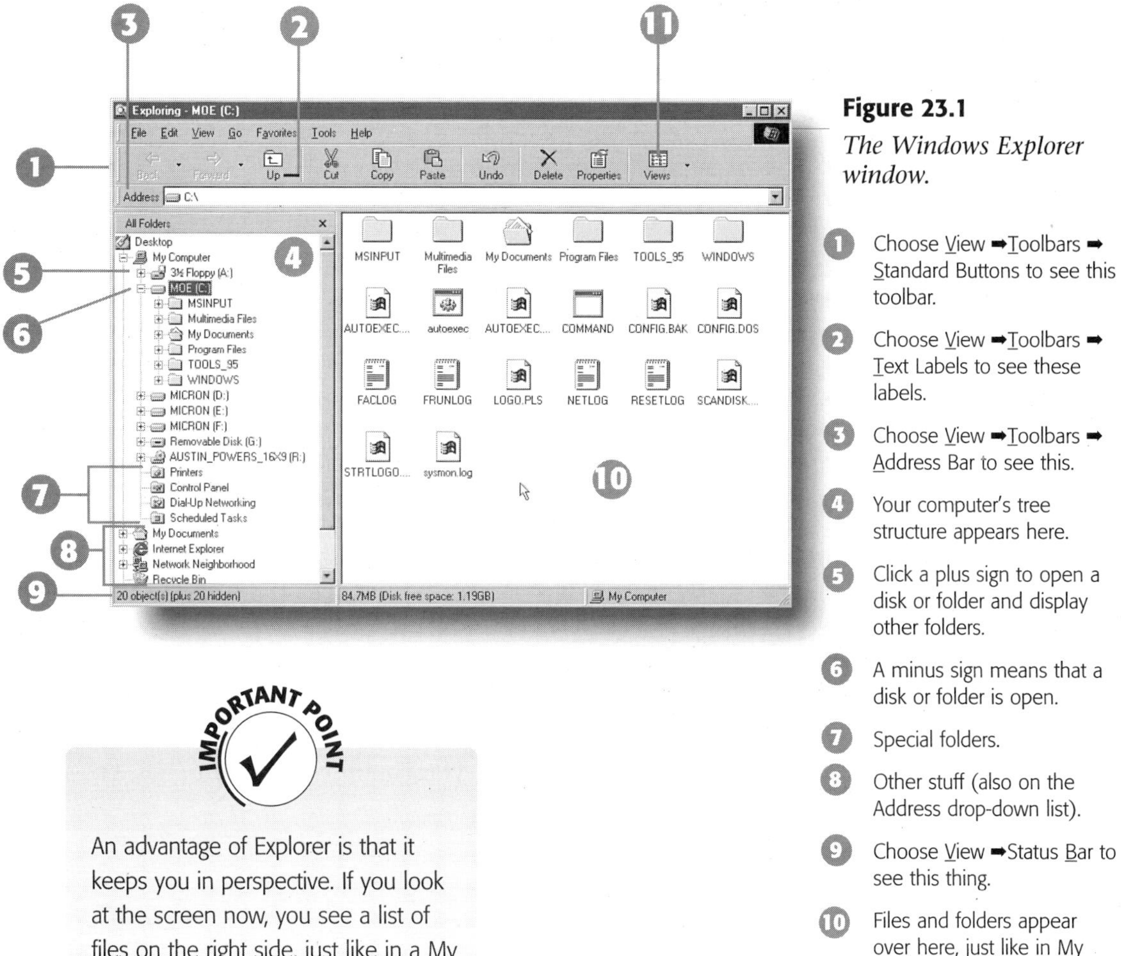

Figure 23.1

The Windows Explorer window.

1. Choose View ➡Toolbars ➡ Standard Buttons to see this toolbar.
2. Choose View ➡Toolbars ➡ Text Labels to see these labels.
3. Choose View ➡Toolbars ➡ Address Bar to see this.
4. Your computer's tree structure appears here.
5. Click a plus sign to open a disk or folder and display other folders.
6. A minus sign means that a disk or folder is open.
7. Special folders.
8. Other stuff (also on the Address drop-down list).
9. Choose View ➡Status Bar to see this thing.
10. Files and folders appear over here, just like in My Computer.
11. Click here to change the way files are displayed in the window below.

IMPORTANT POINT

An advantage of Explorer is that it keeps you in perspective. If you look at the screen now, you see a list of files on the right side, just like in a My Computer window. You can immediately tell on the left that the folder you're viewing is on drive C. Plus, you can see other folders nearby.

Going to a Specific Folder

Explorer makes it easy to go to any specific folder, primarily because you can see more folders at one time.

Continue the last section's tutorial:

▶ **Open the Program Files folder.**

Click the + by the Program Files folder on the folder side of the window. That step opens the "tree" for that section, displaying all the folders inside the Program Files folder. You should see a bunch of them.

The + opens a folder "branch."

The – closes a folder "branch."

Notice how the right side of the window does not change its contents.

▶ **Choose the Accessories folder.**

Click the Accessories folder to open its contents on the right side of the window.

Suppose that you're working along—la, la, la—and you need to go to the Windows folder. Here's how you do it:

▶ **Scroll down the folder side of the Explorer window.**

Scroll until you see the Windows folder.

▶ **Click the Windows folder to select it.**

The contents of the Windows folder appear on the file side of the window.

(If you've been working earlier tutorials in this book, notice that the Windows folder now automatically displays its files. When you turn off the View As Web Page option, no Click Here item exists to prevent the files in the folder from being displayed.)

To move back to the preceding folder (Accessories), you could scroll around, but why not take advantage of Windows?

▶ **Click the Back button.**

Ta-da. You're there.

Suppose that you yearn to see the contents of the My Documents folder.

▶ **Click the mouse on the Address bar.**

This step selects the text that's already there: `C:\Program Files\Accessories`.

▶ **Type** My Documents.

You have to type only **My** and a **D** to see the text *My Documents* displayed in the input box.

▶ **Press Enter.**

You're there!

To go somewhere you've been recently, you use the Back button's drop-down "back list," as shown in Figure 23.2.

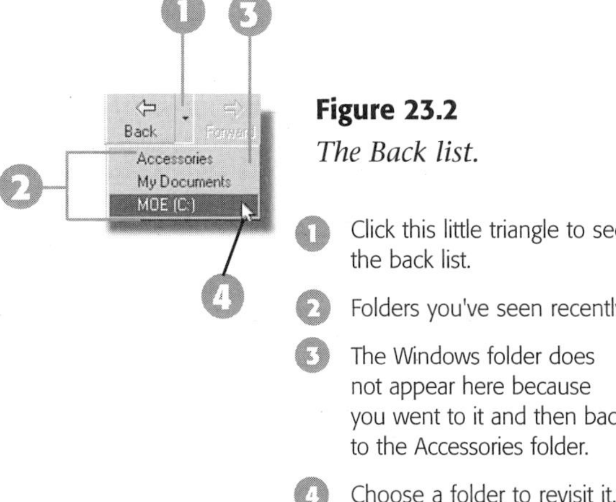

Figure 23.2
The Back list.

1. Click this little triangle to see the back list.
2. Folders you've seen recently.
3. The Windows folder does not appear here because you went to it and then back to the Accessories folder.
4. Choose a folder to revisit it.

- **Click the little triangle to see the Back button's back list.**
- **Choose drive C from the back list.**

You're back on drive C.

Notice that the Windows folder was not on the back list. The reason is that you used the Back button to return from the Windows folder back to the Accessories folder.

When you use the Back button, it removes the previously viewed folder from the list.

None of the folders is now on the list, in fact, because you went back to the first folder, drive C's root folder. Look in the Explorer window. The Back button is dimmed, and the list is empty.

- **Click the Up button.**

The Up button always moves you to the *parent* folder—the folder that contains the current folder. For drive C, the parent folder is My Computer.

The parent folder of My Computer is the desktop, but you don't need to go there.

- **Click the Back button.**

You're back to drive C.

- **Click the Forward button.**

Hey! You're back in the My Computer folder. Back and forth. Back and forth...

Just don't let the gentle back-and-forth action of Explorer put you to sleep.

▶ **Close the Explorer window.**

Enough navigational training for now.

- You can see any folder's contents by selecting the folder from the left side of the Explorer window.
- Click the + to open a folder branch.
- Click the – to close a folder branch.
- Use the Back button to return to a previously viewed folder.
- Use the Back button's list to choose a folder you've been to recently.
- Use the Up button to move to the parent folder.

Finding a Folder When You Know Its Name

No sense in hunting down a folder by clicking endless + signs and searching through the left side of the Explorer window. You can always do things in better ways than the obvious.

Suppose that you're desperate to find the Fonts folder, where Windows keeps all its fonts. (I'm using the Fonts folder for this tutorial because I know that you have a Fonts folder on your hard drive. Most experienced Windows users know that the Fonts folder is in the Windows folder.)

From the Start Thing menu, choose Find ➡Files or Folders.

The Find dialog box appears, as shown in Figure 23.3. You have some customizing to do.

▶ **Click the Advanced tab.**

The Advanced panel appears. You have to tell Windows to look for only folders.

▶ **Press Alt+T to select the Of Type drop-down list.**

▶ **Type** FO.

All you have to type is the first part of the word *folder*, **FO**. The Folder file type appears on the list.

Typing an item's name in a drop-down list is a quick way to get to that item.

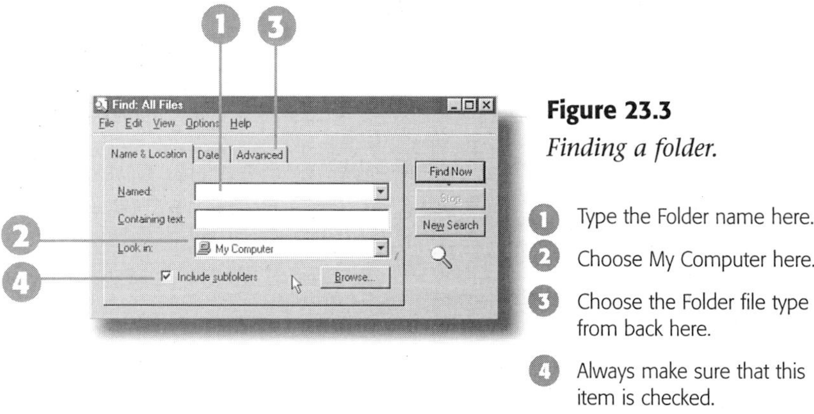

Figure 23.3
Finding a folder.

1. Type the Folder name here.
2. Choose My Computer here.
3. Choose the Folder file type from back here.
4. Always make sure that this item is checked.

Now Windows looks only for folders.

- ▶ **Click the Name & Location tab.**

Tell Windows the name of the folder you're looking for and where to look:

- ▶ **Type** Fonts **in the Named box.**
- ▶ **Choose My Computer from the Look In drop-down list.**
- ▶ **Put a check mark by Include Subfolders (if one isn't there already).**
- ▶ **Click Find Now.**

Windows begins its search.

Eventually one or more folders matching your search are found. They're listed at the bottom of the window, as shown in Figure 23.4.

If no folders were found, you probably made a typo or a wrong selection in the preceding steps. Review what you did and try again.

The folder you want is in the C:\WINDOWS folder.

- ▶ **Double-click the Fonts folder.**

A My Computer type of window opens, displaying the contents of the folder you were looking for.

- ▶ **Close the FONTS window.**
- ▶ **Close the Find window.**

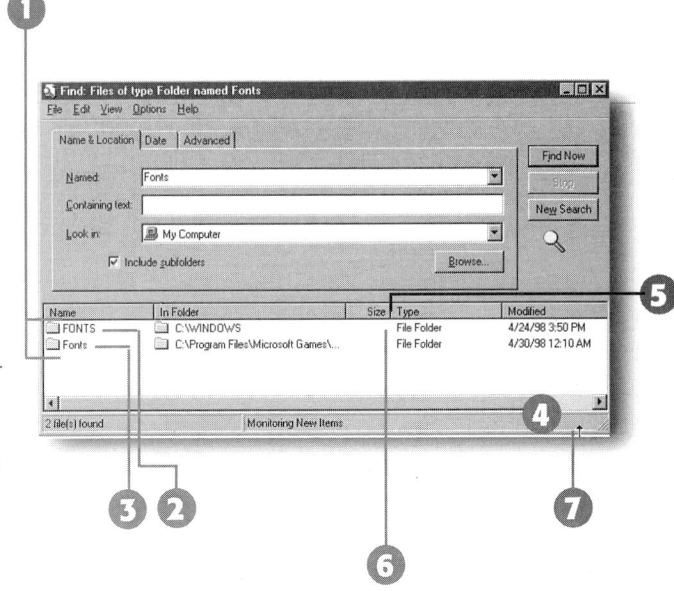

Figure 23.4
Folders in the Find dialog box.

1. Matching folders found.
2. The one you were looking for.
3. Other FONTS folders Windows found (you may or may not have these).
4. Stretch the Find dialog box to the right by dragging here with the mouse.
5. Drag between columns to change their size, or...
6. ...double-click between columns to make them large enough to display all the text.
7. Stretch the Find dialog box down to see more of the files in the list.

- This tutorial was just an exercise. A shortcut to the Fonts folder is in the Control Panel.
- Chapter 42, "Fun with Fonts," covers fonts in Windows in vast detail.

TIP

The key to finding a folder quickly is to choose Folder from the Of Type list in the Find window's Advanced panel. If you don't choose Folder, leaving that item set to All Files and Folders, Windows finds not only folders named FONTS but also any type of file with *FONTS* in its name.

Unlacing a Pathname

Often folder names are shown in *pathname format*. A *pathname* is a DOS term (actually, a UNIX term). It's one word—a long, complex word—that describes exactly where a file or folder is located in your computer.

Normally I wouldn't bring up pathnames, but many programs, including Windows, still use the term. The secret to understanding pathnames is to properly unlace them.

Suppose that you're told to go to this folder:

```
C:\WINDOWS\SYSTEM\VIEWERS
```

This folder isn't that hard to find when you ignore all the symbols and concentrate instead on the text:

```
C
WINDOWS
SYSTEM
VIEWERS
```

The first letter is a disk drive, drive C. The rest of the names are folders, one inside the other.

▶ **From the Start Thing, choose Programs ➡Windows Explorer.**

▶ **Open drive C.**

Click the + sign by drive C to open it, if it's not open already.

▶ **Open the Windows folder.**

▶ **Open the System folder.**

You might have to scroll down to find the System folder.

▶ **Open the Viewers folder.**

Just click the Viewers folder to display its contents; no + is next to the folder because it contains no other folders.

Notice the Address bar. It says C:\WINDOWS\SYSTEM\VIEWERS.

As long as you break up the pathname into words, you can get to that folder.

Here's a typing trick—in case you ever have the urge to type a pathname rather than click folders.

Suppose that you're told to go to this folder:

```
C:\PROGRAM FILES\INTERNET EXPLORER
```

You know how to get there with the mouse, and here's how to get there with the keyboard:

▶ **Click the Address bar.**

This step selects the text.

▶ **Press the Delete key.**

This step deletes the text on the Address bar. You now type the following pathname (yes, with your own fingers):

▶ **Type** C.

Hey! Look at the screen. Windows assumed the `:\` part of the pathname for you.

▶ **Press the right-arrow key on your keyboard.**

This step moves the cursor to the end of the selected text—accepting that text as part of your input.

▶ **Type** P.

Well, hey! If you're lucky, you see the rest of the folder's name (`rogram Files`) displayed for you.

If you don't see `Program Files` displayed, keep typing: **R**, **O**, **G**, **R**, and so on until Windows displays `Program Files`.

▶ **Press the right-arrow key to accept the text.**

Now it should say C:\PROGRAM FILES (although maybe in mixed case).

▶ **Type** \i.

Sometimes a backslash and an *I* are all you need in order to see `Internet Explorer` displayed. If not, keep typing **Internet Explorer** until Windows fills in the rest for you.

The pathname should be typed completely. If you're lucky, you probably pressed only six keys. That's not bad.

▶ **Press Enter.**

Windows displays the C:\PROGRAM FILES\INTERNET EXPLORER folder.

▶ **Close the Explorer window.**

Most of the time, you don't have to sit and stare at a pathname to understand its meaning. Fewer and fewer programs are using them, although they still crop up in the oddest places.

- As long as the Address bar is displayed, you can see the pathname for the current window—just in case a computer nerd walks by and requests that information from you.
- You can also type a pathname in the Run dialog box to display that folder's contents. Choose Run from the Start Thing, although this option requires you to type the entire pathname *exactly*, which can be a pain in the butt.

Organizing Folders

Creating your own folders is necessary for storing your own stuff. You create folders, put your stuff in them, and then maybe create even more folders for more stuff. It's much easier than trying to assemble one of those California Closet organizers.

Summoning a New Folder into Existence

In keeping with the Windows theme, create your new folders in the My Documents folders. You really have no reason to create folders elsewhere, although Windows lets you stick a folder anywhere.

Everyone needs a JUNK folder. It's where you put temporary files or stuff you're just playing with. It might be called JUNK or STO or TEMP or BLAKE—whatever—it just fills up with junk. Put it in your My Documents folder:

- **Right-click the My Documents icon on the desktop.**
- **Choose Explore.**

The Explorer window opens, showing you the contents of the My Documents folder.

- **Choose File ➡New ➡Folder.**

The new folder appears in the window, named New Folder. How dumb. Give it a new name:

- **Type** Junk.
- **Press Enter.**

The name Junk is applied to the new folder. Now you have a Junk folder, where you can put throwaway or temporary files you don't really need long-term.

In fact, all the little temporary files you created in Part I of this book can go there.

- **Move the Jet Trip document to the Junk folder.**

Drag the Jet Trip document to the Junk folder, as shown in Figure 23.5. This step moves the Jet Trip document to the Junk folder.

- **Move the Our Journey document to the Junk folder.**

If you don't have the Jet Trip or Our Journey documents, drag some other meaningless text documents into the Junk folder just because. (You're bound to have some junk text files there; why not put them in an appropriate place?)

Eventually, your My Documents folder should contain lots of folders, neatly organizing your work. As an example of what you can do, I submit Figure 23.6, which shows how deep organization can go.

As an example of the organization, get out a magnifying glass and find the 2000 folder under *Letters* in Figure 23.6. If you follow the path from My Documents, reading each successive folder name, it tells you exactly what you can find there:

- **My Documents, Work, Letters, 2000**

The folder must contain letters written in the year 2000 relating somehow to work. (Did you notice how close that is to a pathname? It can truly be very descriptive.)

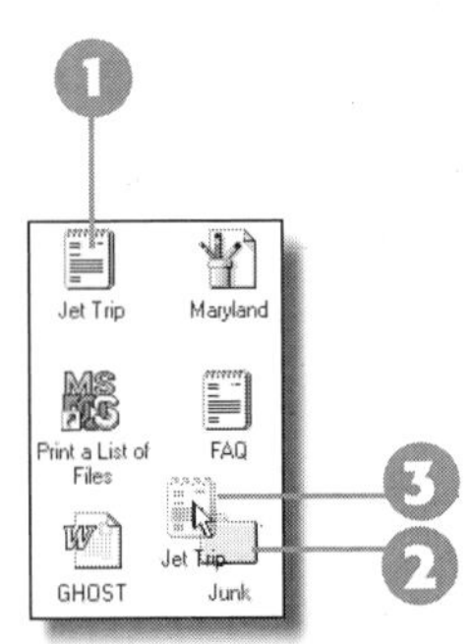

Figure 23.5
Moving a file to the Junk folder.

1. Drag the document from here…
2. …to this folder.
3. Release the mouse button to drop the document into the folder.

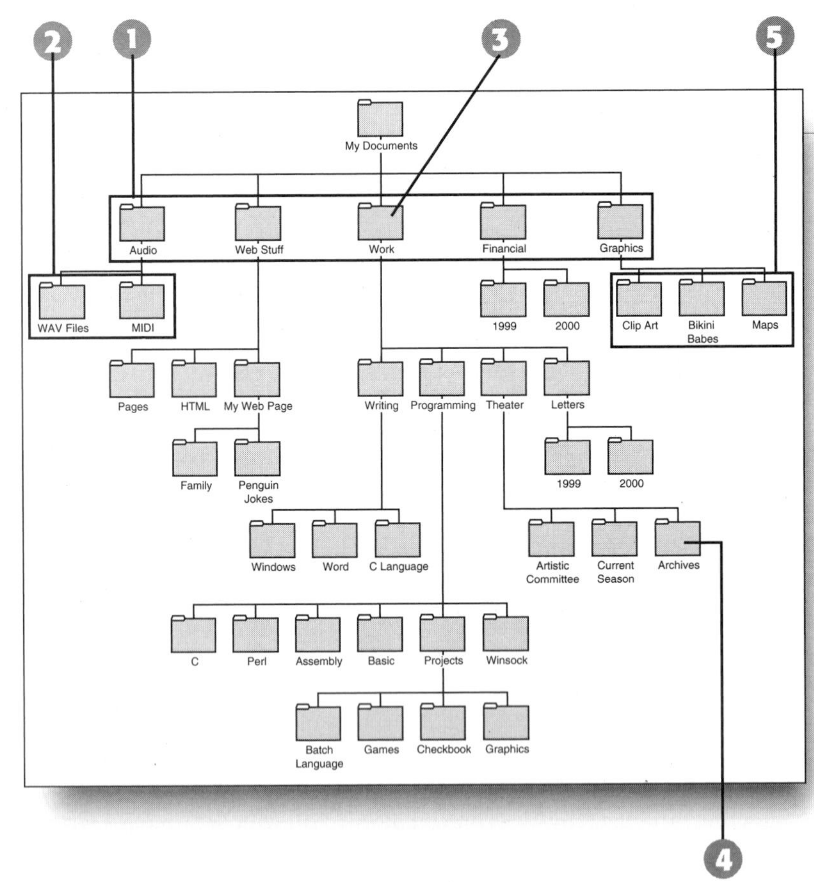

Figure 23.6
An organized folder strategy.

1. Main categories under My Documents.
2. Specific folders for specific types of audio files.
3. General Work folder for business stuff.
4. Archive folders are good for storing old data.
5. Different types of graphics files, organized in their own folders.

Start your organizational theme! Create a Work folder inside the My Documents folder:

▶ **Right-click in the My Documents window.**

Right-click the right side of the window, where the files are. A pop-up menu appears.

▶ **Choose New ➡Folder.**

This method is yet another way to create a folder.

▶ **Rename the new folder** Work.

Type **Work** right after the folder is created to give it that name. You're ready to start putting (and creating) important stuff there.

If you already have a Work folder, Windows doesn't let you create a second one. Rename the New Folder folder as Working instead; or just delete New Folder, which is covered later in this chapter.

▶ **Close the Explorer window.**

I can only *show* you how to organize—I can't do your organization. On your own, you need to create folders for specific files.

Don't expect to build your entire folder structure at once. If you do, in fact, it doesn't work. You have to build it a piece at a time, as you need it. No hurry.

TIP

A good way to start is simply to look at what's in your My Documents folder already. Do you have a bunch of graphics files? If so, create a Graphics folder for them.

- A folder has no minimum file requirement. A folder can contain thousands of files, one, or zero files.
- Of course, a folder with thousands of files probably needs some subfolders to organize things further.
- I have a beef with Microsoft over how disorganized the Windows folder is. Although those folks moved some items (like Fonts) out to their own folder, a bunch of random stuff is still stuck in the Windows folder. (Don't reorganize it! Windows expects those files to be there.)
- Honestly, a keyboard shortcut should exist for creating a new folder. I vote for Ctrl+N. (It's ⌘+-N on the Macintosh, not that I'm comparing or anything.)
- I occasionally create a new folder in places other than the My Documents folder. For example, I created a DOS Utilities folder in the Program Files folder for all my old, favorite DOS utility programs. Nothing is wrong with this method, but still all my documents and graphics files are stored in an elaborately organized scheme under the main My Documents folder.

- The My Documents folder on drive C and the My Documents folder on the desktop are really the same thing. If more than one person logs on to your computer, however, the two folders might be different.
- John Wayne as Wil Anderson in *The Cowboys*: "We're burnin' daylight!"

What? Two My Documents Folders?

It's true; the My Documents folder on the desktop is subtly different from the My Documents folder right off drive C. You might notice that opening one or the other might show you the same files, in a different order. Or maybe the contents between the two are different entirely.

Normally, for one person using a computer, the two folders should be identical, showing the same contents (but maybe not in the same order). If your PC is configured for more than one person to use it (to log in), however, the two folders are different. In that case, the folder on the desktop is the one you should use.

When two or more people use a computer, Windows customizes things for everyone. The My Documents folder on the desktop is the personal one, the one just for you. Its content changes, depending on who logs in to the computer. The other My Documents folder, the one on drive C, is the "group" folder. It reflects changes made by all the users to their individual My Documents folder.

I profusely apologize for the confusion caused by the multiple My Documents folders. I wish that Microsoft had done things another way, but this arrangement is how everyone has to live with things under Windows.

Renaming a Folder

Eventually you might discover that a folder contains stuff which doesn't relate to the folder's name. When that happens, you can rename the folder.

For example, the Junk folder you created earlier in this chapter now contains some text documents you made. The folder isn't really "junk" any more.

- ▶ **Click the Junk folder once to select it.**
- ▶ **Press the F2 key.**

The F2 key is the keyboard shortcut for the Rename command.

- ▶ **Type** Sample Text Files.

The word *Files* might "wrap" to the next line below the icon so that it says

```
Sample Text
Files
```

That's okay; the name is still readable and informative. Although you can rename a folder with as many as 255 characters, shorter and descriptive names are always better.

▶ **Press Enter to lock in the new name.**

Renaming a folder happens all the time. For example, you might be planning a trip to the mountains. Everything about the trip is in your Mountain folder in the Vacations folder. Then you get a *huge* bonus check. Time to rename the Mountain folder as the Disney World folder.

Although renaming folders is easy, I have a warning:

Don't rename a folder if it contains a program! It doesn't matter which type of program it is: DOS, Windows, a game, whatever.

Windows memorizes the names of folders containing programs, and, if you rename them, takes longer to find and start your program. It doesn't "lose" the program, although it takes Windows longer to find the program when you try to run it again.

The purpose of the My Documents folder, and all the folders you create there, is to hold documents, not programs. Therefore, renaming folders in My Documents is always okay.

Never rename a folder containing programs. Sheesh!

- You cannot give a folder the name of another folder in the same window. If you already have a Sample Text Files folder in My Documents, for example, Windows spews a nasty error message at you.
- You can give a folder a name as long as 255 characters, although short and descriptive is always best.
- You can use letters, numbers, and spaces in any combination to name a folder. You can also use periods and other symbols, but not any of these characters:

  " * / : ? \ | < >

Never rename the Windows folder or any folders in that folder. If you do, your computer might not start up.

- You can also rename a selected folder by choosing the File ➡Rename command.
- Right-clicking a folder and choosing the Rename command from the shortcut menu also renames the file.
- Never rename any folders inside the Program Files folder or the Program Files folder itself.

Moving a Folder

Part of organization involves not only putting proper files in proper folders but also keeping those folders organized. For example, because your collection of MIDI files is stored haphazardly in the My Documents folder, you wisely follow my good advice and create a MIDI folder, moving your MIDI files into it.

Then you notice that you also have an Audio folder for sound files. Hey! The MIDI folder should go in there! Eventually you end up with a scheme similar to the one shown in the upper-left part of Figure 23.6. My, how organized.

Because this book is work, the Sample Text Files folder should go in your Work folder.

▶ **Drag the Sample Text Files folder into your Work folder.**

This step works just like moving a file; use Figure 23.5 as a guide, although you drag a folder and not a file.

TIP

Make sure that you can see both the Sample Text Files folder and the Work folder.

Some words of advice:

Moving a folder moves *all* the folder's contents, including any other folders inside that folder and all their contents. It's a massive operation.

Moving a folder isn't a casual thing. Make sure that you're doing so primarily for organizational purposes. That process implies some thought, as opposed to saying, "Well, I'll just drag it here for now."

TIP

A better way to move a folder is with cut and paste because you normally can't see in the window the folder you're moving to, which makes dragging the folder with the mouse unwieldy.

▶ **Press Ctrl+Z, the Undo command.**

The Sample Text Files folder is moved back. This step might take a second or two.

▶ **Click the Sample Text Files folder once to select it.**

▶ **Click the Cut tool.**

The folder icon appears dimmed to indicate that it has been cut and has yet to be pasted anywhere.

▶ **Open the Work folder.**

You can double-click the folder on the right side of the window or just click the folder on the left side of the window once.

▶ **Click the Paste tool.**

The folder is pasted into the Work folder.

This process might seem like a great deal of work—and it is. Normally you just drag the folder to move it. What if the Work folder were on drive D, inside the I Hate folder? Then it would be easier to cut and paste the folder than to attempt a drag operation.

Keep the Explorer window open for the next exciting tutorial.

- Moving folders around is known as "pruning and grafting." It's a pun because the folder structure on your hard drive is called a "tree structure." If you turn Figure 23.6 upside down, it kind of looks like a tree. Sorta.
- MIDI files play music on your computer. Chapter 11 showed you how to play a Brandenburg Concerto MIDI file by using the Run command.

Zapping a Folder to Kingdom Come

Deleting a folder removes not only the folder but also all its contents. It's scary stuff.

Continue the preceding tutorial (in Explorer at the Work folder):

▶ **Drag the Sample Text Files folder to the Recycle Bin.**

You might have to slide the Explorer window over to the right a little to see the Recycle Bin icon on the desktop.

A warning dialog box might appear, asking whether you want to toss the folder and all its contents into the trash. You really don't want to because this section is a tutorial.

▶ **Click No.**

If the message doesn't appear and the folder was thrown away, press Ctrl+Z to get it back.

Remember that deleting a folder deletes not only the folder but also all its contents. That can be a great deal of stuff.

Why delete folders? Because you might no longer need them. For example, you might have a collection of *Babylon 5* videos you grabbed from the Internet, and they're taking up megabytes of disk space, so you just delete the Babylon 5 Video folder to save yourself space.

Now the warning:

Don't delete folders containing programs!

Remember that you're supposed to uninstall programs, not delete them.

Another warning:

Never delete the following folders or any folders within them:

```
C:\Windows
C:\Program Files
```

Don't delete the main My Documents folder. If you do, it deletes all your stuff, and Windows and some applications expect to put your new documents in that folder.

Generally speaking, don't delete any folder you didn't create yourself.

- You can also delete a folder by selecting it and choosing File ➡Delete from the menu or by right-clicking a folder and choosing Delete from the shortcut menu.
- The Delete button on the toolbar also deletes a selected folder.
- You can press the Delete key on your keyboard to delete a folder.
- The Amazing Kreskin can delete a folder simply by using his mind.
- See Chapter 28, "Deleting, Undeleting, and Recycling," which discusses the Recycle Bin in detail.
- See Chapter 14 for information about uninstalling programs.

Making a Folder Shortcut

You probably don't want to make a copy of a folder. When you do, you copy the folder and all its contents—which can be a considerable chunk of disk space. No, rather than copy a folder, you want to create a folder shortcut.

Folder shortcuts are placed mostly on the desktop. For example, your current project folder can be put on the desktop as a shortcut, saving you time when you need to get to your files.

TIP

You can always copy the folder from your hard drive to a floppy disk or ZIP drive.

Continue the preceding tutorial (in the Explorer window, Work folder):

▶ **Right-drag the Sample Text Files folder to the desktop.**

Use the right mouse button to drag the file to the desktop. When you release the mouse button, a pop-up shortcut menu appears, as shown in Figure 23.7.

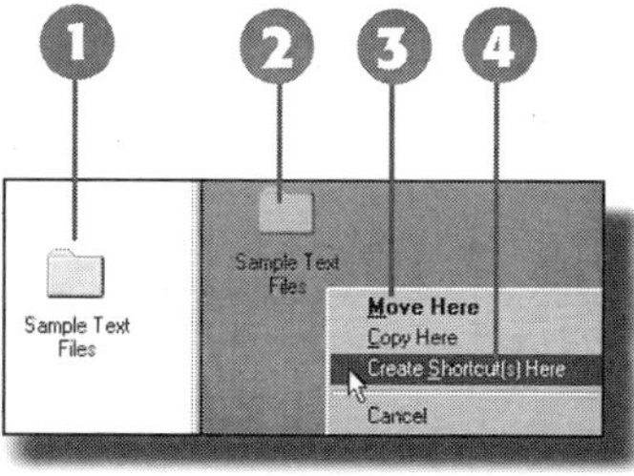

Figure 23.7

Creating a shortcut on the desktop.

1. Right-drag from here...
2. ...to out here.
3. Release the mouse button to see the shortcut menu.
4. Choose this option to create the shortcut.

▶ **Choose Create Shortcut(s) Here.**

▶ **Press F2 to rename the file.**

▶ **Delete the first part of the name: Shortcut To.**

Use the cursor keys on your keyboard to move up to the beginning of the folder's name. Then press the Delete key to edit out "Shortcut To."

▶ **Press Enter.**

TIP

You never really need an icon named Shortcut To because all shortcut icons have the little twisty arrow on them.

The shortcut *represents* the original folder but is not a copy. You save disk space and keep a handy shortcut on the desktop.

▶ **Open the Sample Text Files folder shortcut.**

You see a window containing the text files, the same window you would see had you opened the folder in the Work folder.

▶ **Close the Sample Text Files window.**

Because this section is just a tutorial, you don't need the Sample Text Files shortcut on the desktop.

▶ **Click the Sample Text Files desktop shortcut once to select it.**

▶ **Press the Delete key.**

Click Yes if Windows asks whether you're emotionally ready to delete the shortcut. You are.

Although the shortcut is gone, the original folder remains. Your Sample Text Files folder in the Work folder still lives. In fact, it never changed; only the shortcut to it was zapped to kingdom come.

Deleting a shortcut icon does not delete the original file.

▶ **Close the Explorer window.**

The tutorial ends here, although you can create shortcuts to your project folders and stick them on the desktop for handy access. I find that method quicker than browsing through folders or even using the Start Thing's Documents menu.

- As a real-life example, I created a desktop shortcut to the folder containing the files for *DOS For Dummies* (IDG Books Worldwide, Inc.) when I wrote it back in 1991. It was handy while I was writing that book. When I was done with the book, I dragged the shortcut icon to the Recycle Bin, removing it from the desktop (which doesn't delete the original folder on the hard drive).
- You know, it's amazing that I did all that, considering that Windows 98 didn't come out until seven years later.
- Folder shortcuts don't always have to go on the desktop. For example, using Figure 23.6, you could create a shortcut to the Letters folder in the Writing folder. That would give you quicker access to that folder, if you need it.
- John Wayne as J.B. Books in *The Shootist*: "I won't be wronged, I won't be insulted, and I won't be laid a hand on. I don't do these things to other people, and I require the same from them."

Chapter 24

File Fun

Questions Answered and Thoughts Inspired

- Copying a file
- Making file shortcuts
- Moving files with cut and paste
- Renaming files and icons
- Working with groups of files

Crack your knuckles as though you were Bugs Bunny sitting down to play the Hungarian Rhapsody. Your fingers are about to dance on the keyboard as you learn some basic file-manipulation skills: making shortcuts and copying, duplicating, moving, renaming, and working with groups of files. It's all covered in this chapter.

- All the file-manipulation commands in this chapter apply to folders too. See Chapter 23.
- The only command missing from this chapter is Delete, which is used to remove unwanted files. That command is covered in Chapter 28, "Deleting, Undeleting, and Recycling."
- The tutorials in this chapter use the badtrip file, created in Chapter 3, the Silly Picture file created in Chapter 5, and the desktop map file created in Chapter 17.
- The tutorials also use the Work\Sample Text Files folder you created in Chapter 23.

One final thing: Don't forget the Undo command: Edit➡Undo or Ctrl+Z. It can undo any of the file-manipulation commands covered in this chapter.

Ten Thousand Ways to Copy a File

I suppose that making a copy of a file is important. DOS had the COPY command, and then came the XCOPY and XCOPY32 commands. It's the same in Windows: You can copy a file in probably a half-dozen ways. Choosing how to copy a file depends on where you're copying it. This section explains everything.

First, some configuration. Whenever you work with files, especially copying them, it's best to work with the Windows Explorer window rather than the My Computer window:

- **Right-click the My Documents folder on the desktop.**
- **Choose Explore.**

The Explorer window appears, as shown in Figure 24.1.

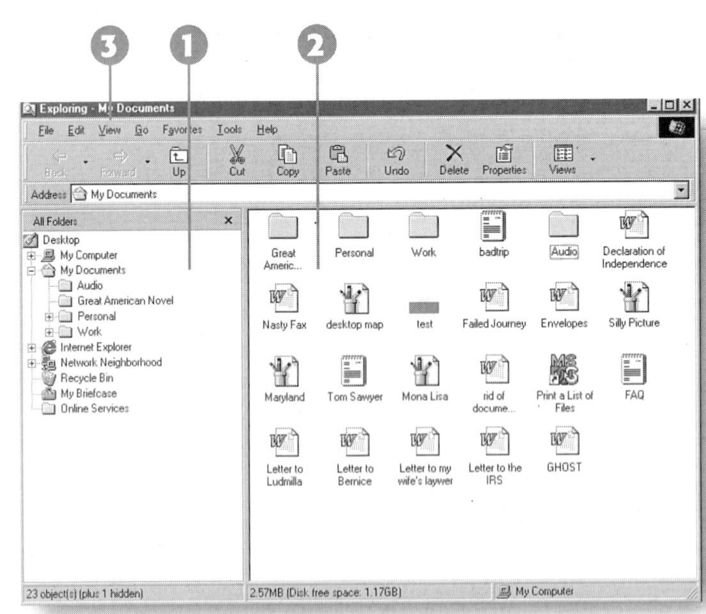

Figure 24.1
Exploring the My Documents folder.

1. Folders and disk drives here.
2. Files in the My Documents folder here.
3. Choose View➡as Web Page to remove any Web page graphics that would otherwise appear right here.

Keep this window open for this chapter's tutorials.

The Essence of Copy and Paste

The easiest way to copy files is to use the Copy and Paste commands. Follow these steps:

1. **Select an icon and copy it.**
2. **Navigate to the folder in which you want the copy.**
3. **Paste the copy.**

Of course, that's just too simple for Microsoft; some *variety* must be in there, as you'll discover.

Here is one way you can copy the badtrip icon from the My Documents folder to the Work\Sample Text Files folder:

- **Click the badtrip icon to select it.**
- **Copy the file.**

Here are your choices:

Choose Edit➡Copy. This option works best if you're whizzing around by using the mouse.

Choose the Copy button on the toolbar. This method is better than using the menu, as long as the toolbar is visible.

Press Ctrl+C, the keyboard shortcut. This method works only if your left hand is glued to the keyboard while your right hand is working the mouse.

The badtrip file has been selected for copying. It sits in the Clipboard, awaiting the moment it will be pasted.

- **Open the Work\Sample Text Files folder.**

On the left side of the window, click the + by the Work folder, and then click the Sample Text Files folder once to open it.

- **Paste the file.**

More options:

Choose Edit➡Paste. Remember that the more times you click your mouse, the more noise you make and the more work others nearby assume that you're doing.

Choose the Paste button on the toolbar. Use this option when no one is around, because it's fast and efficient yet doesn't give the illusion that you're doing too much work.

Press Ctrl+V, the keyboard shortcut. Use this option only if you can figure out how *V* can be associated with the word *paste*.

The file is copied to the new directory. It has the same name and same content as the original. Everything is the same; the next file is a duplicate of the original.

If you're good with two buttons on the mouse, you can shorten things considerably: To copy, right-click an icon and choose the Copy command. In the new location for the file, right-click in the window and choose the Paste command.

- All told, that's 4 ways to copy a file and 4 ways to paste. That's 16 possible copy-and-paste combinations. So far.

Pasting Files for the Anal Retentive

Pasting a file into a window can be an ugly thing; Windows usually tacks the file down wherever you click the mouse. Often this method doesn't bode well for the overall aesthetic look of the window. Some adjustments are necessary.

To arrange icons after a sloppy paste job, choose View➡Line Up Icons from the menu.

If you want the icons arranged in alphabetical order, choose View➡Arrange Icons➡by Name. This arrangement has the bonus result of squaring up the icons with the window's size.

Copying by Ctrl+Dragging

Dragging an icon with the mouse is okay for copying files between two folders or two open windows *you can see*. Beyond that, I recommend copying by using the Copy and Paste commands discussed in the preceding section.

Continue the preceding section's tutorial:

- ▶ **Click the Back button to return to the My Documents folder.**
- ▶ **Ctrl+drag the Silly Picture icon to the Work folder.**

Press the Ctrl key first. Then drag the Silly Picture icon to the Work folder. Release the Ctrl key *after* you release the mouse button.

To copy an icon with the mouse, hold the Ctrl key down. Otherwise, you move the file.

- *Ctrl* refers to the Ctrl key on your keyboard, which is called the *control* key, so "Ctrl+drag" refers to a control-drag.
- Windows assumes that you want to move a file when you drag its icon between two folders on the same hard drive. In that situation you must press the Ctrl key to copy the file instead.

Notice the + while you're Ctrl+dragging? It's your clue that you're copying the icon, not just moving it.

- When you drag a file to another hard drive, Windows assumes that you mean to copy it; you don't have to press the Ctrl key. In fact, the + automatically appears when you drag an icon to another hard drive.

Duplicating a File

Whenever you copy a file, you're creating a duplicate. However, I reserve the phrase "duplicating a file" for creating a copy of a file in the same folder. This stuff can be tricky.

Suppose that you create some piece of artwork and want to mess with it while keeping the original intact:

- ▶ **Open the Work folder.**

You should find the Silly Picture file, copied there from a previous lesson.

- ▶ **Right-click the Silly Picture file.**
- ▶ **Choose Copy.**
- ▶ **Right-click the window.**

Click next to the Silly Picture file to display the window's pop-up menu.

- ▶ **Choose Paste.**

Hey! It's called Copy of Silly Picture, a duplicate of the same file in the same folder.

Windows has to rename the duplicate file because two files in a folder cannot share the same name.

If you were working on a real file, you'd probably rename the duplicate to something else. For example, when I recently used this trick to edit a programming file named a-sort, I cleverly renamed the duplicate b-sort. Then I proceeded to mess with the b-sort file while the original a-sort remained untouched.

Making a File Shortcut

Sometimes you need a copy of a file just to be handy. For example, you're always fishing in the Windows folder for the FAQ file. If you need better access to the file, why not create a shortcut to it someplace handy, such as in My Documents or on the desktop?

Continue this chapter's tutorial by using Explorer:

- **Open drive C.**
- **Open the Windows folder.**

Click the Windows folder on the left side of the Explorer window. The contents of the Windows folder appear on the right side.

Making a shortcut works just like copying a file. The only difference is that you paste the file as a shortcut, not as a full copy.

- **Press the Tab key.**

This step switches the focus to the right side of the window, where the files are.

- **Keep pressing** F **on your keyboard until the FAQ file is highlighted.**

Typing a letter scrolls the list of files, displaying each file starting with that letter. (You can't use this trick to type a file's full name; only the first letter of the filename is used.)

- **Press Ctrl+C to copy the FAQ file.**
- **Return to the My Documents folder.**

You can click the Back button a few times to get there—if you've been working through this chapter's tutorials.

- **Choose Edit➡Paste Shortcut.**

The new file, Shortcut to FAQ, appears in the My Documents window. You now have easy access to the file.

- Shortcuts are easily identified by the little, curly arrow in the icon's lower-left corner (see the icon in the margin).
- Opening the shortcut is the same as opening the original.
- Shortcuts are pasted mostly to the desktop.
- The Start menu is full of program shortcuts (refer to Chapter 10).
- Most people rename shortcut icons, removing the initial Shortcut To part of the name. Renaming a shortcut does not change the original in any way.
- Deleting a shortcut icon does not change the original in any way.
- Moving a shortcut icon does not change the original. (Okay: In any way.)

Opening a shortcut icon and editing the file *does* change the original. Remember that it's a shortcut, not a copy.

Don't Make a Shortcut This Way!

The worst way to create a shortcut is to choose New➡Shortcut from any one of several menus around Windows. When you do, you're faced with a dialog box that forces you to type manually the original file's pathname (barf!) or use a Browse dialog box to hunt down the original file. What a colossal waste of time!

The Copy Warning

Two files of the same type with the same name cannot live in the same folder. When you attempt to copy or move a file to a folder and a file with that name is already there, you see a warning. Be careful.

- Ctrl+drag the Silly Picture icon from the My Documents window to the Work folder.

This step attempts to copy the Silly Picture icon to that folder—although a file named Silly Picture is already there. Because Windows assumes that you want to replace the old one with the one you're pasting, a warning dialog box appears, as shown in Figure 24.2.

Examine the file dates and time in the Confirm File Replace window. If the file you're pasting (on the bottom) is more recent, you probably want to replace the older one. If that's not what you expected, click No.

▶ **Click No.**

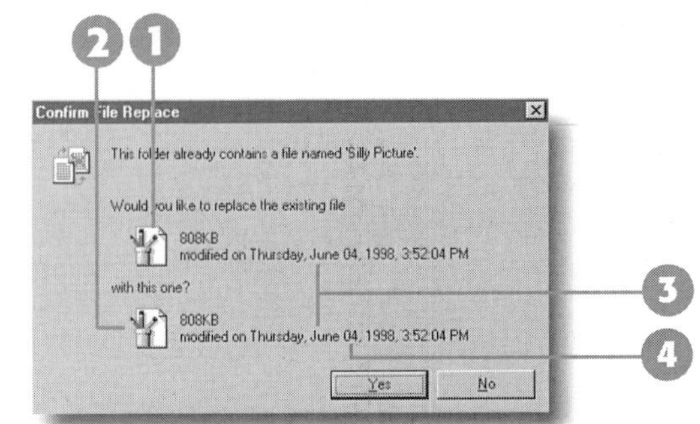

Figure 24.2
A file is about to be replaced. Uh-oh!

1. The file about to be replaced.
2. The file you're replacing it with.
3. Check these dates!
4. If this date is more recent, replacing the file *might* be okay.

If you're copying a group of files, you're asked to confirm each one or you can click Yes To All to replace all the files.

TIP

For example, I routinely send copies of the files I'm working on to a floppy disk as a backup. When I go to paste the files, Windows displays a warning similar to the one shown in Figure 24.2. I click Yes (or Yes For All, which appears when you copy more than one file at a time) to replace the older backup files on the floppy disks with my current work.

- The Confirm File Replace is actually a Paste command warning. It appears whether you've copied or moved files (used the Copy or Cut commands, respectively).
- In addition to filenames, files have types. For example, Silly Picture is a Paint program file, called a *bitmap graphic*. Chapter 26, "Essence of a File," covers file types.

TIP

If you really want to copy the file and not delete the original, rename something. Rename the file that's already in the folder, or rename the file you're pasting.

Moving a File Hither and Thither

Most of the time, you probably move files, not copy them. Ideally this happens during the throes of disk organization. You realize that your Junk folder contains a bunch of doodles you draw while you're on the phone, so you move them from that folder to a special Doodle folder, where you keep them until one day they'll be published and you'll be famous (that happens after you're dead, though, so you never see any money from it).

Moving a File with Cut and Paste

Although copying files is done with the Copy and Paste commands, moving a file is done with Cut and Paste. Here are the steps you take to move a file:

1. **Select an icon and cut it.**
2. **Navigate to the folder to where you want it moved.**
3. **Paste it.**

As with the Copy command, an equal variety of Cut commands exist. It all works similarly; you're just moving the file instead of creating a duplicate.

Suppose that the organizational bug has hit you and now you need a Graphics folder in the My Documents folder:

- **Make sure that the My Documents folder is open in the Explorer window.**

It should be if you've been following through this chapter's tutorials.

- **Choose File➡New➡Folder.**
- **Name the folder** Graphics.

Now you can move some graphics files into that folder.

Moving files is all about organization.

As with copying files, the easiest way to move a file is to drag it, as long as the folder is visible. To move the Desktop Map file to the Graphics folder, all you have to do is drag it.

- **Drag the Desktop Map file to the Graphics folder.**

Releasing the mouse over the Graphics folder "drops" the file into that folder. Confirm that you've done your job:

▶ **Open the Graphics folder.**

There's the Desktop Map file. Great.

▶ **Open the Work folder.**

Use the left side of the window. Locate the My Documents folder, and click the Work folder once to open it.

▶ **Select the Silly Picture icon.**

▶ **Cut the file.**

This step is not a delete operation. Because you're cutting the file to paste it elsewhere, selecting the file and cutting it does not delete the file.

Here are your choices for the Cut command:

Choose Edit➡Cut. Gotta love them menu commands, although I admit that this method is out of the way for most folks.

Choose the Cut button on the toolbar. My personal fave.

Press Ctrl+X, the keyboard shortcut. If you're addicted to keyboard shortcuts, this method is the one you use.

The Silly Picture file is now "cut," and it appears dimmed onscreen. It's not deleted; it's merely flagged as being cut. In fact, if you were to wander off and do something else now (other than Paste), Windows does not move the file.

▶ **Open the Graphics folder.**

Locate the Graphics folder on the left side of the window. Click once to open that folder and display its contents.

▶ **Paste the file.**

Now you can use the standard Paste options, the same ones as for Copy and Paste:

Choose Edit➡Paste. Ah, the menu. Always there. Reliable. Boring.

Choose the Paste button on the toolbar. My favorite.

Press Ctrl+V, the keyboard shortcut. The favorite of keyboard users around the world (where, in some languages, the word for *paste* might start with a **V**).

The file is moved to the new directory. It's the same file; just in a new place.

You can also select a file for cutting by right-clicking the icon and choosing the Cut command from the shortcut menu. When you get to the folder in which you want to paste, right-click in the window and choose the Paste command.

Making Up Your Mind As You Go

Another way to copy or move files is to drag with the *right* mouse button. As I've said, this method works best if you can see the folder to which you're copying or moving a file. If so, the right-drag is great because it lets you copy, move, or create a shortcut in one operation.

After you release the mouse in a right-drag, a pop-up menu appears. From that menu you can select one of these options:

Move here—Moves the file to the new location

Copy Here—Copies the file to the new location

Create Shortcut(s) Here—Makes a shortcut icon in the new location

Or you can choose Cancel to skip the whole operation.

(The reason I'm writing this tip in a sidebar is that it's tricky: You must be able to see the destination folder, and you must use the right mouse button, which throws many people.)

Giving a File a New Name

If we named our children the way we're supposed to name files in Windows, kids would probably be walking around today with names such as Inventive, Stubborn, Cuddly, Independent, Constantly in Trouble, and Tattles About Her Sister. That's a silly method for naming human children but entirely appropriate when you're naming files.

A file's name is assigned when the file is created. Afterward you can rename the file by using one of the various Windows Rename commands.

▶ **Open the Sample Text Files folder.**

It's in the My Documents\Work folder, if you don't have the Explorer window open.

▶ **Rename the Our Journey file as** My First Document**.**

Here are your choices:

Select the file and press the F2 key—This method is the way I rename files: You have to use the mouse to select the file, but the F2 key is handy because your hands are on the keyboard anyway to retype the filename.

Right-click the file and choose Rename—This method is my second favorite because it combines selecting the file with choosing the Rename command. Handy.

Select the file and choose File➡Rename from the menu—I've always thought that this method involved an extra step, so it's my least favorite file-renaming option.

Finally, my not-recommended option, which you might have already stumbled on accidentally:

Click the file once to select it and then again to rename—This step is not a double-click; it's slower. You click the file once to select it. Pause. Then click the file again and the filename becomes selected, ready for replacement or editing. (You'll do this accidentally all the time. Just press the Esc key on your keyboard to cancel.)

▶ **Type the icon's new name.**

Name the file **My First Writing Assignment**.

TIP

You can edit an icon's name just as you edit any text in Windows. Normally you just type a new name, which replaces the old one. However, you can use the cursor keys, Backspace, Delete, and other editing keys.

▶ **Press Enter to lock in the new name.**

If you see a dialog box telling you that the file cannot be renamed, read the message. It generally tells you which of the 72 file-renaming errors you've violated. (The number isn't 72—I just pulled that number out of a hat.) Try renaming again.

See the sidebar "Basic File-Naming Rules and Regulations," later in this chapter for more information about what you can and cannot name a file.

If you're using the As Web Page option on the View menu, you might have trouble renaming some files. For example, a graphics file would be previewed on the left side of the window (the Web page). If you try to rename a file, Windows always switches to preview the file instead. In that case, turn off the As Web Page option.

- Don't rename any file, icon, or folder you didn't create yourself.
- Don't rename any files in the Windows or Program Files folders.
- You cannot rename a file with the same name of another file in the same folder. If you try, Windows displays an ugly warning dialog box. Close the dialog box, and then try renaming your file again.
- You can rename only one icon at a time. You cannot select a group of files and rename them at one time (you could in DOS, but not in Windows). See the section, "Crowd Control (Working with Groups of Files)."

Don't rename programs. Sure, it would be cute to rename WordPerfect as DoodleWriter. Unfortunately, that name might give you some problems when Windows claims that it can no longer find WordPerfect (because it was renamed).

- You can give two files of different types the same name. It's possible, for example, to have both a WordPad and Paint file named Airplane Food in a folder. But two WordPad files named alike? No way.

The rules for naming also apply to folders. With folders I urge you even more so to be brief and descriptive. It's just easier to read the names under the icons and to navigate the various directory collapsible tree structures with shorter names.

- You can rename disk drives—not their letters, but rather the funky label-name (refer to Chapter 20).

Basic File-Naming Rules and Regulations

A filename can contain letters, numbers, and spaces.

A filename cannot contain any of these characters:

" * / : ? \ ¦ < >

A filename can be any number of characters long, from 1 to 255. A 256-character filename is one character too many and probably ridiculous.

Although uppercase and lowercase letters look different onscreen, Windows doesn't notice any difference. You can save a file as May Schedule, and Windows still finds it when you type *may schedule* or even *MAY SCHEDULE*.

Crowd Control (Working with Groups of Files)

You can copy or move groups of files in the same way as you work with single files. The only difference is that you have to select more than one file in the first step. That way, you can treat the files as a group for a gang-copy or gang-cut. Obviously this technique is much more efficient than doing things one file at a time.

The remaining tutorials in this chapter merely select groups of files. To copy or move the group, refer to previous sections in this chapter. The Copy and Cut commands covered in those sections apply to groups as well as to individual files.

Selecting a Ragtag Group of Files with Ctrl+Click

To select more than one file at a time, press the Ctrl key as you click each file. This process is known as a *Ctrl+click* (control-click):

▶ **Open the My Documents window in Explorer (if it's not open already).**

You should have a few files in this folder. If not, go to one of your other folders that contains a large number of files. Go only to a folder you created; don't use any Windows folders.

▶ **Press and hold the Ctrl key.**

As long as the Ctrl key is pressed, Windows remembers which files you click.

▶ **Click an icon to select it.**

▶ **Click another icon to select it.**

Both icons are selected—a group!

▶ **Continue Ctrl+clicking icons to select a group.**

For example, you could Ctrl+click all your graphics icons to select them and then move them to the Graphics folder. Figure 24.3 illustrates this concept.

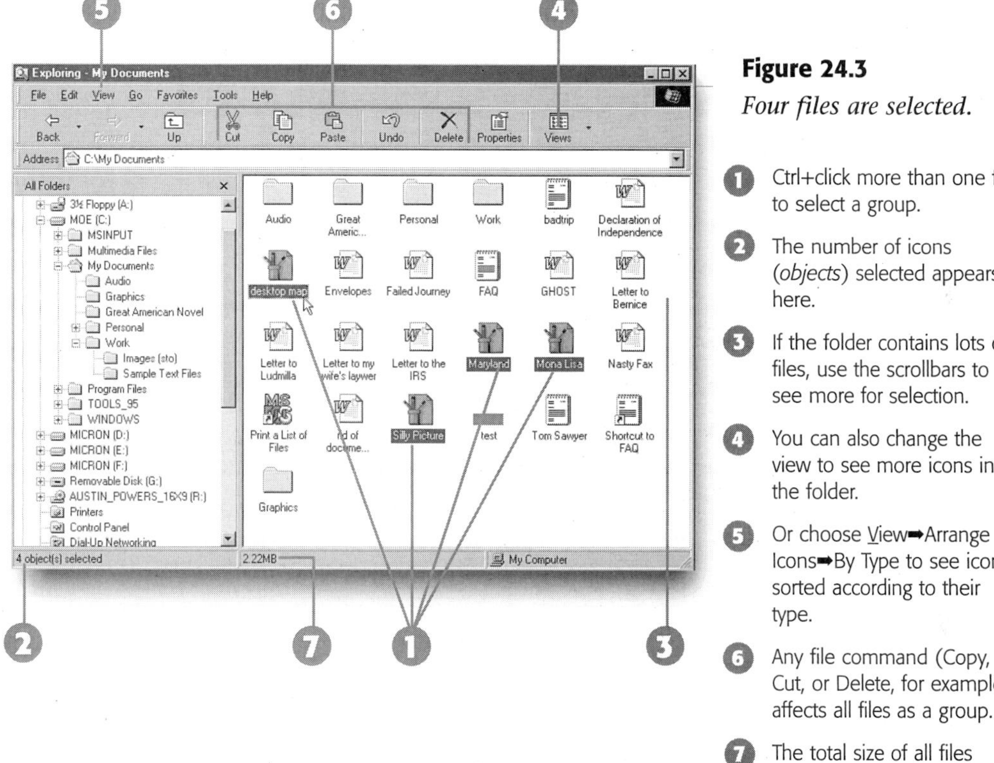

Figure 24.3
Four files are selected.

1. Ctrl+click more than one file to select a group.
2. The number of icons (*objects*) selected appears here.
3. If the folder contains lots of files, use the scrollbars to see more for selection.
4. You can also change the view to see more icons in the folder.
5. Or choose View➡Arrange Icons➡By Type to see icons sorted according to their type.
6. Any file command (Copy, Cut, or Delete, for example) affects all files as a group.
7. The total size of all files selected.

At this point you would use the file command on the group of icons: Copy or cut them (or delete them, which is covered later in this chapter).

- You can select files in only one folder at a time. If you want to work with files in several folders, you must select each group in each folder, work with the files, and then move on to the next folder.
- You can drag the group of files as a unit: Press the button while pointing the mouse at any one of the selected files to drag, Ctrl+drag, or right-drag the group.

You can switch away from the window and do something else, and the files are still selected. Be careful where you click, though! If you click anywhere in the Explorer's right window other than on one of the selected files, you deselect the group and have to start over.

Calf-Ropin' Files

A wholly graphical way to corral a bunch of files into a group is to drag the mouse around them, as shown in Figure 24.4. This technique is good for selecting files when they're grouped together.

▶ **To select a group of files, drag the mouse around them.**

Figure 24.4 explains how to do this step. All files inside the "line of ants" become selected.

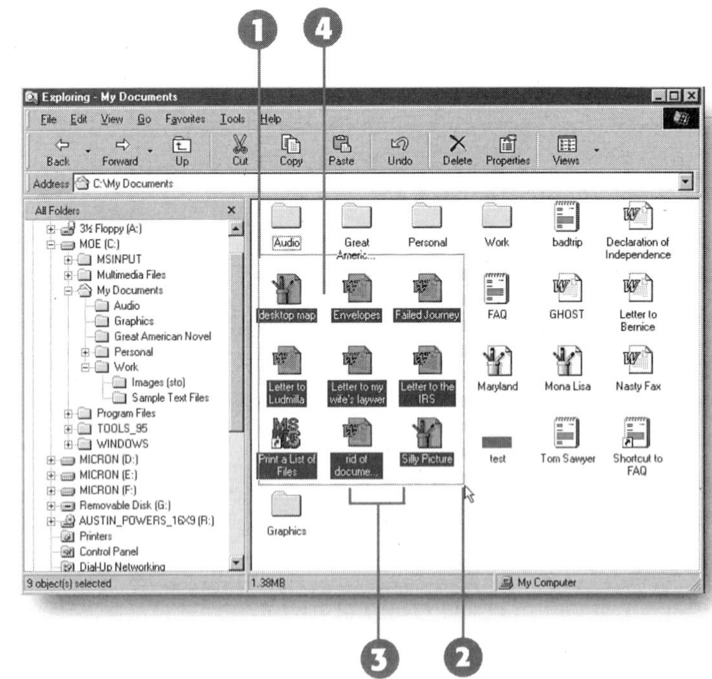

Figure 24.4
Dragging to select a group of files.

1. Start here.
2. Drag down to here.
3. A "line of ants" ropes in the files.
4. Selected files.

Often you're not blessed with having all your file's icons in a neat and nifty rectangle onscreen. If so, you can rope as many as you can, and then you can still Ctrl+click other rogue icons to make them part of the group.

Another trick: Drag to select a group of files. Then, to select another group, press and hold the Ctrl key. That technique selects the second group in addition to the first group. Figure 24.5 shows how to do it.

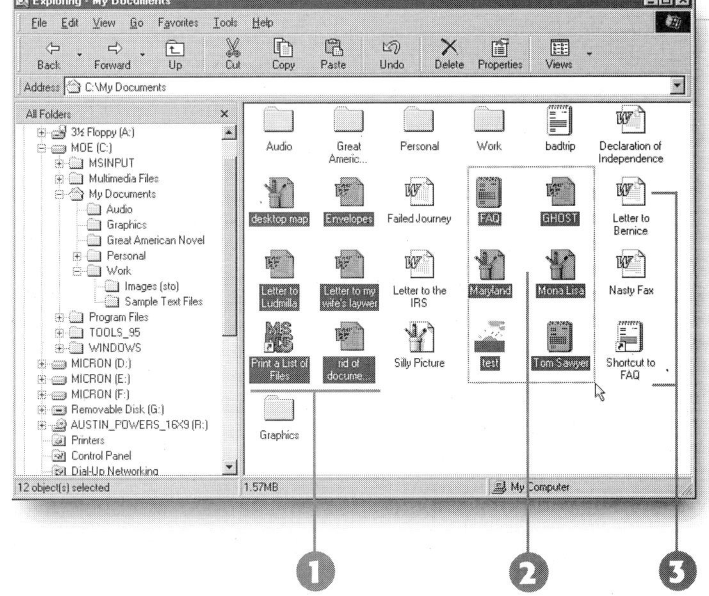

Figure 24.5

Selecting two groups of files.

1. This group is selected, as shown in Figure 24.4.
2. The Ctrl key was pressed as the mouse was dragged to select this group too.
3. You can select additional rogues by Ctrl+clicking them.

Selecting a Line of Files with Shift+Click

Suppose that you want to select all files of a certain type in a window. For example, you want to move all your WordPad documents. You could just Ctrl+click to select each one, but that's a pain. An easier way is to arrange the window to show WordPad documents together:

▶ **Choose View➡Arrange Icons➡by Type.**

Be careful when you're using the Ctrl key while you're dragging over a group of files to select them. If you miss your timing, you *copy* selected files rather than select them. Because Ctrl+drag is a copy operation that affects selected files, make sure that you press the Ctrl key, pause, and then drag to lasso a bunch of files.

The icons appear in the window sorted according to their file type (or which program created them).

If you're using Large Icon view, it might not be possible to see how things are arranged. Better choose List view instead:

- ▶ **Choose View➡List.**

Or you can click the Views button on the toolbar until List view appears, as shown in Figure 24.6.

Figure 24.6

Selecting files by Shift+clicking.

1. Click here to select the first item in the group.
2. Shift-click here to select the final item in the group.
3. All items between the two items are selected.
4. You can choose List view from here.

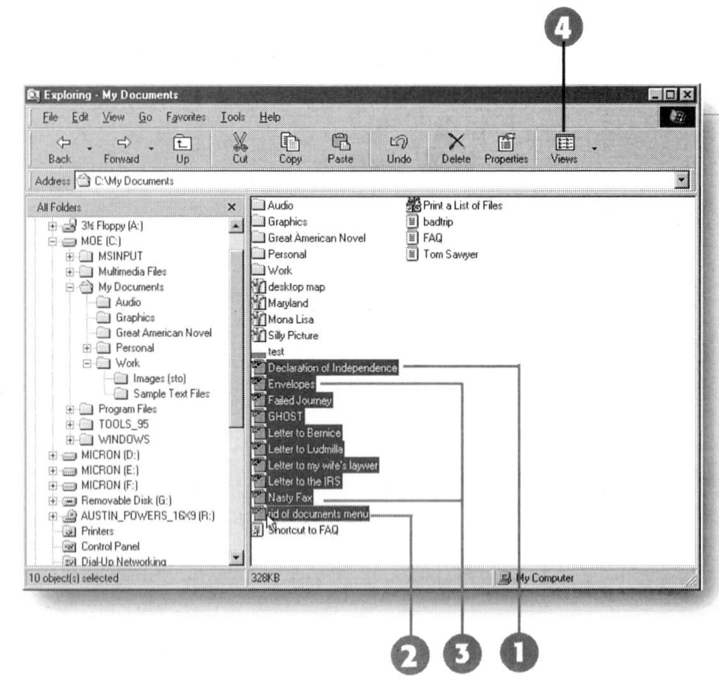

- **Click the first file on the list.**
- **Shift+click the last file on the list.**

All files (of the same type) between them are selected.

This technique works to select files in sequence no matter how the window displays them. If the files are displayed alphabetically, you can select them from *A* to *Z* or from *1* to *9* or from *M* to *X* or whatever.

(To restore the window to the way it was, choose View➡Arrange Icons➡by Type and then View➡List.)

Selecting the Whole Dang Doodle

If you're not discriminating about which files you select, you can select them all (the whole dang doodle)—all the files in a folder. It's easier than it sounds:

Choose Edit➡Select All.

Or you can press the handy Ctrl+A shortcut key combo. Whatever—everything in that window is selected.

If the window contains hidden files or folders, you see a dialog box asking whether you want to select the hidden file or folder too. Choose OK. Because hidden files generally relate somehow to other files in the folder, you should probably move or copy them too.

Leave all the files selected for the next section's tutorial.

Unselecting Selected Files

Suppose that you select your group of files by using one of the techniques mentioned in this chapter (such as Select All), and in addition to all the files in the window, some folders and other whatnot are also selected. Don't fret. Unselecting them is easy:

- **Ctrl+click files to deselect them.**

When you Ctrl+click a selected item, you unselect it.

Unselect the folders in the My Documents window. Ctrl+click each of them until only the documents in that window are selected.

You can also use the Ctrl key when you drag over files to unselect them.

- **Choose Edit➡Select All.**

Again, all the files are selected. You don't want the folders to be selected, however.

▶ **Press the Ctrl key.**

▶ **Lasso the folders.**

Drag the mouse around the folders as though you were selecting them. A-ha! Because you have the Ctrl key pressed, you're deselecting the folders.

▶ **Release the Ctrl key.**

You can also do it backward: Suppose that you want now to select all the folder icons in the My Documents window.

Don't do a thing! Although you can select the folders in a number of ways, you should have all files *except* the folders selected. You can easily reverse that situation:

▶ **Choose Edit➡Invert Selection.**

Whoa! All the deselected files are now selected and vice versa. I use this trick all the time when I want to select all except a single file in a folder: I select the file and then choose Edit➡Invert Selection. It saves time.

You can close the Explorer window now.

- Ctrl+clicking a selected file does not affect other files selected in the window. It merely unselects the file you Ctrl+clicked.
- You can also use the Ctrl key while dragging over selected files to unselect them.

If you accidentally copy files when you're using the Ctrl key to select, press Ctrl+Z to undo the Copy command.

Working with groups of files is one of the major weaknesses in Windows. When it comes to moving or copying a group of files, an experienced DOS user can beat the pants off any Windows user.

Chapter 25

Using the Send To Command

Questions Answered and Thoughts Inspired

- Finding the Send To menu
- Using the Send To menu
- Adding to the Send To menu
- Removing commands from the Send To menu

Every cloud has a silver lining. It took me until the age of 18 to realize what that means. I would rather say that every pile of trash contains some jewels. That's true, you know: Someday the technology will exist to sift through landfills for lost silver, gold, and jewelry—stuff people accidentally throw out all the time.

If you've discovered the Send To menu in Windows, you too have found a jewel in the rubbish heap (not to draw a direct analogy or anything). Windows isn't junk; it's just messy and random. Occasionally, however, a brilliant idea shines through. This chapter is about this type of idea: the Send To menu, which can be oh-so-very handy.

Hello, Send To Menu

Attached to every file and folder in Windows is a pop-up menu. The pop-up menu, or *shortcut* menu, contains lots of common commands for doing things depending on which icon you click.

Common to all folder and file icons is the Send To submenu. It provides a quick way to send the icon to another location or program in Windows. Figure 25.1 sorts things out.

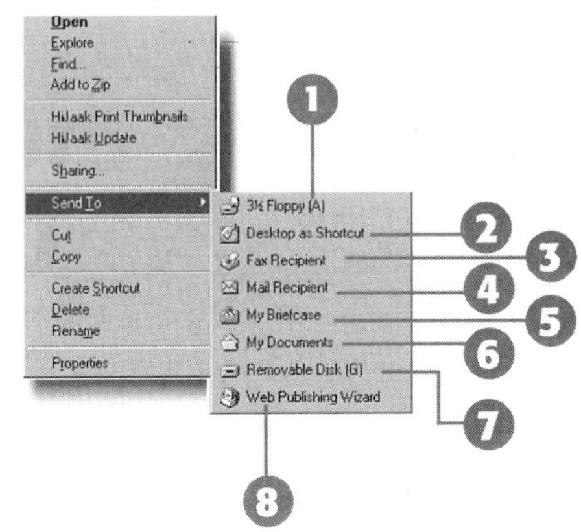

Figure 25.1

The Send To menu in all its glory.

1. Copies a file to drive A.
2. Pastes a copy of the file on the desktop as a shortcut.
3. Sends the file as a fax or starts the Fax Wizard.
4. Sends the file as an attachment to an email message.
5. Briefcase.
6. Moves the icon to the My Documents folder.
7. Copies the icon to drive G (a ZIP drive, on this system).
8. Sends a copy of the file to the Web Publishing Wizard program.

The Send To menu you see on your computer is probably different. The reason is that it's totally customizable. Your programs might add their own items there, and you can add and remove items there. This chapter shows you how.

- The Send To menu's items work differently depending on the item. For example, sending a file to another drive *copies* the file. Sending the file to a folder (such as My Documents) on the same drive, however, *moves* the file.
- Each program on the Send To menu works differently with a file. Choosing the Fax or Email option attaches the document to a fax or email message. In some cases, the Send To menu might send the file to an application for processing, such as a graphics viewer or text-translation utility.

Using the Send To Menu

There's nothing magic about the Send To menu. It's just a shortcut, an easy way to transfer or put a file somewhere else.

Suppose that you're starting a new project and want to create a desktop shortcut for that project's folder:

- **Open the My Documents icon on the desktop.**
- **Open the Work folder.**

You created this folder and the following Sample Text Files folder for a tutorial earlier in this book:

- **Right-click the Sample Text Files folder to display its shortcut menu.**
- **Choose Send To ➡Desktop As Shortcut.**

A shortcut icon to the folder has been placed on the desktop. You probably need to get rid of the Work window, however, to see it.

- **Close the Work window.**

There, on the desktop, is the Shortcut to Sample Text Files folder.

Rename the folder as Sample Text Files, if necessary. Or you can just go ahead and delete the shortcut folder by dragging it to the Recycle Bin.

- The Send To command also appears on the File menu whenever one or more icons is selected.
- You can add your own items to the Send To menu or remove items you never use.

TIP

The number one thing I use the Send To menu for is copying files to drive A. At the end of my workday, I go to my project folder, select all the files, and then choose File ➡Send To ➡3 1/2 Floppy (A). It's much faster than Copy and Paste.

Adding Your Own Command to the Send To Menu

In my opinion, the way Microsoft sets up the Send To menu is merely a suggestion. You can put far more interesting and useful things on that menu than the silly bunch that's already there.

For example, one thing I always put on the Send To menu is Notepad. That way, if I ever find a file and have no idea what's in it, I can send it to the Notepad for a quick peek.

Shhhh! Items on the Send To menu are in the C:\Windows\SendTo folder.

- **Right-click My Computer.**
- **Choose Explore from the shortcut menu.**
- **Open drive C.**
- **Open the Windows folder.**
- **Open the SendTo folder.**

You might have to scroll down a few inches to find that menu. Inside you see all the items on the Send To menu, although here they appear as icons in the window—in fact, that's all they are. Figure 25.2 describes things.

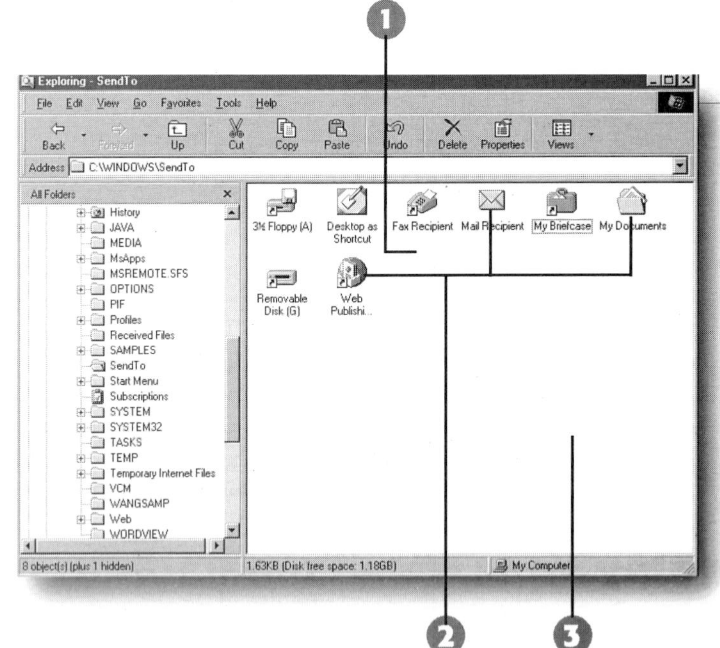

Figure 25.2
The Send To menu in all its glory.

1. Shortcut items have been pasted in here.
2. Some items are not shortcuts; do not delete them.
3. Lots of room for other stuff!

To add the Notepad program to the list of items on the Send To menu, all you have to do is paste in a shortcut. Notepad lives in the Windows directory.

- **Click the Up button.**

Scroll through the file list in the Windows folder to look for the Notepad icon.

▶ **Right-click the Notepad icon.**

▶ **Choose Copy from the shortcut menu.**

▶ **Click the Back button.**

▶ **Choose Edit ➡Paste Shortcut.**

You had better rename the shortcut. The command Send To ➡Shortcut to NOTEPAD reeks of "Amateur!"

▶ **Press F2.**

▶ **Rename the icon as** Notepad.

Now the menu says Send To ➡Notepad, which looks like an okay Windows command to me. Prove it: Right-click the Notepad icon, and choose Send To to view the menu. It should say just Notepad. Nifty.

Now, try out your shortcut.

Lots of mystery files are on your computer. Chapter 26 gives you some hints on how to discover what the files are all about. Some files you just have to peek at, however, to see whether they're worthy of anything.

▶ **Choose drive C.**

On the left side of the window, scroll up and select drive C. You see files in the root folder on the right side of the window.

Among the files you see should be some "log" files: SCANDISK.LOG or SYSMON.LOG. These files have a generic icon, as shown in the margin.

▶ **Right-click SYSMON.LOG.**

If you don't have SYSMON.LOG, you can choose another file, such as AUTOEXEC.BAK or CONFIG.BAK.

▶ **Choose Send To ➡Notepad.**

The file appears in Notepad for viewing. (Or, if the file is huge, WordPad opens it.) What does it mean? I don't know. The Send To command works, though.

Look only! Don't mess with unknown files you might open in Notepad!

▶ **Close Notepad.**

Notepad is only partially useful. I use it to view C language source code files quickly and to edit them if necessary. (Notepad loads more quickly than my C programming software.)

Keep the Explorer window open for the next section's tutorial.

- If you have lots of graphics files, put a shortcut to your graphics file viewer (such as HiJaak) on the Send To menu. That way, you can send files there that might otherwise be opened by the programs that create them.
- You can add folders to the Send To menu: Choose the folder and copy it, and then paste a shortcut in the SendTo folder. For example, create a new folder in My Documents and name it Hell. Then put a shortcut to that folder in the SendTo folder. That way, every shortcut menu boasts a Send To ➡Hell command.
- To put a disk drive on the Send To menu, right-click the drive's icon in My Computer and choose Create Shortcut from the pop-up menu. Although the drive's shortcut icon has to be placed on the desktop first (Windows insists), you can drag it from there in the SendTo folder's window.
- If a file you want to view is too large for Notepad, Windows prompts you to open WordPad instead. This switch is fine; the Send To ➡Notepad command still does its job, and you can preview the file.
- Yes, I know that I told you never to mess with the Windows folder or any of its subfolders. For this particular folder (and others I specifically tell you about), it's okay—within limits, of course.

Removing Commands from the Send To Menu

You can edit the Send To menu as well as add to it. For editing, you can rename an icon to rename the command, or you can delete an icon to utterly remove the command. This feature is handy, especially if your Send To menu has commands you *know* that you'll never use (like, say, that My Briefcase icon).

Continue the preceding section's tutorial:

▶ **Open to the Windows\SendTo folder on drive C.**

The folder has three icons you shouldn't delete (at least it does in Figure 25.2 on my system):

- *Desktop As Shortcut*—Copies the file (or files) as a shortcut on the desktop
- *Mail Recipient*—Attaches the file to an email message
- *My Documents*—Moves or copies the file to the My Documents folder

Notice that none of these icons is a shortcut. They're all in the folder by some other mysterious means, which implies that they would be a bear to replace, so just leave them alone.

Everything else—all the shortcut icons in the SendTo folder, are available for deleting.

▶ **Select the icon you want to remove.**

No one uses My Briefcase. No one! I'm serious. You don't need it. Delete its icon.

▶ **Press the Delete key on your keyboard.**

Press **Y** for Yes if you're asked to confirm deleting the file. You are.

The useless My Briefcase item has been removed from the menu.

Feel free to delete any other icons or menu items from the folder if you feel that you'll never use them. If this advice troubles you, give yourself about six months of using Windows. If, after that, you never use any of those commands, delete them.

No one wants a gallimaufry of things on the Send To submenu.

You can close the Explorer window. The tutorial is over.

Chapter 26

Essence of a File

Questions Answered and Thoughts Inspired

- Determining what's in a file
- Using a file's icon to identify the file
- Using the Quick View command
- Playing an icon
- Viewing an icon's properties
- Understanding file types and extensions
- Discovering file associations

No man (or woman, for that matter) could behold the face of the gorgon and live. One fatal look into Medusa's eyes turned you to stone. Hair stylists would probably faint at the mere sight of her hair. I mean, how do you brush snakes?

Medusa could make life easier on everyone by wearing a mask—maybe a mask with a nice, pleasant picture on it. In Windows, computer information is truly an electronic gorgon: Viewing raw binary data would surely make you turn to stone. Fortunately, Windows has other ways of representing the data in a file. Primarily, it uses icons to put a pleasing face on data. Haven't you noticed that the little picture often has nothing to do with what's in the file? Or how about mystery files? Who really knows what's in them?

This chapter is about basic file ID. What's in a file? How does the icon relate to the file type? If you have snakes for hair, this chapter tells you how to make a stylish hair clip from hose clamps and PVC pipe.

What Is That File?

Who knows what evil lurks in the heart of files? Windows might know. You should know.

Ideally, a file's name and its icon should tell you a great deal. The name should describe the file's contents. The icon should tell you which type of file it is and whether it's a program, a document created by a specific program, or what.

If you're curious about a file's contents, you can pull several tricks to divine what the file is all about:

✓ Try to identify the file by its name or icon.

✓ Use the file's Quick View command to peek inside.

✓ Use the file's Play command to see or hear its contents.

✓ Use the file's Open command to attempt to run it.

Although these items might sate your curiosity, sated or not, you should never delete or move any file you're unfamiliar with. Even if it's just an innocent 'lil 20KB text file.

If you didn't create it, don't mess with it.

- The lesson to learn here is that you should properly name your files short, sweet, and to the point.
- Unfortunately, you can't do anything about the icons and how they identify a file. Windows makes up icons and assigns them as it sees fit. Alas, it's not very good at it.

Identifying Icons

Windows uses a handful of icons to recognize popular types of files. This section lists only a few of them.

Text documents contain plain text. Notepad creates these files, and you can open and save them in WordPad as a text document (plain text, ASCII, or MS-DOS text).

Paint creates *bitmapped* graphics files.

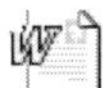

The icons for WordPad documents look the same as the icons for Microsoft Word documents. They're both "doc" (for *doc*ument) files.

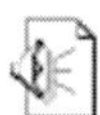

Wave files play sounds on your computer. All sound files have this icon and can be opened (or played) so that you can hear the sound.

MIDI files play music. Opening them runs a MIDI player program that operates your computer's on-board synthesizer and plays beautiful music. La-la-la!

Web pages and other HTML documents appear with the Internet Explorer icon on them. Although these are plain-text documents (you *could* use Notepad to view them), to see them with all their formatting and graphics, you have to view them in Internet Explorer.

DOS batch files have a gear on them. These files contain DOS commands in a list. When a batch file program runs, the DOS commands execute one after the other. Although you can use Notepad to edit this type of file, unless you know batch file lingo, you can do little else.

Some configuration files are special text files. Notice that the icon looks like a text file with a tiny gear on it. Although you can use Notepad to edit or modify these files, unless you know what to change or add in them, it's best not to mess with them.

DOS programs are given a generic "program" icon, which looks like a plain window. You can open these programs to run them, although they run best in DOS mode.

Program files generally have their own unique icons. Chances are that if you see a unique icon, such as old Sol in the margin, it's probably a program you can open and run. Even so, not every program you run does something fun. I run programs all the time just to see what they do and often have to reset my computer to get control again. Be careful!

When Windows doesn't recognize a program, it slaps the generic icon on it. That's a good sign not to mess with the file: Don't open it, rename it, or move it, and especially don't delete it.

Your programs also have their own icons. Although you eventually grow familiar with them—honestly!—it's tough sometimes to tell what a file is by just looking at its icon.

Using Quick View

Every icon in Windows has attached to it a shortcut menu. Most of the shortcut menus have a Quick View command available, which lets you see a preview of the file's contents.

▶ **Right-click the My Computer icon.**

▶ **Choose Explore.**

- **Open drive C.**
- **Open the Program Files folder.**
- **Open the Internet Explorer folder.**

The folder contains a selection of several file types, some of which you should recognize from the preceding section: text files, DOS program files, and regular (Windows) program files. Still, these files are a mystery. Rather than just run them to see what they do, you can use the Quick View command:

- **Right-click the REGEXP file.**
- **Choose Quick View.**

The Quick View window appears, attempting to explain what it found inside the file, as shown in Figure 26.1. Divine what you can from this information. All I see is the top part, Windows Executable, which tells me that it's a program and I probably should leave it alone.

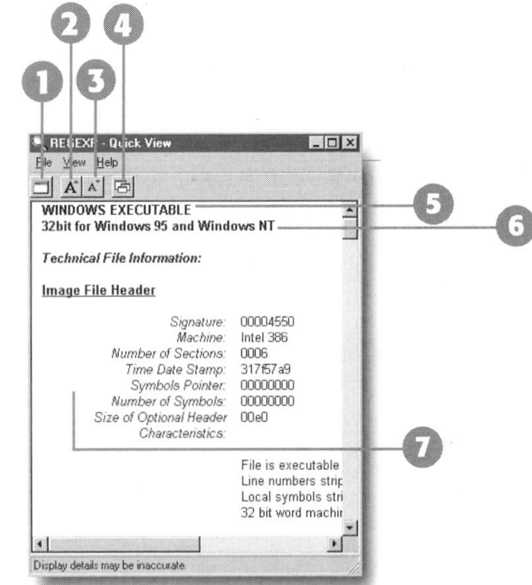

Figure 26.1

The Quick View window looks at a program.

1. Open (run) the icon you're viewing.
2. Zoom in.
3. Zoom out.
4. Tells Windows to use this Quick View window to preview all files as opposed to opening a new Quick View window every time.
5. File contents.
6. This line means that it's a Windows program.
7. Yet, it really is technical.

- **Close the Quick View window.**
- **Choose the My Documents folder from the left side of the window.**

Locate a WordPad icon. (Or, if you know where you've put the WordPad documents you created elsewhere in this book, go to that folder instead.)

- **Right-click the WordPad icon.**
- **Choose Quick View.**

The contents of the WordPad document are displayed in the window as a preview.

- **Close the Quick View window.**

Continue examining icons with Quick View. Keep the Explorer window open for the next section's tutorial.

- Not every icon has a Quick View command.
- If you don't see a Quick View command there, don't bother with the icon; later sections in this chapter tell you how to deal with those icons—what I call the "open with" icons.
- Quick View is actually a program, QUIKVIEW. You can find it in the Windows\System\Viewers folder.

The Play Menu Option

Some types of files don't need a Quick View command. Instead, these *multimedia* files have a Play command on their shortcut menu that lets you see or hear the file as a preview. That can be fun.

- **Open the Windows\Media folder on drive C.**

Open the Windows folder, and then choose the Media folder to display its contents.

If you don't have a Media folder, you can use the Find command to locate WAV or MIDI files on your PC (this subject is covered in Chapter 27).

- **Right-click a MIDI file.**

MIDI files contain digital music that plays on your PC's synthesizer. Locate a MIDI file with an icon like the one shown in the margin. On my PC, I pick the Brandenburg Concerto.

Notice that the Quick View command is gone. Instead you see two options: Play and Open. Play plays the media file, whereas Open might also play it or open it in the program that created it.

- **Choose Play.**

We're rockin'! See Figure 26.2.

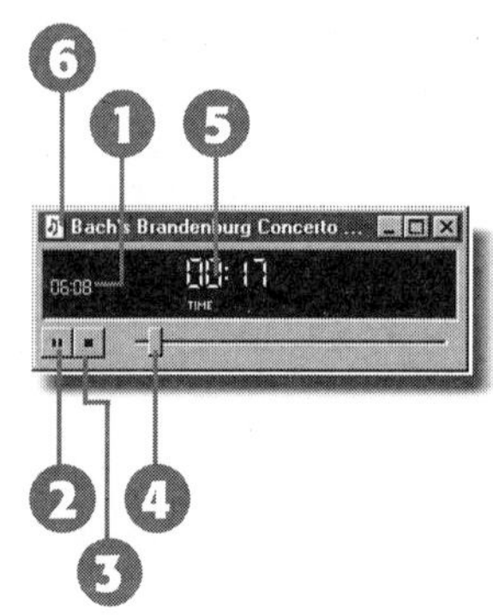

Figure 26.2
A MIDI file fills the halls with music.

1. Total time for the song.
2. Pause/Play button.
3. Stop button.
4. Progress/position slider.
5. Length of time the song has played.
6. Right-click in here to see a control menu.

Stop the song if you want, or wait out the whole 6 minutes and 8 seconds.

▶ **Right-click a sound file.**

Sound (or "wave") files contain recorded audio bits—like on a tape recorder. Some of them are funny sounds, some are music bits, and some are recorded bits of TV shows or films. On my PC, I found the Robotz Close file.

▶ **Choose Play.**

The sound file plays. There. Now you know what's in it.

Now you can spend about the next 15 minutes right-clicking and playing all the sound files in the folder. Go ahead—you have the time.

Keep the Explorer window open for the next tutorial.

- Animation and video files also have a Play command on their shortcut menus . Although you might not have these types of files on your system, some sample videos do come on the Windows 98 distribution CD.
- You can use the Find command to locate audio and video files all over your hard drive (see Chapter 27).
- See Chapter 41, "Sound Advice," for information about setting your PC's volume.

Checking a File's Properties

Another way to gather information about an icon is to examine its properties sheet. Sometimes this sheet can tell you a great deal about the file. Other times it shows you a bunch of trivia and nothing much else.

Continue from the preceding section's tutorial in the Windows\Media folder:

▶ **Right-click a MIDI file icon.**

For example, select the Brandenburg Concerto icon.

▶ **Choose Properties.**

The icon's Properties dialog box appears, as shown in Figure 26.3.

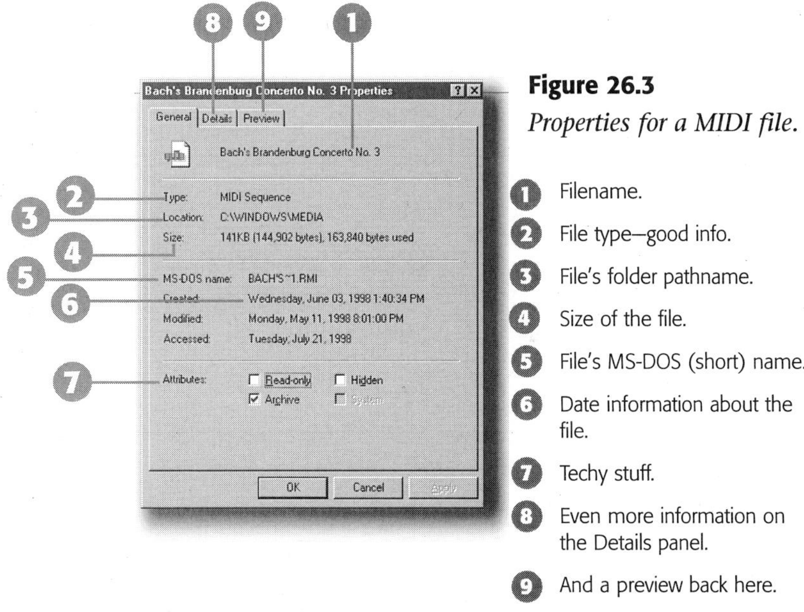

Figure 26.3
Properties for a MIDI file.

1. Filename.
2. File type—good info.
3. File's folder pathname.
4. Size of the file.
5. File's MS-DOS (short) name.
6. Date information about the file.
7. Techy stuff.
8. Even more information on the Details panel.
9. And a preview back here.

A MIDI file is easy to flag, primarily because of its unique icon. You see in the Properties dialog box, however, that the type is a MIDI sequence file—a dead give-away.

▶ **Click the Details tab.**

The Details panel offers even more information about the file, including lots of tidbits in the Other Information area.

▶ **Click the Preview tab.**

Finally, the Properties dialog box even lets you preview the file's contents. Remember that this preview is only for a MIDI file—and a few other multimedia files. Some unknown file types lack all this juicy information.

▶ **Click Cancel to close the Properties dialog box.**

Keep the Explorer window open for the next tutorial.

- Not every file's Properties dialog box gives you the juicy information that a MIDI file does. In fact, the "mystery files" in drive C's root folder have lousy, nondescript Properties dialog boxes.
- A Preview tab appears on sound files, MIDI music files, video clips, and other multimedia files. It enables you to view the file's contents.
- Summary and Statistics tabs appear on certain documents, such as Microsoft Word documents. They offer more information about the document, such as who wrote it, how long it is, and whether it's a good read.
- If you check the properties of a shortcut icon, a special Shortcut tab appears. In that panel you can find out about the original file and change the shortcut file's icon.
- In addition to General, other tabs appear for other files, including the whole half-dozen that appear in a DOS program's properties dialog box.

A shortcut for the Properties command is to press the Alt+Enter key combination. This command is pretty universal throughout Windows for seeing various Properties dialog boxes.

Opening an Icon to See What's Inside

As a last resort, you can always open an icon just to see what it does; just remember the cat.

Curiosity killed the cat.

Curiosity, although it's good and all that, can also crash a computer. I did it just the other day, by opening a file to see what it did. Do you know what happened? Can you guess? I couldn't. Eventually I found out that the program scrambled the Windows graphics, giving the screen a bad case of myopia. (That's probably not what was supposed to happen, but because I was messing around, that's what did happen.) I could use Windows, but I couldn't *see* anything. Not fun. Had to restart.

- If the file you open makes the computer act weird (or dead), reset your PC. Chapter 1 tells you how.
- Get this: Windows doesn't even let you open certain icons. When you make an attempt, an Open With dialog box appears. See the section, "The Mysterious File Associations" later in this chapter, for more information.

If you feel the urge to wantonly open a file, remember to save your work in other windows first.

The Exciting World of File Types and Filename Extensions

Windows assigns icons to files based on the file's type. For example, a MIDI file is a MIDI type, and a text file is a text-type. That's how Windows knows which program to run when you open a file and which icon to display for it. It can also cause some puzzlements:

These two icons apparently share the same name—which is technically not permitted. However, they're two icons of different types. One is a WordPad icon, and the other is a Paint icon. This situation is permissible because the icon's names are, in secret, *not* identical. Shhh!

- **Open the Windows Explorer if it's not open already.**
- **Browse to the My Documents folder.**

You should have the Explorer (and My Computer windows) configured now to display only a file's name. The second part of the name is the *extension*. It's the last part of the name, and it is what tells Windows the file type.

- **Choose View➡Folder Options.**

The Folder Options dialog box appears.

- **Click the View tab.**
- **Remove the check mark by Hide File Extensions For Known File Types.**

On the View panel, in the Advanced Settings area, locate the item Hide File Extensions For Known File Types. Removing the check mark there tells Windows to display the full filename for all files in a window.

- **Click OK.**

The change in the My Documents folder is subtle, primarily because your eye notices the icons more than the text underneath them. Look around. Graphics files end with BMP, WordPad documents end with DOC, and text files end with TXT. That's the filename extension.

The extension is usually a period followed by the last three letters of a filename. It tells Windows which type of file you have.

Viewing the extensions in a filename isn't necessary. In fact, it can be confusing, which is why you should configure Windows not to display the extensions (as I had you originally configure things in Part I).

For example, if you rename a file and forget the extension, Windows loses track of things. Suppose that you rename the Failed Journey file as My Trip. (You created the Failed Journey document in Part I; if it's not in your My Documents folder, use another WordPad file.)

▶ **Rename Failed Journey as My Trip.**

Select the Failed Journey icon. Press F2. Type **My Trip** and press Enter.

Warning! Figure 26.4 shows you the error message you should see. If you rename the file *without* the extension, Windows loses track of it.

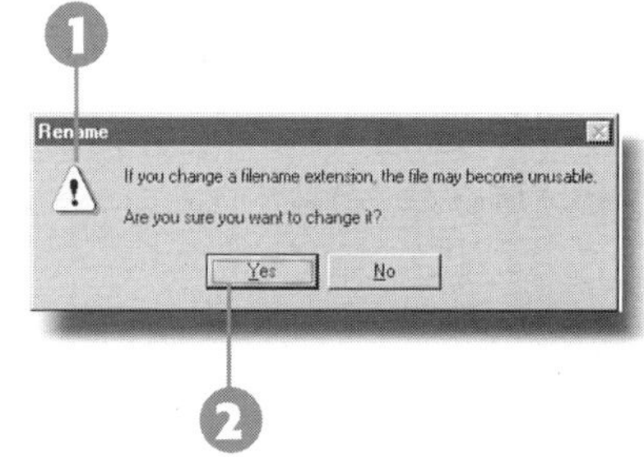

Figure 26.4
Oops! Better not rename the file.

1. You've renamed a file without a filename extension. That's bad.
2. Click here, and rename the file again.

▶ **Click Yes.**

I'm having you mess up on purpose: Clicking Yes renames the file. Now look at the icon. It's the ugly, generic, unknown-file-type icon. Egads!

The contents of the file have not changed; only the name has. Don't panic. You haven't lost information. In fact, you could drag the My Trip icon to the WordPad shortcut icon on the desktop, and it would open just fine. Just the file's name has been changed, although visually it stinks.

▶ **Rename the file as My Trip.doc.**

Select the file, and press the F2 key. Press the End key on your keyboard. Type a period and then **doc** and press Enter.

Ahhh. The icon is associated back to WordPad.

Now you know why I had you configure Windows not to display the extensions.

When Windows hides extensions, you don't have to worry about them when you rename files. In fact, as long as you can recognize their icons, you don't ever have to see their extensions. It just junks things up. With extensions visible, however, you *must* rename the file with the extension, or else you screw things up.

Ummm...

Rehide the extensions, please:

- **Choose View→Folder Options.**
- **Click the View tab.**
- **Restore the check mark next to Hide File Extensions for Known File Types.**
- **Click OK.**

Notice that the option says "Hide File Extensions for Known File Types." That implies that unknown file types *do* in fact display their extensions. Wanna see?

- **Choose drive C from the left side of the window.**

Several random files clutter drive C's root folder. You should see among them some with unknown file type extensions: LOG, BAK, and DOS, for example. Because they're file types Windows doesn't know about, it slaps on the generic icon. Even so, you can often tell what's in a file:

- ✓ *BAK*—Backup file, or a copy of an original. Unfortunately, BAK is generic. For example, if you have Microsoft Word create backups of your documents, it gives them the BAK extension. Even though the backups are Word documents, they have an unknown file type according to Windows.
- ✓ *LOG*—Log file, or a recording of some computer activity. Notepad can read this type of file (usually a text file). Read more about it in the following section.
- ✓ *DOS*—DOS configuration file, usually a backup of an original. This type of file might be used when a computer is started up in DOS mode.

Zillions of unknown file types and extensions exist. I know about the ones in the preceding list because, well, it's my job! Generally speaking, you shouldn't mess with any file of an unknown type. You can peek, but don't modify, move, or delete the file.

Keep the Explorer window open for the next section's tutorials.

- Your programs register their icons and file types with Windows when the programs are installed. That way, Windows can display icons for your programs and their data files.
- Windows knows a file type by examining the file's name, more specifically, its extension.
- The extension is merely the last part of a filename, beginning with a period and having one to three letters.

When you have the Hide File Extensions for Known File Types option set, you cannot change an icon's extension with the Rename command. Only when that option is turned off can you change an icon's extension. The reason you would want to do that is questionable, but my point is that you cannot "force" a text document to become a WordPad document by changing its name.

- Hey! Remember choosing a file type when you're saving a document in WordPad? It's the same thing here: A file's format is associated with a certain three-letter extension known to Windows. Nifty, huh?
- You can find more information about customizing folders in Chapter 39, "A View to a Folder."
- Sorry to keep bringing this subject up, but don't mess with unknown files, even if you feel the urge (which might be as strong as your desire to eat)! If you really want to mess with files, you should learn about the UNIX operating system, where messing with files becomes a passion.

Some four-letter extensions exist. Only one comes to mind: HTML, for identifying Web page documents.

The Mysterious File Associations

When you install new software, it tells Windows about its file types and filename extensions. Although this subject is techy stuff you're normally free to ignore, this chapter is about teaching you what's in a file, so I suppose that you're interested in this sort of thing.

Telling Windows which filename extensions belong to which types of files and mixing in icons makes for a heavy brew. The whole deal is called file association, and it sounds like some brotherly organization, although it's not. *File association* means telling Windows, "This file is a blah-blah type of file, with these contents, edited by this program and with this icon."

See? It's nice that Windows does all this stuff automatically.

Windows uses a file association list to keep track of all the files it knows about. You can review this list from any My Computer or Explorer window.

Continue from the preceding section's tutorial:

- **Choose View➡Folder Options.**
- **Click the File Types tab.**

The list of File Associations is shown in the Folder Options dialog box (see Figure 26.5).

- **Click the Bitmap Image file type.**

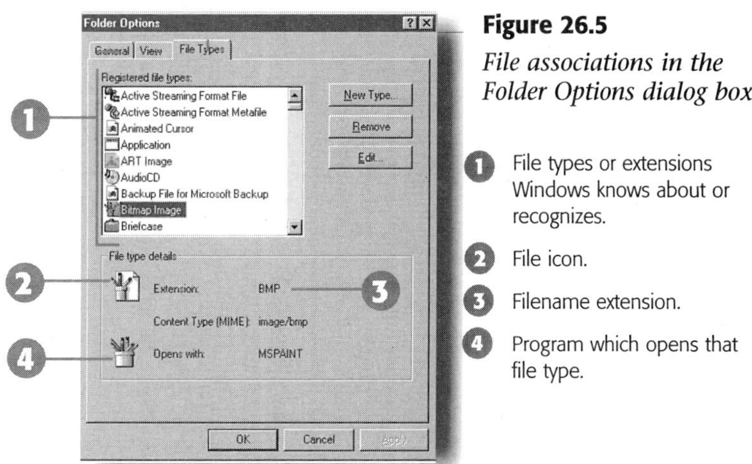

Figure 26.5
File associations in the Folder Options dialog box

1. File types or extensions Windows knows about or recognizes.
2. File icon.
3. Filename extension.
4. Program which opens that file type.

The dialog box tells you bundles about the Bitmap Image file type, as shown in the figure. You can see in the File Type Details area that a bitmap image file has an icon, filename extension, and associated program, Paint. All files ending in BMP share these characteristics.

▶ **Locate Text Document on the list.**

Scroll down to find the Text Document item.

▶ **Click Text Document once to select it.**

Notice how the text document has several extensions associated with it? It means that Notepad can open several types of files. Although they're all text files, they have different extensions.

▶ **Click Cancel to close the Folder Options dialog box.**

▶ **Close the Explorer window.**

As you become more comfortable with Windows and curious about file associations, you might consider picking up a more advanced Windows book that discusses file associations in detail and how you can make up your own or edit existing associations. Although you don't have to know that stuff, if you're curious, it can be fun.

- Doesn't Windows have a great deal of file types? Makes you wonder why it needs them all. (Actually, in the old days, third-party developers sold those programs as utilities, whereas Microsoft supplied only the operating system. It seems that Microsoft is now trying to supply everything. I'm not making legal commentary here or anything—it's just true.)
- New programs install their own icons on the File Types list.

I wouldn't mess with the file type list if I were you. Some people can, although they're usually versed in the way Windows does things and know what they're doing.

Chapter 27

Hunting Down Files

Questions Answered and Thoughts Inspired

- Finding the Find command
- Finding a file by its name
- Finding a file by only part of its name
- Finding a file by its contents
- Finding a file by its file type
- Finding a file by its date

Oh where, oh where, did my little file go? Oh where, oh where can it be?

You should never lose files. Never. Following proper folder organization, as discussed in Chapter 23, means that you should always have a place for everything—even the junk.

Yeah, but everyone loses files now and then. You fumble the Save As dialog box and, lo, the file is stored somewhere else. To find it, whip out the Find command. This chapter tells you how best to employ this powerful tool. Study hard, and maybe the "Oh where, oh where" song will stop playing in your head.

Hello, Find Command!

You can find a file in two ways, whether you're desperate or not. The first way is to use the Find command on the Start Thing menu. Figure 27.1 shows the items on the Find submenu, although more often than not you use the Files and Folders command.

Figure 27.1
The Find submenu.

1. Find files, folders, and icons on your PC.
2. Find a computer on the network (boring).
3. Item put there by a third-party program, probably not on your PC.
4. Search the Internet (I recommend another approach in Chapter 30).
5. Search the Address Book. (I don't recommend that you use the Address Book because this item is useless.)

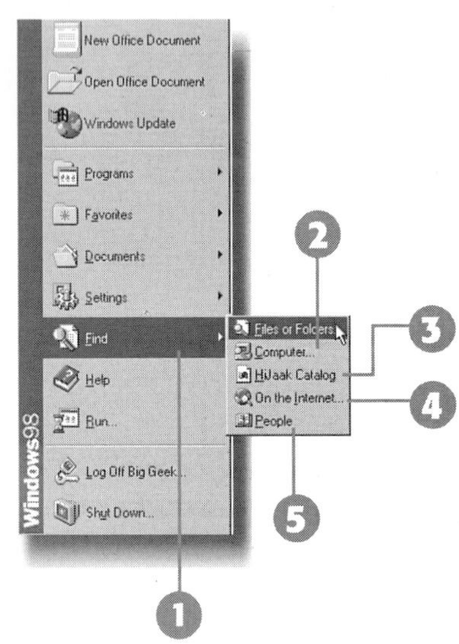

▶ **From the Start Thing menu, choose Find ➡Files and Folders.**

The Find Dialog box appears, as shown in Figure 27.2. Give it a look-see.

▶ **Close the Find dialog box.**

Another way to quickly find files is to press the F3 key. This keyboard shortcut works only when you see the desktop or have a My Computer or Explorer window open.

▶ **Open the My Computer icon.**

▶ **Press F3.**

Lo, it's the Find dialog box again.

▶ **Close the Find dialog box.**

▶ **Close the My Computer window.**

Now you know how to summon the Find dialog box. Finding specific things is covered in the remaining sections of this chapter.

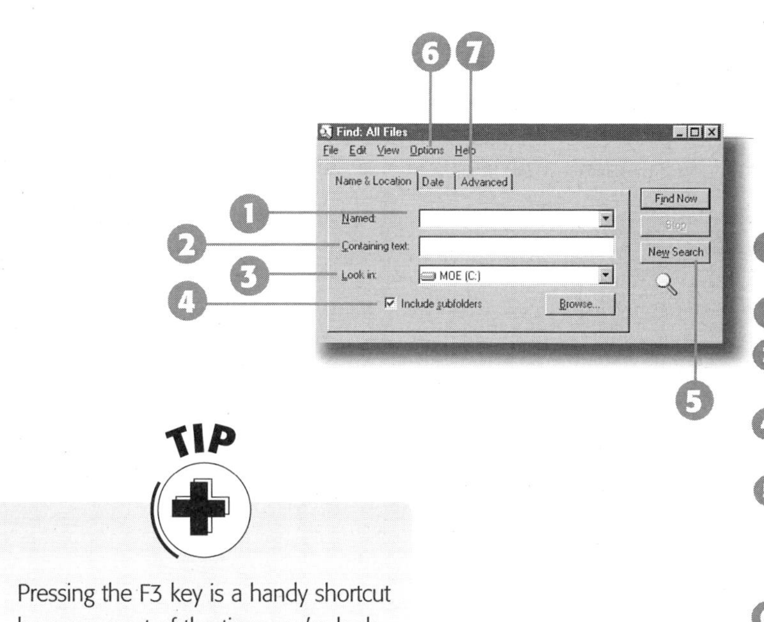

Figure 27.2
The Find dialog box.

1. Type or guess the name of the icon or folder here.
2. Type text to search for here.
3. On which drive to search (disk drives).
4. Always check this box to do a thorough search.
5. The start-over button resets all options (starts over without closing and reopening the dialog box).
6. Options for searching by date.
7. Options for searching by file type and size.

TIP

Pressing the F3 key is a handy shortcut because most of the time you're looking for files you're using the Explorer or My Computer window anyway.

- Lots of items are in the Find dialog box to help you locate a file. The following sections demonstrate the use of the more popular items in the dialog box.
- Every time you use the Find dialog box, all the options are reset. Unlike the Find command in a word processor, which remembers what you found last, the Find command in Windows starts out fresh every time.

You can use the Find command with a variety of options, as described in the following sections. For example, you can use date information along with a partial filename to locate a specific file. Don't think that because I've divided the information into sections in this chapter that you're somehow limited to using one Find technique at a time.

Finding a File When You Know Its Name

As long as you know the exact name of the file you've lost, it's easy to find it. (You don't even have to know the whole name, a subject that's covered in the following section.) Here are the steps to quickly find any lost file whose name you know:

1. Summon the Find dialog box.
2. Type the filename in the Named text box.
3. Choose My Computer from the Look in list.
4. Ensure that a check mark is next to the Include subfolders item.
5. Click Find Now.

The file, if it exists, is found and displayed in the bottom of the Find dialog box. From there you can see where the file is or just open it directly from the Find dialog box.

Alas, the Find command cannot locate your car keys or glasses—unless they're in a file on disk.

Normally you know exactly what you're looking for when it comes to finding a file. For the following tutorial, I've used the README filename. README is a file that usually comes with software or hardware products. It contains additional instructions and information about the product. Your hard drive is bound to have a few README files on it.

- **Summon the Find dialog box.**
- **Type** readme **in the Named box.**

You're looking for a file named readme. You don't have to type upper- or lowercase; Windows finds any matching letter.

- **Choose My Computer from the Look in drop-down list.**

If you're looking just on drive C, you can choose drive C. Or if you want to limit the search to all your PC's hard drives, choose Local Hard Drives from the list.

- **Put a check mark in the Include subfolders box (if one isn't there already).**

If you don't put a check mark there, Windows looks in only the folder you specify.

- **Click Find Now.**

Windows searches for *readme* and displays any matching files—and folders. Figure 27.3 shows the results it found on my computer.

If no files are found, Windows displays the message "There are no items to show in this view" and says "0 file(s) found" at the bottom of the dialog box. Boo-hoo.

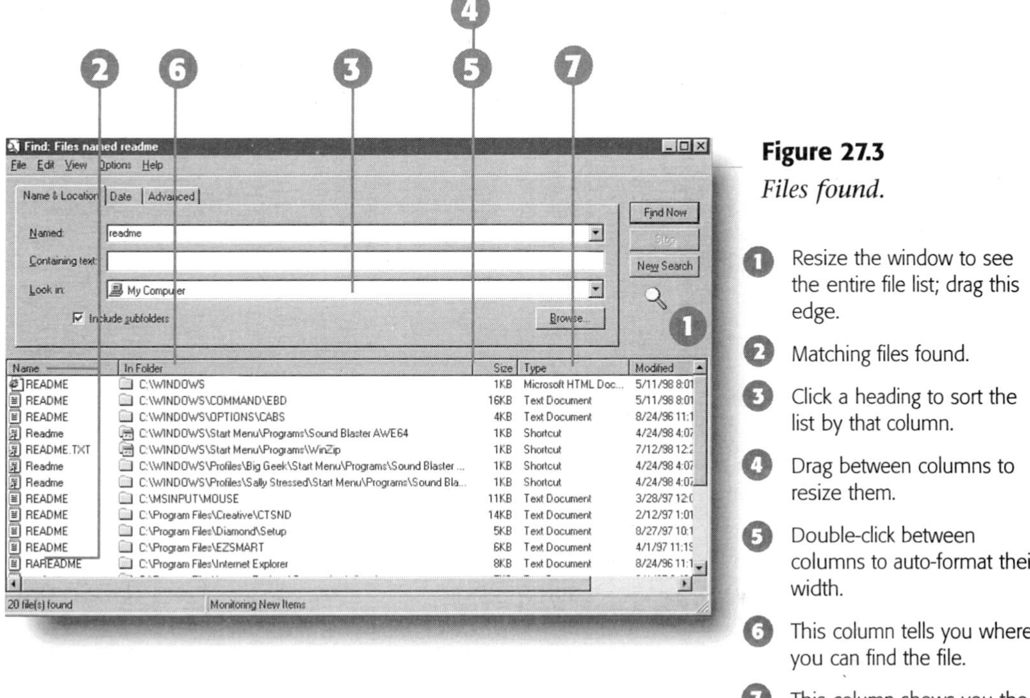

Figure 27.3
Files found.

1. Resize the window to see the entire file list; drag this edge.
2. Matching files found.
3. Click a heading to sort the list by that column.
4. Drag between columns to resize them.
5. Double-click between columns to auto-format their width.
6. This column tells you where you can find the file.
7. This column shows you the file type.

As is often the case, you might see more matches than you were looking for. That's when you use the In Folder and Type columns to confirm that it's the file you're looking for.

TIP

The results displayed in the Find dialog box are like a mini-My Computer window. You can open the files displayed there, drag them to other windows, and cut or copy them. Rename the icons. Delete them. Whatever.

Okay, enough about README files for now.

▶ **Close the Find dialog box.**

Or, if you need to search again, keep the dialog box open. Click the New Search button. Click OK to clear the current search and start all over.

- Did you notice how quick that was? Didn't take any time at all for the Find command to locate dozens of files all over your computer.
- Notice how the Find command found not only README files but also files with longer names that had the letters *README* in them? Call that convenient.

TIP

(Here's another tip, and I'll bet that you didn't know this: You can also use the file lists in the Save and Open dialog boxes like miniature versions of the Windows Explorer program. You can rename, cut, copy, or delete any file listed just about anywhere in Windows.)

- If it's important to you to search for a specifically named file, such as ReadMe rather than README or readme, choose Options ➡Case Sensitive from the menu.
- Personally, I'm a fan of Details view, which is normally how the Find dialog box displays its results (refer to Figure 27.3). However—just like with Explorer—you can change the view by using the View menu (just like with Explorer).

Finding a File When You Know Part of Its Name

I recommend saving files and documents by using brief descriptive names. For example, the name Grocery List for You and Please Don't Forget to Pick Up Junior at the Soccer Rally is a perfectly legal Windows name. (No, you don't go to prison for using that filename). If you forget where you put it, though, and *exactly* how it's written, it might take some time to find it...

Not so fast!

The Find command lets you find files when you know only a small part of the filename. You can use special characters called *wildcards* to substitute any or all of the characters you're fuzzy on.

Windows uses two wildcard characters:

✓ The * replaces a group of any letters, numbers, or characters in a filename.

✓ The ? replaces a single letter, number, or character in a filename.

Table 27.1 shows some examples of how this technique works.

Table 27.1 Using Wildcards

Filename	Matches These Files
win*	Any file that starts with win: wince, windbag, Windsor, windsurfing, wine cellar, wingding, wink, Winnebago, and winter, for example.
data	Any file that contains the word data: data, database, databank, viewdata, and rawdatafile, for example.
*up	Any file that ends in up: group, backup, checkup, cover-up, and go belly up, for example.
p?p	Any three-letter file that starts with p and ends in p: pip, pop, and pup, for example.
*.??t	Any filename and a three-letter extension ending in t: (too many to list).

You'll probably use the * wildcard more than the ? wildcard, as long as you know at least part of the filename.

- **Bring forth the Find dialog box.**
- **Type** *the* **in the Named box.**

You want to find any file with the word *the* in it, at the beginning, middle, or end of the filename.

- **Choose My Computer from the Look in drop-down list.**
- **Put a check mark next to Include subfolders (if one isn't there already).**
- **Click Find Now.**

Lordy! I didn't guess that Windows would find so many. My computer has 122 "the" files on it. That's a bunch.

Finding a filename with *the* in it was only a tutorial. Just the other day, I used this trick to search for a filename with *loan* in it. I knew that I had created that type of file but had no idea what the other part of the name was. (I knew that it was named "something-loan.") Using the Find command as just described, I searched for *loan and was able to locate the file quickly.

Close the Find dialog box if you want, or keep it open for the next section's tutorial. If you keep the dialog box open, click the New Search button. Click OK to clear the current search so that you can start afresh.

Finding a File When You Know What's in It

Sometimes a file's name just flies out the window, even if the window is shut and it's freezing outside. Filenames do that. As long as you remember some tidbit of text inside the file, though, Windows should be able to locate the file—or at least a small group from which you can pick.

The containing text box in the Find dialog box is designed to order the Find command to locate a specific snippet of text inside all the files you're searching. Although this type of search might take longer than a filename-only search, if that's all the information you have to work with, it's better than nothing.

▶ **Conjure up the Find dialog box.**

Because you don't know the filename, you have to leave the Named box blank.

Gads! Will it still work?

▶ **Type your name in the Containing text box.**

This step is known as an *ego search*. For example, I type **Dan Gookin** in the box to look for any file containing my name. You do the same, but with your name. (I would have put your name in this paragraph, but for legal reasons the publisher told me not to.)

▶ **Choose My Computer from the Look in drop-down list.**

▶ **Put a check mark next to Include subfolders (if one isn't there already).**

▶ **Click Find Now.**

This search might take awhile. Rather than find files by name, Windows has to open every file and look inside for the matching text. Depending on the size and number of files on your hard drive, it could take a few minutes.

Doh-dee-doh.

The amazing thing about this search is the strange places your name ends up. Don't panic! The computer doesn't "know things" about you. You entered your name when you first fired up Windows, remember? You're just seeing all the strange places on your hard drive where your name has ended up.

My test system's hard drive has 31 files containing my name, most of which are in my email directories. On my main writing computer are 290 files with my name, most of them containing the text *By Dan Gookin*. My main email computer has 1,719 matches with my name—lots of email. That makes sense. No conspiracy going on...

You can close the Find dialog box if you need a rest. Otherwise, reset it for the next tutorial: Click the New Search button. When you're asked whether you want to clear the current search, click OK.

Finding Files of a Certain Type

Ever wonder where Windows keeps its sound files? How about MIDI music files? Windows comes with lots of those. Video files? Well, you might have some of them on your hard drive too. Why not use the Find command to hunt 'em down?

- **Beckon the Find dialog box.**
- **Click the Advanced tab.**

The Advanced panel contains two options: one for choosing a file type and another for choosing a file size range (see Figure 27.4).

- **Choose MIDI Sequence from the Of type list.**

It's a long list. Remember that you can repeatedly press the M key to scroll to items starting with *M*.

The File Type option is often used in conjunction with another Find dialog box option—unless, well, you really do want to see where all the files of a certain type are located or just want to have them all in one window.

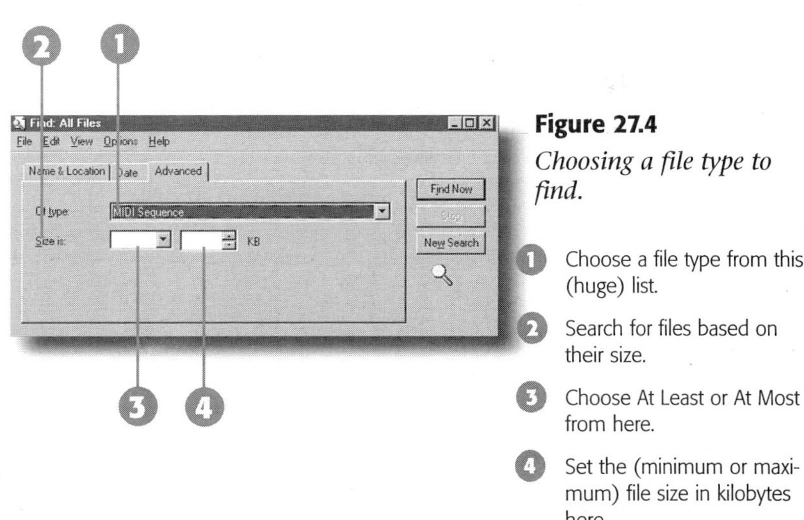

Figure 27.4
Choosing a file type to find.

1. Choose a file type from this (huge) list.
2. Search for files based on their size.
3. Choose At Least or At Most from here.
4. Set the (minimum or maximum) file size in kilobytes here.

- **Click the Name & Location tab.**
- **Choose My Computer from the Look in drop-down list.**

▶ **Put a check mark next to Include subfolders (if one isn't there already).**

▶ **Click Find Now.**

You should see some MIDI files in the Windows\Media folder as well as in folders for your PC's sound card and maybe for some games. If you have MIDI-composition software, you see some MIDI samples in its folder.

To play a MIDI file on the list, right-click it and choose Play.

You can play with the files some more or search again for other multimedia file types: wave sounds and video, sound, and movie clips.

You can close the Find dialog box now. Or, to continue with this chapter's final tutorial, click the New Search button and then click OK (when you're asked to clear the current search), and you're ready to search again.

- Refer to Chapter 26 for information about file types.
- You can choose the type Folder to find only folders, not files.

I use the Size is item on the Advanced panel in the Find dialog box to locate superhuge files on my computer—mostly for disk cleanup operations. For example, I set Size is to At Least and then enter 1000 KB (for one megabyte). The Find command then locates all 1MB (or heftier) files on my hard drive. If it finds any I created, especially if I no longer need them, they're banished to the Recycle Bin.

- The All Files and Folders option is used to match any file or any folder on your computer.
- The Windows 98 distribution CD definitely has WAV, MIDI, and video files. Use the Find command on that CD to locate them.

Finding Files Created in, Oh, Just the Past Few Days or So

You don't know the filename. You don't know the file type. You can't even remember what text you put in it—or maybe it was a graphics file that contains no text. Is the Find command useless? Are you stuck? Hardly.

As long as you know approximately *when* you last saved the file, Windows can still help you find it. You don't even have to know dates or times—just approximately how many days or months ago you remember saving the file.

▶ **Muster the Find dialog box.**

▶ **Click the Date tab.**

The Date panel contains several options for narrowing the date when a file was created, modified, or last accessed, as shown in Figure 27.5.

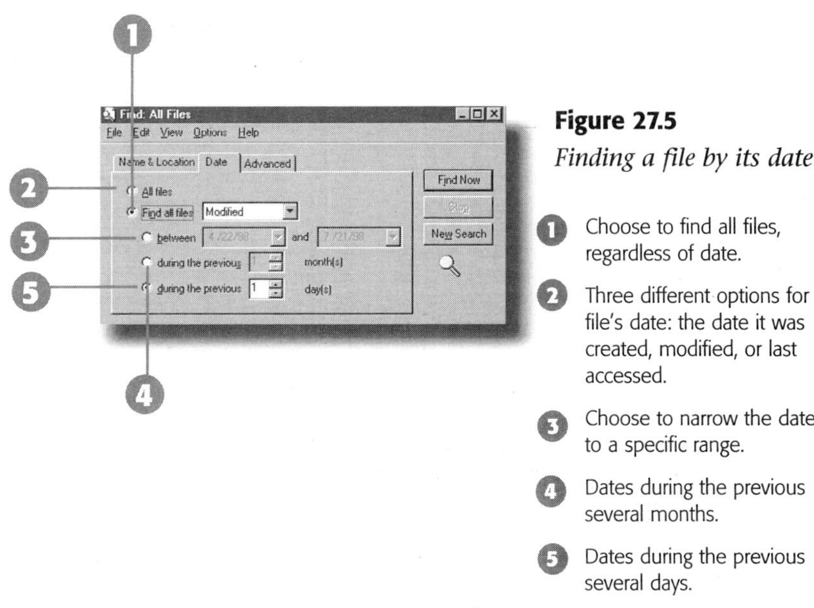

Figure 27.5
Finding a file by its date.

1. Choose to find all files, regardless of date.
2. Three different options for a file's date: the date it was created, modified, or last accessed.
3. Choose to narrow the dates to a specific range.
4. Dates during the previous several months.
5. Dates during the previous several days.

▶ **Choose Find all files and Created from the drop-down list.**

▶ **Choose during the previous.**

▶ **Enter** 2 **for day(s).**

Windows is about to find any file created during the previous two days. Don't forget the name and location information:

▶ **Click the Name & Location tab.**

Leave the Named text box blank. You want to find any file or folder created in the past two days.

▶ **Choose My Computer from the Look in drop-down list.**

- **Put a check mark next to Include subfolders (if one isn't there already).**
- **Click Find Now.**

The list of files found tells you, in a way, how busy you've been these past two days. Me? I'm on a deadline. My screen shows 81 files created! (Most of the files are from being on the Internet during the past few days. They're temporary files used to store images and other information from the Web pages you visit—temporary files, mostly.)

Don't forget that you can mix and match settings in the Find dialog box. The more information you provide for Windows, the more accurately it finds the file you're looking for.

If you were trying to find something on that list, you would simply scroll down and examine the filenames. Somewhere on the list is every file you've created, so if you've lost something on your computer, it's bound to be there. If not, adjust the number of days and search again.

Close the Find dialog box.

Ah. The tutorial is finally over!

Chapter 28

Deleting, Undeleting, and Recycling

Questions Answered and Thoughts Inspired

- Deleting files
- Deleting programs
- Using the deadly Delete command
- Recovering a file you've accidentally deleted
- Making adjustments to the Recycle Bin
- Emptying the Recycle Bin

Although deleting files might seem like a scary proposition, it is part of computer life. You delete files because you no longer need them, to free up disk space, or because they're old and useless. It's all a part of routine file maintenance, which, like sweeping the floor, is something you'd rather have someone else do.

This chapter discusses everything you need to know about deleting files and folders. It also covers the Recycle Bin, which is the hell where files go when they're deleted. Don't fret: You can undelete files when you rescue them from Recycle Bin hell. This chapter shows you how.

- Never delete programs or drag them to the Recycle Bin! Programs must be uninstalled (refer to Chapter 13).
- Don't forget Undo! The Undo command can instantly restore a file (or files) you've accidentally blasted to kingdom come! That's Edit ➡Undo or the Ctrl+Z keyboard shortcut.

Killing Off a File or Two

Deleting files can be scary at first. When I first used a computer, I never deleted anything. Then I filled up my first and only floppy disk. My choice was simple: Delete a few files, or buy another disk. At $8 for a 180KB 5 1/2-inch floppy disk, I began deleting files. I haven't stopped since.

Death to the file!

The choice of which files to delete is up to you. As you use your computer, you accumulate temporary or junk files all the time. Because I urge you to save everything (and you should), eventually you notice that many of those saved files are not necessary anymore. That's when you delete them. Or, if you've copied the files to a ZIP disk, for example, for long-term storage, you can delete the duplicates.

Never delete any file you personally did not create!

Please don't wantonly delete files—even if they're silly old README files off in some lowly folder for a program you think that you'll never use. Stupid old me deleted a README file like that once, and now I have a computer with a CD-ROM drive I can no longer access.

Deleting a File

In the film *Forrest Gump*, the character Bubba Blue goes on and on about how many ways you can fix shrimp: "Shrimp is the fruit of the sea."

Like those several dozen ways to fix shrimp, Windows must have a half-dozen ways to delete a file. Even so, only two steps are involved:

1. Select the icon you want to delete.
2. Kill off the file.

The variety comes in the method of terminating a file:

- **Open the My Documents folder.**
- **Delete a file.**

It doesn't matter which file you delete. Just pick any old random file and then choose one of these methods of execution:

- *Drag the icon to the Recycle Bin*—The best method if you can see the Recycle Bin icon on your desktop.
- *Right-click the icon and choose Delete*—My favorite because it's one quick action.

- *Select the icon, and then click the Delete button on the toolbar*—Not my style, but very toolbar-like if you're a toolbar fan.
- *Select the icon, and then choose File➡Delete*—A method that's too cumbersome for me. In fact, I don't think that I've ever deleted a file this way.
- *Select the icon, and then press the Delete key on the keyboard*—Awkward.

Windows might display a warning dialog box, asking whether you want to delete the file. I find this question insulting; I'm not so dumb as to go through any of the preceding motions and—oops!—make a mistake. On top of that, you can undelete with ease any file you delete, which I show you how to do before the end of this chapter.

▶ **Click Yes to delete the file if Windows warns you about it.**

The file is gone.

No, it's not: The file is not gone. It has been moved to the Recycle Bin for a while. That way, you can easily get it back if you need to. More about that in a few paragraphs.

Always click No when you're faced with the "program delete" dialog box.

Deleting a Program File

Never delete a program file! If you make the attempt, Windows warns you, as shown in Figure 28.1.

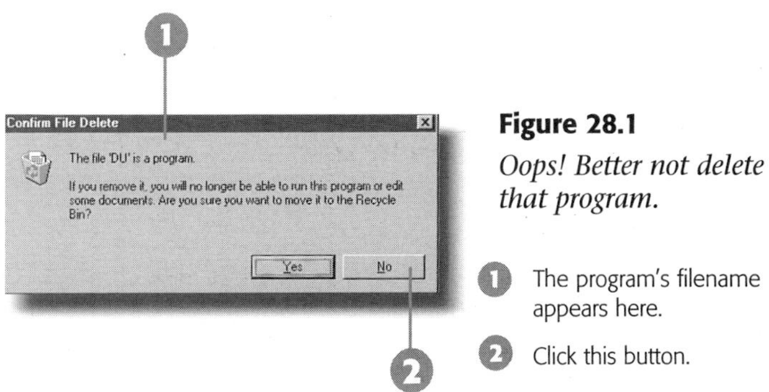

Figure 28.1
Oops! Better not delete that program.

1. The program's filename appears here.
2. Click this button.

Deleting Files en Masse

Deleting a group of files is cinchy: Select the icons as a group, and choose one of the various Delete commands, as covered in the section "Deleting a File," earlier in this chapter.

Another way to delete a group of files is to delete the folder the files are in. This action deletes the folder, all the files in the folder, and all the files in any subfolders. It's mass extinction!

Deleting a folder can be potentially a *massive* operation. You might want to review the contents of the folder before deleting it.

Continue this chapter's tutorial in the My Documents window:

▶ **Right-click the Great American Novel folder and choose Delete.**

You created this folder in Part I of this book. If you don't have this folder, choose another one.

Windows might warn you that deleting the folder deletes not only the folder but also every dang doodle file in the folder. Click Yes.

The folder and all its precious documents are gone. (Don't worry: You restore them soon.)

- Never delete any folder you did not personally create.
- Refer to Chapter 24 for information about selecting files in groups.

Seriously Deleting a File

One more Delete command exists. It's the deadly one. This Delete command does not casually *move* your icon to the Recycle Bin for safekeeping. No, this command obliterates your file, zapping it to Bit Heaven.

▶ **In the My Documents window, choose File➡New➡Bitmap Image.**

This command is one of those I recommend avoiding earlier in this book. The New menu is good for creating new folders but not much else. Now you've created a blank Paint document. To edit the document, you have to open Paint anyway, so why not just open Paint instead? Silly. Silly. Silly.

Anyway, the New command creates a useless document you can use to practice the deadly Delete command:

▶ **Select the New Bitmap Image document.**

▶ **Press Shift+Delete.**

This step works like pressing Shift+S to produce a capital *S*; press and hold the Shift key and tap the Delete key. Release both keys.

Shift+Delete is the deadly delete command. Be careful with it!

An appropriately nasty dialog box is displayed, as shown in Figure 28.2.

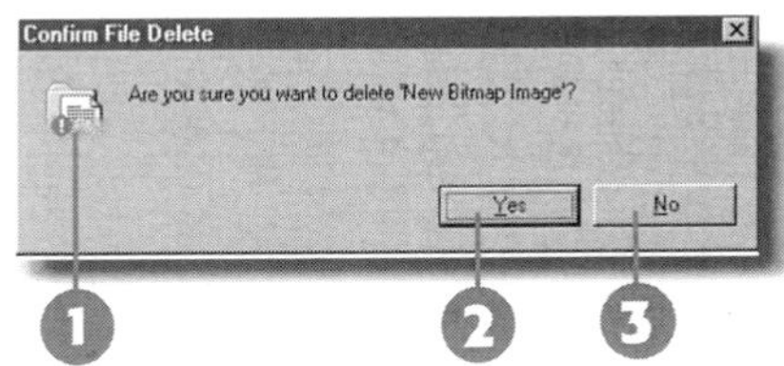

Figure 28.2
Really, seriously, deleting a file.

1. A visual image of the file being disintegrated.
2. Click to banish the file from reality.
3. Click to chicken out and maybe use the normal Delete command instead.

Your only visual clue that the file is being deadly deleted is the vanishing icon in the Confirm File Delete dialog box. Watch for that icon. (If you've turned off the Confirm File Delete dialog box for the regular Delete command, this one still appears. Thank goodness.)

▶ **Click Yes.**

The file is permanently destroyed. You have no way to get it back.

▶ **Close the My Documents window.**

Obviously, the Shift+Delete command isn't something you use casually. In some circumstances, however, you should consider it.

Use Shift+Delete if you're cleaning your hard drive for the purpose of increasing disk space. For example, I found an old video file I made years ago that was consuming 5MB of disk space. I used Shift+Delete to kill off the file and save the 5MB. Otherwise, the file is moved into the Recycle Bin, where it still takes up disk space. I never needed the file again, so Shift+Delete saved me the disk space.

Another circumstance for using the Shift+Delete command is when you don't want a file to be recovered by anyone. Suppose that you draw a picture of the boss on your PC and black out all his teeth. It's a riot, so you keep it around. At the end of the day, though, you use Shift+Delete to get rid of it, in case you get fired and someone looks through your Recycle Bin. (In that case, who would care? But I had to come up with some example for the security-conscious.)

Some utilities might be capable of rescuing a file you've killed off with Shift+Delete. I don't know of any personally, although I do know that the FBI and the IRS successfully recover deleted file information from criminals' hard drives all the time. So it is possible. (Buy the utility first, though; the FBI and the IRS do not recover deleted data as a public service.)

Undeleting a File

Deleting a file doesn't mean that it's killed off indefinitely. That's the idea behind naming the Windows dead-file receptacle the Recycle Bin and not the Trash Can. You can recycle files you might have accidentally thrown out. I do it all the time.

All files you delete on removable disks (floppy disks and ZIP disks, for example) are deadly deleted automatically. (The warning dialog box reminds you about it.) Under Windows you have no way to configure removable disks in any other way.

To recover a deleted file, follow these steps:

1. Open the Recycle Bin icon on your desktop.
2. Select the files you want recovered.
3. Choose File ➡Restore from the menu.
4. Close the Recycle Bin.

The following tutorial rescues the file and folder you deleted in this chapter's previous tutorials:

▶ **Open the Recycle Bin.**

The Recycle Bin icon is located on the desktop. Opening it reveals a window in which you see files in limbo, as shown in Figure 28.3.

To recover files you recently deleted, you should sort the dead by the date they were deleted:

▶ **Choose View ➡Arrange Icons ➡by Delete Date.**

Figure 28.3

Deleted files inside the Recycle Bin.

1. Choose View ➡as Web Page to see this useful information.
2. Previously deleted files and folders.

The icons in the window are now sorted by the date they were deleted, oldest first. The more recent files are at the bottom of the list.

▶ **Scroll to the bottom of the list (if necessary).**

The last two items on the list should be the folder and file you deleted earlier in this chapter.

Now you select the item (or items) you want to recover.

Can you find the New Bitmap Image document? No! It was removed with the deadly delete command, Shift+Delete. You cannot recover it from the Recycle bin.

▶ **Click the folder you deleted to select it.**

See the information on the left side of the window change. Figure 28.4 tells you all about the removed file—where it was originally, the date it was deleted, and other trivia.

▶ **Ctrl+click the icon you deleted to select it too.**

The information on the left side of the window changes to reflect that two files are now selected for recovery. (If you want to see individual information about each icon, just click them one at a time.)

▶ **Choose File ➡Restore.**

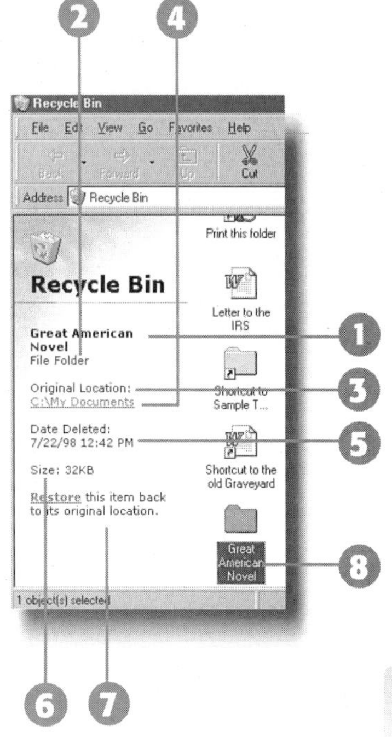

Figure 28.4

Information about the selected deleted file.

1. The name of the file.
2. File type.
3. Where the file was deleted.
4. Click here to browse to that folder in this Window (click Back to return).
5. Termination date and time.
6. File size.
7. Click here to instantly restore the selected file.
8. A folder deleted earlier in this chapter.

The files are resurrected from the Recycle Bin and placed back in their original folder, My Documents.

▶ **Close the Recycle Bin.**

Although restoring files from the Recycle Bin is easy, never use that as an excuse to be lazy when you're deleting files!

Managing the Recycle Bin

Windows designed the Recycle Bin to be easy to use and maintain. You don't ever really have to do anything with it, although this section describes some common Recycle Bin activities you might do from time to time as well as some customization suggestions.

Tweaking the Recycle Bin

To make the Recycle Bin behave the way *you* want it to, you have to access its Properties dialog box and go a-tweakin'.

▶ **Right-click the Recycle Bin icon on the desktop.**

▶ **Choose Properties.**

The Recycle Bin Properties dialog box is displayed, as shown in Figure 28.5.

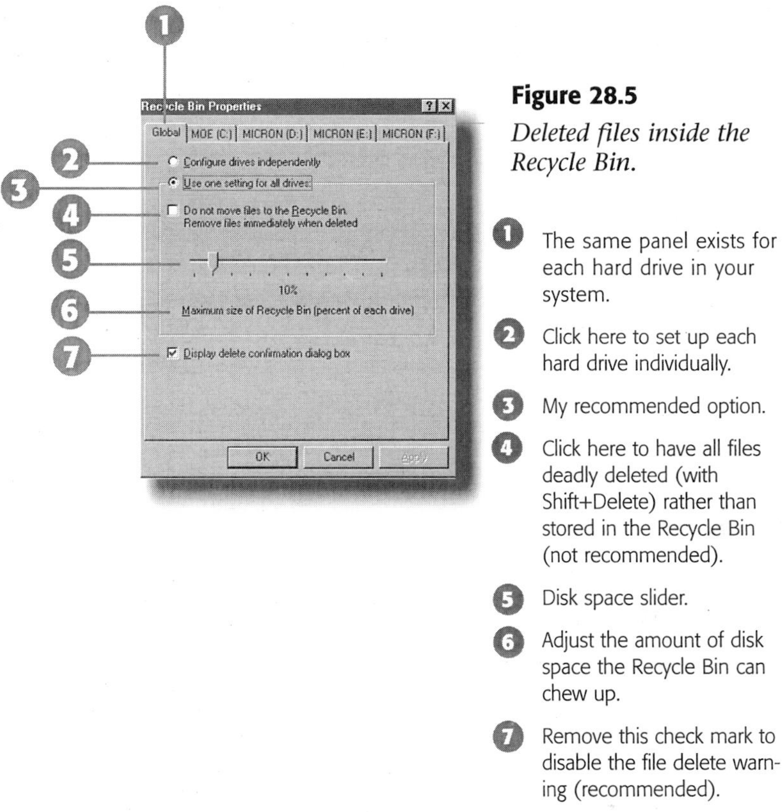

Figure 28.5
Deleted files inside the Recycle Bin.

1. The same panel exists for each hard drive in your system.
2. Click here to set up each hard drive individually.
3. My recommended option.
4. Click here to have all files deadly deleted (with Shift+Delete) rather than stored in the Recycle Bin (not recommended).
5. Disk space slider.
6. Adjust the amount of disk space the Recycle Bin can chew up.
7. Remove this check mark to disable the file delete warning (recommended).

You can set the settings in the Recycle Bin Properties dialog box individually or globally for each hard drive in your system. I recommend globally:

- ▶ **Choose Use One Setting for All Drives if it's not chosen already.**

You have no reason not to use this setting. The only one I can possibly think of is if, for example, drive D were a 9GB hummer. In that case you might want to adjust the Maximum Size slider on that panel to 1% or so. That way, the Recycle Bin doesn't use as much disk space.

Speaking of disk space:

- ▶ **Adjust the disk space slider to** 10% **if it's not at that percentage already.**

This step sets the maximum storage space for files in the Recycle Bin. For example, if you have a 2GB drive, you have 200MB set aside for storage in the Recycle Bin. That's an okay capacity, considering the huge size of today's programs.

If you have a 9GB drive, 10% of that is 900MB. My opinion? That's too big. If you drag the slider down to 1%, it gives you 90MB of storage for the Recycle Bin, a more reasonable amount.

Turning Off the Delete Warning

Should you turn off the delete warning? It depends on the amount of mistakes you make. If you have ten thumbs, for example, you might feel happier with the warning turned on. If you're like me, though, you might tire of the warning dialog box that says, "Are you sure you want to delete this file? I mean, you might have accidentally chosen the Delete command, you big dummy."

If you feel comfortable not having the warning displayed, do this:

▶ **Click to remove the check mark next to the item Display Delete Confirmation dialog box.**

Honestly, the warning isn't necessary when you consider that you can always rescue files from the Recycle Bin.

The deadly delete warning, however, still appears (refer to Figure 28.2).

Making the Recycle Bin into a trash can. If you want all files deadly deleted rather than just moved to the Recycle Bin, choose the Do Not Move Files option. Although this action saves disk space, it utterly eliminates all chance of file recovery in case you make a boo-boo. I do not recommend this option.

▶ **Click OK to close the Recycle Bin Properties dialog box.**

Any changes or new settings you've made take place after you close the dialog box. Or, if you change your mind, choose Cancel instead.

- Although you might have 10% of your hard drive set aside for Recycle Bin storage, the Recycle Bin might never fill up. If its size does concern you, you can adjust the value downward. A value of 5% on a 2GB hard drive is still 100MB of potential storage.

When the recycle bin does fill up, it starts deleting files (permanently), starting with the oldest first.

Emptying the Recycle Bin

Every so often you should flush your Recycle Bin and dump into oblivion all the files stored there. You flush it primarily to free up disk space, although at times you might just want to rid yourself of all those old files. It's a good job for spring.

▶ **Open the Recycle Bin icon.**

▶ **Review the files stored therein.**

Take time to scroll through the list of files and look them over. If you see any files you might want to keep, pluck them out now: Select the file and choose File ➡Restore from the menu. Odds are, however, that you won't find anything worthy of rescuing.

▶ **Choose File ➡Empty Recycle Bin.**

The deadly delete dialog box asks whether you're serious (refer to Figure 28.2). It lists the total number of files in the Recycle Bin and shows you the disintegration icon.

Yes, you're serious. You're about to save some disk space.

▶ **Click Yes.**

The Recycle Bin is empty. For now.

▶ **Close the Recycle Bin window.**

Don't worry. It should fill up again, soon.

- If you have a hard time reviewing the files and you get all choked up remembering them and then don't decide to empty the Recycle Bin, well, you have hope. Right-click the Recycle Bin icon on the desktop. Choose Empty Recycle Bin from the menu. You're done. No reminiscing, no belated good-byes.

If you don't want to delete all the files, select the ones you want to keep. (Ctrl+click to select them.) Then choose Edit ➡Invert Selection to select the files you don't want to keep. Choose File ➡Delete to remove the selected files permanently from the Recycle Bin.

- That's right—any file you delete in the Recycle Bin window is permanently deleted.
- One of the options in the Disk Clean-up tool program is to empty the Recycle Bin (refer to Chapter 21).

Part V

Somewhere, Out There

Chapters in This Part

Part V

Visual Topic Reference A.

1. Browse the Internet with Internet Explorer (Chapter 29).
2. Read email (Chapter 33).
3. The Active Desktop (Chapter 32).
4. Other computers on the network (Chapter 34).
5. A shared network drive (Chapter 35).
6. A network drive mapped to this PC (Chapter 35).

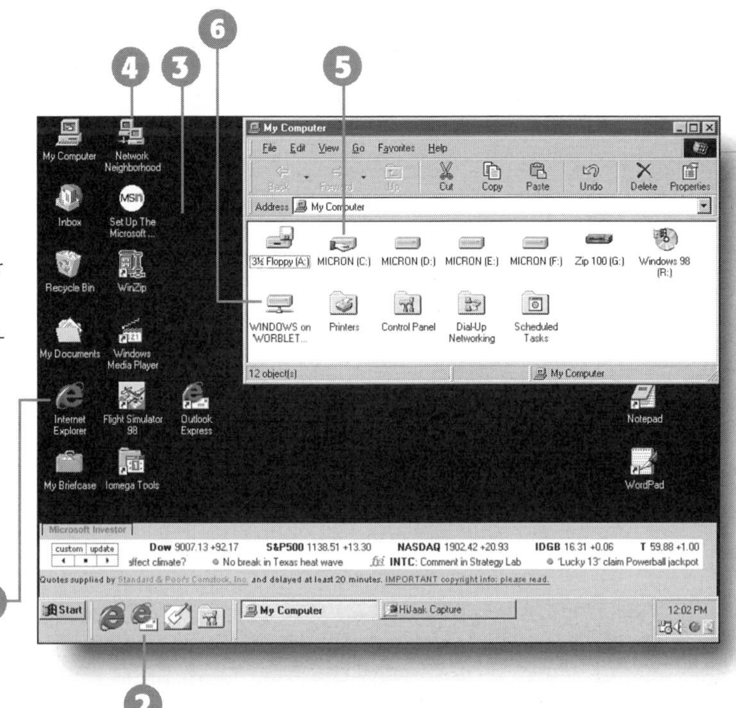

Part V

Visual Topic Reference B

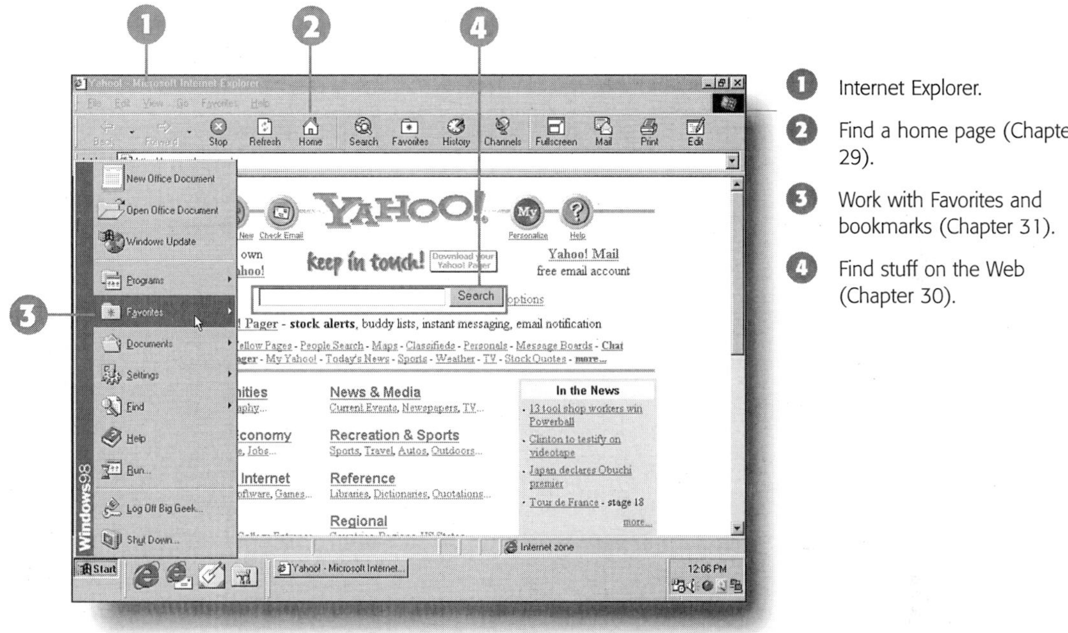

1. Internet Explorer.
2. Find a home page (Chapter 29).
3. Work with Favorites and bookmarks (Chapter 31).
4. Find stuff on the Web (Chapter 30).

Chapter 29

Planet Internet

Questions Answered and Thoughts Inspired

- Using the Internet Explorer
- Setting your home page
- Browsing to a particular address
- Clicking links and typing addresses

"Welcome to the exciting new world of Windows 98, where your computer desktop meets the Internet." That's what it says in the Welcome to Windows 98 startup dialog box. Honestly, I want Windows 98 just to help me meet deadlines, not the whole Internet. That's like saying that you answer the phone to understand long-distance packet switching. No, thanks! I just want to know who's calling.

Whether you like it or not, Windows 98 is melded to the Internet. Microsoft tried to make it *seamless*, where you can't tell where your computer ends and the Internet begins. If you *really* understand how work gets done in life, though, you know the difference. This chapter helps, with a tour of the Windows Web browser, Internet Explorer.

- Refer to Chapter 7 for a general introduction to the Internet.
- This chapter assumes that you connect to the Internet through a modem. If you connect by using your company's network, some things may work differently. Contact your network supervisor if you need assistance.

- Microsoft claims that you can use other Web browsers (that means Netscape) with Windows 98. Yes, you can, although Windows insists that you use Internet Explorer, which is what's covered in this chapter.
- Using Internet Explorer and browsing Web pages involves much more than I can describe in this little chapter. If you want to know more about the Web, consider buying a good book about Internet Explorer or a general Internet title.
- Internet Explorer does not read your email. You use Outlook Express for that, as covered in Chapter 33.
- This chapter uses the abbreviation IE to stand for Internet Explorer. Forgive me, but it's late, and my fingers are tired of typing.

Hello, Internet Explorer!

Honestly, the question isn't *how* to start Internet Explorer (IE) but rather how to *prevent* it from starting. The silly program seems to jump to life just about every time you do anything in Windows. It's almost as unnerving as the happy paper clip in Microsoft Office. But I digress.

When you feel the urge to browse the World Wide Web, you can start IE:

▶ **Open the IE icon on the desktop.**

Or you can click the IE icon on the Quick Launch bar. Or, from the Start Thing menu, choose Programs ➡Internet Explorer ➡Internet Explorer.

If the Dial-up Connection dialog box appears, optionally enter your name and password. Click Connect to have the modem dial. Otherwise, your modem should start dialing automatically.

The Dialing Progress dialog box appears, telling you that your modem is trying to connect with the Internet.

Eventually the IE window appears, as shown in Figure 29.1. Most of the items highlighted in that figure are covered later in this chapter.

▶ **Maximize the IE window.**

It's always best to see the World Wide Web on a full screen, no matter how big your monitor is.

Keep the IE window open for the next section's tutorial.

This chapter assumes that you have Windows configured to dial the Internet automatically. If that's not the case, remember to dial whenever you're prompted to do so.

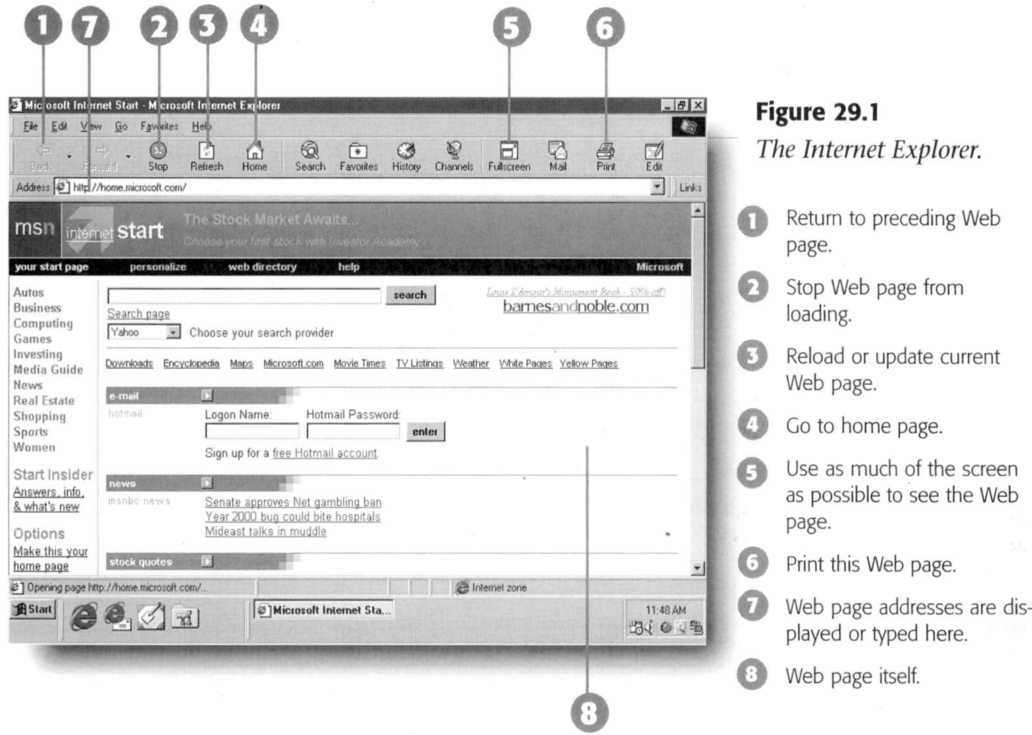

Figure 29.1
The Internet Explorer.

1. Return to preceding Web page.
2. Stop Web page from loading.
3. Reload or update current Web page.
4. Go to home page.
5. Use as much of the screen as possible to see the Web page.
6. Print this Web page.
7. Web page addresses are displayed or typed here.
8. Web page itself.

- Internet Explorer starts up whenever information is requested from the Internet. It can happen at odd and unexpected times, such as when you use Windows Help or create a Web page address in Microsoft Word.
- You don't have to start IE every time you visit the Internet. You could, for example, start your email program instead (see Chapter 33).

- If you see the little connection thing on the system tray, you know that you're connected to the Internet. Watch for it.

- After you're comfortable using IE, you can use it at an even larger size. Click the Fullscreen button on the toolbar. That pretty much eliminates everything else onscreen, except for a tiny toolbar. Click the Fullscreen button again to return everything to normal size.

"Oh, Give Me a Home Page..."

The first Web page you see in the IE window is known as the *home page*. That's merely a location (page) on the World Wide Web where IE goes whenever you first start it up—just as TVs in some hotel rooms always display the pay-movie preview channel when you turn on the TV.

IE is preset to open the Microsoft Internet Start Web page. You can see the name on the window's title bar and see the Web page address listed on the Address bar. In Figure 29.1, it says

`http://home.microsoft.com`

You don't have to use that home page. You can have IE open to any Web page on the Internet and use that page as your home page instead. I suggest two pages:

the CNN home page, at `http://www.cnn.com/`

or

the Yahoo! home page, at `http://www.yahoo.com/`

Both these home pages offer news and links to other places on the Web. They're good places to start. Because Yahoo! is a Web page, in fact, you'll probably be visiting often—why not make it your home page?

The following tutorial sets the IE home page to Yahoo! However, you can specify any Web page you want, and you can change the home page at any time.

▶ **Click in the Address box.**

The text in the Address box—the Web page address—is selected.

▶ **Press the Delete key on your keyboard.**

The text is gone!

▶ **Type** yahoo.com**.**

You don't have to type the full address, `http://www.yahoo.com/`. IE is smart enough to figure out the `http://www` part.

Or you can type the address of any Web page you want to make your home page, such as `cnn.com`.

▶ **Press Enter.**

Eventually, the Yahoo! home page appears. (Using Yahoo! is covered later in this chapter.)

▶ **Choose View ➡Internet Options.**

The Internet Options dialog box appears.

▶ **Click the General tab to bring that panel forward (if it's not already).**

The General tab is described in Figure 29.2. Your area of concentration is at the top, where it says "Home page."

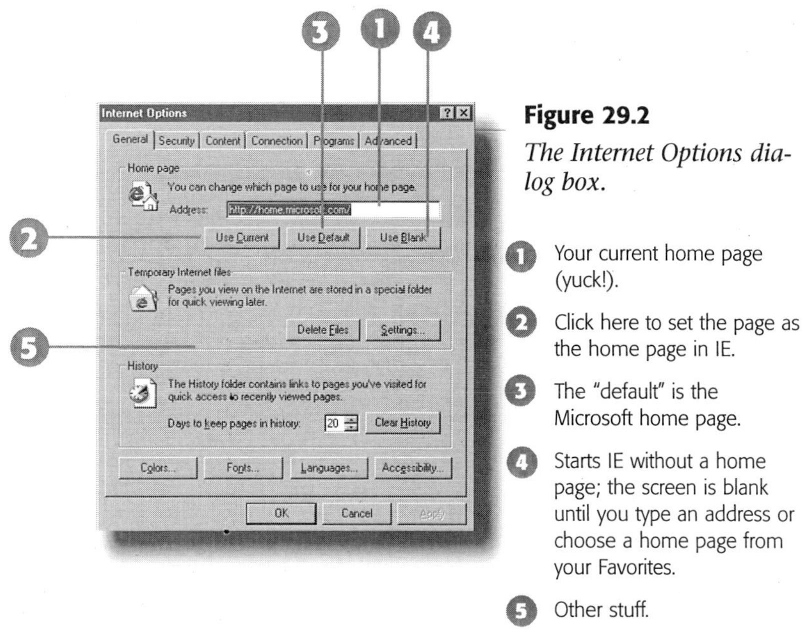

Figure 29.2

The Internet Options dialog box.

1. Your current home page (yuck!).
2. Click here to set the page as the home page in IE.
3. The "default" is the Microsoft home page.
4. Starts IE without a home page; the screen is blank until you type an address or choose a home page from your Favorites.
5. Other stuff.

▶ **Click Use Current.**

The current Web page—the one IE is looking at right now—becomes the home page.

You should see `http://www.yahoo.com/` replace the old home page in the Internet Options dialog box. (If you've selected another home page, its name appears there instead.)

▶ **Click OK.**

The new home page is set. Try it out:

▶ **Click the Back button.**

You return to the preceding Web page, which should be the boring, old Microsoft "home" page. Yawn.

▶ **Click the Home button.**

Ta-da! There's your new home page.

Not only do you now return to the home page every time you click the Home button, but it also appears whenever you start IE.

- The home page is merely the Web page you see when you first start IE (or any Web browser). There's nothing special about it, although any good home page should contain lots of links as well as updated information or news.
- Yahoo! makes a good home page because it really doesn't have anything to sell you. Yahoo! also provides an excellent catalog of other pages on the Web. (The Microsoft Web page doesn't do that; it lists only Microsoft products and concerns.)

- You can return to your home page at any time by clicking the Home button on the IE toolbar.

Quitting IE

When it's time to quit, and you're done wasting time, er, *researching* on the Internet, you simply close the IE window:

▶ **Close the IE window.**

▶ **Click Yes in the Disconnect dialog box.**

If you don't see the Disconnect dialog box, double-click the connection thing on the system tray. Then choose Disconnect from the dialog box that appears.

- The Windows email reader, Outlook Express, is covered in Chapter 33.
- Other Internet programs I've mentioned (FTP and telnet, for example) are included with Windows, but you have to find an Internet-specific book to learn about what they do.

You don't have to disconnect. If you want to start another Internet program, such as an email reader, FTP program, telnet, or whatever, you can do so.

Starting IE By Typing an Address

You can get on the Internet in Windows in lots of ways. The most obvious way is to start IE, which is how most people do it, I suppose. You can also get on the Internet by typing a Web page address.

For example, you can type a Web page address directly in any Address box in the Explorer or My Computer windows.

▶ **Open the My Computer icon on the desktop.**

If the Address box is not visible, choose View ➡Toolbars ➡Address bar.

▶ **Click in the Address bar to select the text.**

The text *My Computer* is selected.

▶ **Type** cnn.com **and press Enter.**

The Dialing Progress dialog box appears, and you're connected to the Internet. Soon the CNN Web page—full of news and other information that some would call news—appears.

Did you notice how the My Computer window quickly transforms into an IE window? Amazing.

Read the news if you want, but remember that you're working a tutorial here.

▶ **Quit IE.**

TIP

Maximize the window if you need to.

Close the window.

▶ **Click No if you're asked to disconnect from the Internet.**

Time to try another trick.

▶ **From the Start Thing menu, choose Run.**

The Run dialog box appears.

▶ **Type** http://www.usatoday.com **in the Open box.**

▶ **Press Enter.**

Wouldn't you expect Windows to try to open a program named `http://www.usatoday.com`? That makes sense. Windows recognizes that gobbledygook as a Web page address, however, so it starts IE and loads that Web page.

Oh, many more ways to start IE are laced throughout the fabric of Windows. Discover them all! In the meantime, get on with your work:

▶ **Close IE.**

Click Yes to disconnect from the Internet, or stay online if you plan to continue this chapter's tutorials.

- An address box also can appear on the taskbar. See Chapter 38, "Toolbars from Beyond Infinity," for more information.
- You can also start the Internet by choosing an item from the Channel bar that might appear on the desktop when Windows starts. (The Channel bar contains pictures of Mickey Mouse and various Warner Brothers cartoon characters.) However, I recommend later in this book that you remove the Channel bar.
- You can also choose a Web page to go to from the Favorites menu on the Start Thing. More about that later in this chapter.

Browsing the World Wide Web

Ever wonder why it's called "the Web?" Could it be because, like a spider web, you get stuck to your computer when you're on the Internet? Or maybe because you never move while you're on the Internet and your toes grow together to give you webbed feet? That might be it.

No, the truth is that it's called the Web because the various pages are *linked* to each other. Visit the Chili Cook-Off page, and you might see a link to the Pepto-Bismol page. If you visualize that (the links, not the Chili Cook-Off), you can see how it makes for a web of information. Okay, enough descriptions!

You can visit another Web page on the Internet in one of two ways:

✓ Click a link to take you to another Web page

✓ Type the Web page's address

The easiest way to visit another Web page is to click a link, which is why having a home page full of links is ideal. Typing a Web page address is more of a pain because you can make a typo, and that's frustrating.

In keeping with my theme of frustrating you during a tutorial, you can start your Web-browsing adventure by typing a link:

▶ **Start IE and connect to the Internet.**

Your home page should contain links to other pages on the Web—the earmark of a good home page. If you've chosen Yahoo! as your home page, it has thousands of links to follow. If you want to go to NASA and you know its address, however, typing it is quicker than finding the link:

▶ **Type** www.nasa.gov **on the Address bar.**

You must type the whole address: type **www.nasa.gov**.

▶ **Press the Enter key.**

You may have to wait awhile.

Waiting is called the "fourth W." (The first three are World Wide Web.)

Lo, the NASA home page is onscreen.

Easier than typing a Web page address is clicking a link:

▶ **Click the Home button.**

Or type the address **www.yahoo.com** to go to Yahoo! if it's not your home page.

▶ **Click the Today's News link.**

The link is near the top of the page, in the middle of two lines of text that contain various links. (I would show you a picture of it, but Yahoo! changes its look too often.)

Clicking the Today's News link takes you directly to the Yahoo! news page. See? That's easier than typing an address. It's also why Web software is called a "browser" and not "practice strange typing lessons."

Continue reading the news (or wander aimlessly about the Web—I do it every day!). Otherwise, the tutorial ends here:

▶ **Close IE.**

A link on a Web page is typically a bit of underlined text. The text is often a different color from the rest of the text, usually blue. Some pictures and graphics are also links. Generally, whenever the mouse pointer is pointing at a link, it changes to a "pointing hand." Click that link to go somewhere else on the Web.

Close the IE window to shut it down. Click Yes to disconnect from the Internet.

- You can have more than one IE window open at a time. Just open an IE icon to start another window. What's going on in one IE window is unaffected by what's going on in another window.

You can also open a link in a new window—if you're reading a Web page, for example, and want to see information about a related link at the same time. To do that, right-click the link and choose Open in New Window from the shortcut menu.

- Rather than type links over and over, you should consider "dropping" a bookmark to remember the Web pages you visit. Chapter 31 explains.

Chapter 30

Finding Stuff on the Web

Questions Answered and Thoughts Inspired

- Looking things up in Yahoo!
- Searching for Web pages
- Using various search engines
- Locating humans on the Internet
- Searching newsgroups

The Web is crawling with information. At least that's how they promote it. In reality, the Web is like a library without a librarian. Although that's good because no one shushes you, it's not good because it's harder to locate the information you want—what they say is out there.

The solution to finding stuff on the Web is to use a *search engine,* a Web page that contains a catalog of other pages on the Internet. It can also be a program that can search through every page on the Internet looking for specific tidbits of text. Knowing how to use these search engines to find information on the Internet is what this chapter is all about.

You might have noticed a Search button on the IE toolbar. Ignore it. The Search button takes you to a Web page Microsoft chose because it made a deal with some other company. That location might be a good place to search for things, but I would rather make my own decisions about how to search the Web.

Yahoo!, the Web Librarian

The closest thing the Web has to a librarian or even a card catalog is Yahoo! It began life as a Web catalog, started by two guys who just wanted to keep track of their favorite Web pages. From there it blossomed into a full-size company worth several million dollars. Even so, Yahoo! is still the best place to find information on the Web. It's my first choice, always.

▶ **Start IE.**

Start Internet Explorer (if it's not open already), and connect to the Internet.

▶ **Browse to Yahoo!, at `http://www.yahoo.com`.**

If Yahoo! is your home page, click the Home button. Otherwise, type **yahoo.com** in the Address box and press Enter.

Yahoo! actually stands for something: Yet Another Hierarchical Officious Oracle.

The Yahoo! main screen appears, as shown in Figure 30.1. Notice that what you see on your screen might be different; Yahoo! changes its look from time to time, although generally you should be able to find the items described in this figure.

You can work Yahoo! in two ways: browse and search.

- A Web page that lets you find information on the Internet is known as a *search engine*.
- Although Yahoo! tries its best, it doesn't catalog everything on the Web. See the section, "Other Web Search Engines to Try," later in this chapter, for more information.

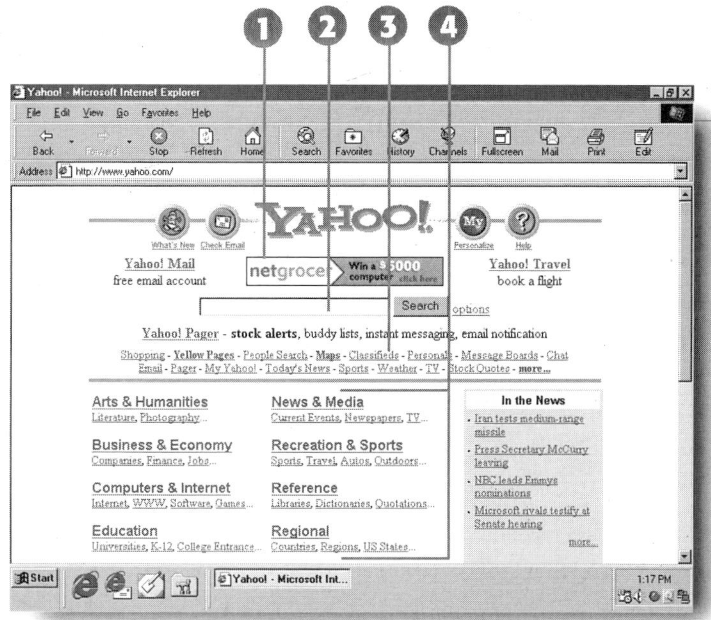

Figure 30.1
Yahoo! The Place to start searching the Web.

1. An ad, which is how Yahoo! makes money.
2. Type something in this box to search for.
3. Yahoo! features and news links.
4. The Yahoo! big catalog of Web pages, organized by category.

Browsing the Yahoo! Catalog

Yahoo! works best like a library's card catalog. You find the catalog links at the bottom of the page: Arts & Humanities, Business & Economy, Computers & Internet, for example. Click the links to see subcategories and Web pages organized into those categories. It's the browser's approach to finding information in Yahoo!

Suppose that you want to lighten up your report with some classic lines from old TV shows:

▶ **Click the News & Media link.**

The next page contains subcategories related to News & Media.

▶ **Click Television.**

You might have to scroll down to find this link.

The Television page appears. The top of the page describes where you are in the Yahoo! catalog: Home:News and Media:Television.

▶ **Click Shows.**

Again, you might have to scroll down to find this one.

The next screen lists various categories of TV shows. See? You're getting deeper and deeper, closer and closer, and you haven't had to walk anywhere.

▶ **Click Comedies.**

Notice how the next page is organized. You're getting close now to seeing a list of Web pages in the categories. First, some visual help, as shown in Figure 30.2.

Figure 30.2
Deciphering Yahoo!

1. Additional subcategories listed up here.
2. Web pages listed down here.
3. The @ indicates that the link takes you to a list of Web pages.
4. The number in parentheses tells you how many Web pages are listed in that category.

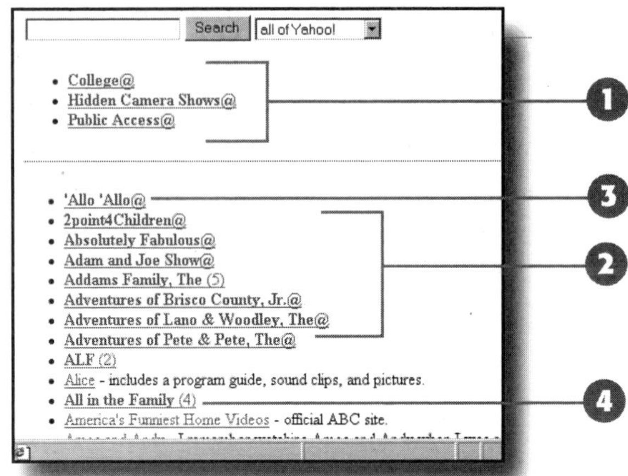

Now you're pretty much on your own. Locate a link or click a category. Eventually you see Web pages related to the TV comedy about which you want more information.

For example, click `I Love Lucy` to see some Web pages dedicated to that show and some links to Lucille Ball Web pages.

Don't stray too long. The tutorial continues with the next section.

Conductor: Madam, did you stop this train by pulling that cord?

Lucy: Well, I didn't do it by draggin' my foot.

Yahoo! updates itself every so often, so some of the links mentioned in this section might have moved. No problem. Remember that this is a *browsing* tutorial. If you know what it is you want, you're better off searching, which is covered next.

Searching for Something in Yahoo!

If you know specifically what you're looking for, you can search through the Yahoo! catalog by using its Search command. For example, if you're interested in seeing what the Golden Gate Bridge looks like right now, you can search for that:

▶ **Return to the Yahoo! main page.**

Use the IE Back button's back list. Click the down arrow next to the Back button to display the Web pages you've visited, as shown in Figure 30.3. You're looking for the page titled "Yahoo!"

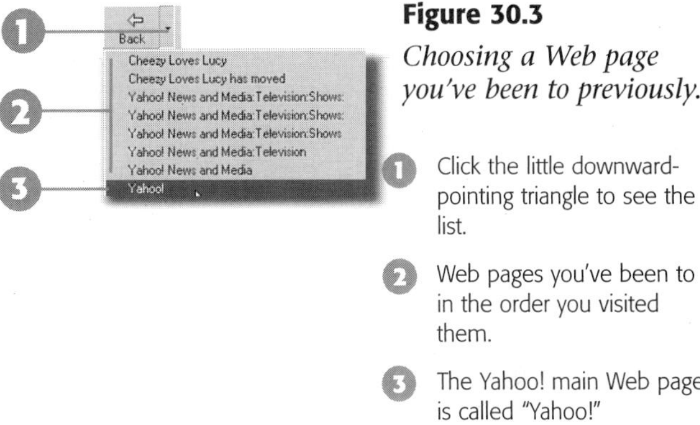

Figure 30.3
Choosing a Web page you've been to previously.

1. Click the little downward-pointing triangle to see the list.
2. Web pages you've been to in the order you visited them.
3. The Yahoo! main Web page is called "Yahoo!"

If you can't find the page listed, you can type `www.yahoo.com` in the Address box or just click the Home button if Yahoo! is your home page.

▶ **Type** Golden Gate Bridge **in the search box.**

The Search box is near the top of the Yahoo! Web page. Click the mouse in the box to place the cursor there, and then type **Golden Gate Bridge**.

▶ **Click the Search button.**

A Security Alert dialog box might scare the pee out of you at this point. Figure 30.4 explains.

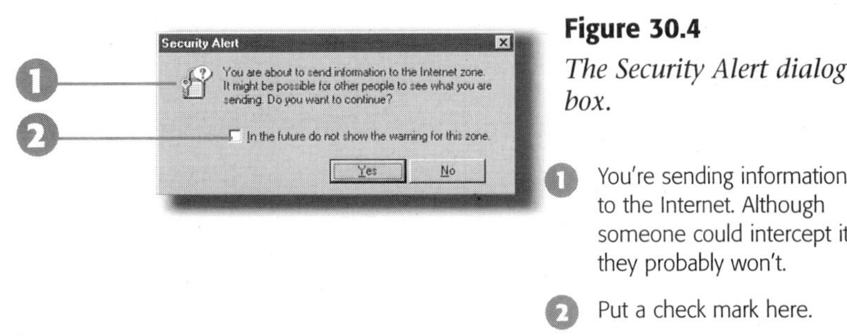

Figure 30.4
The Security Alert dialog box.

1. You're sending information to the Internet. Although someone could intercept it, they probably won't.
2. Put a check mark here.

I recommend putting a check mark in the In the Future box. See the "Security Alerts and Warnings" sidebar, later in this chapter, for more information. Click OK to close the Security Alert dialog box forever.

Soon Yahoo! shows you a list of categories and Web pages that match `Golden Gate Bridge` or whatever text you were searching for. Figure 30.5 explains things.

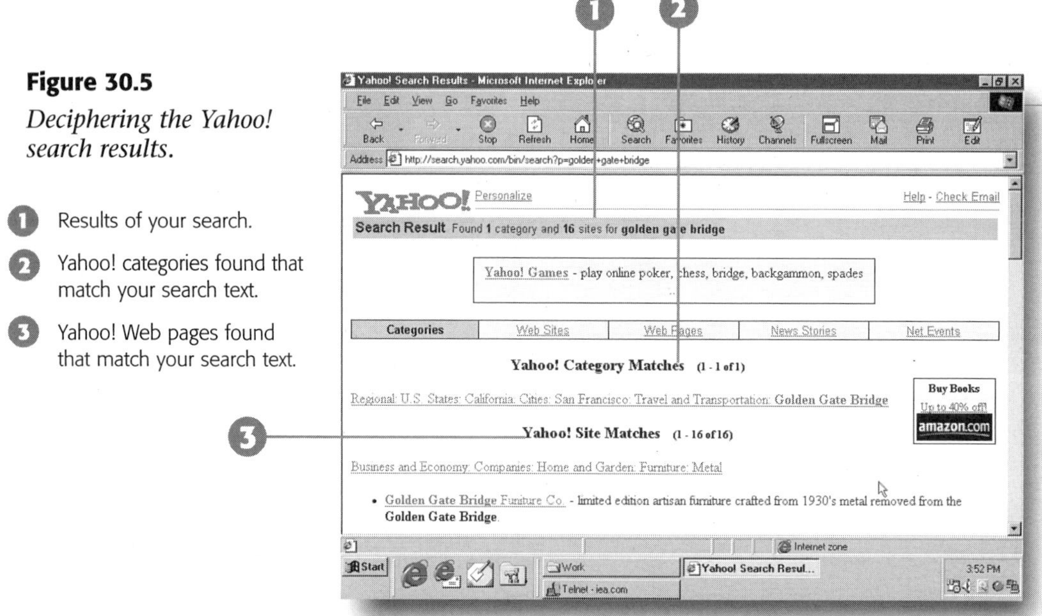

Figure 30.5
Deciphering the Yahoo! search results.

1. Results of your search.
2. Yahoo! categories found that match your search text.
3. Yahoo! Web pages found that match your search text.

▶ **Scroll down to find the Outdoor Cameras category.**

The full name of the category is

```
Computers and Internet: Internet: Interesting Devices Connected to the Next:
Web Cams: Outdoor Cameras
```

That's a category, and within that category are two links (at least when I visited) containing the text you searched for, *Golden Gate Bridge.*

▶ **Choose one of the links.**

I chose the GateCam, although that link might eventually disappear and you might have to pick another one. (Web pages are flighty.)

In a few moments, the Web page should load so that you can see a relatively recent image of the Golden Gate Bridge. (The image on GateCam is updated every five minutes. Also, although it was foggy the day I looked, GateCam keeps a library of better photos.)

Isn't it nice to know someone cares enough to put these things up on the Web?

Keep IE open for the next section's tutorial.

Security Alerts and Warnings

The odds of someone's stealing information you send on the Internet are very, very low. In most cases, the Security Alert dialog box (refer to Figure 30.4) is unnecessary. I mean, do you really mind if someone else sees that you're searching for "Cindy Crawford" on the Internet? Like they can blackmail you with that? It's not a big deal.

Don't fret over credit card numbers! When you visit a site to buy something with a credit card, IE switches over to secure mode. In *secure mode* you can send credit card and other sensitive information without anyone's snooping. Generally, you see the Security Alert dialog box only when you're sending trivial information.

Another type of panic dialog box IE displays is the Security Warning dialog box. It tells you that you're about to "install and run" some program from the Internet. Those dialog boxes are generally okay too.

The only warning dialog boxes I worry about are the ones for strange or unknown programs being saved to my hard drive. Chapter 33 discusses those warnings.

Finding Your Car Keys or Glasses By Using Yahoo!

I'm just kidding. Yahoo! doesn't know everything.

Other Web Search Engines to Try

You can use Yahoo! to find just about anything on the Web. If Yahoo! can't help you find it, it shows you other places to look.

If you've just finished working the tutorial in the preceding section, return to the last Yahoo! page you visited:

- **From the Back list, choose Yahoo! Search Results.**

Refer to Figure 30.3 to see how to access the Back list.

- **Scroll down to the bottom of the Search Results Web page.**

You see, at the bottom of the page, text that says Other Search Engines with some links on the next line. You can click those links to find similar information on other search engines. In fact, you don't even have to type a subject again; Yahoo! sends along Golden Gate Bridge (or whatever you searched for) to the other search engine.

▶ **Click the AltaVista link.**

AltaVista is another search engine, one that contains information about millions of Web pages (although it's not a catalog, like Yahoo!). Yahoo! lists it on their home page because Yahoo! is a fair and generous company that knows its limits.

As soon as the AltaVista page appears, notice how many matches it found. On my screen it says `About 3,148,918 matches were found`. That's more than 3 million bits of *Golden Gate Bridge* text found on the Internet. Whoa.

You can scroll down and view the AltaVista Web page, but remember that this is a tutorial. Time to move on to Search HQ for the Web:

▶ **Browse to `http://www.excite.com/`.**

Type the address **http://www.excite.com/** on the Address bar in IE, and then press the Enter key to visit that Web page.

The Excite search engine searches by the Web page's content—not by the title or subject.

▶ **Type** Lincoln **in the Search box.**

Click in the Search box with the mouse, and then type **Lincoln**.

▶ **Click the Search button.**

The next page displays the results in three different areas.

The top of the screen contains a list of search words to help you refine what you're looking for: Put a check mark next to `abraham` or `mercury` to look for those types of Lincoln Web pages.

I use Excite when I'm looking for some hard-to-find things on the Web—stuff that doesn't appear in any Yahoo! category.

The middle of the screen contains some `Try these first` links to places such as Lincoln, Nebraska, or related books or music titles.

The bottom of the screen shows you matching Web pages with a percentage value. The higher the percentage, the more likely the site deals with the word you're searching for. If you find a match that's close, click the `Search for more documents like this one` link to further refine your search.

To conclude your Web search journey, return to Yahoo:

- **Browse to `http://www.yahoo.com`.**

Unlike other search engines on the Web, Yahoo! isn't afraid to list its competition—and, boy, is there a bunch of it.

- **Click the Computers & Internet link.**
- **Click the Internet link.**
- **Click the World Wide Web link.**
- **Click the Searching the Web link.**
- **Click the Search Engines link.**

There. Now you're down deep in Yahoo! The competition is listed—and it's listed better and more accurately than this or any other book could describe.

I'll leave you on your own to find another search engine. I use Yahoo first and then Excite. After that, I'd probably visit the page you're looking at right now, where Yahoo! lists alternative search engines. Anyway, you're bound to find the information you're looking for.

Millions and millions of Web pages exist. They appear and disappear, and their contents change. No search engine or Web catalog—not Yahoo! or Excite or anything else—lists everything, so don't give up easily if you're looking for information. It might just take time to find it.

- You can use a Start Thing command to find things on the Web: From the Start Thing menu, choose Find➡On the Internet. This command takes you to a Web page that Microsoft set up, but I find it too junky a place to start a Web search.

Finding People on the Internet

Here is something scary: Are you on the Internet? Are you listed? Your name and address and phone number? Probably. If you're in the phone book, chances are that you're also listed in an Internet people search engine.

Don't panic! Most of the people search engines let you remove your name from their database if it freaks you out. If anything, be prepared to freak out.

▶ **Visit Yahoo!**

Browse to `http://www.yahoo.com` if you're not there already.

On the Yahoo! main page, you see a People Search link. You can use People Search to locate humans on the Internet. (Actually, it's one of several ways to find folks you might know on the Internet.)

▶ **Click the People Search link.**

Yahoo! displays its People Search page, where you can look for people's email addresses or phone numbers. Wow. Figure 30.6 shows you how to set things up.

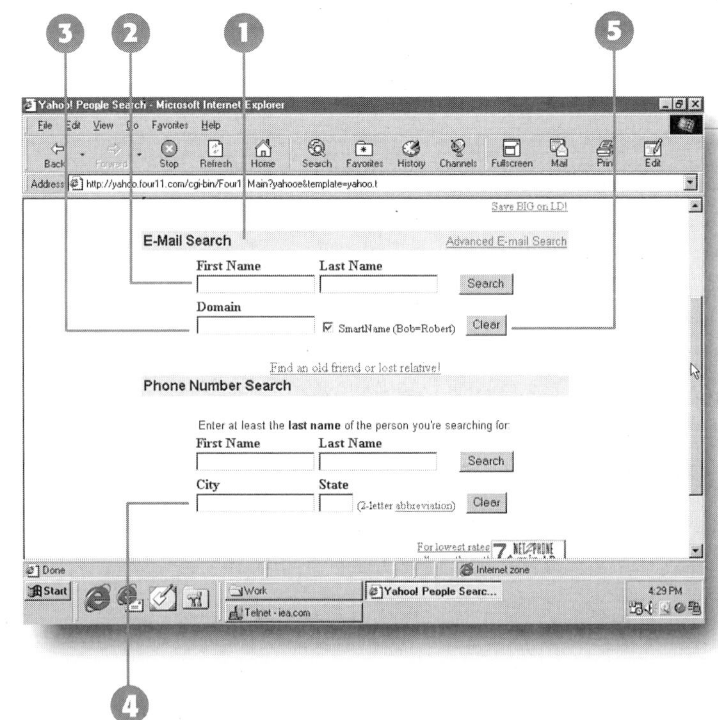

Figure 30.6

Locating a human on the Internet.

1. Finding someone's email address.
2. Type the person's first and last names.
3. Silly. If you know the person's domain (ISP or email computer name, such as `microsoft.com`, `juno.com`, `hotmail.com`, for example), you probably know the address anyhow. Duh.
4. Optionally supply a city and state if you're looking for a human.
5. Click this button to reset and clear the form.

▶ **Type your first name in the First Name box in the Phone Number Search area.**

▶ **Type your last name in the Last Name box.**

- **Enter your city in the City box.**
- **Enter your state in the State box.**

Inhale.

- **Click the Search button on the Web page.**

Did it find you? I just tried with my grandmother's name, and it found her. She's not even on the Internet.

The Yahoo! people search might not find everyone. If you're chagrined at not locating yourself, a loved one, or someone who still owes you money, you can try another people search place. The only other one I've frequented is at `http://www.switchboard.com`.

If you're concerned about your privacy, you can do something about having your name listed on the Internet. Most people-search sites have a feature that lets you suppress your name. These Internet sites are as sensitive about your personal information as you are.

Fishing Through Newsgroups for Information

Newsgroups aren't really news. They are groups, though—groups of people who discuss certain topics, like an open email forum. They're quite popular, and you can use Outlook Express to view them (although I don't cover them here because I believe that that's way too far off the beaten path for a Windows book).

Even though newsgroups might be esoteric, you can get lots of good information there. One way to find that information without having to toil through pointless newsgroup messages is to search the newsgroups. The number-one newsgroup search engine is DejaNews. Type this address in IE to visit that Web page:

- **Browse to `http://www.dejanews.com`.**

The DejaNews Web site looks like any other search engine on the Web (see Figure 30.7). The site contains categories (or *channels*) for some types of information, although mostly you use the Find box near the top of the page.

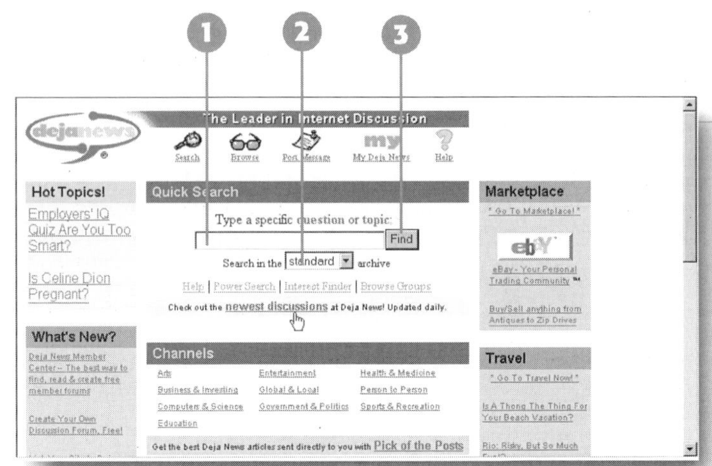

Figure 30.7
Searching newsgroups with DejaNews.

1. Type a subject to search.
2. Choose various archives from here.
3. Click here to find newsgroup messages with your search text.

Suppose that you're a concerned parent, and you want to know about spanking:

▶ **Type** spanking **in the search text box.**

▶ **Click Find on the Web page.**

You see some messages from concerned parents about all sorts of spanking topics. Along with that, you might see some, well, other messages pertaining to spanking. It's all part of the search process; from the message subjects listed, you can usually tell what's important to you and what's, well, only distantly related to the topic.

The results DejaNews displays appear in the IE window. First notice how many matches were found. On my screen it says `Matches 1-20 of exactly 3852 for search`. That line means that the first 20 matches of 3,852 messages are displayed on the Web page.

Each message is displayed in the middle of the page in several columns: Date, Score (or percentage of the file that matches what you searched for), Message subject, the newsgroup to which the message was posted, and the screen name of the person posting the message.

▶ **To view a message, click its subject link.**

The message is displayed like an email message but as a Web page. You see links to view the next or preceding article in the list, or you can email the message to a friend.

▶ **Click the Back button to return to the list of found messages.**

Notice the Next Results link at the bottom of the page. Click that link to see more messages DejaNews found.

Please try to keep an open mind with some of the newsgroups that are available. Some are targeted to specific audiences, which you can usually determine by the newsgroup's name. If the newsgroup's name offends you, don't be appalled by the message content you might see. In newsgroups that don't offend you, don't take to heart everything you read.

Continue searching the newsgroups, or, if you've seen enough, you can quit.

▶ **Close IE and log off the Internet.**

Your search is over.

- If you want more information about newsgroups, refer to a solid Internet text, something that can give you a good introduction and tips for how to work the newsgroups.

Another term for newsgroups is USENET. Many of the old-timers and UNIX people call it that instead.

Chapter 31

Dropping Web Breadcrumbs

Questions Answered and Thoughts Inspired

- Removing unwanted bookmarks from the Favorites menu
- Using the bookmark feature
- Organizing the Favorites menu
- Removing old or dead bookmarks

Remember Hansel and Gretel? It was Grimm. In the original version, it wasn't a witch who fattened them up and tried to eat them—it was their stepmother. Yup. And it was a *children's* story. What would Dr. Laura say?

Of course, pudgy li'l Hansel and plump Gretel never did get eaten. They found their way back home by following a trail of breadcrumbs they had dropped. Like that forbidding forest, the Web can be a dark and mysterious place. It helps if you drop a few electronic breadcrumbs from time to time so that you can find your way back to a favorite Web page. That's what this chapter tells you how to do.

- The birds ate the breadcrumbs only when Hansel and Gretel were led even farther into the forest by their wicked stepmother.
- In the end, the kids tricked the witch and pushed her into a fiery oven. In real life, they would do time for it.

Your Favorite Web Things

When you find a Web page you enjoy, add it to your list of favorites. This process is known as *bookmarking*. Like putting a bookmark in a favorite book, you can bookmark a Web page so that you can more easily return to it later.

Always drop bookmarks!

You should "drop" a bookmark on any Web page you ponder at, even for a short time. That way, you can easily go back to the Web page later. Don't worry about accumulating bookmarks: You can edit them at any time, removing the old ones you never use.

- I use the term *d*rop a bookmark because the command to do so is Ctrl+D.
- Microsoft doesn't call it bookmarking because that's what Netscape calls it. Microsoft makes the only Web browser in the world that does not call it bookmarking.

Cleaning Up the Favorites Menu

Windows stores its bookmarks on an IE menu called *Favorites*. This menu is a duplicate of the Favorites menu on the Start Thing:

▶ **From the Start Thing menu, choose Favorites.**

You see the Favorites submenu, which contains about half a dozen submenus, none of which you created. Each submenu contains Web page links or other submenus. It's a mess, as shown in Figure 31.1.

Let me be honest: You can freely delete any link that has already been put on the Favorites menu. Any of them. All of them. Those links were added by others, usually people who want to sell you something. You really, honestly, truthfully don't ever need to visit any of those Web pages. Ever.

Don't interpret my tirade as saying that the Favorites menu is useless. It's not! It's very handy. It becomes handy, however, only when you delete the crap that Microsoft and others put there and start making the Favorites menu your own.

To clean up the Favorites menu, you have to run IE. You don't have to clean things up, but, as you browse the Web and create your own bookmarks, you realize that you *never* visit most of the places already on the Favorites menu more than once. Cleanup is only prudent:

▶ **Start IE and connect to the Internet.**

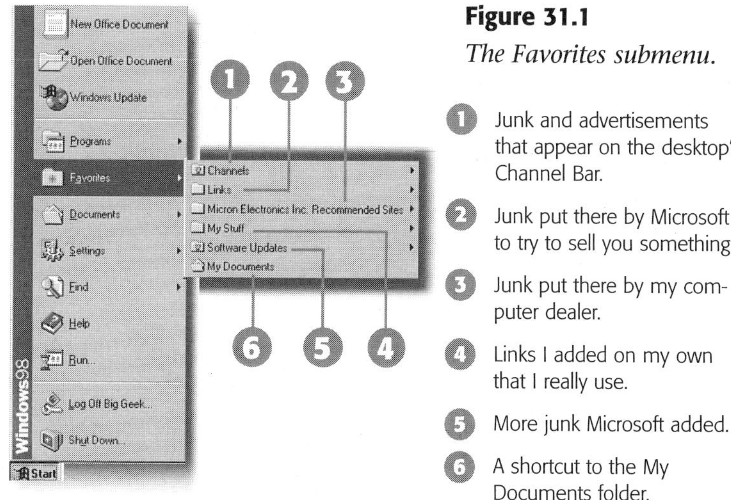

Figure 31.1

The Favorites submenu.

1. Junk and advertisements that appear on the desktop's Channel Bar.
2. Junk put there by Microsoft to try to sell you something.
3. Junk put there by my computer dealer.
4. Links I added on my own that I really use.
5. More junk Microsoft added.
6. A shortcut to the My Documents folder.

You don't have to connect to perform this operation, although you should be online to continue with the other tutorials in this chapter.

▶ **Choose Favorites ➡Organize Favorites.**

The Organize Favorites dialog box appears. Figure 31.2 shows you some tips for using it. It helps if you think of it as a cross between a Browse dialog box and an Explorer window.

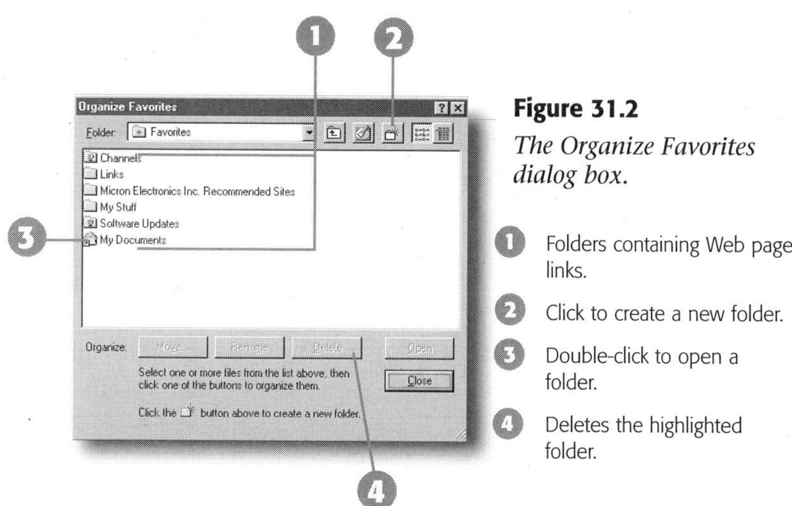

Figure 31.2

The Organize Favorites dialog box.

1. Folders containing Web page links.
2. Click to create a new folder.
3. Double-click to open a folder.
4. Deletes the highlighted folder.

▶ **Select all the folders that you didn't personally create.**

For example: Select Channels, Links, Software Updates, and any other folders you didn't put there. In Figure 31.2 I also chose the Micron Electronics entry. I left the My Stuff folder because I've been using it.

If you plan to use the Channel Bar, don't delete the Channel Bar folder. I don't like the thing hovering on my desktop and find that it clutters Windows. You really don't need it.

If you've *imported* (copied) bookmarks from another Web browser, do not remove those links. Those are your bookmarks, and you probably want to keep them.

You can leave the shortcut to the My Documents folder, although it's just a shortcut and you can repaste another shortcut icon there later.

Ctrl+click to select multiple folders in the dialog box.

▶ **Click Delete.**

The folders you've chosen are moved to the Recycle Bin.

There. Now you can make the Favorites menu your own.

I know, I know! I've written repeatedly that you should never delete anything you didn't personally create. This time is an exception. You do not need those bogus links messing up your Favorites bookmark list.

▶ **Click Close.**

Now you can start making the Favorites menu truly useful by dropping some bookmarks that mean something to you.

Keep IE open and stay online for the next section's tutorial.

- The IE Favorites menu duplicates the Start Thing's Favorites menu, with a few extra items.
- Don't mess with the Favorites button on the IE toolbar. It opens a miniwindow to the left of the IE main browser window. That button gets in the way more than it helps.

Adding to Favorites (Dropping Bookmarks)

Whenever you visit any Web page remotely interesting, drop a bookmark. An example is the Internet Movie Database.

- **Start IE if it's not open already.**
- **Browse to `www.imdb.com`.**

The `imdb` stands for Internet Movie Database.

- **Click your country's flag.**

TIP

I find it best to use the Favorites menu on the Start Thing. In fact, choosing an item from there is a great way to start IE and get on the Internet.

For example, if you're in the United States, click the U.S. flag to use the U.S. version of the IMDB.

The Internet Movie Database is a great source of information for anyone who enjoys films. Better drop a bookmark after your country's version of the IMDB page appears.

- **Press Ctrl+D.**

Although you get no visual feedback, you can check to confirm that a bookmark has been dropped:

- **Open the Favorites menu.**

At the bottom of the menu, the Internet Movie Database is displayed. It worked!

A necessary place to visit is the Internet hoaxes Web page. You can find information about various rumors and hoaxes floating around the Internet. It's a good place to check whenever you get a frantic email from your friend Reed that says "Don't do such-and-such on the Internet, or else your computer will explode!"

- **Browse to `http://ciac.llnl.gov/ciac/CIACHoaxes.html`.**

Yup, that's a lot to type. Look at it this way, though: CIAC appears three times. CIAC stands for Computer Incident Advisory Capability. The `llnl` thing is two lowercase *l*s, an *N*, and another L.

Check your typing before you press the Enter key. (Fortunately, because you're adding the link to your Favorites bookmark list, you never have to type it again.)

When you get to the CIAC page, which is part of the U.S. Department of Energy, drop a bookmark:

- **Press Ctrl+D.**

Now when your friend Jerry writes to warn you about the "Good Times" email virus, you can proudly tell him that no such thing exists.

Drop bookmarks all over the Web, wherever you go.

The next section tells you how to clean up bookmarks and organize them if you need to. Keep IE open and stay online for that tutorial.

- You can also drop a bookmark by choosing Favorites ➡Add to Favorites from the menu. But isn't Ctrl+D easier?
- You don't have to wait for a Web page to completely *load* (appear) before pressing Ctrl+D.
- The Web pages you bookmark are stored at the bottom of the Favorites menu. To put them on a submenu (in a folder), you must edit the Favorites list, which is covered in the next section.
- By the way, in Netscape you use the same Ctrl+D command to drop a bookmark.

Organizing Your List-o-Favorites

If you follow my advice and drop bookmarks like there's no tomorrow, you eventually end up with a Favorites menu several feet long. Time for some organization and cleanup:

▶ **Start IE if it's not open already.**

▶ **Choose Favorites ➡Organize Favorites.**

See Figure 31.2 for a description of the dialog box, although what you might see on your screen is a whole lotta Web pages and no folders.

Organize your favorites like you organize your folders.

The idea behind organizing your bookmarks is the same as for organizing your folders (that story is told in Chapter 23). Suppose that you have a number of news links: `cnn.com`, `usatoday.com`, your local newspaper, the news links in Yahoo!, and the *Wall Street Journal*, for example. Why not create a News folder?

▶ **Click the Create New Folder button.**

The new folder, named New Folder, appears in the Organize Folders window. (The Organize Folders window is really a mini-Explorer window. In fact, the Favorites you're editing are in the Windows\Favorites folder.)

▶ **Rename the New Folder as** News.

Press Enter to lock in the new name.

The News folder is a submenu of the Favorites folder on the Start Thing.

▶ **Drag your news bookmarks to the News folder.**

You may have to scroll the window to do it. Drag to the News folder `cnn.com`, `usatoday.com`, and any other link that's related to news.

Repeat these steps to create more subfolders for your bookmarks.

▶ **When you're done with your organizational frenzy, close the Organize Folders dialog box.**

Go to the Favorites menu on the Start Thing to check your work. Organizing things really helps you get to your favorite bookmarks quickly.

▶ **Close the IE window.**

Or you can keep IE open for the next section's tutorial.

- You can organize items in the Start Thing's Favorites menu by dragging the bookmarks around—similar to the way Chapter 10 teaches you to organize the Start Thing's Programs menu by dragging things around.

Try to work with the Organize Folders dialog box at least once a month to edit and organize your bookmarks.

Removing Unwanted Bookmarks

Web pages die. If you encounter any bookmarks you no longer want or especially bookmarks for Web pages that are no longer online (called *cobweb* pages), you can delete them. You do that in the Organize Favorites dialog box.

▶ **Start IE if it's not open already.**

Before you delete a bookmark, it's a good idea to ensure that it's no longer living. For example, those bookmarks you dropped a few months back may no longer be valid. (Web pages die, remember?) Before you go on a whirling deleting frenzy, choose a few old bookmarks from the Favorites menu just to be sure that they're dead.

Web pages don't have to be dead, of course, to have their bookmarks deleted. You can also delete bookmarks for Web pages you never visit anymore:

▶ **Choose Favorites ➡Organize Favorites.**

If the bookmark you want to remove is in a folder, open the folder by double-clicking it.

▶ **Select the bookmark link you want to delete.**

Click the link once to select it.

▶ **Click the Delete button.**

A confirmation dialog box may appear; if so, click Yes to delete the bookmark.

Continue whacking away at unwanted bookmarks. When you're done, close the Organize Favorites dialog box and even IE itself.

▶ **Close the Organize Folders dialog box.**

▶ **Close the IE window.**

Or you can continue to stay on the Internet and do "research."

- It's a good idea to review your Favorites list for dead bookmarks every month or so, lest they start piling up.
- If you're leery of deleting bookmarks, create a Near Death folder in your Favorites menu. Drag into that folder any bookmarks you want to delete—but are not yet certain. Then, later, when you are certain, you can find those bookmarks quickly.

Chapter 32

Activating the Desktop

Questions Answered and Thoughts Inspired

- Switching on the Active Desktop
- Downloading a new Active Desktop item
- Removing an Active Desktop item
- Removing the Active Desktop

Where does the desktop stop and the Internet begin? Can you tell? I can. Although Microsoft tried to make it smooth, the actual spot where Internet and desktop meet has a big, ugly welding scar on it. Legal arguments aside, an Internet browser and a computer operating system are two different animals. But I digress.

One feature of Windows 98 that truly blurs the line between "desktop" and "Internet" is the Active Desktop. It's not a life-or-death feature, although it's interesting in what it can do and how others react when they see it. Maybe in the future it will be a must-have deal, but until then it's something I'm compelled to cover here, lest I get kicked out of the Windows 98 Computer Book Authors' Union.

An Active Desktop Overview

Active Desktop is the Microsoft buzzword for a desktop that displays content from the Internet. For example, your desktop can show a news and stock ticker—just like at the bottom of the screen on *CNN Headline News*. Or you can see a weather map, updated every hour by using information from the Internet. Those are examples of Active Desktop programs.

An Active Desktop program runs on your computer by using information from the Internet.

Sounds weird, right? Sounds unnecessary? Whatever—it exists, and some people rave about the Active Desktop and others can leave it alone. Consider it nice that Microsoft gives you a choice.

Using the Active Desktop works like this:

1. **You tell Windows to display the desktop as an Active Desktop.**
2. **You visit the Display Properties dialog box to add or remove Active Desktop Programs.**
3. **Optionally you visit the Microsoft Active Desktop Gallery on the Internet to download new Active Desktop programs.**
4. **You watch the Active Desktop programs dance on your desktop.**
5. **Every so often your computer dials up the Internet to update the Active Desktop programs.**

Most of the time, you work step 4, watching the Active Desktop programs busy themselves onscreen. It's a great distraction, especially when you have other work to do.

Don't fret over step 5: To update information on some Active Desktop programs, your computer spontaneously dials the Internet. This task takes maybe one minute and happens throughout the day. When you're running an Active Desktop, don't fear that your computer will spend all day online.

None of the Active Desktop programs I've seen are *productivity* programs, which means that they're all trivial and not related to getting any work done. Although that might change later, for now the Active Desktop is more of a toy than a must-have tool. At least that's how I see it.

Activating Your Desktop

Before you can run an Active Desktop program, you have to properly configure your computer. The desktop must be changed from regular desktop mode to Active Desktop mode. Only then can you add or activate the tiny Active Desktop programs.

- **Right-click the desktop.**
- **Choose Active Desktop.**

The Active Desktop submenu is displayed, as shown in Figure 32.1.

- **Choose View➡As Web Page.**

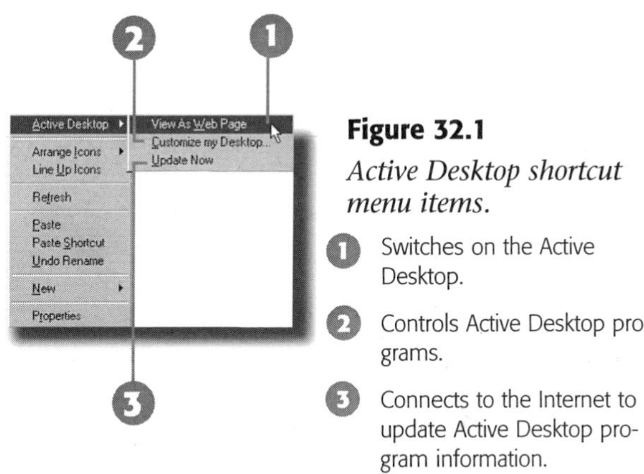

Figure 32.1
Active Desktop shortcut menu items.

1. Switches on the Active Desktop.
2. Controls Active Desktop programs.
3. Connects to the Internet to update Active Desktop program information.

Your desktop might change to display a Web page. It's not a Web page on the Internet, but rather a Web page document (an HTML document, in fact) stored on your PC's hard drive. It's necessary in order for Windows to place Active Desktop programs on the desktop.

If you don't notice any change, your desktop has been configured not to display Web page information. Chapter 37, "A New Face on the Interface," describes how to display a Web page as the background on the desktop.

I prefer to have lots of shortcut icons on my desktop. If you like the Active Desktop in Windows, you'll realize that you can't have a bunch of shortcut icons on the desktop because they clutter things up too much. You either have to rearrange the shortcut icons or just do without them.

- An *HTML document* is a Web page document. When you look at a Web page, what you're seeing is an HTML document as displayed by IE or whichever browser you're using.
- Windows lets you create or modify HTML documents, although doing so is a bit beyond the scope of this book. Any good Internet book, or any book about HTML or the Microsoft FrontPage program, should tell you how to work with HTML documents.

Activating an Active Desktop Program

The second step in your journey to Active Desktopland is to activate your Active Desktop programs. Just viewing the desktop as a Web page isn't enough. The second step is to add some programs to the desktop.

Any Active Desktop programs already installed on your computer are listed on the Web panel in the Display Properties dialog box. Windows comes with one program preinstalled: the Channel Bar. You can also add other Active Desktop programs, a subject that's covered later in this chapter.

To activate any Active Desktop programs you have already, follow these steps:

▶ **Right-click the desktop again.**

▶ **Choose Active Desktop ➡Customize my Desktop.**

You're taken to the Web panel of the Display Properties dialog box, as shown in Figure 32.2.

Any Active Desktop programs you have in your repertoire are displayed on the list. Unless you've added some on your own, you probably have only the Internet Explorer Channel Bar item available. (I added the *Fortune* Stock Chart and MSNBC Weather programs shown in Figure 32.2.)

To add a program, click in its box to put a check mark there. For example:

▶ **Click to put a check mark in the box next to Internet Explorer Channel Bar (if a check mark isn't there already).**

Placing a check mark in the program's box switches that program on and displays it on the desktop. You see a preview of where and how the program will sit on the desktop, as shown in the dialog box's preview screen.

Add other programs if you want.

If you want to remove a program, click to remove its check mark. This step removes the program from the desktop but does not delete the program from your computer. You can always reactivate the program later.

▶ **Click OK.**

After the Active Desktop program's window is visible, you can move it around the desktop like any other program. You'll probably want to reposition or even resize various Active Desktop programs. For example, I resized the stock ticker by stretching it across the bottom of the desktop—like it looks on CNBC.

The title bar on each Active Desktop program contains two buttons, as shown in Figure 32.3. The drop-down menu button (item C) displays a menu of commands to control the Active Desktop program. The X button in the upper-right corner closes the program, removing it from the desktop.

Unfortunately, the Channel Bar lacks anything interesting in its drop-down menu, although you can peek at it if you want.

▶ **Close the Channel Bar by clicking its X button.**

The Channel Bar goes bye-bye.

To resummon the Channel Bar (or any Active Desktop program), you have to return to the Display Properties dialog box. Remember: The program hasn't been deleted; it has just been removed from the desktop.

- Honestly, you don't need the Channel Bar. It's just an advertisement. In fact, it's a poor example of an Active Desktop program. (It's a rather *inactive* program.) Better examples of Active Desktop programs are introduced in the next few sections.

The title bar shows up only when you point the mouse at the top of the Active Desktop program's window.

Adding an Active Desktop Item

The Active Desktop makes sense only if you have real Active Desktop programs floating around: a stock ticker, sports score update program, weather map, local news, audio jukebox, and satellite-tracking program, for example. (Those are all real-life Active Desktop programs, and more are available. Had I made any of them up, I would have said "the UCSD RoachCam, a program to measure the thickness of the earth's crust in your backyard, and a tool that translates a Web page into Morse code data.")

The easiest way to add a new Active Desktop program is to use the New button on the Web panel of the Display Properties dialog box (refer to Figure 32.2). This step takes you to the Active Desktop Gallery at the Microsoft Web page. (Other Active Desktop programs should be available elsewhere eventually; for now, the Gallery from Microsoft is all that's available.)

▶ **Right-click the Desktop.**

▶ **Choose Active Desktop ➡Customize my Desktop.**

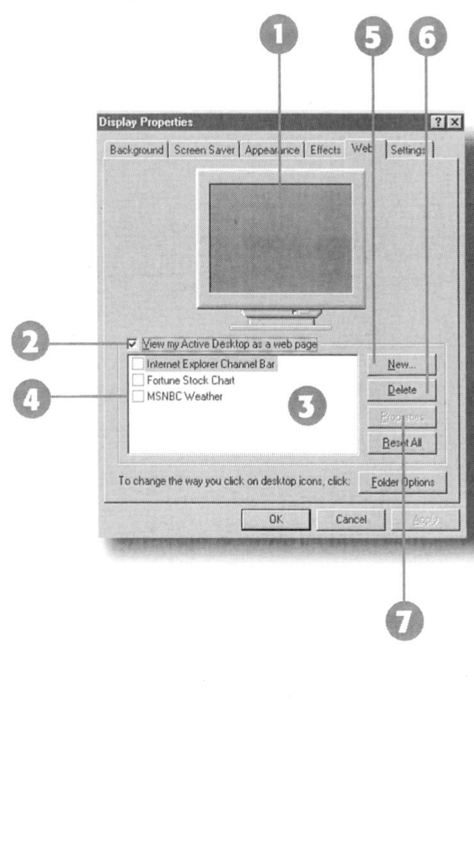

Figure 32.2
The Web panel in the Display Properties dialog box.

1. Preview screen.
2. This is selected when you've chosen to have your desktop display a Web page.
3. Active Desktop programs are listed here.
4. Put a check mark here to display or activate a program. The program window's size and position are shown on the preview screen.
5. Click here to hunt for Active Desktop programs on the Microsoft Web page.
6. Delete a highlighted Active Desktop program.
7. Display the Properties dialog box for a highlighted program.

After the Display Properties dialog box closes, you see the application floating on the desktop.

The next section covers rearranging the Active Desktop programs.

- Removing the check mark from an Active Desktop program in the Display Properties dialog box does not delete the program. However, if you select the program and click the Delete button, the program is gone for good.
- Too many Active Desktop programs and not enough desktop? Consider increasing your screen's real estate. See Chapter 40, "Tweaking Your Monitor."

Rearranging Active Desktop Programs

Each Active Desktop program on the desktop appears in a window, although it's not like any other window in Windows. To see the Active Desktop program's window, you must carefully point the mouse at the program, and then its window appears. After the window is visible, you can move it or resize it for some Active Desktop programs.

As an example, if you've made the Channel Bar visible, notice that it lacks the border it has in normal desktop mode. In Active Desktop mode, you have to point the mouse at the Channel Bar to see its window. This technique works for all Active Desktop programs:

▶ **Point the mouse at the Channel Bar.**

Notice that a window appears, as shown in Figure 32.3. If you cannot see the top *title bar* part of the window, point the mouse up near the top of the Channel bar. (It takes some getting used to; this stuff isn't easy.)

▶ **Drag the Channel Bar around.**

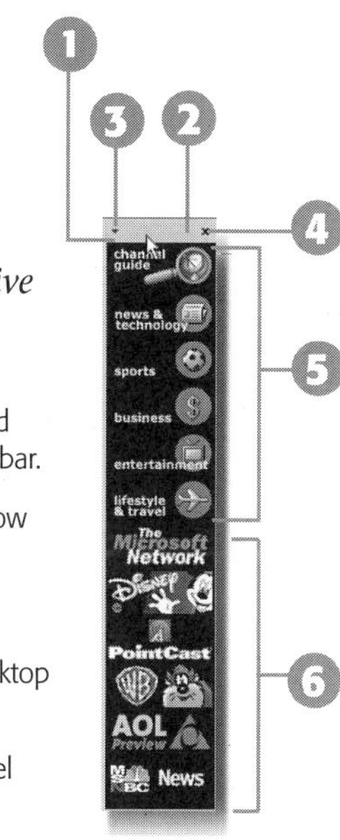

Figure 32.3
The window of an Active Desktop item.

1. Hover the mouse around this area to see the title bar.
2. You can move the window by dragging its title bar.
3. Drop-down menu list.
4. Removes the Active Desktop item from the desktop.
5. Submenus listing channel providers.
6. Companies who most likely paid Microsoft to have their logos flashed here.

The Display Properties dialog box appears, with the Web panel front and center.

▶ **Click the New button.**

If a New Active Desktop Item dialog box appears, click Yes. You want to connect to the Internet and grab a new Active Desktop program.

The Display Properties dialog box vanishes, and an IE window opens (if you don't have one open already). Maximize the IE window, if necessary.

Windows connects you to the Internet. (Connect to the Internet as you normally do.)

If you're not connected to the Internet, you must connect manually. For example, if you see the text "Working Offline" on the IE title bar, choose File ➡Work Offline from the IE menu and click the Refresh button on the toolbar.

The IE window takes you to the Microsoft Web page that contains a "gallery" of Active Desktop items you can download.

▶ **Browse through the various Active Desktop programs that are available.**

If you see any security-warning dialog boxes explaining that you're about to install and run some program from Microsoft Corporation, click Yes. These programs make getting the Active Desktop controls easier.

Because the content of the Active Desktop Gallery changes from time to time (it has changed twice since I started writing this book), I won't confuse you with a figure here, even though it would be helpful. Instead, use the links on the gallery's Web page to find Active Desktop items.

You should see a list of categories on the Web page somewhere: News and Sports, for example.

You might also see a list of content providers (*channels*), such as ESPN and MSNBC. If so, you might have to click a channel link to visit that page, where you see the Active Desktop program link.

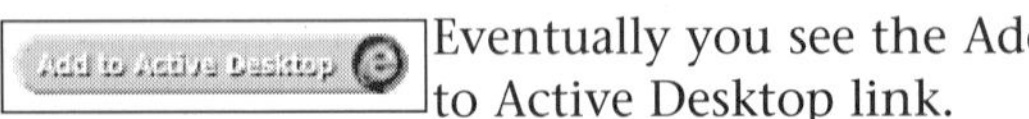

Eventually you see the Add to Active Desktop link. That's the one you click to download the program, copying it from the Internet to your PC's desktop.

Some Active Desktop programs might have descriptions next to them. If so, read the descriptions to see what the program does.

▶ **Click the Add to Active Desktop link.**

▶ **Click Yes if you see a Security Alert dialog box.**

You do want to add the item to your Active Desktop.

The Add Item to Active Desktop dialog box appears. It contains strange and unreadable information about the Active Desktop program you're adding.

▶ **Click OK to download the Active Desktop item.**

Downloading Subscriptions

This step might take a few moments, or it might quick.

When the transfer has been completed, check out the desktop to view your new item.

▶ **Minimize IE.**

Lo, you see your Active Desktop item.

▶ **Quit IE.**

Restore the IE window and quit if you want, disconnecting from the Internet. The next few sections in this chapter deal with customizing Active Desktop programs (you don't necessarily need to be connected to the Internet to do that).

- Active Desktop programs run whether or not you're connected to the Internet.
- The information displayed in some Active Desktop programs does have to be updated from time to time. When that happens, your computer automatically dials in to the Internet, downloads the necessary information, and then disconnects.
- The following section shows you how to customize when an Active Desktop program dials in to the Internet for updating.

Make sure that the link you click is the Add to Active Desktop link. Similar-looking links might be available. Don't be confused!

If you're using the Quick Launch Bar, as described in Chapter 11, click the Desktop button to quickly minimize all windows.

You can move or resize the Active Desktop program if you need to. Point the mouse at the program so that you can see its window. Stretch or move the window as you would any other program's window. See the section, "Rearranging Active Desktop Programs," earlier in this chapter for more information.

Adjusting the Active Desktop Program's Update Schedule

The key word in the term *Active Desktop program* is *active*. The program has to display meaningful information to be of any use to you. How the program gets that information is by stealthily dialing in to the Internet every so often.

The Active Desktop program actually dials in to the Internet automatically? That's scary!

Fear not, noble Windows user!

Most Active Desktop programs are set to automatically dial the Internet at preset times. You can change those times, even going so far as to make everything update manually. Of course, the more often some Active Desktop programs are updated, the handier they are; if you want to see a stock ticker, it makes sense to see *today's* stock prices as opposed to last week's.

Don't worry about an Active Desktop program connecting you to the Internet and staying online, maybe chatting with its friends over at the university. Most Active Desktop program updates take less than a minute.

Follow these steps to change or review how often your Active Desktop programs are updated. These steps assume that you have Active Desktop programs spinning happily away right now on your desktop.

▶ **Click the Active Desktop program's drop-down menu.**

See Figure 33.2 for information about displaying this list. You must point the mouse at the Active Desktop program's window until you see the downward-pointing triangle. Then click that triangle to see a drop-down menu.

▶ **Choose Properties.**

The Properties dialog box for your Active Desktop program appears.

▶ **Click the Scheduling tab.**

The Scheduling panel is where you set how often the Active Desktop program will be updated, if at all. Figure 32.4 explains things.

▶ **Choose Scheduled.**

As opposed to Manual, the Scheduled option allows you to let Windows automatically update the Active Desktop program's information.

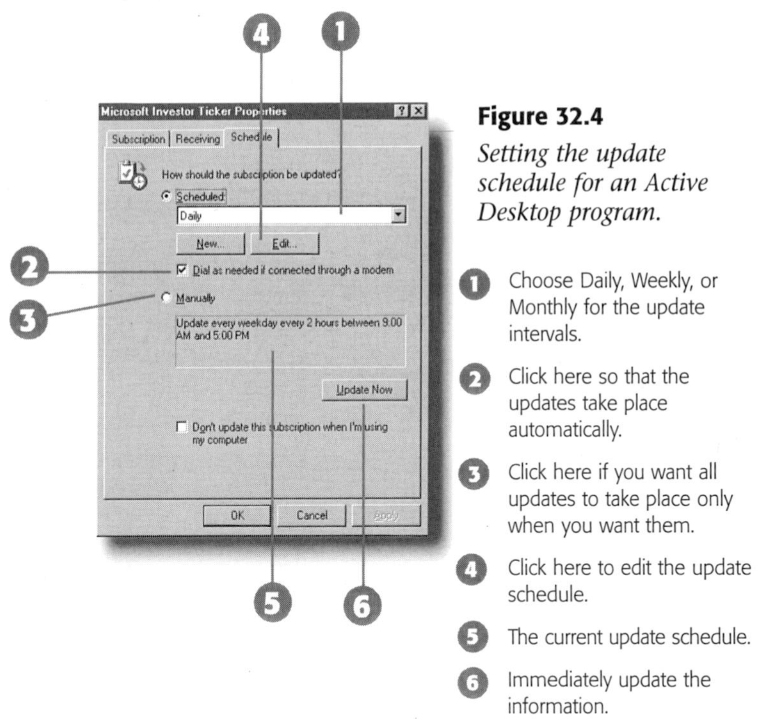

Figure 32.4
Setting the update schedule for an Active Desktop program.

1. Choose Daily, Weekly, or Monthly for the update intervals.
2. Click here so that the updates take place automatically.
3. Click here if you want all updates to take place only when you want them.
4. Click here to edit the update schedule.
5. The current update schedule.
6. Immediately update the information.

If you choose Manual instead, the information is updated only when you choose an Update Now command, such as the one shown in item F in Figure 32.4. (An Update Now command is also on the Active Desktop submenu, as shown in Figure 32.1.)

▶ **Choose Daily.**

This step tells Windows to update the Active Desktop program's content on a daily schedule. Or, if the content doesn't change much, you can choose Weekly or even Monthly instead.

▶ **Click Edit (if available) or New to adjust the schedule.**

If the Edit button is available, click it to adjust the update schedule; otherwise, you have to click New to set a schedule.

The Custom Schedule dialog box appears, offering you several hundred ways to have Windows dial in to the Internet and update the Active Desktop program's content.

You can select a specific time of day or have updating repeated throughout the day or just during office hours.

When you're done setting the schedule, close the Custom Schedule dialog box.

▶ **Click OK.**

The new schedule you've set appears in the program's Properties dialog box, as shown in Figure 32.4. In the figure, you can see how I'm updating my stock ticker: every 2 hours from 9:00 a.m. through 5:00 p.m. on weekdays.

▶ **Click OK.**

The Active Desktop program's Properties dialog box closes, and the new update schedule is set.

Don't be alarmed when your computer automatically dials the Internet to update Active Desktop information. In fact, it's kind of a nifty thing to see; computers should do more things automatically, in my opinion.

- Not all Active Desktop programs require constant updating. For most, a quick check at noon or midnight is all they need. Some programs might need updating only once a week.

Use the ? (question mark) button in the upper-right corner of the dialog box to get some point-and-click help, if you need it.

You can always do a manual update: Right-click the desktop and choose Active Desktop ➡Update Now. Windows dials the Internet, connects, and then updates your Active Desktop items. This process takes, maybe, the blink of an eye. Then Windows disconnects from the Internet.

Undoing Thy Active Desktop Sins

If you tire of the Active Desktop, you can remove it or just remove items from the desktop. I suppose that it depends on how much of what tires you.

You can customize most Active Desktop items. For example, you can load the stock ticker with symbols from your personal stock portfolio.

Removing Items from the Active Desktop

After downloading every dang-doodle Active Desktop item in the gallery, you decide that a few of them are really too much. For example, that spinning Java 3-D clock gives you vertigo. You hate it. But you still like the phase-of-the-moon Active Desktop program. There is a solution:

▶ **Right-click the desktop.**

▶ **Choose Active Desktop ➡Customize my Desktop.**

The Web panel of the Display Properties dialog box appears, as shown in Figure 32.2.

▶ **To remove an item from the desktop, click in its box to remove the check mark.**

For example, to remove the Java Clock, find Java Clock on the list and click in its box to remove the check mark.

Notice that the preview window is updated to show that the clock has gone bye-bye.

▶ **Click OK.**

The Display Properties dialog box goes away, and so does the Active Desktop item you no longer want to view.

Removing the Active Desktop and Reverting to "Normal"

The Active Desktop might be pointless, but it sure can be fun. In fact, if you ever want to impress someone with what Windows 98 can do, a preview of the Active Desktop screen does the trick. If the trick grows stale, you can go back to the way things were.

▶ **Right-click the Desktop.**

▶ **Choose Active Desktop ➡View As Web Page.**

This step removes the check mark there and restores your desktop to the way it looked before it was activated.

Reason number one for admiring Microsoft: It always gives you an undo command.

The changes you made while the desktop was activated aren't lost. Whenever you want, you can switch back to the Active Desktop by repeating the two preceding steps. You might have to reactivate or update some of the Active Desktop items (covered earlier in this chapter), but Windows 98 remembers all your settings.

Chapter 33

Mail Call!

Questions Answered and Thoughts Inspired

- Starting Outlook Express
- Reading your mail
- Replying to your email
- Forwarding email
- Using the Address Book
- Sending email
- Dealing with email attachments

Getting an electronic message—email—is the number one thing people do on the Internet. In fact, women (the more practical half of the species) use email more than they use the Web. And why not? Email is cool. An email address on a business card is a must. And getting lots of email means bragging rights (even though most of it is junk).

This chapter covers mail: inbox and outbox. Specifically, the program I cover here is Microsoft Outlook Express. Although it's not, in my opinion, the best email program (I prefer Eudora), it's free and it's what you have automatically if you use Windows.

- You cannot get email unless you set up an email account (refer to Chapter 7).
- I prefer Eudora because, like many non-Microsoft programs, it does one thing and does it well. Eudora does email and doesn't pretend to be anything else. You can download an evaluation copy of Eudora Light from `http://www.eudora.com`.
- This chapter has less of a tutorial nature than other chapters in this book. Although you can work the sections in this chapter if you have email, it's probably best just to read through the chapter to get an idea of what's going on and then come back here for specific information later.

Outlook Express, In and Out

The first thing most people do when they connect to the Internet is check their email. "Did anyone send me any messages?" "Do people like me enough to send me a message?" "Am I worthy?" "Am I interesting?" "Or am I just so despondent about email that I bore everyone and *that's* why I never get any email?"

A-hem.

When someone sends you email, it sits on your Internet service provider's (ISP) computer until you dial in to pick it up. The program you use for that task is Outlook Express:

▶ **Outlook Express.**

You can click the Outlook Express icon on the Quick Launch bar, open the Outlook Express shortcut icon on the desktop, or choose Programs ➡Internet Explorer ➡Outlook Express.

If you see the Dial-up Connection dialog box, enter your name and password if necessary. Click Connect to hook up to the Internet.

Outlook Express appears onscreen, looking something like Figure 33.1.

▶ **Maximize the window.**

If you have email waiting, Outlook Express tells you. You might hear some chimes, and, if you have any mail, you definitely see the text `You have ?? unread message(s) in your Inbox`. Yippee!

If you don't have any email waiting, well, aren't you pitiful?

Seriously, you don't always have mail. If you do, great. If not, check back later.

Reading mail (if you've received any) is covered in the following section. Skip over there and continue reading if you want.

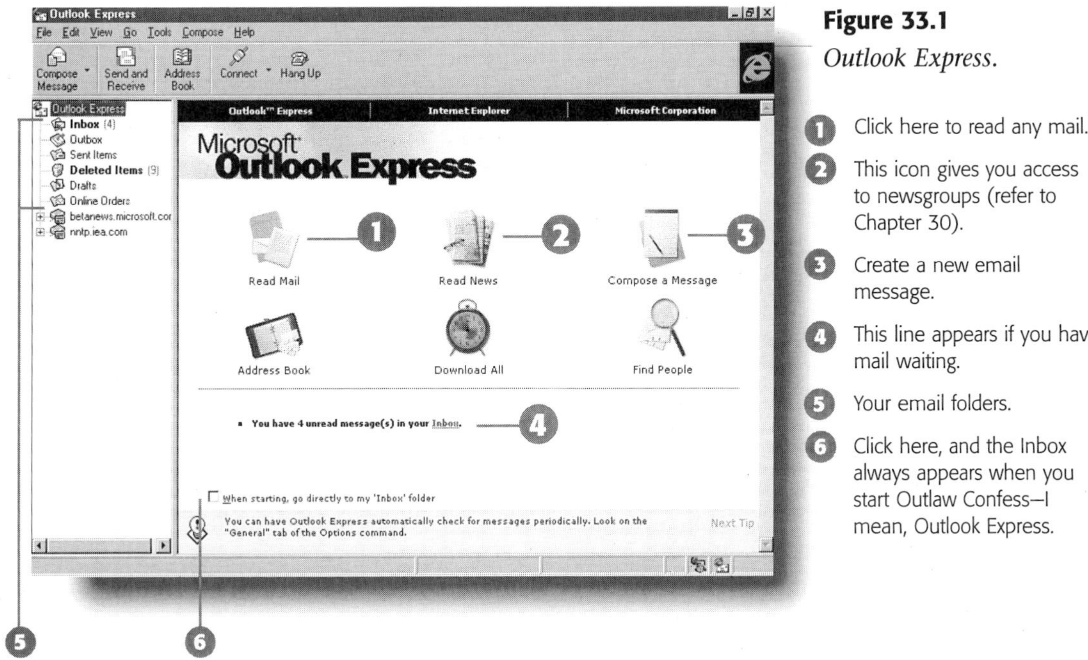

Figure 33.1
Outlook Express.

1. Click here to read any mail.
2. This icon gives you access to newsgroups (refer to Chapter 30).
3. Create a new email message.
4. This line appears if you have mail waiting.
5. Your email folders.
6. Click here, and the Inbox always appears when you start Outlaw Confess—I mean, Outlook Express.

When you're done reading your mail, or if you don't have any mail because no one really likes you, you will want to quit Outlook Express.

▶ **Close any open mail-reading windows you might have.**

Any messages you've been reading are open in their own windows (more about this subject in the next section). Use the taskbar to switch to any open message-reading windows, and then close them.

▶ **Choose File ➡Exit.**

A dialog box might appear, asking whether you want to disconnect from the Internet. Choose Yes if you're done for the day.

- Don't be discouraged if you don't get much mail. Few people do. Those who brag about it are usually in a position that requires them to get a great deal of email.
- Check your mail at least once a day. People who respond quickly to email get more email than people who ignore it.

TIP

The best way to get email is to send it. Find out which of your friends and coworkers have email accounts. Send them email. Then, when they answer you, *write back*! Remember that email is communication, and communication has to go both ways in order to work.

- Other fun names for Outlook Express:

  Outlook Distress

  Outlook Clueless

  Outhouse Express

  Outguess the Mess

  Output for Less

  Outward Abscess

  Awkward Undress

Reading Your Mail

When you have mail waiting, Outlook Express lets you know. Figure 33.1 shows you the cheery `You have ?? unread message(s) in your Inbox` message, meaning that you have email waiting to be read.

▶ **Click the Read Mail item.**

Your inbox opens to reveal any messages that are waiting. Figure 33.2 explains things.

The first unread message you have is already displayed onscreen, as shown in Figure 33.2. However, that's not the best way to read the message. (As usual, Microsoft offers several ways.)

▶ **Double-click the message's envelope icon.**

See the item labeled 7 in Figure 33.2 to see where to click. When you do, a special message-reading window appears, which I think offers a better way to read the message than reading it in the main window. Figure 33.3 explains how the window works.

Double-click your messages to open them in their own message-reading window.

▶ **Read the message.**

After you're done reading a message, you can choose to reply to that message, forward the message along to someone else, delete the message, move the message to a folder for storage, or just skip along and read the next message. The following sections tell you how each of these options works.

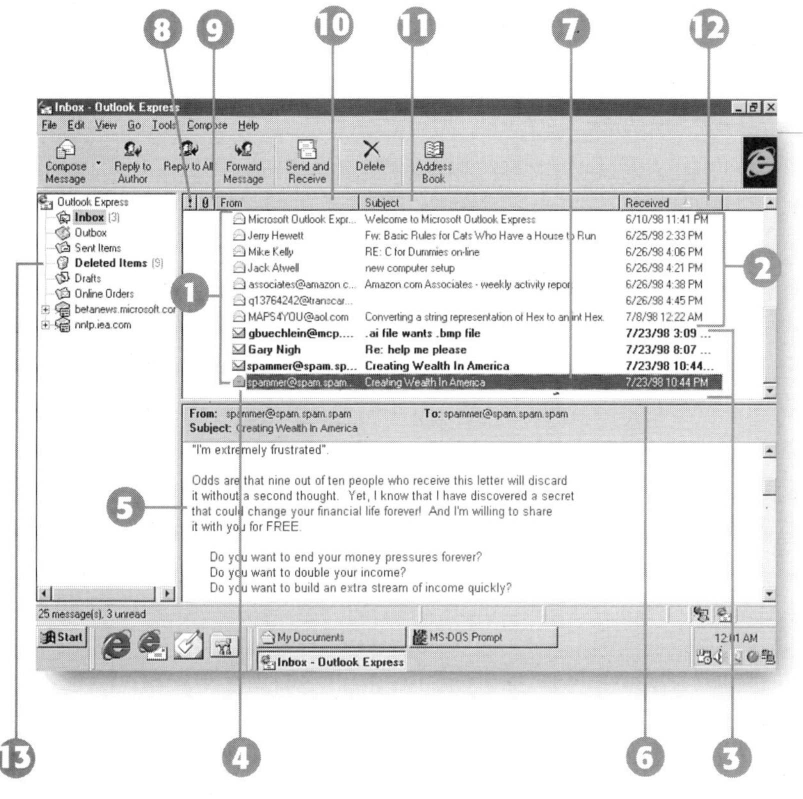

Figure 33.2
Reading mail.

1. Contents of your inbox.
2. Mail you've read appears dimmed.
3. Unread mail appears in bold type.
4. The message you're reading is highlighted.
5. Current message (real, spam, or junk email).
6. You can drag here to adjust the inbox/message window size.
7. Double-click here to open the message for reading.
8. Priority column.
9. Attachments are flagged here.
10. Person sending the email (his email address, actually).
11. Message subject.
12. Time received.
13. Email Recycle Bin.

If you would rather "hold" on a message and just read the next message in the list, click the Next button in the mail-reading window. All messages stay in your inbox until you delete them or move them to a folder.

- If you're ever asked for your password when you're using Outlook Express, type it in there. Note that you can always check-mark an item to tell Windows to remember your password. Check it. I do.

TIP

If you're using Outlook Express online and want to check your mail again, click the Send and Receive button.

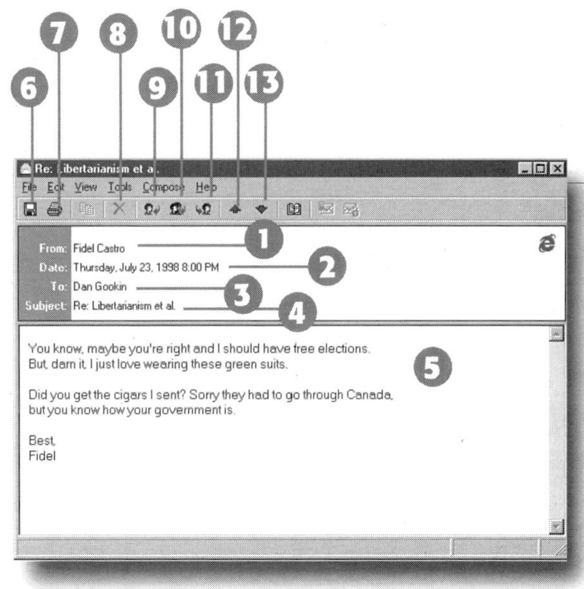

Figure 33.3
Reading a message.

1. Person who sent the message.
2. Time it was received.
3. You! Actually, it's me—you would be listed here instead.
4. Message subject.
5. Message contents.
6. Save the message as a file on disk.
7. Print this message.
8. Delete the message.
9. Reply to the sender.
10. Reply to the sender and all CC people.
11. Forward this message to someone else.
12. Read the preceding message.
13. Read the next message.

TIP

Another nifty thing you should consider doing when you're reading a message is adding that person's name to your email program's address book. This subject is covered in the section, "Adding Someone's Name to Your Address Book," later in this chapter.

- Junk email is commonly called *spam*, after the Hormel meat product.
- Yes, you will get some spam email. Just delete it. No one outside of Wall Street "makes money quick" on the Internet.

Replying to a Message

In email-speak, a *reply* is an answer to an email message. You don't have to reply to all the messages. For example, it's common not to reply to someone who says "Thank you" or "I'll see you next Tuesday" or "You're a dork." Most of the time, however, a reply is considered a courteous acknowledgment or response.

To reply to a message you're reading, do the following:

▶ **Click the Reply to Author button.**

The keyboard shortcut for the Reply to Author button is Ctrl+R, which I use instead of clicking the button because it's quicker and my hands are already on the keyboard.

"Reply to Author" refers to the author of the email message, not the author of this book. The message's "author" and the "sender" are usually the same person.

The Reply window appears, as shown in Figure 33.4. That's where you enter your email reply.

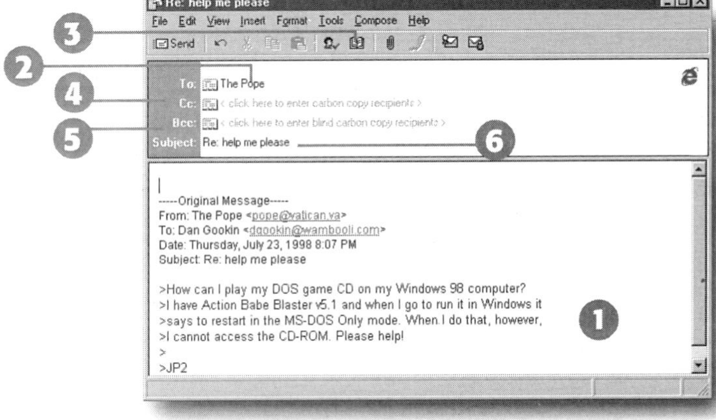

Figure 33.4
Replying to a message.

1. The original message appears "quoted" here. Quoting is a courtesy to the recipient to remind her of the original message's content.
2. The To field automatically contains the name of the person who wrote the message you're replying to.
3. You can add other names to the list by clicking here.
4. You can send carbon copies of the message to others here.
5. Blind carbon copies go here.
6. The message subject.

▶ **Type your reply.**

Enter your message in the lower half of the reply window.

Notice that a copy of the original message is kept at the bottom of the window, which is common in most email programs. The copy helps keep the reader aware of the original message's content.

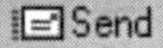

▶ **Click the Send button to send the message.**

Off it goes, into cyberspace.

If the copy of the original message is overly long, you can cut it out or edit it. For example, people every so often send me their C programs for debugging. When I reply, I edit out the C program to keep my reply short and to the point.

You can press the F7 key to spell-check your message when you're done composing it. This check helps you avoid some spelling errors, although they're common in email messages and no one really thinks any less of you for it.

The Reply window closes and your inbox returns, where you can store or delete the original or just skip over it and continue reading new messages. (More about this subject in the following sections.)

- If you want to cancel the message before sending it, just close the Reply window. A dialog box asks whether you want to save the message. Click No, and the message isn't sent.
- You can send a *carbon copy*, or courtesy copy, of the message to others in the message's CC field. That way, people can be informed of the message without thinking that the message is directed to them.
- The BCC (blind carbon copy) field sends the message to others, although their names are not visible when the message is read by folks listed in the To and CC fields. This way, you can keep someone in the loop about a message without letting the other folks know about it. It's sneaky.
- Mail delivery over the Internet is usually instantaneous. I've sent messages back and forth to a reader in Australia, and he read them just seconds after I sent them.

Forwarding a Message to Someone Else

Occasionally you get email you want to resend to someone else. For example, if Jerry sends you a humorous story about firefighters and you want to send a copy of it to your friend Mike the Fireman, what you need to do is *forward* the message.

Update the Subject line if the message content changes.

Forwarding is different from replying. When you reply, you send a message back to the person who wrote you. When you forward, you take a message someone has sent to you and send it along to someone else.

After reading a message, take these steps to forward it:

▶ **Click the Forward Message button.**

As with replying to a message, the Reply window appears. The original message appears quoted in the lower half of the window, just as though you were replying to the message. Don't think that you've screwed up, though! On close examination, you notice some differences. For example, the To field is blank.

The keyboard shortcut for forwarding a message is the logical Ctrl+F.

▶ **Type an email address in the To field.**

For example, type Mike the Fireman's email address. Type the whole email address, which usually fits into the format `name@place.something`. No spaces are allowed in an email name.

If you've been saving email addresses, you can click the little Rolodex card to view your address book and automatically insert an address. (See the section, "Adding Someone's Name to Your Address Book," later in this chapter.)

▶ **Type a brief message (if necessary).**

Type something like **I thought you would want to see this**. The original message—the one you're forwarding—appears in the bottom half of the window, underneath whatever you type.

▶ **Click the Send button to send the message.**

You don't *have* to type any message. Check the Subject line onscreen. It has the letters *FW* in it, which is a sign that the message you're sending has been forwarded. All astute email readers will pick up on that immediately.

Your message has been forwarded. No, wait! It looks like it's being held in the Outbox. Ohhh—now it's gone!

Deleting a Message

More often than not, you end up deleting the messages you get. Sure, you can save them, but the majority of email is spam, which is junk you don't want to reply to or even keep. Trash it!

▶ **Click the Delete button to delete a message you're reading.**

The message is moved into the Outlook email Recycle Bin.

- Getting and deleting spam is part of email life.
- How do you get on a spam emailer's list? Dumb luck. You increase your chances if you post to a newsgroup, display your email address on a Web page, or order something from a Web page. Even if you avoid all those chances, though, one or more of them still might find you and send you spam.
- Messages are merely moved to the Recycle Bin, not fully deleted. If you open the Recycle Bin folder in Outlook Express, you can get the messages back. Only if you delete the messages in the Recycle Bin folder are they truly gone.

Please don't respond to any spam or unsolicited email! It's a trick: If they can get you to respond, they know that you're a real person and they send you *even more* spam. Don't ever respond to spam!

Adding Someone's Name to Your Address Book

After reading a message from some guy named Bill Clinton, you decide that it's a good idea to add him to your address book. In the message-reading window, do the following:

▶ **Choose Tools ➡Add to Address Book ➡Sender.**

You don't have to do this step for every message—just for the folks you plan to communicate with regularly: friends, coworkers, business associates, family, and people like that.

After choosing the preceding menu item, you see the person's Properties dialog box, which is part of the Outlook Express address book. Figure 33.5 explains things.

▶ **Enter a nickname in the Nickname box.**

After reading the message, consider adding the sender's name and email address to your address book. Although this step is optional, it's a good idea for anyone with whom you plan to correspond regularly.

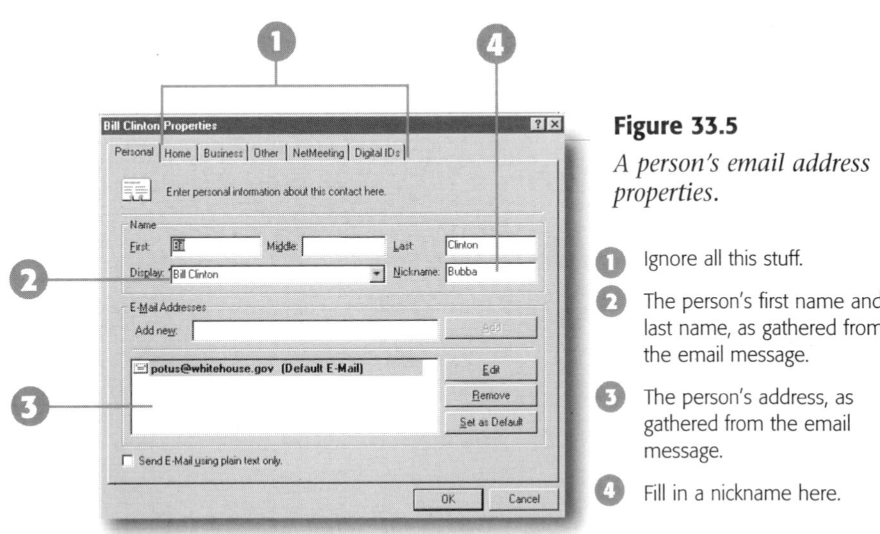

Figure 33.5

A person's email address properties.

1. Ignore all this stuff.
2. The person's first name and last name, as gathered from the email message.
3. The person's address, as gathered from the email message.
4. Fill in a nickname here.

For example, my editor has a long, complex email name that I'll never memorize. However, her address book entry has a nickname: Grace. When I want to send Grace a new message, I type only **Grace** in the To field, and Outlook Express automatically figures out the rest.

Nicknames are very handy to have. Everyone to whom I send mail has a nickname. That way, I can send mail to Matt or Jerry or even Bubba, and it always gets to the right person.

▶ **Click OK.**

The person's Properties dialog box closes, and you're back at the message-reading window.

- Put in the address book the names of people with whom you frequently correspond.
- You have to do this only once for everyone.
- No, the person receiving the email message doesn't see the nickname. Outlook Express replaces the nickname with the person's real name and email address as it sends the message.
- It's unnecessary to update *all* the information in the address book. (The program is kind of kooky.)
- Yes, it's the same Address Book program used to fax information to people. You can ignore it for faxing, although it's ideal for storing email names and nicknames.

Composing a New Email Message

To send an email message to someone else, you need only two things: the person's email address and something to write about. It's similar to sending someone a letter, although in this case no paper is involved and you have nothing to lick. (Well, if you're in the habit of licking your PC monitor to send an email message, don't let me stop you.)

To send some human an email message, do the following:

▶ **Start Outlook Express.**

Refer to the section, "Outlook Express, In and Out," at the beginning of this chapter for the details about starting Outlook Express.

▶ **Choose Compose a Message from the main screen.**

Or press the keyboard shortcut, Ctrl+N, to start a new message. This technique works if you're already using Outlook Express and cannot see the main screen.

The New Message window appears, as shown in Figure 33.6.

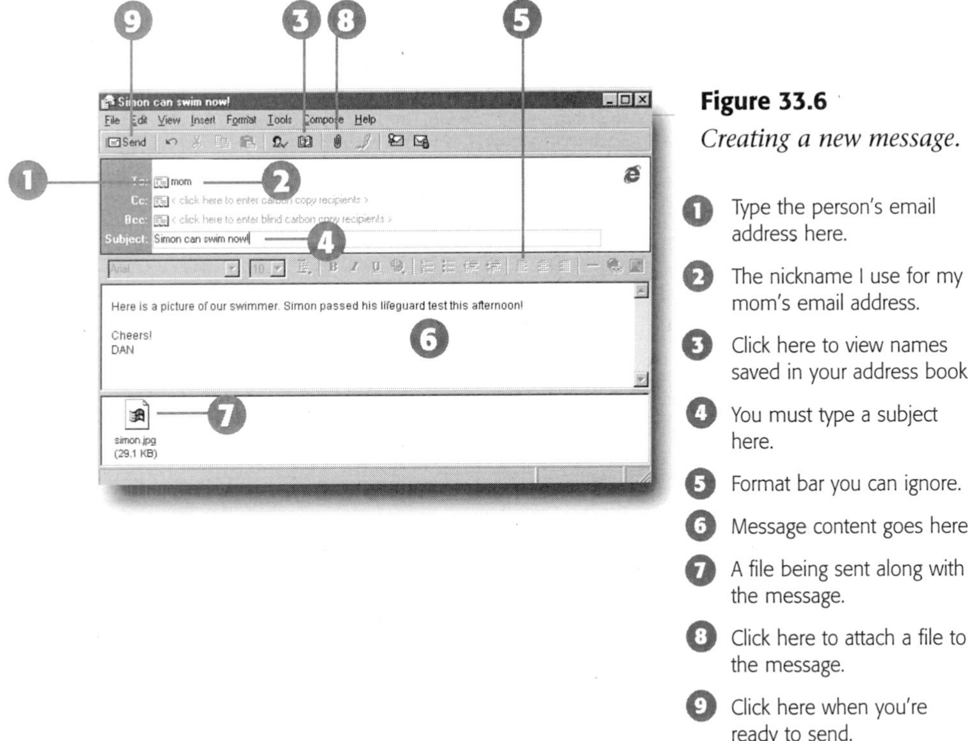

Figure 33.6
Creating a new message.

1. Type the person's email address here.
2. The nickname I use for my mom's email address.
3. Click here to view names saved in your address book.
4. You must type a subject here.
5. Format bar you can ignore.
6. Message content goes here.
7. A file being sent along with the message.
8. Click here to attach a file to the message.
9. Click here when you're ready to send.

- **In the To field, type the email address of the person to whom you're sending the message.**

If you've been saving email names in the address book, you can type a nickname rather than the full address.

Also, if you've been using the address book, you can click the Rolodex icon to view names in the address book and copy them to the To field.

- **Enter any CC names.**

These people are the ones to whom you want to send a carbon copy of the message, such as "FYI, but it's not directed at you." As with the To field, you can type multiple names; separate each with a comma.

- **Enter any BCC name.**

The Blind Carbon Copy field contains the email names and addresses of folks whom you want to see the message; however, the other folks in the To and CC fields don't see these names.

TIP

You can send a message to more than one person. The secret is to type everyone's email addresses in the To field. Separate each email address by using a comma, like this:

```
potus@whitehouse.gov,bgates@microsoft.com,dave@lateshow.cbs.com
```

Each email address is written in the To field, separated by a comma.

Or, if you're using nicknames, you might type

```
bubba,geek,dl
```

Again, everything is separated by a comma.

▶ **Type a subject.**

The message subject is required. Make it short and descriptive of the message's contents:

▶ **Type the message content.**

No limit exists on how much you can type. Some email messages can get quite long. Then again, no rule exists about replying with just one word or a sentence, if that's all it takes.

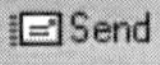

▶ **Click the Send button.**

Your message is whisked off into the ether, sent through the Internet to the recipient.

- Try not to format your message with bold or fancy fonts or backgrounds. Not every email program can understand the formatting, so the person you're sending to might not get the formatted message. Because email traditionally consists of just plain text, avoid using the format toolbar unless you're certain that the person you're sending to also uses Outlook Express.
- Outlook lets you create a message by using "stationery." The drop-down list that's displayed when you click the Compose Message button contains some samples if you want to play. Not everyone receiving the message will see the pretty stationery. In fact, some people might not even be able to read the message.

All About Email Attachments (Sending Files with Your Email)

Many email messages have, in addition to plain text, *attachments*. They're files people send along with a message. Sending an attachment is like sending someone a file on a floppy disk through the mail, although the file is being sent from another computer to your computer through the Internet.

In Outlook Express you can send files and receive them. Sending is easier. I cover that one first.

Sending an Email Attachment

To send an email attachment, simply compose an email message, as described earlier in this chapter in the section, "Composing a New Email Message." Just like with any other message, you have to send the message to someone, supply a subject, and maybe write a few lines of text explaining the attached file.

Before you go to send your email message, you have to attach the file:

▶ **Click the Insert File button on the toolbar.**

The Insert File button is the little paper clip on the toolbar. After clicking it, you see the Insert Attachment dialog box. It works like any Open dialog box.

▶ **Find the file you want to send by using the Insert Attachment dialog box.**

Browse through your hard drive, looking for the file you want to send.

Send only "real" files. Do not send shortcuts! Sure, on your PC, a shortcut works just like the original file. If you attach a shortcut to an email message, however, you're attaching only the shortcut file—not the original.

Always attach "real" files, not their shortcuts.

When you've found the file you want to send, click the Attach button in the Insert Attachment dialog box:

▶ **Click Attach.**

The file's icon appears in the bottom half of the window.

You can attach multiple files: Just keep clicking the little paper clip button and finding files to send. Keep in mind that more files make for a *very large* email message, which some people don't like. (I send multiple files in separate messages.)

▶ **Send the message.**

At this point, sending the email message with an attachment works just like sending any other email message. The only difference is that you're sending a file, and it might take awhile longer than usual to send the message, depending on the file's size.

- When you're sending an attachment, ensure that the person your're sending the message to can deal with it. For example, don't send a WordPerfect document file to someone who doesn't have WordPerfect.
- Another attachment consideration: Try to avoid sending *huge* attachments to people. For example, my friend Reed once sent me a 2MB graphics file. Ugh. Write a message beforehand, and ask the person whether it's okay to send a file that large.
- The To and Subject fields are always required in an email message, even when you're sending a file.
- You don't *have* to write any text when you're sending a file, although you should. Explain what the file is and why you're sending it.
- I used email to send to my editor in Indiana every file I wrote for this book. I printed not one page, licked no stamps, and incurred no exorbitant FedEx bills.
- If you decide not to send an attachment you've already attached, right-click its icon at the bottom of the new message window. Choose Remove from the shortcut menu, and the file is unattached.

Receiving an Email Attachment

Getting a file with your email is simple—as long as you're not using America Online (AOL) for email. I get many letters from AOL users asking about attachments, so I suppose that the AOL email program can't deal with them. (Keep that in mind when you send attachments.) Fortunately, Outlook Express handles attachments with ease. You should have no problems.

Attachments are received along with your regular email.

▶ **Read your mail.**

Reading an email message with an attachment works just like reading any email message. You should see some subject and message content in addition to the attachments. (Refer to the section "Reading Your Mail," earlier in this chapter, for information about reading email.)

Figure 33.7 shows an email message I received containing an attachment. The attachment is a JPEG graphics file. The graphics file (which you saw in Figure 33.6) appears as a picture when the message is shown as received (see Figure 33.7).

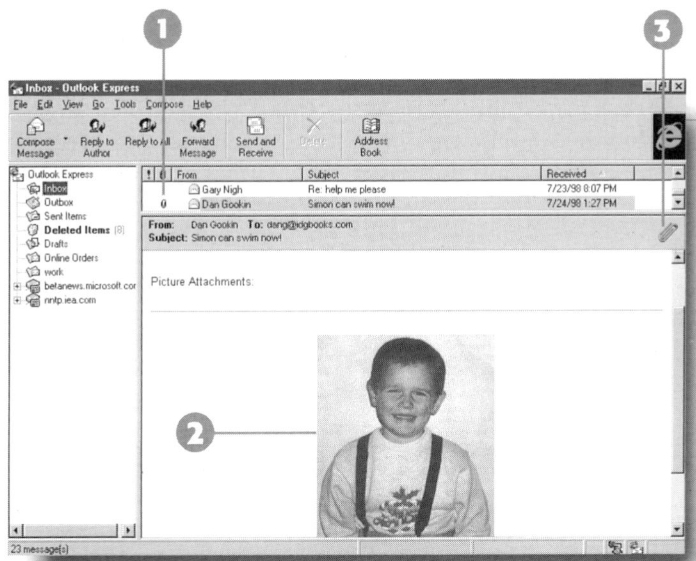

Figure 33.7

A graphics attachment in a message.

1. The little paper clip indicates that the message has an attachment.
2. The graphics image is displayed at the end of the message.
3. You can access other attachments with the big paper clip icon.

If the file isn't a graphics image or other type of file that can be displayed in the message, you have to click the big paper clip icon in the upper-right corner of the message.

Keep an eye out for the big paper clip button. It's your clue that you have an email attachment.

▶ **Click the big paper clip button.**

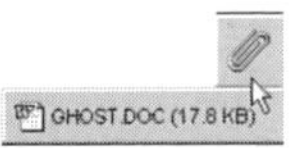

When you click the big paper clip, a list of attached files appears, as shown in the margin.

▶ **Choose an item from the list to open it.**

The program that created the file opens it, and you can see its contents.

Or, if you would rather not open the files now, choose File ➡Save Attachments and choose the attachment from the submenu. A Save Attachment As dialog box appears, which you can use to save the attachment as a file anywhere on your computer.

Beware of mystery attachments!

Some people might send you files you're unfamiliar with. A common file type is the ZIP archive. Unless you have an unzipping program, such as WinZIP, you cannot use that type of file. In that case, delete the message and don't bother opening or saving the attachment.

When you get files of an unknown type, reply to the sender. Tell the person that you're unable to read the attachment, and then ask for more information. Don't fret over this situation; it happens all the time.

Never, ever, open any *program* sent to you by anyone you don't know. *That's* how your computer can get a virus from email. Reading an email message does not give your PC a virus (it's impossible). Opening and running an unknown program, however, *can* possibly give your PC a virus. Do not run programs sent to you from strangers!

Figure 33.8

An attachment warning dialog box.

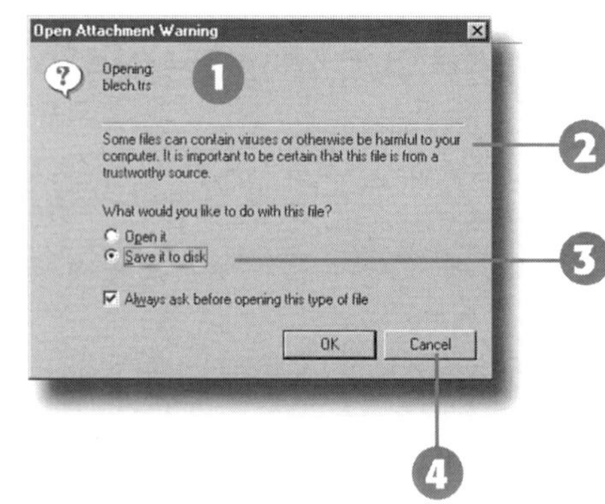

1. Windows does not recognize this type of file.
2. Never open an unknown file type.
3. I even recommend against saving an unknown file type to disk.
4. Click here to cancel the whole thing.

Sometimes you might see a warning dialog box when you try to open a file of an unknown type, as shown in Figure 33.8. My advice? Click Cancel and be rid of the file.

- If you receive a ZIP file, you need an unzipping program to read it. If you don't yet have a copy of WinZIP, get one. Visit the WinZIP Web page, at `www.winzip.com`, and download an evaluation copy. If you use the program frequently, buy it! I did. The registered version has much nicer features, and it's only $29. Cheap!

If someone you know sends you a program and you trust that person, it's okay to open the program. Sending files through email is very common, so don't get paranoid. If someone you don't know, or someone you don't trust, sends you a program file, however, delete that message.

Any attachments you receive are not saved as files on disk until you tell Outlook Express to do so. Until then, the attachments are secretly encoded in each email message.

Chapter 34

The Network 'Hood

Questions Answered and Thoughts Inspired

- Using the Network Neighborhood
- Finding files and computers on the network
- Using the Open and Save As commands on the network
- Running programs from another computer (advice only)

"It's a beautiful day in the Network Neighborhood..."

The *Network Neighborhood* is one of those icons, like My Computer and the Recycle Bin, you might find lurking on your desktop. Its purpose is to give you a window into other computers on your *local area network* (*LAN*). It lets you see which other computers are on the network and optionally use their hard drives and printers. This chapter tells you how to do all that stuff.

- See Appendix B for more general information about networks. This chapter assumes that you already have a network "up" and installed in your office (or home).
- If you don't see the Network Neighborhood icon on your desktop, your computer is not networked. You can skip this chapter and the next.
- An odd chance exists that you might see the Network Neighborhood icon on the desktop of a nonnetworked PC. It happens when your computer is configured to connect to the Internet. (It can also happen when the manufacturer uses a network card to install the computer's software and fails to remove the card's drivers

after the installation.) In that case you cannot use the Network Neighborhood icon. No loss.

The information in this chapter is specific to a peer-to-peer Windows 98 network. If you have another type of network, things will doubtless look different to you, and other networking commands and options might be available. The network administrator at your office should be able to help you.

Hello, Network Neighborhood!

If you have a computer network, what you have is an office (or home, if you're eccentric) with several computers all connected to each other with network cabling. The computers can talk, share information, and join together for the occasional network crash. Networking can be fun.

To help you access files, folders, disk drives, and printers on other computers, Windows 98 comes with a special icon: Network Neighborhood. Opening that icon reveals a window kind of like the My Computer window, except that what you see is the entire network and not just one computer.

▶ **Open the Network Neighborhood icon on the desktop.**

Double-click the Network Neighborhood icon to splay it open. What you should see is a list of every other computer on your network, as shown in Figure 34.1.

The list of computers you see is particular to your workgroup. For example, you might be in a cluster of people in the Torture and Anguish division. If so, you see only computers in the Torture and Anguish workgroup. Other workgroups, and computers in those groups, are accessed through the Entire Network icon:

▶ **Open the Entire Network icon.**

The Entire Network icon shows you which workgroups are on your network, as shown in Figure 34.2.

Your computer is assigned to one of the workgroups for a reason. You probably won't venture into the other workgroups often, if ever. (If you do, you probably should change workgroups. Have your network system administrator set that up for you.)

▶ **Click the Back button.**

You return to the main Network Neighborhood window.

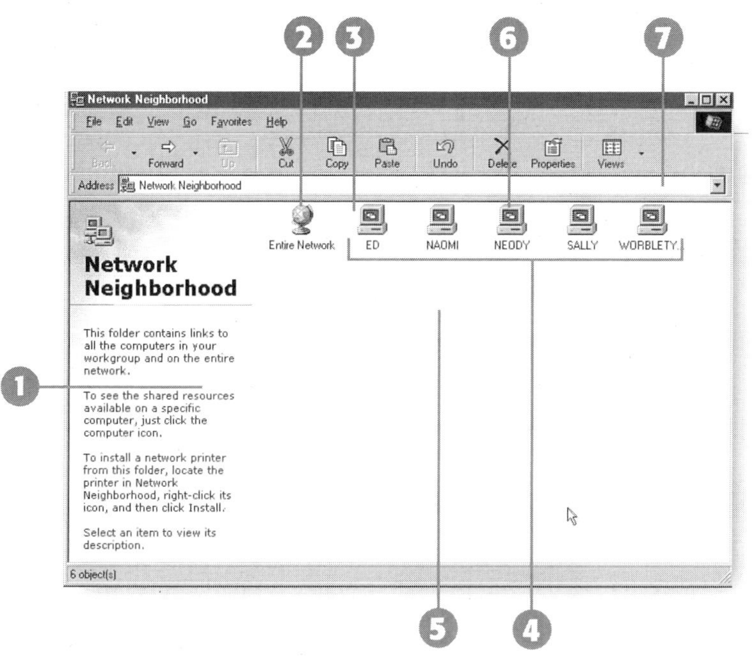

Figure 34.1

The Network Neighborhood window.

1. Choose View ➡As Web Page to see this information displayed.
2. Represents the entire network (all workgroups).
3. Only computers logged in to the current workgroup appear here.
4. Individual computers on the network.
5. If any printers are directly connected to the network, they appear here too.
6. Open a computer to see what resources it's sharing.
7. You can also display this folder by choosing Network Neighborhood from this list.

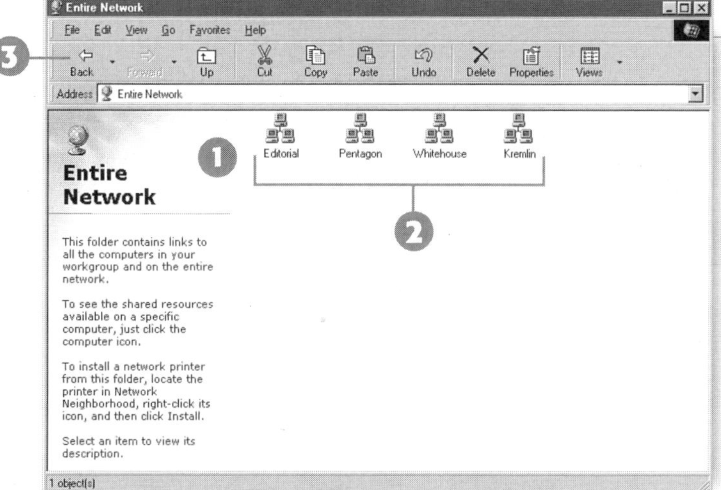

Figure 34.2

All the workgroups on your LAN.

1. All workgroups on the network.
2. Open one of these to see the computers in that workgroup.
3. Click here to return to the Network Neighborhood.

When you're done with the Network Neighborhood, you close its window:

▶ **Close the Network Neighborhood window.**

Your network journey continues in the following section.

- If you get an "Unable to browse the network" error message after opening the Entire Network icon, your computer is probably not on the network. The network might be down, or you might not be connected in the first place. See the nearby "Network Troubleshooting" sidebar.
- Don't be surprised if you don't see your computer listed in the Network Neighborhood window. Only if your computer is sharing a printer or a hard drive (or folder) does it show up. This subject is covered in Chapter 35.
- You can also view computers in the Network Neighborhood window from any Open or Browse dialog box.
- For a computer to appear in the Network Neighborhood window, it must be connected to the network *and* have resources available for sharing. Sharing resources is covered in Chapter 35.

Network Troubleshooting

Networks crash. They go down. It's a part of life. Don't blame anyone. It's just a cruel twist of fate, probably some ancient curse. (That means just the network in your office; this information doesn't apply to crashes on the Internet.)

Your office should have a network administrator whose job it is to ensure that the network goes down all the time—uh, I mean, makes sure that the network *gets back up* all the time. If your office lacks a network administrator, try these tricks:

- Make sure that the network cables are all properly connected.
- If you're using thin Ethernet, make sure that both ends of the network are terminated with those little, round, twisty plugs (*resistors*).
- If you don't see other computers in the Network Neighborhood window, check to make sure that those computers are turned on.
- A big mistake most people make is not using the proper protocols when they're configuring the network. All your network protocols must be the same on *all* computers on the network, or else the sucker just doesn't work (see Appendix B).

You can also run the Network Troubleshooter, which might help in desperate situations: Choose Help from the Start Thing. Then, on the Contents panel, choose Troubleshooting, Windows 98 Troubleshooters, and Networking. Follow the directions the Network Troubleshooter gives to try to solve your problem.

Browsing Your Network

Like My Computer, the Network Neighborhood is a place to browse. Of course, you're browsing on others' computers—which seems kind of sneaky. Remember, though, that anything you can see on another computer is made available voluntarily. You cannot peek where you're not allowed.

The following tutorial is rather sketchy because I don't know which computers you have available on your network. Follow along loosely:

▶ **Open the Network Neighborhood icon on the desktop.**

The Network Neighborhood window opens, as shown earlier in this chapter, in Figure 34.1.

▶ **Open a computer on the network.**

On my network, I open Worbletyme, which is my multimedia workstation (until I retire it next year and replace it with a Macintosh). You can see the Worbletyme icon in Figure 34.1. Figure 34.3 shows what I see when I open that icon. What you see on your screen will be different, although many of the same elements might appear.

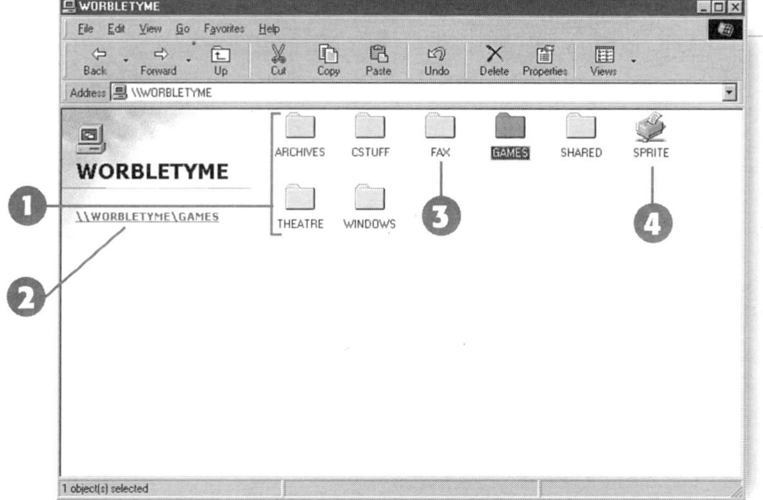

Figure 34.3

Folders and printers shared by another PC.

1. Each of these is a folder or hard drive shared by the other computer.
2. Information about the selected folder, the folder's network pathname (ugh).
3. A folder named FAX might indicate the presence of a network fax modem.
4. A printer is also being shared on this computer.

The folders you see have been selected for sharing by the other computer. (Sharing folders is covered in Chapter 35.) The folders represent a folder or even a whole disk drive on the other computer. It depends on what the other computer is sharing.

If you see a printer, it too has been flagged for sharing by the other computer. You can install that network printer for use by your computer: Right-click the printer and choose Install from the shortcut menu. (Refer to Chapter 18 for information about network printer installation.)

▶ **Open a folder on the network computer.**

Double-click any folder to open it. On my screen, I chose, natch, the Games folder. Opening that folder displayed a list of files, icons, and other folders—just like the My Computer window displays files on your computer. The only difference is that the icons represent items on another computer on the network.

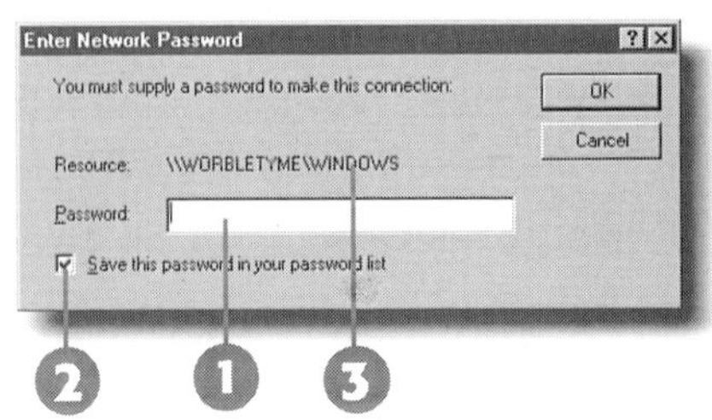

Figure 34.4

You must supply a password to access some folders.

1. Type the access password here.
2. If you keep this check mark here, you never have to type the password again to access the folder.
3. Cryptic network pathname.

If an Enter Network Password dialog box appears, you have to type a password to access the files in a specific folder, as shown in Figure 34.4.

You can use two types of passwords. One is a full-access password, which allows you to delete or move files from the network computer. The other is a read-only password, which allows you to read and copy files but not change them. Type the proper password and click OK to be given access to the network folder.

▶ **Close the Network Neighborhood window.**

Browsing the files and folders on a network hard drive works just like browsing them on your own computer. You can do anything in the Network Neighborhood that you would normally do in a My Computer or Windows Explorer window. In fact, if you prefer the Explorer, use it instead to browse the Network Neighborhood: Just scroll down and open the Network Neighborhood icon on the left side of the Explorer window. You're in business.

- The read-only and full-access passwords are set by the network computer's owner when she shares a given disk drive or folder. Read more about this subject in Chapter 35.
- Yes, the Save This Password in Your Password List item is a security breach; it means that anyone else using your computer can access the same network folder without ever knowing the password. If you ask Microsoft about this matter, it tells you to buy Windows NT.
- Worbletyme is a name I fabricated in college. The name of my radio drama "company" in my radio production class was *The Sterling, Worbletyme, and Grockmeister Radio Theater.*

Accessing Files on Another Computer

Files in a network folder work just like they do on your computer. From the Network Neighborhood window, you can work with the files just as you would on your own computer: You can copy and open them and (as long as read-only access hasn't been set) move, change, delete, and rename them.

The following tutorial opens a graphics file on another computer and assumes that the computer is sharing its C drive. If that's not the case with your LAN, follow along closely, absorbing knowledge like a sponge.

- **Start Paint.**
- **Choose File ➡Open.**

The standard Open dialog box appears, although you won't be using it to open a file on your computer. Instead, you're venturing out on the network to locate a graphics file on another PC. Sneaky.

- **Choose Network Neighborhood from the Look In drop-down list.**

The computer takes a few moments to find all the computers available on the network. They soon appear, just as shown in Figure 34.1, although in List view, not Large Icons view.

- **Open a network computer that shares its C drive.**

On my network, the list includes just about every computer (except Worbletyme). I open ED instead, my editing computer (which is very nice, so a Macintosh won't replace it any time soon).

Open the computer in the Open dialog box's window by double-clicking its icon. Figure 34.5 shows what I see on my screen.

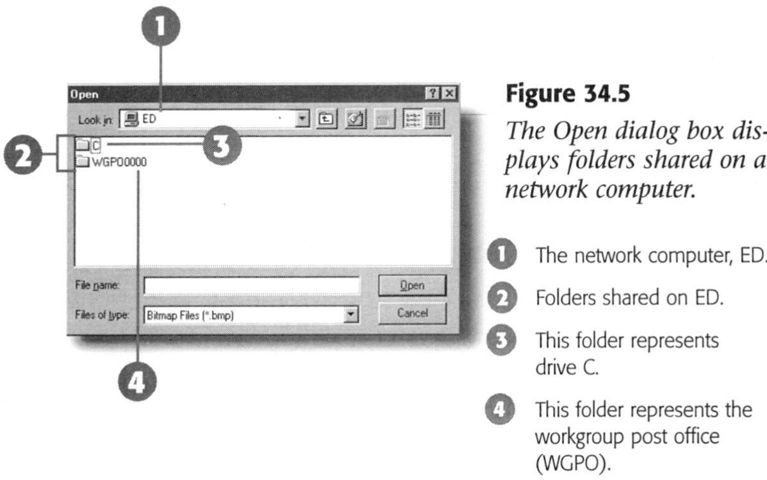

Figure 34.5

The Open dialog box displays folders shared on a network computer.

1. The network computer, ED.
2. Folders shared on ED.
3. This folder represents drive C.
4. This folder represents the workgroup post office (WGPO).

▶ **Open the drive C folder.**

The folders and files you see in the Open dialog box now reflect the folders and files on the other computer's drive C. On my screen I see the folders and files on my ED computer.

Now you have to look for a graphics file to open. On my ED computer, I know that they're stored in the My Documents folder. However, you can find many graphics files in the Windows folder:

▶ **Open the Windows folder.**

▶ **Open a graphics file.**

You might have to scroll right to find the files listed. On my screen I found the *moonguy* graphics file, so I selected it and clicked Open. The image—from the network computer—appears in Paint for editing.

You probably shouldn't edit the file. Because this is a tutorial, you should edit only those files you need to edit. Work with me here.

You have two choices for saving the file: Choose the File ➡Save command, which saves the file on the network hard drive from which it was opened, or choose File ➡Save As to save the file in another location, such as on your own hard drive.

▶ **Choose File ➡Save As.**

The files in the Save As dialog box are still those on the network computer—the same folder from which you opened the graphics file. (Windows always remembers the last folder from which you opened a document.)

To save the file on your own computer, use the Save In drop-down list to find the My Documents folder:

▶ **Choose My Documents from the Save In drop-down list.**

▶ **Click Save.**

The document is saved on your computer. (This technique works even if the network hard drive was read-only; although you cannot write new information to that hard drive, you can copy files from it.)

If you didn't modify the graphics image, all you've done, of course, is copy the file from a network computer to your own PC. You could also do that with the Copy and Paste commands in the Network Neighborhood window.

▶ **Close Paint.**

I use the Open and Save As dialog boxes to open and save documents all over the network in my office. In fact, the images in this book were "taken" on my Windows

98 test computer and then saved on the network computer Worbletyme by using the exact techniques mentioned in this section.

- You can use the Open or Save As dialog boxes to open or save a file on any network hard drive—as long as the hard drive is shared as full access.
- You cannot use the Save As dialog box to save a document on a read-only network hard drive.
- You can open a document on a read-only hard drive and alter or edit that document. You cannot save it back to a read-only hard drive, however. You must save it elsewhere (on your own hard drive, for example) if you want to save the modified file.

Running Programs on Another Computer

Here's a tricky one: Can you run on your own computer a program that lives on a network computer? For example, your computer doesn't have Excel. Tina's computer does have Excel. Can you run Excel on your computer from her copy? (And why does Tina have Excel, huh? Is she so much better than you?)

Generally, you shouldn't run a program on another computer. You can try! For example, I tried to run Excel from another computer, and it worked. I'm just not sure whether it worked because I already had Excel installed on my computer. (Other programs I tried to run didn't work.)

It's best to run only programs installed on your computer.

A few programs may be available on your network for running remotely. For example, you might have a database of some sort available on a central computer, and you can use a program to access that database. Or all network computers might run the same email program on another computer. These are examples of programs you can run on the network. As for going into the Network Neighborhood and fishing for files to run, however, don't even try.

- Some older DOS programs and games can be run on the network.
- Some programs can be installed from the network. For example, you might be able to install a copy of Excel from a central file server.

Chapter 35

Stealing and Sharing on the Network

Questions Answered and Thoughts Inspired

- Confirming your network setup
- Making your printer available on the network
- Making your hard drive or a folder available on the network
- Mapping a network drive or folder

A potluck dinner works only if everyone brings something. Everyone knows that, so everyone shows up with a casserole or Jell-O™ salad—even if no one else eats it. Computer networking works similarly, although sharing your own stuff is optional.

Being on a computer network means that you can borrow resources (printers and hard drives) from other computers on the network. It also means that you can share your own computer's resources. As with a potluck dinner, you can share everything. Unlike with a potluck, you don't have to share and can just be a borrower. This chapter shows you how to share and how to borrow stuff on a network.

- This chapter assumes that your computer has already been configured for networking. See Appendix B if it's not.
- You don't have to share any of your computer's resources. It's not like a potluck: No one scowls if you don't share.

How to Be Network Friendly

Before you can share your PC's hard drives and printer, you have to tell Windows that you're open to the concept (it's like the first stage of one of those 12-step programs):

- **Open the Control Panel.**
- **Open the Network icon.**

The Network dialog box appears.

- **Click the File and Print Sharing button.**

The File and Print Sharing dialog box appears, as shown in Figure 35.1.

Figure 35.1

File and Print Sharing dialog box.

1. Click here to share your disk drives, folders, and files.
2. Click here to share your printer.

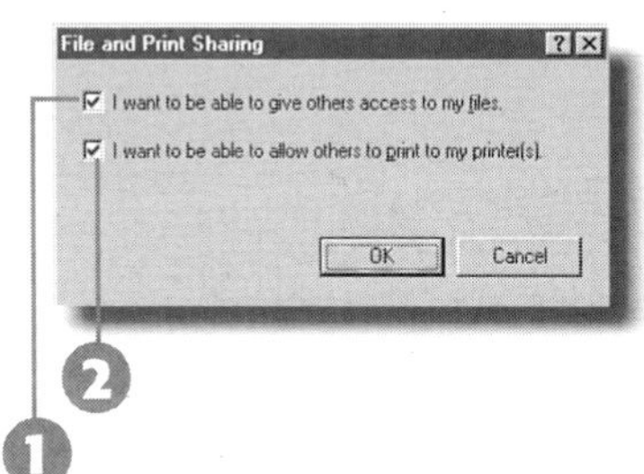

Ensure that both items have check marks. If not, place check marks there.

Telling Windows that you want to give others access to your files doesn't mean that everyone is automatically granted access. It's not like planting on your PC's network icon a sign proclaiming, "Wild 24-hour file orgy here!" No, you must manually select a disk drive or folder to share, and then you have the option of adding passwords or read-only protection.

- **Click OK.**
- **Click the Identification tab to bring that panel forward.**

The Identification panel describes how the rest of the network sees your computer. Review the items in the dialog box, as shown in Figure 35.2.

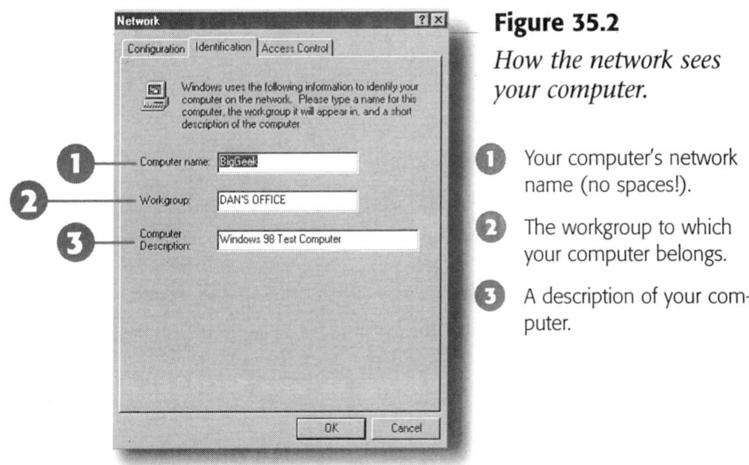

Figure 35.2
How the network sees your computer.

1. Your computer's network name (no spaces!).
2. The workgroup to which your computer belongs.
3. A description of your computer.

You can change any individual item if you want.

The Computer Name box cannot contain any spaces, so if you want to call your PC Monkey King on the network, you have to settle for MonkeyKing instead.

Your network administrator sets the name in the Workgroup box—do not change it. Ask your network administrator for the name of another workgroup and tell him/her why you feel you're worthy to join it.

The Computer Description box can contain anything you want. I don't know where the text pops up, but it's not anywhere obvious. I usually leave this one blank.

▶ **Click OK to close the Network dialog box.**

▶ **Close the Control Panel.**

Everything is now set to enable your PC to share its folders and printers on the network. The following section details how to do that.

- Your computer's name and icon don't appear in the Network Neighborhood window until you actually share a printer or a hard drive or folder, a subject covered in the following section.
- Funny: Windows 3.11 let you give your computer a network name with a space in it. Windows 95 and 98 don't let you do that.
- You can access other computers' resources without sharing any yourself. It's computer networking. It doesn't have to be fair.
- If you have any networking troubles, ask your network administrator for help. (This advice isn't a cop-out on my part; it's just a rehash of what the Windows online networking help information says.)

Sharing Your Printers and Hard Drives

Time to cough up some resources for others on the net. You can share your printer, an entire hard drive, or just selected folders. On top of that, you can restrict access to read-only or slap on a few passwords. It's all up to you.

Sharing Your Printer

The easiest thing to share on the network is your printer. You do that in the Printers folder. It assumes that a printer is connected to your computer. No printer? Then you can't share one. This isn't communism, you know.

▶ **From the Start Thing, choose Settings ➡Printers.**

The Printers folder appears, listing any printers attached to your PC (and maybe some network printers and a fax machine).

▶ **Right-click the icon of the printer you want to share.**

The printer you want to share can be any printer connected to your computer (if you have more than one). It does not have to be the default, or favorite, printer.

▶ **Choose Sharing from the shortcut menu.**

The printer's Properties dialog box appears, similar to the one shown in Figure 35.3.

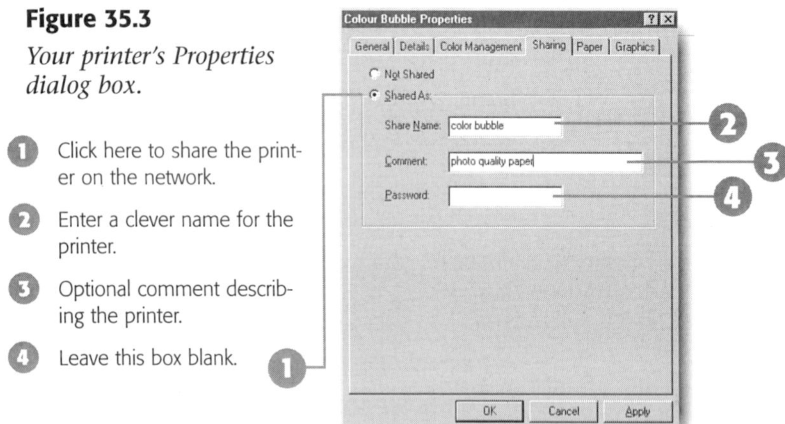

Figure 35.3
Your printer's Properties dialog box.

1. Click here to share the printer on the network.
2. Enter a clever name for the printer.
3. Optional comment describing the printer.
4. Leave this box blank.

▶ **Choose Shared As.**

This step is the key that unlocks the printer on your network. (Conversely, choosing Not Shared means that the printer is no longer available for use by others on the network.)

▶ **Fill in the blanks.**

Give your printer a nice, short, descriptive name in the Share Name text box. You can type as many as 12 characters. (Windows might have suggested a name already; it's probably dumb, so you can replace it.)

Optionally type a comment in the Comment field. That information appears only if someone else on the network displays your printer's Properties dialog box. The comment can be descriptive. For example, you can list the printer's location or maybe any special paper (letterhead or photo quality) that's loaded in the printer.

Leave the Password box blank. Only if you want to restrict access should you type a password there.

▶ **Click OK.**

The printer's Properties dialog box closes. The printer is now available for use by others on the network.

In the Printers folder window, you should notice the little "sharing hand" under your printer's icon. That's the dead ringer indicator that your printer is available for sharing on the network.

▶ **Close the Printers window.**

The real way to confirm that the printer is "up" and on the network is to visit someone else's computer. Open her Network Neighborhood icon, and then open your computer's icon. You should see your printer there, ready for action.

- If you're going to share your printer, you should leave the printer turned on all the time. That way, no one has to wait for you to turn the printer on so that he can get his documents.
- When the printer is turned off, the documents waiting to be printed sit in the queue (refer to Chapter 18) until you turn the printer back on and printing resumes.
- Refer to Chapter 18 for more information about the Printers folder, including information about setting a default (favorite) printer.
- Oh, and refer to Chapter 18 also for information about installing a network printer. (You should just read Chapter 18 after you read this chapter, you know?)

Sharing a Lonely Folder or an Entire Hard Drive

Windows lets you share everything you have or just a small portion of it. It's all up to you. If you would rather let everyone see everything on your hard drive, that's okay. If you want to limit access to a folder, that's fine too.

▶ **Open the My Computer icon on the desktop.**

To share drive C and all its files, you can right-click that drive. Or if you want to share only a handful of folders, just browse to them in the window. For this tutorial, I share drive C.

- **Right-click drive C.**
- **Choose Sharing.**

A Properties dialog box for the disk drive appears, as shown in Figure 35.4.

If you're trying to share a folder, click the Sharing tab to display the Sharing panel, as shown in Figure 35.4.

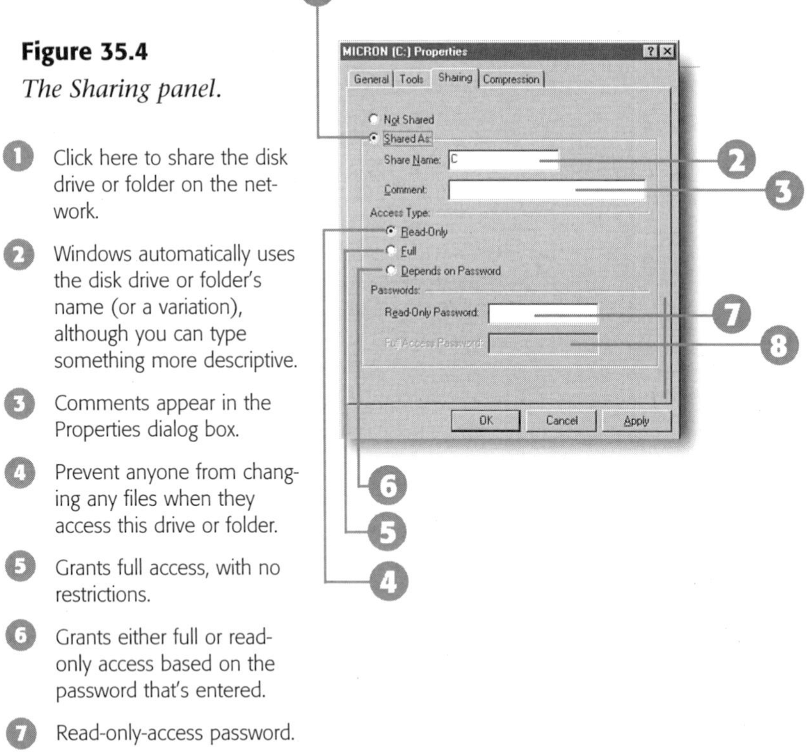

Figure 35.4
The Sharing panel.

1. Click here to share the disk drive or folder on the network.
2. Windows automatically uses the disk drive or folder's name (or a variation), although you can type something more descriptive.
3. Comments appear in the Properties dialog box.
4. Prevent anyone from changing any files when they access this drive or folder.
5. Grants full access, with no restrictions.
6. Grants either full or read-only access based on the password that's entered.
7. Read-only-access password.
8. Full-access password.

- **Click Shared As.**

The name supplied in the Share Name text box might be okay, or you might want to type something better. On my screen, for example, Windows has displayed `C` for drive C. Replacing that with `Drive C` is much more descriptive.

Typing a comment is unnecessary.

▶ **Choose an Access Type.**

If you don't want anyone messing with your hard drive, choose Read-Only. Otherwise, if you want others to access and modify files, choose Full.

Optionally, if you want to have some form of password protection, choose Depends on Password.

Fill in the Password boxes with passwords if necessary. The passwords are not displayed onscreen; asterisks appear instead.

Don't forget the passwords!

▶ **Click OK.**

If you select passwords, a confirmation dialog box appears. Type the passwords again so that Windows is certain that you won't forget them. (Yeah.)

The disk drive (or folder) is now shared. You see its icon appear in the My Computer window with a little sharing hand beneath it. Others on the network can now see and access the files therein. Nifty.

▶ **Close the My Computer window.**

As with sharing a printer, the only true way to confirm that your disk drive or folder is up for grabs on the net is to use another computer to find out. You should be able to open your computer's icon in the Network Neighborhood window and then see any printers or folders being shared.

- You can also share a disk drive or folder from Windows Explorer.
- Windows lets you share CD-ROMs and other types of removable drives.
- Some older CD-ROM drives cannot be shared on the network. Although you can share them fine, other computers cannot access their data.

Stealing from Others (Mapping a Network Drive or Folder)

The Network Neighborhood icon lets you access files and folders on other network computers. Or you can use any Open or Save As dialog box to get to some other folder on the network. That method works fine. If you notice that you often use a particular network disk drive or folder, though, you should make a permanent connection. This process is known as *mapping*.

Don't ask me why it's called mapping. I prefer using the term theft.

Suppose that you always access the ClipArt folder on the network computer Worbletyme. Rather than wade through the Network Neighborhood every time you want to do that, you could *map* the network folder to your own hard drive—like a shortcut. Call the ClipArt folder drive M instead. That way, you always have easy access to it. The following tutorial explains:

▶ **Open the Network Neighborhood icon on the desktop.**

▶ **Open the computer containing the folder you want to map.**

For example, I would open Worbletyme to find the ClipArt folder.

You have to open the computer and see whether it has folders available for sharing. You can map only a folder (which might represent a folder or an entire hard drive). You cannot map a computer.

▶ **Right-click the folder you want to map.**

You can right-click any folder on the network computer, whether it represents a disk drive or just a single folder. It doesn't matter.

A shortcut menu appears.

▶ **Choose Map Network Drive.**

The Map Network Drive dialog box appears, as shown in Figure 35.5.

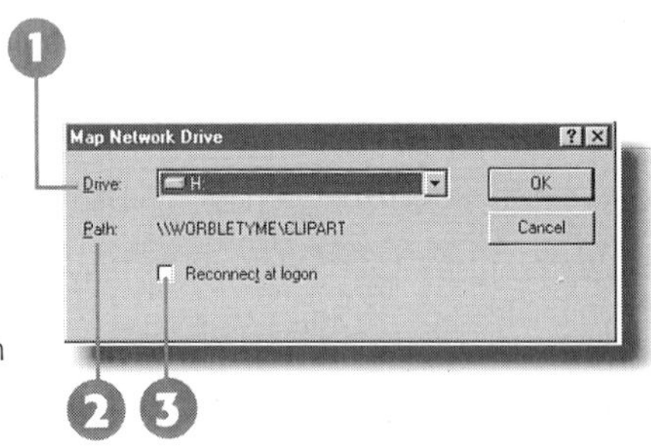

Figure 35.5
The Map Network Drive dialog box.

1. Choose the drive letter from this list.
2. The network pathname.
3. Click here so that your computer always maps this drive every time it starts up.

▶ **Choose a drive letter from the Drive drop-down list.**

The Drive list displays only the drive letters available on your computer, from the last hard drive on up to Z (minus any network mapping you've already done).

If the network connection is one you always plan to use, be sure to click Reconnect at Logon to put a check mark there.

TIP

Try to pick a letter that matches the intent of the drive you're mapping; for example: G for games, P for programs, and W for work files. Because Windows lets you pick from a number of drive letters, you might as well try to weave some sense into things.

▶ **Click OK.**

If a password is required in order to access the folder or disk drive, you see an Enter Network Password dialog box. Type the proper password for full or read-only access. Click OK.

A window appears, showing you the files on the new disk drive you've mapped. That window doesn't describe your new situation, however, as well as the new look of the My Computer window.

▶ **Close the newly mapped drive's window.**

The window should be the top one on the screen.

▶ **In the My Computer window, choose My Computer from the Address drop-down list.**

The newly mapped network drive appears in the My Computer window along with your PC's own hard drives and special folders, as shown in Figure 35.6. The plumbing is the clue that it's a network drive.

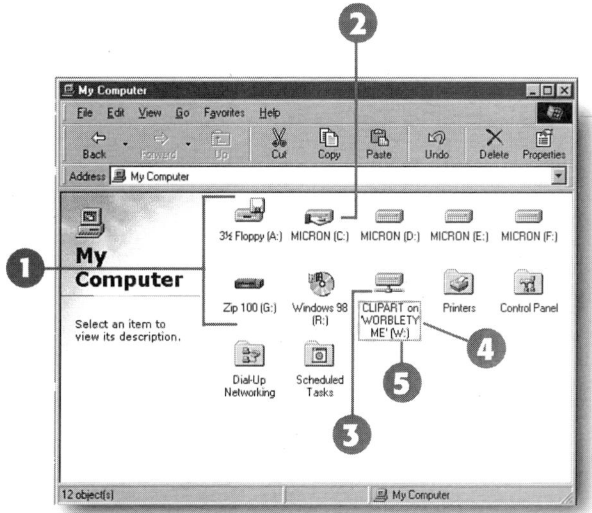

Figure 35.6

A mapped network drive in the My Computer window.

1. Disk drives appear in order.
2. You're sharing this drive.
3. The plumbing indicates a mapped network drive.
4. The drive is the folder CLIPART on the network computer WORBLETYME.
5. Drive letter, W.

▶ **You can close the My Computer window.**

Accessing a mapped network drive is as easy as accessing any drive on your computer. You no longer have to wade through the Network Neighborhood; just use the drive letter directly.

- You can map as many disk drives and folders as your computer has drive letters available.
- The other computer has to be running and available on the network before you can access files from a mapped network drive. If the other computer isn't available, a proper warning dialog box appears.
- If you tire of a mapped hard drive, you can unmap it. Right-click the mapped icon in My Computer and choose Disconnect from the shortcut menu.

Another Map Network Drive command is available by right-clicking the My Computer or Network Neighborhood icons on the desktop. Don't use that command. Its dialog box requires you to know the full network pathname for the folder you're mapping. It's just much easier to browse for the folder, right-click, and then map it.

Part VI

The Tweak Master

Chapters in This Part

Part VI

Visual Topic Reference A

1. Tweak Central for your PC (Chapter 36).
2. Change the look of your screen (Chapters 37 and 40).
3. Add and remove toolbars (Chapter 38).
4. Change the look of a folder (Chapter 39).
5. Adjust the sound volume (Chapter 41).
6. Change your system sounds (Chapter 41).
7. Change the mouse pointer (Chapter 43).
8. Schedule tasks (Chapter 44).
9. Add new hardware (Chapter 45).
10. Tweak the keyboard (Chapter 36).
11. Add a joystick (Chapter 36).
12. Set the date and time (Chapter 36).

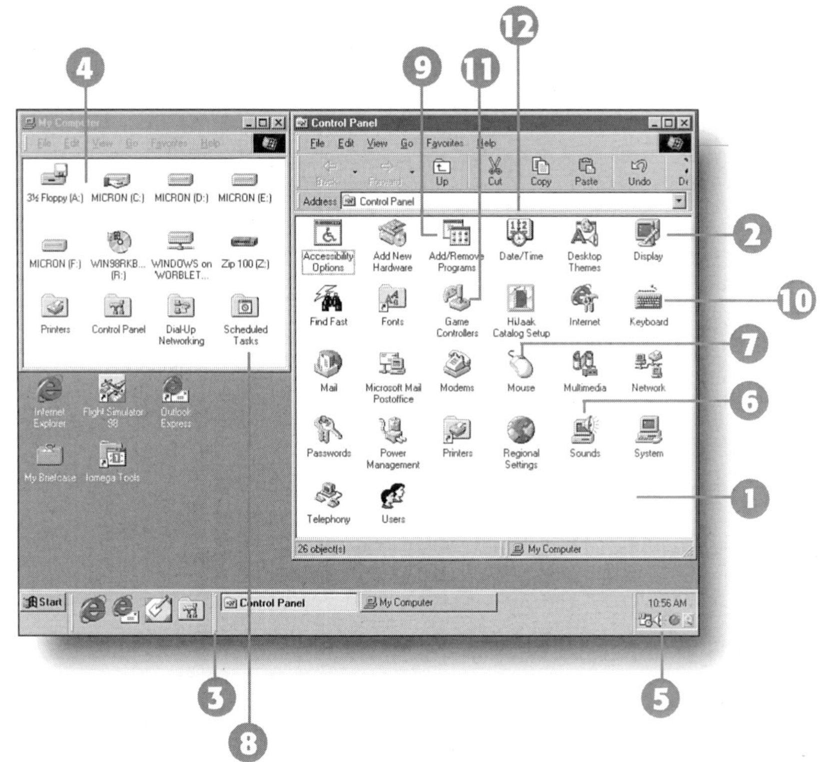

Chapter 36

The Control Panel

Questions Answered and Thoughts Inspired

- Finding the Control Panel
- Using icons in the Control Panel
- Setting the PC's date and time
- Configuring your PC's joystick
- Adjusting your keyboard
- Setting up Windows for more than one user

You can do three things in Windows: You can work, you can dink, and you can play.

Working is what you're supposed to do. It's the reason you have a computer. It's the important stuff. The other two things you can do with Windows distract from your business: Playing, well, that's obvious. The Solitaire and FreeCell games are banned on many corporate computers. But dinking?

Dinking is the chore of messing with Windows for Windows' own sake. You tweak. You adjust. You fiddle. It's required, yet it takes away from your work. Because it's a major part of Windows, I have to cover it, not only in this chapter—which covers Tweak Central, the Control Panel—but also in this entire part of the book. Yup. It's a big deal.

Wherefore Art Thou, Control Panel?

The Control Panel contains lots of icons for changing lots of system settings. Because it's one of those places in Windows you visit every so often, finding it is not a problem.

My favorite way to display the Control Panel is from the Start Thing menu:

- **Choose Settings➡Control Panel.**

Ploop! There's the Control Panel, as shown in Figure 36.1.

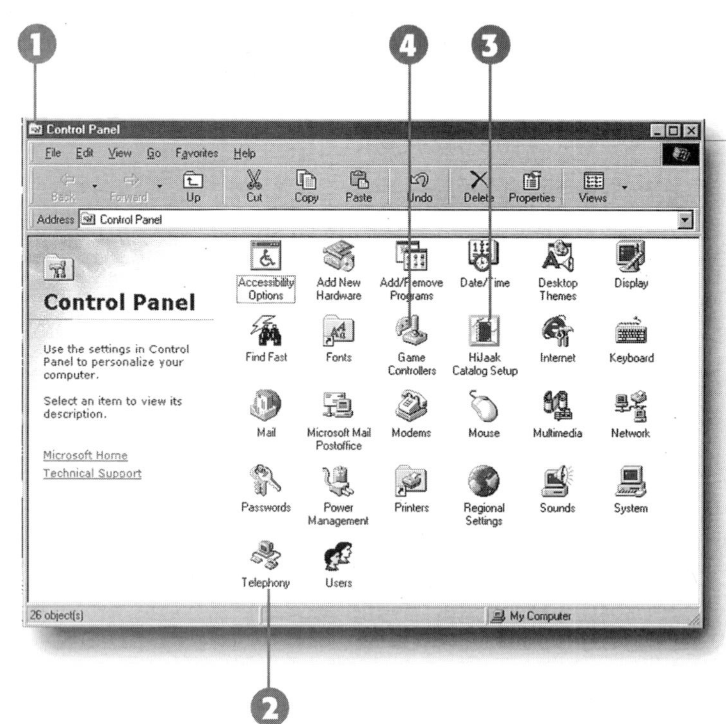

Figure 36.1
The Control Panel.

1. Choose View➡As Web Page to see this information.
2. Select an icon to see information about it displayed here.
3. Some icons are placed here by other programs.
4. Some icons appear here only if you have certain hardware installed.

- **Close the Control Panel window.**

Another place to find the Control Panel is in My Computer:

- **Open the My Computer icon on the desktop.**

The My Computer window displays disk drives plus a handful of special folders. One of them is the Control Panel. Handy.

If you want to make the Control Panel even more handy, you can create a shortcut to its folder. You can then put the shortcut right on the desktop or on the Quick Launch bar if you have it visible.

- **Right-click the Control Panel folder.**
- **Choose Create Shortcut.**

A dialog box pops up, telling you that because the shortcut cannot be created in the My Computer window, Windows will put the shortcut on the desktop. Talk about ESP.

- **Click Yes.**

The icon Shortcut to Control Panel appears on the desktop.

- **Close the My Computer window.**
- **If necessary, rename the Shortcut to Control Panel as** Control Panel**.**

Select the icon, press the F2 key, and then edit the name to read just *Control Panel.* Press Enter to lock in the new name.

If you want to have the Control Panel shortcut icon on the Quick Launch bar, just drag it down to the bar. That copies the icon from the desktop to the Quick Launch bar for ready access. If you like the icon better on the Quick Launch bar, delete it from the desktop (or vice versa).

You can delete the Control Panel shortcuts: Just drag them to the Recycle Bin. That does not remove the Control Panel from your computer. You can always get to the Control Panel through the Start Thing's Settings menu or the My Computer window.

- The Control Panel isn't a folder like My Documents or the Windows folder. No, it's more of a program than a folder—a program that displays other programs you can use to tweak your PC.
- The Quick Launch bar is covered in Chapter 11.
- If you accidentally drag the Control Panel shortcut to the taskbar, you end up creating a Control Panel toolbar. If that's what you want, okay; for me, it takes up too much room. Refer to Chapter 38, "Toolbars from Beyond Infinity!" for information about removing the extra toolbar.

What's Important and What's Odd in the Control Panel

Like most gathering places, the Control Panel has some parts that warrant more attention than others. Like stores at the mall, some icons in the Control Panel you use all the time; others, like foo-foo girly shops, you rarely ever visit.

The following list briefly describes items in the Control Panel, what they do, and where you can get more information about them.

If your Control Panel contains any items other than the ones listed in Table 36.1, yours are particular to some piece of software you have. For example, as shown in Figure 36.1, Microsoft Office has placed the Find Fast icon in the Control Panel, and the HiJaak graphics program I use has added the HiJaak Catalog.

Table 36.1 Control Panel Greeblies.

Icon	Description
Accessibility Options	Features for the auditory or visually impaired. This icon must be added (refer to Chapter 15, "Adding More of Windows").
Add New Hardware	Runs the Hardware Installation Wizard in case Windows doesn't recognize your new hardware right away. (See Chapter 45, "Installing New Hardware.")
Add/Remove Programs	The proper way to uninstall programs or add new software or add or remove Windows components (refer to Chapters 14 and 15).
Time/Date	Adjust the time or date as kept by Windows and your PC (covered later in this chapter).
Desktop Themes	Change all aspects of the desktop and sound options to match some specific theme: the 1960s, Jungle, Nature, or Science, for example. (See Chapter 37, "A New Face on the Interface.")
Display	Change screen attributes; color, resolution, and other screeny things. (See Chapter 40, "Tweaking Your Monitor.")
Fonts	Preview, add, or remove fonts. Chapter 42, "Fun with Fonts," says it all.
Game Controllers	Add, remove, or adjust joysticks and paddles or other "scientific instruments" (covered later in this chapter).

Icon	Description
Internet	Adjust various Internet settings and whatnot. Basically, the Internet Connection Wizard (refer to Chapter 7) provides this information. It's worth checking out, but nothing worthy of a chapter or section in this book.
Keyboard	Adjust the keyboard or select a foreign-language keyboard layout (as covered later in this chapter).
Mail	A setup icon for the old Microsoft Exchange email program. A holdover from Windows 95 upgrades. Feel free to ignore this one.
Microsoft Mail Postoffice	Used to tweak the network post office for LAN email only. A holdover from Windows 95 upgrades. You can ignore this one too.
Modems	Adjust your modem's settings, long-distance dialing rules, and so on.
Mouse	Boy, you can do a bunch of things to adjust the mouse. Chapter 43, "Messing mit der Mouse," covers just about all of them.
Multimedia	Another one to ignore, it has a few settings you can look at but nothing worthy of explanation in this book.
Network	See Chapters 34 and 35 and Appendix B for anything important that goes on with this icon.
Passwords	Sets or changes your Windows password and (like communism) allows several people to use one Windows 98 computer. (It's covered later in this chapter.)
Power Management	Settings for computers that can "sleep" and for laptop computers. Self-explanatory.
Printers	A shortcut to the Printers folder (see Chapter 18).
Regional Settings	Allows you to change some things if you ever move to another country. (This information was entered when you first set up Windows.) No need visiting this one again—until you make that move to the Grand Caymans for tax reasons.
Sounds	A mirthful place to play and waste serious time. Chapter 41, "Sound Advice," starts the party.
System	Boring system settings. Nothing fun there.

continued

Table 36.1 Continued

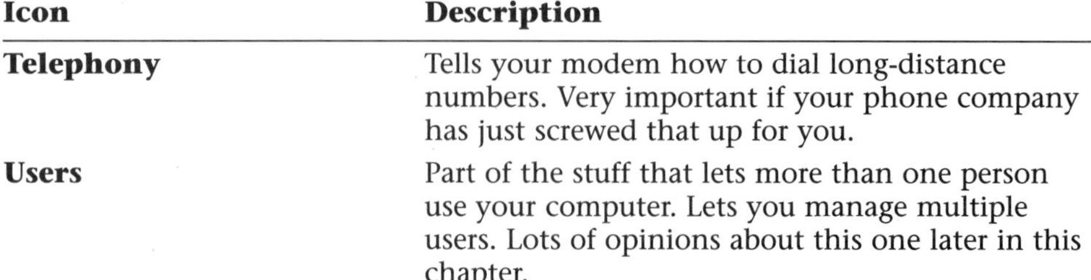

Icon	Description
 **Telephony**	Tells your modem how to dial long-distance numbers. Very important if your phone company has just screwed that up for you.
Users	Part of the stuff that lets more than one person use your computer. Lets you manage multiple users. Lots of opinions about this one later in this chapter.

Some Quick Tinky-Dinks to Get Out of the Way

Some icons in the Control Panel are worthy of note but not worthy of an entire chapter. They include the following:

- ✓ Date/Time
- ✓ Game Controllers
- ✓ Keyboard
- ✓ Passwords and Users

This section touches on what's important or worthy of looking into with each of these icons.

Computers Make Lousy Clocks

Your computer can keep track of the time...barely. Generally, you'll probably have to reset your computer's clock every month or so—more often if you're a stickler for the exact time.

Computers have too much to do to keep track of the time properly.

The truth is that computers make lousy clocks. Because they do so much and do it immediately, the time often slips—especially computers with power-saving features (computers that "sleep"), which often lose a few minutes every day, for some reason. Why? Who knows. What you should know is how to reset the clock if necessary:

- **Open the Control Panel.**
- **Open the Date/Time icon.**

The Date/Time Properties dialog box is displayed, as shown in Figure 36.2.

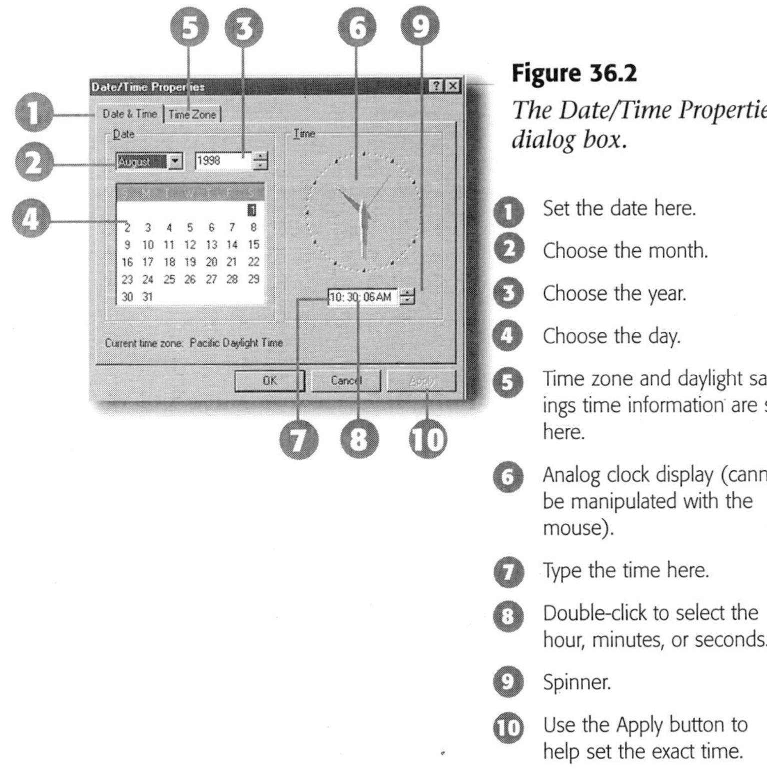

Figure 36.2
The Date/Time Properties dialog box.

1. Set the date here.
2. Choose the month.
3. Choose the year.
4. Choose the day.
5. Time zone and daylight savings time information are set here.
6. Analog clock display (cannot be manipulated with the mouse).
7. Type the time here.
8. Double-click to select the hour, minutes, or seconds.
9. Spinner.
10. Use the Apply button to help set the exact time.

The following technique is the way I set the time. You might want to read through these steps before you set the time, because the, uh, timing of the steps is important:

- **Observe what time it is now, as a reference.**

"Does anybody really know what time it is? Does anyone care?"

I use a digital clock as a reference. (Unlike a computer's clock, a digital clock shows me the exact time.) You can dial up the Time Lady on the phone (if your phone company still offers that service) or just use a nearby clock to see what time it is. Use it as your "reference clock."

- **Enter the current hour in the Time/Date dialog box.**

Double-click the hour that's displayed (it's `10` in Figure 36.2), and type the hour or use the spinner.

If the current hour is already set, leave it alone.

▶ **Enter the *next* minute.**

Don't enter the current minute; enter the next one. For example, if your clock says that it's 2:45 in the afternoon, enter **46** in the minute part of the Time/Date dialog box.

▶ **Enter 00 for the seconds.**

Type **00** for the seconds.

Wait until your reference clock—the one you're using to set the time—reaches `00` seconds.

▶ **Click Apply.**

Now the computer's clock is set to exactly the same time as your reference clock. For now, anyway.

▶ **Close the Control Panel.**

If you want to set your PC's time to the most accurate clock in the universe, you can visit the "Atomic" clock Web page, run by the National Institute of Standards and Technology:

`http://www.bldrdoc.gov/doc-tour/atomic_clock.html`

As it says on the Web page, the time you see is slightly less than true because of Internet traffic and the time it takes to display the information—but it's pretty darn close!

You can also download special Internet software that sets your PC's clock according to the atomic clock. This software is much more accurate than just viewing the time on the Web page:

`http://www.boulder.nist.gov/timefreq/javaclck.htm`

Browse to this address to get the NISTIME program. Be sure to run the NISTIM32 version after downloading. (Refer to Chapter 10 for information about adding the program to the Start Thing menu.)

- The average PC's clock slips from 10 to 40 seconds per day. Sorry!

Don't feel bad: Some early PC "clones" actually dragged several days behind real time. A bug in the PC's chip prevented the day from turning over at midnight. On those computers you would have, for example, two Mondays in a row. Weird.

- You can also display the Date/Time Properties dialog box by double-clicking the time on the system tray.
- If you live where they celebrate daylight savings time, your computer reminds you when its clock needs to be changed one hour ahead or back, and then it makes the change automatically. Amazing devices.

They're Not Joysticks—They're Scientific Instruments!

When IBM introduced its PC back in 1981 it came with a small variety of expansion cards: one to add memory, one to give you color graphics, one with a serial port on it, and one with an "analog/digital," or A-to-D, port. The IBM documentation explained that the A-to-D port allowed you to connect certain "scientific instruments" for data collection and analysis. Uh-huh.

The A-to-D port is a joystick port.

Sure, you could connect something like a model train set or weather anemometer to your PC's A-to-D port. Because its name has changed to *joystick port*, however, the thing you're most likely to plug into it is a joystick.

- **Open the Control Panel.**
- **Open the Game Controllers icon.**

Yeah, "game controllers" is much more sophisticated than "joystick." And maybe it's more accurate; have you seen the buttons and gizmos on a typical joystick? Anyway, the Game Controllers dialog box appears onscreen (see Figure 36.3).

To add a joystick to your PC, plug it in. Then click the Add button and choose your joystick from the list. Or click the Add Other button and then the Have Disk button to install your joystick by using any floppy disk that came with it.

Figure 36.3

The Game Controllers dialog box.

1. Any joysticks you already have installed.
2. Click to install another joystick.
3. Calibrate the joystick here.

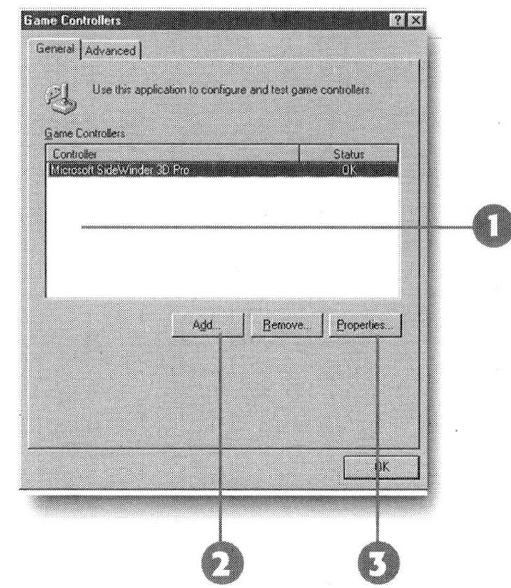

You can use the Properties button to calibrate and test your joystick.

▶ **Click OK to close the Game Controllers dialog box.**

▶ **Close the Control Panel.**

Most games still use DOS, and those games usually have a joystick setup or calibration option. Use that rather than the Windows Control Panel calibration option when you play the DOS game.

- Adding a joystick to your computer is simple: Plug it in. You do not have to run the New Hardware Wizard or make any additional adjustments. In some cases you might have to install some joystick software, although that's about it.
- USB joysticks are the easiest to install: Just plug them in.

Make sure that your game supports whichever joystick you're using. If you haven't yet bought a joystick, look in your game's documentation. It tells you exactly which joystick works best. Buy that one.

- The joystick port is also where you plug in a MIDI device, keyboard, or other musical instrument. Although you can use both a MIDI device and a keyboard, it's best to unplug one when you're using the other.

Making Keyboard Adjustments

You can use the keyboard icon in the Control Panel to adjust the speed and feel of your keyboard as well as to give you access to certain foreign-language characters. If you feel the urge, therefore, to type *à la française* or if the keys on the keyboard ssss-stick, do the following:

- **Open the Control Panel.**
- **Open the Keyboard icon.**
- **Click the Speed tab (if the Speed panel is not visible).**

The Keyboard Properties dialog box shows itself, looking much like Figure 36.4. Refer to the figure to change your settings.

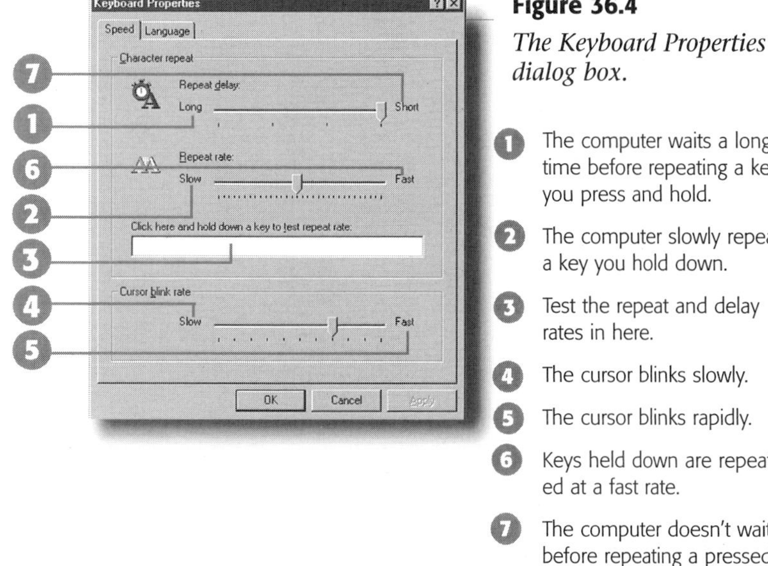

Figure 36.4
The Keyboard Properties dialog box.

1. The computer waits a long time before repeating a key you press and hold.
2. The computer slowly repeats a key you hold down.
3. Test the repeat and delay rates in here.
4. The cursor blinks slowly.
5. The cursor blinks rapidly.
6. Keys held down are repeated at a fast rate.
7. The computer doesn't wait before repeating a pressed key.

- **Click the mouse in the Click Here box.**
- **Press and hold the A key.**

Wait for the A key to start repeating: AAAAAAAA.

- **Release the A key.**

The pause before the A key repeats is set on the Repeat Delay slider.

The speed at which the A key repeats is set on the Repeat Rate slider.

Make adjustments as necessary. (The settings I prefer appear in the figure.)

▶ **Click the Language tab.**

The Language panel appears, as shown in Figure 36.5.

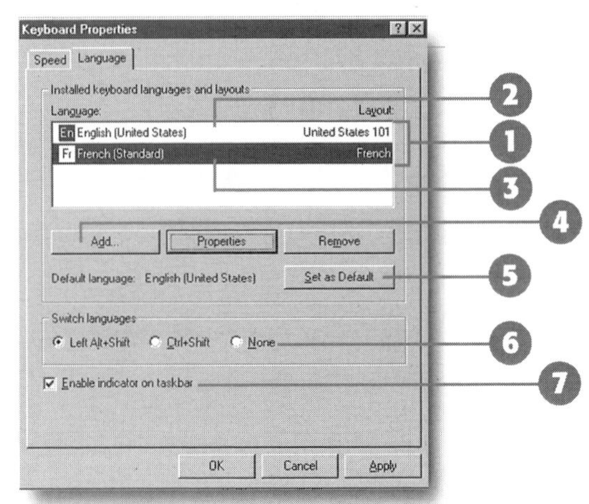

Figure 36.5
Set your foreign language keyboard here.

1. Keyboard languages and layouts you have installed.
2. English (United States) is the keyboard layout used in the United States.
3. The standard French keyboard layout used in France.
4. Click here to add another keyboard layout.
5. Sets the highlighted keyboard as the default.
6. Keyboard shortcuts used to switch keyboard layouts on-the-fly.
7. Click here to put a keyboard layout indicator on the system tray (recommended).

To add a French keyboard, follow these steps:

▶ **Click Add.**

The Add Language dialog box appears.

▶ **Choose a keyboard layout from the Language drop-down list.**

Be aware of language variations. For example, the English (British) keyboard has the £ symbol above the 3 rather than the American #. The French (Canadian) and French (Swiss) ones have differences between them, too.

For this example, choose French (Standard) if you're at a loss.

▶ **Click OK to close the Add Language dialog box.**

The language and keyboard layout you chose appears in the Language list.

- **Choose Left Alt+Shift as your Switch Languages key.**
- **Ensure that the Enable indicator on the taskbar item is on.**
- **Click OK.**

You might need the Windows CD in order to install some files. Otherwise, everything is set.

Notice the blue square on the taskbar? It should say `En`, which means that you're using the standard English keyboard layout.

- **Press the Alt+Shift key combination, by using the Alt and Shift keys on the left side of your keyboard.**

This step switches keyboards to your alternative choice: the *French* keyboard. See the little `Fr` on the system tray?

- **Start Notepad.**
- **Type** Oo-la-la, see how I type in French?

Hmmm...

```
Oo)lq)lq; see hoz I type in French§
```

Did you notice that the French keyboard layout is different from your made-in-the-USA keyboard layout? The A is where the Q key is, for example.

Also, did you notice that what you typed wasn't automatically translated into French? It's a *keyboard layout* feature, not a translation program.

- **Close Notepad.**

No, you don't have to save the file.

- **Press the Left Alt+Shift key combination to switch back to an English keyboard.**
- **Right-click the blue EN on the system tray.**
- **Choose Properties from the shortcut menu.**

Lo, you're back in the Keyboard Properties dialog box, on the Language panel.

If you want to remove the French (Standard) keyboard, click it once to select it and then click Remove. That option is gone.

- **Click OK to close the Keyboard Properties dialog box.**
- **Close the Control Panel.**

The question you're probably asking right now is, "Where are the maps of the foreign-language keyboards?" To tell you the truth, I don't know. Microsoft used to include them with its documentation. The last half of the DOS manual consisted of keyboard layouts, for example. Windows comes with scant documentation, though, and the online help doesn't show you the keyboard layouts. Sorry.

Another missing item: the Dvorak keyboard layout. It was developed decades ago to simplify typing and improve speed. Honestly, if you want to use a Dvorak keyboard layout, buy a Dvorak keyboard. It usually comes with setup software so that Windows understands the new keyboard layout.

One PC, Many Humans

If a Windows computer will be shared by more than one human, you can set it up so that everyone can customize the Windows desktop and other items to suit their fancy. That should make people happy (as happy as they can be while all sharing the same computer).

To configure Windows to be shared and customized by several users, heed the following steps:

▶ **Open the Control Panel.**

▶ **Open the Passwords icon.**

▶ **Click the User Profiles tab.**

The User Profiles panel appears, as shown in Figure 36.6.

Follow these steps only if you want more than one person to use your computer. Otherwise, things will change that might annoy you.

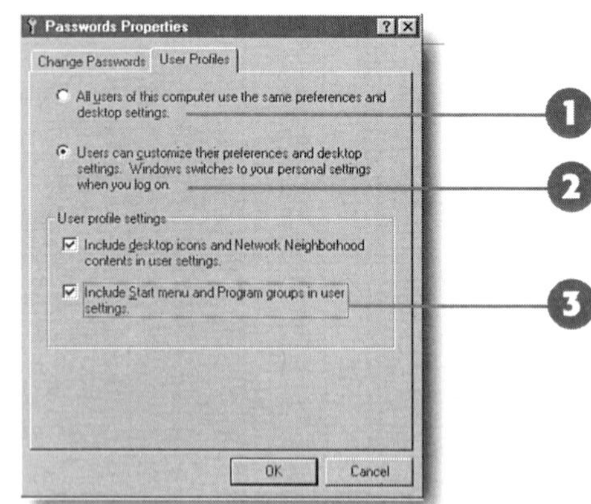

Figure 36.6
The User Profiles panel in the Passwords Properties dialog box.

1. Choose this for multiple users.
2. Allows everyone to have their own desktop settings.
3. Allows everyone to have their own Start Thing menus.

▶ **Choose Users Can Customize.**

This step enables the bottom two items in the dialog box, allowing you to choose one or the other or both.

▶ **Choose both user profile settings.**

▶ **Click OK.**

▶ **Click Yes to restart Windows.**

Windows restarts. (Play calming music here.)

After telling Windows to accept multiple users, you're prompted for a login name and password every time it starts up—even if your computer isn't on a network.

Each user now has to log in to Windows. If you're a new user (which means that Windows doesn't recognize you), type your name and password, and then confirm your password.

- When Windows is set up for multiple users, it remembers any changes any user makes to the desktop or to the Start Thing menu or wherever he might roam.
- Also: You're just another user when you set up Windows for multiple users. Any settings you've made—desktop, colors, whatever—are probably reset whenever the computer restarts.
- New users can add themselves by simply typing a new name and password in the Logon dialog box when Windows starts up. Or you can manually add users by using the Users icon in the Control Panel.

Chapter 37

A New Face on the Interface

Questions Answered and Thoughts Inspired

- Changing the desktop wallpaper (background)
- Using a Web page as wallpaper
- Tweaking Windows's windows
- Replacing Windows's popular icons
- Building your own icon
- Working with desktop themes

Henry Ford is rumored to have said, "They can have the car in any color, as long as it's black." Sounds rude, right? Well, what color is your PC now? Kind of a fawn white, maybe? Case closed. Color limitations don't have to apply to the outside of your PC, however. You can change the colors, fonts, and all sorts of other stuff in the Windows interface. This chapter tells you what you can change and how to do it.

- Microsoft workers sing happy songs in praise of Chairman Bill.

This chapter is a serious time waster. The options and settings it presents give you an opportunity to tweak and tune for hours—if you let the time get away from you.

A New Background to Match Your Mood

The desktop is Windows's front door, so to speak. It doesn't have to be so dull, though. You can replace the desktop with another image or pattern—or even a Web page document. You can even create your own images, patterns, or Web page documents to cover Windows's ugly doorstop:

- **Right-click the desktop.**
- **Choose Properties.**

The Display Properties dialog box appears.

- **Click the Background tab to bring that panel forward (if it isn't already).**

Figure 37.1 shows the Background panel, where you choose the wallpaper—a graphics image, pattern, or Web page to appear on the desktop.

You can also see the Display Properties dialog box by opening the Display icon in the Control Panel.

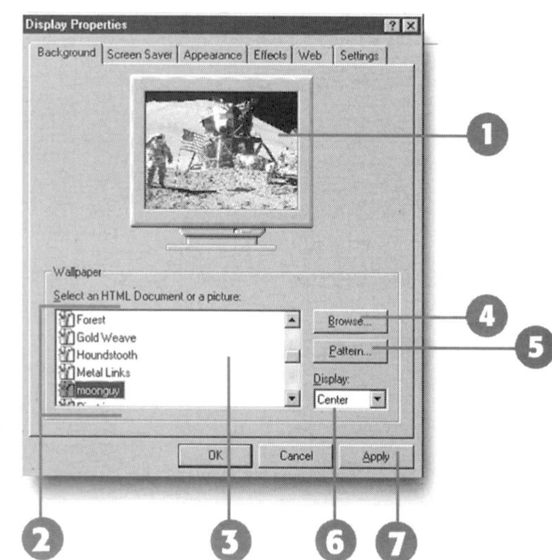

Figure 37.1

Setting the desktop's wallpaper.

1. Preview screen.
2. Choose a graphics file or Web page document from this list.
3. Files shown here are in the C:\Windows folder.
4. Click here to find another graphics or Web page document to display.
5. Click here to select a pattern rather than an image or Web page.
6. Adjusts the graphic to centered, tiled, or stretched.
7. Click here to preview your changes.

The following sections describe the various things you can do in this dialog box to change the way the desktop looks.

Using a Desktop Pattern as Wallpaper

Patterns are the simplest and often the best thing to have as your desktop wallpaper. Unlike graphics images and Web page documents, patterns take the least amount of time to display. Because they're boring and not splashy, however, few people bother. (Except me!)

▶ **Open the Display Properties dialog box.**

Refer to the instructions in the preceding section if the dialog box isn't open.

▶ **Click Pattern.**

The Pattern dialog box appears, as shown in Figure 37.2.

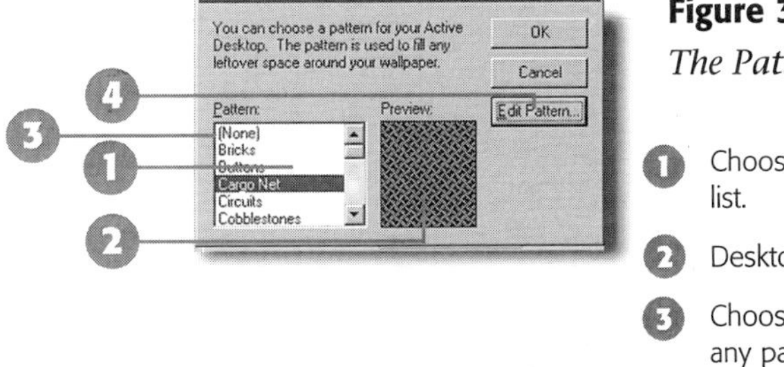

Figure 37.2
The Pattern dialog box.

1. Choose a pattern from this list.
2. Desktop pattern preview.
3. Choose (None) not to have any pattern.
4. When a pattern is selected, click here to edit it.

Windows comes with an array of preset patterns you can choose.

▶ **Preview a pattern by choosing it from the Pattern list.**

For example, Cargo Net, previewed in Figure 37.2, displays a hypnotic, manly, seagoing pattern. At least to me it does.

Windows lets you pick a preset pattern or fashion your own. To fashion your own, choose any pattern from the list to modify it. (You cannot modify `(None)` because it isn't a pattern.)

▶ **Click Edit Pattern.**

The Pattern Editor window appears, which I just *have* to show you in Figure 37.3.

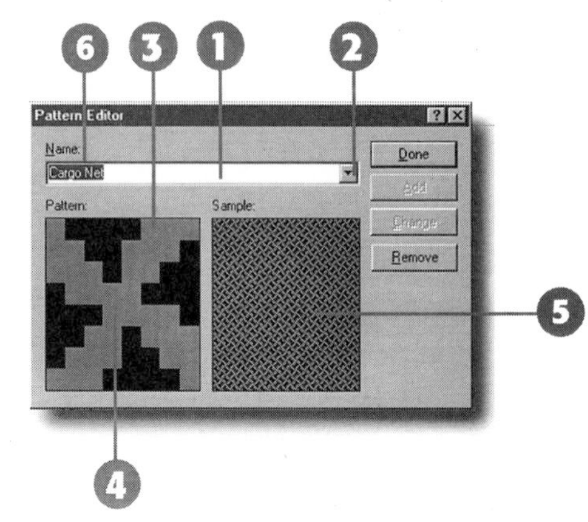

Figure 37.3
The Pattern dialog box.

1. Pattern name.
2. Choose a pattern from here.
3. Click once to set a block, and click again to reset it.
4. You can also drag in here to change colors in full strokes.
5. Preview window.
6. Enter a new name and click here to add the pattern to the list.

Feel free to waste time here. Figure 37.3 offers instructions and tips on how to edit a pattern or create your own. If you create your own, remember to type its name in the Name box and then click Add.

When you're done, click the Done button:

- ▶ **Click Done.**

The Pattern Editor closes and you're back at the Pattern dialog box.

- ▶ **Choose the Cargo Net pattern from the list.**

Or choose any pattern you might have just created. (I created an interesting pattern that I can't show in a family book.)

- ▶ **Click OK.**

In the Display Properties dialog box, notice that your pattern probably doesn't show up in the image preview. That means that you've selected an image or Web page document to display instead. (They have priority.)

- ▶ **Choose None from the top of the Select window.**

Now you should see your pattern previewed.

- ▶ **Click Apply.**

The Apply button makes the changes you suggest but leaves the Display Properties dialog box open, in case you want to make more changes.

Keep the Desktop Properties dialog box open for the next section's tutorial.

Of all the things you can have on the desktop, a pattern is the fastest to display an update. (If you've ever noticed Windows taking too long to redraw the desktop, it's probably due directly to the complexity of the desktop wallpaper image.)

- The foreground color for the pattern is always black. The background color is set in the Display Properties dialog box, on the Appearance panel, in the Color drop-down list.

Using a Desktop Image As Wallpaper

The most popular thing to slap on the desktop is a graphics image. It can come from several sources:

- ✓ Windows has a store of graphics images in its C:\Windows folder.
- ✓ You can create the image yourself by using Paint or any graphics program that produces bitmap image (BMP) files as output.
- ✓ You can "scan in" the image—such as a picture of your kids—by using a scanner. Just save the image as a bitmap image (BMP) file and, you're set.

Files must be BMP files to be used as a desktop image.

If you do create your own bitmap image file, save it in the Windows folder. (It's one of the few times when you *should* save something in that folder.) If you save it there, you see it in the list of options in the Display Properties dialog box. Otherwise, you have to use the Browse button to find the document elsewhere on disk.

▶ **Open the Display Properties dialog box (if it's not already open).**

▶ **Click the Background tab (if that panel is not already forward).**

Choose a bitmap image from the list of files. The tiny Paint icon next to the name (refer to Figure 37.1) flags the bitmap images.

▶ **Choose a picture file.**

You see two different types of files. One of them needs to be tiled; the image is so small that it takes up only a tiny square in the preview window. The second type of image file fills the screen, or else it might have to be stretched to fill the screen.

▶ **To tile, center, or stretch an image, use the Display drop-down list.**

As an example, I picked the `officialpenguin` graphic, which I downloaded from the `www.linux.org` Web page on the Internet. The three settings shown in Figure 37.4 illustrate how the penguin is centered, tiled, and, finally, stretched.

Figure 37.4
The centered, tiled, and stretched images.

1. A centered image.
2. Pattern background (None).
3. Tiled image, which works better with smaller images.
4. Stretched, the image fills the screen.

Although the preview window shows you generally how everything looks, it's always best to use the Apply button.

▶ **Click Apply.**

The desktop wallpaper changes to the image you selected.

You'll probably want to goof around with more options. Use the Browse button to try some desktop wallpaper patterns by using your own graphics files.

▶ **Close the Display Properties dialog box.**

If you create your own wallpaper image file, it's best to make it the same size as your screen. In the Display Properties dialog box, on the Settings panel, the screen's size is listed in the Screen Are box. Setting your graphics program to that same resolution (`800 by 600` or `1024 by 768`) ensures that the image fits perfectly on your desktop.

The next section's tutorial assumes that the dialog box is closed.

- You can convert JPEG graphics files (commonly found on the Internet) to BMP files by using the Paint program: Open the JPEG file, choose File➡Save As, and then choose a Bitmap item from the Save As Type drop-down list. (You see three bitmap items of varying color resolution. The 256 Color Bitmap option is a good all-purpose option to choose.)
- To capture a JPEG file from a Web page, right-click the image and choose Save Picture As from the shortcut menu. Remember to convert the JPEG image to a BMP image, as described in the preceding bullet.
- GIF is another popular graphics format found on the Web. Alas, you cannot convert GIF images to BMP images by using Paint. Other programs, such as HiJaak, can do so.

Using an HTML Document (Web Page) As Wallpaper

The final type of image you can place on the desktop is a Web page image, also known as an *HTML* document. It's the same as a Web page you see on the Internet, although it's not being sent by the Internet; the document is stored on your computer and displayed on the desktop.

You can create an HTML document for use as a Web page, or you can steal a Web page (HTML) document from the Internet. To steal (I should really say "borrow") a Web page document from the Web, you merely have to save it to disk:

▶ **Close the Display Properties dialog box if you have it open.**

▶ **Start IE.**

You can pick any Web page you want as your desktop pattern; just remember that the Web page is static on the desktop. It cannot be updated unless you save a new copy to disk. (The desktop is not a Web browser.)

▶ **Browse to `http://www.yahoo.com`.**

Type the Yahoo! address, or just wait a few seconds for Yahoo! to load if it's already your home page.

- **Choose File➡Save As.**

The Save HTML Document dialog box appears.

- **Browse to the My Documents folder from the Save In drop-down list.**

You have to do this step only if My Documents isn't already the folder you're looking at.

- **Type Yahoo's Home Page in the File Name box.**
- **Click Save.**

The Web page is saved to disk: graphics, text, and all.

- **Close IE and disconnect from the Internet.**

The HTML document is now stored on disk. Time to display it as your desktop's wallpaper:

- **Right-click the desktop.**
- **Choose Properties.**
- **Click the Background tab (if that pane is not shown already).**

Because the HTML document was saved in the My Documents folder, it doesn't appear on the list of images in the Display Properties dialog box.

- **Click the Browse button.**
- **Choose My Documents from the Look In drop-down list.**
- **Choose the Yahoo's Home Page file.**
- **Click Open.**

You see the Yahoo home page in the preview window. Pretty nifty, huh?

Depending on the size of your screen, you might see only the top part of the Web page. Notice that you cannot stretch the image; the Display drop-down list is dimmed. Even so, it's possible to change the screen resolution. See Chapter 40, "Tweaking Your Monitor," for more information.

▶ **Click OK.**

If a warning box appears, telling you that the Active Desktop must be enabled, click Yes.

Wow! Talk about a busy desktop!

Lo, there's the Yahoo home page as your desktop background, as shown in Figure 37.5.

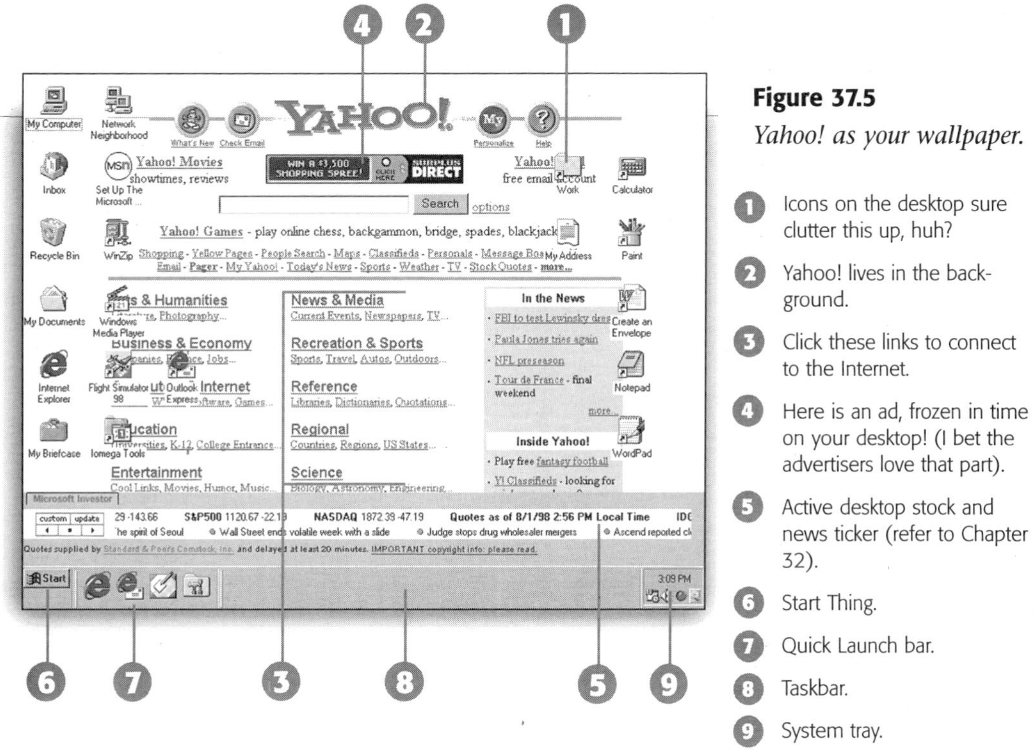

Figure 37.5
Yahoo! as your wallpaper.

1. Icons on the desktop sure clutter this up, huh?
2. Yahoo! lives in the background.
3. Click these links to connect to the Internet.
4. Here is an ad, frozen in time on your desktop! (I bet the advertisers love that part).
5. Active desktop stock and news ticker (refer to Chapter 32).
6. Start Thing.
7. Quick Launch bar.
8. Taskbar.
9. System tray.

And now, for the fun:

▶ **Click a link on the Web page.**

Yes, the links work. The Web page is a document on your computer, although the links point Windows's nose out into cyberspace.

IE starts and Windows connects you to the Internet so that you can view the link you clicked.

Notice that IE starts in its own window—not on the desktop. The desktop is not IE.

Continue playing on the Internet, or close the IE window and disconnect.

If you're not happy with having a junky Web page as your desktop wallpaper, open the Display Properties dialog box again and choose a boring old pattern instead. That's what I do.

Remember that what you see is not a real Web page; it's just a document (an HTML document). In fact, you could create your own HTML document and use it instead.

- Refer to Part V of this book for more information about Internet Explorer (IE).
- You have to refer to a book specifically about HTML documents for information about creating such beasts. It's a big topic, although creating an HTML document is much like working in a word processor.
- The Yahoo! document you used as wallpaper in this tutorial is not updated—unless you download a new copy every day. It isn't like an Active Desktop program, which is updated. The two things are different animals. See Chapter 32 for more information about the Active Desktop.
- Windows comes with a program called FrontPage Express, which you can use to create HTML documents. It's on the Start Thing menu (click Programs➡Internet Explorer➡Front Page Express).

Be careful as you're right-clicking the desktop when an HTML document is showing. You want to click the document's background, not a link. If you right-click a link, you get that link's shortcut menu, not the desktop's shortcut menu.

To get rid of the icons when you're viewing the desktop as a Web page, open the Display Properties dialog box, go to the Effects panel, and put a check mark next to Hide Icons When the Desktop Is Viewed As a Web Page. Click OK.

New Colors, Fonts, and Stuff

I'm always surprised at how many Windows users don't bother changing the window colors and fonts. It's always the same boring, old, blue windows and stick fonts. Yuck. You spend all that time picking out your clothes, finding a car in the right color, and even mulling over furniture, but you leave Windows in the same boring color.

- **Right-click the desktop.**
- **Choose Properties.**

The Display Properties dialog box shows up.

- **Click the Appearance tab (if that panel isn't already showing).**

The Appearance Panel (see Figure 37.6) is where you're allowed to change the Windows color and font scheme. Really! You can change it. Figure 37.6 shows you what's what.

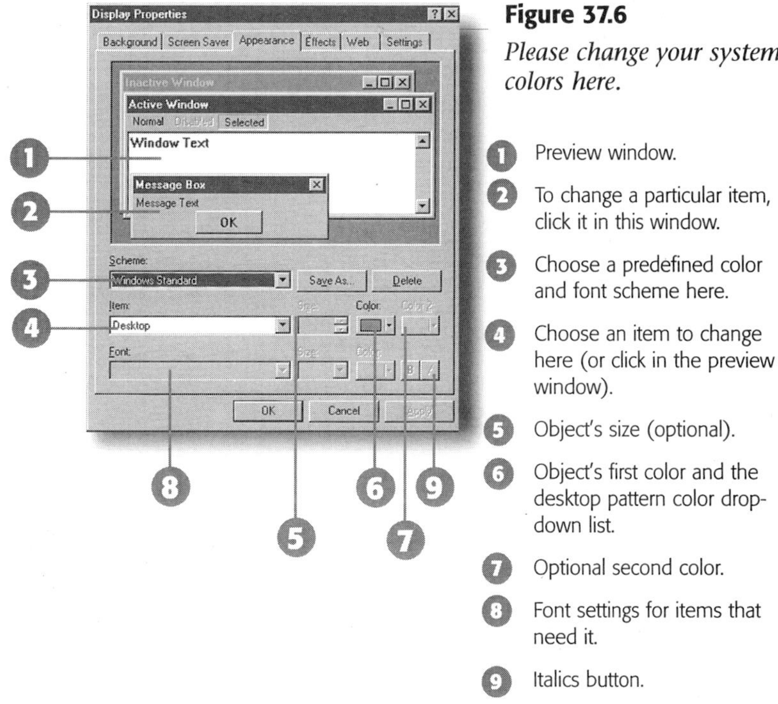

Figure 37.6
Please change your system colors here.

1. Preview window.
2. To change a particular item, click it in this window.
3. Choose a predefined color and font scheme here.
4. Choose an item to change here (or click in the preview window).
5. Object's size (optional).
6. Object's first color and the desktop pattern color drop-down list.
7. Optional second color.
8. Font settings for items that need it.
9. Italics button.

Play! Have fun! Change things! To get you in the mood, take this swift step:

- **Choose Red, White And Blue (VGA) from the Scheme list.**

The Scheme list contains a bunch of settings already made for you: fonts and colors. See how the windows are red and the text is shown in a fun font in the preview screen?

- **Choose Desktop from the Item list (if it's not chosen already).**
- **Click the Color drop-down list.**

A wee little color palette appears.

- **Pick a Gold color from the drop-down list.**

See how the background changes color?

- **Click the text *Message Box* in the preview window.**

The Font area at the bottom of the screen is active.

- **Choose Comic Sans MS from the Font drop-down list.**

If you don't have Comic Sans MS, choose another font.

- **Click the font's Color drop-down list.**

Oops. That shade of pale green isn't there.

- **Click Other.**

Whoa! Whole lotta colors going on!

- **Choose a pale green color.**

Choose the color from the Basic Colors palette or from the color curtain on the right side of the color.

- **Click OK when you've found your pale green.**
- **Click the text *Active Window* in the preview window.**
- **Use the spinner next to the Size box to increase the size way up.**

Notice how the Active Window title bar changes?

The number of colors you have is determined by how your monitor is set up. Changing the colors to a higher number is covered in Chapter 40, "Tweaking Your Monitor."

Okay! Enough goofing around!

▶ **Click Cancel to close the Display Properties dialog box.**

You get the idea. You know the feel. If you really want to tweak the Windows colors and fonts, return to the Appearance panel in the Display Properties dialog box and go mad!

- If you become enamored with your selections, click the Save As button to save your color and font scheme along with those that come with Windows. Aren't you nifty?

If you totally and utterly goof things up, choose Windows Standard from the Scheme drop-down list. That returns your settings to the way they were when you first set up Windows.

The possibility exists that you can screw things up to the point where you cannot control the windows on the screen (which implies that you shouldn't get careless). If so, start the computer with the Ctrl key pressed and choose Safe Boot from the menu that appears. After Windows starts, revisit the Appearance panel in the Display Properties dialog box, and reset Windows as described in the preceding bullet.

Changing the Main Icons

You can pull some other tricks with the way Windows shows itself. They're minor tricks, and if you're in the mood for play and have the time, you can certainly have some fun changing the Windows look some more.

▶ **Right-click the desktop.**

▶ **Choose Properties.**

▶ **Click the Effects tab (if that panel isn't already showing).**

The Effects Panel contains the last few things you can tweak on the desktop, as shown in Figure 37.7.

You can set the items in the Visual Effects part of the dialog box on your own. They're self-explanatory.

Changing an icon is quite easy; unfortunately, the icons to choose from are rather boring:

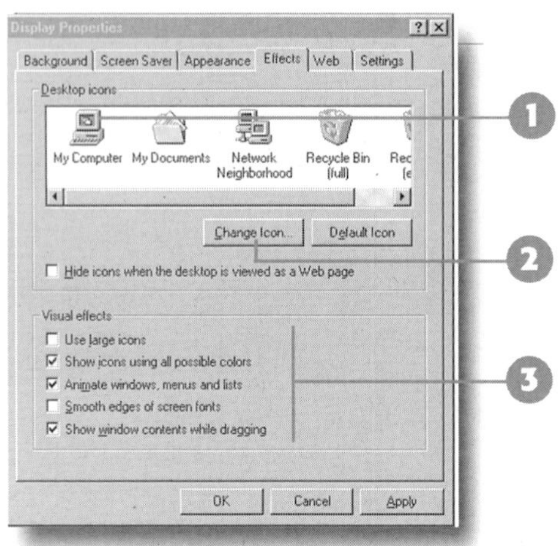

Figure 37.7
Other things to change.

1. Select a standard icon from here.
2. Click here to change the selected icon.
3. Self-explanatory options.

- **Click the Recycle Bin (Full) icon to select it.**
- **Click Change Icon.**

A list of icons appears—most of which you probably recognize. They're Windows "system" icons, and they're boring as hell.

Better create your own icon.

You can create icons by using the Paint program—and some imagination and drawing skill.

- **Click Cancel to close the Change Icon dialog box.**
- **Click Cancel to close the Display Properties dialog box.**
- **Start Paint.**

You have to reset the image size to the exact size of an icon.

- **Choose Image➡Attributes.**
- **Type 32 in the Width box.**
- **Type 32 in the Height box.**
- **Choose Pixels from the Units area.**

All icons measure 32X32 pixels.

- **Click OK.**
- **Click the magnifying-glass tool and choose 8X from below the tool palette.**

This step magnifies the image to a very large size, as shown in Figure 37.8. You want to work "under magnification" so that you can better see what you're doing. The lines and dots you draw then look larger. This is a good thing.

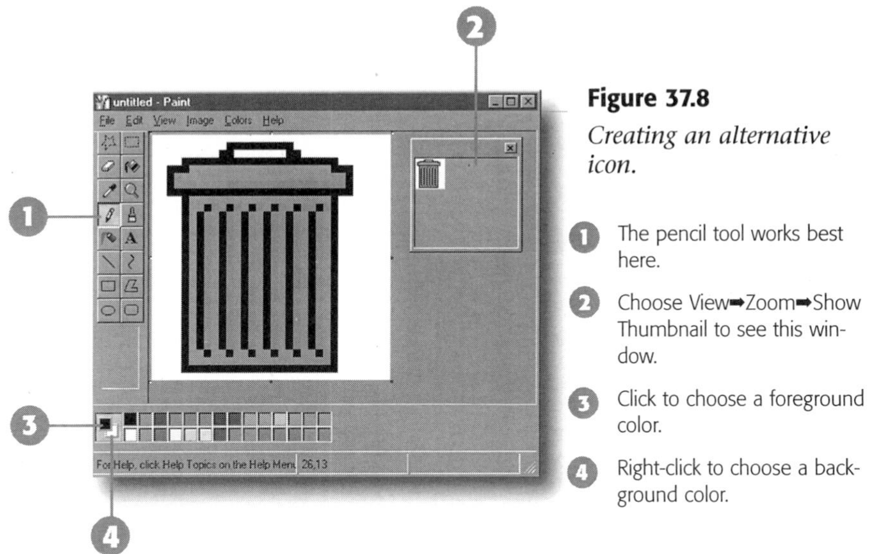

Figure 37.8

Creating an alternative icon.

1. The pencil tool works best here.
2. Choose View➡Zoom➡Show Thumbnail to see this window.
3. Click to choose a foreground color.
4. Right-click to choose a background color.

▶ **Draw a pretty trashcan.**

Go ahead! Draw the Macintosh trashcan. Do what Bill Gates' lawyers told him he couldn't do!

Boy! This is hard!

If you're stuck, use the Rectangle tool to drag a tall, trashcan-like rectangle. Fill it with gray. Draw some vertical lines with the Line tool. Use the Pencil tool to draw a thick lid. It doesn't have to be pretty. Remember that the icon drawers at Microsoft make something like $400 an hour!

▶ **Choose File➡Save As.**

▶ **Choose the My Documents folder from the Save in drop-down list.**

▶ **Choose 256 Color Bitmap (*.bmp, *.dib) from the Save As Type list.**

▶ **Type Trash icon as the File name.**

▶ **Click Save.**

You might see a warning that some color information will be lost. No problem. You've just set your desktop to more than 256 colors, but the icon is *only* 256 colors. Click OK to continue.

- **Close Paint.**

Now you can choose the icon you created to replace the Recycle Bin on the desktop:

- **Right-click the desktop.**
- **Choose Properties.**
- **Click the Effects tab (if that panel isn't already showing).**
- **Click the Recycle Bin (Full) icon to select it.**
- **Click Change Icon.**
- **Click the Browse button in the Change Icon dialog box.**
- **Browse to the My Documents folder.**
- **Choose All Files from the Files of Type drop-down list.**
- **Select Trash Icon from the list.**
- **Click Open.**

You see your icon in the Change Icon window. Nifty.

- **Click OK.**

Check it out! The Recycle Bin is replaced by your own icon.

You cannot change the icon right now *on-the-fly*. You have to restart Windows in order to see the icon. If that's what you want, click OK and then restart Windows. Otherwise, you probably want the old Recycle Bin icon back:

- **Click the Recycle Bin (Full) icon to select it.**
- **Click Default Icon.**

The cruddy old icon is back.

- **Click OK to close the Display Properties dialog box.**

Remember that you can change any icon back to the way it was by clicking the Default Icon button.

- Any Paint image saved to disk that's only 32-by-32 pixels in size can be used as an icon.
- Icon drawers don't really make $400 an hour. In fact, they're not even called "icon drawers" because a drawer is where you put your underwear. They're icon *illustrators*. They make minimum wage, plus $2 million in stock perks.

If you change the Paint image's extension from *.BMP to *.ICO, Windows recognizes it as an icon file all the time. (You might have to use DOS to do that if you're viewing your folders with the filename extensions hidden.)

Using a Desktop Theme

Tired of doing it all a little at a time? Wish that the "experts" would design a desktop theme for you—one that includes fonts, colors, a background image, and even sounds?

Consider it done:

- **Open the Control Panel.**
- **Open the Desktop Themes icon.**

An off-chance exists that you might not have this icon available in the Control Panel. In some versions of Windows, you need the Plus! package in order to get the Desktop Themes icon. If you don't have the package, don't worry: You're missing only a few silly and some interesting options—nothing absolutely necessary.

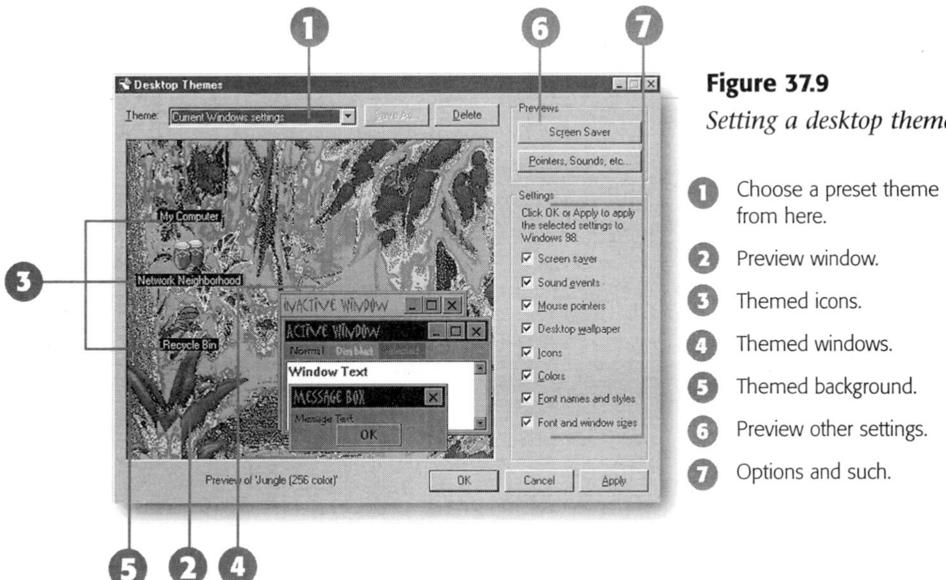

Figure 37.9
Setting a desktop theme.

1. Choose a preset theme from here.
2. Preview window.
3. Themed icons.
4. Themed windows.
5. Themed background.
6. Preview other settings.
7. Options and such.

- **Pick a theme from the Theme drop-down list.**

Some of them are fun. Some are way too busy.

Enough! I'm wasting too much time here!

- **Click the Screen Saver button to see the theme's screen saver in action.**

See? They think of everything.

- **Wiggle the mouse when you're done watching the screen saver.**
- **Click the Points, Sounds, Etc. button.**

A Preview window appears, as shown in Figure 37.10.

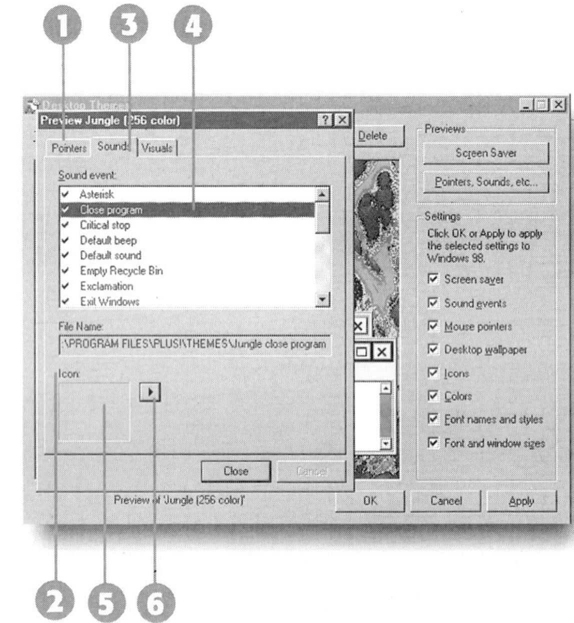

Figure 37.10
Previewing various audio and visual settings.

1. Mouse pointers previewed here.
2. Icons previewed here.
3. Sounds previewed here.
4. Click an item to preview it below.
5. Icons and mouse pointers appear here.
6. Click to hear a sound preview.

Notice that some of the mouse pointers are animated. Nifty!

- **Click Close when you're bored with previewing.**

Now you really have no other settings to make or change in the Desktop Themes dialog box. You merely pick and preview a theme:

▶ **Close the Desktop Themes dialog box.**

To update your desktop with a specific theme, click OK. All the various changes are made: wallpaper, icons, sounds, mouse pointers, and so on. Or, if you don't want to change your desktop, click Cancel.

- Don't be anal! The desktop themes don't "waste" that much space on your hard drive. True, if you're running low on space, you can delete them. See Chapter 15 for information about adding more of Windows. If you remove the check mark next to the Desktop Themes item, the themes are uninstalled from your system.
- You can also download new themes directly from Microsoft as well as from other manufacturers. See Chapter 15 for information about accessing the Windows Update program, which usually offers some new or different desktop themes.
- Other desktop themes are available all over the Internet. Use Yahoo! to search for the phrase *desktop themes*, and you might find some associated with your favorite sports team, TV show, or computer book author. All of them are free.
- Feel free to modify your settings after choosing a desktop theme. Suppose that you choose the Nature theme and find that the sound settings are too quiet. No problem—just change the sounds to something else (see Chapter 41).

The changes you make can also be undone individually. Simply return to the proper icon in the Control Panel (Display, Sounds, or Mouse, for example) to reset or tweak any options.

Chapter 38

Toolbars from Beyond Infinity

Questions Answered and Thoughts Inspired

- Making the taskbar disappear
- Moving and resizing the taskbar
- Finding a lost taskbar
- Working with toolbars
- Putting a Web page on the toolbar (nuts)
- Making a toolbar into a floating palette

In the beginning was the taskbar. It not only listed buttons for every open program or window but also had the Start Thing to the left and the system tray to the right. And it was good.

Then along came the Quick Launch bar. And it too was good. But things started to get cramped. This chapter introduces you to taskbar overload. Windows has a total of four optional toolbars you can meld into the taskbar. Plus, you can put any folder (that's on the desktop) on the taskbar. Heck, why not just put Windows itself on the taskbar and forget about it? But I digress.

Wrestling with the Taskbar Bar

There's no point in wrestling with the taskbar unless you know a few key moves and pressure points. Figure 38.1 is your taskbar lexicon for the rest of this chapter. Study the figure. Return to this section when you encounter some taskbar or toolbar jargon you're not familiar with.

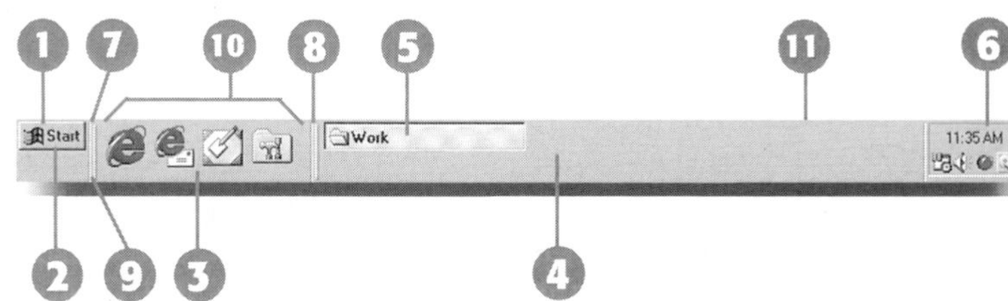

Figure 38.1
Sweet spots on the taskbar.

1. Start Thing.
2. Right-click here for a Start Thing shortcut menu.
3. Quick Launch bar.
4. Taskbar.
5. Button on the taskbar.
6. System tray.
7. Handle; drag here to move or resize the toolbar.
8. Right-click here to see the taskbar's shortcut menu.
9. Right-click here to see the toolbar's shortcut menu.
10. Right-clicking these displays their own, unique shortcut menus.
11. Upper lip; used to resize the taskbar.

- Keep in mind those right-click points on the taskbar. The best place to right-click for a particular toolbar is the handle.
- Right-clicking a taskbar icon displays the shortcut menu for that icon or program.

Bye-Bye, Taskbar

The taskbar has various degrees of invisibility. You can make it vanish between programs or hide it altogether. Let me tell you that just about everyone likes having the taskbar visible. In fact, a major frustration many folks face is not being able to get to a hidden taskbar.

▶ **Right-click the taskbar.**

Click a blank part of the taskbar, or click the taskbar's handle, if it has one (refer to Figure 38.1).

▶ **Choose Properties.**

The Taskbar Properties dialog box appears, as shown in Figure 38.2.

▶ **Put a check mark by Auto Hide.**

▶ **Click OK.**

▶ **Start WordPad.**

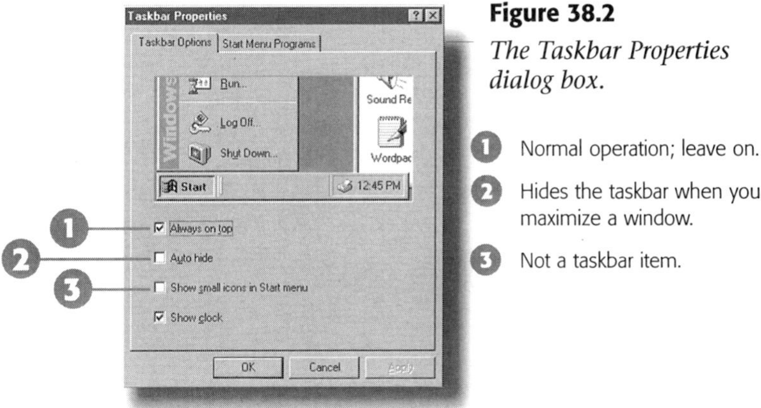

Figure 38.2
The Taskbar Properties dialog box.

1. Normal operation; leave on.
2. Hides the taskbar when you maximize a window.
3. Not a taskbar item.

See how the taskbar gets out of the way? It's just a little gray strip at the bottom of the screen.

▶ **Point the mouse at the taskbar.**

Vloop! Up it pops.

▶ **Move the mouse away from the taskbar.**

Vloop! Down it goes.

It's the taskbar version of the hokey pokey!

▶ **Close WordPad.**

You don't need to have a program open. The taskbar just hides itself all the time.

I feel that this option is horrible. I need to see the taskbar to determine whether everything is working properly on my computer. Also, the taskbar lets me see whether I have any open windows and confirms whether I'm on the Internet, by displaying the connection thing on the system tray.

Another way to get the taskbar to pop up is to press the Alt+Esc key combination on your keyboard. If your keyboard sports a Windows key, you can press it to pop up the taskbar.

If you prefer to have the taskbar hidden, move on to the following section. Otherwise, repeat the preceding steps to remove the check mark next to Auto Hide in the Taskbar Properties dialog box.

▶ **Point the mouse at the taskbar.**

Get the sucker to pop up.

▶ **Right-click the taskbar.**

- **Choose Properties.**
- **Remove the a check mark by Auto Hide.**
- **Click OK.**

Ahhh. Back to normal. For now.

- You can configure Internet Explorer to run "full screen," in which case the taskbar disappears. However, you can still move the mouse to the bottom of the screen to make the taskbar pop up.
- Some DOS games run in a full-screen mode where you cannot see the taskbar. That's good.
- Some Windows games also hide the taskbar. That's better.

Changing the Taskbar's Size

Most people I know run the taskbar at the same size: the same height as a button on the taskbar. That's okay, but you can change its size. For example, if you're running the Quick Launch bar with full-size icons, you probably want a thicker taskbar. If you have lots of windows open, a thicker taskbar lets you see more windows at a time.

Follow these steps to resize the taskbar:

- **Point the mouse at the top of the taskbar, its "upper lip."**

The upper lip is pointed out in Figure 38.1. It's the entire top part of the taskbar, not just the part pointed to in the figure.

- **Drag the mouse up.**

Press the mouse button and drag 'er up. The taskbar resizes itself as you drag.

Notice how dragging is done in specific increments. Drag until the taskbar is about three button heights tall.

- **Release the mouse button.**

If you have the Quick Launch bar (or any other toolbar) visible, you might notice that the taskbar has automatically rearranged itself, displaying the toolbars horizontally, as shown in Figure 38.3.

You can still have the Quick Launch bar and taskbar (and other toolbars) arranged from right to left rather than from top to bottom. See the section, "Arranging the Toolbars," later in this chapter.

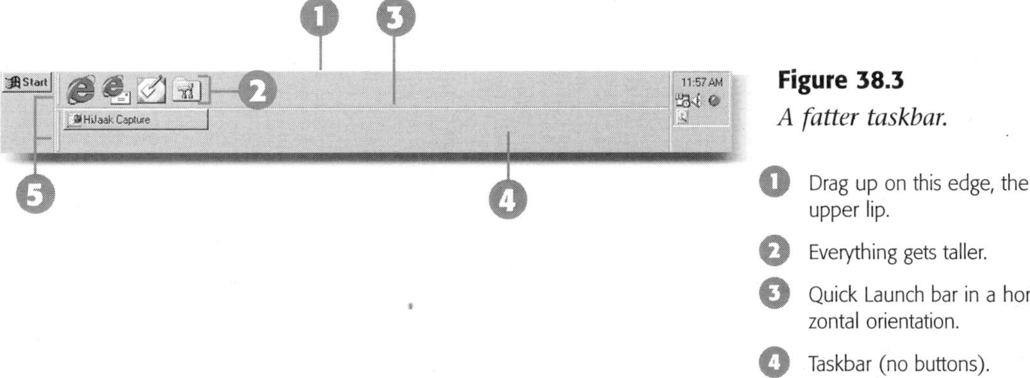

Figure 38.3
A fatter taskbar.

1. Drag up on this edge, the upper lip.
2. Everything gets taller.
3. Quick Launch bar in a horizontal orientation.
4. Taskbar (no buttons).
5. Handles.

To resize the taskbar to make it smaller, just reverse the preceding steps:

▶ **Point the mouse at the taskbar's upper lip.**

▶ **Drag the mouse down.**

Remember this basic move you've just done! It's important. Although you might not be able to imagine it now, there will be times when you resize the taskbar to enormous sizes. Keep in mind that you can always resize it again. It's flexible.

Moving the Taskbar

Normally the taskbar rests on the bottom of the screen, away from your programs lurking on the desktop. The taskbar isn't glued down there, though. Although few people ever move the taskbar, it can be done. All you do is drag the taskbar to another edge of the screen.

To drag the taskbar, point the mouse at an empty part of the taskbar. Don't point at a program or window's button, and you cannot drag by using the Quick Launch bar. Find an empty spot on the taskbar.

▶ **Drag the taskbar up to the top of the screen.**

Don't release the mouse button until you see the taskbar's outline at the top of the screen.

There. Doesn't that look stupid?

▶ **Drag the taskbar over to the right side of the screen.**

Hmmm. Maybe it needs some resizing. Okay, but resize it only if you plan to keep it over there. Otherwise:

▶ **Drag the taskbar back to the bottom of the screen.**

Although this little demonstration might seem pointless, I'm about to transform you into a Windows troubleshooting guru. Do this:

▶ **Drag the taskbar back up to the top of the screen.**

▶ **Resize the taskbar to make it a thin strip.**

Grab the taskbar's upper lip (well, now it's the lower lip), and drag it up as far as you can, almost off the screen. What you should see is a desktop that looks like it doesn't have a taskbar—just a mysterious, gray strip at the top of the screen.

What you've done is re-create a nasty trick many "experts" would pull on new and unsuspecting Windows users. "Where's my taskbar!" they'd squeal. Of course, now you can rescue those folks:

▶ **Resize the taskbar.**

▶ **Drag the taskbar back to the bottom of the screen.**

You're a genius!

Restoring a Lost Taskbar

In keeping with the theme from the preceding section, sometimes the taskbar utterly disappears and you just can't get it back. Now you know a secret, of course, but I want to tell you another surefire way of restoring a lost taskbar.

When someone bemoans that she has lost her taskbar, you can first check the Taskbar Properties dialog box. See whether she has the Auto Hide option on. If not, you can try the following:

▶ **Resize the taskbar to a thin strip along the bottom of the screen.**

You want to re-create the person's situation. In fact, if she has her monitor set up in such a way that the image overscans the screen, she can't see the taskbar strip at all.

▶ **Press Ctrl+Esc.**

This step pops up the Start Thing menu, and it also switches the Windows focus to the invisible taskbar.

▶ **Press Alt+Spacebar.**

This keyboard shortcut pops up the taskbar's control menu.

▶ **Choose Size.**

Press **S** for Size.

You might not see it, but the mouse pointer has moved to the taskbar's upper lip. It has changed to an up-down "resizing" arrow.

▶ **Press the up-arrow key a few times.**

The taskbar is fattened up to visible size.

If the up-arrow key doesn't work, try the left-, right-, and down-arrow keys. (Some joker might have moved the taskbar to another edge of the screen.)

▶ **Press Enter to lock in the taskbar's new size.**

Now you're a hero.

Adding More Toolbars

Windows comes with an assortment of fun toolbars you can stuff on the taskbar. In addition to adding the Quick Launch bar, which I find useful (it's covered in Chapter 11), you can add one or all of the following:

✓ The Address bar

✓ The Links bar

✓ The Desktop bar

✓ Any folder

✓ Any Internet address

Yes, you *can* add any or all of the preceding items, but the real question is *should* you? I've already voiced my opinion about the Quick Launch bar and how useful it is. The other toolbars, eh?

To add a toolbar, follow these steps:

▶ **Right-click the taskbar.**

Or you can right-click any handle on the taskbar to see the shortcut menu.

▶ **Choose Toolbars.**

The Toolbars submenu appears. The four alternative toolbars are listed at the top of the menu, as shown in Figure 38.4.

▶ **Choose Address.**

The Address bar appears on the taskbar (making things rather crowded, but if you've read this chapter so far, you know one way to remedy that). It's the same Address bar used in Internet Explorer. Typing an address there starts up IE (if it's not already) and takes you to that Web page.

Handy? Who knows. I don't use it.

Figure 38.4
The Toolbars submenu.

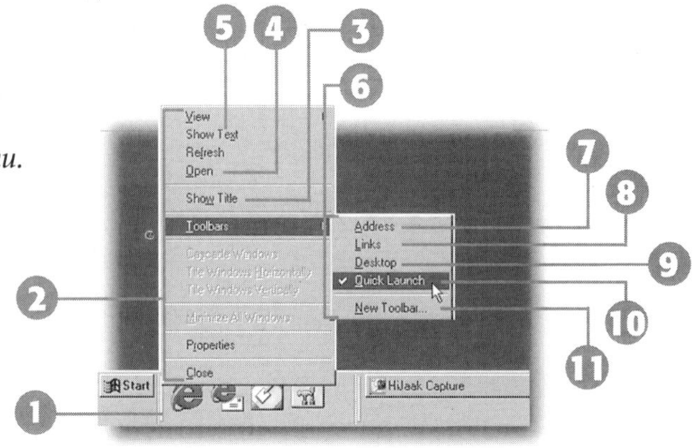

1. Right-click the handle to see the shortcut menu.
2. Toolbar menu items.
3. Displays the toolbar's title (wastes space).
4. Opens the toolbar as a window.
5. Displays each icon's name (also wastes space).
6. Toolbars submenu.
7. Address bar, like in My Computer.
8. Links submenu from the Favorites menu.
9. Toolbar with all your desktop icons on it.
10. See Chapter 11.
11. Allows you to add a folder or Web page as a toolbar.

- **Right-click the Address bar's handle.**
- **Choose Toolbars ➡Address.**

This step removes the Address bar.

- **Right-click the taskbar.**
- **Choose Toolbars ➡Desktop.**

On my screen, the Desktop toolbar is displayed with its title and captions visible, making the toolbar far too long, as shown in Figure 38.5.

- **Right-click the Desktop toolbar's handle.**
- **Choose Show Title to remove the check mark.**

Almost done:

- **Right-click the Desktop toolbar's handle a second time.**
- **Choose Show Text to remove the captions.**

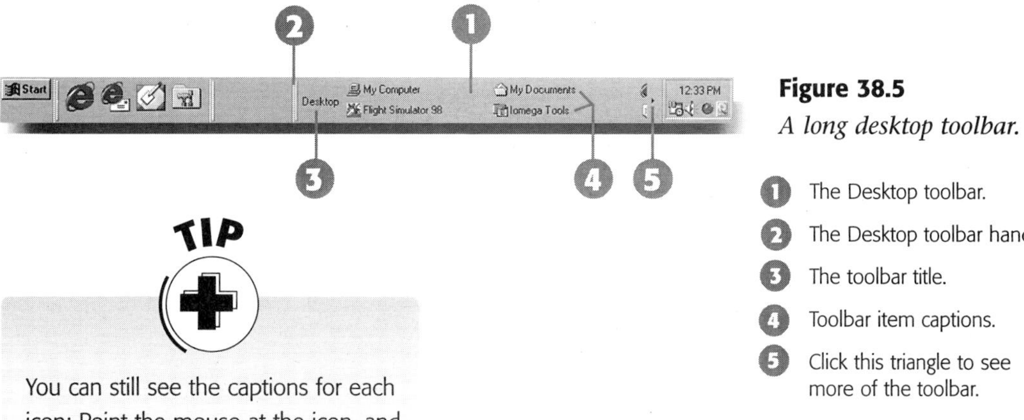

Figure 38.5
A long desktop toolbar.

1. The Desktop toolbar.
2. The Desktop toolbar handle.
3. The toolbar title.
4. Toolbar item captions.
5. Click this triangle to see more of the toolbar.

TIP

You can still see the captions for each icon: Point the mouse at the icon, and eventually the caption appears in a pop-up balloon.

Now the toolbar should fit (more or less) onscreen. What I see are a bunch of mini-icons representing everything on the desktop.

Although the Desktop toolbar isn't important (I don't use it; I use the Desktop button on the Quick Launch bar instead), it illustrates how Windows displays a folder on the taskbar.

Suppose that you want to add your My Documents folder as a toolbar on the desktop. First remove the Desktop folder:

- **Right-click the taskbar.**
- **Choose Toolbars ➡Desktop.**

The Desktop toolbar is gone.

- **Right-click the taskbar.**
- **Choose Toolbars ➡New Toolbar.**

The New Toolbar dialog box appears, as shown in Figure 38.6.

- **Browse to the My Documents folder.**

Open drive C, and then select My Documents.

- **Click OK.**

The folder appears on the desktop.

To remove the My Documents toolbar, follow these steps:

- **Right-click the My Documents toolbar's handle.**
- **Choose Close.**

Figure 38.6
The New Toolbar dialog box.

1 Type a Web page address here.

2 Tree-structure thing.

3 Pick a folder, a disk drive, My Computer—whatever—from here.

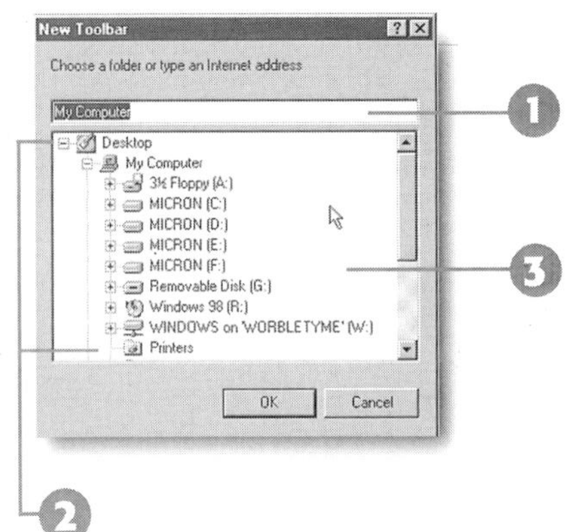

A warning dialog box might appear. It tells you that if you close the toolbar, you have to use the New Toolbar command on the Toolbars submenu whenever you want to add the toolbar again. Whatever. Click OK.

For your final tutorial in this chapter, it's time to see how adding a Web page toolbar affects things. This should be obtusely interesting.

TIP

You'll probably want to remove the new toolbar's title and captions. The proper steps for removing that text are covered earlier in this section.

- **Right-click the taskbar.**
- **Choose Toolbars ➡New Toolbar.**

The New Toolbar dialog box appears.

- **Type** http://www.yahoo.com/ **in the top text box.**

Type the Yahoo! address in the text box, as just shown.

- **Click OK.**

Windows connects to the Internet (if you're not online already). Soon you see—believe it or not—the Yahoo! Web page appear on the taskbar. Don't the scrollbars seem pitiful?

I don't know about you, but to me, a Web page on the taskbar seems really, really, really dumb.

Get rid of it now, before it drives you nuts!

- **Right-click the Yahoo! toolbar's handle.**
- **Choose Close.**

Disconnect from the Internet if you're not asked to do so automatically.

My advice: If you want to see a Web page, use IE, although I know that Microsoft must have some hidden plan in store somewhere for the Web-page-on-the-taskbar feature. Still, seems silly, right?

Adding a folder to the taskbar can prove useful—if you customize a folder for that specific purpose. For example, create a folder called Projects. Inside the Projects folder, put shortcuts to all your project folders—the things you do all the time. Then stick the Projects folder on the taskbar as a toolbar.

- You can also choose the Control Panel as a toolbar. From the New Toolbar dialog box, browse down to the Control Panel and click OK.

Arranging the Toolbars

Even if you have just two toolbars floating on the taskbar, arranging them is something you have to deal with. For some reason, Windows slips around the toolbars like they're attached with Vaseline. Ugh.

To move or rearrange a toolbar, you must drag it around by its handle.

Unfortunately, I cannot show a tutorial for this because Windows's behavior is rather inconsistent when it comes to laying down toolbars.

If you want to play on your own, open about three toolbars, which is discussed in the preceding section. Then practice moving them around by dragging their handles. (Sorry I can't do better, but my test tutorials never worked the same way twice.)

Floating a Toolbar

One final trick—and it's a trick because I can't find any practical use for it: You can *drag* any toolbar from the taskbar to create a floating palette on the desktop. Why would one do this? I have no idea. Like putting a Web page on the taskbar, though, it can be done:

- **Right-click the taskbar.**
- **Choose Toolbars ➡Desktop.**

The Desktop toolbar appears, scrunched on the taskbar like 5 o'clock traffic on the Ventura freeway.

▶ **Drag the Desktop toolbar to the desktop.**

You must drag by using the toolbar's handle. The mouse pointer changes to a "copy" pointer (with the little, gray rectangle). When you release the mouse, a *palette*, or tiny window, appears, containing all the toolbar's commands, as shown in Figure 38.7.

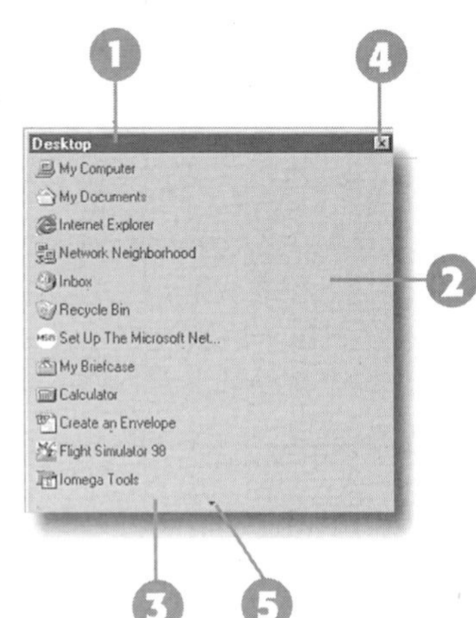

Figure 38.7
A floating-palette toolbar.

1. Drag using the handle.
2. The floating palette.
3. Right-click here for the palette's shortcut menu.
4. Close the palette.
5. You can drag the palette back to the taskbar.

Although a desktop palette on the desktop is redundant, other palettes might be useful.

Notice that Figure 38.6 shows the Desktop palette with small captioned icons. You can change that on the taskbar, but not when you convert the toolbar to a floating palette.

▶ **Drag the Desktop palette back to the taskbar.**

Drag the palette by its title bar and release the mouse button when the pointer is over the taskbar.

▶ **Right-click the Desktop toolbar's handle.**

▶ **Choose View ➡Large.**

The toolbar changes to display large icons rather than small icons.

The captions are a little redundant. Better remove them:

▶ **Right-click the Desktop toolbar's handle.**

▶ **Choose Show Text.**

Now you're ready to re-create the palette:

▶ **Drag the Desktop toolbar up on the desktop to create a palette.**

Drag by using the toolbar's handle.

The palette now looks like a bunch of icons—more like a palette than a menu.

▶ **Close the Desktop palette by clicking its X close button.**

A warning dialog box appears. Yadda-yadda-yadda. Click OK.

- You cannot drag the taskbar up to create a floating palette.
- A floating palette has the same attributes as a toolbar, except that you can change them only in toolbar mode.
- Does all this stuff seem a little much? Yup. Keep in mind that all this stuff is optional. It's there if you need it, but you most likely won't.

Chapter 39

A View to a Folder

Questions Answered and Thoughts Inspired

- Changing a window's background
- Manipulating a folder's options

Windows has many options for changing the way it displays icons in a folder. Some of these options are nifty; others are obtuse. But hey! You should be expecting that by now!

This chapter covers folders. Specifically, you learn how to change the way a folder displays information. As usual, you have more options than you'll probably use in a lifetime. So I'd better hurry.

Adding a Pretty Background to a Folder

Folders don't have to be boring. Look at the desktop. You can add any image to the desktop, creating a fun and engaging look for your computer and also wasting mountains of time. Guess what? You can do the same for each folder in Windows.

To start with, the following tutorial creates a Personal folder in the My Documents folder—a place where you can experiment before trying this stuff out on more serious folders on your hard drive.

- **Open the My Documents folder on the desktop.**
- **Choose File ➡New ➡Folder.**
- **Rename the new folder as** Personal.
- **Open the Personal folder.**

The folder doesn't yet have any icons in it, but that's okay. It's best to try this trick out on an empty folder.

▶ **Choose View ➡Customize This Folder.**

The Customize This Folder dialog box has two options for setting a folder's background plus an option for removing any settings you've made previously.

▶ **Choose the middle option, labeled Choose a Background Picture.**

▶ **Click Next.**

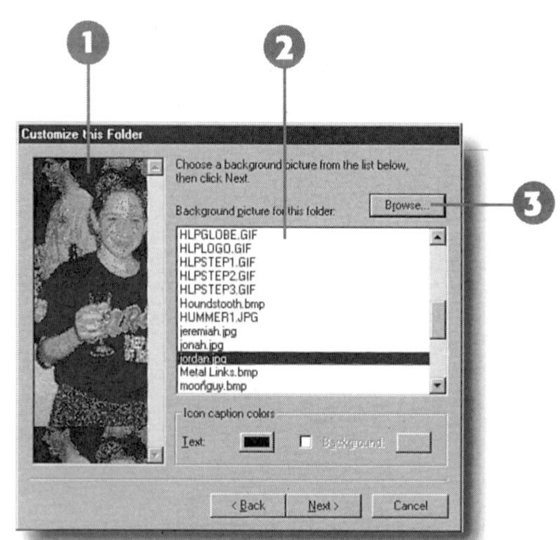

Figure 39.1
The Customize This Folder dialog box.

1. Image preview (you can't scroll left or right).
2. All the graphics files on your hard drive.
3. Browse for more images.

The next panel in the Wizard is really nifty. It lists all the graphics files Windows has found on your hard drive—very convenient.

▶ **Choose a background image.**

Scroll through the list to find a suitable image for the folder's background. All the graphics files are tiled to fill in the folder (unlike the desktop, no centered or stretch options are available).

If you can't find a particular image, use the Browse button to search for one. The image types are BMP (Windows bitmap graphic or Paint file format), JPEG, and GIF (two standard Web page graphics file formats).

▶ **Click Next.**

▶ **Click Finish.**

You see your graphics file appear as the folder's background. In an empty folder, that looks nifty. With icons floating over the image, however, you might consider choosing a different image. For example, the pictures of my kids obscure the icons in the window—even though my kids are very cute.

If you just want to change the background *color* of a folder, refer to Chapter 37. The Appearance tab in the Display Properties dialog box lets you change the folder's background color. Choose Window from the Item list and pick a color from the Color drop-down list.

Simple, boring background graphics work best.

If you have chosen View ➡As Web Page, the background image appears only on the right side of the window.

▶ **Click the Up button.**

Notice that the My Documents folder was not affected by your background change in the Personal folder.

- You can change any or all of your folders in this way. Windows remembers the background image you've selected no matter which folder you visit. That can be fun.

The first option in the Customize This Folder dialog box is Create or Edit an HTML Document. Do not choose this option if you're unfamiliar with HTML editing. Honestly, it took me by surprise that Microsoft would start Notepad with raw HTML text for editing when this option is selected. I would assume that you could pick a Web page for a background, similar to what can be done with the desktop, but no. This option is way, *way* too advanced for most people. Avoid it. Sorry!

Removing a Folder's Background Image

If the fun ever grows dull, you might want to reset things back to normal. Follow these steps:

▶ **Open the folder you want to change back to "normal."**

In this case, it's the Personal folder you play with in the preceding section.

- **Choose View ➡Customize This Folder.**
- **Choose the bottom option, Remove Customization.**
- **Click Next.**
- **Click Next.**
- **Click Finish.**

The folder goes back to its normal dull appearance.

You can close the Personal folder window now or keep it open for the next section's tutorials.

Setting Folder Options

You can train your folders to exhibit certain behaviors, customizing the way they act and display information. And all this training can be done in one dialog box. You don't have to feed your folders fish like they feed the seals at the zoo to get them to bark and clap and catch a ball on their noses.

- **Open the Personal folder (if it's not open already) created in the preceding section's tutorial.**
- **Choose View ➡Folder Options.**

The Folder Options dialog box appears, as shown in Figure 39.2.

You have three options for setting up the way your folders work. The preview window at the top of the dialog box shows you what you get with each option.

- **Choose Web Style.**

Each window looks like a Web page. The icons and folders become like "links" you can click to open—only one click, by the way.

Soak it in.

- **Choose Classic Style.**

Yawn! Check out that preview window. And you *paid money* to get Windows 98. Yup.

- **Choose Custom.**

Ahhh. I like it when you have a choice. (Note to Microsoft: That's *a* choice, not *40* choices.) The Custom, Based on Settings You Choose is my favorite. It allows you to set individual options the way you like, mixing the best of Web and Classic styles.

- **Click Settings.**

The Custom Settings dialog box appears, where you can tailor the way Windows displays its folders, picking and choosing options as you go. Figure 39.3 deciphers the commands for you, showing you which settings I use.

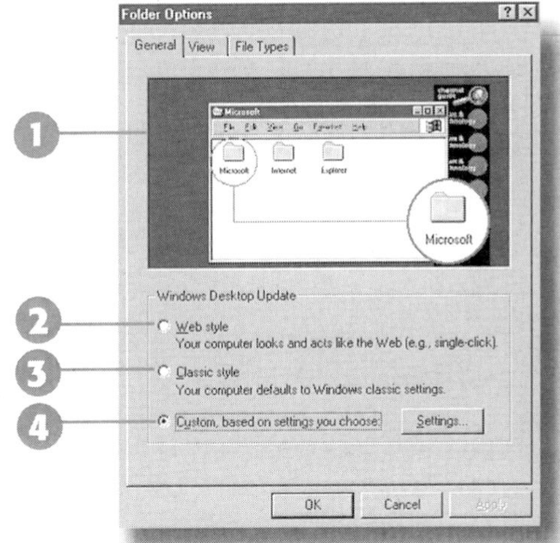

Figure 39.2

The Folder Options dialog box.

1. Preview window.
2. Web style—as though you're not sick of the Internet already.
3. Windows 95 style; nothing classic about it.
4. Ahhh, you choose the options. I like this one the best.

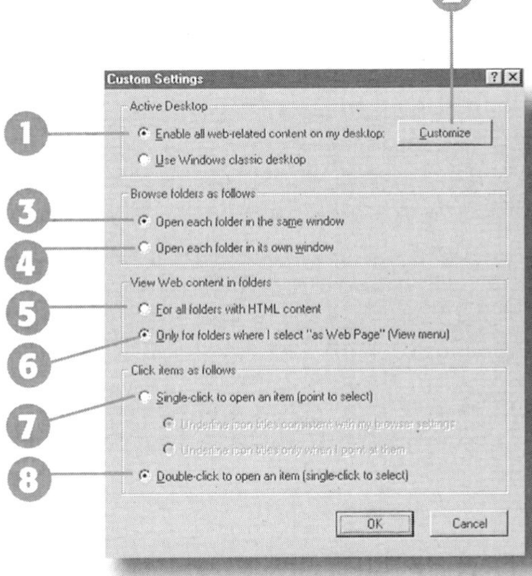

Figure 39.3

The Custom Settings dialog box.

1. Allows you to view Web page information on the desktop.
2. Takes you to the Web panel in the Display Properties dialog box.
3. I prefer to browse using only one window.
4. Choose this option to have folders and disk drives open in new windows. **Warning:** It clutters your desktop quickly.
5. Automatically choose Web view when you open a folder configured that way (which I find annoying).
6. Lets you switch Web view on and off.
7. Single-clicking or pointing to select is nontraditional and not what has been discussed in this book. It causes you to open many files accidentally.
8. I prefer the old-fashioned double-click to open an icon.

Avoid the Single-Click to Open an Item (Point to Select) choice! If you've been using Windows for any time, you're used to the "classic" way; a single-click selects and a double-click opens. All the Windows books, manuals, courses and all the experienced users expect Windows to behave the classic way.

You can make any adjustments here, or use the settings that were shown in Figure 39.3.

After you're done making any settings, you can leave the dialog box. Or you can leave without making any changes:

▶ **Click OK to close the Custom Settings dialog box.**

▶ **Click Cancel to close the Folder Options dialog box.**

You can close the Personal folder window too, if you're done with it. The tutorial has ended.

- Part I of this book discusses folder options for viewing icons: Large Icons view and List view, for example, in addition to options for sorting the icons as they're displayed in a folder window.
- You can always choose View ➡As Web Page to display a window in Web page mode.

Chapter 40

Tweaking Your Monitor

Questions Answered and Thoughts Inspired

- Changing monitor color and resolution
- Using a screen saver
- Password-protecting your screen saver
- Using two monitors (advice only)

As an apprentice computer book writer back in 1985, I had to learn the difference between the monitor, the screen, and the display. They're not the same, you know.

The *monitor* is the box that sits on top of or alongside your computer. It's the TV-set-like thing. The *screen* is the glassy part of the monitor, where the image is displayed. The *display* is the image that's displayed. Even knowing that, I still titled this chapter "Tweaking Your Monitor" rather than "Tweaking the Display." Maybe it should have been titled "Tweaking Your Old Boss."

Changing Screen Size and Colors

Every monitor has the capability to display an image with a specific number of *pixels*—those tiny dots you see when you press your nose against the screen. The dots are measured by vertical and horizontal values, so you can have a screen with 480,000 pixels—800 pixels across (horizontal resolution) by 600 pixels high (vertical resolution). Lots of pixels.

Then there are colors. Each pixel can be configured to display a certain number of colors: 16 colors, 256 colors, more than 1 million colors, 16 million colors, and even more.

Together, these two values make up the screen size and color settings for your monitor. You can change the settings, increasing the resolution and number of colors, as much as your PC's video adapter and monitor will let you. It's all done in the Display Properties dialog box.

▶ **Right-click the desktop.**

▶ **Choose Properties.**

The Display Properties dialog box rears its ugly head.

▶ **Click the Settings tab.**

The Settings panel is shown in Figure 40.1.

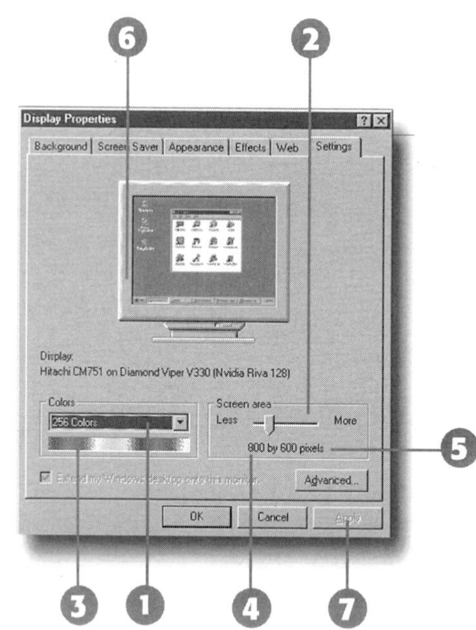

Figure 40.1

The Settings panel in the Display Properties dialog box.

1. Set the number of colors here.
2. Set the screen area (pixels) here.
3. Color preview.
4. Horizontal (across) resolution.
5. Vertical (up and down) resolution.
6. Preview screen.
7. More on this feature later in this chapter.

In Figure 40.1, you see that I've chosen the rather lame settings of 256 colors and a resolution of 800X600 pixels. My monitor is capable of much more—in fact, some of my software demands that I set the number of colors to 16 million or more. Because the publisher's production department wants the chosen settings, though, I'm stuck with them (until I finish this book—ha-ha!).

▶ **Slide the Screen Area bar one notch to the right.**

This step increases your available screen real estate. On my screen, the values jumped from 800-by-600 up to 1024-by-768. Likewise, the preview window shows more available screen space. Yippee!

▶ **Slide the Screen Area bar all the way over to the right.**

How big is big? On my screen, it can go all the way up to 1600-by-1200 pixels. Wow. Of course, a drawback to that size is that you cannot display as many colors.

High resolution usually means fewer colors.

With the resolution set as high as it goes, choose a high color value:

▶ **Choose the highest color value from the Colors drop-down list.**

On my screen the value is True Color (32-bit). When I choose that value, however, the Screen Area slider slides back to a resolution of 1152-by-864 pixels. The computer is telling me that that's the highest resolution I can have with 32-bit colors. The values on your screen might be different—it all depends on your video adapter.

Why the difference in colors at high resolution? It's a trade-off. The video adapter has only so much memory. Together, a high resolution and many colors require lots of memory, so you have to trade off: You can have lots of colors, but not an ultimately high resolution, or you can have a high resolution but not that many colors.

Put another way: A high resolution usually implies a clear picture. However, you can use lots of colors to fool the eye into thinking that the resolution is higher when it's not. For example, a TV has very low resolution but an infinite number of colors. That fools the eye into thinking that the resolution is higher than it is.

To preview your new resolution, you click the Apply button. Windows attempts to preview the resolution for 15 seconds and then switches you back to your current screen resolution.

▶ **Click Apply.**

A warning dialog box appears. Don't panic. It's giving you a choice: Reset and preview or preview now without resetting. (In the old days, it just reset.)

▶ **Ensure that the Apply the New Color Settings Without Restarting? option is chosen.**

In fact, you could put a check mark in the Don't Ask This Question Again box and be perfectly safe.

▶ **Click OK.**

'Nother warning.

If the resolution is high, the text onscreen is *tiny*. If you can't see the text, just wait, and your screen will be restored to normal.

▶ **Click OK.**

Twang! The screen tweaks to its new resolution and color values.

A Monitor Settings dialog box appears. Do you like the new look?

▶ **Click Yes to keep the new settings, or just sit there if you can't stand 'em.**

If you click Yes, you're in business. Otherwise, wait, and Windows switches you back to the way things were. (Me? I had to wait because the publisher's production department enjoys the lower resolution more than I enjoy it.)

You can keep the Display Properties dialog box open for the next section's tutorial. Or close the dialog box if you're ready to take a brisk walk and get some air.

Honestly, higher resolutions look best on monitors with a diagonal measurement of 19 or more inches.

- Did you get more screen space, or did the images onscreen just get smaller? Actually, it's both. To get more stuff onscreen, you have to make things smaller—science has yet to figure out a way to increase the size of the monitor (unless you buy a huge monitor to begin with).

One way to improve the visibility of your icons at a high resolution is to open the Display Properties dialog box, display the Effects panel, and put a check mark by Use Large Icons.

- For some strange reason, many children's games require a very low color value: 256 colors. If you run those games without setting the low color value, your screen might appear in all black or with black areas.
- Newer programs that require a higher color value might reset the value automatically for you when they run. I know that the Intel Create & Share Camera Pack does that. Other programs might, also.
- It's possible to change colors without changing resolution and vice versa. However, keep in mind that higher resolutions might not display all the colors you need.
- High resolutions are great! You can see lots of open windows and have lots of screen space. Most Windows programs generally have a zoom feature that enlarges the text you're editing. It's a great way to run a computer.
- High resolutions work really well on large-format monitors. In fact, I don't buy any monitor anymore unless it has at least a 19-inch diagonal.
- If you have just pressed your nose against your screen, you probably have a greasy mark on your monitor. Spray some Windex or glass cleaner on a paper towel or a soft cloth and wipe the screen. Don't take me so literally next time.

The Screen Needs Saving

A *screen saver* is an archaic program designed to prevent something called "phosphor burn-in." It was a malady that affected early monochrome and color PC monitors; if you left the monitor on for any length of time, eventually the screen image would "burn" into the phosphor. Many such monitors had a hollow image of WordPerfect or VisiCalc visible onscreen—even with the monitor turned off!

What the screen saver did was to blank out the monitor, "saving" it from being burned by an image. At first screen savers merely blanked the screen, turning it black until you pressed a key. Then fancier screen savers offered images—floating toasters and flying toast, for example. Watching a screen saver was more like playing a game.

- Monitors are now better made than the earlier monochrome and RGB color monitors. Phosphor burn-in is no longer a problem (it rarely if ever happens), although the screen saver program survives as a sort of fun thing to do anyway.
- A screen saver in Windows is the only practical way to put a password on your system.
- If you download a screen saver from the Internet, save it in your C:\WINDOWS\SYSTEM folder. That way, it appears on the list of screen savers along with what Windows normally offers.

Setting a Screen Saver

Windows comes with a gaggle of screen savers you can choose from. To set one up on your PC, you use the Display Properties dialog box:

- ▶ **Open the Control Panel.**
- ▶ **Open the Display icon.**
- ▶ **Click the Screen Saver tab to bring that panel forward.**

The Screen Saver panel in the Display Properties dialog box is shown in Figure 40.2.

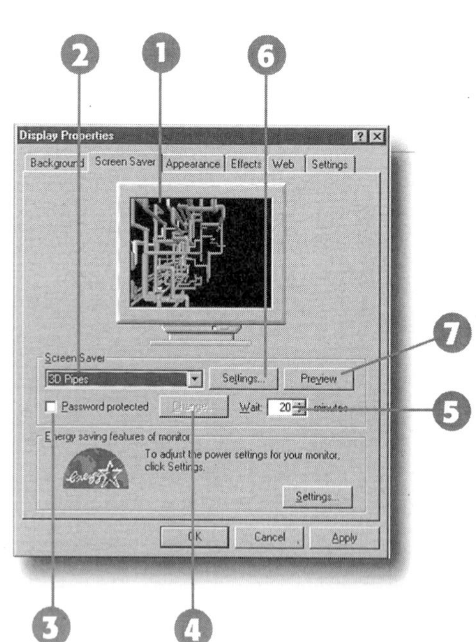

Figure 40.2
Save your screen here.

1. Screen saver preview window.
2. Choose a screen saver from this list.
3. Activate password protection.
4. Set or change the screen saver's password.
5. Delay before the screen saver kicks in.
6. Adjust the screen saver.
7. Preview what it will look like.

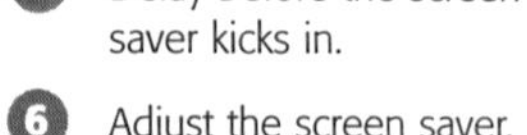

As with other parts of the Display Properties dialog box, the Screen Saver panel encourages play. Let me take you on a tour of the ground rules before you set off on your own:

- **Choose 3D Pipes from the Screen Saver drop-down list.**

Or choose any screen saver you find interesting. Or, heck, choose them all!

If you choose (None), the screen saver is disabled.

You see the screen saver preview—such as animated pipes—in the preview window. That's a pitiful way to enjoy a screen saver, though.

- **Click Preview.**

The screen saver appears full-screen—just like it does when it finally takes over your computer.

- **Press the Ctrl key.**

You have two ways to restore the screen after a screen saver kicks in: Press any key on the keyboard, or jiggle the mouse. If you want to press a key on the keyboard, the Ctrl key is the safest one to press. Press Enter, Esc, or even the Alt key to trigger some application. Because the Ctrl key doesn't affect any application, it's the best key to press.

After you've chosen your screen saver, you have to tell Windows when to kick it in. The value in minutes is specified in the Wait box. If you don't move the mouse or type anything from the keyboard for that number of minutes, Windows kicks in the screen saver.

- **Enter** 15 **in the Wait box.**

Windows waits for 15 minutes of inactivity before it switches on the screen saver. I usually set the screen saver to this amount of time, adjusting it up or down depending on how often I use my computer.

- **Click OK.**

The Display Properties dialog box goes away. Your screen saver is set, and now you have to wait to see it in action. (Go outside and take a walk. When you come back, the screen saver should be on.)

- The Settings button can be used to adjust certain aspects of each screen saver. The dialog box you see when you click the Settings button is different for most screen savers, yet the controls in that dialog box are fairly obvious.
- Even though the original purpose of the screen saver was to prevent the same image from appearing on your monitor, quite a few screen savers do, in fact, display a static image. Oh, well. So much for progress.

If you're in a habit of just sitting there and reading Web pages on the Internet, you might want to choose a value higher than 15 minutes.

- My choice is not to use a screen saver at all! My PC sports an energy-efficient monitor. Rather than save the screen, I tell the computer to turn the monitor off after a specified amount of time. This topic is covered in the section "Sleep, Monitor, Sleep..." later in this chapter.

Password-Protecting Your Screen Saver

The only truly secure password Windows 98 offers is the screen saver password. The logon password is a joke; it doesn't prevent people from accessing your computer. The screen saver password cannot be bypassed.

- ▶ **Open the Control Panel.**
- ▶ **Open the Display icon.**
- ▶ **Click the Screen Saver tab.**

You must use a screen saver in order to have a screen saver password. I know: That sounds dumb. If you choose None from the list of screen savers, though, the Password Protected option becomes unavailable. I assume that you have already chosen a favorite screen saver.

- ▶ **Click to put a check mark in the Password Protected box.**

This step enables the Change button.

- ▶ **Click Change.**

Windows displays the Change Password dialog box. You must type the screen saver's password *twice* to lock it into memory.

- ▶ **Type the password in the New Password box.**

Type something short and sweet—something that you'll remember. Try to stick with letters and numbers, although not something obvious, like your name.

All characters you type are displayed as asterisks.

▶ **Type the password again in the Confirm New Password box.**

Type the same password again. Asterisks onscreen replace the characters you type.

▶ **Click OK to close the Confirm New Password dialog box.**

Windows pops up a dialog box saying that the password has been changed.

▶ **Click OK.**

The password is set.

To try it out, wait awhile. (You cannot test the password by clicking the Preview button.)

▶ **Click OK to close the Display Properties dialog box.**

Wait.

When the screen saver kicks in, only typing the proper password lets you regain access to your computer.

You must remember the screen saver password. If you forget it, you cannot use your computer.

Figure 40.3 shows the password dialog box. Type your password there, or else you'll never get back into Windows!

Figure 40.3
Reenter windows by typing your password.

▶ It doesn't matter which screen saver you're using; password protection works the same for all of them.

▶ The only way to get back into Windows if you forget your password is to reset your computer. I know that I told you that was a no-no back in Chapter 1, but this is one of those few desperate situations when you can't do anything else and are compelled to reset.

▶ We keep passwords on all our computers at home, primarily to keep our little kids out. The passwords for all the computers are `none`, and it works quite well—at least until Simon is old enough to read this book.

Sleep, Monitor, Sleep...

Rather than bother with a password, you can put your monitor to sleep. This feature is on most newer PC monitors. They can turn themselves off and go into a special low-power mode. The screen goes blank—just like a screen saver—and you save energy.

- **Open the Control Panel.**
- **Open the Display icon.**
- **Click the Screen Saver tab.**

If your monitor is capable of sleeping, you see a special section labeled Energy Saving Features of Monitor at the bottom of the Display Properties dialog box (refer to Figure 40.2).

- **Click Settings.**

The Power Management Properties dialog box appears, as shown in Figure 40.4. (It's the same dialog box you see if you choose the Power Management icon in the Control Panel.)

I have my monitor sleep after 30 minutes of computer inactivity (no typing or mouse movements).

- **Choose After 30 Mins from the Turn Off Monitor drop-down list.**
- **Click OK to close the Power Management Properties dialog box.**
- **Click OK to close the Display Properties dialog box.**

Now your monitor is configured to turn itself off after 30 minutes (or whatever value you choose).

You can always use a screen saver and turn your monitor off. For example, set the screen saver to kick in after ten minutes and the monitor to turn itself off after an hour.

Then again, you can always just turn your monitor off by pushing its button. Naaah, that's too much effort.

By the way, if you have a screen saver that plays sounds, the sounds continue to play if your monitor sleeps. That's because the monitor, not the computer, is turned off. If you've set the computer to sleep as well, it doesn't play the sounds. (Some of those sounds can get to you after awhile.)

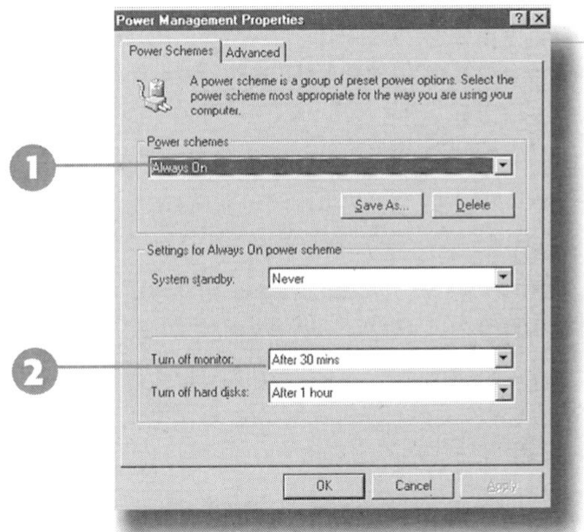

Figure 40.4

The Power Management Properties dialog box.

1. Set the power scheme here; for example, for a laptop computer.
2. Choose a time after which you want your monitor to sleep.

Dealing with Dual Monitors

Here's a little-known fact: The PC has always had the capability to have two monitors running at one time. It's true! Every PC, from the first IBM model on up to whatever they're selling at Costco (probably some lame Packard Bell model) has the capability to have *two*—yes, two—monitors attached. Cool.

The downside was that, although one of the monitors could be a color model, the other had to be monochrome. Also, only a few programs could display information on both monitors at one time; notably, some old CAD software—but I'm talking ancient history here. (When I visited Microsoft World Headquarters once, I saw some programmers using both monitors.)

Most people have forgotten about the dual-monitor capability of a PC. The Macintosh has had it since the Mac II came out. I had a Mac SE with a large "portrait" monitor alongside the SE's internal monitor. It was great! The Macintosh I have now has two monitors. My friend Bruce Webster once hooked up eight monitors to his Mac II for an article in the old *BYTE* magazine. (I miss you, old *BYTE*!)

Oh, but I'm rambling.

I suppose that the point is that having two monitors on a PC isn't new and isn't much of a big deal, unless you're stupid like me and you run out and buy another monitor and another VGA video adapter card (the spendy, 4MB, 3D graphics model) and try to hook it up *before* you take the following steps:

- **Open WordPad.**
- **Choose File ➡Open.**
- **Browse to the Windows folder on drive C.**
- **Choose Text Documents (*.txt) from the Files of Type list.**

▶ **Open the file named DISPLAY.**

▶ **Scroll down to the heading Multiple Display Support.**

It's about halfway through the document.

What you're looking at is a list of video adapter cards that Windows 98 cherishes. Only those cards can be used with a second (or third) monitor on your PC.

Do you see listed the Diamond Viper card I bought for my PC? No, you do not see it listed. Instead, you see a number of ATI cards. ATI-this. ATI-that.

So now you are smarter than the author of this book. Buy an ATI card to do dueling monitors.

So I'm a dork. I bought the wrong video adapter, and I cannot run multiple monitors. If you choose to do so, print the DISPLAY document *right now*. Use it as your buying and installation guide.

If you continue reading the DISPLAY file on multiple monitors, you find out how techy and tricky it is to install several monitors on a PC. Definitely a task for the truly nerdy among us.

▶ **Close WordPad.**

▶ **Open the Control Panel.**

▶ **Open the Display icon.**

The Display Properties dialog box appears. When you're running multiple monitors, they appear in this dialog box next to each other.

▶ **Click the Settings tab.**

The Settings panel contains one item that clues you into being a successful dual-monitor Windows 98 person. See the item near the bottom that says Extend My Windows Desktop onto This Monitor (refer to Figure 40.1)? Yup. That's it.

The Settings panel is also where you arrange the multiple monitors by dragging them around. That way, you can drag icons or windows between two monitors, and it looks contiguous. Really nifty. (Then again, I've been doing that on a Macintosh since 1987.)

▶ **Close the Display Properties dialog box.**

▶ **Close the Control Panel.**

Maybe rather than extol the virtues of having two monitors, I should now just explain how arrogant a thing it is. (I'm trying to make you forget that it's a subject not really covered in this book.) You know: one head, one monitor. It makes sense. Two monitors? Isn't that just a feeble admission that you didn't buy a large enough monitor in the first place? Or maybe it's saying something about your inner feelings. You know, "I'm not much of a man, so I need dual monitors to make up for my personal inadequacies." That sort of thing.

I'm working on it.

- When my friend Bruce did his multiple-monitor text for *BYTE*, he had to arrange the monitors in a pattern on the floor, face up. There's just no way to arrange four or more monitors around a PC—unless you devise some sort of musical instrument tubing and mount the monitors on it. Hey! That would look nifty. I think that's what Batman had in the Batcave.
- You know, I didn't have to check any documentation for the Macintosh when I added a second monitor. In fact (and this is the last time I mention the Mac in this book), the monitor I bought for my PC to do the dual-monitor test is now being used on the Macintosh. So there!

BYTE magazine was the granddaddy of all computer magazines, dating back to the heyday of the hobbyists in the mid-70s. I had been a subscriber since 1983 but recently canceled my subscription when *BYTE* was sold, folded, and almost killed off. I haven't seen the "new" *BYTE* magazine, so I don't know what's up with it anymore.

Chapter 41

Sound Advice

Questions Answered and Thoughts Inspired

- Adding sounds to system events
- Creating and using a sound scheme
- Recording your own sounds
- Adjusting the volume

For some people, a happy computer is one that sits still, doing its work by feeling the gentle taps on the keyboard and quietly displaying text on the monitor. The soft warbling of the computer's fan adds a nice high-tech touch. Productivity swells.

For other people, a silent computer is a boring computer. They want to hear a slippery squeak when a window is maximized to fill the screen. They ache to hear Big Ben at the top of each hour. They chortle at the sound of an ill wind when Windows is shut down. To those people I dedicate this chapter. May your computer be silent no more. May you now add sound to everything you do.

- This chapter assumes that your PC is properly equipped with a sound card. If your system lacks a sound card, you can do nothing here; feel free to skip this chapter.
- The easiest way to tell whether your PC has a sound card it to check its rump. On the back of your computer should be several connectors (miniplugs) into which a set of speakers or a microphone plugs.
- You must connect speakers to most models of PCs in order to hear their sounds. Some PCs can play the sounds internally or through the monitor.

Adding Sound to the Point of Annoyance

Face it: Sounds make a computer fun. They add a level of life that's often lacking in the sterile computer world.

Windows lets you play with sounds in the Control Panel. You can set or remove sounds for a number of Windows activities as well as sounds for a handful of other programs.

- **Open the Control Panel.**
- **Open the Sounds icon.**

The Sounds Properties dialog box appears, ready for you to play. Figure 41.1 shows you which knobs to twist and which buttons to punch.

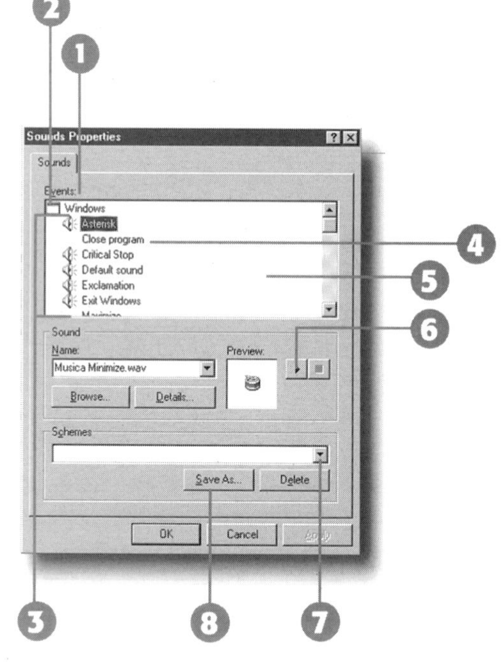

Figure 41.1

The Sounds Properties dialog box.

1. Events to which sounds can be assigned are listed here.
2. Program.
3. Program's sounds.
4. No speaker means that no sound has been assigned to that event.
5. Pick a sound here.
6. Preview the sound.
7. Choose a predefined sound scheme.
8. Save your own sound scheme.

The following sections discuss a few popular activities that take place in the Sounds Properties dialog box.

Toward a More Cacophonous PC

To assign a sound to an event, scroll through the list of events in the Sounds Properties dialog box. Events with speaker icons beside them already have sounds, although you can change the sound if you want. No speaker means that no sound is yet associated with that event (refer to Figure 41.1).

▶ **Select the Exit Windows event.**

If a sound is associated with that event, click the Play button beside the Preview icon to hear the sound.

To assign a new sound, follow these steps (they work for any event):

▶ **Choose a new sound from the Name drop-down list.**

Several dozen or so sounds should be listed.

▶ **Pick the DING.WAV sound.**

Your screen might just say `DING`. That's okay. It's the same file.

▶ **Click the Play button to preview the sound.**

Hey! Now *that* is boring. (I feel like I just correctly answered a question on a quiz show: "What's the capital of Uruguay?" "Bob, that would be Montevideo." DING.WAV!)

You could choose another sound, but because this is a tutorial, you have to go browsing for more sounds:

▶ **Click Browse.**

A special sound-browsing Browse dialog box appears, as described in Figure 41.2.

Windows stores its sound files in one of three possible places, depending on how your system is set up.

The first place to look is in the C:\Windows\Media folder, which is probably where the Browse dialog box is pointed right now. If not, use the Look In drop-down list to visit drive C, and then open the \Windows folder and then the \Media folder (if it exists) to find your sound files.

The second place to visit is the \Windows folder itself.

▶ **Click the Up button in the Browse dialog box.**

Figure 41.2

A special sound-browsing dialog box.

1. Only sound files are displayed here.
2. The sound file type is WAV.
3. Click to play the highlighted sound file. This feature is nifty 'cause you can preview a sound before you open it.
4. Stop!

From the Media folder, the Up button takes you to the \Windows folder, in which you might find some sound files. Scroll the window to the right to find any sound files. (I didn't.)

The third place Windows might stuff sound files is in the C:\Program Files\Plus!\Themes folder. This folder exists only if you or your dealer has installed the Microsoft Plus! package on your PC.

▶ **Browse to C:\Program Files\Plus!\Themes.**

Choose drive C from the Look In drop-down list. Open the Program Files folder, and then the Plus! folder, and then the Themes folder. If none of these folders exist, return to the \Windows\Media or \Windows folder or wherever you previously found sound files.

The Themes folder has lots of files, specifically those used in desktop themes (covered in Chapter 37).

Have some fun! Start plucking through the sound files, picking one and then clicking the Preview Play button.

You can install "missing" themes by adding the rest of Windows, as covered in Chapter 15. Add the Desktop Themes item.

This could take hours.

Keep in mind which sound you're choosing. In this tutorial, it's the new Exit Windows sound. On my computer, I've chosen the Baseball Restore Down file—even though I'm not using any other baseball sound themes. I just like the drum roll effect when Windows exits.

▶ **Choose your sound and click OK.**

The sound appears in the Sounds Properties dialog box and is associated with the Exit Windows event.

Repeat the preceding steps to assign several more sounds to Windows events. Just go nuts!

When you're done, you can close the Sounds Properties dialog box (and the Control Panel) or continue with the next section's tutorial.

- You can also use the Find command to locate sound (WAV) files on your PC. Refer to Chapter 27, "Hunting Down Files."
- To remove a sound from an event, choose None from the Name drop-down list in the Sound area of the Sounds Properties dialog box.
- Volume too soft or too loud? See the section "Adjusting Just How LOUD It Gets," later in this chapter.

Using a Sound Scheme

Windows comes with a swarm of predefined sound schemes. Pick a sound scheme, and it sets all your sounds in Windows to a particular theme—if you want. I like to mix and match. Even then, Windows lets you save your choices as your own sound theme.

▶ **Open the Sounds Properties dialog box if it's not open already.**

If you've been going nuts selecting your own personal sounds for various events, it's time that you save your choices as a sound scheme:

▶ **Click Save As in the Sounds Properties dialog box.**

The Save Scheme As dialog box appears. It's rather boring. No figure is necessary.

▶ **Type** My Sounds **in the box.**

After all, they are your sounds. If you can think of something more clever, type it instead.

▶ **Click OK.**

If you don't see any schemes, they probably weren't installed with Windows. Refer to Chapter 15 to add the Multimedia, Multimedia Sound Themes, and Desktop Themes items to Windows.

Your sound scheme is safe and saved. Now you can mess around and preview another scheme without fear of losing what you've created already.

▶ **Display the Schemes drop-down list.**

Various sound schemes are displayed.

▶ **Choose Musica Sound Scheme.**

The sounds in the Events area are changed all at one time to the predefined Musica theme.

Try a few sounds! Choose an event and click the Play button. See how the Musica theme works.

If you find a scheme you like, choose it and click OK to set it in place. Or you can mix and match themes—again wasting hours of valuable time in the Sounds Properties dialog box.

To restore your own theme, choose My Theme from the drop-down list.

▶ **Click OK to close the Sounds Properties dialog box.**

▶ **Close the Control Panel.**

Some third-party hardware and software developers have concocted their own themes. Also, bonus themes are available at the Windows Update Web page (refer to Chapter 15). You might find sound themes on the Internet too. Use Yahoo! to search.

From Whence Cometh Thy Sounds?

No, don't look to the hills for your sounds. If a sound file can't be found on your computer, you have two options: Create the sound file yourself, or use a sound file someone else has created.

To create your own sound file, you need two things. First, you need a microphone connected to your computer. Some PCs have built-in microphones, which you should be able to see (typically) on the monitor somewhere. Other PCs have a mic port in back, into which you can plug a cheap microphone.

Second, you need a special piece of software to record sounds. Windows comes with this type of program, called the Sound Recorder.

The following tutorial assumes that you have a microphone properly connected to your PC's rump:

▶ **From the Start Thing, choose Programs ➡Accessories ➡Entertainment ➡Sound Recorder.**

The Sound Recorder appears, as shown in Figure 41.3.

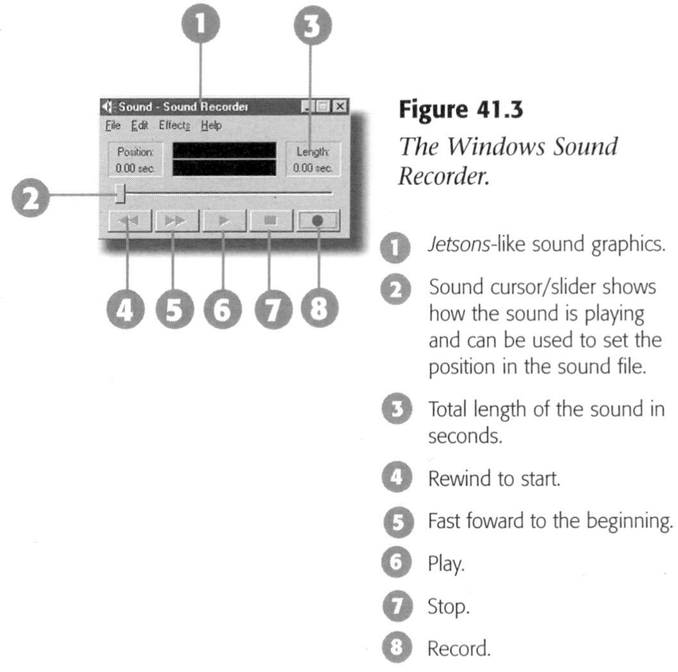

Figure 41.3
The Windows Sound Recorder.

1. *Jetsons*-like sound graphics.
2. Sound cursor/slider shows how the sound is playing and can be used to set the position in the sound file.
3. Total length of the sound in seconds.
4. Rewind to start.
5. Fast foward to the beginning.
6. Play.
7. Stop.
8. Record.

Unlike Aunt Debra, who just points the videocamera in your face and says, "Say something nice about Thanksgiving," I'll give you a break. Here's what you should recite into the microphone: "I love Windows! Ha-ha-ha-ha-ha-ha."

The "ha-ha-ha-ha-ha" part is laughter, although if you cannot laugh on cue, just say "ha-ha-ha-ha-ha" very fast. Trust me. This will be good.

Stand by.

▶ **Click the Record button.**

▶ **Say out loud, "I love Windows! Ha-ha-ha-ha-ha."**

▶ **Click the Stop button.**

Don't worry now about the quality of the recording. This is a tutorial. You can come back later and record something more meaningful and with better quality.

Listen to how the computer thinks you sound:

- **Click the Play button.**

Not bad. Well, it could be better. For example:

- **Choose Effects ➡Add Echo.**
- **Click the Play button.**

Echoes always add authority, don't you think? So does having a nice, rich, sonorous radio voice. The Sound Recorder can help:

- **Choose Effects ➡Decrease Speed.**
- **Click the Play button.**

Very jolly. Very green.

This next one is tricky:

- **Choose Effects ➡Increase Speed (by 100%).**

This step resets the sound to normal speed (trust me).

- **Choose Effects ➡Increase Speed (by 100%).**

Yes, a second time.

- **Click the Play button.**

Where is the Lollipop Guild when you need it?

- **Choose Effects ➡Decrease Speed.**

Your settings are back to normal again (still with the echo).

- **Choose Effects ➡Reverse.**
- **Click the Play button.**

Now you know what you sound like to Satan.

- **Choose Effects ➡Reverse.**

Back to normal again.

Time to save the sound!

- **Choose File ➡Save As.**

A standard Save As dialog box appears. On my screen, the Save As dialog box shows the My Documents folder. You can save your sound file there, if you want. Or, if you plan to collect lots of sound files, create a new folder called Sounds or Audio for the sound files. Use the Create New Folder button in the Save As dialog box to do that.

Because the Sound Recorder has no Undo command, the best way to restore your sound is to save it all the time. Save before you try out any effect. Then reopen the file if you mess up.

▶ **Type** me **in the File Name text box.**

▶ **Click Save.**

Your sound is saved for all history!

▶ **Close the Sound Recorder.**

Now you can return to the Sounds Properties dialog box and apply witty sayings and various body noises to all the things Windows does. Enjoy yourself.

- You can also find sounds on the Internet. Go to Yahoo! and search for `sounds`. Visit the various Web pages it displays to hear the sounds. Right-click a sound link and choose Save Target As to download the sound to your computer.
- Most sound cards come with their own sound-recording and manipulation programs. Although the Windows Sound Recorder is great, I believe that you'll find many more useful features in your sound card manufacturer's own software.

If you're handy with audio gadgets, you can hook up any stereo, VCR, TV set, or other audio device directly to your computer for recording. You have to patch the device's output with a mini-din cable into the PC's line-in jack. You can record sounds directly from the device, eliminating any ambient room noises.

Adjusting Just How LOUD It Gets

Your computer can have two or more volume switches. One is a control on the taskbar's system tray. The others, if they exist, are on your computer's external speakers.

I'll trust that you can figure out on your own how to adjust your external speakers' volume.

Changing the Master Volume

To adjust a sound as Windows plays it, you use the sound control on the system tray:

▶ **Click the sound control on the system tray.**

Click once. If you click twice, close the Volume Control window, go back to the system tray, and *click once* on the little sound-control guy.

A pop-up sound control appears, as shown in Figure 41.4.

▶ **Slide the bar up.**

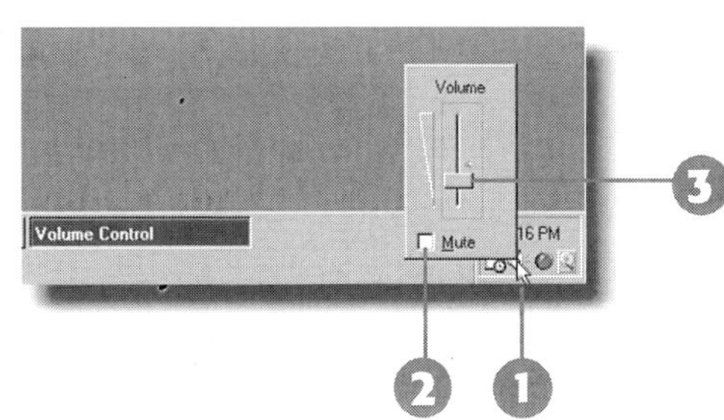

Figure 41.4
The Sound Control pop-up.

1. Click here.
2. Disables all sounds.
3. Slide up to increase volume and down to decrease it.

When you release the mouse button, you hear a sound, indicating how loud the volume level is.

▶ **Slide the bar down.**

Releasing the mouse button plays the sound, which is now softer.

Find a comfortable sound level. Click the slider a few times to hear how loud the beep is.

To hide the sound control when you're done, just click the mouse anywhere outside the sound control, such as on the desktop:

▶ **Click on the desktop.**

Don't forget that your PC usually has a second volume control on the speakers. The volume control on the system tray only goes up so high. Your speakers, on the other hand, might go all the way up to 11.

- If you choose the Mute option on the sound control, the sound icon on the system tray appears with the universal "no" symbol superimposed.

A better way to test the volume is to have a Sound Recorder window open with a sound opened and ready for playing. For me, a simple beep doesn't do it. I need *more sound* to hear if it's really too loud or too soft.

Changing the Volume for Individual Sound Devices

Before I knew about the Volume Control window, I had to manually reset my computer's volume every time I played a music CD. I had the volume set low for the computer's own sounds. Whenever I played a CD, though, I pumped up the volume. After playing the CD, whenever Windows beeped at me, I would jump out of my chair.

Why is it we as a species don't force computers to do more of the work?

The volume control on the system tray is a master. It controls all the sounds your PC plays. Inside your PC are several things that generate sound. To control their volumes individually, you have to accidentally discover the Volume Control window, just like I did:

▶ **Double-click the sound icon on the system tray.**

The Volume Control window appears, as shown in Figure 41.5. You can also access the Volume Control window by choosing Programs ➡Accessories ➡Entertainment ➡ Volume Control from the Start Thing menu.

Suppose that you want to play a WAV file quietly. You can turn the volume down in the Wave part of the dialog box. If you really want to hear your CDs play loudly, bump that volume control way up (kind of like it is in the figure).

▶ **Choose Options ➡Properties.**

The Properties dialog box sets which volume controls you see (or don't see). In the bottom of the dialog box is a scrolling list of volume controls Windows deals with.

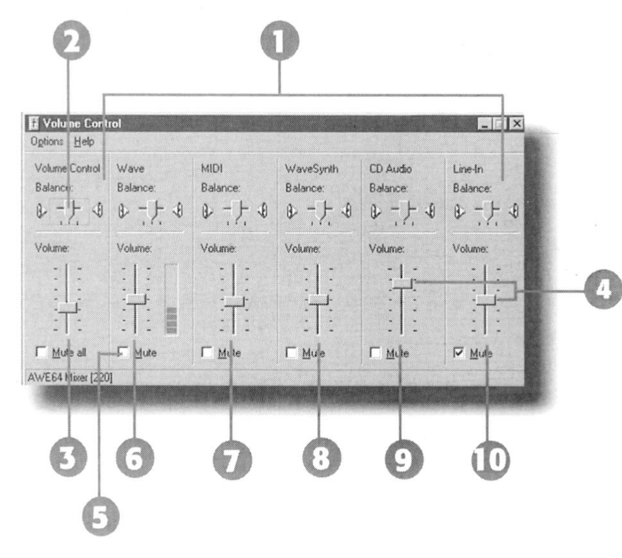

Figure 41.5
The Volume Control window.

1. Sound sources inside your PC.
2. Adjust the balance of the left and right speakers.
3. Main volume control (same as on the system tray).
4. Individual volume controls for each sound source.
5. Mute an individual sound source.
6. Volume for WAV files.
7. MIDI music file volume.
8. I don't know what this one is.
9. CD audio (music) volume.
10. Any sounds coming into the sound card's line-in jack.

To see a control displayed, click to put a check mark in its box. Likewise, to remove a control from the Volume Control window, click to remove the check mark.

▶ **Click OK to close the Properties dialog box.**

▶ **Close the Volume Control window.**

Now you know the secret and can have the computer do the work of adjusting the volume whenever you play a CD or MIDI file and want the WAV (sound) files played at a different volume.

Chapter 42

More Fonts for You

Questions Answered and Thoughts Inspired

- Finding the Fonts folder
- Previewing your fonts
- Making a hard-copy list of fonts
- Adding fonts
- Removing fonts
- Using the Character Map program

You can't really have much fun with fonts. They're basically different styles of type you can see onscreen, use in documents, and send off to the printer. Hubcaps are more interesting (especially when they pop off on the freeway and transform themselves into spinning metal disks of death).

Although fonts add pizzazz, that's not the subject of this chapter. The key here is unlocking the secrets of fonts; they live all by themselves in the Fonts folder. You can preview fonts, add new ones, or remove old ones. It's all cinchy, although I had to write a chapter about the topic anyway.

Hello, Fonts Folder!

All Windows fonts (almost all of them, anyway) are kept in their own Font folder. It's a special folder sitting right beneath Windows' own folder on your hard drive. You don't have to wade through My Computer or the Explorer to get there; a handy shortcut to the Fonts folder lives inside the Control Panel:

- ▶ **Open the Control Panel.**
- ▶ **Open the Fonts folder.**

The Fonts folder window is displayed, as shown in Figure 42.1. This folder is customized, so don't blow me off and skip over the figure. You have important things to note there.

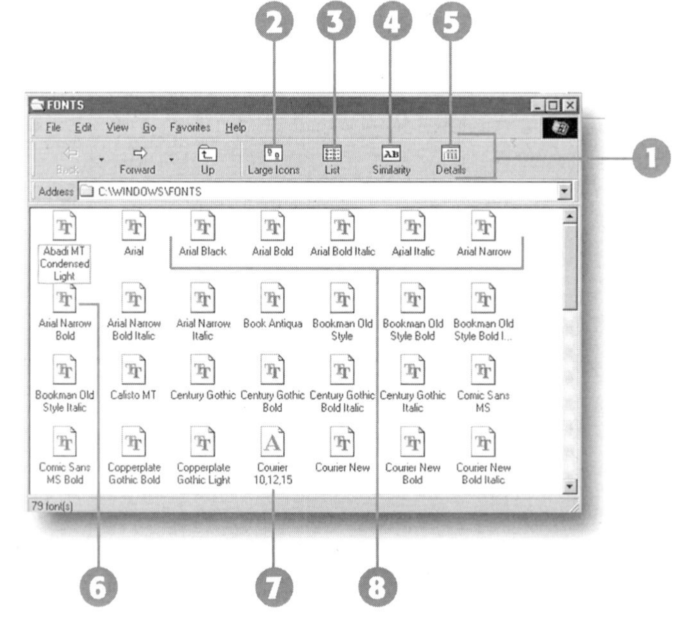

Figure 42.1
The Fonts folder.

1. Special views.
2. Large icons.
3. List view.
4. Group fonts by their similarity.
5. Show all font file details.
6. A TrueType (resizable) font.
7. A system (fixed size) font.
8. Notice how different fonts have different weights and styles (choose View ➡Hide Variations to eliminate the Black, Bold, and other descriptions).

You'll discover that the Fonts folder is your beehive of activity for anything to do with Windows fonts. The following sections go over the many things that take place there.

Keep the Fonts folder open for the next section's tutorial.

- Only Windows fonts live in the Fonts folder. If you're using other fonts, such as PostScript fonts for use with the Adobe ATM software, they live in another folder. (Use the ATM program to manage those fonts.)

- *TrueType* fonts have the TT icon. You can resize these fonts from small to large without affecting the font's appearance onscreen or in printed documents. Most of your fonts are TrueType.
- *System* fonts are used internally by Windows, usually in dialog boxes or error messages. These fonts are also called *fixed* fonts because they're displayed only in specific sizes. You probably won't use these for your word processing.

Try using TrueType whenever you can. TrueType fonts look good at any size and on any printer.

A Font Sneak Peek

Windows lets you preview any font in the Fonts folder. To see the preview, just open a font file.

▶ **Open the Arial font.**

Locate the Arial font in the Fonts folder, and double-click its icon for a preview. You see something similar to Figure 42.2.

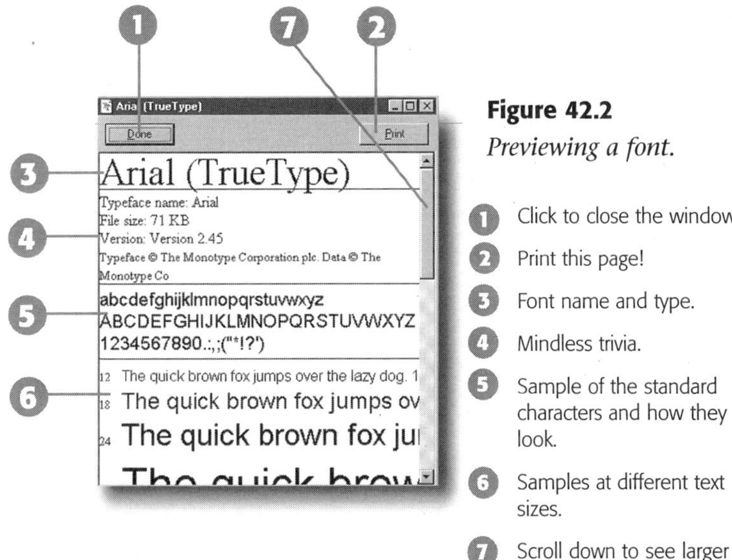

Figure 42.2
Previewing a font.

1. Click to close the window.
2. Print this page!
3. Font name and type.
4. Mindless trivia.
5. Sample of the standard characters and how they look.
6. Samples at different text sizes.
7. Scroll down to see larger text sizes.

Absorb the font.

When you're previewing a font, you should see which type of font it is. Different fonts have different uses based on their type:

- *Serif fonts*—These fonts have curlies and pointies on the ends of the letters. Choose a serif font for text that people read (the serifs make it easier to read the text). Good serif fonts are Times, Garamond, and Bookman. My favorite serif font is Souvenir.
- *Sans serif fonts*—These fonts are typically blocky and square. A sans serif font is best used for a headline. Good sans serif fonts are Arial, Helvetica, and Monogramma. My favorite sans serif font is Optima.
- *Decorative fonts*—You might see these fancy fonts in advertisements or as illustrations. They're used primarily as decorations or logos. Writing a report in this type of font would be tiresome and, well, strange. Examples of decorative fonts are Wingdings, Zapf Dingbats, and Bocklin. My favorite decorative font is Fajita.

Also, look for unique characters in the font. Three characters to look for are the lowercase *g* and the uppercase *W* and *Q*. Although two fonts might appear similar, if you look at their little *g* and big *W* and *Q*, you'll definitely find some differences.

▶ **Click the Done button to close the Arial font.**

Open other fonts and take a look at their previews.

Previewing All Your Fonts

One common question I get is, "How can I see all my fonts at once?" It's a logical request. Often you have to repeatedly use the Font command to change a font over and over to see which one you like the best. Wouldn't it be nice if Windows would let you print all your fonts in one fell swoop?

Alas, Windows offers no way to preview all your fonts at once. You can do some other things instead:

▶ **Open the Fonts window (if it's not open already).**

▶ **Open the first font listed in the window.**

On my PC, it's Adabi MT Condensed. (I suppose that if I add water, it would expand to full size—I'm making a joke.)

▶ **Click the Print button.**

A Print dialog box appears

▶ **Click OK.**

The font preview is printed.

- **Close the font preview window.**

Repeat these steps for every font in the Fonts folder.

Egads! I have more than 100 fonts!

Why pull yourself through that hell? Instead, try the second way:

- **Open WordPad.**
- **Type the following text:**

```
This is the Adabi MT Condensed Font
ABCDEFGHIJKLMNOPQRSTUVWXYZ
abcdefghijklmnopqrstuvwxyz
1234567890!@#$%^&*()
```

- **Select the text.**

Drag the mouse from the *T* to the final *)* to select all the text.

- **Choose Adabi MT Condensed from the Font drop-down list.**

The Font drop-down list is the first drop-down list on the Format bar. If you don't see the Formatting toolbar, choose View ➡Format Bar.

- **Choose 14 for the font size.**

Gotta make it easier to see:

- **Press Ctrl+C.**

Copy the text.

- **Click the cursor down to the next line.**
- **Press Ctrl+V.**

Paste in the same text.

- **Edit the line that contains the font name to reflect the new font's name.**

On my screen I changed *Adabi MT Condensed* to read *Albertus Medium.*

Repeat these steps for the fonts you plan to use.

Figure 42.3 shows my progress in WordPad with the fonts file.

You don't have to document *every* font. Just choose those you plan to use. Other fonts, you can delete (which is shown later in this chapter). Yes, this is still a long process, but you'll use the output forever.

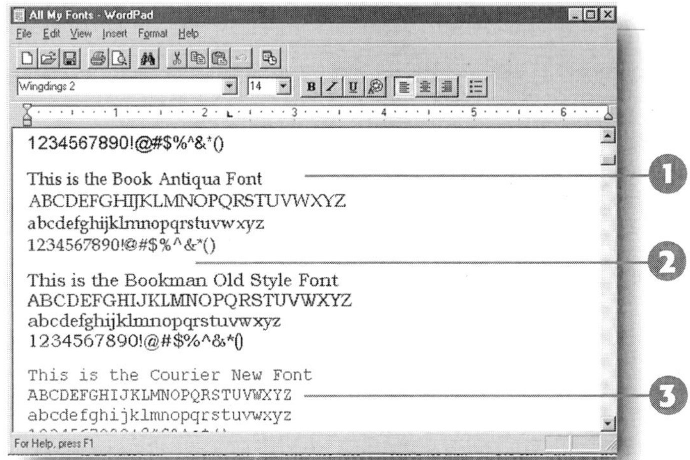

Figre 42.3
My personal fonts file.

1. Each font has its own bit of text pasted in.
2. A line between each font is nice.
3. I skipped some of the more unusual fonts, putting down only what I plan to use.

When you're done, save your document to disk.

- **Choose File ➡Save As.**
- **Type** All My Fonts **in the File Name box.**
- **Click Save.**

You have to update the file as you add or remove fonts, although that isn't as much of a hassle as creating the file in the first place.

Use the Print command when you're ready to print your font lists:

- **Choose File ➡Print.**
- **Click OK.**

Keep the hard copy in a folder near your computer as a handy reference.

- **Close WordPad.**

Keep the Fonts window open for the next section's tutorial.

- Yes, I'm sorry that this process seems like a pain in the butt; it's the best way, however, to get a listing of all your fonts.
- It's *not* a pain to create the file, as long as you're adept at copy-and-paste.
- Another way to preview fonts, although it's not personal, is to get a font book. For example, if you add fonts to your system from one of those "2 Billion Fonts on a CD" programs, keep the booklet handy so that you can see what the fonts look like. You can preview many popular Adobe offers on the Image Club Web page, at `http://www.imageclub.com/fonts/`.

Adding a New Font to Your Font Font

Microsoft made one trick really easy: To add a new font, you simply copy the font files to the Fonts folder. Suddenly, every Windows program knows about the new font. It's that easy.

▶ **Have your font disk or CD ready.**

In my hot little hands, I have a font CD containing the font ITC Benguiat. I just ordered it from Image Club (800-661-9410; `http://www.imageclub.com`).

▶ **Open the Fonts window (if it's not open already).**

▶ **Stick your font disk into drive A, or the font CD into the CD-ROM drive.**

▶ **Choose File ➡Install New Font.**

The Add Fonts dialog box appears, as shown in Figure 42.4.

▶ **Choose the fonts disk's disk drive from the Drives list.**

I chose drive A. Choose your CD-ROM drive if the font CD is in there.

▶ **Open the font's folder (if necessary).**

No folder was available to open on drive A (refer to Figure 42.4). On a CD, however, you might have to open a Fonts folder.

It takes Windows awhile to read in the font names and such. Be patient.

When the font names appear in the List of Fonts window, you have to pick and choose which ones you want:

▶ **Select the fonts you want to install.**

Click a font name to install only that font.

Don't bother with the Network button. It brings up one of those "you have to know the network pathname first" type of dialog boxes—a waste of time.

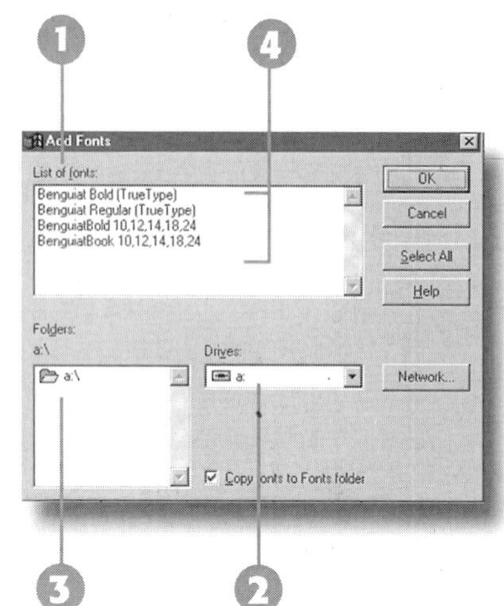

Figure 42.4
The Add Fonts dialog box.

1. List of fonts on the disk you've chosen.
2. Pick the disk drive from here.
3. Pick the folder from here.
4. Click or Ctrl+click to select fonts to install.

Ctrl+click to select more than one font. Or click the Select All button to install all the fonts.

▶ **Click OK.**

Chugga-chugga. The fonts are copied to the Fonts folder, where they live safely on your hard drive. You have no need to reset; the fonts are ready to use.

Keep the Fonts window open for the next section's tutorial.

If several fonts are in a group, such as the variations on Benguiat shown in Figure 42.4, choose them all. You don't have to choose every font on the disk, although choosing all fonts of one type is okay.

- You have to quit some Windows programs and then reopen them so that they can "see" the new fonts.
- Even though you can copy the font files manually by dragging or copying a font icon from one folder to the Fonts folder, it's best to use the Install New Font command.
- Fonts are cheap and freely available all over. You can find them on the Internet, at a software store, or they might even come with programs and applications you install.

If you get one of those "Two Billion Fonts on a CD" disks, don't install all the fonts! Just pick and choose the ones you need *as you need them.* Avoid font bloat.

Killing Off an Underused Font

Fonts are cheap, and just about every application seems to come with its own clutch of font files, all automatically installed for you. Eventually your programs' Font menu is longer than the Empire State Building. Welcome to font glut.

You have two choices: Just delete the font you don't plan to use or drag it to another folder for storage. I show you the kill option first:

- **Open the Fonts folder (if it's not open already).**
- **Select the icons for fonts you want to kill off.**
- **Choose File ➡Delete.**

A warning box appears, asking whether you're sure that you want to delete the fonts.

- **Click Yes.**

The fonts are rubbed out.

If you see a warning dialog box telling you that the font you're deleting is being used, choose another font. Obviously you want to delete fonts you *don't* use.

"But you say never to delete anything I didn't create myself."

Yes, I said never to delete any file you personally didn't create. Fonts are a rare exception. If you have font bloat, you *need* to delete fonts you don't use. Or, if it sits better with you, use the second option, described next.

Notice that the Undo command does not rescue your font. Go ahead and check: The Undo command is dimmed. You can still get your font back from the Recycle Bin. You must restore it manually. See Chapter 28, "Deleting, Undeleting, and Recycling," for more information.

Your second option, as opposed to deleting fonts, is to move the unwanted ones elsewhere for storage:

- **Open the My Documents icon on the desktop.**
- **Choose File ➡New ➡Folder.**
- **Rename the folder as** Font Storage**.**

Press Enter to lock in the new name.

- **Open the Font Storage folder.**

Now you can drag font icons from the Fonts folder over to your Font Storage folder. This *must* be a drag operation; you cannot use the Cut command in the Fonts window. Drag the font icon from the Fonts window into the Font Storage window. (See Chapter 12 for information about arranging windows on the desktop.)

Storing your spare fonts in another folder means that the fonts are still available (you can even open them for a preview), although they don't appear in any Windows program's Font menu.

- **Close the Font Storage window.**
- **Close the Fonts window.**

To reinstall the font icon, just drag it from the Font Storage window back to the Fonts window. Or you can use the Add Fonts dialog box. The result is the same.

- If the font icon came from a CD, I delete it from my system as opposed to storing it elsewhere on my hard drive. After all, it's already stored on the CD.
- Having too many fonts can slow down your system. If you've noticed that the Font menu takes awhile to appear, you probably have font glut working against you. Delete them fonts!

Snipping Out Characters with the Character Map Program

Opening a Font icon lets you preview the font, although it doesn't let you use any of the amazing characters you can find there. For example:

- **Open the Fonts folder.**
- **Open the Wingdings icon.**

The preview window shows you many of the delightful characters in this decorative font. Nifty.

See the happy face? Would he be cool to insert into a memo telling your kids to clean their rooms? Alas, you cannot select the character in the window, and, even if you could, no Copy command is available. Drat!

- **Click the Done button to close the font preview window.**
- **Close the Fonts window.**

To your rescue comes the Character Map program. It lets you not only preview all the characters in a font but also copy and paste them.

- **From the Start Thing menu, choose Programs ➡Accessories ➡System Tools ➡Character Map.**

The Character Map program appears, looking similar to Figure 42.5.

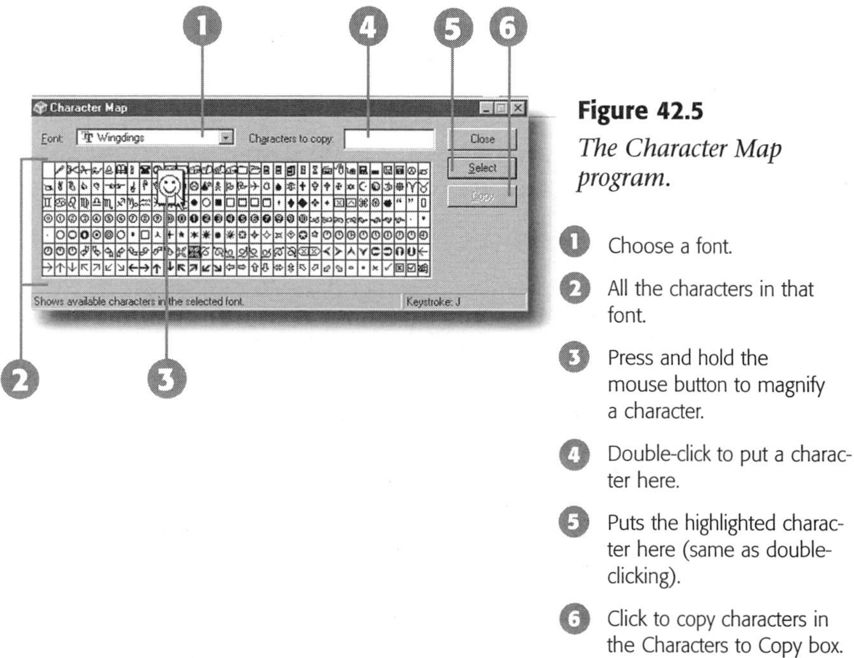

Figure 42.5
The Character Map program.

1. Choose a font.
2. All the characters in that font.
3. Press and hold the mouse button to magnify a character.
4. Double-click to put a character here.
5. Puts the highlighted character here (same as double-clicking).
6. Click to copy characters in the Characters to Copy box.

- **Choose Wingdings from the Font drop-down list.**

All the characters in the Wingdings font appear on the Character Map grid.

- **Point the mouse at a character, and then press and hold the mouse button.**

The character you're pointing at is magnified so that you can better see it. In Figure 42.5, I'm highlighting the smiley-face guy.

- **Double-click the smiley-face guy.**

Refer to Figure 42.5 to narrow down his location.

After you double-click, the character appears in the Characters to Copy text box. You can double-click additional characters to insert into the text box. (In fact, you could use the Character Map program rather than the keyboard to type—but that method would be ridiculous.)

▶ **Click Copy.**

The smiley character is copied to the Windows Clipboard.

▶ **Click Close.**

The Character Map program goes away.

▶ **Start WordPad.**

Before you type, some formatting:

▶ **Click the Center tool.**

▶ **Choose a font size of 48.**

Gotta make it big.

▶ **Choose Arial from the Font drop-down list.**

Sans serif fonts seem more urgent.

▶ **Type** Please Remember to Make Your Bed!

▶ **Press Enter to start a new line of text.**

▶ **Press Ctrl+V to paste the smiley face.**

If the smiley face shows up too small, select him and choose **48** from the Font Size drop-down list. (Be careful when you're selecting the happy face; select only that character.)

The result of your labor should look something like Figure 42.6.

Save your masterpiece. Print it. Use it! Maybe someone will listen.

▶ **Close WordPad.**

Remember that *three* faces are in the Wingdings font file: happy, nonplused, and sad. Pick a face to match your mood!

- If the Character Map program isn't installed on your computer, see Chapter 15 for information about adding it.

Figure 42.6
The resulting file in WordPad.

1. Arial font; 48-point text size.
2. Wingding font; 48-point text size.
3. Character pasted in from Character Map program.

In Microsoft Word you can choose Insert ➡Symbol from the Word menu to see a dialog box similar to the Character Map window. You can use that dialog box to insert special characters directly into your document.

Chapter 43

Messing mit der Mouse

Questions Answered and Thoughts Inspired

- Using an animated mouse pointer
- Converting the mouse to left-handed use

No one does much toying with their mouse in Windows, although I had to write a chapter about it, if anything, to show you all the amazing animated mouse pointers you can play with. Oh, and other things in the Mouse Properties dialog box are worthy of note. I touch on them here and there in this wee chapter.

The Mouse Properties dialog box isn't covered in serious depth in this chapter. That's because most of the stuff in there is fun stuff you can play with on your own. While you're in the dialog box, play around! Some nifty and often useful mouse features are available.

- If one is a mouse and two are mice, why can't one be a house and two be hice?

Animate Your Mouse Pointer

See the mouse? See the mouse pointer? Dumb mouse pointer. Dumb. Dumb. Dumb. The mouse pointer moves on the screen. Up and down. Back and forth. The pointer is dumb. Dumb. Dumb. Dumb.

- **Open the Control Panel.**
- **Open the Mouse icon.**

The Mouse Properties dialog box appears.

Things get weird here. If you're using the new Microsoft IntelliMouse (the "wheel" mouse), you see a different Mouse Properties dialog box than folks without the IntelliMouse. In fact, different mouse manufacturers have different Mouse Properties dialog boxes. Finding the similar areas in each, therefore, might require some effort on your behalf. Bear with me.

- **Click the Pointers tab to bring that panel forward.**

The Pointers panel is shown in Figure 43.1. (The panel should look the same regardless of which mouse you have.)

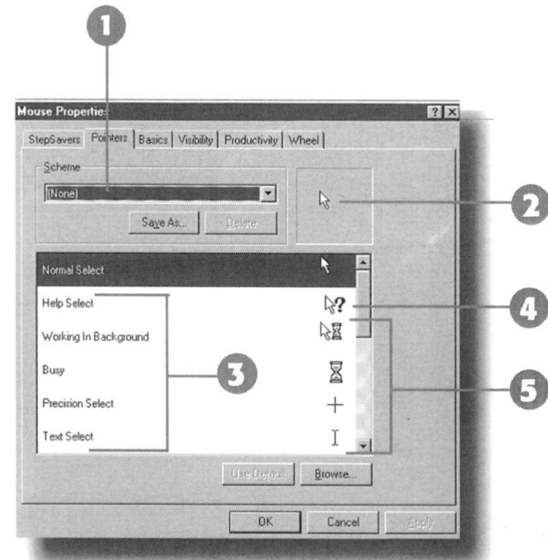

Figure 43.1

Change your mouse pointer here.

1. Choose a pointer scheme from here.
2. Pointer preview.
3. Various mouse or Windows conditions to which the pointer reacts.
4. The selected pointer for that condition.
5. Double-click to change the pointer.

Suppose that you want to find something more interesting for the Busy pointer—something amusing to watch while the computer toidles:

▶ **Double-click the Busy cursor icon.**

A special Browse dialog box appears, one with a cursor preview window in the bottom-left corner, as shown in Figure 43.2.

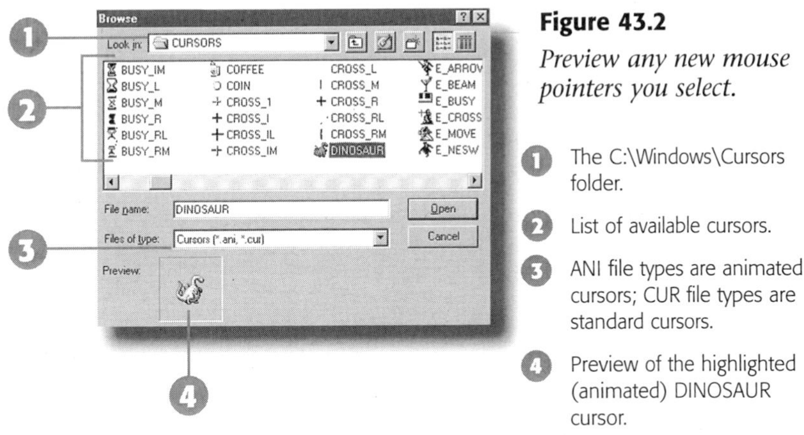

Figure 43.2
Preview any new mouse pointers you select.

1. The C:\Windows\Cursors folder.
2. List of available cursors.
3. ANI file types are animated cursors; CUR file types are standard cursors.
4. Preview of the highlighted (animated) DINOSAUR cursor.

▶ **Browse to the C:\WINDOWS\CURSORS folder.**

Use the Look In drop-down list to go to drive C, the \Windows folder, the Cursors folder—if you're not taken there automatically.

To choose a new cursor, find a cursor file in the window and click it once to highlight it.

▶ **Click the DINOSAUR cursor file once to select it.**

You might have to scroll the window left to find the DINOSAUR file. When you do, select it to see a preview of the animated dinosaur trumbling along. What a prefect replacement for the "busy" cursor.

If you don't have the DINOSAUR, choose something else.

▶ **Click Open.**

The Browse dialog box closes, and you see the Dinosaur cursor replace the hourglass on the scrolling list. Also, a preview of the cursor appears in the upper-right corner of the dialog box.

Continue choosing and replacing cursors, or, if you want to do things all at once, you can use a cursor Scheme:

▶ **Choose Food from the Schemes drop-down list.**

Corny, huh? Check out the "busy" apple.

When you're done playing in the Mouse Properties dialog box, click OK to lock in your settings and use the new cursors. Otherwise, click Cancel, and Windows restores everything to the way it was.

You can close the Control Panel now or leave it open for the next section's tutorial.

- If you pick and choose your cursors, you can save them as a scheme. Use the Save As button. Also see Chapter 41 for information about saving a Sound Scheme—it works similarly.
- Third-party programs are available to help you create your own cursors. Visit `http://www.shareware.com` on the Internet, and search for Windows programs by using the keyword `cursor`.
- The Windows Resource Kit contains a program called ANIEDIT, which you can use to create your own animated cursors.

Are You a Southpaw?

Maybe you're left-handed. Gauche, say the French. Don't fret. My mother, brother, and two of my sons are lefties. Mom uses the mouse like a right-hander, though (she's so talented), so she never takes advantage of the southpaw mouse features in Windows.

If you're left-handed and would prefer to work the mouse left-handed, Windows can accommodate you. Or maybe you're right-handed, like my friend Wally Wang, and use the mouse left-handed. (Don't ask.) Whatever, prepare to reverse your polarity:

- **Open the Control Panel.**
- **Open the Mouse icon.**
- **Click the Basics tab.**

If you don't have the Basics tab, click the Buttons tab instead.

The Basics/Buttons panel contains items to help a left-handed person work the mouse without having to rewire her brain. Basically, it lets you choose which mouse button is the main button: the left or the right.

This book assumes that the "main" mouse button is the left one, which a right-handed person would use.

A left-handed person might be better off using the *right* mouse button as the main button, which is the button under your index finger when you hold the mouse in your left hand.

Follow these steps only if you want to change your mouse!

- **To create a left-handed mouse, click the Right button on the Basics panel.**

Or, if you have the original mouse (not a wheel mouse):

- **Click the Left-Handed button to select the left-handed mouse.**

Your mouse buttons have been reversed. You click with the right mouse button, and what's called a right-click in this book (and elsewhere) is now a left-click.

- **Click OK to close the Mouse Properties dialog box.**

Click with the right button if you just switched them.

- **Close the Control Panel.**

Using the mouse should seem more natural to you now. The only caveat I can offer is that books, manuals, and Web pages use the term *right-click*, which is now a left-click for a left-handed mouse. Watch out for that.

Chapter 44

Scheduling Activities

Questions Answered and Thoughts Inspired

- Finding the Scheduled Tasks folder
- Adding a task
- Running a task
- Changing a task's scheduled time
- Removing tasks

Like a real operating system, Windows has the capability to let you schedule certain activities to take place at certain times. The technical term is to *automate tasks*. It's only logical that computers should do that: They keep track of the time and, therefore, should be able to start certain activities at certain times.

It's the job of the Task Scheduler in Windows to start or run certain programs at specified times or intervals. This chapter tells you how to use the Task Scheduler to automate compudrudgery.

- The Task Scheduler is a descendant of the old System Agent program in the Windows 95 Plus! package.
- Whenever you hear someone talk about a "real" operating system, he usually means UNIX. It's an arrogant thing to say, so if you want to feel superior, say, "UNIX is the only *real* computer operating system."
- If you want to appear better than superior—nay, *holy*—remark that BeOS ("BEE-os") is also a real operating system. Because few people are familiar with Be, they'll have to agree with you and marvel at your advanced knowledge of the subject.

Hello, Scheduled Tasks Folder!

Windows keeps all the tasks it has scheduled in the Scheduled Tasks folder, yet another one of those special folders lurking throughout Windows:

- **Open the My Computer icon on the desktop.**
- **Open the Scheduled Tasks folder.**

The Scheduled Tasks folder window appears, as shown in Figure 44.1.

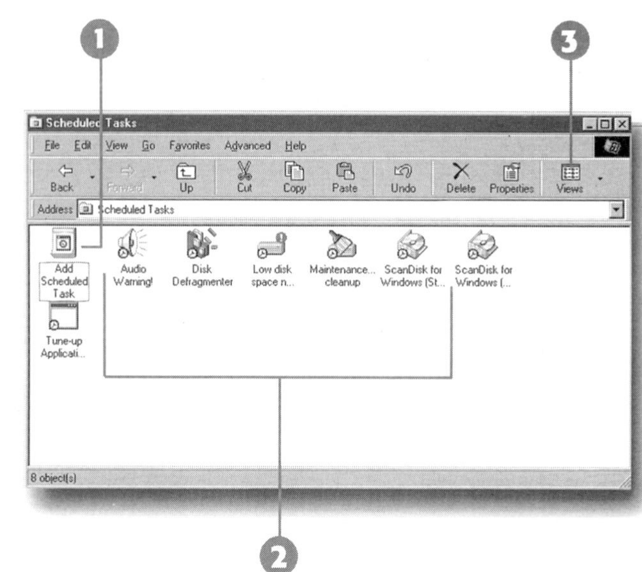

Figure 44.1
The Scheduled Tasks folder.

1. Open this to add a new task to the list.
2. Icons represent *tasks* to take place at a specific time, not the programs that run.
3. Change the view.

- **Click the Views icon until the window looks like Figure 44.2.**

Details view displays more information about the icons in the Scheduled Tasks window.

In Figure 44.2, you see a list of tasks and their scheduled times, plus the times they last ran. They're all programs that Windows starts automatically, listed with the time they'll run next and when they ran last.

Keep the Scheduled Tasks window open for the next section's tutorial.

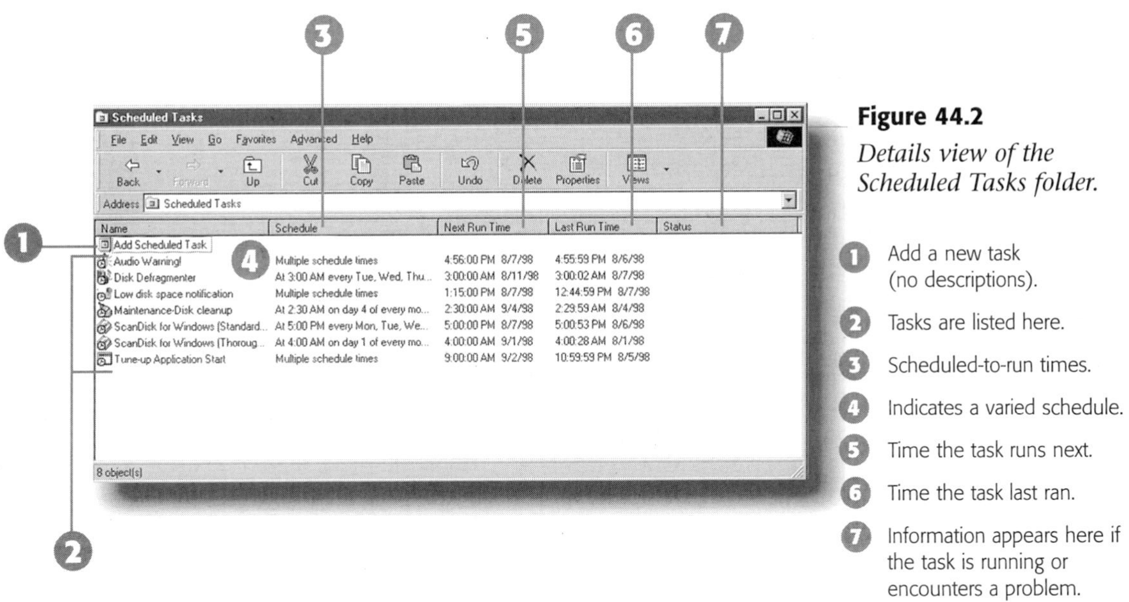

Figure 44.2
Details view of the Scheduled Tasks folder.

1. Add a new task (no descriptions).
2. Tasks are listed here.
3. Scheduled-to-run times.
4. Indicates a varied schedule.
5. Time the task runs next.
6. Time the task last ran.
7. Information appears here if the task is running or encounters a problem.

Making Up Your Own Task

The tasks listed in the Scheduled Tasks window represent programs elsewhere on your hard drive. The icons you see are merely the "tasks," or information Windows uses to automatically start the programs.

Notice that most of the programs in the window are disk utilities: Defragmenter and ScanDisk, for example. You can have any program start automatically, though. All you do is run the Add Scheduled Task program. The Scheduled Task Wizard sets everything up for you.

First create a sample task. How about a nice audio warning? You can use the sound file you created in Chapter 41 and have it play every day at noon on your computer. (Or you can record another sound file—for example, "Time to quit!"—and play it at 5 o'clock.)

▶ **Open the Add Scheduled Task icon.**

The Scheduled Task Wizard starts. Yadda-yadda.

▶ **Click Next.**

The next screen in the wizard lists all the programs available on your computer, allowing you to schedule any of them. Figure 44.3 shows how it works.

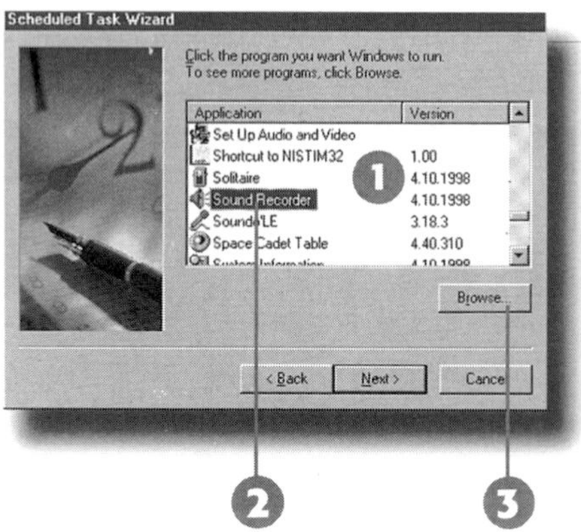

Figure 44.3
Choosing a program to schedule.

1. Applications listed alphabetically.
2. Sound Recorder (refer to Chapter 41).
3. Click here to find a program if it's not listed.

Choose a program to run, not a document. For example, this tutorial sets things up to run the ME file created by the Sound Recorder. The Task Scheduler does not "run" the ME file, even though you can run it by opening it on the desktop. No, you have to run Sound Recorder and tell it to run that file.

▶ **Choose the Sound Recorder.**

You have to scroll down the list to find this program.

▶ **Click Next.**

The next panel in the wizard allows you to name the task and assign the interval at which you want it to run.

▶ **Type** Audio Alert! **in the text box.**

▶ **Choose Daily.**

You want the task to run once a day.

▶ **Click Next.**

The next screen allows you to pick the exact time at which you want the program to run, as described in Figure 44.4.

Although the Task Scheduler can run a program more than once a day, you have to make that modification after creating the task in the wizard. Alas, there's no easy way to say "Run this program every hour." There should be, but there isn't.

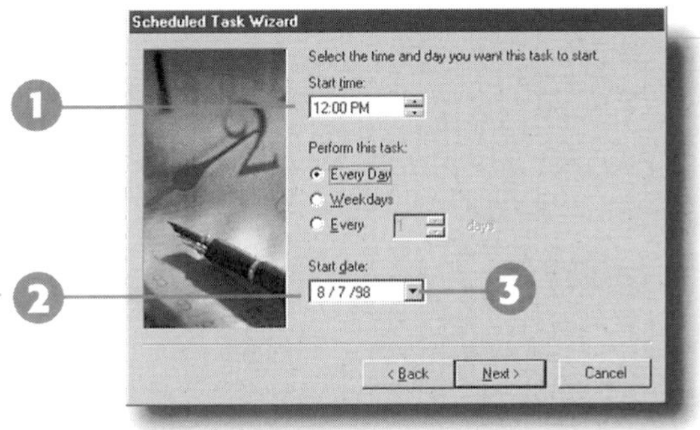

Figure 44.4

Picking a start time and date.

1. Double-click to select hours or minutes, and then type a new value.
2. Today's date, to start the program right now.
3. Displays a nifty calendar.

▶ **Enter** 12:00 PM **in the Start Time box.**

▶ **Click Next.**

The final page of the wizard displays a summary of what you've done. Whatever.

▶ **Click Finish.**

The Wizard dialog box vanishes, and you're back at the Scheduled Tasks window. In a few moments, you see your task appear on the list. (Notice that the Last Run Time is Never.)

You could wait around for the task to run later in the day (or tomorrow) at noon. Instead, you can cheat and rush things, just to see how it works. This topic is covered in the following section.

- See Chapter 21, "Caring for Your Hard Drive," for more information about disk utilities.
- You can automate many programs without using the Scheduled Tasks window. For example, your backup program might have a scheduling tool that sets automatic backups for midnight once a week. You can schedule Active Desktop programs to automatically connect to the Internet to download information (refer to Chapter 32, "Activating the Desktop").

Test-Running a Task

Rather than wait around to see whether a task runs, you can direct the Task Scheduler to run a task Right Now. This feature is great for testing out new tasks you're trying to assign.

▶ **Open the Scheduled Tasks window (if it's not open already).**

Refer to the section, "Hello, Scheduled Tasks Window!" at the beginning of this chapter for more information about opening the window.

▶ **Right-click the icon of the task you want to test-run.**

If you're continuing this chapter's tutorial, right-click the Audio Alert! icon.

▶ **Choose Run from the pop-up menu.**

The task runs as it normally would when scheduled.

"Uh, no, it didn't! I didn't hear anything!"

For testing some types of programs, these steps work just fine. Because your program runs, you can trust that it will run on schedule from now on. Okay. The Sound Recorder—and possibly other programs—require additional tweaking, though. In the case of the Sound Recorder, you must tell it to "play" a specific sound file on disk. Some modifications are in order:

▶ **Close the Sound Recorder.**

▶ **Open the Audio Alert! task.**

Double-click its icon to display the task's dialog box, as shown in Figure 44.5.

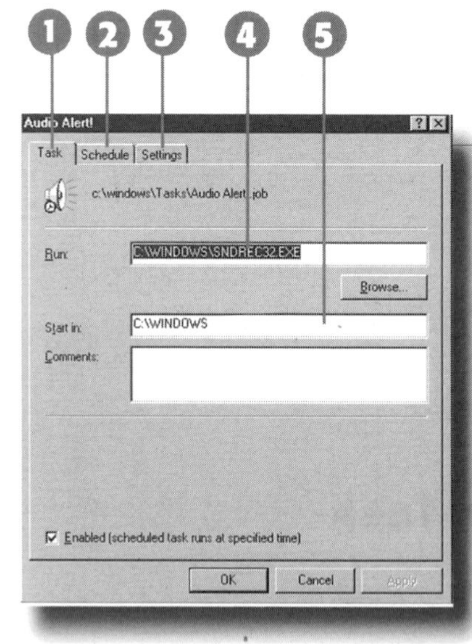

Figure 44.5
The task's dialog box.

1. General information about the task.
2. View or modify the task's schedule.
3. Advanced settings and options.
4. The command line.
5. The folder in which the program runs.

To tell the Sound Recorder to play a sound, you have to do two things: Specify the `/play` option after SNDREC32.EXE, and specify the name of the sound to play:

▶ **Click the mouse in the Run Text box.**

▶ **Press the End key.**

This step moves the cursor to the end of the command line, right after the EXE part.

▶ **Type** /play c:\my documents\me.wav.

Type a space, **/play**, another space, and then the pathname of the sound file you want to play.

If you saved the ME sound file in the My Documents folder, type the command as just shown. You must add a period and `WAV` so that Sound Recorder can find the file.

Or, if you saved the ME sound file in the AUDIO folder, type **c:\my documents\audio\me.wav** instead.

The full command in the Run text box should look like this:

```
C:\WINDOWS\SNDREC32.EXE /PLAY C:\MY DOCUMENTS\ME.WAV
```

▶ **Click OK.**

Time to test it again:

▶ **Right-click the Audio Alert! icon.**

▶ **Choose Run from the pop-up menu.**

"I love Windows. Ha-ha-ha-ha-ha!"

Be prepared to hear that every day at noon from now on!

▶ **Close the Sound Recorder program.**

You must close the Sound Recorder manually every time it runs. Other programs, such as the disk utilities, close automatically (or display a summary screen) when they're done.

You can close the Scheduled Tasks window now or leave it open for the next section's tutorial.

- You must follow the Sound Recorder program's name (SNDREC32.EXE) with the `/play` option and then the pathname of the sound file you want it to play. (Refer to Chapter 23 for more information about pathnames.) This is actually a DOS command.
- Don't specify documents in the Scheduled Tasks window; run programs instead. If you want to run a document, you have to type the document's name after the program's name in the Run text box, as shown in this section.

- If you try to run a document file and it doesn't work, you're told so in the Scheduled Tasks window. In Details view (refer to Figure 44.2), the final Status column displays the text `Could Not Start` if a program or document cannot be run.

Modifying a Task's Time

The Scheduled Task Wizard can set things up for you, although it often doesn't let you set as many options as you want. For example, you might want to play your audio warning every hour. Or maybe on the first of the month you want to run the Disk Cleanup program in addition to running it on Sundays at 4:00 a.m. These modifications are easy to make:

▶ **Open the Scheduled Tasks window (if it's not open already).**

▶ **Right-click the task you want to reschedule.**

For this tutorial, use the Audio Alert! task created earlier in this chapter.

▶ **Choose Properties from the shortcut menu.**

The task's Properties dialog box appears.

▶ **Click the Schedule tab.**

The Schedule panel appears, as shown in Figure 44.6.

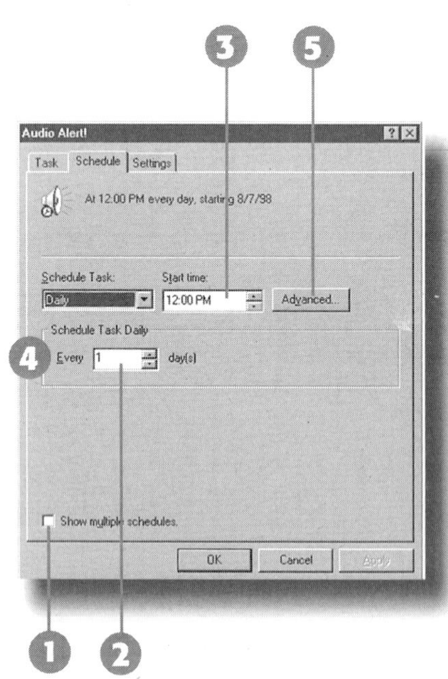

Figure 44.6
The task's schedule.

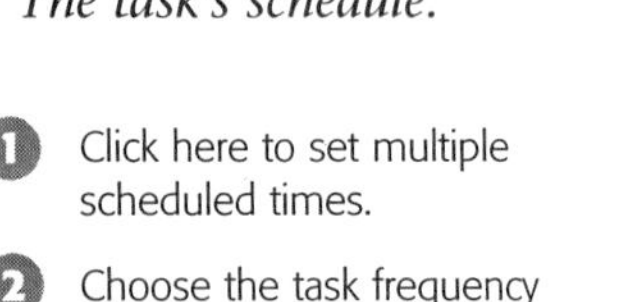

1. Click here to set multiple scheduled times.
2. Choose the task frequency here.
3. Time of day.
4. This area changes depending on the task frequency.
5. Specify even more times to run.

Suppose that you want to run the task every hour on the hour:

- **Click Advanced.**

The Advanced Schedule Options dialog box appears.

- **Click Repeat Task to put a check mark there.**
- **Enter** 1 **in the Every box.**
- **Choose Hours from the drop-down list.**
- **Click Duration.**
- **Enter** 24 **in the Hour(s) box.**

Egads!

- **Click OK.**

Read the top of the Schedule panel. It should say something like this:

```
Every 1 hour(s) from 12:00 PM for 24 hour(s) every day, starting [today's date]
```

Finally, you have your hourly clock.

If you click OK, the task begins running, playing your sound every hour on the hour. This is a tutorial, however, and you don't get off that easy:

- **Click Advanced.**
- **Click Repeat Task to remove the check mark.**
- **Click OK.**

To have the task run at only preset times during the day, you must specify multiple schedules. This technique works the same for any preset times during the day, week, or month.

- **Click Show Multiple Schedules to put a check mark in that box.**

A new drop-down list appears at the top of the Schedule panel. It shows the current schedule (which should revert to `At 12:00 PM` every day, starting whenever).

To have the task also run at 4:59 p.m. every day, do the following:

- **Click New.**

Notice the new text in the drop-down list at the top of the dialog box. Ignore it for now.

- **Choose Daily from the Schedule Task drop-down list.**

If you have time, choose other options from that list to see how they affect the appearance of the Schedule panel: Weekly, Monthly, When Idle—each has its own settings. Return to the Daily item when you're done looking.

▶ **Enter** 4:59 PM **into the Start Time box.**

▶ **Ensure that 1 is chosen in the Every Day(s) box.**

Notice how the text in the drop-down list changes to reflect the new time? You're all set.

▶ **Click OK.**

The Schedule column in the Scheduled Tasks window (Details view) now shows that the Audio Alert! task runs at multiple scheduled times.

Now you can sit and wait for noon or 4:59 p.m. to fly by, at which time your computer reminds you of just how much you love Windows.

You can close the Scheduled Tasks window now or leave it open for this chapter's final section.

- If you choose Weekly on the Schedule panel, the dialog box changes to show days of the week.
- Choosing Monthly on the Schedule panel lets you pick a specific day of the month or any day of the week for any week in the month. You can even select in which months you want the task to run.
- Tasks can even be scheduled to run when the computer has been idle for a specified number of minutes. *Idle* is defined as no keyboard or mouse action by the person using the computer. You could have the computer pop up with an audio alert that says "Are you still alive?" after any 20 minutes of inactivity.

You can schedule any task by using the preceding steps, not just the Sound Recorder as shown in the tutorial.

Killing Off Tasks

If you want a task to run only once, you can set it up that way. Or, if you want a task to run once a year, you can set it up that way. If you sicken of a task, you can just zap it off the Scheduled Tasks window.

Removing a task does not delete the program.

- **Open the Scheduled Tasks window (if it's not open already).**
- **Select the task or tasks you want to delete.**

Click a task to select it. Use Ctrl+click to select multiple tasks.

For this tutorial, select the Audio Alert! task.

- **Click the Delete button on the toolbar.**

If the Are You Sure warning dialog box appears, choose Yes to delete the task icon.

Zap! The task is gone.

Actually, the task is merely sitting in the Recycle Bin, waiting to be restored, if necessary.

- **Close the Scheduled Tasks window.**

Your task lesson is over.

You can run any program on your computer at any time by opening its icon or choosing it from the Start Thing menu. Remove the program from the Scheduled Tasks window does not delete that program.

Chapter 45

Beefing Up Your PC with New Hardware

Questions Answered and Thoughts Inspired

- Adding hardware to your computer
- Installing an expansion card
- Configuring Windows to "see" your hardware
- Running the Add New Hardware Wizard

Adding a new toy to your PC is fun. Well, having the toy is fun, but installing it can be a pain. Microsoft has tried its best to make hardware installation easy for you. In the old days, you had to run complex setup programs and modify your CONFIG.SYS or AUTOEXEC.BAT files. There were chants and animal sacrifices. It was messy.

Windows now greets new hardware toys with a wink and a smile. Almost everything is done automatically. This chapter provides you with a gentle overview of the process.

How to Add Hardware to Your PC

Installing most goodies on your PC involves two parts: the hardware part and the software part.

The hardware part is the physical installation, either attaching some goodie to your PC's rump or opening up the PC's case and installing some gizmo. Generally this stuff isn't tough; it just requires some patience and money to pay someone else to do it for you.

The software part used to drive people nuts, which is where Windows 98 has become a blessing. When Windows sees the new hardware, it instantly recognizes it and sets everything up for you. It blows you away the first time it happens.

Beyond the software part might be installation of a program to run a hardware goody. For example, although installing a scanner is cinchy, you need an application to run the scanner and display the images onscreen.

- As long as you buy hardware that is *Plug and Play* or "Designed for Windows 98 (or Windows 95)," the software experience isn't that difficult.
- Installing hardware isn't truly difficult. Anyone with a screwdriver can manage it. Good illustrations help. Oh, and unplugging the computer before you open the case is a big bonus.

Outside the Box

Any hardware installed outside the computer box is referred to as a *peripheral*. The printer, joystick, external modem—they're all peripherals. Oddly, though, the keyboard, mouse, and monitor aren't true peripherals because they're considered essential to the computer's operation.

Installing a USB Peripheral

USB stands for Universal Serial Bus. The devices that plug into a USB port are perhaps the most exciting things to install in a PC. Windows 98 is geared specifically to crave USB stuff. You'll know why whenever you plug a USB something-or-other into your PC. It's magical.

First you have to be sure that your PC has USB support. The easiest way to tell is to look on the back of your PC for a USB socket. It's about the same size as a breath mint (but don't plug a breath mint into the hole), and it has the USB symbol alongside, as shown in the margin.

Second, you need a USB device. They tell us that all printers, keyboards, modems, mice, and other standard devices eventually will plug into the USB port. As I sit here typing this paragraph, only certain types of speakers, a few keyboards, and a videocamera plug into the USB port.

Finally, you install the USB device. You don't even have to turn off your PC. Just plug the sucker in. Windows recognizes it instantly and installs software, and you're done.

"Is that it?"

Okay, you're not *really* done. Although you've completed the hardware installation, you still have to install software for the USB device. For example, although I installed a little videocamera as just described, I still had to install the video software so that I could play with the camera. (That's the second, software side of installation, covered later in this chapter.)

If you have a USB port and have the option of buying a USB version of some device, buy the USB version. It's just easier to set up.

- Newer computers will sooner or later come with a USB port as standard equipment. If your PC lacks a USB port, you can always buy one on an expansion card.

Installing Other Types of Peripherals

Beyond the USB port, you can install peripherals on your PC's serial port, printer port, or SCSI port (if your PC has one). Windows might or (most likely) might not recognize the devices. You have to follow whatever instructions came with the device in order to continue the installation so that Windows recognizes whatever it was you plugged in.

Inside the Box

Scarier than installing something outside the box, installing something inside the computer console requires a great deal of patience and often some dexterity. If installing anything *inside* your computer worries you, have someone else do it. I'm serious! Even though the PC is designed so that anyone can install an option or more memory, it's really cheap to have your dealer or a "consultant" do it for you.

This section outlines each hardware-upgrading procedure. This information isn't overly detailed. In most cases whatever piece of hardware you're buying comes with detailed instructions, sometimes with nice illustrations right next to the original Chinese instructions.

Always unplug your PC before you open its case. It's not just a matter of turning the thing off. You must also unplug it. That avoids any unintentional power inside the case, which could be deadly to either you or your computer's innards.

Installing Memory

Upgrading your PC with more memory is beneficial, and sometimes it's a cinch. After plugging in the memory-expansion cards (little suckers called *SIMMs* or *DIMMs*), you just turn the computer back on. It should instantly recognize the memory and start using it right away.

- After you install memory, your computer might urge you to run its setup program. A message appears—well before the Welcome to Windows screen—asking whether you want to run the setup program. Do so. Tell the computer about the extra memory in whatever manner the setup program has you do it. Then save the setup program's information and restart the computer. (The exact steps vary from system to system.)
- One problem you might have with installing memory is if you're out of memory slots inside the computer. For example, your PC might have four memory slots each with 8 megabytes (MB) of RAM, for a total of 32MB. To upgrade to 64MB, you have to remove *all* the memory in your system and buy one 64MB RAM expansion card. I know that it sounds absurd, but it's the cheapest way to go.

Although I realize that it's too late to give you this tip, the best way to buy a computer is to have *all* its memory put in one expansion slot. You must ask for this setup specifically, which avoids the problem presented in the preceding bullet point. (Just keep it in mind for your next PC purchase.)

- Most of the larger computer magazines have ads in back from companies that sell computer memory. Most of the memory is sold in "kits," depending on which computer you own and how much memory you want to add. You can also shop for memory online; use Yahoo! to search for online computer stores.

Installing Another Hard Disk Drive

All PCs can instantly have more storage by adding a second hard drive. It's physically easy to install but difficult to set up, software-wise.

Most hard drive kits you can buy come with detailed and often fun instructions for how to set them up. Physically, installing a hard drive is almost as easy as assembling a Lego toy.

The following steps are generic. They might have subtle variations, depending on your PC and the hard drive you're installing:

- **Turn off your PC.**
- **Unplug your PC.**
- **Open your PC's case.**

Each PC case opens differently. See the manual that came with your computer (the one you never read) for details.

- **Locate a drive bay for the hard drive.**

The hard drive is installed in a disk drive *bay* inside the computer. Several of these bays should be available near the front of the computer box.

- **Slide the hard drive into the bay.**

Most hard drives slide in from the back (inside the case). Some hard drives have to be slid in from the front of the case.

- **Screw the hard drive into the mounting brackets.**

Four screws, two on each side, anchor the hard drive to the case.

- **Connect the hard drive to the power cable.**

The power cable has three or four colored wires, all of which connect to your PC's power supply. Connect the cable to the hard drive's rump. (You have only one way to plug it in.)

- **Connect the hard drive to the data cable.**

The data cable should already be attached to your PC's first hard drive. Between the first hard drive and your PC's motherboard is another connector stuck on the cable. Plug the new hard drive into that connector.

- **Close up your PC.**

The hardware setup is complete.

For the software side, Windows requires that the disk be configured and formatted before you use it. That does not happen automatically. The hard drive should come with instructions for how to use the FDISK and FORMAT programs to configure and format the hard drive. If not, any competent computer dealer or consultant can set things up for you.

- Two types of hard drives are popular in PCs: IDE and SCSI. Ensure that you buy the proper type for your computer. If your system already has an IDE hard drive, buy one of those. If your system uses a SCSI hard drive, buy a second SCSI drive.
- No easy way exists to tell whether you have IDE or SCSI drives, other than to find your PC's invoice and see what the dealer installed.
- You do not have to match the capacity of the first hard drive to the second. For example, if your first hard drive stores 4 gigabytes (GB), your second hard drive can store 9GB—or any value. It doesn't matter.

Adding a new hard drive rearranges your disk drive letters! If your CD-ROM was drive D, for example, it is drive E (or F or even G) after installing a second hard drive. To avoid this peripatetic CD-ROM drive letter, I recommend setting your CD-ROM drive letter to something "high up" in the alphabet. Chapter 22 explains how.

Installing a New Microprocessor

I do not recommend doing a microprocessor upgrade. I know that lots of companies make big bucks installing new microprocessors in old PCs. In my opinion, however, it's just cheaper to buy a new PC. The new PC has not only the newer microprocessor but also a newer hard drive, memory, and other options you have to upgrade eventually anyway. And it's cheaper in the long run.

Installing an Expansion Card

Expansion cards allow you to expand your PC's capability. They add new circuitry and allow a mild-mannered, meek PC to become a super PC, with just a few twists of a screwdriver.

With an expansion card, you can add a second monitor to your PC or add a network adapter, TV tuner, SCSI controller, or a host of other options and goodies.

When you're ready to install the expansion card, follow these steps:

▶ **Check the card for any switches that have to be set.**

Most expansion cards sold today lack switches; they're configured by software instead. Even so, check the expansion card's manual to ensure that the card has switches and, if so, determine which way they should be set.

Make sure that you unplug the thing and not just turn it off. Newer PCs have pushbutton switches on their front panel, not the heavy-duty on-off switches hidden 'round back on earlier models. My tummy has many a time turned on a PC as I've reached over it to remove its lid.

- **Unplug your PC and remove its cover.**
- **Locate an empty expansion slot.**

It can be any expansion slot. No rule says, "Video cards go in slot 2" or anything anymore (such a rule did once exist). Just make sure that the slot is suitable for the card: ISA types of cards plug into only ISA slots, and PCI cards plug into PCI slots. You can't goof this stuff up. If the card doesn't fit, you're trying the wrong slot.

- **Remove the back plate cover for the slot.**

A small screw attaches the cover to the slot. You can throw away the slot cover, but keep the screw.

I'm serious about throwing away the slot cover. You don't need them. I have a drawer full of 'em.

- **Insert the card.**

Slide the card into the slot, gently but firmly. Ensure that it's fully seated; the card should not rock from front to back when you push on its front or back edge.

- **Connect any internal cables (if necessary) .**

Some expansion cards might have cables that connect to internal devices. If so, connect them and optionally install the internal devices now. The instruction manual for the card tells you what goes where.

- **Screw the card to the PC's case.**

Use the same screw you removed when you took off the slot cover.

- **Close 'er up.**

You might have to connect external cables now, if necessary. For example, if you installed a network card, you might have to attach the network hose. If you're installing a second monitor, you have to hook it up to the back of the card.

▶ **Turn on the computer.**

What happens next depends on what you're installing. For most expansion cards, Windows should recognize the card instantly and prompt you to install software. The software comes from either the Windows CD or any disk that came with the expansion card.

The Software Setup

Windows is designed to recognize 95% of new computer hardware immediately after it's installed. (The missing 5% is supposed to be other things that might still exist.) After you install your hardware, you should be able to turn your PC on and, lo, whatever you installed is instantly recognized. That's when you read the following section, "Everything Works Right." Read the section after that, "It Didn't Go As Planned," when Windows fails to recognize your new hardware.

Everything Works Right

After installing the hardware, Windows starts up and immediately recognizes the hardware. A dialog box appears, proclaiming that "new hardware" has been found. Windows then proceeds to install the necessary software to run that hardware.

Windows might ask for the Windows CD to be inserted. Get ready for that.

Because Windows sometimes might not find a proper driver, check to see whether your hardware came with a driver. If so, you have to keep that CD or floppy disk handy. Insert it when (or if) you're asked.

If a dialog box appears, prompting you to restart your computer, do so.

That's it for hardware installation. Windows has all the software necessary to run your new hardware. Keep in mind, however, that you might have to install an application to use the hardware. For example, although Windows instantly recognized my PC's new videocamera, I still had to install the application that uses the camera in order to take videos and still pictures.

It Didn't Go As Planned

If Windows acts stupid after you start your PC with the new hardware installed, don't get frustrated. You simply have to tell Windows to go out and hunt for your hardware. It's an extra step, that's all.

A tiny category of hardware exists that Windows cannot recognize. Stuff in that category includes

- ✓ External modems
- ✓ Joysticks
- ✓ Tape backup drives
- ✓ Some SCSI peripherals

You must install modems and joysticks from the Control Panel's Modems or Game Controllers icons, respectively. Open the icon and click the Add button to choose a new modem, or install a modem from disk.

Tape backup drives are recognized by only your backup software—nothing else. When you run your backup program, it recognizes the tape drive, even though Windows might not.

You must set up SCSI peripherals by using a program that came with your SCSI adapter card. Most of the time, the SCSI card recognizes the device, although you might have to run a special format program or install some other option to get the hardware to work.

Anything not in the preceding categories is installed by using the Add New Hardware Wizard in the Control Panel.

If you've just added new hardware to your PC and Windows has not recognized it, do the following:

- ▶ **Open the Control Panel.**

- ▶ **Open the Add New Hardware icon.**

The Add New Hardware Wizard starts up. It does a thorough examination of your PC's guts to see whether any new hardware is attached.

- ▶ **Click Next.**

- ▶ **Click Next.**

Windows scours your PC for Plug and Play items. This search might take awhile, or it could be quick.

If something is found, Windows proceeds with the installation. (Really, though, Windows probably would have found the new item when it started.)

If Windows finds nothing, the next panel in the wizard is displayed, as shown in Figure 45.1.

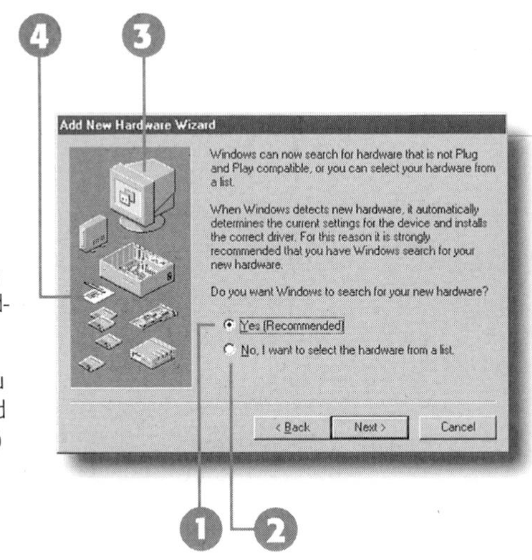

Figure 45.1
The Add New Hardware Wizard.

1. Choose this option to have Windows look for new hardware.
2. Choose this one only if you know the manufacturer and product name (or number) of whatever it is you installed or if the hardware came with an installation disk.
3. If the console is open, it should be unplugged with no image on the monitor.
4. Should be a screwdriver.

- **Choose Yes (if it's not chosen already).**
- **Click Next.**
- **Click Next.**

Windows takes a few minutes to search for new hardware.

To properly tell whether the computer has "stopped responding," just wait. You should see no movement on the Detection progress bar, no hard drive light flickering, and *no* computer activity—for at least four minutes. Only then should you consider resetting your computer.

If Windows finds any new hardware, it is displayed on a list onscreen. Choose the hardware you want to install in order to continue. Windows might ask for an installation disk. If so, stick it in the drive. You're done.

If no hardware has been found, you get a chance to search manually.

▶ **Click Next.**

The Add New Hardware Wizard presents a screen full of peripherals you might have installed, as shown in Figure 45.2. Your job is to select which one you installed for a manual setup.

▶ **Choose the device you installed from the list.**

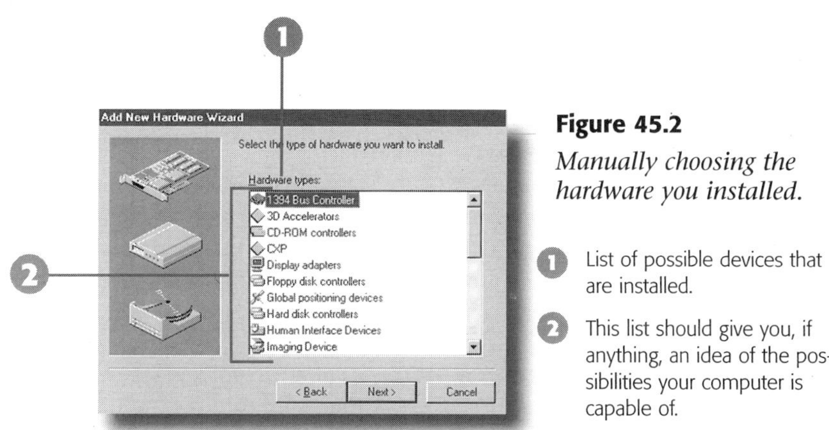

Figure 45.2
Manually choosing the hardware you installed.

1. List of possible devices that are installed.
2. This list should give you, if anything, an idea of the possibilities your computer is capable of.

Suppose that you've installed an older SCSI card, one that Windows couldn't recognize. You would select SCSI Controllers from the list.

▶ **Click Next.**

The next screen (my favorite) is shown in Figure 45.3. It's where you must know the manufacturer and product name for the device you've installed. Or, if the manufacturer isn't listed, click the Have Disk button to install from the setup floppy disk that came with the hardware.

▶ **Click Next.**

If you're running this tutorial just to see what happens, please do not choose any hardware from the list! You do not want to burden your PC with extra drivers for software you do not own. Click Cancel to quit the Add New Hardware Wizard now.

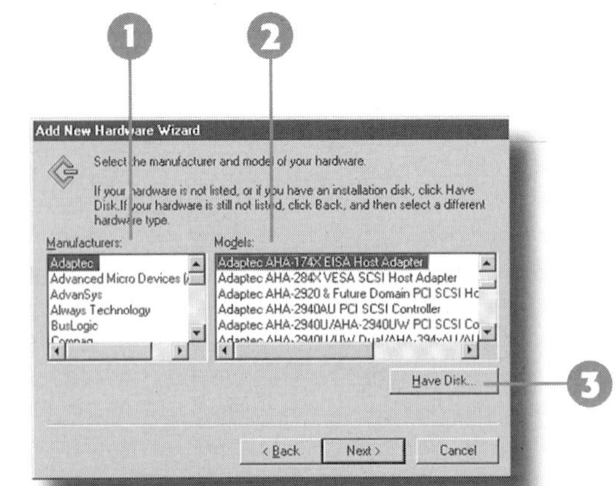

Figure 45.3
Find your hardware here.

1. Find your hardware manufacturer here.
2. List of their products over here.
3. Click here if it's not listed but you have an installation disk.

The next screen might ask for additional information about the hardware. This process might get technical, although whatever Windows has listed should generally be okay settings.

▶ **Click Next.**

You might be asked now to insert the Windows CD. Then your computer might reset. (Actually, whatever happens after this varies depending on what type of hardware you're installing.)

Eventually the Add New Hardware Wizard finishes its operation, and your PC should be set up and installed with its new hardware. (Unfortunately I can't offer any more detailed information at this point without knowing exactly what it is you're installing.)

TIP

If you have any problems, don't hesitate to use the technical-support number for whatever hardware you're installing. Many hardware technical-support lines aren't as busy as the software-support lines.

Part VII

Problem Solving

Chapters in This Part

Part VII

Visual Topic Reference A

1. The System Info program (Chapter 46).
2. Troubleshooting (Chapter 47).
3. Other irksome things (Chapter 48).

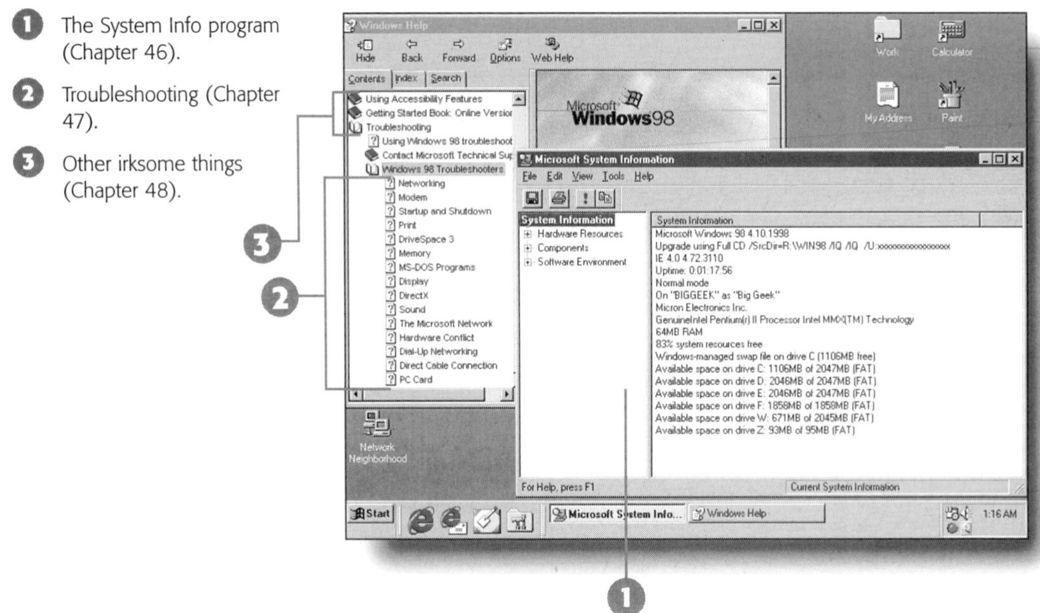

Chapter 46

Tools to Help You

Questions Answered and Thoughts Inspired

- Using the Microsoft System Information program
- Checking your system files
- Checking for version conflicts
- Scanning for viruses (advice only)
- Creating an emergency boot disk

Being a doctor is easier than being a veterinarian, which is easier than fixing computers. A doctor can always ask you, "Where does it hurt?" Even if you don't know the name, you can point and go "Ouch." A vet can look at a sad cow or lumpy kitty and figure out some possibilities. But a computer doctor? If the PC is goofing up, how can you trust it to tell you what's wrong?

This chapter covers some helpful programs that come with Windows. You can use these programs in times of woe to help determine what is wrong with your system. Also covered is creating an *emergency boot disk*, which can help you start and diagnose a dead computer.

Microsoft System Info

Your first response to a weird, ailing, or silly computer is to call the tech-support people. Start with your computer dealer. You paid those folks the most money and from them you should get the most help. Especially if you bought from a national dealer, it probably has teams of eager young people, cheerfully dressed in white lab coats, yearning to assist you.

Whenever you phone for help, the support folk probably want to know some general information about your computer. To get that info, you should run the Microsoft System Information program. It acts as a central storage place for all sorts of trivial tidbits about your computer. It also contains a menu full of help-me-now programs.

▶ **From the Start Thing menu, choose Programs ➡Accessories ➡System Tools ➡System Information.**

The Microsoft System Information program shows itself on your computer, which should look similar to Figure 46.1. The information shown in the figure details my computer's basic setup. What you see on your system is different (unless you sneak into my office and run the System Information program on BIGGEEK).

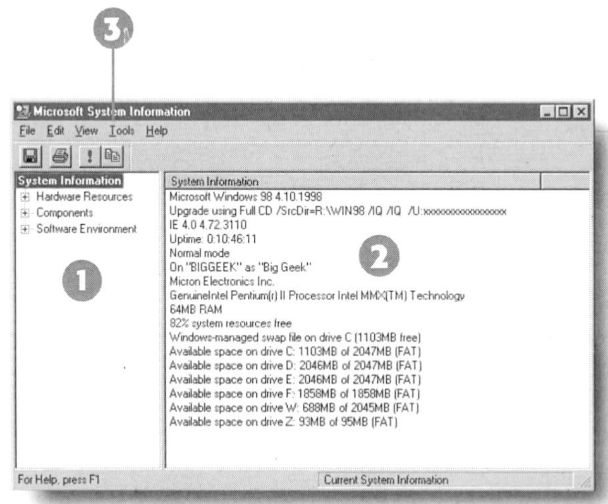

Figure 46.1
The Microsoft System Information program.

1. Categories and subcategories.
2. Information is displayed here.
3. Helpful Tools menu.

The System Info program (which is what I call it because typing the words *Microsoft System Information* at this late point in the book would take too much time) isn't magic. The program is not designed to *cure* any ills. For that, you use troubleshooters, as described in Chapter 47.

No, the job of the System Info program is to provide tech-support people—or your computer guru—with an overview of how your PC is set up.

On your screen you should see some basic PC information: the amount of RAM, number of hard drives, type of microprocessor, and other stuff it would otherwise be tough to tell just by looking at your computer's case.

By opening and selecting items on the left side of the window, you can see additional information:

▶ **Click the + next to Hardware to open it.**

A list of hardware trouble spots appears, although you can do nothing there other than poke around.

A tech-support person might ask you to choose one of the categories listed just to be sure that nothing unusual is going on with your PC's setup.

Keep the System Info program window open for the following section's tutorial.

- Write down all the tech-support phone numbers (computer dealer, computer manufacturer, Microsoft) on this book's Quick Reference card.
- The System Info program isn't magic. It just provides a review of your system's setup plus any additional information the tech-support people might need.

System File Checker

Nestled on the System Info program's Tools menu are a bunch of scanning and reporting tools. Some of them display information, and others actively try to fix common problems.

▶ **Open the System Info program (if it's not open already).**

▶ **Choose Tools ➡System File Checker.**

The System File Checker is a program that reviews Windows's own programs to see whether everything is okey-doke. Figure 46.2 shows what it looks like.

▶ **Click Start.**

Windows checks out its own files, similar to the way ScanDisk operates (refer to Chapter 21).

If Windows finds any files that are corrupted or missing, a dialog box is displayed. Insert the Windows 98 CD in your CD-ROM drive, and the file will be fixed for you.

If everything is okay, you eventually see a dialog box telling you, "System File Checker has finished scanning your system files." Otherwise, Windows replaces any corrupt files it finds.

- ▶ **Click OK.**
- ▶ **Click Close to close the System File Checker window.**

You return to the System Info window. Keep it open for the next section's tutorial.

You have no reason to run the System File Checker on a regular basis; it's not the same as running the Defragmenter or ScanDisk. Use the System File Checker only if you sense that Windows is somehow acting strange (or at least stranger than usual).

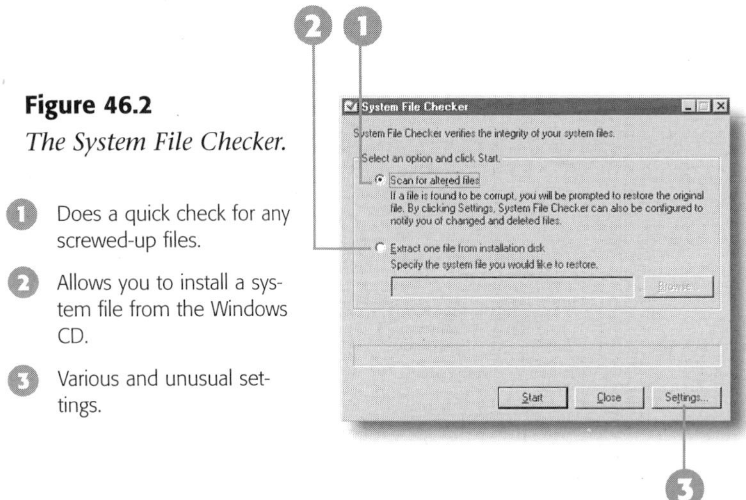

Figure 46.2
The System File Checker.

1. Does a quick check for any screwed-up files.
2. Allows you to install a system file from the Windows CD.
3. Various and unusual settings.

Version Conflict Manager

A major in-the-news item when Windows 98 was first released was the Version Conflict Manager. It's a necessary program because many applications in Windows rely on the same files. If those files are changed, some programs don't run.

For example, most Windows programs use the COMMDLG.DLL program file to display the standard Save and Open dialog boxes. Suppose that one program relies on Version 4.2 of the COMMDLG.DLL file and a newer program you install overwrites Version 4.2 with Version 4.0 of the COMMDLG.DLL file. Sounds dumb? It happens all the time. In fact, the biggest criminal is Windows itself.

How rude of Windows to do that!

When Windows 98 is installed, it overwrites many newer files with older versions—on purpose. To deal with this problem, you have the Version Conflict Manager, which lets you restore the newer version of the common file.

▶ **Open the System Info program (if it's not open already).**

▶ **Choose Tools ➡Version Conflict Manager.**

The Version Conflict Manager window appears, as shown in Figure 46.3. It lists any system files that Windows itself has replaced with older versions.

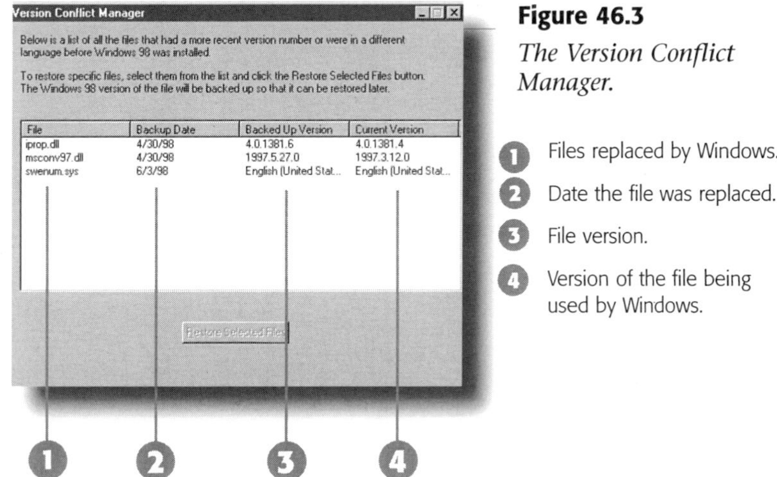

Figure 46.3
The Version Conflict Manager.

1. Files replaced by Windows.
2. Date the file was replaced.
3. File version.
4. Version of the file being used by Windows.

If everything is running fine on your PC, you have nothing to fear. You should consider restoring the newer version only if you encounter problems when a program runs—consistent problems often accompanied by an error message claiming that a certain DLL file is out of date.

For example, if you receive a message that the MSCONV97.DLL file (refer to Figure 46.3) is out-of-date or corrupted, you can highlight that file and click the Restore Selected Files button. Do that only if you're having problems, though.

▶ **Close the Version Conflict Manager window.**

I've had no problems with version conflicts—at least so far. Others, however, have reported lots of problems with specific programs. If that's you, the Version Conflict Manager is your hero.

▶ **Close the System Info window.**

Microsoft is quite adamant about Windows 98 overwriting newer files. The company produced a strangely worded press release about how older versions of important files were better than the newer versions, or something like that. Weird. At least now you know how to fix it.

Virus Scanning

One of the sad parts of computer life is that some nasty people have written even nastier programs called computer *viruses*. Oh, they have other names, although *virus* is the one everyone is familiar with.

A virus can really ruin your day. The program, when it's run, erases files or causes general mayhem—a bad situation. Fortunately, you're not a helpless babe in the woods.

Generally speaking, you never get a computer virus if you follow two simple rules:

- ✓ Never start your computer by using a floppy disk someone else gives you.
- ✓ Never run a program emailed to you from someone you don't or barely know.

People who steal software break the first rule. It happened to a fellow I knew who got a "free" game from a buddy at work. The game was an illegal copy of commercial software, and it had a virus. Booting from the floppy disk infected this guy's system, and he lost everything.

The second rule is easier to obey. Never, under any circumstances, accept a program from someone you don't know—especially if it's sent by email. I'm not talking about graphics images or ZIP files or any nonprogram file attachments. However, a *program* file—a COM or EXE file—is suspect, especially if someone you don't or barely know has sent it.

Reading email does not infect your computer.

Even if you get a bad program as an email attachment, it infects your computer only when you run the program. At that point, the only resource you have is a piece of software called a *virus scanner,* or *antivirus software*.

Windows 98 includes no antivirus software (which is dumb, in my opinion). The Windows 98 Plus! package has a virus scanner. You can also get a virus scanner from the Web. Visit this site:

`http://www.mcafee.com`

The McAfee antivirus software is the most popular and most effective method for checking any file on your computer for signs of infection. If McAfee finds a bad file, the program can remove the file quickly and safely. I highly recommend that you visit the company's Web page and download an evaluation copy. Pay for it if you use it.

Creating an Emergency Boot Disk

During moments of sheer panic, you *must* have an *emergency boot disk*. It's a floppy disk you can use to start your computer in times of woe.

To create an emergency boot disk, you need a floppy disk. Go grab one now. Label it. Write *emergency boot disk* on the label. Write the computer's name on the label. Date the label.

- **Open the Control Panel.**
- **Open the Add/Remove Programs icon.**
- **Click the Startup Disk panel in the Add/Remove Programs Properties dialog box.**
- **Stick your floppy disk in drive A.**
- **Click Create Disk.**

If you're asked to insert the Windows 98 CD into your CD-ROM drive, do so.

Windows asks you to insert the floppy disk into drive A. Hey! You've already done that.

- **Click OK.**

Wait while Windows copies files to the floppy disk.

Wait. Wait. Wait.

When the thermometer disappears on the dialog box, it's done!

- **Click OK to close the Add/Remove Programs Properties dialog box.**
- **Close the Control Panel.**
- **Put your emergency boot disk in a safe yet handy place for whenever you might need it. Whenever you have serious disk trouble, use the emergency boot disk to start your computer.**
- **When the emergency boot disk starts up, it displays a menu asking you which type of CD-ROM drive you have: IDE or SCSI. Choosing the proper option (most likely IDE, unless you're sure that you have a SCSI drive) allows you to access files on the CD-ROM drive, which can help you reinstall Windows.**
- **Notice that the emergency boot disk installs most of its fix-up programs on a RAM drive. When you read the startup screen (after choosing a CD-ROM drive), it tells you the RAM drive's letter, on which you find the fix-up programs.**

- **Now the bad news: The fix-up programs are all DOS programs. They're exactly what a computer guru needs in order to fix things, but nothing I can explain to you now that would be of any help.**
- **All PCs can be started from a floppy disk. Before hard drives were created, that's how everyone started up a PC.**
- **Floppy disks are good for about a year, sometimes less. Make sure that you create a new emergency boot disk every year or so. That way, whenever you need it, you can be sure that it works.**

Chapter 47

Hardware Troubleshooting

Questions Answered and Thoughts Inspired

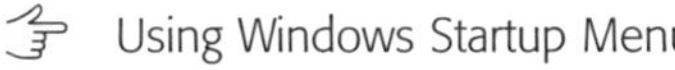

- Using Windows Startup Menu
- Running a Troubleshooter

When the problem isn't Windows, it's your PC's hardware. Things go wrong. The modem decides to walk in the park. Memory disappears. Two expansion cards duke it out, and you lose several system features. Nasty stuff. Or maybe not-so-nasty stuff: You rearrange your desktop, and suddenly you can't click any buttons because you've made them too small or too big. Ugh.

This chapter has two hardware solutions for some general PC woes. The first is using the Windows Startup menu to run in Safe mode. The second solution is to run one of the Windows hardware troubleshooters to fix or at least narrow down some common hardware problems.

Hello, Startup Menu!

If you ever screw up Windows to the point that you can't see anything onscreen, or maybe you've added some device that suddenly makes Windows less than usable, you have hope. You can start Windows in Safe mode. The following steps take you on a brief preview:

▶ **From the Start Thing, choose Shut Down.**

▶ **Choose Restart.**

▶ **Click OK.**

Your computer shuts itself down. Glub, glub, glub.

When it starts up again, wait for the beep.

Listen for the beep!

▶ **After the beep, press the F8 key.**

If you're too late, Windows starts up as it normally does. Oops! Try again.

If your timing is good, you see the Windows 98 Startup menu, as shown in Figure 47.1.

Figure 47.1
The startup menu.

1. Boot up as you normally do.
2. Create a log of startup events (might be required if a guru is troubleshooting your PC).
3. Run in Safe mode, which recovers most screen disasters.
4. Don't bother.
5. Start the MS-DOS prompt rather than Windows.
6. Start the Safe mode MS-DOS prompt.

```
Microsoft Windows 98 Startup Menu
=================================


   2. Logged (\BOOTLOG.TXT)
   3. Safe mode
   4. Step-by-step confirmation
   5. Command prompt only
   6. Safe mode command prompt only

Enter a choice: 1













F5=Safe mode  Shift+F5=Command prompt  Shift+F8=Step-by-Step confirmation [N]
```

- **Press 3 to start in Safe mode.**
- **Press Enter.**

Your computer continues to start up, but when you see the desktop, you notice that Windows is running in a low-resolution, plain-vanilla mode. This mode is the best way to recover if you've changed screen sizes or colors and cannot get anything back.

A warning dialog box is displayed. Read it.

- **Click OK.**

If your screen's size, color, or whatever was screwed up, fix those items now. Use the Control Panel to make your adjustments.

Do not make any adjustments if you're just cruising through this section on a tutorial. Your system is restored to normal when you reset later in this section. Fix something only if it's broken!

After making necessary changes (if any), restart the computer:

- **From the Start Thing, choose Shut Down.**
- **Choose Restart.**
- **Click OK.**

Your computer restarts as normal. If you had to make any adjustments in Safe mode, you see them reflected when you restart your computer. Hopefully, things should be better. If not, you can run a troubleshooter, as described in the following section.

Safe mode prevents some devices from working. Remember that it's not the normal way you use your computer. Safe mode is designed to help you recover things.

Running a Troubleshooter

Windows has some great programs to help you narrow down and fix various hardware problems. These troubleshooting wizards have often prevented me from tossing a computer through a window.

Several troubleshooters are available, depending on which piece of hardware you're having a fit with.

▶ **From the Start Thing menu, choose Help.**

The Windows Help window appears. (See Chapter 8 for more information about using Windows Help.)

▶ **Click the Contents tab to bring that panel forward (if necessary).**

▶ **Choose Troubleshooting.**

Click Troubleshooting once with your mouse to "open it up."

▶ **Choose Windows 98 Troubleshooters.**

A full list of hardware troubleshooters appears, as shown in Figure 47.2.

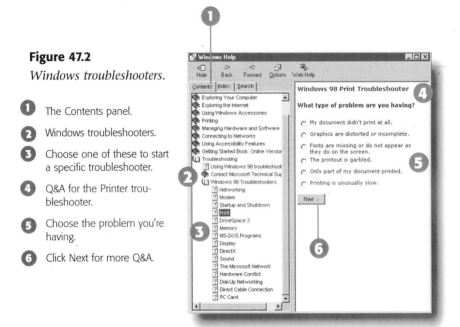

Figure 47.2
Windows troubleshooters.

1. The Contents panel.
2. Windows troubleshooters.
3. Choose one of these to start a specific troubleshooter.
4. Q&A for the Printer troubleshooter.
5. Choose the problem you're having.
6. Click Next for more Q&A.

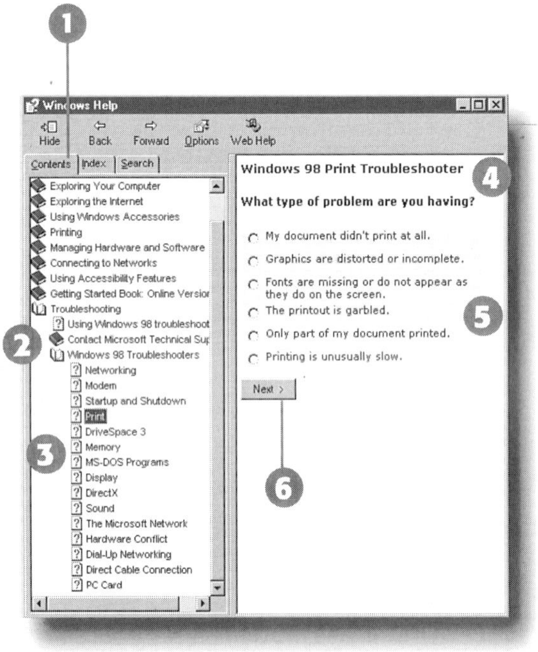

Pick your problem! Whatever you're having trouble with, click that item on the list to start up a troubleshooter.

The troubleshooter presents a list of situations or solutions. Choose one that matches your problem. Click the Next button, and continue to answer questions or try solutions.

Most computer problems are common and easy to solve. Microsoft is very clever in the way they present information in the troubleshooters. I would guess that a majority of the problems you might have can be easily fixed by following the steps in the troubleshooter.

Some troubleshooters run other programs in Windows. Try to move the Help window over so that you can see both the instructions and the window you're working in.

▶ **Close the Help window.**

When you're done with the troubleshooter, close the Help window.

Chapter 48

Irksome Things

Questions Answered and Thoughts Inspired

- Soothing words of wisdom
- Fixing a slow-running system
- Removing annoying startup messages
- Finding a lost window
- Undoing the sins of the Auto Arrange command
- Removing a dead program

Because I put my email address in all my books, people write. Sometimes they say "I'm just writing to see whether you really answer all your email." I do. Sometimes they say "Where they heck is my window?" and I try to help them. I don't mind. If you buy one of my books and the answer you need isn't in there, I feel that I owe you some help. It's only fair.

Over the years I've saved some of the more interesting bits of email I've gotten, dragging those messages and my replies to a special folder. This chapter contains a majority of those questions and answers, mostly the common problems people encounter when they're using Windows and my suggested solutions. If you can't find the answer here, you can always write me, and maybe your question and its answer will appear in the next edition of this book.

- My email address is `dgookin@wambooli.com`, and I answer every message.
- Even though I answer every letter, I can't help everyone. It's always best to try your dealer first. Be sure to read all the chapters in this part of the book first because the answer to your question might already be in here. Thanks.
- Also refer to the Index for more items not specifically mentioned here. This book is full of troubleshooting information.

General Advice

I don't have a list of ten commandments for you, although if I were on my deathbed and saw you start up Windows, I might utter the following words of wisdom before logging off this big, blue ball:

- ✓ "Don't reinstall Windows to fix a problem."
- ✓ "Don't upgrade to the next version of Windows."
- ✓ "Resetting your PC fixes most weirdness."

Because I'm not on my deathbed and the little machine that goes "boop" is still "booping," I can elaborate on these knowledge nuggets.

Don't Reinstall Windows

There's this bozo on the radio where I live (no, I don't name names, although the clever among you will figure it out). His solution for every PC woe is to have listeners reformat their hard drives and reinstall Windows.

What a jerk.

You never have to reformat your hard drive. Also, because reinstalling Windows is a pain, I do not recommend it. A solution exists for every Windows problem. Sure, reinstalling Windows might fix the problem, but why go through such an ordeal? I mean, if *I* were on the radio, I'd either say "I dunno" or give the proper answer. But reformatting a hard drive and reinstalling Windows? Sheesh.

First, try to find your problem in this part of the book, in either this or the preceding two chapters.

Second, phone your dealer for support. Phone Microsoft. Or visit its Web page for support. You're probably not the first or only person to have the problem. A fix exists, or at least an answer does.

Third, never mess with your PC's operating system. Sure, I admit that Mr. Computer Radio Head isn't entirely wrong about reinstalling Windows. I have a Windows 95 computer that I bought in 1994. It started life as a DOS/Windows 3.11 computer, and then I upgraded. Big mistake. Although reinstalling Windows would probably fix some problems, I really don't have the time.

Never Upgrade Your Operating System

Your operating system (Windows) is the most important piece of software on your PC. As long as it does everything you need, you never have any reason to buy a newer version. This rule applies to *all* your software, not just the operating system.

Upgrading an operating system means that you're putting all your software at risk. After all, if the stuff works now, why fix it? Windows 98 is okay, but if you're happy with Windows 95, don't upgrade! When Windows 2000 comes along, don't bother with it either!

The secret is to wait until you buy a new computer. The new computer will have the new operating system preinstalled and set up perfectly. You can continue to use your old system just fine.

- Most people's problems with Windows stem from the fact that they've upgraded from an older operating system. I'm serious! Upgrading leads to trouble.
- If any software you're using does the job, you don't need to upgrade. You should consider an upgrade only if the new version has features you absolutely need.
- I did a special edition of *DOS For Dummies* published by IDG Books Worldwide for Microsoft, one that was packaged with the last version of MS-DOS, 6.22. The only thing Microsoft made me edit in the book was this remark: "Do not upgrade DOS!" Apparently it wasn't good for the company's bottom line. I can't lie to you: You don't need to upgrade Windows!

Reset!

Restarting your computer often fixes much of its weirdness. For example, if the mouse cursor is gone or you can't paste to the desktop or drag an icon to the Recycle Bin, a quick reset fixes the problem. Always try that method first.

Your System Is Running Slowly

Computers run slowly only when they have a lot to do. Are you making your PC do a lot? How many buttons are on the taskbar?

The more programs you run, the slower your PC runs.

Even though Windows is capable of running more than one program at a time, doing so slows things down. Especially big, clunky programs, such as Microsoft Word and Excel. Running them along with other programs can cause out-of-memory errors and general slowness.

The solution: Shut down some programs.

Alas, shutting down programs doesn't help when the Internet is slow. The Internet can slow down—no matter how fast your modem is—depending on the number of people online at the time. For example, when the "dancing baby" animation was hot, it took the dancing-baby home page *hours* to load.

The solution: When the Internet is slow, disconnect and try again some other time.

"I Changed My Screen (Somehow), and Now I Can't See or Get at Anything"

A guy wrote me complaining that he couldn't see a thing he was typing. He'd gone into the Display Properties dialog box and made all his Windows controls *really huge*. (Ha-ha!) Okay, that happens. And it's an innocent mistake. That dern Apply button is just too tempting, I suppose. Anyway...

Refer to the Chapter 47 for information about starting Windows in Safe mode whenever you can't see the screen. That method enables you to see the screen and make changes to fix things. It's all described in Chapter 47.

"I See Some Annoying Startup Messages"

On my computer, the beautiful "Starting Windows" graphics image (the one with the clouds) is interrupted by the following ugly text:

```
SET BLASTER=A220 I5 D1 H5 P330 E620 T6
```

I assume that it means only that aliens have taken over my PC and are ready for attack.

Seriously, that's one of many annoying startup messages you can see when you run Windows (which is still based on DOS, which is where the preceding message comes from).

To fix the preceding line of text, do the following:

- **From the Start Thing menu, choose Run.**
- **Type** SYSEDIT **in the Open box.**
- **Click OK.**

The System Configuration Editor runs, as shown in Figure 48.1.

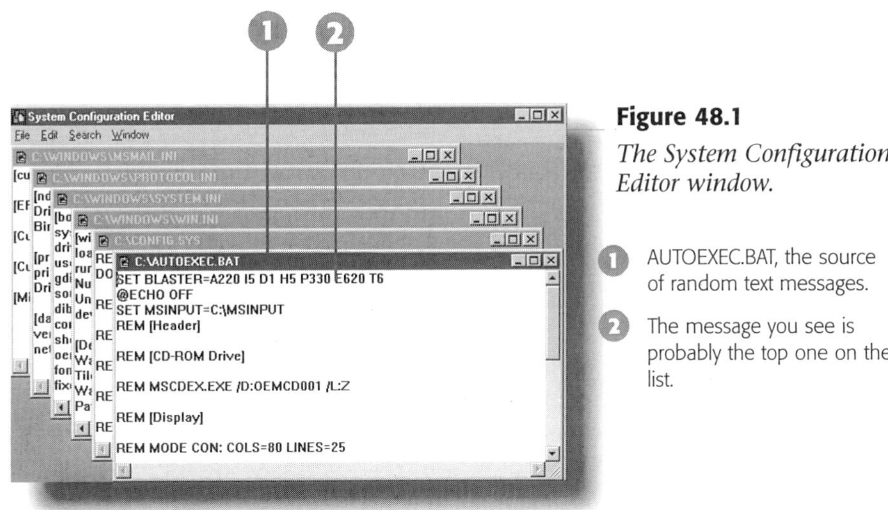

Figure 48.1

The System Configuration Editor window.

1. AUTOEXEC.BAT, the source of random text messages.
2. The message you see is probably the top one on the list.

▶ **Choose Window ➡C:\AUTOEXEC.BAT.**

This step brings the AUTOEXEC.BAT file window to the front (if it's not there already).

The cursor should be blinking at the top of the window. If not, press the Ctrl+Home key combination.

▶ **Type** @ECHO OFF**.**

Type the **@** symbol, and then **ECHO**, a space, and **OFF**.

▶ **Press the Enter key.**

This step inserts the line `@ECHO OFF` as the first line of text in the file. (It's okay if the line of text is already in the file; `@ECHO OFF` should be the first line in AUTOEXEC.BAT no matter what.)

▶ **Close the System Configuration Editor window.**

A warning dialog box appears, asking whether you want to save your changes to AUTOEX-EC.BAT.

▶ **Click Yes.**

You're done. The next time your PC starts up, you don't see the annoying text message.

TIP

If you're handy with the Cut and Paste commands, you can just cut any existing `@ECHO OFF` line in AUTOEXEC.BAT and paste it as the first line in the file.

Oops! Floppy in the Drive

Another error message you might see when the system starts up goes like this:

```
Non-system disk or disk error
Replace and strike any key
```

Duh! You left a floppy disk in drive A. Oops! Remove it. Press Enter. You're done.

ScanDisk Rears Its Ugly Head

If your computer was improperly shut down—for example, you just turned it off or a power outage hit—Windows runs the ScanDisk program when you restart, to ensure that everything is okay.

Don't panic! It's a good thing that ScanDisk runs. It ensures that any open files don't clutter the hard drive. If you're prompted to run ScanDisk, do so.

If you notice that ScanDisk runs *every time* you start your computer, you're improperly shutting down your PC. Always use the Shut Down command on the Start Thing menu to quit Windows. See Chapter 1.

Finding a Lost Window

You can easily locate wandering windows. Just look for the window's button on the taskbar. As long as the button is there, you should be able to find a window somewhere nearby.

If you cannot see the window or cannot "grab" it with the mouse, do the following:

▶ **Click the window's button on the taskbar.**

This step ensures that Windows is focusing its attention on the errant window.

▶ **Press Alt+Spacebar.**

This step activates the window's control menu, which you might or might not see, depending on how lost the window is.

▶ **Press M (for Move).**

The window is now in a special Move mode. You can press the cursor keys on the keyboard to move the window up, down, left, or right.

▶ **Press the up-, down-, left-, or right-arrow cursor keys to move the window.**

This step should slide the window into view.

▶ **Press the Enter key when you're done moving the window.**

If the window is lost in a program that uses multiple document windows (such as Word or Excel), choose the missing window from the Windows menu. Press Alt+- (Alt plus the hyphen key). Then type **M**, and move the window as just described.

Don't let the window wander off again.

"I Can't Drag Items in a Window!"

Stuck icons usually mean that you've accidentally chosen the Auto Arrange item for a window. This problem can be maddening. It took me two days to figure out the problem on my Windows 98 laptop.

▶ **Right-click the window with the stuck icons.**

This step also works on the desktop.

▶ **Choose Arrange Icons.**

Look on the Arrange Icons submenu. If a check mark appears next to Auto Arrange, you have to remove that check mark:

▶ **Choose Auto Arrange to remove the check mark.**

The icons shall be stuck no more.

If the preceding steps don't work (no check mark appears next to Auto Arrange), resetting your computer should do the trick.

Closing a Dead Program

Nothing is more amusing to me than when some Windows program crosses its eyes and nods off into oblivion. Its window stays put on the desktop. You can still work.

The taskbar works. Other programs slide their windows around just fine. That one program is a booger, though. Here's how to get rid of it:

▶ **Press Ctrl+Alt+Del.**

Yes, this step is the "three-finger salute," the Vulcan nerve pinch that resets the computer under DOS. In Windows, you can press the Ctrl, Alt, and Del keys simultaneously to summon the Close Program window, as shown in Figure 48.2.

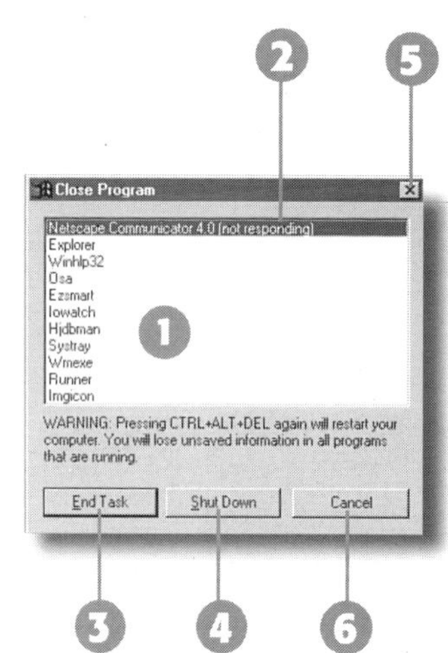

Figure 48.2
The Close Program window.

1. Tasks (programs) running on your PC.
2. The "not responding" part is your clue that you've found a dead task.
3. Remove the highlighted task.
4. Instantly shut down your computer—watch out!
5. Close this window.
6. Heed this warning!

▶ **Look for any programs "not responding."**

If you find one, click it once to select it, and then click End Task. After a short time, Windows might display another warning dialog box, asking whether you really want to shut down the program. Click Yes.

▶ **Click Cancel to close the Close Program window.**

If you ever have to close a program that has run amok, do so as just described. Then shut down Windows. Although you can continue to use your computer, my advice is always to play it safe. Shutting down Windows ensures that all your files are saved to disk and that any memory used by the dead program isn't wasted.

Playing DOS Games

DOS lives. Okay, not as a real operating system anymore. DOS lives in a window inside Windows. This arrangement enables you to run your old DOS software, use a command prompt (if you're that crazy), and play games, most of which are still written for DOS. This chapter touches on DOS in Windows.

- Quite a few newer games no longer require DOS. For example, the latest Microsoft Flight Simulator runs in Windows, not in DOS.
- DOS is a big nut to crack. It has much more to it than I could describe in this wee li'l chapter. Visit your bookstore or library for books about DOS if you decide to dive in to the command prompt in any depth.

A Look at the DOS Window

In Windows, DOS lives in a window onscreen.

- **From the Start Thing menu, choose Programs s➡MS-DOS Prompt.**

A DOS prompt window opens onscreen, looking much like Figure A.1.

If you see instead a full-screen DOS prompt (not in a window), press the Alt+Enter key combination.

- **Close the DOS window.**

DOS windows close just like any other window in Windows. You can click the Close button (the X) in the window's upper-right corner to rid yourself of the DOS window.

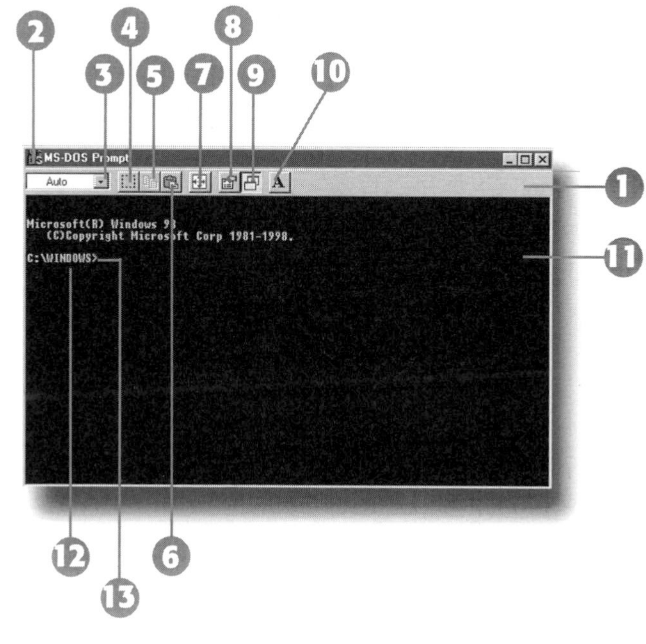

Figure A.1
The DOS prompt window.

1. The toolbar.
2. Choose Toolbar from this menu if you don't see the toolbar.
3. Set the font size for DOS text.
4. Select DOS text.
5. Copy selected DOS text.
6. Paste text.
7. Switch to Full-Screen mode.
8. Properties dialog box for this program.
9. Enable or disable background multitasking.
10. Display Fonts panel in the DOS window's Properties dialog box.
11. DOS program runs here.
12. DOS prompt.
13. Type DOS commands here.

- ▶ **Start the MS-DOS Prompt again.**
- ▶ **At the DOS prompt, type** EXIT **and press Enter.**

You can also use the EXIT command to close the DOS window. Why is this method handy? Because you work DOS by typing on the keyboard. Often it's much easier to type the EXIT command than to reach for the mouse to close the window.

Running a DOS Program at the Prompt

To run a DOS program, you type the program's name at the DOS prompt:

- ▶ **Start the MS-DOS Prompt program.**

To run the MS-DOS Editor, you type **EDIT** at the prompt:

▶ **Type** EDIT **at the prompt and press Enter.**

The MS-DOS Editor appears in the window.

If you're running MS-DOS programs, this method is exactly how you start them from the prompt. Or, if you've installed the programs on the Start Thing menu, they appear in MS-DOS prompt windows, just as the Edit program appears on your screen right now.

Although running a DOS program in a window is nice, you can also run the program full-screen—just like in the old days, when DOS ruled the PC:

▶ **Press Alt+Enter.**

The Alt+Enter key combination switches between Full-Screen and Window mode for any DOS program. The Editor now appears on your monitor in Full-Screen mode.

▶ **Press Alt+Enter again.**

The Alt+Enter keystroke combo switches you back to Window mode.

▶ **Close the DOS window by clicking the X Close button.**

Whoops! Unlike in a Windows program, you cannot just close any old DOS program.

Always quit your DOS programs before you close the DOS prompt window.

In some instances, the DOS prompt window goes away when you quit a program. Sometimes you have to close the window yourself. Sometimes you have to type **EXIT** at the DOS prompt to close the window.

▶ **Click No.**

The only time you click Yes is when a DOS program has run amok and you're unable to close the window in any other way.

▶ **Choose File➡Exit from the MS-DOS Editor's menu.**

Yes, the mouse works in a DOS window. Any DOS program that recognizes the mouse in DOS recognizes it in a window also.

Now you can close the window without fear:

▶ **Click the X to close the DOS prompt window.**

If you start a program directly, such as the MS-DOS Editor, you don't have to close the window when it quits:

▶ **From the Start Thing, choose Run.**

▶ **Type** EDIT **in the Open text box and press Enter.**

Typing **EDIT** starts the MS-DOS Editor program in a DOS prompt window.

▶ **Choose File➡Exit from the MS-DOS Editor's menu.**

The window closes automatically when the program quits. Most DOS prompt programs exit that way whenever you start them directly, either from the Run dialog box or if you've placed the program on the Start Thing menu.

One more demo:

▶ **From the Start Thing, choose Run.**

▶ **Type** CHOICE **in the Open text box and press Enter.**

The CHOICE command isn't really a program; it's a batch file command. Still, the CHOICE command shows you how some DOS programs might quit when they're done.

All CHOICE does is ask a yes-or-no question and wait for you to press Y or N:

▶ **Press Y.**

Notice the title bar for the DOS window. It says `Finished`. It's your clue that the program has stopped running and that it's okay to close the DOS prompt window. In fact, because the window is now "dead," closing it is the only thing you can do.

▶ **Close the DOS prompt window.**

Quite a few DOS games end with the Finished DOS prompt window. When that happens, click the Properties button in the window (which you can still do, even though the window is dead). On the Program panel, put a check mark in the box next to Close on Exit. Click OK, and you never see the Finished window for that program again.

- Always quit your DOS programs properly—never by just closing the DOS prompt window.
- Some DOS programs close their windows automatically when they're done running.
- To close a DOS window from the DOS prompt, type the **EXIT** command.

Running DOS Games

Generally, any DOS game should run just fine under Windows 98. Starting the game, either at a DOS prompt or by opening its icon, should pull Windows into the proper game mode. No problem.

Few items are available to check when you're configuring a DOS game, just to make it easy.

The following tutorial assumes that you have a DOS game you want to configure.

▶ **Locate the DOS program's icon.**

Use Windows Explorer or My Computer to find the program's icon. In this example, I'm using DOOM II, which lives in the \Program Files\DOOM2 folder on my computer's drive C.

▶ **Right-click the icon and choose Properties from the pop-up menu.**

▶ **Click the Program tab to bring that panel forward.**

Figure A.2 explains how to work the Programs panel.

▶ **Click the Screen tab.**

▶ **Choose Full-Screen.**

Microsoft boasts that most DOS games can run in a window with no problem. However, my experience is that the "problem" is really how smoothly the game runs. In a window, games are jerky and hard to see. After all, does not the game *milieu* require a full screen? I mean, who wants to see Windows when you're zapping imps on Deimos?

▶ **Click the Misc tab.**

Figure A.3 describes the Misc panel.

▶ **Make whatever settings are necessary on the Misc panel.**

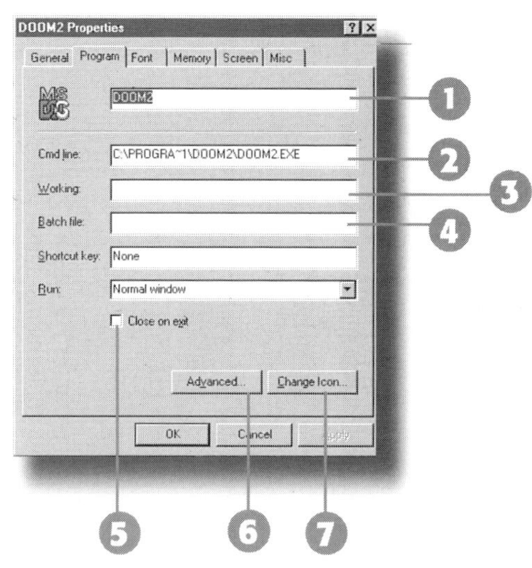

Figure A.2

The Program panel in a DOS game's Properties dialog box.

1. Type the icon's name here (can be anything).
2. The command that runs the game.
3. The game's directory (if required).
4. The batch file (if required) used to run the game.
5. Put a check mark here to have the game's DOS window close automatically.
6. Used to configure stubborn DOS games to run in MS-DOS Only mode.
7. Click here to browse for a new icon for the game.

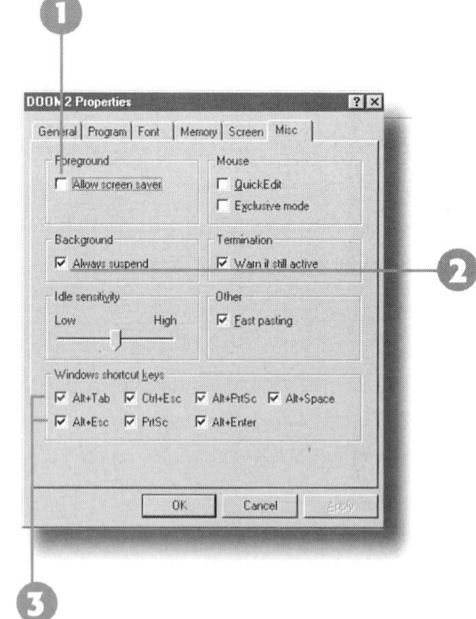

Figure A.3

The Misc panel in a DOS game's Properties dialog box.

1. Keep this one blank; no, you do not want the screen saver interrupting your game.
2. Check here; no point in running the game when you're not there.
3. Remove the check mark for the key combinations the game uses.

How can the screen saver interrupt your game? Easy: Most of the time, you're shooting things with a mouse or joystick. The screen saver probably doesn't notice. Besides, it's just rude.

Also, be sure to check the Always Suspend box; if the program is a real-time game, you might return to find that your man was eaten by gnarfs while you were answering email.

In the area labeled Windows Shortcut Keys, remove the check marks next to the key commands the game uses. For example, if pressing Alt+Spacebar in your game drops a bomb, you want to see a bomb drop when you press that key combination. You do not want to see your game morphed into a window with the control menu hanging down.

▶ **Click OK.**

Your game is properly configured.

If you elect to run your game in MS-DOS Only mode, go to the Programs panel in the game icon's Properties dialog box and click the Advanced button. Put a check mark next to MS-DOS Mode. What this step does is essentially shut down Windows, restart DOS, and run your game that way. When the game is done, DOS shuts down and Windows restarts.

If you're having lots of trouble with your game, you can configure the game to run in MS-DOS Only mode.

MS-DOS Only mode might or might not solve your problems. Several old games utterly refuse to run in Windows, amen. When that happens, your only option is to start up in DOS mode instead.

Making a Network

This appendix tells you how to set up a local area network (LAN) in your office by using ethernet hardware and Windows' own software. It's setup and how-to information. Chapters 34 and 35 cover network operations.

- The peer-to-peer network described in this appendix meets the needs of most small businesses.
- Larger, more sophisticated networks are available, most of which are centered around the Windows NT operating system. Those types of network, and other file-server-based networks, are not covered here.

"Why Do I Need a Local Area Network?"

Most people don't need a local area network, or LAN. If you have just one computer and you're sitting in a one-person office or at home, a LAN would be a waste of time. Go on! Get out of here.

Suppose that you're in a small office and you have two computers. You might need a network. Here's how to tell:

If the person using the "nice" laser printer keeps getting requests from the other person to borrow the printer, you need a network. (You can share the printer between both computers on the network.)

If anyone ever walks around your office carrying a floppy disk, you need a network. (You can copy files to other computers on the network without walking anywhere.)

If one computer has the big database program everyone uses—so that when you need to use that program, you have to walk to that computer—you need a network. (You can run the program or access files over the network from your own computer.)

Basically, a network enables you to share—like in elementary school. You can share your computer's disk drives and printer with other computers on the network, and you can use others' hard drives and printers. A network can be a boon to productivity.

A Local Area Network Overview

Figure B.1 illustrates the type of network this chapter helps you set up. Known as a *thin ethernet* type of network, it's the least expensive yet quite an effective network for a small office. It's exactly the type of network I have set up in my home office.

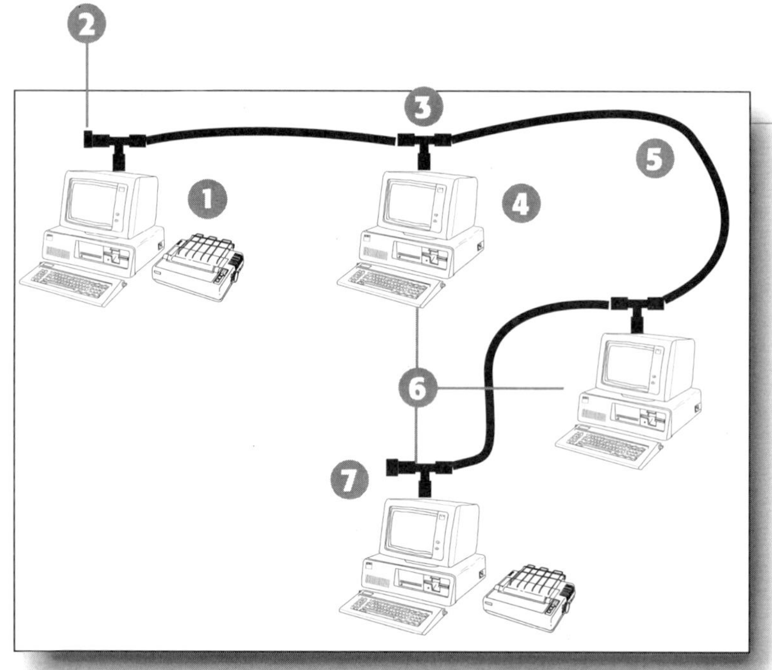

Figure B.1

A thin ethernet, peer-to-peer network (not to scale).

1. Computer and printer on the network.
2. Terminator.
3. T connector.
4. Computer has a network card.
5. Network hose.
6. Other computers on the network.
7. Other terminator.

For each computer on your network, you need these items:

- ✓ *Network adapter (expansion card)*—Get a 10Base-2 network card. It's the type of card that has a BNC adapter, which is designed to plug into a thin ethernet cable. A *combo card*, one that has both 10Base-2 and 10Base-T connectors on it, is also okay.
- ✓ *T connector*—Typically comes with the network adapter, although you can pick some up at any Radio Shack. A T connector hooks the network adapter card to the network hose.

- ✓ *Network adapter software*—Comes with the adapter itself.
- ✓ *Network software*—Comes with Windows.

For the network itself, you also need these items:

- ✓ *Network hose (cable)*—The hose is necessary in order to connect one PC to another. It's something extra you have to buy; it doesn't come with your network adapter. Get thin ethernet or 58 Ohm cable with BNC connectors on each end. The guy at Radio Shack will know what you mean.
- ✓ *Two terminators*—Each end of the network must be terminated. A *terminator* is a small resistor that twists onto the end of the T connector on the last computer on the network (both ends; refer to Figure B.1). The network doesn't work without these things.

TIP

To figure out how long the cable should be, measure the distance between your computers and then double it. If two computers are 10 feet apart, for example, you need 20 feet of cable.

Your Shopping List

For each computer, buy a network adapter with a *10Base-2* connector. It's also called a *BNC*, or *thin ethernet*, adapter.

You also need network hose in order to connect each computer, as shown in Figure B.1.

Get two thin ethernet resistors to cap off the ends of your network.

- If you can, try to buy the PCI (not ISA) type of ethernet card. A PCI card is faster, although it works only if your computer has a spare PCI slot.
- The 10Base-T connector, which looks like a big phone plug, is faster and better than the 10Base-2 (thin ethernet) connector. However, setting up that type of network requires more hardware and works best when the wiring is preinstalled in the wall.

How You're Going to Set Up the Friggin' Network

Setting up a network is a pain, but you do it only once for each computer. My advice is to start small, with just two computers. Then add other computers to the network one at a time, making sure that everything works along each step of the way.

Here are the steps to follow to add any computer to the network:

1. Install the network adapter card.
2. Install the network adapter card's software.

3. Set up the network adapter in Windows (if necessary).
4. Configure Windows for networking.
5. Configure the network.

Yeah, it seems like a bunch of redundant steps, but that's the way it goes. Remember that you do it only once.

Installing the Network Adapter Card

Setting up a network adapter card is a snap. The software setup *after* that is where you start to lose your marbles. Don't worry. Just getting through this section means that you deserve some type of award.

The Hardware Setup

The following instructions offer an overview of what you're doing (the instructions that come with your network card are more specific and should be your true guide):

- **Install the network adapter card in one of your PC's expansion slots.**

Instructions for this step are in Chapter 45, "Beefing Up Your PC with New Hardware," in the section "Installing an Expansion Card."

The network adapter card is the easiest type of expansion card to install because you have no internal cables to connect.

- **Close up the computer box.**
- **Connect the T connector to the rear of the network adapter.**

The T connector twists and locks into place, attaching to the nub of the network adapter card sticking out the back of your computer.

The T connector must attach directly to the nub on the network adapter. Do not use a cable to connect the T connector to the adapter; that method just doesn't work.

Thin ethernet networks have two ends, both of which are terminated with a twist-on cap on the T connector. The network is not a loop.

- **Hook on the network hose.**

Attach the network cable to one or both ends of the T connector. If this computer is on one end of the network (refer to Figure B.1), attach the cable to one end of the T connector and the resistor/terminator to the other end.

- **Turn on the computer.**

Windows *should* recognize the network adapter right away. The New Hardware Found dialog box is displayed as the computer sets itself up to recognize the network adapter.

- If you're asked to insert the Windows CD, do so.
- If files aren't found on the Windows CD, try the directory C:\Windows\Options\Cab.
- You might also try searching for any missing files on the floppy disk that came with your expansion card.
- If you see a Version Conflict dialog box, always go with the current or newer file.

▶ **Reset your computer if you're prompted to do so.**

Be patient.

▶ **Log in.**

Because you now have a network, you're required to log in, as shown in Figure B.2.

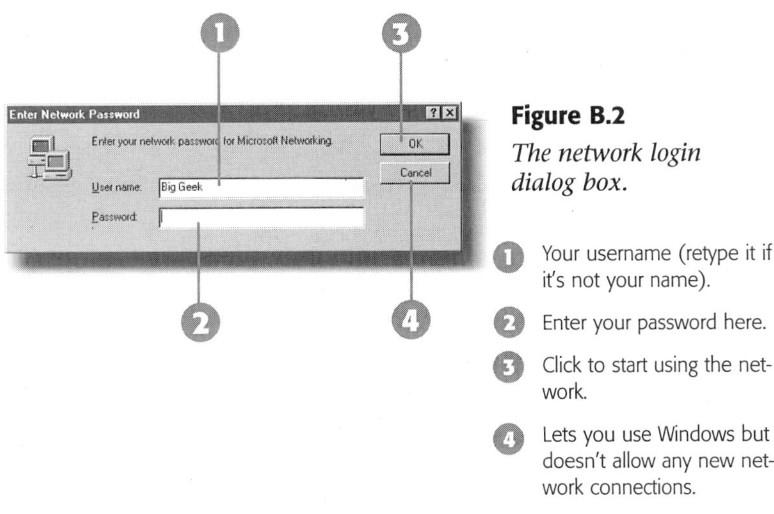

Figure B.2
The network login dialog box.

1. Your username (retype it if it's not your name).
2. Enter your password here.
3. Click to start using the network.
4. Lets you use Windows but doesn't allow any new network connections.

Type your username and password. If the computer doesn't recognize you, you're asked to confirm your password in a second dialog box.

Installing the Software Disk

Most network adapters come with an installation disk. Windows doesn't really need the disk, although it's a good idea to review the disk just in case it has useful information on it.

- **Insert the network adapter's disk into drive A.**
- **Browse to drive A on My Computer.**

Open My Computer, and then open drive A.

- **Open any README files.**

On my computer, the README file basically says that all the files on the disk are for operating systems other than Windows.

- **Run any additional installation programs (if necessary).**

In some cases you might have to run additional setup programs to finish installing the adapter card. The manual (or the README file) that came with the card should explain when that's necessary. For example, your card might require a setup program or drivers newer than the ones Windows offers.

- **Copy any necessary files to your hard drive.**

The setup program might do this step for you. If not, consider copying all the files from the floppy disk to a folder on your hard drive: Create the folder in the Program Files folder. Name the new folder `Network Card` or something clever. Then copy all the files from the floppy disk to that folder. That way, your adapter's files are handy whenever you need them.

- **Remove the floppy disk from drive A.**

Keep the disk in a safe place, where it's handy if you need it later.

Configuring Window's Networking Software

Don't think that you're done just because the network adapter is installed and connected and Windows has installed software for it. That's merely the hardware part of the installation. Next you must tell Windows which type of network you're connecting to and how you want to share your computer's goodies with others on the network.

You have to do essentially four things:

1. Confirm that your network adapter software has been properly installed.
2. Confirm that the Client for Microsoft Networks is installed.

3. Add file- and printer-sharing.
4. Describe your computer and network.

Check the Configuration

Confirm that your network hardware is properly installed:

- ▶ **Open the Control Panel.**
- ▶ **Open the Network icon.**

The Network dialog box appears, with the Configuration panel looking similar to what you see in Figure B.3.

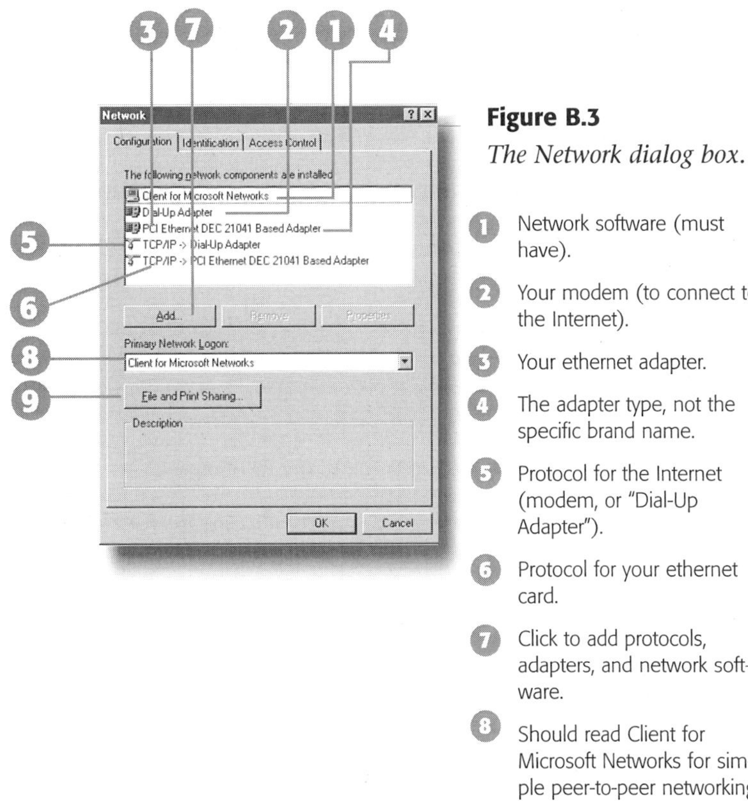

Figure B.3
The Network dialog box.

1. Network software (must have).
2. Your modem (to connect to the Internet).
3. Your ethernet adapter.
4. The adapter type, not the specific brand name.
5. Protocol for the Internet (modem, or "Dial-Up Adapter").
6. Protocol for your ethernet card.
7. Click to add protocols, adapters, and network software.
8. Should read Client for Microsoft Networks for simple peer-to-peer networking.
9. Click here to share your hard drives and printers with others on the network.

Three different types of items appear on the Configuration panel:

Network software—Controls the network hardware

Network hardware (adapters)—The ethernet card and your modem if you dial in to the Internet

Network protocols—Control how information is sent through the network

For the Internet, you need a Dial-Up Adapter (your modem) and the TCP/IP protocol for the Dial-Up Adapter. Don't mess with those two items right now.

For your thin Ethernet network, you need the Client for Microsoft Networks, your ethernet adapter, and some type of protocol for the adapter, such as the TCP/IP protocol shown in Figure B.3.

▶ **Add your adapter, if it's not already showing.**

If Windows did not install your adapter automatically, add it now. Click the Add button. Choose Adapter from the list and click Add. Choose your adapter's manufacturer from the first list, and then choose the adapter type from the second list. If your adapter isn't listed, insert its disk in drive A and click the Have Disk button.

When you're done, click OK to back out of the various dialog boxes and return to the Network dialog box.

▶ **Add the Client for Microsoft Networks, if it's not already showing.**

Click the Add button. Choose Client from the list and click Add. Choose Microsoft from the list of manufacturers, and then choose Client for Microsoft Networks from the clients list. Click OK.

▶ **Remove the TCP/IP protocol for your ethernet adapter (if you don't plan to use TCP/IP on your network).**

If you're using only a thin ethernet network between PCs running Windows, you don't really need TCP/IP for your ethernet adapter. However, if you have a network with other computers and use TCP/IP to communicate with those alien computers, keep the protocol. (This chapter does not discuss TCP/IP setup for your local area network.)

▶ **Add the NetBEUI protocol, if it's not already showing.**

Click the Add button. Choose Protocol from the list and click Add. Choose Microsoft from the list of manufacturers, and then choose NetBEUI from the Network Protocols list. Click OK.

NetBEUI (whatever it stands for) is the protocol that allows peer-to-peer networking for Windows computers.

Do not leave the Network dialog box.

Add File- and Printer-Sharing

Continuing from the last section:

- **Click the Add button.**

The Select Network Component Type dialog box appears.

- **Choose Service and click Add.**

The Select Network Service dialog box appears.

- **Under Manufacturers, choose Microsoft.**
- **Under Network Services, choose File and Printer Sharing for Microsoft Networks.**
- **Click OK.**

The File and Printer Sharing for Microsoft Networks item should be added to the list on the Configuration panel.

To take advantage of the file- and printer-sharing:

- **Click the File and Print Sharing button.**

The File and Print Sharing dialog box appears. It's where you allow others on the network to access to your PC's hard drive and printers. Both check boxes should be checked already.

This dialog box only allows you to share your hard drive and printer. Because you must still manually select a drive and printer for sharing before anyone has access, you have no reason to uncheck the boxes in the File and Print Sharing dialog box.

- **Click OK.**

You're almost done. Keep the Network dialog box open for the following section.

Describe Your Network

Every network has a name, and every computer on the network needs a name. Using the Identification panel in the Network dialog box, you tell your computer to which network it belongs and assign your computer a name:

- **Bring up the Identification panel.**

Click the Identification tab in the Network dialog box to bring that panel forward. What you see looks something like Figure B.4.

- **Enter the computer's name.**

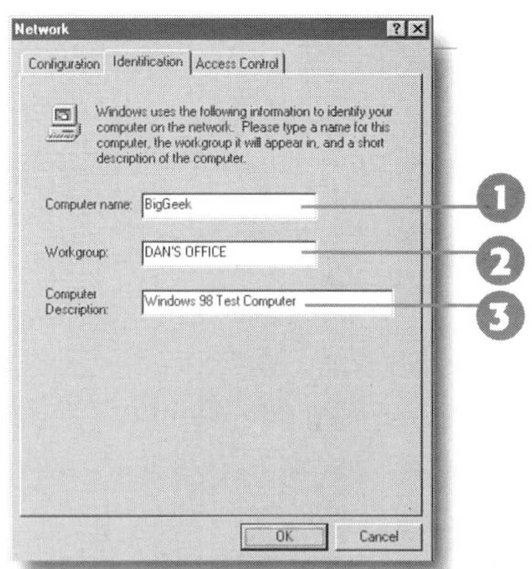

Figure B.4

Identifying your network computer.

1. Give your computer a name (15 characters max, no spaces).
2. The workgroup name.
3. A description of this computer.

I've named all my computers since my first one, in 1982. My Windows 98 test computer is Big Geek, although because you cannot use spaces in the Computer Name input box, I typed `BigGeek` instead. Press the Tab key.

▶ **Type the workgroup name.**

It's the same name for every computer on the network. In fact, you can call it Network, if you want, or Workgroup. Press the Tab key.

▶ **Type a description.**

The words you type appear when someone else on the network views information about this computer. Something like The Old 486 at the End of the Hall That No One Uses would be an appropriate name.

▶ **Click OK.**

You're done configuring the software side of the network installation.

Because Windows might copy a few files from its CD, be sure to have the CD handy or already in your CD-ROM drive.

Windows wants to reset itself because you've added new software; the System Settings Change dialog box appears.

▶ **Click Yes to restart Windows.**

Click! Windows stops. Windows starts. You log in again, and the network should be up and running.

The next step is to test the network, making sure that your computers are talking with each other.

- You can have multiple network names on a single network; for example, one network name for the salespeople and another for the research-and-development department. For most small offices, however, multiple names aren't necessary.
- Some people give their computers the same name as the logon name that's used when Windows starts up. Nothing wrong with that.

The computer name is used when other computers access your computer's hard drive or printer. Be careful not to change that name later, or else those other computers lose their connection.

Testing the Network

Assuming that everything went well with the hardware and software installation, your computer should now be part of a local area network. To confirm that everything is connected, you use the Network Neighborhood icon. Every other computer on the network should appear as an icon there.

▶ **Open the Network Neighborhood icon on the desktop.**

Every computer on the network should be represented. (If not, see the bullet point, at the end of this section, about running the Network Troubleshooter.) What I see on my screen is shown in Figure B.5.

▶ **Close the Network Neighborhood window.**

You're ready to use your network.

- Chapters 34 and 35 discuss the Network Neighborhood as well as how to access and share resources on your network.
- If you have any trouble with the Network Neighborhood or with your network, run the Network Troubleshooter. Choose Help from the Start Thing menu. On the Contents panel, choose Troubleshooting, and then Windows 98 Troubleshooters, and then Networking. Answer the questions on the right side of the window; if the troubleshooter doesn't help solve your problem, it at least narrows down the possible causes.

Figure B.5

All is well in the Network Neighborhood.

1. Other computers on the network.
2. Select a computer to see its description.
3. Opening a computer displays whatever resources it has for sharing.

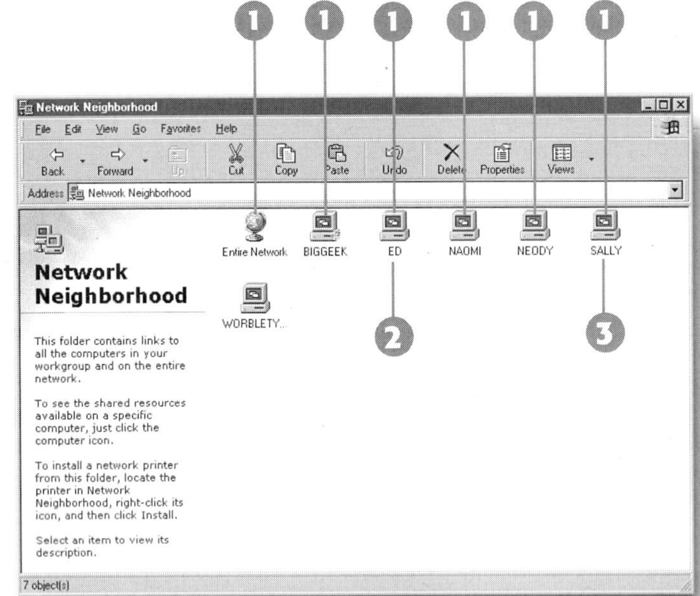

Index

Symbols

A

D

E

F

G

H

I

J–K

L

M

P

Q

T

U

V

W

X-Y-Z